Xlib Programming Manual

Volume One

Xlib Programming Manual

---

for Version 11 of the X Window System

by Adrian Nye

O'Reilly & Associates, Inc.

Xlib Programming Manual

by Adrian Nye

Editor: Adrian Nye

Printing History:

August 1988:	First Edition.
November 1988:	Minor revisions.
May 1989:	Release 3 updates added. Minor revisions.
April 1990:	Second Edition covers Release 3 and Release 4.
July 1990:	Minor revisions.
October 1990:	Minor revisions.
December 1991:	Minor revisions.
July 1992:	Third Edition covers Release 4 and Release 5.
March 1993:	Minor revisions.
July 1993:	Minor revisions.
January 1995:	Minor revisions.

Volume 1, Third Edition: ISBN 1-56592-002-3

[9/96]

Table of Contents

Chapter 12 Interclient Communication 403

Chapter 15 Other Programming Techniques 495

Chapter 16 Window Management 511

Figures

Examples

Tables

Preface

In The Preface:

Preface

About This Manual

This manual describes the X library, the C Language programming interface to Version 11 of the X Window System. The X library, known as Xlib, is the lowest level of programming interface to X. This library enables a programmer to write applications with an advanced user interface based on windows on the screen, with complete network transparency, that will run without changes on many types of workstations and personal computers.

Xlib is powerful enough to write effective applications without additional programming tools and is necessary for certain tasks even in applications written with higher-level "toolkits."

There are a number of these toolkits for X programming, the most notable being the DEC/MIT toolkit Xt, the Andrew toolkit developed by IBM and Carnegie-Mellon University, and the InterViews toolkit from Stanford. These toolkits are still evolving, and only Xt is currently part of the X standard. Toolkits simplify the process of application writing considerably, providing a number of *widgets* that implement menus, command buttons, and other common features of the user interface.

This manual does not describe Xt or any other toolkit. That is done in Volumes Four and Five of our X Window System series. Nonetheless, much of the material described in this book is helpful for understanding and using the toolkits, since the toolkits themselves are written using Xlib and allow Xlib code to be intermingled with toolkit code.

Summary of Contents

This manual is divided into two volumes. This is the first volume, the *Xlib Programming Manual*. It provides a conceptual introduction to Xlib, including tutorial material and numerous programming examples. Arranged by task or topic, each chapter brings together a group of Xlib functions, describes the conceptual foundation they are based on, and illustrates how they are most often used in writing applications (or, in the case of the last chapter, in writing window managers). Volume One is structured so as to be useful as a tutorial and also as a task-oriented reference.

The second volume, the *Xlib Reference Manual*, includes reference pages for each of the Xlib functions, organized alphabetically for ease of reference; a permuted index; and numerous appendices and quick reference aids.

Volume One and Volume Two are designed to be used together. To get the most out of the examples in Volume One, you will need the exact calling sequences of each function from Volume Two. To understand fully how to use each of the functions described in Volume Two, all but the most experienced X "hacker" will need the explanation and examples in Volume One.

Both volumes include material from the original Xlib and X11 protocol documentation provided by MIT, as well as from other documents provided on the MIT release tape. We have done our best to incorporate all of the useful information from the MIT documentation, to correct code references we found to be in error, to reorganize and present it in a more useful form, and to supplement it with conceptual material, tutorials, reference aids, and examples. In other words, this manual is not only a replacement but is a superset of the MIT documentation.

Those of you familiar with the MIT documentation will recognize that each reference page in Volume Two includes the detailed description of the routine found in Gettys, Newman, and Scheifler's *Xlib–C Language X Interface*, plus, in many cases, additional text that clarifies ambiguities and describes the context in which the routine would be used. We have also added cross references to related reference pages and to where additional information can be found in Volume One.

How to Use This Manual

Volume One is intended as an introduction to all the basic concepts of X programming and also as a useful reference for many of the most common programming techniques. It is divided into 14 chapters, which describe and demonstrate the use of the X programming library, and numerous appendices.

You will find it necessary to read at least Chapters 1, 2, and 3 before attempting to program with the X library. Chapter 1, *Introduction*, provides a discussion of the context in which X programs operate. Chapter 2, *X Concepts*, describes the conceptual foundations underlying X programming. Chapter 3, *Basic Window Program*, presents a simple program.

Chapters 4 through 9 (*Window Attributes*, *The Graphics Context*, *Drawing Graphics and Text*, *Color*, *Events*, and *The Keyboard and Pointer*) discuss various programming techniques that are used in all X programs. These chapters can be read as a tutorial and consulted for reference later.

Chapter 10, *Internationalization*, and Chapter 11, *Internationalized Text Input* describe the Xlib features for making an application usable in any language without changes to the application binary. These features were added in Release 5.

Chapter 12, *Interclient Communication*, is a description of communication between applications and between applications and the window manager, including properties and selections.

Chapter 13, *Managing User Preferences*, describes the facilities provided for database management, parsing the command line, and managing user preferences. Xlib calls this the resource manager.

Chapter 14, *A Complete Application*, provides an example of a complete application. This chapter is especially useful in demonstrating managing user preferences with the resource manager.

Chapter 15, *Other Programming Techniques*, describes programming techniques that will be useful to some but not all programs. It should be scanned for applicable techniques and read in detail when needed for a particular project.

Chapter 16, *Window Management*, describes what window managers do and how they work. This information should provide a more complete knowledge of the variety of contexts in which X applications may function. It also describes the Xlib functions that are intended primarily for window management. A simple window manager program is described.

Appendix A, *Specifying Fonts*, describes how the programmer should specify default font names.

Appendix B, *X10 Compatibility*, describes the routines supported in X11 for compatibility with X Version 10.

Appendix C, *Writing Extensions to X*, is a guide to writing extensions to X. This is for experienced X programmers only. It is provided so that this manual can serve as a complete replacement for the MIT Xlib documentation.

Appendix D, *The basecalc Application*, presents the complete code for *basecalc*, the complete application described in Chapter 12, *A Complete Application*.

Appendix E, *Event Reference*, describes each event type in a reference page format. Included is how to select the events, when they are generated, the contents of the event structures, and notes on how to use them. This information is vital in using the numerous events.

Appendix F, *The Xmu Library*, describes the routines in this miscellaneous utilities library that are useful in Xlib programming. This library is not an X Consortium standard but is widely available.

Appendix G, *Sources of Additional Information*, lists where to get the X software, companies that offer training in X programming, and descriptions of additional published books on the subject.

Appendix H, *Release Notes*, describes the changes between Releases 3, 4 and 5. This manual describes Release 4 and Release 5.

The *Glossary* gives you somewhere to turn should you run across a term with which you are unfamiliar. Some care has been taken to see that all terms are defined where they are first used in the text, but this assumes a sequential reading of the manual.

Volume Two consists of a permuted index, reference pages to each library function, and appendices that cover macros, structures, function groups, events, fonts, colors, cursors, keysyms, and errors. Finally, Volume Two concludes with at-a-glance charts that help in setting the graphics context (GC) and the window attributes. This volume should be consulted to obtain the specifics of calling each Xlib function.

Getting the Example Programs

The example programs in this book are available electronically in a number of ways: by ftp, ftpmail, bitftp, and uucp. The cheapest, fastest, and easiest ways are listed first. If you read from the top down, the first one that works for you is probably the best. Use *ftp* if you are directly on the Internet. Use ftpmail if you are not on the Internet but can send and receive electronic mail to internet sites (this includes CompuServe users). Use BITFTP if you send electronic mail via BITNET. Use UUCP if none of the above works.

FTP

To use FTP, you need a machine with direct access to the Internet. A sample session is shown, with what you should type in boldface.

```
% ftp ftp.uu.net
Connected to ftp.uu.net.
220 FTP server (Version 6.21 Tue Mar 10 22:09:55 EST 1992) ready.
Name (ftp.uu.net:kismet): anonymous
331 Guest login ok, send domain style e-mail address as password.
Password: kismet@ora.com (use your user name and host here)
230 Guest login ok, access restrictions apply.
ftp> cd /published/oreilly/xbook/xlib/
250 CWD command successful.
ftp> binary (Very important! You must specify binary transfer for compressed files.)
200 Type set to I.
ftp> get xlibprgs4.tar.Z
200 PORT command successful.
150 Opening BINARY mode data connection for xlibprgs4.tar.Z.
226 Transfer complete.
ftp> quit
221 Goodbye.
%
```

The file is a compressed tar archive; extract the files from the archive by typing:

```
% zcat xlibprgs4.tar.Z | tar xf -
```

System V systems require the following tar command instead:

```
% zcat xlibprgs4.tar.Z | tar xof -
```

If *zcat* is not available on your system, use separate uncompress and tar commands.

FTPMAIL

FTPMAIL is a mail server available to anyone who can send electronic mail to and receive it from Internet sites. This includes any company or service provider that allows email connections to the Internet. Here's how you do it.

You send mail to *ftpmail@online.ora.com*. In the message body, give the FTP commands you want to run. The server will run anonymous FTP for you and mail the files back to you. To get a complete help file, send a message with no subject and the single word "help" in the body. The following is an example mail session that should get you the examples. This command sends you a listing of the files in the selected directory, and the requested example files. The listing is useful if there's a later version of the examples you're interested in.

```
% mail ftpmail@online.ora.com
Subject:
reply-to jerry@ora.com          (where you want files mailed)
open
cd /published/oreilly/xbook/xlib
dir
mode binary
uuencode                        (or btoa if you have it)
get xlibprgs4.tar.Z
quit
```

A signature at the end of the message is acceptable as long as it appears after "quit."

All retrieved files will be split into 60KB chunks and mailed to you. You then remove the mail headers and concatenate them into one file, and then *uudecode* or *atob* it. Once you've got the desired file, follow the directions under FTP to extract the files from the archive.

BITFTP

BITFTP is a mail server for BITNET users. You send it electronic mail messages requesting files, and it sends you back the files by electronic mail. BITFTP currently serves only users who send it mail from nodes that are directly on BITNET, EARN, or NetNorth. BITFTP is a public service of Princeton University. Here's how it works.

To use BITFTP, send mail containing your ftp commands to *BITFTP@PUCC*. For a complete help file, send HELP as the message body.

The following is the message body you should send to BITFTP:

```
FTP  ftp.uu.net  NETDATA
USER  anonymous
PASS your Internet email address (not your bitnet address)
CD  /published/oreilly/xbook/xlib/
DIR
BINARY
GET  xlibprgs4.tar.Z
QUIT
```

Once you've got the desired file, follow the directions under FTP to extract the files from the archive. Since you are probably not on a UNIX system, you may need to get versions of *uudecode*, *uncompress*, *atob*, and *tar* for your system. VMS, DOS, and Mac versions are available. The VMS versions are on *gatekeeper.dec.com* in */archive/pub/VMS*.

Questions about BITFTP can be directed to Melinda Varian, *MAINT@PUCC* on BITNET.

UUCP

UUCP is standard on virtually all UNIX systems, and is available for IBM-compatible PCs and Apple Macintoshes. The examples are available by UUCP via modem from UUNET; UUNET's connect-time charges apply.

You can get the examples from UUNET whether you have an account or not. If you or your company has an account with UUNET, you will have a system with a direct UUCP connection to UUNET. Find that system, and type:

```
uucp uunet\!~/published/oreilly/xbook/xlib//xlibprgs4.tar.Z yourhost\!~/yourname/
```

The backslashes can be omitted if you use the Bourne shell (*sh*) instead of *csh*. The file should appear some time later (up to a day or more) in the directory */usr/spool/uucppublic/yourname*. If you don't have an account but would like one so that you can get electronic mail, then contact UUNET at 703-204-8000.

It's a good idea to get the file */published/oreilly/xbook/xlib//ls-lR.Z* as a short test file containing the filenames and sizes of all the files in the directory.

Once you've got the desired file, follow the directions under FTP to extract the files from the archive.

Compiling the Example Programs

Once you've got the examples and unpacked the archive as described above, you're ready to compile them. The easiest way is to use *imake*, a program supplied with the X11 distribution that generates proper Makefiles on a wide variety of systems.) *imake* uses configuration files called Imakefiles which are included. If you have *imake*, you should go to the top-level directory containing the examples, and type:

```
% xmkmf
% make Makefiles
% make
```

All the application-defaults files are in the main examples directory. The application-defaults files are not automatically installed in the system application-defaults directory (usually */usr/lib/X11/app-defaults* on UNIX systems). (See Chapter 9, *Resource Management and Type Conversion*, for details.) If you have permission to write to that directory, you can copy them there yourself. Otherwise, you can set the XAPPLRESDIR environment variable to the complete path of the directory where you installed the examples. The value of XAPPLRESDIR must end with a / (slash). (Most of the examples will not function properly without the application-defaults files.)

Assumptions

Readers should be proficient in the C programming language, although examples are provided for infrequently used features of the language that are necessary or useful when programming with X. In addition, general familiarity with the principles of raster graphics will be helpful.

Font Conventions Used in This Manual

Italic is used for:

- UNIX pathnames, filenames, program names, user command names, and options for user commands.
- New terms where they are defined.

`Typewriter Font` is used for:

- Anything that would be typed verbatim into code, such as examples of source code and text on the screen.
- The contents of include files, such as structure types, structure members, symbols (defined constants and bit flags), and macros.
- Xlib functions.
- Names of subroutines of the example programs.

`Italic Typewriter Font` is used for:

- Arguments to Xlib functions, since they could be typed in code as shown but are arbitrary.

Helvetica Italics are used for:

- Titles of examples, figures, and tables.

Boldface is used for:

- Chapter and section headings.

Related Documents

The C Programming Language by B. W. Kernighan and D. M. Ritchie.

The following documents are included on the X11 source tape:

Xt Toolkit Intrinsics by Joel McCormack, Paul Asente, and Ralph Swick
Xt Toolkit Widgets by Ralph Swick and Terry Weissman
Xlib−C Language X Interface by Jim Gettys, Ron Newman, and Robert Scheifler
X Window System Protocol, Version 11 by Robert Scheifler

The following other books on the X Window System are available from O'Reilly and Associates, Inc.:

Volume Zero — *X Protocol Reference Manual*
Volume Two — *Xlib Reference Manual*
Volume Three — *X Window System User's Guide*
Volume Four — *X Toolkit Intrinsics Programming Manual*
Volume Five — *X Toolkit Intrinsics Reference Manual*
Volume Six — *Motif Programming Manual*
Volume Seven — *XView Programmer's Guide*
Volume Eight — *X Administrator's Guide*
PHIGS Programming Manual
PHIGS Reference Manual
Pexlib Programming Manual
Pexlib Reference Manual
Quick Reference — *The X Window System in a Nutshell*

We'd Like to Hear From You

We have tested and verified all of the information in this book to the best of our ability, but **you may** find that features have changed (or even that we have made mistakes!). Please let us **know** about any errors you find, as well as your suggestions for future editions, by writing:

```
O'Reilly & Associates, Inc.
101 Morris Street
Sebastopol, CA 95472
1-800-998-9938 (in the US or Canada)
1-707-829-0515 (international/local)
1-707-829-0104 (FAX)
```

You can also send us messages electronically. To be put on the mailing list or request a catalog, send email to:

info@ora.com   (via the Internet)
uunet!ora!info   (via UUCP)

To ask technical questions or comment on the book, send email to:

bookquestions@ora.com   (via the Internet)

Bulk Sales Information

This manual is being resold by many workstation manufacturers as their official X Window System documentation. For information on volume discounts for bulk purchase, call O'Reilly and Associates, Inc. at 617-354-5800, or send e-mail to linda@ora.com (uunet!ora!linda).

Source licensing terms for online documentation are also available.

Acknowledgements

The information contained in this manual is based in part on *Xlib–C Language X Interface*, written by Jim Gettys, Ron Newman, and Robert Scheifler, and the *X Window System Protocol, Version 11*, by Robert Scheifler (with many contributors). The X Window System software and these documents were written under the auspices of Project Athena at MIT. In addition, this manual includes material from Oliver Jones' Xlib tutorial presentation, which was given at the MIT X Conference in January 1988, and from David Rosenthal's *Inter-Client Communication Conventions Manual*. I owe a great debt to the X Consortium policy allowing others to build on their work.

I would like to thank the people who helped this book come into being. It was Tim O'Reilly who originally sent me out on a contract to write a manual for X Version 10 for a workstation manufacturer and later to another company to write a manual for X Version 11, from which this book began. I have learned most of what I know about computers and technical writing while working for Tim. For this book, he acted as an editor, he helped me reorganize several chapters, he worked on the *Color* and *Managing User Preferences* chapters when time was too short for me to do it, and he kept my spirits up through this long project. While I was concentrating on the details, his eye was on the overall presentation, and his efforts improved the book enormously.

This book would not be as good (and we might still be working on it) had it not been for Daniel Gilly. Daniel was my production assistant for critical periods in the project. He dealt with formatting issues, checked for consistent usage of terms and noticed irregularities in content, and edited files from written corrections by me and by others. His job was to take as much of the work off me as possible, and with his technical skill and knowledge of UNIX, he did that very well.

This manual has benefitted from the work and assistance of the entire staff of O'Reilly and Associates, Inc. Sue Willing was responsible for graphics and design, and she proofed many drafts of the book; Linda Mui tailored the troff macros to the design by Sue Willing and myself and was invaluable in the final production process; John Strang figured out the resource manager and wrote the original section on that topic; Karen Cakebread edited a draft of the manual and established some conventions for terms and format. Peter Mui executed the "at-a-glance" tables for the inside back cover; Tom Scanlon entered written edits and performed copy fitting; Donna Woonteiler wrote the index of the book; Valerie Quercia, Tom Van Raalte, and Linda Walsh all contributed in some small ways; and Cathy Brennan, Suzanne Van Hove, and Jill Berlin fielded many calls from people interested in the X manual and saved me all the time that would have taken. Ruth Terry, Lenny Muellner, and Donna Woonteiler produced the Second Edition, with graphics done by Chris Reilley. Mike Sierra produced the Third Edition. A special thanks to everyone at O'Reilly and Associates for putting up with my habits of printer and terminal hogging, lugging X books around, recycling paper, and for generally being good at what they do and good-natured to boot.

David Flanagan wrote much of the material on X11R5, which appeared originally in his book *Programmer's Supplement for Release 5*. I'm sincerely grateful to him for doing such a great job.

I would also like to thank the people from other companies that reviewed the book or otherwise made this project possible: John Posner, Barry Kingsbury, Jeff MacMann and Jeffrey Vroom of Stellar Computer; Oliver Jones of Apollo Computer; Sam Black, Jeff Graber, and Janet Egan of Masscomp; Al Tabayoyon, Paul Shearer, and many others from Tektronix; Robert Scheifler and Jim Fulton of the X Consortium (who helped with the *Color* and *Managing User Preferences* chapters), and Peter Winston II and Aub Harden of Integrated Computer Solutions. Despite the efforts of the reviewers and everyone else, any errors that remain are my own.

— *Adrian Nye*

1

Introduction

This chapter gives the big picture: what X is all about and some fundamentals of how it works. Everyone should look at this chapter, though readers who are already familiar with X may only want to skim it.

In This Chapter:

1
Introduction

In September 1987, the Massachusetts Institute of Technology released the first snapshot of what may well become one of the most significant software technologies of the 1990s: Version 11 of the X Window System, commonly referred to as X11. X11 may not change the world, but it is likely to change the world of workstations.

The X Window System is being adopted as a standard by nearly every workstation manufacturer and should eventually replace or be supported under their proprietary windowing systems. Versions will also be available for personal computers and supercomputers.

For the first time, portable applications can be written for an entire class of machines rather than for a single manufacturer's equipment. Programmers can write in a single graphics language and expect their applications to work without significant modifications on dozens of different computers.

What's more, since X is a network-based windowing system, applications can run in a network of systems from different vendors. Programs can be run on a remote computer, and the results displayed on a local workstation. Proprietary networks have been around for a while. However, network cooperation of *different* computers has been held up by the lack of a common applications language. Now there is one.

Vendors hope that X will lead to a software explosion similar to the one that occurred in response to the PC standard on microcomputers.

1.1 Versions of X

X was developed jointly by MIT's Project Athena and Digital Equipment Corporation, with contributions from many other companies. It was masterminded by Robert Scheifler and colleagues at MIT, though it owes some debt to the "W" windowing package developed by Paul Asente at Stanford.

There have been numerous research versions of X. Version 10, Release 4 (popularly known as X10.4), which was released in 1986, became the basis for several commercial products. Development of most X10.4 products was curtailed, however, when it became apparent that Version 11 would not be compatible with it. Version 11, Release 1 became available in September 1987, Release 2 in March 1988, Release 3 in February 1989, Release 4 in January 1990, and Release 5 in August 1991.

Version 11 is a complete window programming package. It offers much more flexibility in the areas of supported display features, window manager styles, and support for multiple screens and provides better performance than X Version 10. It is fully extensible. But just as important, the X11 subroutine library (Xlib) is expected to be stable for several years and to be at least a de facto industry standard. That means that programs written with this library will not need major revisions because of software updates. While there may be additions to this library, there will not be incompatible changes to it.

With X11 Release 2, control of X passed from MIT to the X Consortium, an association of major computer manufacturers who plan to support the X standard. The Consortium was formed in January 1988 and includes virtually all large computer manufacturers. Many software houses and universities are associate members, who also have a voice in controlling the standard and receive advance access to newly released software.

1.2 X Window System Concepts

The X Window System is complex, but it is based on a few premises that can be quickly understood. This section describes these major concepts.

1.2.1 Displays and Screens

The first and most obvious thing to note about X is that it is a windowing system for bit-mapped graphics displays.* It supports color as well as monochrome and gray-scale displays.

A slightly unusual feature is that a *display* is defined as a workstation consisting of a keyboard, a pointing device such as a mouse, and *one or more* screens.† Multiple screens can work together, with mouse movement allowed to cross physical screen boundaries. As long as multiple screens are controlled by a single user with a single keyboard and pointing device, they comprise only a single display, as shown in Figure 1-1.

---

*In bitmapped graphics, each dot on the screen (called a *pixel*, or picture element) corresponds to one or more bits in memory. Programs modify the display simply by writing to display memory. Bitmapped graphics are also referred to as raster graphics, since most bitmapped displays use television-type scan line technology: the entire screen is continually refreshed by an electron beam scanning across the face of the display tube one scan line, or raster, at a time. The term bitmapped graphics (or memory-mapped graphics) is more general, since it also applies to other dot-oriented displays, such as LCD screens. We assume that you are familiar with the basic principles of bitmapped graphics.
†As of Release 5, there is a standardized extension called the X Input Extension that supports multiple input devices other than keyboards or mice.

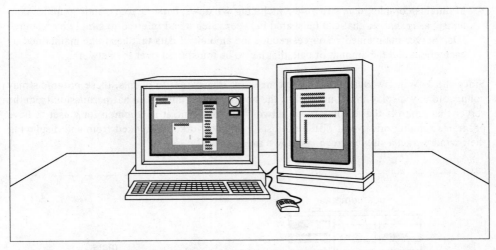

Figure 1-1. A display consisting of more than one screen

1.2.2 The Server–Client Model

The next thing to note is that X is a network-oriented windowing system. An application need not be running on the same system that actually supports the display. While many applications can execute locally on a workstation, other applications can execute on other machines, sending requests across the network to a particular display and receiving keyboard and pointer events from the system controlling the display.

At this point, only TCP/IP and DECnet networks are supported by the X Consortium and most vendors, though that may change before long.

The program that controls each display is known as a *server*. At first, this usage of the term server may seem a little odd—when you sit at a workstation, you tend to think of a server as something across the network (such as a file or print server) rather than the local program that controls your own display. The thing to remember is that your display is accessible to other systems across the network, and for those systems, the code executing in your system does act as a true display server.

The server acts as an intermediary between user programs (called *clients* or *applications*) running on either the local or remote systems and the resources of the local system. The server (without extensions) performs the following tasks:

- Allows access to the display by multiple clients.

- Interprets network messages from clients.

- Passes user input to the clients by sending network messages.

- Does two-dimensional drawing—graphics are performed by the display server rather than by the client.

- Maintains complex data structures, including windows, cursors, fonts, and "graphics contexts," as *resources* that can be shared between clients and referred to simply by resource IDs. Server-maintained resources reduce the amount of data that has to be maintained by each client and the amount of data that has to be transferred over the network.

Since the X Window System makes the network transparent to clients, these programs may connect to any display in the network if the host they are running on has permission from the server that controls that display. In a network environment, it is common for a user to have programs running on several different hosts in the network, all invoked from and displaying their windows on a single screen, as shown in Figure 1-2.

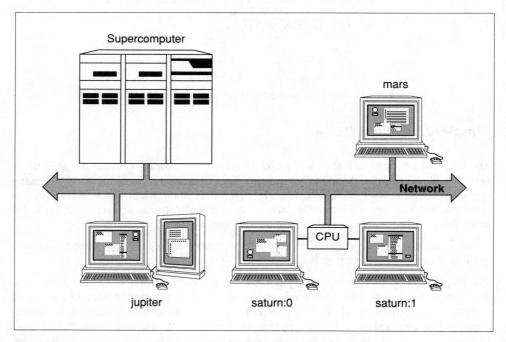

Figure 1-2. Applications can run on any system across the network

In practice, each user is sitting at a server and can start applications locally to display on the local server or can start applications on remote hosts for display on the local server, if the remote hosts have permission to connect to the local server. All other users in the network are in a similar situation—they can run applications on their own system or on yours, but they will, for the most part, be displaying on their own server. This use of the network is known as *distributed processing*. Distributed processing helps solve the problem of unbalanced system loads. When one host machine is overloaded, the users of that machine can arrange for some of their programs to run on other hosts.

One extreme of this arrangement is the PC server or X terminal. Because these single-task systems can run only the X server (and sometimes a window manager), a user sitting at one of these servers must run all clients on systems across the network, with their results displayed on the PC or X terminal screen. This makes the single-tasking PC or X terminal look and work just like X on a multitasking workstation.

1.2.3 Window Management

Another important concept in X programming is that applications do not actually control such things as where a window appears or what size it is. Given multiprocessor, multiclient access to the same workstation display, clients must not be dependent on a particular window configuration. Instead, a client gives *hints* about how long and where it would like to be displayed. The screen layout or appearance and the style of user interaction with the system are left up to a separate program, called the *window manager*.

The window manager is just another program written with Xlib, except that it is given special authority to control the layout of windows on the screen. The window manager typically allows the user to move or resize windows, start new applications, and control the stacking of windows on the screen, but only according to the window manager's window layout policy. A *window layout policy* is a set of rules that specify allowable sizes and positions of windows and icons.

Unlike citizens, the window manager has rights but not responsibilities. Programs must be prepared to cooperate with any type of window manager or with none at all (there are fairly simple ways to prepare programs for these contingencies). The simple window manager *twm* does not enforce any window layout policy, but clients should still assume that there could be one. For example, the window manager must be informed of the desired size of a new window before the window is displayed on the screen. If the window manager does not accept the desired window size and position, the program must be prepared to accept a different size or position or be able to display a message such as "Too small!"

If you are having trouble visualizing this situation, imagine a window manager where no windows are allowed to overlap. This is known as a *tiled* window manager. The Siemens RTL tiled window manager lets only transient windows (such as pop-up menus) overlap. The *twm* window manager, on the other hand, is referred to as *real-estate-driven* because keyboard input is automatically assigned to whatever window the pointer currently happens to be in.

There is at least one other window manager variety that you will encounter, called a *listener* or *click-to-type*. Its distinguishing feature is that it assigns all keyboard input to a single window when that window is selected by clicking on it with the pointer. A listener may or may not allow windows to overlap. Apple Macintosh™ users will recognize this type of interface.

X is somewhat unusual in that it does not mandate a particular type of window manager. Its developers have tried to make X itself as free of window management or user interface policy as possible. And, while the X11 distribution includes *twm* as a sample window manager, individual manufacturers are expected to write their own window managers and user interface guidelines. In fact, two commercial window managers with user interface guidelines are already becoming established. They are *olwm*, the OPEN LOOK™ window manager from AT&T and Sun, and *mwm*, the Motif™ window manager from Open Software Foundation. The OSF Motif window manager *mwm*, and OPEN LOOK window manager *olwm* both can be configured to be real-estate-driven or click-to-type.

In the long run, the developers of X may well have made the right choice, in that the lack of clear user interface guidelines will allow a period of experimentation in which the marketplace could come up with better designs than are presently available. Some industry observers, however, decry this move, pointing out that it undercuts X's appeal as a standard user platform—X *programs* may be portable across systems from multiple vendors, but if users have to deal with a different user interface on each system, half the benefit of that portability will be lost. Until a clear user interface standard emerges from the marketplace, developers must be careful to write their programs in such a way that they can run under different window managers and user interface conventions.

1.2.4 Events

As in any mouse-driven window system, an X client must be prepared to respond to any of many different *events*. Events include user input (keypress, mouse click, or mouse movement) as well as interaction with other programs. (For example, if an obscured portion of a window is exposed when another overlapping window is moved, closed, or resized, the client must redraw it.) Events of many different types can occur at any time and in any order. They are placed on a queue in the order they occur and usually are processed by clients in that order. Event-driven programming makes it natural to let the user tell the program what to do instead of vice versa.

The need to handle events is a major difference between programming under a window system and traditional UNIX or PC programming. X programs do not use the standard C functions for getting characters, and they do not poll for input. Instead there are functions for receiving events, and then the program must branch according to the type of event and perform the appropriate response. But unlike traditional programs, an X program must be ready for any kind of event at any time. In traditional programs the program is in control, asking for certain types of input at certain times. In X programs, the user is in control most of the time.

1.2.5 Extensions to X

The final thing to know about X is that it is *extensible*. The code includes a defined mechanism for incorporating extensions, so that vendors are not forced to hack up the existing system in incompatible ways when adding features. These extensions are used just like the core Xlib routines and perform at the same level. Some extensions are standards of the MIT X Consortium, such as the Shape extension, which supports non-rectangular windows, and the X Input extension, which supports input devices other than keyboard and mouse. There is also a standard 3-D graphics extension called PEX, with two APIs called PHIGS and PEXlib. Other extensions are under development.

Extensions have both client-side and server-side code. A server vendor is not required to provide support for all the standard extensions. Therefore, before using an extension, you must query the server to see if the extension is supported. At this writing, only the Shape extension is widely supported.

1.3 X Window System Software Architecture

By now, we have described enough to draw a simple picture of the X Window System architecture (see Figure 1-3).

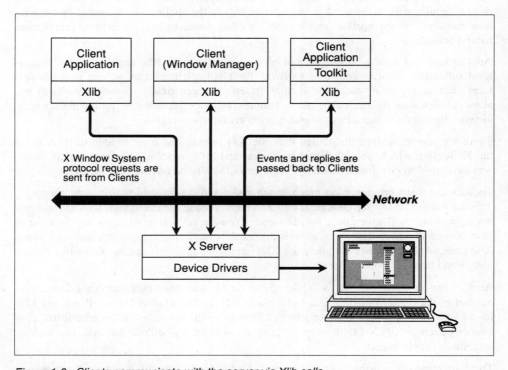

Figure 1-3. Clients communicate with the server via Xlib calls

A display server is a program that runs on each system that supports a graphics display, keyboard, and mouse. The X release from MIT includes sample monochrome and color servers for Sun, DEC, Hewlett Packard, IBM, Apple Macintosh, and many other systems. Commercially developed servers are available for virtually all major workstation vendors. In addition, companies such as Graphics Software Systems, Interactive Systems, and Locus Computing offer server implementations for IBM-compatible PCs. Finally, there are X terminals, which are screens controlled by an X server running in ROM. X terminals are available from companies such as Visual, Network Computing Devices, and GraphOn.

Applications communicate with the server by means of calls to a low-level library of C language routines known as *Xlib*.* Xlib provides functions for connecting to a particular display server, creating windows, drawing graphics, responding to events, and so on. Xlib calls are translated to protocol requests sent via tcp/ip either to the local server or to another server across the network. Some of the many sample applications available on the X release include *xterm* (a terminal emulator), *xcalc* (a calculator), *xmh* (a mail handler), *xclock* (a clock), and a troff previewer.

The window manager is just another program written with the X library, except that by convention it is given special authority to control the layout of windows on the screen.

Client is a slightly more general term than application, although they are almost synonymous. All clients except the window manager are called applications. When a statement in this manual applies only to the window manager or only to the applications managed by the window manager, the appropriate term is used. In other instances, whichever term seems more natural is used.

Applications and window managers can be written solely with Xlib or with a set of higher-level subroutine libraries known as *toolkits*. Toolkits implement a set of user interface features such as menus or command buttons (referred to generically as toolkit *widgets*) and allow applications to manipulate these features using object-oriented programming techniques. Toolkit *intrinsics* allow programmers to create new widgets.

There are several toolkits distributed with the X11 release, the most notable of them being the Xt Toolkit, which was developed by Digital and MIT, and the Interviews toolkit, which was developed by Stanford University. Xt is now officially part of the X11 standard.

Toolkits can make programming much, much easier and the finished project more thorough. Toolkits have built-in user configurability and built-in code for interaction with the window manager, which will save you a lot of trouble. You are advised to use a toolkit for most of your X programming. However, all existing toolkits in C also require or allow you to use Xlib code. And, more than that, they use Xlib internally; so understanding Xlib will help you understand how the toolkits work.

Another reason to use a toolkit is to take advantage of established user interface conventions. Several of these are available, such as OSF's Motif and Sun's OPEN LOOK. If you use Xlib for all your X programming, either you will have to reimplement one of the established conventions such as OPEN LOOK or your program will be an oddball that will not look or respond as people expect.

There are tradeoffs in using toolkits, however. One is that the executable for a given program using a toolkit is considerably larger than the equivalent program written using Xlib. Another is that the toolkits utilize highly abstract concepts and require strict programming conventions because of their object-oriented design. These take time to learn.

This manual describes how to write programs with Xlib. Other volumes in our X Window System series cover the toolkits.

---

*A low-level analog to Xlib exists for Lisp.

1.4 Overview of Xlib

Just what does the X library contain? Table 1-1 groups the Xlib routines according to their major function and lists the chapter in which the group is discussed.

Table 1-1. Xlib Routines by Function

Function Group	Description	Chapter
Color	Routines to change the way colors drawn by an application are interpreted on the screen.	Chapter 7
Cursors	Routines to change the shape and colors of the image that tracks the pointer around the screen.	Chapter 6
Data Management	Several mechanisms to associate data with windows or numbers.	Chapter 15
Display Connection	Routines to connect and disconnect an application with a display, possibly across the network.	Chapter 3
Display and Server Specifications	Macros and equivalent functions are provided that provide information about a particular server implementation and the connected display hardware.	Volume One, throughout; Volume Two, Appendix C
Drawing	Routines to draw dots, lines, rectangles, polygons, and arcs, and an analogous set to fill the last three.	Chapter 6
Errors	Routines to set the functions called when errors occur.	Chapter 2
Events	Routines to get input from the user, from other applications, and from the server. In X, these are collectively called events.	Chapter 8
Extensions	Routines to find out what extensions are available on a particular server and get information about how to use one.	Chapter 15
Fonts	Routines to list available fonts, load fonts, and find out their characteristics.	Chapter 6
Geometry	Routines to manipulate and translate geometry specifications.	Chapter 13
Graphics Context	Routines to set the way drawing requests are interpreted.	Chapter 5
Host Access	Routines to control access to a server from other machines connected in a network.	Chapter 15
Images	Routines to get, display, or manipulate screen images.	Chapter 6

Table 1-1. Xlib Routines by Function (continued)

Function Group	Description	Chapter
Interclient Communication	Routines enabling any client to make available information for any other client to read.	Chapter 12
Internationalization	Functions to handle user input and draw text independent of language.	Chapters 6, 10, and 11
Keyboard	Functions to modify the way keyboard input is handled, including the keyboard mapping.	Chapter 9
Pointer	Functions to modify the way pointer input is handled.	Chapter 9
Regions	Routines to perform mathematical operations on polygonal regions.	Chapter 6
Resource Management	Routines to make managing user preferences and command line arguments easier.	Chapter 13, Chapter 14
Screen Saver	Routines to set the operating characteristics of the daemon that blanks the screen when the keyboard and pointer have been idle for a time.	Chapter 15
Text	Routines for drawing text and for determining the size of a string to be drawn.	Chapter 6
User Preferences	Routines for setting and getting the keyboard click and auto-repeat settings.	Chapter 9
Window Attributes	Routines for setting and getting the current characteristics of a window.	Chapter 4
Window Life	Routines to create or destroy a window.	Chapter 3
Window Management	Routines to allow the manipulation of windows around the screen, changing their size, their visibility on the screen, and their apparent position above or below other windows.	Chapter 16

As you can see, Xlib provides a lot of functionality. X was designed to allow any style of user interface, and that requires a very flexible set of routines. But not all the routines are necessary or intended for writing normal applications. Many are intended for window management or for other specialized purposes.

A more detailed listing that provides the name and a brief description of the routines in each group can be found in Appendix A, *Function Group Summary*, of Volume Two, *Xlib Reference Manual*.

2

X Concepts

This chapter introduces the concepts that underlie X programming. You should read this chapter even if you are the type of person who likes to jump right into the code. (If you are desperate, you can skip ahead to Chapter 3 and return to this chapter when you get confused.) "An hour or so spent reading about the system in general can save many hours of programming that leads to a dead end when the approach turns out to be wrong."

In This Chapter:

2
X Concepts

When learning a new programming language, many programmers prefer to look at a few code samples and then begin programming right away, looking up more information as they need it. This manual is organized so that most of it is useful both as a tutorial and as a reference. There are lots of code samples and fragments in this manual to help the person who likes to read code more than words. Around the code they will find many of the concepts described that are necessary for understanding that particular example.

The "just-look-at-the-examples" approach works up to a point. It allows a sharp individual to get "something" running in a very short time. Eventually, however, programmers find that in order to get the most out of a system—and sometimes even to get it do anything useful—a lot of underlying issues must be understood. In X, there are a lot of interrelated concepts and assumptions that are so basic that the programmer should know them cold. An hour or so spent reading about the system in general can save many hours of programming that leads to a dead end when the approach turns out to be wrong.

This chapter describes those underlying issues and assumptions that are so important to programming with Xlib. It goes into considerably more detail than the brief conceptual overview provided in Chapter 1, *Introduction*. After reading this chapter, you will be well prepared to understand the rest of this manual and will have a sound idea of what is required to write an X application. This chapter describes how Xlib works, including a description of window concepts and characteristics, graphics, and events, and reviews the issues that you will need to think about in order to program.

2.1 How Xlib Works

Let's start by describing the problem that X was designed to solve and then describe how it goes about solving it.

First of all, X was designed to provide windows on bitmapped terminals. This has been done before but not in a way designed to be easily portable to many different brands of hardware, from PCs to supercomputers. The code was designed to stress easy portability, even between different operating systems, but still to allow high performance.

Second, X was designed to allow many different types of machines to cooperate within a network. This was one of the major innovations in the X design. There are several standard networking protocols, but there was lacking a widely adopted standard for a higher-level protocol specifying what should be sent over the network to drive a window system. The first thing that was determined about X was the protocol used to communicate across the network.

Third, the developers of X decided that it should not require (or even imply) a particular style of user interface. Practically speaking, X would not have been adopted as a standard by many companies if it had implied a user interface incompatible with their proprietary window systems. In addition, the developers of X felt that the issues surrounding the design of a window-based user interface for X were not sufficiently worked out at present. An important design goal was thus to make X "policy free."

To accomplish these goals, the X Window System had to be designed from the bottom up. To work over a network, there had to be programs running at both ends of the connection to send and receive the information and to interpret it. The end that controls the display and input devices was named the server. At the other end are clients—programs written using Xlib to interface with the X protocol. This is shown in Figure 2-1.

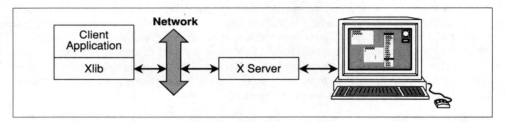

Figure 2-1. Clients and servers

Actually, although this manual describes Xlib, the C language interface to the X protocol, there is also a Lisp interface, and there are likely to be others. Any language binding that can generate and receive X protocol requests can communicate with a server and be used with the X Window System. But, at present, Xlib is the most popular low-level programming interface used with X, because C is so widely available.

2.1.1 The X Protocol

The X protocol specifies what makes up each packet of information that gets transferred between the server and Xlib in both directions. Even when the server and Xlib are running on the same machine, the protocol is used for communication, through some internal channel instead of the external network. There are four types of packets that get transferred via the protocol: requests, replies, events, and errors.

A protocol *request* is generated by Xlib and sent to the server. A protocol request can carry a wide variety of information, such as a specification for drawing a line or changing the color value in a cell in a colormap or an inquiry about the current size of a window. Most Xlib routines generate protocol requests. The exceptions are routines that only affect data structures local to Xlib and do not affect the server (regions and the resource manager are the primary examples of these exceptions).

A protocol *reply* is sent from the server to Xlib in response to certain requests. Not all requests are answered by replies—only the ones that request information. Requests that specify drawing, for example, do not generate replies. When Xlib receives a reply, it places the requested data into the arguments or returned value of the Xlib routine that generated the request. An Xlib routine that requires a reply is called a *round-trip request*. Round-trip requests have to be minimized in clients because they lower performance when there are network delays.

An *event* is sent from the server to Xlib and contains information about a device action or about a side effect of a previous request. The data contained in events is quite varied, because it is the principal method by which clients get information. Events are kept in a queue in Xlib and can be read one at a time by the client. The range of types of events that the server sends to a client is specified by the client.

An *error* tells the client that a previous request was invalid. An error is like an event, but it is handled slightly differently within Xlib. Errors cannot be read by the Xlib calls that read events. Instead, errors are sent to an error-handling routine in Xlib. The default error handler simply prints a message and exits; it can be replaced by a client-specific error-handling routine.

2.1.2 Buffering

Xlib saves up requests instead of sending them to the server immediately, so that the client program can continue running instead of waiting to gain access to the network after every Xlib call. This is possible because most Xlib calls do not require immediate action by the server. This grouping of requests by the client before sending them over the network also increases the performance of most networks, because it makes the network transactions longer and less numerous, reducing the total overhead involved.

Xlib sends the buffer full of requests to the server under three conditions. The most common is when an application calls an Xlib routine to wait for an event but no matching event is currently available on Xlib's queue. Since, in this case, the application must wait for an appropriate event anyway, it makes sense to flush the request buffer. Second, Xlib calls that get information from the server require a reply before the program can continue, and therefore, the request buffer is sent and all the requests acted on before the information is returned. Third, the client would like to be able to flush the request buffer manually in situations where no user events and no calls to query the server are expected. One good example of this third case is an animated game, where the display changes even when there is no user input.

Let's look at how this works in practice. When the application starts up, all the requests that create the initial appearance of the application are queued up by Xlib. Then the application goes into its event loop and calls **XNextEvent()**. Since nothing has yet been sent to the server, there are no windows and therefore no events have yet been generated. So **XNext-Event()** causes all the requests to be sent to the server, displaying the application. Meanwhile, the application is still waiting for the first user input. When the user moves the mouse or presses a button or key, the server, sends the events to Xlib as soon as the network allows—it does not queue them or group them (except under rare conditions involving grabs discussed in Section 9.4). Normally, once an event arrives, the application generates more requests to draw—for example, highlighting the border of a button. These stay queued in Xlib until all the events that have already arrived have been processed. Once the application arrives at `XNextEvent( )` and no more events are in the queue, the queued requests are sent to the server and the process starts again.

Using Xlib calls, the client can flush the connection in three ways: by calling a routine that requires an immediate reply (a routine with `Query`, `Fetch`, or `Get` in its name); by calling certain event-reading routines when no matching event exists on Xlib's queue; or by calling the routines `XFlush` or `XSync( )`.* The first of these actions says to the server, "I need some information; please act on these requests right away and then give me the information." The second says, "I'm waiting for a certain kind of event, so I'll check if you already sent the event over to Xlib. If not, please act on these requests immediately, and then I'll be waiting for the event." The last one says, "I don't need any information from you now, but I need you to act on these requests immediately." Normally, the last method is not used much because there are enough of the first two types of Xlib calls in the client to make the transactions frequent enough.

You should already know that Xlib maintains a queue of the events for each server to which an application is connected, as shown in Figure 2-2. Whenever events arrive from the server, they are queued until the client reads them.

The fact that Xlib queues both input and output is very important in application programming and especially in debugging. It means that drawing requests will not appear in a window until the request buffer is flushed. It means that errors are not discovered by the server until the requests arrive at the server and are processed, which happens only after Xlib flushes the request buffer. Once discovered, the error is reported immediately to the client. In other words, several Xlib routines may be called before an error caused by an earlier routine is reported. These are two of the most visible examples of the effects of buffering. See Section 2.6.3 for more details on how buffering affects programming and debugging.

2.1.3 Resources

X uses several techniques to reduce network traffic. One major technique is to have the server maintain complex abstractions such as windows or fonts and have the client allocate an integer ID number for each one as a nickname. Each of these abstractions is called a *resource*. A resource can be a window, pixmap, colormap, cursor, font, or graphics context (these will be described in a moment).

---

*In this manual, whenever you see typewriter font (such as that used for the routine `XSync( )`), it means this word would be typed verbatim into C code as a symbol, structure name, structure member, or Xlib routine. Italic typewriter font is used for dummy arguments to Xlib routines, since they could be typed into code as shown but are arbitrary. The argument names used in this volume are the same as the names used on the reference pages in Volume Two, *Xlib Reference Manual*.

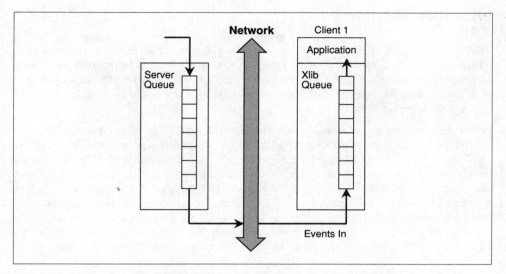

Figure 2-2. The server's event queue and a client's event queue

Whenever an operation is to be performed on a window (or any other resource), the ID of the window is used in one argument to the Xlib routine. This means that instead of an entire structure full of data being sent over the network with an Xlib routine call, only a single integer that refers to that structure need be sent. Remember that since the client and the server may be running on different machines, pointers cannot be used to refer to structures. The caveat of the resource approach is that the client must query the server when it needs information about resources, which, as mentioned above, leads to network delays. As it turns out, clients normally do not need to query the server very often, and the resource abstraction greatly simplifies programs.

If any client knows the ID of a resource, that client can manipulate that resource even if some other client created the resource. That means that more than one client can draw into the same window, although that is not often desirable. More importantly, this is how window managers are implemented—they can move and resize application windows because they know the IDs.

Be warned that there is another use of the term "resource" in X that pertains to the resource manager. A resource in the context of the resource manager is a user-preference specification that controls user-customizable elements of an application. Fortunately, these two uses of the term resource apply to different parts of X and therefore are not too difficult to keep separate. One use applies to server-maintained data structures, and the other to user customization of an application.

2.1.4 Properties and Atoms

The developers of X needed a way to allow clients to communicate arbitrary data with each other, and they came up with properties. A *property* is a packet of information associated with a window, made available to all the clients running under a server. Properties are used by clients to store information that other clients might need or want to know and to read that information when set by other clients.

Properties have a string name and a numerical identifier called an atom. An *atom* is an ID that uniquely identifies a particular property. Property name strings are typically all upper case, with words separated by underscores, such as "WM_COLORMAP_WINDOWS". Atoms are used to refer to properties in routine calls so arbitrary-length property name strings do not need to be sent over the network. An application gets the atom for a property by calling `XInternAtom()`. You specify the string name for the property as an argument to `XInternAtom()`, and it returns the atom. From this point on, the application uses only the atom to refer to that property. Every application that uses this procedure will get the same atom for the same property name string, if it is connected to the same server (that has not been reset).

Some atoms, called *predefined atoms*, are defined when the server initializes. An application does not need to use `XInternAtom()` to get these atoms. Instead, these atoms are available as symbolic constants beginning with `XA_`. These atoms identify properties whose contents have a certain meaning known by convention to all clients. The properties themselves do not have any contents until a client or the window manager sets them. Some of the properties described in this manual have predefined atoms and others do not, for historical reasons. Where predefined atoms are available, such as `XA_WM_HINTS`, we will use them in the text to refer to the property. For properties with no predefined atoms, we will use the string property name such as WM_COLORMAP_WINDOWS, which does not begin with XA_ and is not in Courier typeface. This tells you whether you will need to call `XInternAtom()` before using the property.

A group of related clients or an extension may define other properties and atoms that will have a meaning known to all the clients in the group or using the extension.

Atoms for properties are analogous to the IDs used to refer to server resources, except that both an atom and a window are needed to uniquely identify a property. The same atom would be used to identify a property on one window as on another—only the window is different in the calls to set or read this property on two windows. Only the type `Atom` is ever used in client code; properties are the underlying data managed by the server.

One of the most important uses of properties is to communicate information from applications to the window manager and vice versa. The application sets the *standard properties* on its top-level window to specify the range of sizes it prefers for its top-level window and other information. These properties are called "standard" because they are the minimum set that an application should specify. Properties also communicate the other way; for example, the window manager specifies what sizes of icon pixmaps it prefers.

For more information on properties and atoms, see Section 12.1.

2.1.5 The Window Manager

The window manager is just another client written with Xlib, but by convention, it is given special responsibilities. It mediates competing demands for the physical resources of a display, including screen space and the colormap. Usually it has a user interface to allow the user to move windows about on the screen, resize them, and start new applications.

Most window managers decorate the main windows of all applications with a titlebar and various tools for iconifying and resizing the application. The window manager does this by creating a separate window that fits behind the main window of each application. It is this separate window that has the decorations on it. This is important mainly because your application code does not need to handle this drawing. Figure 2-3 shows the titlebar added to an application by *twm*, the standard window manager in the MIT distribution as of R4.

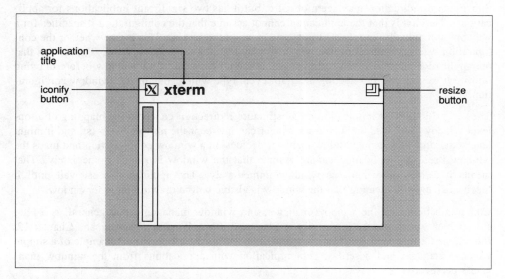

application title

iconify button

resize button

Figure 2-3. Titlebar added to applications by the twm window manager

Much of the communication between clients and the window manager and vice versa occurs through properties (the rest occurring through events). Many of the properties are known as *hints* because they may not necessarily be honored by the window manager, even if one is running. An application must be prepared for the window manager to ignore, modify, or honor the preferences it indicates through the window manager hints. The properties themselves do not have valid contents until applications or the window manager set them.

Quite a few of the features of Xlib (and the X protocol) exist only to give the window manager the mechanism to enforce its authority. These are described in Appendix L, *Interclient Communication Conventions*, of Volume Zero, *X Protocol Reference Manual* (as of the second printing). They will not be needed by normal applications.

One such feature is called *substructure redirection*. Substructure refers to the size, position, and overlapping order of the children of a window. Redirection refers to the requests by applications to change the configuration of these windows being sent to the window manager for approval instead of actually getting acted upon by the server. Substructure redirection allows a window manager to intercept any request by an application to change the size, position, border width, or stacking order (known collectively as the window configuration) of its top-level windows on the screen. Any application request to change the configuration of its top-level window will be canceled, and instead an event will be sent to the window manager indicating the arguments used in the reconfiguration request. The window manager can then decide what size, position, and stacking order to grant the application, and the window manager will reconfigure the window to those dimensions. For temporary windows such as pop-up menus and dialog boxes, the substructure redirect feature can be turned off using a window attribute.

Substructure redirection may seem obscure, but it has two significant implications for applications. The first is that the application cannot assume that the configuration it specifies for a window will actually be reflected in the window on the screen. This is true whether the configuration was set by creating the window or by reconfiguring the window. That means that the application must always determine the new configuration of the window before drawing into it. It can do this by selecting a certain event type which contains the window configuration.

The second important implication of substructure redirection concerns the mapping of a top-level window. Because the window manager can intercept the mapping request, and it might take some time before the window manager decides on a window configuration and maps the window itself, an application cannot assume that the window is visible immediately. That means it cannot draw into the window immediately. The application must wait until it receives an event indicating that the window is visible before drawing into the window.

Communicating with the window manager, and window management in general, is a long story which we'll describe more fully in Chapter 3, *Basic Window Program*, and Chapter 12, *Interclient Communication*. Chapter 16, *Window Management*, gives an example of a simple window manager and describes communication with applications from the window manager's perspective.

Most window managers today also have the ability to start and kill applications. This is known a session management. However, they can usually start only *xterm* and a few other basic clients. A true *session manager* can be a separate client. It would be able to start any client and control its command line arguments and save the state of a whole group of clients (before the user logs out) and later restore them to the same position on the screen (when the user logs back in). This level of capability is not yet available (but people are working on it). Each application supplies its command line as a hint so that the window or session manager has enough information to restart it in its current state.

Now you should have an idea of how Xlib works. Let's move on to a description of windows.

2.2 What are X Windows?

An X server controls a bitmapped screen. In order to make it easier to view and control many different tasks at the same time, this screen can be divided up into smaller areas called windows. A window is a rectangular area that works in several ways like a miniature screen. Windows on the screen can be arranged so they all are visible or so they cover each other completely or partially. A window may be any size greater than zero.

Each window (on a screen running X) can be involved in a different activity, and the windows currently in use are placed so they are at least partially visible. The window manager lets you move a different window to the top when necessary or rearrange the size and position of the windows.

What you may not have realized is that some of these windows, such as the ones created by the mail handler *xmh*, are made up of many layered windows of various sizes. The scrollbars, titlebar, command buttons, and other features of the user interface are actually separate windows that provide information to the user or allow for input providing convenient control, as shown in Figure 2-4. There is more here than meets the eye.

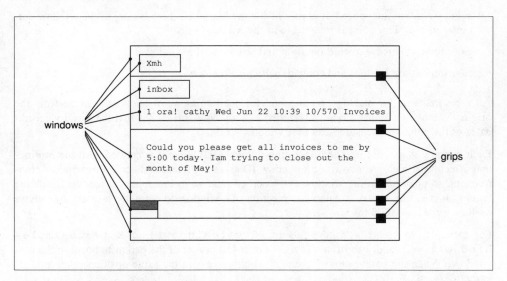

Figure 2-4. The windows used to create an instance of the xmh application

2.2.1 Window Characteristics*

What are the characteristics of a window? There are many.

First of all, a window always has a *parent* window, which is assigned as the window is created. Each window is contained within the limits of its parent. The window cannot display output in areas outside itself and cannot receive input from the keyboard or the pointer while the pointer is outside itself (unless a *grab* or *keyboard focus* is in effect, as described in Sections 8.3.2.1 and 8.3.2.2). Every window fits in a hierarchy set up by its children, its parent, its parent's parent, and so on. The very first window, the only one that has no parent, is called the root window and fills the entire screen. The root window is created by the X server as it starts up.

Second, each window has its own coordinate system. As shown in Figure 2-5, the origin of a window is the top-left corner of the window and the x and y coordinates increase to the right and bottom.

In the X Window System:

* The horizontal axis is x, and the vertical axis is y.

* x and y are 0 at the upper-left corner inside the border (if there is one) of the window currently in use. This point is referred to as the window's *origin*.

* Coordinates increase toward the right and bottom of the window.

* Coordinates are integral and coincide with pixel centers.

All measurements for placing graphics and for positioning subwindows are made from the origin. When we say that a point is *relative to* a window, this means that the x and y coordinates of the point are measured from the window's origin.

Each window is given a unique identifying number (ID) when it is created. All the routines that affect a particular window use a window ID as an argument and act in this window environment, so positions in the window are specified relative to the upper-left corner inside the border. It is not necessary to know the position of a window to correctly locate subwindows or draw graphics within the window.

For example, to create a window using **XCreateWindow()** or **XCreateSimple-Window()**, you supply an offset from the upper-left corner of the parent to position the new window. When the parent moves, the new window stays in the same position relative to its parent.

Third, a window has a *position*, which locates its upper-left corner relative to its parent's corner, a certain *width* and *height* of usable pixels within the border, and a *border width*. These characteristics are shown in Figure 2-5. By convention, the window width and height do not include the border. Since several windows may have the same parent, a window must also have a *stacking order* among these windows to determine which will be visible if they over-

---

*Do read this section even if you are already familiar with windowing systems, to make sure you understand X's particular implementation of windowing.

lap. These four characteristics are collectively known as the *window configuration* because they affect the layout of windows on the screen.

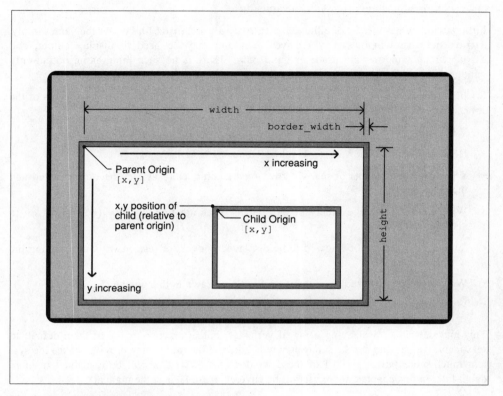

Figure 2-5. Elements of the window configuration

To summarize, the window configuration includes:

- A window's width and height in pixels, not including the border.

- A window's border. It can vary in width; zero makes the border invisible.

- A window's particular position on the screen, specified by *x* and *y* in pixels, measured from the origin of the parent (the upper-left corner, inside the border) to the upper-left corner of the child, outside its border.

- A window's particular stacking order among the windows with the same parent.

The width, height, and position are collectively called the window *geometry*. Applications often allow users to specify the geometry and border width of the window as a command line argument or through the user defaults mechanism.

Fourth, a window has characteristics referred to as *depth* and *visual*, which together determine its color characteristics. The depth is the number of bits available for each pixel to represent color (or gray scales). The visual represents the way pixel values are translated to produce color or monochrome output on the monitor.

Fifth, a window has a *class* of either `InputOutput` or `InputOnly`. As the names imply, `InputOutput` windows may receive input and may be used to display output, and `InputOnly` windows are used for input only. There is no such thing as an output-only window because certain types of input, called events, are needed by all windows.

Sixth, a window has a set of *attributes*. The window attributes control many aspects of the appearance and response of the window:

- What color or pattern is used for the border and background of the window?

- How are partial window contents relocated during resizing?

- When are the contents of the window saved automatically as they become covered and then exposed?

- Which event types are received, and which types are thrown away (not passed on to ancestor windows)?

- Should this window be allowed to be displayed, moved, or resized without notifying the window manager?

- Which colormap is used to interpret pixel values drawn in this window?

- Which cursor should be displayed when the pointer is in this window?

This may seem like a dizzying array of variables, but in practice, many of them default to reasonable values and can be safely ignored. And the flexibility they provide makes the system much more powerful. All of these window characteristics will be explained in more detail later in this chapter, and most will be covered again later in the manual.

But first, a little more detail is necessary on the basic framework of X: the window hierarchy, the stacking order, and the concept of wrapping. These are the subjects of the next three sections.

2.2.2 Window Hierarchy

Windows are arranged in a hierarchy like a family tree, except that only one parent is required to create a child window. There is a separate hierarchy for each screen. At the top is the *root* window, which fills the entire screen and is created when the server initializes. The first windows to be created by each client are children of the root window. In the client's first call to `XCreateWindow()` or `XCreateSimpleWindow()` (either of which creates a new window), the root window is the parent.

The children of the root window are special, because they are the top-level windows of each application and they are managed by the window manager. Chapter 3, *Basic Window Program*, describes the special procedures required of a client before displaying, moving, or resizing this window.

Each child may also have its own child windows. These child windows of the top-level windows are used to create application features like command buttons and scrollbars.

Figure 2-6 shows a window hierarchy as it might appear on the screen, and Figure 2-7 shows the same hierarchy in schematic form. Note that the windows A through G represent subwindows of each application, which may not overlap like this in real applications. Normally the subwindows are used as command buttons or panes which are laid out in non-overlapping fashion, as was shown in Figure 2-4. However, this hypothetical hierarchy serves to demonstrate the effects of the stacking order and the window hierarchy.

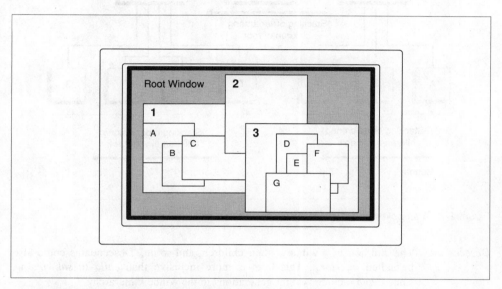

Figure 2-6. A sample window hierarchy on the screen

A child may be positioned partially or completely outside its parent window, but output to the child is displayed and input received only in the area where the child overlaps with the parent. Figure 2-6 shows that the child windows do not extend beyond the borders of the parent even when they are positioned in such a way that they would otherwise overlap the parent's edge. (For example, in Figure 2-6, window G will not be drawn beyond the bottom of window 3 even if its height would suggest that it should.) If a window is moved in such a way that it would extend beyond the parent, it is clipped, so that only the part overlapping the parent is displayed.

These are the terms used to describe subsets of the window hierarchy:

Parent   The window used when creating a child window.

Child   A window created with another window as parent.

Subwindow   Synonymous with child. Not the same as descendant.

Siblings   Windows created with the same parent (brothers and sisters).

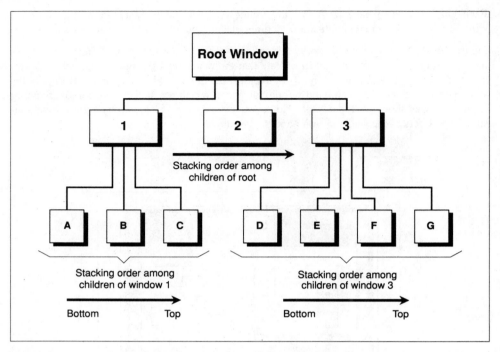

Figure 2-7. A sample window hierarchy in schematic form

Descendants The children of a window, their children, and so on. Descendants could also be called *inferiors*. This term is more inclusive than *child* or *subwindow*, since it can include several generations in the window hierarchy.

Ancestors The parent of a window, its parent, and so on, including the root window. Ancestors could also be called *superiors*.

2.2.3 Window Stacking Order

When one window overlaps one of its sibling windows, the one on top obscures part of the other. The stacking order determines which window appears on top. This order can be changed with various routines to raise, lower, or circulate windows relative to their siblings. These routines affect only a group of siblings and their descendants but not their ancestors.

Child windows always stay in front of their parent. When a window with children is moved in the stacking order, all its child windows move with it, just as they do (because of the window-based coordinate system) when the parent is moved around the screen.

Figures 2-6 and 2-7 showed a set of windows on the screen and their hierarchy, and if you look carefully, you can see how the stacking order affects each group of sibling windows. Notice that window *2* is above window *C* and all the other children of window *1*.

2.2.4 Mapping and Visibility

A newly created window does not immediately appear on the screen. It is an abstract entity that cannot be drawn to (unless a backing store feature—discussed later in this section—is implemented on that server and turned on with the appropriate window attribute). *Mapping* marks a window as eligible for display. If it is not obscured by siblings or siblings of ancestors, it may be visible, and only then can it be drawn to.

`XMapWindow()` maps a window in its current position in the stacking order, while `XMap-Raised()` places the window at the top of the stacking order of its siblings before mapping it. For a new window never mapped before, these two calls are equivalent, since the initial stacking position of a new window is on top.

You must map a window before you have any chance of seeing it, but that alone is not enough. A number of factors can affect whether any window, newly created or already mapped, is visible:

1. The window must be mapped with `XMapWindow()` or related routines.

2. All of the window's ancestors must be mapped.

3. The window must not be obscured by visible sibling windows or siblings of ancestors. If sibling windows are overlapping, whether or not a window is obscured depends on the stacking order. The stacking order can be manipulated with `XCirculate-Subwindows()`, `XConfigureWindow()`, and `XRestackWindows()`.

4. The request buffer must be flushed by a routine that gets events, with a call to `XFlush()`, or by a function that requests information from the server. More information on this topic was provided in Section 2.1.2.

5. The initial mapping of a top-level window is a special case, since the window's visibility may be delayed by the window manager due to substructure redirection that was briefly described in Section 2.1.5. For complicated reasons, a client must wait for the first `Expose` event before assuming that its window is visible and drawing into it. It is not important to understand why this is true at this point.

An important consequence of these rules, and one of the reasons for them, is that unmapping a window (with `XUnmapWindow()`) erases the window and all its descendants from the screen. X allows you (or, actually, the window manager) to control the placement and visibility of an entire client made up of a hierarchy of windows simply by manipulating the top-level window.

The window configuration and window attributes are maintained when a window is unmapped. But it is important to remember that the X server does not automatically preserve the visible contents of a window. Graphic operations on a window that is not visible or that is unmapped have no effect. Graphics visible in a window will be erased when that window is obscured and then exposed. For these reasons, it is important for the client to be prepared to redraw the contents of the window on demand, as described in Section 2.5.

On some high performance servers, a "backing store" feature is available that maintains the window contents when a window is unmapped or covered by other windows, so that the window is automatically refreshed with the current contents when it becomes visible again.

This feature is expensive in terms of computing resources and should be invoked only for windows whose contents are difficult to recreate. On many types of equipment, this feature is not supported, so for the sake of portability, programs should be capable of recreating the contents of their windows in other ways. This portability is particularly important in X, because network environments often employ various brands of equipment.

Mapping is done with the **XMapWindow()** or **XMapSubwindows()** routines. Unmapping is done with the **XUnmapWindow()** or **XUnmapSubwindows()** routines.

2.3 Introduction to X Graphics

This section provides a brief introduction to the terms and concepts used in graphics under the X Window System. You will see these terms used in Chapters 3 and 4 before we get to a serious treatment of graphics in Chapters 5, 6, and 7.

2.3.1 Pixels and Colors

The X Window System is designed to control bitmapped graphics displays. In the simplest black-and-white display, there is a single bit per pixel: the state of that bit determines whether the pixel will be black or white. In color systems or on monochrome systems allowing gray-scale displays, there are multiple bits per pixel.

The state of the multiple bits assigned to each pixel does not directly control the color or gray-scale intensity of that pixel. Instead they are used as an index to a lookup table called a *colormap*, as shown in Figure 2-8. On a color display, a pixel consists of separate red, green, and blue phosphors, each sensitive to a separate electron beam; the relative intensity of these three colors fools the eye into thinking it sees a single color. Accordingly, the colormap contains an array of red, green, and blue (RGB) triples. In other words, if the value of the bits for a given pixel (a *pixel value*) is 14, the RGB values of the fourteenth member of the colormap will be displayed at that location on the screen.

Each member of a colormap is called a *colorcell*, each of which translates a pixel value into a specified set of red, green, and blue values. All bitmapped displays have at least one hardware colormap, though in the case of a single-plane monochrome screen, it may consist of only two colorcells. In most cases, all clients share the single colormap by allocating only the number of colorcells they need and sharing as many as possible. When clients have special requirements, however, X allows them to have private colorcells or to create virtual colormaps which are then swapped into the hardware colormap (if it is writable) when necessary.

Note that each window can potentially specify a different colormap. This is the significance of the fact that the colormap is a window attribute.

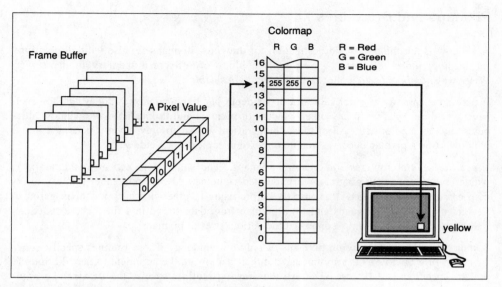

Figure 2-8. Mapping of pixel value into color through colormap

2.3.2 Pixels and Planes

The number of bits per pixel is also referred to as the number of *planes* in the graphics display. Black-and-white systems have a single plane, color displays have from 4 to 28 planes, and gray-scale displays usually have from 2 to 4 planes. X11 supports up to 32 planes.

As can be inferred from the previous discussion of bits per pixel as an index to the colormap, the number of possible colors or shades of gray that can be *simultaneously* displayed on the screen is 2^n, where *n* is the number of planes in the display. (Of course, additional colors can be made available even on a system with only a few planes, at the cost of existing colors, simply by loading different RGB values into the hardware colormap if it is writable.)

All graphics calculations are performed on the pixel values before they are translated into RGB. The *source* pixel values specified in a drawing request and the *old destination* pixel values are combined according to a plane mask, clip mask, and logical function to arrive at the final *destination* pixel values. The plane mask, clip mask, and logical function are aspects of a structure called the graphics context (GC) and are described in Chapter 5, *The Graphics Context*.

The macros `BlackPixel()` and `WhitePixel()` return pixel values that map to black and white using the default colormap for that screen. These macros are intended for use in monochrome programs so that they will work on monochrome, gray-scale, or color displays. On color hardware, the colors of black and white may not actually be black and white, but they are guaranteed to be contrasting.

2.3.3 Pixmaps and Drawables

A window is not the only valid destination for drawing. Pixmaps are also valid destinations for most graphics requests. A *pixmap* is a block of off-screen memory in the server. Windows and pixmaps are collectively known as *drawables*.

A pixmap is an array of pixel values. It has a depth just like a window. It does not, however, have a position relative to any other window or pixmap, and it does not have window attributes such as a colormap. All of those things affect a pixmap only when it is copied into a window. And a pixmap becomes visible only when copied to a window.

There are several routines for creating pixmaps. The simplest is **XCreatePixmap()**, which creates an empty pixmap with undefined contents. Always remember to clear a pixmap created with **XCreatePixmap()** before using it, otherwise it may contain garbage. Several others create pixmaps and fill a pixmap from data stored in a file. These functions will be mentioned later in the context of the various uses of pixmaps.

Some routines operate only on pixmaps or only on windows. These routines specify either **Pixmap** or **Window** as the argument. If either is allowed, the argument to the Xlib routine will be specified as a **Drawable**. All the drawing routines specify the **Drawable** argument type.

A pixmap is not susceptible to being covered by other windows. Windows, on the other hand, may only be drawn to usefully when they are visible, since their contents are not maintained when they are obscured or unmapped (unless the backing store feature is available and in effect).

To be copied to a window with **XCopyArea()**, a pixmap must have the same depth as the window it is to be copied to. Once copied, the colormap associated with the window is used to translate the pixel values from the pixmap to visible colors. After copying, additional drawing into the pixmap does *not* appear in the window. A single plane of a pixmap of any depth can be copied into any window with **XCopyPlane()**.

In short, windows have the disadvantage that, when they are not visible, drawing to them will not do anything. A pixmap, which represents an area of the screen, resides in memory and can be drawn to at any time. Unfortunately, pixmaps must be copied into a visible window before the user can see them. This copying can have performance penalties. Perhaps more importantly, off-screen memory in the server used for pixmaps may be limited in quantity. Therefore, programs that use a lot of pixmaps may not work on PC servers and X terminals.

A pixmap of depth 1 is known as a *bitmap*, though there is no separate type or resource called Bitmap. A bitmap is a two-dimensional array of bits used for many purposes including cursor definitions, fonts, and templates for two-color pictures. Each bit represents a single pixel value that is either set (1) or unset (0). Depending on the visual type, these pixel values can be interpreted as two colors or simply as black and white.

2.3.4 Drawing and the Graphics Context

As in any graphics language, X provides routines for drawing points, lines, rectangles, polygons, arcs, text, and so on. Routines that draw graphics are generically called *graphics primitives*. But in X, a given graphics primitive does not contain all the information needed to draw a particular graphic. A server resource called the *graphics context* (GC) specifies the remaining variables, such as the line width, colors, and fill patterns. The ID of a GC is specified as an argument to the drawing routine and modifies the appearance of everything that is drawn into the drawable.

The GC must be created by the client before any drawing is done. The created GC is stored in the server, so that the information it contains does not have to be sent with every graphics primitive—only its ID is passed. This improves the performance of drawing significantly since it reduces the traffic over the connection between Xlib and the server. All GC settings apply to all graphics drawn using that GC.

More than one GC can be created, and each can be set with different values. This allows a program to switch between GCs and get different effects with the same graphics primitive.

2.3.5 Tiles and Stipples

When pixmaps are used for patterning an area, such as for the background of a window or in a GC, they are often referred to as tiles or stipples.

A *tile* is a pixmap with the same depth as the drawable it is used to pattern. The tile is typically 16 by 16 pixels but can be other sizes—certain sizes are drawn faster—depending on the hardware (see `XQueryBestTile()`). It is typically composed of only two different pixel values since this is the easiest type to create, but multiple pixel values are permitted. Areas drawn by any of the drawing routines can be tiled by placing certain values in the GC. The background and border of windows can be tiled by specifying a pixmap in the window attributes.

A *stipple* is a pixmap of depth 1. A stipple is used in conjunction with a foreground pixel value and sometimes a background pixel value to pattern an area in a way similar to a tile. There are two styles of stippling that can be set in the graphics context. In one, set bits in the stipple are drawn in the foreground color and unset bits are drawn in the background color. In the other, only the set bits in the stipple are drawn in the foreground pixel value, and the pixels in the destination represented by unset bits in the stipple are not changed. Like tiling, stippling affects only those pixels that are selected by the graphics request, such as the pixels drawn for a line or a character. Stipples are only present in the GC and cannot be used for window backgrounds.

Figure 2-9 shows how a tile is used to pattern the background of a window.

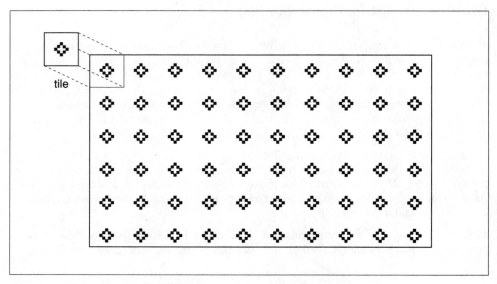

Figure 2-9. Tiling of a window background

2.4 More on Window Characteristics

This section expands on the overview of window characteristics in Section 2.2.1 and describes in more detail the window attributes, window configuration, class, and depth and visual.

2.4.1 Window Attributes

The window attributes consist of information about how a window is to look and act. Each window has a separate set of attributes, which can be set with **XChangeWindow-Attributes()** or, in some cases, with routines that change individual attributes. The attributes control the following window features:

Background   Can be a solid color, a tiled pixmap, or transparent.

Border   Can be a solid color or a tiled pixmap.

Bit Gravity   Determines how partial window contents are preserved when a window is resized.

Window Gravity   Determines how child windows are relocated when a window is resized.

Backing Store   Provides hints about when a window's contents should be automatically saved while the window is unmapped or obscured, which display planes should be saved, and what pixel value is to be used when restoring unsaved planes. Not all servers are capable of backing. Check the value returned from the `DoesBackingStore()` macro to determine whether this feature is supported on a particular screen on your server.

Saving Under
Provides hints about whether or not the screen area beneath a window should be saved while a window, such as a pop-up menu, is in place to save obscured windows from having to redraw themselves when the pop up is removed. Not all servers can save under windows. You can find out whether this feature is supported on a particular screen with the `Does-SaveUnders()` macro.

Events
Indicate which events should be received and which events should not be sent to ancestor windows.

Substructure Redirect Override
Determines whether this window should be allowed to be mapped on the screen without intervention by the window manager. This override is usually done for menus and other windows that are frequently mapped and then almost immediately unmapped again.

Colormap
Determines which virtual colormap should be used for this window.

Cursor
Determines which cursor should be displayed when the pointer is in this window.

It may clarify the picture to describe the features that window attributes *do not* affect. Setting the window attributes does not determine the size or position of a window, its parent, or its border width; these comprise the window configuration. Setting the window attributes does not affect the depth, class, or visual of a window; these are permanently set when the window is created. Attributes do not determine how graphics requests are interpreted; this is the job of the graphics context (GC).

2.4.2 Window Configuration

A window's configuration consists of its position, width and height, border width, and stacking position, as described in Section 2.2.1. These factors are handled differently from the window attributes (even though they are stored internally in the `XWindowAttributes` structure) for an important reason: changing the configuration of a top-level window (a child of the root window) must be done in cooperation with the window manager.

We will not go into detail here about how the application must interact with the window manager when attempting to map a window or change a window's configuration. For now, suffice it to say that there are certain rules the application must follow so that the window manager can be responsible for controlling what is on the screen and where. See Chapter 3, *Basic Window Program*, for an introduction to client-window manager interaction and Chapter 12, *Interclient Communication*, for a complete description.

2.4.3 Class: InputOutput and InputOnly Windows

The X Window System provides two classes of windows: `InputOutput` and `Input-Only`. The main difference between the two classes is that an `InputOnly` window cannot be used as a drawable (a destination for a graphics request). Consequently, `InputOnly` windows have a more limited set of window attributes, have no border and a transparent background, and cannot have `InputOutput` windows as children.

`InputOnly` windows make an invisible area of the screen in which input has a different purpose but the display is not changed. `InputOnly` windows usually are assigned a different cursor to distinguish them. `InputOnly` windows are rarely used.

The class of a window is assigned at creation and cannot be changed.

2.4.4 Depth and Visual

The depth and visual of a window are assigned at creation and cannot be changed. The depth is the number of planes that are to be used to represent gray scales or color within a window; depth is also the number of bits per pixel. The maximum depth allowable for an `Input-Output` window is the number of planes supported by the screen with which it is associated. If a screen has 12 planes, a window may have at most 12 bits per pixel, and therefore there are at most 2^{12} possible different shades of gray or color.

The depth of an `InputOnly` window is always 0. For `InputOutput` windows, the symbol `CopyFromParent`, when used as the *depth* argument in `XCreateWindow()`, copies the depth of the parent window. Most windows use the default depth, inherited from the root window.

The visual accounts for the differences between various types of display hardware in determining the way pixel values are translated into visible colors within a particular window. A screen may support only one visual or several types of visuals. An `XVisualInfo` structure contains all the information about a particular visual. One member of `XVisualInfo` is the visual class, which has one of the values `DirectColor`, `GrayScale`, `PseudoColor`, `StaticColor`, `StaticGray`, or `TrueColor`. These values specify the characteristics of the colormaps that can be used with the window—whether the colormap is read-only or read/write, color or monochrome, split into three primary colors or composite. Other members of `XVisualInfo` specify the valid range of pixel values; how many bits of the pixel are allocated to red, green, and blue; and several other variables.

Both the depth and visual are inherited from the parent when a window is created with `XCreateSimpleWindow()`. For more information on the visual class, see Chapter 7, *Color*.

2.4.5 Icons

An *icon* is a small marker window that indicates that a larger "main" window exists and is available but is not currently mapped on the screen.

Most window managers allow the user to *iconify* an application to get it out of the way without destroying it. Deiconifying an application is faster and more convenient than running the application from scratch. Also, the iconified application keeps running whatever processes it was at work on when iconified (unless the application is programmed to halt when it is iconified). When input is required, the program may either wait until the window is deiconified or accept input in the icon.

Figure 2-10 shows an *xterm* window before and after it is iconified. The *xterm* application does not create an icon pixmap, and therefore, the window manager *uwm* simply draws its icon name into the icon. The appearance and placement of icons varies between window managers.

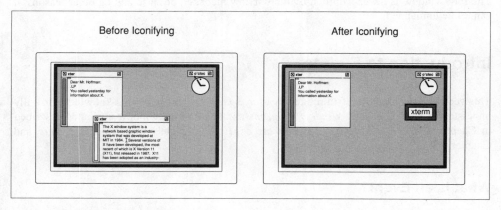

Figure 2-10. An application and its icon

Icon windows are managed and, in many cases, created by the window manager. Through the window manager hints (which will be detailed in Section 3.2.8 and Chapter 12, *Interclient Communication*), an application passes its icon's name and pixmap to be displayed in the icon window. If an application needs to perform operations on its own icon window (perhaps to be able to change the background at any time, as the mail handler *xmh* does to indicate that mail has arrived), it can create its own icon window and pass the window ID to the window manager. Otherwise, the window manager will create the icon window.

The window manager may specify in a property on the root window what sizes of icon pixmaps it prefers. If this property is set, the application should attempt to provide an icon pixmap of an acceptable size. The window manager may also specify where icons will be placed. These are optional features of the window manager that may not be present. In fact, most current window managers do not specify icon sizes or control icon location.

2.4.6 Special Characteristics of the Root Window

The root window is created when the X server program is initialized. The root window's characteristics differ slightly from those of other windows.

The root window is an **InputOutput** window. It is always mapped. Its size cannot be changed. Its upper-left corner is always at the upper-left corner of the screen, where the global coordinates are (0,0). The root window has a zero-width border. Its size is accessible through macros that will be described in Chapter 3, *Basic Window Program.*

The default window attributes of the root window include a background pixmap with diagonal cross-hatchings, the default colormap, and a default cursor that is a large X. Any of these can be changed. The event mask attribute can be changed, but by default, no events that occur in the root window are sent to any client. None of the other attributes are applicable to the root window. See Chapter 4, *Window Attributes*, for more information on setting window attributes.

The root window is never iconified by the window manager, because among other reasons, it cannot be unmapped.

2.5 Introduction to Events

This section provides a brief introduction to events. You will need this knowledge to fully understand Chapter 3, *Basic Window Program*, and some of the window attributes described in Chapter 4, *Window Attributes*. Events are covered completely in Chapter 8, *Events*, and Chapter 9, *The Keyboard and Pointer*.

2.5.1 What is an Event?

Moving the pointer or pressing a keyboard key causes an input event to occur. These are two of the simplest and most common event types, but there are many others. An event is a packet of information that is generated by the server when certain actions occur and is queued for later use by the client. The queued events can be read at any subsequent time in any order, but they are usually read and processed in the order in which they occurred.

Here are some other sorts of events:

- Mouse (or other pointer) button pressed or released. (**ButtonPress, Button-Release**)

- Window mapped or unmapped. (**MapNotify, UnmapNotify**)

- Mouse crossing a window boundary. (**EnterNotify, LeaveNotify**)

These event types are usually used for user input and to control a user interface.

A second group of events reports side effects of window operations. For example, when a window becomes visible after being obscured, it receives an **Expose** event. When window gravity (a window attribute that controls the position of a window when the parent is resized) takes effect, a `GravityNotify` event is generated.

A third purpose of events is to allow various clients to communicate with each other and with the window manager. The events that report the following actions are usually used for the second purpose.

• A client may request that all keyboard input be sent to a particular window regardless of the pointer position; this is called a *keyboard focus* window. Changing keyboard focus from one window to another causes **FocusIn** and **FocusOut** events, indicating to the client whether or not it can expect further keyboard events.

• Changing the mapping between keyboard keys and codes they generate causes a `MappingNotify` event to be sent to all clients.

• Reparenting a window is sometimes done by the window manager to add a frame to windows on the screen. This action causes a `ReparentNotify` event.

• A `PropertyNotify` event is generated when a client changes a property on a window.

• `SelectionClear`, `SelectionNotify`, and `SelectionRequest` events are used to communicate back and forth between a client that is allowing a user to select a section of text (or other information) and a client that is allowing the user to place the information in its window. Some of these events are sent with **XSendEvent**.

At this point, it is only important to understand in general what events are, not precisely what each one is for or how to use them. Chapter 8, *Events*, and Chapter 9, *The Keyboard and Pointer*, will provide complete details.

2.5.2 Selection and Propagation of Events

A client must select the event types that it wants the server to send for each window. The selection is made by calling **XSelectInput()**, which sets the **event_mask** window attribute, by setting that attribute with the more general **XChangeWindow-Attributes()** routine, or when calling **XCreateWindow()**.

For example, a scrollbar may require mouse button events but not keyboard events, while the main window of an application may require keyboard but not mouse events. One would select different event types on each of these windows.

Keyboard and pointer events are generated in the smallest window enclosing the pointer (or grabbing the pointer, as discussed in Section 8.3.2.2). Then an event of one of these types (only) propagates upward through the window hierarchy until the event type is found in the **event_mask** or **do_not_propagate_mask** attributes of the window. If the event is found in an **event_mask** first (or in both on the same window), then the event is sent as if it occurred in that window, and if it is found in a **do_not_propagate_mask** first, then it is never sent. The ID of the window that finally received the event (if any) is put in the `window` member of the event structure.

The `do_not_propagate_mask` can only be set with `XChangeWindow-Attributes()` or `XCreateWindow()`. Events other than keyboard and pointer events do not propagate. They occur in the window in which they were selected when the appropriate action occurs.

For most types of events, a copy of an event can be sent to more than one client if each client has selected that event type on that window. Each client has its own event mask for each window. The client that created the window need not do anything to cooperate. The second client that wants to get an event from a window that it did not create simply needs to find out the ID of the window and then select the desired event types with `XSelectInput()` on that window. A duplicate event is sent to each window, and these events propagate independently up through the hierarchy in the two applications. This is rarely done, because there is usually no reason for any program other than the window manager to play with another application's windows.

2.5.3 The Event Queue

What do we mean when we say that an event is queued? Each client has its own event queue which receives the selected events in the order they are sent by the server, as was shown in Figure 2-2.

The client then can remove each event at any time and process it according to its type and the other information in each event structure. There are several functions that get input, and they differ in how many windows are monitored and what types of events are sought. The client can also read events on the queue without removing them, remove one and then put it back, or clear the queue by throwing away all the events. Events can also be created by a program and sent to the window manager or other programs.

2.5.4 An Event Structure

`Expose` is one of the most important event types, and its event structure is shown in Example 2-1. It is generated when an area of a window becomes visible on the screen and indicates that the client must redraw that area. This happens when a window is mapped, moved, resized, or deiconified or when an obscuring window is unmapped. Exposure events are common and can happen at any time, since they may be caused by the actions of other clients.

Example 2-1. An event structure

```
typedef struct {
    int type;
    unsigned long serial;      /* # of last request processed by
                                * server */
    Bool send_event;           /* True if this came from a SendEvent
                                * request */
    Display *display;          /* Display the event was read from */
    Window window;
    int x, y;
    int width, height;
    int count;                 /* If nonzero, more expose events
                                * follow */
} XExposeEvent;
```

The type of event is reported in every event structure—in the **XExposeEvent** structure, the *type* field would be the symbolic constant **Expose**. The window to which the event propagated is reported in the *window* member, present in all but five event types (those dealing with selections and graphics exposure). All other information in the event structures is specific to certain event types and is described in detail in Appendix E, *Event Reference*.

2.5.5 The Event Loop

Because events can arrive in any order, the structure of code to handle them is predetermined. Every program contains an event loop in which each event is received and processed. Normally this loop is implemented as an infinite **while** loop, beginning with an event-getting routine and followed by a **switch** statement that branches according to the event type. Within each branch for an event type, there may be additional branches corresponding to the window in which the event occurred or other fields in the event structure.

The loop will almost always include exposure events. X does not normally keep track of the contents of the obscured regions of windows. It is the responsibility of the program to make sure that the window contents can be redrawn when exposure occurs. The program must be prepared to receive and act on an exposure event at any time, meaning at every invocation of the event-gathering routine. A program may work perfectly as long as there are no other programs running, but that is not good enough in a window environment!

When a window is first mapped, the first function of the program must be to read the exposure event that is generated by mapping the window. Then the program can draw the window's contents. As it turns out, this is also how the program should respond when an exposure event arrives at any later time. The first drawing and later redrawing are done in exactly the same way, using the same code.

Note, however, that another type of event, **ConfigureNotify**, must be handled in case the window manager modified the size of the application before mapping it and in case the user later resizes the window. More will be said about this in Chapter 3, *Basic Window Program*.

2.6 How to Program with Xlib

This section reviews what is important to know about X programming before you write any code. Describing what goes into the designing, writing, and debugging of X programs should give you a better start when you begin your own programming.

The basic program described in Chapter 3 illustrates many of the issues described here.

2.6.1 Designing an X Application

Let's begin by outlining the major tasks any X application must perform.

From the user's standpoint, almost any application under any window system will do the obvious things: create a window on the screen of an appropriate size, determine a position for some text and/or graphics within the window, draw into the window, and accept keyboard and/or pointer input, changing the screen accordingly. Essentially, the top-level window of the application is treated very much like the whole screen would be treated on a PC. These tasks are straightforward and most programmers should find them familiar.

There are, of course, a few complications resulting from the unique features of window systems in general and the X Window System in particular. These complications determine the design requirements for an application that is to run under X.

2.6.1.1 Design Requirements

The following four paragraphs describe the things X applications must do that are not obvious. These are things that must be done for the application to operate properly under X but that the average user might not notice or know about.

First, X allows workstations to be connected in a network in which any host or node may run X programs and display them on any other node, given permission. This means that the program must be able to accept the user's specification of which display to use. (Remember that each display has its own server, so choosing the display is equivalent to establishing the connection between the client and a particular server.) This requirement turns out to be built in and requires virtually no programming, as is described in Section 3.2.2.

Second, the application must be responsible in its use of the limited resources of the display, chiefly screen space and colormaps. This is because there may be many applications running concurrently on a single screen, sharing those limited resources. The client in charge of managing these limited resources is the window manager. There are certain requirements for communication between each application and the window manager to ensure that competing needs can be fairly arbitrated and to help make sure that the user sees a consistent user interface. These requirements are not difficult to meet for simple applications, but they get more complex for serious applications. This area is described in Chapter 12, *Interclient Communication*.

Third, other clients may be moved over your client and then moved away, requiring your client to redraw its window or windows. X cannot maintain the contents of an unlimited number of overlapping windows, and it is inefficient for it to try to maintain even a few. Your client will be told when redrawing is necessary and in what areas. This requirement is not hard to meet, but it encourages programming in a way that records the current "state" of each window so that it can be redrawn. The handling of exposure is described in Section 3.2.13.

Fourth, the user may resize your application, so it should be capable of recalculating the dimensions and placement of subwindows and graphics to fit within the given window.

In a nutshell, these four aspects are all that is required of an X program beyond its basic functionality. Fortunately, for most clients without unique needs such as a custom colormap, these requirements are straightforward to satisfy.

2.6.1.2 The User Interface

The first step in designing an application will be to determine what its features will be. Determining how the user will invoke those features is probably the next step. This means designing a user interface.

X was purposely designed to be "policy free," and therefore it does not come with a standard user interface like many other window systems do. You will have to write all parts of the user interface yourself, unless you choose to use one of the toolkits that are available. Using a toolkit makes building a user interface much easier and is strongly recommended. Otherwise, you must write menus, command buttons, dialog boxes, and so forth and determine how they are to be used. Although there are many ways to write these user interface features, there is a simple implementation of a menu in the *winman* program shown in Chapter 16, *Window Management*, and an example of a dialog box routine in Chapter 9, *The Keyboard and Pointer*. The writing of a command button routine should be straightforward.

The key elements that interact in the design of a user interface are the hierarchy of windows and the selection and processing of events, chiefly pointer and keyboard events. Since these device events propagate through the hierarchy depending on whether they are selected for each window, both the hierarchy and the selection together determine how events are received. For every user action, there must be a path (possibly unique, possibly common for several different user actions) through the event-handling code that yields some sort of response to the user, either by a visible change, a message, or a beep. Therefore, the job of the event loop is to distinguish all the possible user actions and invoke the proper code. In the main event loop, each case statement for an event type must then have another switch, depending on the window which received the event, before calling the function that performs the action the user requested. The event type and the window in which it occurred are only two of the most common event structure members—there may be additional switch statements based on other members, too, such as which keys or buttons were being held while a key or button press occurred.

Especially for complex programs, a careful design of the window hierarchy and selection of events can simplify the code and save hours of debugging. We recommend drawing out the hierarchy of windows and the types of events selected by each one and then drawing in the events that will be propagated to ancestor windows. This helps find problems before any code is written.

2.6.2 Writing an X Application

The best way to start writing an X application is probably to copy the existing application that is most similar to your intended purpose or to start from a skeleton program such as *basicwin*, described in Chapter 3, *Basic Window Program*. Select one from the core portion of the standard distribution from MIT, because these are the most likely to follow current conventions.

The following sections describe some basic facts about the actual process of coding and compiling an application.

2.6.2.1 Resources and User Customizability

An application should not hardcode all the options that are possible under X, such as colors and fonts. It should allow the user to specify the colors of all windows, the font to use, the display and screen to use, the initial size and position of the application, and a large number of other standard and application specific options.

An application should provide command line options, but there are too many variables to support all of them as command line options. The developers of X have designed a better way for the user to specify options, called resources. The user places the desired options in a file using a particular format and runs the X application *xrdb* specifying this file as a command line argument. *xrdb* places a property on the root window whose value is the contents of this file. Applications use a set of Xlib routines collectively called the resource manager to return a setting for each variable required. The routine `XGetDefault()` makes this process quite easy for the application. If the user has not called *xrdb* to set the property on the root window, `XGetDefault()` reads in a file called *.Xdefaults* in the user's home directory. The application itself should contain a default value for each variable in case neither of these sources contains a value for one of them.

This use of the term resource is completely different from the term *server resource*, which refers to windows and GCs.

A resource specification is a key/value pair. A key/value pair may apply only to a particular window within a particular application, to an entire application, to a certain class of applications such as editors, or to all applications. The algorithm used to find the value for a particular variable operates quite differently from a normal database manager. Given an incomplete specification of a key, it uses an algorithm to determine which of the keys in the resource database is the best match and returns the indicated value. It always returns only one value. This is much different from a normal database manager which would return many values if the key were too general.

The resource manager and providing user customizability are described in detail in Chapter 13, *Managing User Preferences*.

2.6.2.2 Compiling and Linking X Programs

To use all the functions in the X library, you need to include *<X11/Xlib.h>*, *<X11/Xutil.h>*, *<X11/keysym.h>*, and *<X11/Xresource.h>*. These files define data structures, macros, and symbols and declare the types of functions. It is also a good idea to include *<X11/Xos.h>*, which includes certain header files commonly used in C programs that differ in name or location between various operating systems, notably System V and BSD. To compile and link your program with all the available Xlib libraries, including a symbol table for a symbolic debugger, use:

```
cc -g -o outputfile inputfile.c -lX11
```

The *-lX11* option specifies linking with the standard X library, Xlib.

A set of routines to make it easier to port programs from X Version 10 to Version 11 is provided in a separate library. To use the X Version 10 compatibility functions, include *<X11/X10.h>* in your source file and link with both the *-lX11* and *-loldX* options to your *cc* command. You may wish to include *<X11.Xos.h>* if you use system calls, file manipulation, or string manipulation utilities. This header file includes the right files for various operating systems.

Several other libraries are available in the X distribution from MIT: Xmu, the miscellaneous utilities library, and Xext, the extensions library (which requires additional server-side software in order to function). These are not yet adopted standards of the X Consortium but are widely available. If you use *-lXmu*, it must be placed before Xlib on the compiling command line. All toolkit libraries based on Xlib such as Xt must also appear before *-lX11* on the command line. *-lXext* can appear before or after *-lX11* because it does not use Xlib.

If, when compiling, you get errors about header files in *<X11/Xos.h>* not being found, you are probably on a System V system that does not define the symbol **SYSV**. To solve this problem, add *-DSYSV* to the command line.

You will probably want to use *make*(1) when compiling time could be saved by compiling smaller functions separately before linking. (For more information, see the Nutshell Handbook *Managing Projects with Make*.) Even better is to use *make* in combination with *imake*, which generates makefiles from a portable description file. *imake* is provided with the X distribution. For more information see *The X Resource*, Issue 2, Spring 1992.

2.6.2.3 Naming Conventions

There are a number of conventions for the naming of Xlib functions and constants. You should be familiar with these conventions in order to name your own functions and constants properly. The major conventions are:

*   The names of all Xlib functions begin with an X (capital x). Compound words are constructed by capitalizing the first letter of each word. For example, a typical function name is **XAllocColor( )**.

*   The names of most user-visible data structures and structure types begin with an X. The only exceptions are **Depth**, **Display**, **GC**, **Screen**, **ScreenFormat**, and **Visual**.

Pointers to these six structures are quite commonly used in programs, but their members should not be accessed except through pre-existing macros.

- The names of all members of data structures use lower case. Compound words, where needed, are constructed with underscores (_).

- The names of macros do not begin with an X. To distinguish macros from user symbols (which are all caps), the first letter of each word in the macro is capitalized. (The macros used for quarks are an exception to this rule, perhaps because they were once part of a separate library. Their names begin with **Xrm**.)

- The names of symbolic constants defined in X header files (**#defined**) use mixed case, with the first letter of each word capitalized, and do not begin with X. Lowercase symbols are reserved for variables and all uppercase for user symbols, according to existing convention. The only exception is that predefined atom names use all uppercase letters, with underscores separating the words. Atom names begin with **XA_** to distinguish them from user symbols.

You should choose constants and routine names that will not be confused with standard Xlib functions, macros, or constants. User function names should not begin with X and perhaps should have the first letter of the first word lower case to avoid confusion with Xlib macros. User constants should be all upper case. Variable names can be lower case as usual, with underscores separating the words if desired, since X structure member references will always be accompanied by the variable declared as the structure.

2.6.2.4 Using Structures, Symbols, and Masks

Xlib programming takes advantage of many structure definitions and defined constants. This style of programming may be unfamiliar to some programmers. We will describe how structures and constants are typically used so that the idea will be familiar when you see the examples.

Pointers to structures are the major way of specifying data to and returning data from Xlib routines. If the routine returns data, the returned value will be a pointer to the data structure, unless the routine returns more than one structure, in which case one or all of the structures will be arguments. In some routines (primarily those concerning color), a pointer-to-structure argument specifies some information and returns some other information.

When setting the characteristics of a server resource, such as a set of window attributes, a graphics context, the cells in a colormap, or a hardware characteristic (such as key click), both a structure and a mask are specified as arguments. The *mask* specifies which values in the specified structure should be read when updating the resource values. One bit in the mask is assigned to each member in the structure, and a special constant is defined in the Xlib header files to represent that member when constructing the mask. Each of the mask constants has one bit set. The mask argument is made by combining any number of the mask constants with the bitwise OR operator (|). For example, the **CWBackgroundPixmap** constant is used to indicate that the **background_pixmap** member of the specified window attributes structure is to be read and the corresponding member in the resource changed.

The other major use of defined constants in Xlib (other than for masks) is as values for structure members themselves. They indicate which of a number of alternatives is true. For example, several of the structure members can have only the values **True** or **False**. As another example, the **type** member of each event structure can have one of 33 different values, each represented by a different defined constant such as **Expose**. Defined constants are also used as returned values.

Defined constants are also used for predefined atoms. As described in Section 2.1.4, an atom is an integer value identifying a property. Atoms are used to avoid passing arbitrary-length property name strings back and forth between the client and the server.

2.6.2.5 Performance Optimizing

While designing, writing, and debugging your application, you can look for ways to improve its performance.

Whenever possible, you should use Xlib functions that do not require protocol replies. That is, in functions that are called frequently, especially in the event loop, avoid Xlib routines with names containing **Fetch**, **Get**, or **Query**. Most of these functions return information from the server, and as such, they are subject to network delays and will slow down your application. Much of this information can be had from events.

In general, keep the feedback loop between the user's action and the program's response as short as possible.

2.6.2.6 ANSI-C and POSIX Portability

The MIT Release 5 X distribution is compliant with ANSI-C and POSIX standards, and portable across a wide variety of platforms. While the goal of the ANSI-C and POSIX standards is portability, many systems do not implement these standards, or do not implement them fully, so the MIT R5 distribution defines new header files that attempt to mask the differences between systems. The header files are *<X11/Xfuncproto.h>*, *<X11/Xfuncs.h>*, *<X11/Xosdefs.h>*, and *<X11/Xos.h>*. The contents and usage of these header files are described in Chapter 15, *Other Programming Techniques*. None of these files are part of the official R5 standard, so they may not be shipped with your system. But they can be very useful in writing portable applications, so we have included them with the code from this book, which you can get as described in the *Preface*.

2.6.3 Debugging an X Application

All programmers know that debugging is by far the most difficult and time consuming aspect of programming. This is where you catch all the problems caused during the writing stage and often also problems in the design stage. One can rarely foresee all the issues when designing a program.

There are some techniques that make debugging X applications easier. One, of course, is to have good tools. The C program checker *lint* helps find problems such as mismatches in the number of arguments to a function, variables declared but not used, or misused pointers. Although it often finds something to complain about that you do not consider an error, it also provides useful information.

Use of a good debugger such as *dbx* avoids the need to continually place `printf` statements in the code and recompile.

The standard application *xwininfo* is good for displaying information about a window, including its window ID and name, parent and children IDs and names, all the window attributes, and the window manager hints set for that window. Use the *-all* option or see the *xwininfo* reference page in Volume Three, *X Window System User's Guide*, for information on printing just the needed information.

The standard application *xprop*, which displays the name, type, and value of each property set on a window, is useful in debugging applications that set or read properties. It can also display font properties. This application is also described in Volume Three.

If your application generates protocol errors during debugging, it is easier to locate the error if you turn off Xlib's request buffering (described in Section 2.1.2). This is done with the `XSynchronize()` call placed immediately after the call to connect with the sever (`XOpenDisplay()`).

One of the most common places to have difficulty debugging is in event handling. For this reason, we recommend that all programs under development contain `printf` statements at the beginning of each branch of their event handling, so that the programmer can watch the sequence of events in one window and the visible performance of the application in another. This print statement can be placed within a compile-time `#ifdef DEBUG`, `#endif` pair. Then define this symbol on the compiling command line. Later, all the print statements can be taken out of the compiled code by simply changing the command line when recompiling. Although the event types are coded as numbers and will normally be printed that way by the `printf` statements, they are easily translated back into strings that match their symbols using the technique described in Section 8.2.5.

X applications are difficult to test thoroughly. Here are some of the miscellaneous tests you should put your application through:

- Be sure to try all combinations of raising and lowering different windows to test the application's response to exposure. Does it redraw unnecessarily?

- Try all combinations of pressing and releasing different pointer buttons to see if anything breaks.

- Try operating the program in a busy network environment.

- Try the application on a variety of different servers. Does it work on both color and monochrome systems?

- Try running the application on machines with different architectures and bit and byte orders.

- What happens when you type function keys or other unique keys on a particular keyboard?

- Is it possible to crash the application by specifying the wrong set of resources or command line arguments?

If your application can pass all these tests, you have done a good job.

2.6.3.1 Errors

There are really three levels of error handling in programs using Xlib. The first level you implement yourself by monitoring the return status of the routines that create server resources. This allows the client to modify the arguments of the request and try again. The second level, protocol errors, is usually caused by a programming error, and the third by a fatal system error such as a crash of the machine running the server or network failure. The second two types are handled by two separate error-handling functions that can be set by the client but, by default, simply print a message and exit the client.

As an example of the first level of error handling, a client should always check to see whether it was successfully connected to the display server with `XOpenDisplay()` before proceeding. If this connection did not succeed, the client should print a message to *stderr* indicating what happened and which server it attempted to connect to. This process will be demonstrated in Chapter 3, *Basic Window Program*.

X protocol errors occur when routine arguments do not conform to accepted ranges or when IDs do not match existing resources, etc. These types of errors are sent to `XError-Handler`. Fatal errors, such as a broken connection with the server, are unrecoverable conditions and invoke the `XIOErrorHandler`. Both error handlers by default display an intelligible (if not intelligent) message and then exit.

The possible X protocol error messages and their general causes are listed in Appendix B, *Error Messages and Protocol Requests*, of Volume Two, *Xlib Reference Manual*. These error messages also specify which protocol request caused the error, which you can also look up in Volume Two, Appendix B to determine which Xlib routine may have caused the error. This mapping is not unique because several Xlib routines often generate the same protocol request.

User-defined error-handling routines will be called from the error handlers if you pass procedure names to `XSetIOErrorHandler()` or `XSetErrorHandler()`. If either is passed a NULL function pointer, the respective default handler will be reinstated.

If you write your own error-handling routines, it is recommended that you use `XGet-ErrorText()` or `XGetErrorDatabaseText()` to get the string describing an error code, so that the codes of extensions can be handled properly. `XGetErrorDatabase-Text()` uses the resource manager to provide error messages from the file *XErrorDB*, located by default in */usr/lib/X11*.

Only the error-handling routine `XErrorHandler` (or the one you define) receives error events. These events cannot be selected or received by windows.

2.6.3.2 The XErrorEvent Structure

Example 2-2 shows the **XErrorEvent** structure and its members. The value of each member of this structure is displayed by the default X protocol error handler.

Example 2-2. The XErrorEvent structure

```
typedef struct _XErrorEvent {
    int type;
    Display *display;         /* Display the event was read from */
    XID resourceid;          /* Resource ID */
    unsigned long serial;    /* Serial number of failed request */
    unsigned char error_code;   /* Error code of failed request */
    unsigned char request_code; /* Major opcode of failed request */
    unsigned char minor_code;   /* Minor opcode of failed request */
} XErrorEvent;
```

The following list describes each member of the **XErrorEvent** structure in detail:

- The **serial** member is the number of requests sent over the network connection since it was opened, starting from 1. The difference between **serial** and the last request processed as reported in error messages tells you how many requests to count back in order to find the request that caused the error.

- The **request_code** is a protocol representation of the name of the protocol request that failed; these are decoded in Appendix B, *Error Messages and Protocol Requests*, of Volume Two, *Xlib Reference Manual*.

- The **error_code** is one of the items described in Volume Two, Appendix B, such as **BadWindow**.

- The **minor_code** is zero unless the request is part of an extension. If it is, the **minor_code** indicates which request in the extension caused the error.

- The **resource_id** indicates one of the server resources (window, colormap, etc.) that was associated with the request that caused the error.

2.6.3.3 Synchronizing Errors

Since error events are not displayed precisely when they occur, it is often informative to look up the protocol request as well as the error code to determine which function the error occurred in. You cannot rely on the debugger to indicate where the error occurred because of Xlib's request buffering and other delays.

It is useful to use **XSynchronize()** to make sure that protocol errors are displayed as soon as they occur. When **XSynchronize()** is invoked, the performance of graphics will be drastically reduced. The same result occurs by setting the global variable **_Xdebug** to any nonzero value when running a program under a debugger (UNIX only).

2.6.3.4 Software Interrupts

Xlib does not handle software interrupts. Therefore, if you recursively call back into Xlib from a signal handler, the program will hang or crash. This is mostly an issue on systems that feature threads or multiple processors. The correct way to handle signals is to never make Xlib calls from signal handlers.

X Concepts

3

Basic Window Program

Every Xlib program has a similar structure. This chapter shows a simple program that puts up a window and handles events in that window. You can use this simple application as a template for your own more complex applications.

In This Chapter:

basicwin

3
Basic Window Program

This chapter presents a simple program that demonstrates the fundamentals of programming with the X library. All clients will use the techniques described and demonstrated here.

The basic program presented in this chapter fulfills all the requirements for a basic application outlined near the end of Chapter 2, *X Concepts*, and illustrates some of the most important X concepts and programming issues. You should have read Chapter 2 before proceeding.

The program will perform these operations:

* Connect the client to an X server with **XOpenDisplay()**, and exit gracefully if the connection could not be made.

* Get information about the physical screen, and use it to calculate the desired size of the window.

* Create a window with **XCreateSimpleWindow()**.

* Set standard properties for the window manager.

* Select the types of events it needs to receive.

* Load the font to be used for printing text.

* Create a graphics context to control the action of drawing requests.

* Display the window with **XMapWindow()**.

* Loop for events.

* Respond to the **Expose** event resulting from mapping the window (and any other **Expose** event that might come along later) by calling routines to draw text and graphics. If the window is too small to perform its intended function, it will display an appropriate message.

* Receive **ConfigureNotify** events, indicating that the window has been resized by the window manager. The new window size is provided in the event structure.

* Keep handling events until a **KeyPress** or **ButtonPress** event arrives, then close the display connection and exits.

The program does not perform the following operations, which are required of a robust X client:

- Allow the user to specify command line options and read the resource database.

- Handle colors.

For more information on these topics, see Chapter 7, *Color*, and Chapter 14, *A Complete Application*.

3.1 Running the Program

If you have the sample programs (see the *Preface* for how to get them) and a workstation that runs X, you can try out this program by compiling *basic/basicwin.c*. See the description of how to compile X programs in Section 2.6.2.2.

The program just displays a window with some text and graphics drawn into it. Figure 3-1 shows the output of the program. The one useful thing it does is tell you the size and depth of the current screen.

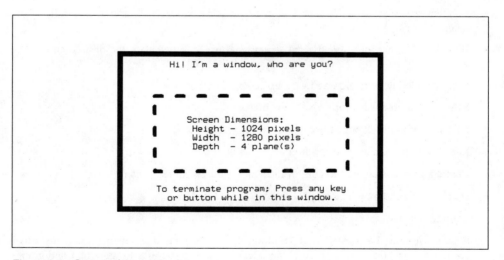

Figure 3-1. Output of the basicwin program

Without further ado, let's begin to look at the code.

3.2 The Main of basicwin

As usual, the code is composed of a main program and several subroutines. The main does everything described at the start of this chapter except create the GC, load the font, and draw the text and graphics. These tasks are done in the `draw_graphics`, `draw_text`, `get_GC`, and `load_font`, routines, which are shown with the complete code in Section 3.2.20 but not described fully until Chapter 6, *Drawing Graphics and Text*. You can get the general idea of what they do just by looking at them, though.

In the following sections, the code is shown and described in small pieces. In some cases, the relevant declarations of variables are shown again in each segment of the code as well as at the top of the program (where they would normally appear). This has been done to increase clarity when showing the individual pieces of the program.

3.2.1 Include Files and Declarations

Example 3-1 shows the include files and declarations from *basicwin.c*.

Example 3-1. basicwin — include files and declarations

```
/* Xlib include files */
#include <X11/Xlib.h>
#include <X11/Xutil.h>
#include <X11/Xos.h>
#include <X11/Xatom.h>

/* Standard C include file */
#include <stdio.h>

/* Bitmap data for icon */
#include "bitmaps/icon_bitmap"

#define BITMAPDEPTH 1

/* Values for window_size in main -- is window big enough to be
 * useful? */
#define TOO_SMALL 0
#define BIG_ENOUGH 1

/* Display and screen_num are used as arguments to nearly every
 * Xlib routine, so it simplifies routine calls to declare them
 * global; if there were additional source files, these variables
 * would be declared "extern" in them */
Display *display;
int screen_num;

/* Name this program was invoked by; this is global because
 * it is used in several places in application routines, not
 * just in main */
static char *progname;

void main(argc, argv)
int argc;
char **argv;
{
```

Example 3-1. basicwin — include files and declarations (continued)

```
Window win;
unsigned int width, height;          /* Window size */
int x = 0, y = 0;                    /* Window position */
unsigned int border_width = 4;       /* Border four pixels wide */
unsigned int display_width, display_height;
char *window_name = "Basic Window Program";
char *icon_name = "basicwin";
Pixmap icon_pixmap;
XSizeHints *size_hints;               /* Preferred sizes for window man */
XEvent report;                        /* Structure for event information */
GC gc;                                /* ID of graphics context */
XFontStruct *font_info;               /* Structure containing
                                       * font information */
char *display_name = NULL;            /* Server to connect to */
```

Let's begin with the include files. The three include files *<X11/Xlib.h>*, *<X11/Xutil.h>*, and *<X11/Xos.h>* are needed in virtually all Xlib programs. The *<X11/Xlib.h>* file contains declarations of structure types used in Xlib functions. *<X11/Xlib.h>* in turn includes *<X11/X.h>*, which sets up many defined constants. *<X11/Xutil.h>* contains more structure definitions and defined constants for certain groups of Xlib functions. Many of the structures and constant definitions from these include files are described in this manual with the functions in which they are used. Structures and constants are also presented on many of the reference pages in Volume Two, *Xlib Reference Manual*, if the routine on that page uses a structure or defined constant as an argument or return value. Appendix F, *Structure Reference*, of Volume Two, *Xlib Reference Manual*, provides an alphabetical listing of structures; Appendix G, *Symbol Reference*, of Volume Two, *Xlib Reference Manual*, provides the definitions of constants.

The final include file referenced in the Example 3-1 is *<X11/Xos.h>*, which attempts to make programs as portable as possible by including certain files depending on the operating system for which the program is being compiled. This include file is not standard and is not absolutely necessary, but it is useful.

Now let's move on to all the strange new types that appear in Example 3-1. The `Window`, `Display`, `Pixmap`, `XSizeHints`, and `XEvent` types used in this program are all defined in *<X11/Xlib.h>*. A brief description of each is given here, but you will need to see the code that uses each variable to fully understand them.

Window
: A unique integer identifier (ID) that is returned by `XCreateWindow()` or `XCreateSimpleWindow()` and is thereafter used by the program to refer to the created window resource.

Display
: A large structure that contains information about the server and its screens. It is filled only after this program connects to a server by calling `XOpenDisplay()`.

Pixmap
: An integer ID like `Window` but for a pixmap resource. The pixmap in this case is a picture to display in the icon for the window.

XSizeHints
: A structure that is used to provide the window manager with information about the preferred sizes and size increments for the top-level window of the application.

XEvent   A union that stores information about an event. It can be interpreted as one of many individual structure types depending on the type of event.

These declarations are repeated in the sections of code below in which they are used to avoid the need to flip back and forth.

3.2.2 Connecting to a Server

XOpenDisplay() connects an Xlib program to a server. The code shown in Example 3-2 that calls XOpenDisplay() will appear in all Xlib programs.

Example 3-2. basicwin — connecting to the server

```
char *display_name = NULL;
Display *display;
int screen_num;
Screen *screen_ptr;
        .
        .
        .
progname = argv[ 0 ];

/* Connect to X server */

if ( (display=XOpenDisplay(display_name)) == NULL )
{
    (void) fprintf( stderr, "%s: cannot connect to X server %s\n",
            progname, XDisplayName(display_name));
    exit( -1 );
}
screen_num = DefaultScreen(display);
screen_ptr = DefaultScreenOfDisplay(display);
```

The *display_name* argument to XOpenDisplay() specifies which server to connect to. This may be any server on the network and could be specified on the command line in a more complete application than this one. (See Section 2.6.2.1 and Chapter 13, *Managing User Preferences*, for a discussion of how to process command line arguments and user-specified default values in an X program.) When *display_name* is not specified by the user, it should be set to NULL, which causes XOpenDisplay() to connect to the server specified in the UNIX environment DISPLAY variable. You can view the current contents of the DISPLAY environment variable by using the UNIX command:

    echo $DISPLAY

It can be changed by typing:

    setenv DISPLAY *display_name*   (C Shell)

or:

    DISPLAY=*display_name*; export DISPLAY   (Bourne Shell)

You must be careful to set the DISPLAY variable when you login to a remote machine to make sure that when you execute X applications from that terminal, your output will be displayed on the screen from which you typed the command.

Both the DISPLAY environment variable and the *display_name* argument to **XOpen-Display( )** have the same format. The format is *host:server.screen*, in which *host* refers to the name of the machine running the server; *server*, the server number on that machine; and *screen*, the screen number on that server.*

The server number can be thought of as the number of the user on a particular host. The *server* number is always zero on a single-user workstation and may be nonzero only if a single host has a separate keyboard, pointer, and display for more than one user, all connected by wires (not networks) to the central host. Systems that run multiple X servers are rare.

The *.screen* part is optional and only specifies which screen is returned by the **Default-Screen( )** macro (more on macros in a minute). You can still use any or all of the screens controlled by the specified server. For example, **Perseus:0.1** instructs the server you are running the program on to connect to server **0** on the host called **Perseus** and that the default screen on that server for this program will be screen **1**.†

The **XOpenDisplay( )** routine returns a pointer to a structure of type **Display**. If the connection is successful, the structure will be filled with information about the server and each of its screens. If the attempt to create a connection fails, **XOpenDisplay( )** returns **NULL**. The code in Example 3-2 above checks to make sure this returned pointer is not **NULL** before proceeding. The message printed when the connection fails includes the text returned by the **XDisplayName( )** function. This function returns *display_name* or, if that is **NULL**, the UNIX environment DISPLAY variable. **XDisplayName( )** is necessary, since without it, there would be no way to tell the user to what server an attempt to connect was made.

The client might not succeed in connecting to a server for a number of reasons. Most likely, the *display_name* variable or DISPLAY environment variable does not specify a valid server that is connected via the network to the machine on which you are running the program. Or perhaps the network is out of order. Another possibility is that the server and client use different versions of the X protocol. X Version 11 programs are not compatible with X Version 10 and vice versa, so that if such a connection is attempted, an error message such as "protocol mismatch" should be printed, since the connection will partially succeed. All releases of X Version 11, however, *are* compatible since they use the same protocol.

The connection will also fail if the host you are running the client on is not on the *host access list* of the server you are trying to display on. The host access list is a simple permission mechanism. A server reads the list of hosts as it starts up and may be connected only to clients running on these hosts. There are commands to add and remove hosts from the access list, but these can be called only from clients running on the host whose list is being changed. In all these cases, the code shown in Example 3-2 will simply print the name of the server to which the connection failed and no further information.

---

*MIT's manual describes this format as *host:display.screen*, using *display* instead of *server*. Since most people think of screens and displays as virtually the same thing, their description leads to confusion. The second member in the string really identifies which server on a particular host to connect to. Each of these servers would support a user.
†Note that most servers only control a single screen. However, an X server can support multiple screens. The most common example is probably the Apple MacX server for the Macintosh.

In R4, a simple authorization scheme has also been implemented. If the person operating the server has turned authorization on, Xlib must know a secret code in order to connect to that server. Xlib gets this code from a file, and the server puts it there to grant access.

If Example 3-2 executes successfully past opening the display, we can begin to set up variables for use in the rest of the program. The first of these is the global variable *screen_num*, set to the return value of the DefaultScreen() macro. *screen_num* will be used throughout the program to indicate which screen on the server our operations are to affect. It is important to use the DefaultScreen() macro rather than to hardcode 0 as the screen used by the client, because even without command line parsing in the client, this allows the user to set the default screen by setting the *.screen* element of the DISPLAY environment variable.

The variable *screen_num* can actually be any integral value between 0 and the value returned by (ScreenCountdisplay – 1), inclusive. The ScreenCount macro returns the number of screens on the connected server. Since we only intend to use one of the screens, we can be satisfied with using the default screen.

3.2.3 Display Macros

We have just described all the macros used in the context of connecting with a display. They all get their information from the Display structure returned by XOpenDisplay(). But this is not the only useful information we can get from the Display structure. There are numerous other macros that supply information about the characteristics of the server and its screens. We will describe these macros where they come in handy in this manual. The complete set of macros that access the members of the Display structure is listed and described in Appendix C, *Macros*, of Volume Two, *Xlib Reference Manual*. They tell you whether the server supports certain features like backing store and motion history buffers, the protocol version and release and the name of the server vendor, and much more. The Display structure also provides information about each screen, such as the root window dimensions and the number of planes.

The macros are provided both for convenience and because the Display structure is intended to be opaque; clients should not access its members directly. The reason for it being opaque is that Xlib's authors want to retain the option to change the members in the Display structure without making existing clients obsolete.

3.2.4 Getting Window Information

Most clients need to know the size of the screen so that the output can be tailored to look the same—or to look good—on any display. There are two ways to get this information: you can access members of the Display structure to get information about the root window or you can use XGetGeometry() or XGetWindowAttributes() to get the root window's dimensions. The first method, using the macros for accessing information from the Display structure, works only for the root window but is more efficient. The second and third methods, reading the window geometry or attributes, work for any window.

To get the dimensions of a screen in pixels, you can use the macros `DisplayWidth()` and `DisplayHeight()`. The macros `DisplayWidthMM()` and `DisplayHeightMM()` return the screen dimensions in millimeters. These four macros get their information locally from the `Display` structure, so they are fast and efficient. The ratio of width in millimeters to width in pixels gives you a measurement of the spacing between pixels horizontally, and the same process can be used to determine the vertical pixel spacing. This can be important because when you draw a circle, it will look more like an ellipse on screens that do not have the same pixel spacing in both directions (usually inexpensive PC servers). You can tailor your drawing to compensate for this effect.

The second and third ways to get the geometry of a window are to use `XGetGeometry()` or to get all the window attributes using `XGetWindowAttributes()`. The difference between these two routines is that `XGetWindowAttributes()` gets much more information and actually calls `XGetGeometry()` itself. These methods have the disadvantage that they get information from the server, requiring a round-trip request that is subject to network delays. We show this method here because, for any window other than the root window, this is the only way to get window information.

The following code fragments demonstrate the three ways of getting root window information. *basicwin* uses the macros method because, in this case, we need information about the root window, and this is the most efficient way to get it.

Example 3-3 shows the macros method; Example 3-4, the `XGetGeometry()` method; and Example 3-5, the `XGetWindowAttributes()` method.

Example 3-3. Code fragment for getting display dimensions — using macros

```
Display *display;
int screen_num;
unsigned int display_width, display_height;
        .
        .
        .
/* Open display */
screen_num = DefaultScreen(display);
        .
        .
        .
/* Display size is a member of display structure */
display_width = DisplayWidth(display, screen_num);
display_height = DisplayHeight(display, screen_num);
```

Example 3-4. Another way to get window size — using XGetGeometry()

```
Display *display;
int screen_num;
Window root;
int x, y;
unsigned int width, height;
unsigned int border_width;
unsigned int depth;
        .
        .
/* Open display */
        .
```

```
        .
/* Get geometry information about root window */
if (XGetGeometry(display, RootWindow(display, screen_num), &root,
            &x, &y, &width, &height, &border_width, &depth) == False)
        {
        fprintf(stderr, "%s: can't get root window geometry\n",
                    progname);
        exit(-1);
        }
display_width = width;
display_height = height;
```

Note that the `root` argument of **XGetGeometry()** returns the root window at the top of the hierarchy of the window being queried. This happens to be useless in this case, because it is the root window we are querying!

Example 3-5. A third way to get window size — using XGetWindowAttributes()

```
Display *display;
int screen_num;
XWindowAttributes windowattr; /* (This declaration at top) */

        .
/* Open display */
screen_num = DefaultScreen(display);

        .
/* Fill attribute structure with information about root window */
if (XGetWindowAttributes(display, RootWindow(display, screen_num),
            &windowattr) == 0) {
        fprintf(stderr, "%s: failed to get window attributes.\n",
                    progname);
        exit(-1);
}
display_width = windowattr.width;
display_height = windowattr.height;
```

3.2.5 Creating Windows

The next step is to create and place windows. Actually, a window's position relative to its parent is determined as the window is created, since these coordinates are specified as arguments to the routine that creates the window.

The *basicwin* application has only one window. Creating the first window of an application is a special case, because that window is a child of the root window and, therefore, is subject to management by the window manager. An application can suggest a position for this window, but it is very likely to be ignored. Most window managers allow the user to position the window as it appears on the screen. So most simple applications create the first window with its position set to (0,0). Example 3-6 shows the simplest call to create a window.

basicwin

In Chapter 14, *A Complete Application*, we will show you a more complete approach that processes command line arguments to get the position of the top-level window. When the user specifies a position, there is a technique for making sure that the window manager will honor the position.

Example 3-6. basicwin — creating a window

```
Window win;
int border_width = 4;          /* Border four pixels wide */
unsigned int width, height;    /* Window size */
int x,y;                       /* Window position */
        .
        .
        .
/* Open display, determine screen dimensions */
screen_num = DefaultScreen(display);
        .
        .
/* Note that in a real application, x and y would default to 0 but
 * would be settable from the command line or resource database */
x = y = 0;

/* Size window with enough room for text */
width = display_width/3, height = display_height/4;

/* Create opaque window */
win = XCreateSimpleWindow(display, RootWindow(display, screen_num),
          x, y, width, height, border_width, BlackPixel(display,
          screen_num), WhitePixel(display, screen_num));
```

The only new thing in Example 3-6 is the use of several new macros in the call to create a window.

Let's talk about the `RootWindow()` macro. Each screen has its own root window. To create the first of your application's windows on a particular screen, you use the root window on that screen as the parent. That window can then only be used on that screen. The ID of the root window on a particular screen is returned by the `RootWindow()` macro. The first generation of windows on a screen (known as the top-level windows) should always use this macro to specify the parent. `XCreateSimpleWindow()` makes a new window given arguments for specifying it parent, size, position, border width, border pixel value, and background pixel value. All other attributes of the window are taken from the parent, in this case the root window. If we wanted to specify any or all the attributes instead of inheriting them from the parent, we would have to use `XCreateWindow()` instead of `XCreateSimpleWindow()`.

3.2.6 Color Strategy

Applications do not choose pixel values, they choose colors and are returned pixel values by a routine they call that allocates colors or they get pixel values from the display macros `BlackPixel()` and `WhitePixel()`.*

---

*`BlackPixel()` and `WhitePixel()` are no longer constants as they were in X Version 10. Pixel values must not be hardcoded.

This example is a monochrome application, but it will work on both monochrome and color screens. We use the `WhitePixel()` macro to specify the background pixel value (in the call to create the window) and set the foreground in the GC to be the contrasting value returned by `BlackPixel()`. The border pixel value is also set to `BlackPixel()`. The background and border pixel values are set with the last two arguments of `XCreate-SimpleWindow()`. The foreground pixel value is set in the `get_GC` routine in the manner described in Section 5.1.

As you may recall from Chapter 2, *X Concepts*, pixel values represent colors, but they will be translated by a colormap before being displayed on the screen. `BlackPixel()` and `WhitePixel()` return the pixel values corresponding to two contrasting colors in the default colormap, which might not actually be black and white.

Every application should be made to work in monochrome, because many people have only monochrome screens.

How to add color handling to *basicwin* (or any application) is described in Chapter 7, *Color*.

3.2.7 Preparing an Icon Pixmap

An application should create an icon design for itself, so that if a window manager is running and the user iconifies the application, the icon will be recognizable as belonging to the particular application. Exactly how to tell the window manager about this pixmap will be described in the next section, but first let's talk about how to create the pixmap.

The program should take two steps in creating the pixmap: it should find out what sizes of icon are acceptable to the window manager and then create a pixmap of an appropriate size. Since most current window managers do not specify icon sizes, and it is difficult to know how to respond in a reasonable way, this issue can be ignored for the present. Eventually, when standard window managers specify standard icon sizes, applications would use `XGet-IconSizes()` to determine which window manager was in operation and have a icon bitmap for each one.

Example 3-7 shows the simple process of creating a pixmap for the icon.

Example 3-7. basicwin — creating an icon pixmap

```
#include "bitmaps/icon_bitmap"

void main(argc, argv)
int argc;
char **argv;
{
    /* Other declarations */
        .
        .
        .
    Pixmap icon_pixmap;

    /* Open display, create window, etc. */

    /* Might someday want to use XGetIconSizes to get the icon
     * sizes specified by the window manager in order to determine
```

Example 3-7. basicwin — creating an icon pixmap (continued)

```
 * which of several icon bitmap files to use, but only when
 * some standard window managers set these */

/* Create pixmap of depth 1 (bitmap) for icon */
icon_pixmap = XCreateBitmapFromData(display, win,
        icon_bitmap_bits, icon_bitmap_width,
        icon_bitmap_height);
    .
    .
    .
```

An icon design can be created using the standard X application *bitmap*. You run *bitmap* with a filename and dimensions as command line arguments, like so:

```
% bitmap icon_bitmap 40x40
```

Then you use the pointer to draw your bitmap. For more information on the *bitmap* editor, see Volume Three, *X Window System User's Guide*. Normally the icon carries some symbolic representation of the application, so use your imagination. *bitmap* creates an ASCII file that looks like Example 3-8. This particular bitmap is a bit small for an icon, being only 20 pixels on a side. A more typical size would be about 40 pixels on a side.

Example 3-8. Format of bitmap files

```
#define icon_bitmap_width 20
#define icon_bitmap_height 20
static char icon_bitmap_bits[ ] = {
    0x60, 0x00, 0x01, 0xb0, 0x00, 0x07, 0x0c, 0x03, 0x00, 0x04, 0x04, 0x00,
    0xc2, 0x18, 0x00, 0x03, 0x30, 0x00, 0x01, 0x60, 0x00, 0xf1, 0xdf, 0x00,
    0xc1, 0xf0, 0x01, 0x82, 0x01, 0x00, 0x02, 0x03, 0x00, 0x02, 0x0c, 0x00,
    0x02, 0x38, 0x00, 0x04, 0x60, 0x00, 0x04, 0xe0, 0x00, 0x04, 0x38, 0x00,
    0x84, 0x06, 0x00, 0x14, 0x14, 0x00, 0x0c, 0x34, 0x00, 0x00, 0x00, 0x00};
```

The bitmap format shown in Example 3-8 is not used only in **XCreateBitmapFrom-Data()**. It is also used by the Xlib functions **XWriteBitmapFile()** and **XReadBitmapFile()**. An application can also read from a file the data used to create a pixmap, instead of including the data, but this is more complicated because it requires processing of filenames.

3.2.8 Communicating with the Window Manager

Before mapping the window (which displays it on the screen), an application must set the standard properties to tell the window manager at least a few essential things about the application.

You may remember from Chapter 2, *X Concepts*, that a property is a collection of information that is readable and writable by any client and is usually used to communicate between clients. The standard properties are part of the convention for communication between each application and the window manager.

You may also remember that a property is associated with a particular window. The standard properties are associated with the top-level window of the application. This is how the server keeps track of the standard properties of all the different applications and has them ready for the window manager to read them.

Several routines are provided that allow the application to easily set these properties; analogous routines allow the window manager to read them. The routine designed to set all the most important properties for a normal application is `XSetWMProperties()`.

The document describing the standard for communication between the application and the window manager is called the *Inter-Client Communication Conventions Manual*; it is reprinted in Appendix L, *Interclient Communication Conventions*, of Volume Zero, *X Protocol Reference Manual*. More information on the conventions can be found in Chapter 12, *Interclient Communication*, of this manual.

The minimum set of properties that an application must set are:

- Window name

- Icon name

- Icon pixmap

- Command name and arguments (the command line)

- Number of arguments

- Preferred window sizes

- Keyboard focus model

We'll say more about each of these after you have seen the code that sets them. Example 3-9 shows the code that sets the standard properties.

Example 3-9. basicwin — setting standard properties

```
void main(argc, argv)
int argc;
char **argv;
{
    XWMHints *wm_hints;
    XClassHint *class_hints;
    XTextProperty windowName, iconName;
        .
        .
        .
    /* To be displayed in window manager's titlebar of window */
    char *window_name = "Basic Window Program";

    /* To be displayed in icon */
    char *icon_name = "basicwin";
    Pixmap icon_pixmap;

    XSizeHints *size_hints; /* Structure containing preferred sizes */
    if (!(size_hints = XAllocSizeHints())) {
        fprintf(stderr, "%s: failure allocating memory\n", progname);
        exit(0);
```

Example 3-9. basicwin — setting standard properties (continued)

```
        }
        if (!(wm_hints = XAllocWMHints())) {
            fprintf(stderr, "%s: failure allocating memory\n", progname);
            exit(0);
        }
        if (!(class_hints = XAllocClassHint())) {
            fprintf(stderr, "%s: failure allocating memory\n", progname);
            exit(0);
        }

        /* Open display, create window, create icon pixmap */
            .
            .
            .

        /* Before mapping, set size hints for window manager */
        /* Note that in a real application, if size or position were
         * set by the user, the flags would be USPosition and USSize,
         * and these would override the window
         * manager's preferences for this window.  */

        /* x, y, width, and height hints are taken from the
         * actual settings of the window when mapped; note that
         * PPosition and PSize must be specified anyway */
        size_hints->flags = PPosition | PSize | PMinSize;
        size_hints->min_width = 300;
        size_hints->min_height = 200;

        /* These calls store window_name and icon_name into
         * XTextProperty structures and set their other fields
         * properly */
        if (XStringListToTextProperty(&window_name, 1, &windowName) == 0) {
            (void) fprintf( stderr, "%s: structure allocation for \
                    windowName failed.\n", progname);
            exit(-1);
        }


        if (XStringListToTextProperty(&icon_name, 1, &iconName) == 0) {
            (void) fprintf( stderr, "%s: structure allocation for \
                    iconName failed.\n", progname);
            exit(-1);
        }

        /* Whether application should be  normal or iconified
         * when first mapped */
        wm_hints->initial_state = NormalState;
        /* Does application need keyboard input? */
        wm_hints->input = True;
        wm_hints->icon_pixmap = icon_pixmap;
        wm_hints->flags = StateHint | IconPixmapHint | InputHint;

        /* These are used by the window manager to get information
         * about this application from the resource database */
        class_hints->res_name = progname;
```

Example 3-9. basicwin — setting standard properties (continued)

```
    class_hints->res_class = "Basicwin";

    XSetWMProperties(display, win, &windowName, &iconName,
            argv, argc, size_hints, wm_hints,
            class_hints);
```

It is important to realize that these properties are only hints. A hint is information that might or might not be used. There may be no window manager running, or the window manager may ignore some or all of the hints. Therefore, an application should not depend on anything having been done with the information provided in the standard properties. For example, take the window name hint. Some window managers will use this information to display a titlebar above or beside each top-level window, showing the application's name. The proper and obvious thing for the application to do would be to set the window name to be the application's name. But if the application were an editor, it could try to set its window name to the name of the current file. This plan would fall through if no window manager were running.

The icon name and icon pixmap should both set to allow the window manager to use either or both. Most current window managers often display just the icon pixmap, unless no pixmap is specified, in which case they use the icon name. If the icon name is not set, the convention within window managers is to use the window name as the icon name; if the window name is not specified either, then they will use the first element of the command line.

The UNIX shell command name and arguments are passed into *main* in the standard fashion from the command line, as `argv` and `argc`. These can be used directly as arguments in the call to set the standard properties. This information might be used by the session manager to restart or duplicate the application when so instructed by the user.

And last but not least, the window size hints property is a structure that specifies the sizes, positions, and aspect ratios preferred by the user or the program for this application. The `XSizeHints` structure is shown in Example 3-10.

Example 3-10. The XSizeHints structure

```
typedef struct {
        long flags;                     /* Marks defined fields
                                         * in this structure */
        int x, y;                       /* Obsolete as of R4 */
        int width, height;              /* Obsolete as of R4 */
        int min_width, min_height;
        int max_width, max_height;
        int width_inc, height_inc;
        struct {
                int x;                  /* Numerator */
                int y;                  /* Denominator */
        } min_aspect, max_aspect;
        int base_width, base_height;    /* New in R4 */
        int win_gravity;                /* New in R4 */
} XSizeHints;
```

You might ask, "How would the user be involved in specifying the size hints when they have to be set even before a window appears?" The answer: applications can be written to let the user specify the position and size of the top-level window through command line arguments or the resource database. A more complete application would get these values, use them to set the size of the window. To tell the window manager that the user, not the application, supplied these values, the application would set the **flags** field to **USSize | USPosition** instead of **PSize | PPosition**.

All this arranges a priority for the different settings of the position and size of a top-level window. The lowest priority is the application itself. Next higher is the window manager, and highest of all is the user. In Example 3-9, the symbols used to set **flags** are **PSize** and **PMinSize**. These indicate that the program is specifying its desired size and its minimum useful size. The symbols used for other members of **XSizeHints** are shown on the reference page for **XSetWMProperties()** in Volume Two, *Xlib Reference Manual*.

Let's describe the other members of **XSizeHints**. The **x**, **y**, **width**, and **height** members are simply the desired position and size for the window. In R4 and later, these fields should not be set.

The rest of the size hints give the window manager information about how to resize the window. The **min_height** and **min_width** fields should be set to the minimum dimensions (in pixels) required so that the application can still function normally. Many window managers will not allow the user to resize the window smaller than **min_width** and **min_height**. **max_width** and **max_height** are analogous to **min_width** and **min_height** but are less critical for most applications.

In R4, the **base_width** and **base_height** fields have been added to the **XSizeHints** structure. They are used with the **width_inc** and **height_inc** fields to indicate to the window manager that it should resize the window in steps—in units of a certain number of pixels instead of single pixels. The window manager resizes the window to any multiple of **width_inc** in width and **height_inc** in height, but no smaller than **min_width** and **min_height** and no bigger than **max_width** and **max_height**. If you think about it, **min_width** and **min_height** and **base_width** and **base_height** have basically the same purpose. Therefore, **base_width** and **base_height** take priority over **min_width** and **min_height**, so only one of these pairs should be set.

The *xterm* application provides a good example of size increments. It wants its window to be resized in multiples of the font width and height, since it uses only constant-width fonts. This way, there are no partial characters along the edges of the window. What's more, the application can then interpret dimensions specified by the user in multiples of **width_inc** and **height_inc**, instead of pixels. The user specifies dimensions in characters (24 by 80 for a standard size terminal), which the application then translates into pixels by multiplying them by **width_inc** and **height_inc**. Most window managers display the dimensions of the window when the user is resizing it, and if **width_inc** and **height_inc** are set, they will use multiples instead of pixels as units.

In R4, the **win_gravity** field has also been added to the **XSizeHints** structure. This field suggests to the window manager how the window should be placed when mapped or, more accurately, how the position for the window specified by the user should be interpreted. Normally, when the user specifies a position, either by clicking a pointer button to position a window or through command line arguments, the window manager places the top-left corner of the application's top-level window at that point. The **win_gravity** field requests the window manager to place a different part of the window at that point. The values of this field are **Center, East, North, NorthEast, NorthWest, South, SouthEast,**

SouthWest, and West. These refer to a corner or edge of the window that should be placed at the specified point. As mentioned, the default is NorthWest, which positions the top-left corner of the window at the specified point. Few applications need to use this feature.

3.2.9 Selecting Desired Event Types

The next step is to select the event types the application will require. Our simple program must receive events for three reasons: to redraw itself in case of exposure, to recalculate its contents when it is resized, and to receive a button or key press indicating that the user is finished with the application.

The program must select these types of events specifically since, by default, it will not receive the kinds of input it needs. Example 3-11 shows the line of code that selects events.

Example 3-11. basicwin — selecting desired event types

```
/* Select event types wanted */
XSelectInput(display, win, ExposureMask | KeyPressMask |
    ButtonPressMask | StructureNotifyMask);
```

The crucial argument of **XSelectInput()** is the event mask. Each symbol used here selects one of more event types. The event mask constants are combined with a bitwise OR since they are really setting bits in a single argument.

ExposureMask selects **Expose** events, which occur when the window is first displayed and whenever it becomes visible after being obscured. **Expose** events signal that the application should redraw itself.

X provides separate events for depressing and releasing both keyboard keys and pointer buttons and separate symbols for selecting each of these types of events. **KeyPressMask** selects only **KeyPress** events, and **ButtonPressMask** selects only **ButtonPress** events. **ButtonRelease** and **KeyRelease** events can also be selected with **ButtonReleaseMask** and **KeyReleaseMask**, but they are not needed in this application.

StructureNotifyMask selects a number of event types, specifically **CirculateNotify**, **ConfigureNotify**, **DestroyNotify**, **GravityNotify**, **MapNotify**, **ReparentNotify**, and **UnmapNotify**. The only one of these we need for our application is **ConfigureNotify**, which informs the application of its window's new size when it has been resized. However, there is no way to select just this one event type. We could get away without selecting this event type, but any real application would use it because it allows an increase in performance. Without this event type, on every **Expose** event the application would have to use **XGetGeometry()** to find out its current size. This is a request that requires a reply from the server and therefore is subject to network delays.

The rest of the event types selected by **StructureNotifyMask** are described in Chapter 8, *Events*.

XSelectInput() actually sets the **event_mask** attribute of the window. If you create the window with **XCreateWindow()** (as opposed to **XCreateSimpleWindow()**), you can select events at the same time by setting the **event_mask** attribute in the last two arguments of the call. This is slightly more efficient than calling **XSelectInput()** separately. You can also set this attribute through **XChangeWindowAttributes()** if, for some other reason, you need to call this function anyway.

3.2.10 Creating Server Resources

The next step in the application is to create any other server resources that are needed. Server resources are collections of information managed by the server and referred to in the application by an ID number. Items with the types **Colormap**, **Cursor**, **Font**, **GC**, **Pixmap**, and **Window** are server resources. They should be created once and the ID kept rather than creating and deleting them in frequently called subroutines. That is why they are normally created in **main** or in a subroutine called only once from **main**.

In this program, we have already created two resources: a window and the icon pixmap. We still need to load a font for the text and to create a graphics context to draw both text and graphics into the window. These operations are done in the routines **load_font** and **get_GC**, called just before mapping the window. We are going to delay describing these routines until Chapters 5 and 6, in order to keep this chapter to manageable proportions. However, the complete code for *basicwin*, including these functions, is listed at the end of this chapter, in case you want a sneak preview.

3.2.11 Window Mapping

Finally we are ready to display the window. Note that we have done all that preparation before mapping the window for good reason. The window manager hints must be set so that the window manager can handle the mapping properly, and events must be selected so that the first **Expose** will arrive and tell the application to draw into its window.

Example 3-12 shows the code that maps the window.

Example 3-12. basicwin — mapping the window

```
/* Display window */
XMapWindow(display, win);
```

You may remember from Chapter 2, *X Concepts*, that in order for a window to be visible, it must meet five conditions. These are so important that they bear repeating:

1. The window must be mapped with **XMapWindow()** or related routines.

2. All its ancestors must be mapped. This condition is always satisfied for the children of the root window, the top-level windows of each application.

3. The window must not be obscured by visible sibling windows or their ancestors—this depends on the stacking order. When first mapped, a window appears on top of its siblings, which will be on top of all windows if its parent is the root window.

4. The request buffer must be flushed. This topic will be described in the next section.

5. The initial mapping of a top-level window is a special case, since the window's visibility may be delayed by the window manager. For complicated reasons, an application must wait for the first `Expose` event before assuming that its window is visible and drawing into it.

3.2.12 Flushing the Output Buffer

`XMapWindow()` causes an X protocol request that instructs the server to display the window on the screen. Like all other X protocol requests, this one is queued until an event-reading routine such as `XNextEvent()`, a routine that queries the server (most routines whose names contain `Fetch`, `Get`, or `Query`), or a routine such as `XFlush()` or `XSync()` is called. The server operates more efficiently over the network when X protocol requests are sent in groups.

The `XNextEvent()` call performs the flushing frequently enough in applications that take user input. The routines that query the server should be called as infrequently as possible because they reduce performance over the network. The `XFlush()` command instructs the server to process all queued output requests right away. `XFlush()` is generally necessary only when an application needs to draw periodically even without user input.

3.2.13 Setting Up an Event-gathering Loop

X programs are event-driven, which means that after setting up all the server resources and window manager hints as described up to this point, the program performs all further actions only in response to events. The event-gathering loop is the standard way to respond to events, performing the appropriate action depending on the type of event and the information contained in the event structure.

The event loop is normally a closed loop, in which one of the event types with certain contents defined by the application indicates that the user wants to exit. In some existing applications such as *xclock*, the loop is completely closed, and therefore the only way to terminate the program is to find the process ID from the shell and kill it or use the window or session manager, but this can be inconvenient.

The choice of which events are received by the application was made earlier when the application selected input or set the `event_mask` attribute. The event loop must make sure to properly handle every event type selected. One of the most common debugging problems is for there to be a difference between the events handled and those selected.

Have a look at the code in Example 3-13, before we describe it in more specific terms.

Example 3-13. basicwin — processing events

```
        .
        .
        .
/* Get events, use first Expose to display text and graphics
 * ConfigureNotify to indicate a resize (maybe even before
 * first Expose); ButtonPress or KeyPress to exit */
while (1)   {
     XNextEvent(display, &report);
     switch  (report.type) {
     case Expose:
          /* Unless this is the last contiguous expose,
           * don't draw the window */
          if (report.xexpose.count != 0)
               break;

          /* If window too small to use */
          if (window_size == TOO_SMALL)
               TooSmall(win, gc, font_info);
          else {
               /* Place text in window */
               place_text(win, gc, font_info, width, height);

               /* Place graphics in window */
               place_graphics(win, gc, width, height);
          }
          break;
     case ConfigureNotify:
          /* Window has been resized; change width and height
           * to send to place_text and place_graphics in
           * next Expose */
          width = report.xconfigure.width;
          height = report.xconfigure.height;
          if ((width < size_hints->min_width) ||
                    (height < size_hints->min_height))
               window_size = TOO_SMALL;
               else
               window_size = BIG_ENOUGH;
          break;
     case ButtonPress:
          /* Trickle down into KeyPress (no break) */
     case KeyPress:
          XUnloadFont(display, font_info->fid);
          XFreeGC(display, gc);
          XCloseDisplay(display);
          exit(1);
     default:
          /* All events selected by StructureNotifyMask
           * except ConfigureNotify are thrown away here,
           * since nothing is done with them */
          break;
     } /* End switch */
} /* End while */
```

Example 3-13 is framed by an infinite while loop. Just inside the top of the loop is the **XNextEvent( )** statement, which gets an event structure from the queue Xlib maintains for the application and puts the pointer to it in the variable **report**. You might assume that the event loop could have been written:

```
    while (XNextEvent(display, &event)) {
        .
        .
        .
    }
```

but this is not the case. **XNextEvent()** returns void; it only returns when there is an event to return. Errors are handled through a separate error-handling mechanism, not through the returned value. So it is necessary to write the event loop:

```
    while (1) {
        XNextEvent(display, &event);
        .
        .
        .
    }
```

Right after **XNextEvent()** is a switch statement that branches depending on the event type. There is one case for each of the four types of events: **ButtonPress**, **ConfigureNotify**, **Expose**, and **KeyPress**.

The **ConfigureNotify** branch, in all applications, will calculate the values of variables based on the new window size. These variable values will then be used to calculate where to draw things in the **Expose** branch the next time an **Expose** event occurs. A **ConfigureNotify** event is always followed by one or more **Expose** events.

2.13.1 Repainting the Window

Expose events occur when a window becomes visible on the screen, after being obscured or unmapped. They occur because the X Window System does not normally save the contents of regions of windows obscured by other windows or not mapped. The contents of windows need to be redrawn when they are exposed.

The code for **Expose** events draws or redraws the contents of the application's window. This code will be reached when the window is first mapped, and whenever a portion of the window becomes visible.

An application can respond to **Expose** events by refreshing only the parts of the window exposed, or by refreshing the entire window. The former is possible because the event structure for each **Expose** event carries the position and dimensions of a single rectangular exposed area, as shown in Example 3-14.

Example 3-14. The XExposeEvent structure

```
typedef struct {
    int type;
    unsigned long serial;/* # of last request processed by server */
    Bool send_event;    /* True if this came from SendEvent request */
    Display *display;    /* Display the event was read from */
    Window window;
    int x, y;
    int width, height;
    int count;          /* If nonzero, at least this many more */
} XExposeEvent;
```

Several **Expose** events can occur because of a single window manager operation, as shown in Figure 3-2. If window *E* were raised, four **Expose** events would be sent to it. The **height** and **width** members in each event structure would correspond to the dimensions of the area where each of the windows overlapped window *E*, and the **x** and **y** members would specify the upper-left corner of each area relative to the origin of window *E*. All the **Expose** events generated by a single action are guaranteed to be contiguous in the event queue.

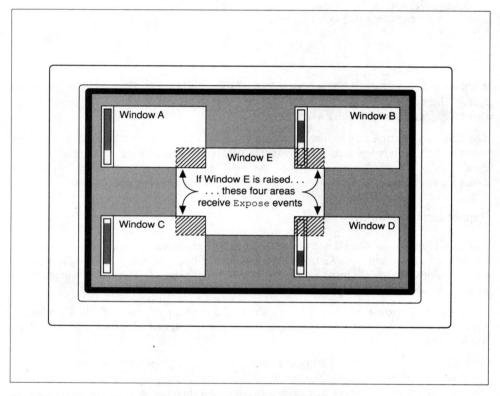

Figure 3-2. Multiple Expose events generated from a single user action

Whether an application should draw the whole window or just the exposed parts depends on the complexity of the drawing in the window. If all of the window contents are simple for both the application and the server to draw, the entire window contents can be redrawn without a performance problem. This approach works well as long as the window is only redrawn once, even if multiple **Expose** events occur because of a single user action. One trick is to monitor the **count** member of the **Expose** event structure and ignore the **Expose** events (do not redraw the window) until this member is **0**. It might seem an even better method to search the entire queue, removing all **Expose** events that occurred on the window, before redrawing. But this is illegal because there may be intervening **ConfigureNotify** events in the queue, and responding to an **Expose** event that follows a

`ConfigureNotify` event too early will result in redrawing the wrong area or not redrawing at the right time. Only *contiguous* `Expose` events can be skipped.

On the other hand, if a window has any elements that can be time consuming for either the application or the server to redraw, then the application should only redraw the time-consuming elements if they are actually within the exposed areas.

The issue here is redrawing time, which has two components under the application's control: the time the application takes to process the redrawing instructions, and the time it takes for the server to actually do the redrawing. On most servers, a user must wait for the server to complete drawing before he or she can move the pointer or go on to other actions. Therefore, the time taken by the server is critical, since it translates directly into waiting by the user. Since the system running X clients is normally multitasking, the time taken by the application to minimize redrawing is not as important, since the user can still do work.

There are two approaches to assisting the server in redrawing exposed regions quickly. One is to avoid redrawing items in regions that have not been exposed. Doing this in an application requires identifying any items to be drawn that do not extend into any of the exposed areas and eliminating these drawing requests. There are a set of routines that perform intersecting calculations on regions that may help you implement this.

The second approach is to set the clip mask in the GC to draw only in the exposed areas. This second approach is much simpler in code, but it delegates the job of eliminating unnecessary drawing to the server. Many servers may not do this elimination, because there is again a tradeoff between the time saved in eliminating requests and the time spent in calculating which requests to eliminate.

If you are now confused and wondering which redrawing approach to take in your application, the general rules should be as follows:

- If the window is fast to draw, the whole window can be drawn in response to the last **Expose** event in a contiguous series; this means drawing only when **count** is zero. The definition of *fast* will vary from server to server, but anything that uses the more complex features of the GC, such as wide lines or join styles, or that may have lots of drawing requests should probably be considered slow.

- For windows that are slow to draw, the application should avoid drawing areas that were not exposed. If the application can figure out which slow drawing requests would draw only into areas that were not exposed and these calculations are not time consuming in themselves, then it should eliminate these requests.

- For windows that are slow to draw, the second best approach is to set a clip mask to allow the server to eliminate unnecessary requests. (This will work only if the server has been designed to do so.) The application can combine all the areas in a contiguous series of expose events into a single clip mask and set this clip mask into the GC. The code for this is only slightly more complex than the approach for the window that is fast to draw.

Since the image used by the *basicwin* application is simple, the application can redraw the entire window upon receiving the last contiguous **Expose** event with little performance penalty. But we will also show you the other approach, as if the window were more complex. Example 3-13 shows the first method from the list above, and Example 3-15 shows the third method.

The second method in the list above is not shown here because it is hard to demonstrate in a way that is transferable to other applications. We will just describe it in a little more detail instead. Let's say that we are writing a spreadsheet application and designing the exposure event handling. In the spreadsheet, it would be easy to determine which cells were affected by the exposure, because the cells are arranged along horizontal rows and in columns. Upon getting an **Expose** event, the application could easily determine which cells overlapped the exposed area and then redraw only those. The same could not be said of a painting program, in which some drawing primitives could be diagonal or drawn with weird line styles. It would be very hard to determine whether a particular primitive drawn in the painting program intersects with an exposed region. In general, any application that draws most or all of its graphics horizontally or vertically can benefit from this technique. One example of an application written this way is *xterm*, and you can look at the code for that if you can get it. *xterm* redraws only the characters that are in exposed areas.

Example 3-15 shows a technique that could be used for more complicated windows. It creates a single **Region** composed of the union of the rectangles in all the **Expose** events. Regions are described fully in Chapter 6, *Drawing Graphics and Text*, but you should be able to understand this example anyway.

Example 3-15. Handling Expose events for complex window contents

```
int window_size = BIG_ENOUGH;   /* Or TOO_SMALL to display contents */
Region region;                  /* Coalesce rectangles from all Expose
                                 * events */
XRectangle rectangle;           /* Place Expose rectangles in here */
        .
        .

/* Create region for exposure event processing */
region = XCreateRegion();

while (1)  {
    XNextEvent(display, &report);
    switch  (report.type) {
    case Expose:
        if (window_size == TOO_SMALL) {
            TooSmall(win, gc, font_info);
            break;
        }
        /* Set rectangle to be exposed area */
        rectangle.x = (short) report.xexpose.x;
        rectangle.y = (short) report.xexpose.y;
        rectangle.width = (unsigned short) report.xexpose.width;
        rectangle.height = (unsigned short) report.xexpose.height;

        /* Union this rect into a region */
        XUnionRectWithRegion(&rectangle, region, region);

        /* If this is the last contiguous expose in a group,
         * set the clip region, clear region for next time
         * and draw */
        if (report.xexpose.count == 0) {
            /* Set clip region */
            XSetRegion(display, gc, region);
            /* Clear region for next time */
            XDestroyRegion(region);
```

```
                region = XCreateRegion();
                /* Place text in window */
                place_text(win, gc, font_info, width, height);

                /* Place graphics in window */
                place_graphics(win, gc, width, height);
        }
        break;
```

Being able to redraw the contents of its windows is important for most applications, but for a few applications, it might be very difficult or impossible. There is another method that might be used in such a situation. The application could draw into a pixmap and then copy the pixmap to the window each time the window needs redrawing. That way the complete window contents would always be available for redrawing the window on **Expose** events. The disadvantage of this approach is that the server might not have sufficient memory to store many pixmaps in memory (especially on color displays) or it might be slow about copying the pixmap into the window. But this would be a logical way to handle exposure in an application that performs double-buffering.* On high performance graphics workstations, a feature known as a backing store might also be available to assist in redrawing windows. When available, this feature can be turned on for any window that really requires it. With the backing store on, the server can maintain the contents of the window when it is obscured and even when it is unmapped and capture drawing to the window while it is in one of these states. The one situation that the backing store cannot fully take care of is resizing the window. This is because it is assumed that most applications need to recalculate the dimensions of their contents to fit a new window size. The application can set an attribute called bit gravity to retain part of the window during a resize, but part of the window is still going to need redrawing if the window is resized larger.

In case you might be wondering, we have intentionally not described the `draw_text` and `draw_graphics` routines here. They are described in Sections 6.2.7 and 6.1.3. But if you are still curious, they are included in the listing of *basicwin* at the end of this chapter.

.2.14 When Can I Draw?

There is often confusion about when an application is permitted to draw into its windows. You might think it would work to draw immediately after the `XMapWindow()` request that displays a window on the screen. But that will not work with most styles of window manager. The rule is that no drawing is allowed until the first **Expose** event arrives.

The reason involves a feature of X called substructure redirection, introduced in Section 2.1.5 and described more fully in Section 16.2.

basicwin

---

*Double-buffering is an animation technique that hides the drawing process from the viewer. In one implementation, a pixmap is drawn into and then copied to a window when the image is complete. Another technique called overlays is described in Chapter 7.

3.2.15 When Will My Drawing Appear?

Another characteristic of X that often confuses newcomers is the fact that graphics drawn may not appear on the screen immediately. It is easy to write a program that properly performs a number of drawing calls but that never makes anything appear on the screen. This is a side effect of the fact that X is designed to buffer communications over a network, as was described in theoretical terms in Section 2.1.2. We will describe it in more practical terms here.

What happens is that the requests (to create windows, to map windows, or to draw into them) are queued up in Xlib, waiting for something to happen that requires an immediate communication with the server. Xlib will not send requests of any kind to the server until such an occurrence. The requests are saved up as a packet so they can be sent over the network more efficiently.

The queue of requests waiting to be sent to the server is called the *request buffer*. The requests are accumulated in the request buffer until a call to:

1. Any routine which requests information from the X server (for example, **XGetWindow-Attributes()**, **XLoadQueryFont()**, **XQueryPointer()**)

2. Certain requests for getting events (**XMaskEvent()**, **XNextEvent()**, **XPending()**, **XWindowEvent**)

3. **XFlush()**

4. **XSync()**

Actually, a routine in number 2 above that gets events triggers a communication with the server only if there is no event on Xlib's event queue that matches what the routine is looking for. Only if the routines are waiting for an event do they trigger the exchange. Any of these actions is said to *flush* the request buffer, which means that all requests up to this point will be acted on by the server. Novice programmers who neglect to call one of these routines will notice that their drawing requests have not been honored. They do not realize that perhaps *none* of their X requests that require communication with the server have been honored.

But does it really take a lot of care to make sure that the request buffer gets flushed? Not usually. Since X programs are event-driven, they often call routines that get events. If an application handles event types that occur frequently, such as pointer or keyboard events, there is nothing to worry about. If the application needs to get information from the server by making a call containing the word **Fetch**, **Get**, or **Query**, no problem is likely. On the other hand, an output-only application that handles only **Expose** events would certainly need to call **XFlush()** once in a while to make sure that its drawing was honored in a timely fashion.

Handling Resizing of the Window

The `ConfigureNotify` event tells the application that the window was resized. In this program, we pass this information to the routines that draw, so that they can position things properly. We also see if the new size is less than the minimum useful size that we set as a size hint for the window manager. If it is smaller in either dimension, then we set the flag `window_size` so that the next time an `Expose` event arrives, we display the message "Too Small" instead of the usual text.

Example 3-16 shows the code that handles the `ConfigureNotify` event.

Example 3-16. basicwin — the ConfigureNotify event

```
       .
       .
       .
case ConfigureNotify:
        /* Window has been resized; change width and height to
         * send to place_text and place_graphics in next Expose */
        width = report.xconfigure.width;
        height = report.xconfigure.height;
        if ((width < size_hints->min_width) ||
                (height < size_hints->min_height))
                window_size = TOO_SMALL;
        else
                window_size = BIG_ENOUGH;
        break;
       .
       .
       .
```

If the window manager resizes the window before it is first mapped, the `Configure-Notify` event appears on the queue *before* the first `Expose` event. This means that the code works even if the window manager modifies the window's size before allowing it to be displayed. The initial `ConfigureNotify` updates the application's knowledge of the window size, and the following `Expose` event allows the application to draw the window's contents.

If we had not selected `ConfigureNotify` events, the code for `Expose` would have to be modified to check the dimensions in the first `Expose` event, so that it knew the correct window size. It would also have to query the server for the window size in response to subsequent `Expose` events, because these events describe only the exposed area, not the entire window.

.2.17 Exiting the Program

This program uses a key or button press to exit. This is not a very demanding use of `Key-Press` and `ButtonPress` events. For a description of how to use keyboard and pointer events for more advanced purposes, see Chapter 9, *The Keyboard and Pointer*.

basicwin

To cleanly exit, a client should free all the memory it has allocated, particularly X resources, and then close the display connection with `XCloseDisplay()`. Example 3-17 shows the code that performs these functions in *basicwin*.

Example 3-17. Closing the display connection and freeing resources

```
case ButtonPress:
        /* Trickle down into KeyPress (no break) */
case KeyPress:
        XUnloadFont(display, font_info->fid);
        XFreeGC(display, gc);
        XCloseDisplay(display);
        exit(1);
```

It is good practice to use `XCloseDisplay()` even though the connection to the server is closed automatically when a process exits. Otherwise, pending errors might not be reported.

3.2.18 Error Handling

Although there does not appear to be much in the way of error-handling code in this example, the question of error handling has been fully considered:

- On the `XOpenDisplay()` call, we check for the error return, tell the user what server the attempt was made to connect to, and exit gracefully.

- For all other errors, we depend on the default error-handling mechanisms. These errors might be a protocol errors caused by a programming error (all of which we hope to eliminate), a protocol error caused by the server running out of memory (the chance of which we cannot eliminate), or an IO error such as losing the connection with the server due to network failure. For protocol errors, the client gets an error event from the server, and Xlib invokes an error handler function. The client is free to provide its own error handler to replace the default handler, which prints an informative message and exits. For IO errors, there is a separate error handler function, which can be separately replaced by the application. But for this example, we have simply relied on the default handlers.

It is important to note that not all protocol errors cause the error handler to be invoked, though this fact does not show itself in *basicwin*. Some errors, such as failure to open a font, are indicated by returned values of type `Status` on the appropriate routine (in this case, `XLoadFont()`). The returned values are zero on failure and nonzero on success. In general, any routine that returns `Status` will need its return value tested, because it will have bypassed the error-handling mechanism.

3.2.19 Summary

The basic steps that were taken in this program are as follows:

- Open connection to server.

- Make sure connection succeeded, print error and exit if not.

- Get display dimensions.

- Calculate desired size of window and create window.

- Create pixmap for icon.

- Initialize `XSizeHint` structure.

- Set standard properties for window manager.

- Select desired event types.

- Map window.

- Set up event gathering loop.

- If event is of type `Expose`, draw contents of window.

- If event is of type `ConfigureNotify`, recalculate dimensions of window.

- If event is `ButtonPress` or `KeyPress`, close the display and exit.

The order of these steps is important up to the point where the window is mapped. Within the event loop, the order of events cannot be completely predicted.

3.2.20 Complete Code for basicwin

Now look at the complete code for *basicwin* and make sure you understand everything. Note that the `draw_graphics`, `draw_text`, `get_GC`, and `load_font` routines have not yet been described but will be covered in later chapters.

Example 3-18. basicwin — in its entirety

```
#include <X11/Xlib.h>
#include <X11/Xutil.h>
#include <X11/Xos.h>
#include <X11/Xatom.h>

#include <stdio.h>

#include "bitmaps/icon_bitmap"

#define BITMAPDEPTH 1
#define TOO_SMALL 0
#define BIG_ENOUGH 1

/* These are used as arguments to nearly every Xlib routine, so it
 * saves routine arguments to declare them global; if there were
 * additional source files, they would be declared extern there */
Display *display;
int screen_num;

/* progname is the string by which this program was invoked; this
 * is global because it is needed in most application functions */
static char *progname;

void main(argc, argv)
int argc;
```

Example 3-18. basicwin — in its entirety (continued)

```
char **argv;
{
    Window win;
    unsigned int width, height;      /* Window size */
    int x, y;                        /* Window position */
    unsigned int border_width = 4;   /* Four pixels */
    unsigned int display_width, display_height;
    unsigned int icon_width, icon_height;
    char *window_name = "Basic Window Program";
    char *icon_name = "basicwin";
    Pixmap icon_pixmap;
    XSizeHints *size_hints;
    XIconSize *size_list;
    XWMHints *wm_hints;
    XClassHint *class_hints;
    XTextProperty windowName, iconName;
    int count;
    XEvent report;
    GC gc;
    XFontStruct *font_info;
    char *display_name = NULL;
    int window_size = 0;             /* BIG_ENOUGH or TOO_SMALL to
                                      * display contents */

    progname = argv[0];

    if (!(size_hints = XAllocSizeHints())) {
        fprintf(stderr, "%s: failure allocating memory\n", progname);
        exit(0);
    }
    if (!(wm_hints = XAllocWMHints())) {
        fprintf(stderr, "%s: failure allocating memory\n", progname);
        exit(0);
    }
    if (!(class_hints = XAllocClassHint())) {
        fprintf(stderr, "%s: failure allocating memory\n", progname);
        exit(0);
    }

    /* Connect to X server */
    if ( (display=XOpenDisplay(display_name)) == NULL )
    {
        (void) fprintf( stderr, "%s: cannot connect to X server %s\n",
                    progname, XDisplayName(display_name));
        exit( -1 );
    }

    /* Get screen size from display structure macro */
    screen_num = DefaultScreen(display);
    display_width = DisplayWidth(display, screen_num);
    display_height = DisplayHeight(display, screen_num);

    /* Note that in a real application, x and y would default
     * to 0 but would be settable from the command line or
     * resource database */
    x = y = 0;

    /* Size window with enough room for text */
```

Example 3-18. basicwin — in its entirety (continued)

```
    width = display_width/3, height = display_height/4;

    /* Create opaque window */
    win = XCreateSimpleWindow(display, RootWindow(display,screen_num),
            x, y, width, height, border_width, BlackPixel(display,
            screen_num), WhitePixel(display,screen_num));

    /* Get available icon sizes from window manager */

    if (XGetIconSizes(display, RootWindow(display,screen_num),
            &size_list, &count) == 0)
        (void) fprintf( stderr, "%s: Window manager didn't set \
                icon sizes - using default.\n", progname);
    else {
        ;
        /* A real application would search through size_list
         * here to find an acceptable icon size and then
         * create a pixmap of that size; this requires that
         * the application have data for several sizes of icons */
    }

    /* Create pixmap of depth 1 (bitmap) for icon */
    icon_pixmap = XCreateBitmapFromData(display, win,
            icon_bitmap_bits, icon_bitmap_width,
            icon_bitmap_height);

    /* Set size hints for window manager; the window manager
     * may override these settings */

    /* Note that in a real application, if size or position
     * were set by the user, the flags would be USPosition
     * and USSize and these would override the window manager's
     * preferences for this window */

    /* x, y, width, and height hints are now taken from
     * the actual settings of the window when mapped; note
     * that PPosition and PSize must be specified anyway */

    size_hints->flags = PPosition | PSize | PMinSize;
    size_hints->min_width = 300;
    size_hints->min_height = 200;


    /* These calls store window_name and icon_name into
     * XTextProperty structures and set their other fields
     * properly */
    if (XStringListToTextProperty(&window_name, 1, &windowName) == 0) {
        (void) fprintf( stderr, "%s: structure allocation for \
                windowName failed.\n", progname);
        exit(-1);
    }

    if (XStringListToTextProperty(&icon_name, 1, &iconName) == 0) {
        (void) fprintf( stderr, "%s: structure allocation for \
                iconName failed.\n", progname);
        exit(-1);
    }

    wm_hints->initial_state = NormalState;
    wm_hints->input = True;
    wm_hints->icon_pixmap = icon_pixmap;
```

basicwin

Example 3-18. basicwin — in its entirety (continued)

```
    wm_hints->flags = StateHint | IconPixmapHint | InputHint;

    class_hints->res_name = progname;
    class_hints->res_class = "Basicwin";

    XSetWMProperties(display, win, &windowName, &iconName,
            argv, argc, size_hints, wm_hints,
            class_hints);

    /* Select event types wanted */
    XSelectInput(display, win, ExposureMask | KeyPressMask |
            ButtonPressMask | StructureNotifyMask);

    load_font(&font_info);

    /* Create GC for text and drawing */
    getGC(win, &gc, font_info);

    /* Display window */
    XMapWindow(display, win);

    /* Get events, use first to display text and graphics */
    while (1)  {
        XNextEvent(display, &report);
        switch  (report.type) {
        case Expose:
            /* Unless this is the last contiguous expose,
             * don't draw the window */
            if (report.xexpose.count != 0)
                break;

            /* If window too small to use */
            if (window_size == TOO_SMALL)
                TooSmall(win, gc, font_info);
            else {
                /* Place text in window */
                place_text(win, gc, font_info, width, height);

                /* Place graphics in window */
                place_graphics(win, gc, width, height);
            }
            break;
        case ConfigureNotify:
            /* Window has been resized; change width
             * and height to send to place_text and
             * place_graphics in next Expose */
            width = report.xconfigure.width;
            height = report.xconfigure.height;
            if ((width < size_hints->min_width) ||
                    (height < size_hints->min_height))
                window_size = TOO_SMALL;
            else
                window_size = BIG_ENOUGH;
            break;
        case ButtonPress:
            /* Trickle down into KeyPress (no break) */
        case KeyPress:
            XUnloadFont(display, font_info->fid);
            XFreeGC(display, gc);
            XCloseDisplay(display);
```

Example 3-18. basicwin — in its entirety (continued)

```
                exit(1);
        default:
            /* All events selected by StructureNotifyMask
             * except ConfigureNotify are thrown away here,
             * since nothing is done with them */
            break;
        } /* End switch */
    } /* End while */
}

getGC(win, gc, font_info)
Window win;
GC *gc;
XFontStruct *font_info;
{
    unsigned long valuemask = 0; /* Ignore XGCvalues and
                                    * use defaults */

    XGCValues values;
    unsigned int line_width = 6;
    int line_style = LineOnOffDash;
    int cap_style = CapRound;
    int join_style = JoinRound;
    int dash_offset = 0;
    static char dash_list[] = {12, 24};
    int list_length = 2;

    /* Create default Graphics Context */
    *gc = XCreateGC(display, win, valuemask, &values);

    /* Specify font */
    XSetFont(display, *gc, font_info->fid);

    /* Specify black foreground since default window background
     * is white and default foreground is undefined */
    XSetForeground(display, *gc, BlackPixel(display,screen_num));

    /* Set line attributes */
    XSetLineAttributes(display, *gc, line_width, line_style,
                cap_style, join_style);

    /* Set dashes */
    XSetDashes(display, *gc, dash_offset, dash_list, list_length);
}

load_font(font_info)
XFontStruct **font_info;
{
    char *fontname = "9x15";

    /* Load font and get font information structure */
    if ((*font_info = XLoadQueryFont(display,fontname)) == NULL)
    {
        (void) fprintf( stderr, "%s: Cannot open 9x15 font\n",
                    progname);
        exit( -1 );
    }
}

place_text(win, gc, font_info, win_width, win_height)
Window win;
```

Example 3-18. basicwin — in its entirety (continued)

```
GC gc;
XFontStruct *font_info;
unsigned int win_width, win_height;
{
        char *string1 = "Hi! I'm a window, who are you?";
        char *string2 = "To terminate program; Press any key";
        char *string3 = "or button while in this window.";
        char *string4 = "Screen Dimensions:";
        int len1, len2, len3, len4;
        int width1, width2, width3;
        char cd_height[50], cd_width[50], cd_depth[50];
        int font_height;
        int initial_y_offset, x_offset;

        /* Need length for both XTextWidth and XDrawString */
        len1 = strlen(string1);
        len2 = strlen(string2);
        len3 = strlen(string3);

        /* Get string widths for centering */
        width1 = XTextWidth(font_info, string1, len1);
        width2 = XTextWidth(font_info, string2, len2);
        width3 = XTextWidth(font_info, string3, len3);

        font_height = font_info->ascent + font_info->descent;

        /* Output text, centered on each line */
        XDrawString(display, win, gc, (win_width - width1)/2,
                    font_height,
                    string1, len1);
        XDrawString(display, win, gc, (win_width - width2)/2,
                    (int)(win_height - (2 * font_height)),
                    string2, len2);
        XDrawString(display, win, gc, (win_width - width3)/2,
                    (int)(win_height - font_height),
                    string3, len3);

        /* Copy numbers into string variables */
        (void) sprintf(cd_height, " Height - %d pixels",
                    DisplayHeight(display,screen_num));
        (void) sprintf(cd_width, " Width  - %d pixels",
                    DisplayWidth(display,screen_num));
        (void) sprintf(cd_depth, " Depth  - %d plane(s)",
                    DefaultDepth(display, screen_num));

        /* Reuse these for same purpose */
        len4 = strlen(string4);
        len1 = strlen(cd_height);
        len2 = strlen(cd_width);
        len3 = strlen(cd_depth);

        /* To center strings vertically, we place the first string
         * so that the top of it is two font_heights above the center
         * of the window; since the baseline of the string is what
         * we need to locate for XDrawString and the baseline is
         * one font_info -> ascent below the top of the character,
         * the final offset of the origin up from the center of
         * the window is one font_height + one descent */
```

Example 3-18. basicwin — in its entirety (continued)

```
        initial_y_offset = win_height/2 - font_height -
                font_info->descent;
        x_offset = (int) win_width/4;
        XDrawString(display, win, gc, x_offset, (int) initial_y_offset,
                string4,len4);

        XDrawString(display, win, gc, x_offset, (int) initial_y_offset +
                font_height,cd_height,len1);
        XDrawString(display, win, gc, x_offset, (int) initial_y_offset +
                2 * font_height,cd_width,len2);
        XDrawString(display, win, gc, x_offset, (int) initial_y_offset +
                3 * font_height,cd_depth,len3);
}

place_graphics(win, gc, window_width, window_height)
Window win;
GC gc;
unsigned int window_width, window_height;
{
        int x, y;
        int width, height;

        height = window_height/2;
        width = 3 * window_width/4;
        x = window_width/2 - width/2;   /* Center */
        y = window_height/2 - height/2;
        XDrawRectangle(display, win, gc, x, y, width, height);
}

TooSmall(win, gc, font_info)
Window win;
GC gc;
XFontStruct *font_info;
{
        char *string1 = "Too Small";
        int y_offset, x_offset;

        y_offset = font_info->ascent + 2;
        x_offset = 2;

        /* Output text, centered on each line */
        XDrawString(display, win, gc, x_offset, y_offset, string1,
                strlen(string1));
}
```

4

Window Attributes

The window attributes control a window's background and border pattern or color, the events that should be queued for it, and so on. This chapter describes how to set and get window attributes and provides a detailed description of each attribute. Everyone should read this chapter.

In This Chapter:

4

Window Attributes

Now that you know the basic X concepts and you have seen the code for an X application, we can go back and start to describe various aspects of Xlib in full detail. This chapter describes the window attributes thoroughly. The window attributes were introduced in Section 2.2.1 and described in more detail in Section 2.4.1. You should read those sections before proceeding.

The setting of window attributes becomes necessary when you use **XCreateWindow()** instead of the simpler **XCreateSimpleWindow()**. However, it is not essential that you set any window attributes other than the window background and border. Therefore, this chapter is mainly about optional features that you may find useful.

You will continue to find this chapter useful as a reference even when you are an experienced X programmer. A useful quick reference to the window attributes is also provided inside the back cover of Volume Two, *Xlib Reference Manual*.

4.1 Setting Window Attributes

Window attributes can be set while creating a window with **XCreateWindow()** or afterward with a call to **XChangeWindowAttributes()**. When creating a window with **XCreateSimpleWindow()**, most of the attributes are inherited from the parent. There are also several routines for changing individual window attributes, including the **event_mask**, background and border.

The procedure for setting the attributes is the same with **XCreateWindow()** or **XChangeWindowAttributes()**. You set the members of an **XSetWindow-Attributes** structure to the desired values, create a mask indicating which members you have set, and call the routine to create the window or change the attributes.

4.2 The Window Attribute Structures

There are actually two structures associated with window attributes. **XWindow-Attributes** is a read-only structure that contains all the attributes, while **XSetWindowAttributes** is a structure that contains only those attributes that a program is allowed to set. We will not show you **XWindowAttributes** until Section 4.4, since it is used in programming only for getting the values of the window attributes.

Example 4-1 shows the structure that is used to set the window attributes.

Example 4-1. The XSetWindowAttributes structure

```
typedef struct _XSetWindowAttributes {
    Pixmap background_pixmap;       /* Pixmap, None, or ParentRelative */
    long background_pixel;          /* Background pixel value */
    Pixmap border_pixmap;           /* Pixmap, None, or CopyFromParent */
    long border_pixel;              /* Border pixel value */
    int bit_gravity;                /* One of the bit gravity symbols */
    int win_gravity;                /* One of the window gravity symbols */
    int backing_store;              /* NotUseful, WhenMapped, or Always */
    long backing_bitplanes;         /* Planes to be preserved, if possible */
    long backing_pixel;             /* Value to use in restoring planes */
    Bool save_under;                /* Should bits under window be saved */
    long event_mask;                /* Events that should be queued */
    long do_not_propagate_mask;     /* Events that shouldn't propagate */
    Bool override_redirect;         /* Override redirected configuration
                                     * requests */
    Colormap colormap;              /* Colormap associated with window */
    Cursor cursor;                  /* Cursor to be displayed or None */
} XSetWindowAttributes;
```

To set the window attributes, you need to set the elements of the **XSetWindowAttributes** structure to the desired values and then set a **valuemask** argument that represents which members are to be changed in the server's internal structure. A symbol specifying each member to be changed is combined with the bitwise OR operator (|). These symbols are shown in Table 4-1. They begin with the letters **CW** ("Create Window" or "Change Window") because the routines they are used in have those capital letters in their names.

Table 4-1. Window Attribute Mask Symbols

Member	Flag	Bit
background_pixmap	CWBackPixmap	0
background_pixel	CWBackPixel	1
border_pixmap	CWBorderPixmap	2
border_pixel	CWBorderPixel	3
bit_gravity	CWBitGravity	4
win_gravity	CWWinGravity	5
backing_store	CWBackingStore	6
backing_planes	CWBackingPlanes	7
backing_pixel	CWBackingPixel	8

Table 4-1. *Window Attribute Mask Symbols* (continued)

Member	Flag	Bit
override_redirect	CWOverrideRedirect	9
save_under	CWSaveUnder	10
event_mask	CWEventMask	11
do_not_propagate_mask	CWDontPropagate	12
colormap	CWColormap	13
cursor	CWCursor	14

For example, if you want to set the initial values of the background and border pixel values, you would follow the procedure shown in Example 4-2.

Example 4-2. Setting window attributes while creating a window

```
Display *display;
Window parent, window;
int x, y;
unsigned int width, height, border_width;
int depth;
int screen_num;
Visual *visual;
unsigned int class;
XSetWindowAttributes setwinattr;
unsigned long valuemask;

/* (Must open display) */

screen_num = DefaultScreen(display);
valuemask = CWBackPixel | CWBorderPixel;
setwinattr.background_pixel = WhitePixel(display, screen_num);
setwinattr.border_pixel = BlackPixel(display, screen_num);
window = XCreateWindow(display, parent, x, y, width, height,
    border_width, depth, class, visual, valuemask, &setwinattr);
```

If the window already exists, you can change those same attributes with the procedure shown in Example 4-3.

Example 4-3. Changing window attributes of existing window

```
Display *display;
Window window;
XSetWindowAttributes setwinattr;
unsigned long valuemask;

/* (Must open display, create window) */

valuemask = CWBackPixel | CWBorderPixel;
setwinattr.background_pixel = WhitePixel(display, screen_num);
setwinattr.border_pixel = BlackPixel(display, screen_num);
XChangeWindowAttributes(display, window, valuemask, &setwinattr);
```

You can also use separate calls to **XSetWindowBackground()** and **XSetWindow-Border()** to set these particular attributes. These and a few other attributes have routines for setting them individually. (These routines are referred to as *convenience routines*. They are provided for the attributes that most often need to be set without modifying any other attributes.) Table 4-2 lists the attributes that can be set individually and the routines that set them. But it is important to realize that each of these routines would generate a separate protocol request to the server, so if more than one attribute is to be set, it is more efficient to use the procedures shown above in Examples 4-2 and 4-3.

Table 4-2. Attributes that can be Set Individually

Attribute	Routine for Setting It
background_pixmap	XSetWindowBackgroundPixmap()
background_pixel	XSetWindowBackground()
border_pixmap	XSetWindowBorderPixmap()
border_pixel	XSetWindowBorder()
event_mask	XSelectInput()
colormap	XSetWindowColormap()
cursor	XDefineCursor() or XUndefineCursor()

Section 4.3 describes all of the attributes and the routines for setting them.

4.3 Settable Attributes

The sections that follow describe the options and default values for each member of the XSetWindowAttributes structure. The attributes control a wide variety of ways for a window to act. They can be grouped loosely to help you understand when you might want to set each attribute.

One group of attributes controls the appearance of a window. These are background_pixel, background_pixmap, border_pixel, border_pixmap, colormap, and cursor. Most clients will set the border, background, and cursor but use the default colormap.

A second group is provided to allow clients to improve their redrawing performance under certain conditions. These are backing_pixel, backing_planes, backing_store, bit_gravity, and save_under. These attributes do not affect the appearance or operation of a client. It is advisable to consider bit_gravity when designing a client, but the code for using these attributes can be added after a client's functionality is complete.

The event_mask and do_not_propagate_mask attributes control the selection and propagation of events. These attributes are described briefly in this chapter but also in much more detail in Chapter 8, *Events*.

The win_gravity attribute provides a means for relocating a window automatically when its parent is resized. Applications can take advantage of this feature to simplify the code that positions their subwindows when they are resized.

The `override_redirect` attribute controls whether requests to map or reconfigure the window can be intercepted by the window manager. `override_redirect` is meant to be set for the most temporary types of windows such as pop-up menus. In practice, this attribute only affects the top-level windows of an application (all children of the root window).

As described in Chapter 2, there are two window classes: `InputOutput` and `InputOnly`. The class of a window is specified in the call to `XCreateWindow()`, or is `InputOutput` if the window is created with `XCreateSimpleWindow()`.

`InputOutput` windows have all of the attributes described in the sections below. `InputOnly` windows have only the following subset of attributes:

- `win_gravity`
- `event_mask`
- `do_not_propagate_mask`
- `override_redirect`
- `cursor`

Any attempt to set attributes other than these five on an `InputOnly` window will cause an X protocol error (`BadMatch`).

4.3.1 The Window Background

The background of a window is the drawing surface on which other graphics are drawn. It may be a solid color, or it may be patterned with a pixmap. This choice is mostly an aesthetic decision for the programmer. However, users expect to be able to specify the background color on the command line or in the resource database. Therefore, if a pixmap is used, the code for creating the pixmap should use two colors specified by the user (see Section 6.1.5 for information on creating pixmaps).

The two attributes that control the background are `background_pixmap` and `background_pixel`, set by `XSetWindowBackgroundPixmap()` and `XSetWindowBackground()`, respectively.

These two attributes are not independent since they affect the same pixels. Either attribute can take precedence over the other, the winner being the one that is set last. If both are set in the same call to `XCreateWindow()` or `XChangeWindowAttributes()`, the `background_pixel` value is used.

The background of exposed areas of windows is automatically repainted by the server, regardless of whether the application selects `Expose` events.

However, changes in background attributes will not take effect until the server generates the next `Expose` event on that window. If you want the new background to be visible immediately, call `XClearWindow()` and flush the request buffer with `XFlush()`.

Applications must set one or the other for all windows. Otherwise, the results are undefined. Most applications set backgrounds to a solid color by setting the `background_pixel` attribute. The easiest way to do this is by setting the last argument of `XCreateSimple-Window()` to `BlackPixel` or `WhitePixel()`.

4.3.1.1 background_pixmap

If the background is set to a pixmap, the background is tiled with the pixmap. *Tiling* is the laying out of a pixmap to cover an area. The first pixmap is applied at the origin of the window (or its parent's origin if using the parent's background pixmap by specifying `Parent-Relative`, as described below). Another copy of the same pixmap is applied next to that one and another below it and so on until the window is filled.

The pixmap may be any size, though some sizes may be tiled faster than others. To find the most efficient tile size for a particular screen, call `XQueryBestTile()`.

A pixmap must be created with `XCreatePixmap()` or `XCreatePixmapFrom-BitmapData()` before being set as the `background_pixmap` attribute. The pixmap must have the same depth as the window and be created on the same screen. These characteristics are assigned to a pixmap as it is created. (For more information on creating pixmaps for tiles, see Section 6.1.5.)

The `background_pixmap` attribute has the following possible values:

None (default) Specifies that the window has no defined background pixmap. The window background initially will be invisible and will share the bits of its parent but only if the `background_pixel` attribute is not set. When anything is drawn by any client into the area enclosed by the window, the contents will remain until the area is explicitly cleared with `XClearWindow()`. The background is not automatically refreshed after exposure. The main purpose of the setting **None** is a minor performance improvement. If the application is simply going to cover the entire window with graphics (i.e., there is no reasonable "background" that the application can set), then why bother forcing the server to spend time painting the background? **None** might also be useful for a subwindow when that subwindow will never be moved in relation to its parent.

a pixmap ID The background will be tiled with the specified pixmap, but not until the next **Expose** event or `XClearWindow()` call. The background tile origin is the window origin. If the pixmap is not explicitly referenced again, it can be freed, since a copy is maintained in the server. Because the server copies the pixmap, changes to it after you set the `background_pixmap` attribute are not guaranteed to be reflected in the window background. For consistent results, therefore, you need to reset the attribute after each change to the pixmap.

ParentRelative Specifies that the parent's background is to be used and that the origin for tiling is the parent's origin (or the parent's parent if the parent's `background_pixmap` attribute is also **Parent-Relative** and so on). The difference between setting **Parent-Relative** and explicitly setting the same pixmap as the parent is the origin of the tiling. The difference between **Parent-Relative** and **None** is that for **ParentRelative**, the background is automatically repainted on exposure.

The window must have the same depth as the parent, or a **Bad-Match** error will occur. If the parent has background **None**, then the window will also have background **None**. The parent's background is re-examined each time the window background is required (when it needs to be redrawn due to exposure). The window's contents will be lost when the window is moved relative to its parent, and the contents will have to be redrawn.

Changing the `background_pixmap` attribute of the root window to **None** or **Parent-Relative** restores the default background, which is server-dependent.

By the way, the symbol **CopyFromParent** is not used for setting the background, but it will not cause an error, since its value is the same as **None**.

4.3.1.2 background_pixel

If the background pixel value is specified, the entire background will take on the color (or shade of gray) indicated for that pixel value in the current colormap.*

The `background_pixel` attribute has the following possible values:

undefined (default)   Indicates that the background is as specified in the `background_pixmap` attribute. This value is possible only by creating a window with **XCreateWindow()** and not setting the `background_pixel` attribute.

a pixel value   The background is filled with the specified pixel value. This can be set with the last argument of **XCreateSimpleWindow()**, **XCreateWindow()**, or **XChangeWindowAttributes()**.

4.3.2 The Window Border

Like the window background, the window border may have a solid color or may be tiled with a pixmap. This choice is again up to the programmer, though the user should be allowed to determine the color or colors.

---

*We should inform you here that a pixel value is not something you choose yourself; you choose a color name, and the pixel value is returned to you from **BlackPixel** or **WhitePixel()** or one of the routines that allocate colors. We go into this subject in detail in Chapter 7, *Color*.

Unlike changes to the window background, changes to a window's border attributes are reflected immediately. No call to **XClearWindow()** or call to flush the request buffer is necessary. This feature makes it possible to use the window border for indicating a client's state. But you cannot use the border of the top-level window, since some window managers manipulate this border to indicate the keyboard focus window (see Section 8.3.2.1 for a description of the keyboard focus).

The design of a pattern for the border will be different from the background pixmap, because the border width is usually narrow (at most four pixels).

The two attributes that affect the border are **border_pixmap** and **border_pixel**. **XSetWindowBorderPixmap()** and **XSetWindowBorder()** can be used to set these attributes. Like the window background, whenever one of these routines is called, it overrides the previous setting of the border. If they are both set simultaneously with **XCreateWindow()** or **XChangeWindowAttributes()**, the **border_pixel** attribute takes precedence.

Most applications simply set the **border_pixel** to **BlackPixel** or **WhitePixel()** in the next-to-last argument of **XCreateSimpleWindow()**.

4.3.2.1 border_pixmap

If the **border_pixmap** is set to a pixmap, the border is tiled with the pixmap. Tiling is performed as described previously for the background pixmap; the border tile origin is the same as the background tile origin.

The **border_pixmap** attribute has the following possible values:

CopyFromParent (default)
> Specifies that the border pixmap is to be copied from the parent. (Note that **CopyFromParent** will cause protocol errors if the window's depth is different from its parent's.) Subsequent changes to the parent's border attributes do not affect the child, but changes to the pixmap used by the parent may be reflected in the child border (server-dependent).

None
> Specifies that the window has no border pixmap. If the window has no border pixel value either, then it uses the same border pixel value as the parent.

a pixmap ID
> Specifies a pixmap to be tiled in the border. The border tile origin is always the window origin; it is not taken from the background tile origin. If the pixmap is not explicitly referenced again, it can be freed since a copy is maintained in the server.

For the root window, **CopyFromParent** indicates that the default border will be inherited by subsequently created children of the root window, instead of any other border that was set for the root window. Setting the **border_pixmap** of the root window to **CopyFrom-Parent** restores the default border pixmap for later inheritance.

4.3.2.2 border_pixel

If a border pixel value is specified, the entire border will take on the color (or shade of gray) indicated for that pixel value in the current colormap.

The `border_pixel` attribute has the following possible values:

undefined (default)   Indicates that the border is as specified in the `border_pixmap` attribute. This value is possible only by creating a window with `XCreateWindow()` and not setting the `border_pixel` attribute.

a pixel value   Overrides the default and any `border_pixmap` given, and fills the border with the specified pixel value. This is set by the next-to-last argument of `XCreateSimpleWindow()`.

4.3.3 Bit Gravity

When an unobscured window is moved, its contents are moved with it, since none of the pixel values need to be changed. But when a window is enlarged or shrunk, the server has no idea where in the resulting window the old contents should be placed, so it normally throws them out. The `bit_gravity` attribute tells the server where to put the existing bits in the larger or smaller window. By instructing the server where to place the old contents, bit gravity allows some clients (not all can take advantage of it) to avoid redrawing parts of their windows.

Bit gravity is never *necessary* in programs. It does not affect the appearance or functionality of the client. It is used to improve performance in certain cases. Some X servers may not implement bit gravity and may throw out the window contents on resizing regardless of the setting of this attribute. This response is the default for all servers. That is, the default bit gravity is `ForgetGravity`, which means that the contents of a window are always lost when the window is resized, even if they are maintained in backing store or because of a `save_under` (to be described in Sections 4.3.5 and 4.3.6).

The window is tiled with its background in the areas that are not preserved by the bit gravity, unless no background is defined, in which case the existing screen is not altered.

There is no routine to set the `bit_gravity` individually; it can be set only with `XChangeWindowAttributes()` or `XCreateWindow()`.

The `bit_gravity` attribute has 11 possible values:

`ForgetGravity` (default)   Specifies that window contents should always be discarded after a size change. Note that some X servers may not implement bit gravity and may use `ForgetGravity` in all cases.

`StaticGravity`   Specifies that window contents should not move relative to the origin of the root window. This means that the area of intersection between the original extent of the window and the final extent of the window will not be disturbed.

Each constant below specifies where the old window contents should be placed in the resized window.

NorthWestGravity	Upper-left corner of the resized window.
NorthGravity	Top center of the resized window.
NorthEastGravity	Upper-right corner of the resized window.
WestGravity	Left center of the resized window.
CenterGravity	Center of the resized window.
EastGravity	Right center of the resized window.
SouthWestGravity	Lower-left corner of the resized window.
SouthGravity	Bottom center of the resized window.
SouthEastGravity	Lower-right corner of the resized window.

Here are two examples of applications that could take advantage of bit gravity. Figure 4-1 shows a fictional application that draws a two-axis graph in a window, with the origin at the lower-left corner. If that window were resized, the application would want the old contents to be placed against the new lower-left corner, no matter which sides of the window were moved in or out. That application would set the **bit_gravity** attribute of this window to **SouthWestGravity**. Figure 4-1 shows the response of this window to resizing with this bit gravity setting.

Each compass constant, such as **SouthWestGravity**, indicates the placement of the retained region in the window after resizing. In this case, the lower-left corner of the existing pixels is placed against the lower-left corner of the resulting window. When an **Expose** event arrives, the application need only redraw the two new strips of the window at the top and right side. No **Expose** event will be generated on the area that was saved because of **bit_gravity**.

For another example, think of a window containing centered text. If that window were resized either larger or smaller, we would still like the text to be centered. In this case, the **bit_gravity** should be set to **CenterGravity**. Then only if the window is resized smaller than the length of the text would we have to redraw the area and only then to break the line or use a shorter message. We could see whether changing the message would be necessary by looking at the **ConfigureNotify** event that occurs as a result of the resize (see *basicwin* in Chapter 3, *Basic Window Program*). The window would still have to be redrawn if it were obscured and then exposed, of course—bit gravity only saves *some* of the redrawing that would otherwise have to be done.

If the constant were **NorthGravity**, the top center of the pixels in the window before the resize would be placed against the top center of the resulting window. This would be appropriate if we had a line of text centered at the top of the window that we wished to preserve when possible.

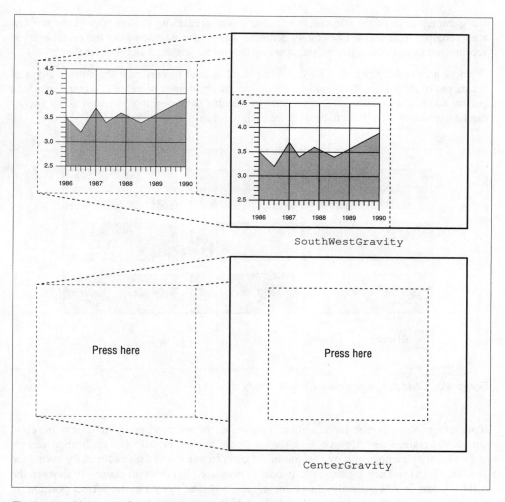

Figure 4-1. bit_gravity for a graphing application

4.3.4 Window Gravity

The `win_gravity` attribute controls the repositioning of subwindows when a parent window is resized. The attribute is set on the children. Normally, each child has a fixed position measured from the origin of the parent window. Window gravity can be used to tell the server to unmap the child or to move the child an amount depending on the change in size of the parent. The constants used to set `win_gravity` are similar to those for bit gravity, but their effect is quite different.

`NorthGravity` specifies that the child window should be moved horizontally by an amount one-half as great as the amount the window was resized in the horizontal direction. The child is not moved vertically. That means that if the window was originally centered along the top edge of the window, it will also be centered along the top edge of the window after resizing. If it was not originally centered, its relative distance from the center may be accentuated or reduced depending on whether the parent is resized larger or smaller.

Window gravity is only useful for children placed against or very near the outside edges of the parent or directly in its center. Furthermore, the child must be centered along one of the outside edges or in a corner. Figure 4-2 shows the nine child positions where window gravity can be useful and the setting to be used for each position.

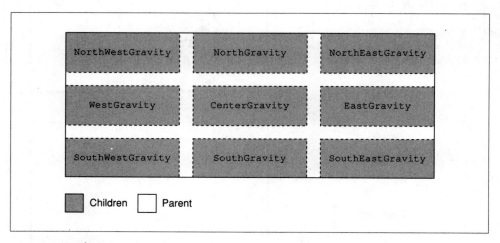

Figure 4-2. Child positions where window gravity is useful

If any other setting is used for any of these positions, the window gravity may move the child outside the resized parent, since there are no checks to prevent this. The application can try to prevent it by getting the new position of the child from a **ConfigureNotify** event (see Section 3.2.16) and moving the child inside if necessary. But this will cause a flash when the child window is automatically placed incorrectly and then moved to the correct position by the application. And if an application has to go to the trouble to check the position and move the child, it might as well just forget about window gravity and place the child itself.

NorthWestGravity (the default) indicates that the child (for which this attribute is set) is not moved relative to its parent.

UnmapGravity specifies that the subwindow should be unmapped when the parent is resized. This might be used when a client wishes to recalculate the positions of its children. Normally, the children would appear in their old positions before the client could move them into their recalculated positions. This can be confusing to the user. By setting the **win_gravity** attribute to **UnmapGravity**, the server will unmap the windows. They can be repositioned at the client's leisure, and then the client can remap them (with **XMap-Subwindows()**) in their new locations.

There is no routine to set the `win_gravity` attribute individually; it can be set only with `XChangeWindowAttributes()` or `XCreateWindow()`.

The `win_gravity` attribute has the following possible values:

`UnmapGravity` Specifies that the child is unmapped (removed from the screen) when the parent is resized, and an **UnmapNotify** event is generated.

`StaticGravity` Specifies that the window contents should not move relative to the origin of the root window.

One of the compass constants below

The list below shows the distance the child window will be moved; W is the amount the parent was resized in width, and H is the amount the parent was resized in height:

`NorthWestGravity` (default)	(0, 0)
`NorthGravity`	(W/2, 0)
`NorthEastGravity`	(W, 0)
`WestGravity`	(0, H/2)
`CenterGravity`	(W/2, H/2)
`EastGravity`	(W, H/2)
`SouthWestGravity`	(0, H)
`SouthGravity`	(W/2, H)
`SouthEastGravity`	(W, H)

4.3.5 Backing Store

A *backing store* automatically maintains the contents of a window while it is obscured or even while it is unmapped. Backing is like having a copy of the window saved in a pixmap, automatically copied to the screen whenever necessary to keep the visible contents up to date. Backing store is only available on some servers, usually on high performance workstations.

These servers can be instructed when to back up a window and which planes to save, through the backing store attributes. Even when it is available, the backing store should be avoided since it may carry a heavy performance penalty on the server. You can find out whether backing is supported on a particular screen with the **DoesBackingStore()** macro.

A client might use this feature to back up a window the client is incapable of redrawing for some reason or to be able to draw into a window that is obscured or unmapped.

Three separate attributes control backing: `backing_store`, `backing_planes`, and `backing_pixel`. There are no routines for setting these attributes individually (use `XChangeWindowAttributes()` or `XCreateWindow()`). The `backing_store` attribute determines when and if a window's contents are preserved by the server. The `backing_planes` attribute specifies which planes must be preserved, and `backing_pixel` specifies the pixel value used to fill planes not specified in `backing_planes`. The X server is free to save only the bit planes specified in `backing_planes` and to regenerate the remaining planes with the specified pixel value.

When the backing store feature is active and the window is larger than its parent, the server maintains complete contents, not just the region within the parent's boundaries. If the server is maintaining the contents of a window, `Expose` events will not be generated when that window is exposed.

Use of the backing store does not make a window immune to the other window attributes. If the `bit_gravity` is `ForgetGravity`, the contents will still be lost whenever the window is resized.

The `backing_store` attribute has the following possible values:

`NotUseful` (default) — Advises the server that maintaining contents is unnecessary. A server may still choose to maintain contents.

`WhenMapped` — Advises the server that it would be beneficial to maintain contents of obscured regions when the window is mapped.

`Always` — Advises the server that it would be beneficial to maintain contents even when the window is unmapped.

The `backing_planes` attribute specifies a mask (default all 1's) that indicates which planes of the window hold dynamic data that must be preserved in the backing store.

The `backing_pixel` attribute specifies a pixel value (default 0) to be used in planes not specified in the `backing_plane` attribute.

4.3.6 Saving Under

The `save_under` attribute controls whether the contents of the screen beneath a window should be preserved just before the window is mapped and replaced just after it is unmapped. This attribute is most useful for pop-up windows, which need to be on the screen only briefly. No `Expose` events will be sent to the windows that are exposed when the pop-up window is unmapped, saving the time necessary to redraw their contents.

Pop-up windows are usually children of the root window and, therefore, are not constrained to appear within the application's top-level window. Therefore, without `save_under` both your application and other applications on the screen would need to redraw areas when the pop-up window is unmapped.

Setting `save_under` is never necessary, but it can improve the performance of the server running clients that frequently map and unmap temporary windows. The user would otherwise have to wait for the area under the menu to be redrawn when the menu was unmapped.

There is no routine for setting the `save_under` attribute individually; it can only be set with `XChangeWindowAttributes()` or `XCreateWindow()`.

The `save_under` attribute is different from the backing store; `save_under` may save portions of several windows beneath a window for the duration of the appearance of the window on the screen, while the backing store saves the contents of a single window while it is mapped or even when unmapped, depending on the attributes.

Not all servers are capable of saving under windows. You can find out whether this feature is supported on a particular screen with the **DoesSaveUnders()** macro.

The **save_under** attribute has the following possible values:

False (default)   Specifies that covered clients should be sent **Expose** events when the window is unmapped, unless they are preserved in the backing store.

True   Specifies that the server should save areas under the window and replace them when the window is unmapped.

Setting the **save_under** attribute to **True** does not prevent all **Expose** events on the area underneath. For example, assume there is a window whose **bit_gravity** is **ForgetGravity**, and this window lies under a window that has the **save_under** attribute set to **True**. The contents of the obscured window will be lost if the underlying window is resized while partially obscured, and **Expose** events will be generated even on the saved area.

4.3.7 Event Handling

The **event_mask** and **do_not_propagate_mask** attributes control the propagation of events through the window hierarchy. The **event_mask** attribute is normally set with **XSelectInput()**, but it can also be set directly with **XChangeWindow-Attributes()** or **XCreateWindow()**.

The **event_mask** attribute specifies which event types are queued for the window when they occur. The **do_not_propagate_mask** attribute defines which events should not be propagated to ancestor windows when the event type is not selected in this window. Both masks are made by combining the constants listed below using the bitwise OR operator (|).

Button1MotionMask	KeyPressMask
Button2MotionMask	KeyReleaseMask
Button3MotionMask	LeaveWindowMask
Button4MotionMask	NoEventMask
Button5MotionMask	OwnerGrabButtonMask
ButtonMotionMask	PointerMotionHintMask
ButtonPressMask	PointerMotionMask
ButtonReleaseMask	PropertyChangeMask
ColormapChangeMask	ResizeRedirectMask
EnterWindowMask	StructureNotifyMask
ExposureMask	SubstructureNotifyMask
FocusChangeMask	SubstructureRedirectMask
KeymapStateMask	VisibilityChangeMask

Much more information on setting the event masks, including examples, is presented in Chapter 8, *Events*. This is a very important topic.

4.3.8 Substructure Redirect Override

A feature called *substructure redirect* allows a window manager to intercept any requests to map, move, resize, or change the border width of windows. This allows the window manager to modify these requests, if necessary, to ensure that they meet its window layout policy.

Setting the `override_redirect` attribute `True` for a window allows a window to be mapped, moved, resized, or its border width changed without the intervention of the window manager. This override is usually done for menus that are frequently mapped and almost immediately unmapped again.

Under properly designed window managers, there is a property you can set to tell the window manager to allow a window to pop up with minimal intervention (`XA_WM_TRANSIENT_FOR`). This is used for dialog boxes, as described in Section 12.3.1.4.6.

There is no routine for setting the `override_redirect` attribute individually; it must be set with `XChangeWindowAttributes()` or `XCreateWindow()`.

The `override_redirect` attribute has the following possible values:

`False` (default)   Specifies that map, move, and resize requests may be processed by the window manager.

`True`   Specifies that map, move, and resize requests are to be done verbatim, bypassing any window manager involvement.

4.3.9 Colormap

The `colormap` attribute specifies which colormap should be used to interpret the pixel values in a window.

For the large majority of clients without special color needs, this attribute can be left in its default state. By default, the `colormap` attribute from the parent is taken, which, if all ancestors of the window have used the default, will be the default colormap. This means that the default colormap for the screen will be used to translate into colors the pixel values drawn into this window.

If the client requires its own colormap for some reason, the client can create a colormap and set the `colormap` attribute to the ID of the new colormap. A colormap ID is of type `Colormap`.

The window manager will read this attribute and install the specified colormap into the hardware colormap when the user indicates that the application should be active. If the system only has one hardware colormap, all other applications will appear in false colors. This is one good reason that applications are encouraged not to create their own colormaps but to use the default colormap instead.

To understand this process, you need to know more about colormaps in X, and for that, see Chapter 7, *Color*.

`XSetWindowColormap()` sets the `colormap` attribute, which can be set to the following values:

`CopyFromParent` (default)
        Specifies that the colormap attribute is to be copied from the parent (subsequent changes to the parent's attribute do not affect the child), but the window must have the same visual type as the parent and the parent must not have a colormap of `None` (otherwise a `BadMatch` error occurs).

a colormap ID   The specified colormap will be used for displaying this window, at least while the window manager considers the application active.

.3.10 Cursor

The cursor is the object that tracks the pointer on the screen, sometimes called the sprite. In X, a *cursor* is a server resource which defines a cursor pattern, its colors, and the point within the pattern that will be reported in events (called the *hotspot*). The ID of a cursor is of type `Cursor`.

Most clients will define a suitable cursor for their top-level window and other cursors for each subwindow if needed. For example, *xterm* specifies the thin text cursor for the main window and a vertical bidirectional arrow for the scrollbar.

A cursor can be associated with any `InputOutput` or `InputOnly` window using the `cursor` attribute. Then the specified cursor will track the pointer while the pointer is within the window's borders.

A primary purpose for having a different cursor in a window is to indicate visually to the user that something different will happen to keyboard or button input while in the window. Another reason might be to change a cursor's color to increase its visibility over the background of certain windows (although there is another way to obtain contrast, with the cursor mask). There are probably other uses for a separate cursor.

A call to `XDefineCursor()` sets this attribute to a `Cursor`, and a call to `XUndefine-Cursor()` sets it back to `None`, which means that the cursor of the parent is used. The resource `Cursor` must be created before calling `XDefineCursor()`. This can be done with `XCreateFontCursor()`. `XCreateGlyphCursor()`, or `XCreatePixmap-Cursor()`, as described in Section 6.5.1. The `cursor` resource can be freed with `XFreeCursor()` when no further explicit references to it are to be made.

The `cursor` attribute has the following possible values:

`None` (default)   Specifies that the parent's cursor will be used when the pointer is in the window.

a cursor ID   Specifies a cursor that will be used whenever the pointer is in the window.

The cursor of the root window is initially a large X, but this may be changed like the cursor in any other window if desired. However, this should only be done by the window manager or by the user using the *xsetroot* application. See Volume Three, *X Window System User's Guide*, for a description of *xsetroot*.

4.3.11 Default Attributes

Table 4-3 summarizes the default attributes for an `InputOutput` window. Only five of the attributes are relevant for `InputOnly` windows: `cursor`, `do_not_propagate_mask`, `event_mask`, `override_redirect`, and `win_gravity`. These attributes have the same defaults as for `InputOutput` windows.

The background, border, and `event_mask` attributes need to be set for virtually all windows.

Table 4-3. Default Window Attributes

Member	Default Value
background_pixmap	None
background_pixel	Undefined
border_pixmap	CopyFromParent
border_pixel	Undefined
bit_gravity	ForgetGravity
win_gravity	NorthWestGravity
backing_store	NotUseful
backing_planes	All 1's (ones)
backing_pixel	0 (zero)
override_redirect	False
save_under	False
event_mask	0
do_not_propagate_mask	0
colormap	CopyFromParent
cursor	None

4.4 Information from the XWindowAttributes Structure

We have been describing the programmable window attributes stored in the **XSetWindow-Attributes** structure. Many of the other window characteristics described in Chapter 2, *X Concepts*, including the window configuration, are also stored with the window attributes by the server but are not programmable using **XChangeWindowAttributes()**. For example, depth, class, and visual are assigned at window creation and cannot be changed. The window size, position, and border width are changed with a separate mechanism, because for top-level windows there must be cooperation from the window manager.

The current state of most of the programmable attributes, the read-only attributes, and the window configuration can be read with **XGetWindowAttributes()**. All this information is returned in an **XWindowAttributes** structure (not an **XSetWindow-Attributes** structure).

Example 4-4 shows the fields of the **XWindowAttributes** structure that are not present in **XSetWindowAttributes**.

Example 4-4. Read-only XWindowAttributes members

```
typedef struct {
      /* Members writable with XChangeWindowAttributes omitted */
      .
      .
      .

      /* Window geometry -- set by window configuration functions
       * in cooperation with window manager */
      int x, y;                /* Location of window */
      int width, height;       /* Width and height of window */
      int border_width;        /* Border width of window */

      /* This is the event_mask attribute set by XSelectInput */
      long your_event_mask;    /* My event mask */

      /* Set when the window is created, not changeable */
      Visual *visual;          /* The associated visual structure */
      int class;               /* InputOutput, InputOnly */
      int depth;               /* Depth of window */
      Screen *screen;          /* Pointer to screen the window is on */

      /* Server sets these members */
      Window root;             /* Root of screen containing window */
      Bool map_installed;      /* Is colormap currently installed */
      int map_state;           /* IsUnmapped, IsUnviewable, or
                                * IsViewable */
      long all_event_masks;    /* Events all clients have interest in */
} XWindowAttributes;
```

As you can see, the members of **XWindowAttributes** that cannot be directly written with **XChangeWindowAttributes()** are separated into four groups.

The first group provides a way to get the window geometry. This information is returned by **XGetGeometry()**, but it might be useful to use **XGetWindowAttributes()** instead if you need both the geometry and a few attributes.

The **your_event_mask** member can be useful if you want to add event mask symbols to those already selected. In a call to **XSelectInput()**, you must always specify all the desired event masks. If you do not know which event masks are already selected or do not want to bother passing an **event_mask** argument into one of your routines, you could read the existing event mask here. Then you could OR in any additional event mask symbols before calling **XSelectInput()** or **XChangeWindowAttributes()**. See Chapter 8, *Events*, for more information on the use of event masks.

The **depth**, **class**, **visual**, and **screen** members are set when the window is created. If the window was created with **XCreateSimpleWindow()**, they were inherited from the parent. If the window was created with **XCreateWindow()**, these members were specified as arguments, except **screen**, which is indirectly specified by the *parent* argument. The **screen** member points to a structure that tells you about the screen on which this window was created. This is one of the **Screen** structures from the list in the **Display** structure, and therefore, the information it contains can also be gotten from the macros as described in Section 3.2.3 and Appendix C, *Macros*, of Volume Two, *Xlib Reference*

Window Attributes

Manual. Again, these should only be needed for convenience to avoid having to pass around these values as arguments or global variables.

The `root` member tells you the ID of the root window on the screen on which your window was created. It is usually more convenient to use the `RootWindow()` macro.

The `map_installed` member can be monitored to tell your application whether the color-map it has set in its `colormap` attribute is currently installed. If not, the application may be displayed in false colors. See Chapter 7, *Color*, for more details.

The `map_state` member can be monitored by a program and used to turn off processing while a window is unviewable. Some applications that continuously poll for input or draw (such as in action games) can stop doing so and save processor cycles when there is no chance of getting input or no point in drawing.

The `all_event_masks` member tells you all the event types that are selected by all clients on the window requested. This is the OR of all the `event_mask` attributes for that window for all clients. By contrast, `your_event_mask` specifies only the events selected by *your* client.

Also note that `XWindowAttributes` is missing a few fields that are present in `XSetWindowAttributes`. This means that there are some fields that can be set but not queried. These fields are the background and border pixel value and pixmap and the cursor. The designers of X decided to make these fields nonreadable to reduce restrictions on the implementation of backgrounds, borders, and cursors in the server.

5

The Graphics Context

The graphics primitives supplied with X are quite simple. Most of the details about how graphics are to be drawn are stored in a resource called a graphics context (GC). GCs are stored in the server, thus reducing the amount of information that needs to be transmitted for each graphics request. This chapter describes how to use GCs and provides details on each member of the XGCValues structure. Everyone should read this chapter.

In This Chapter:

5
The Graphics Context

The X routines that draw graphics are called *graphics primitives*. They draw dots, lines, text, images, and tile or fill areas, and will be described fully in Chapter 6, *Drawing Graphics and Text*. But a given graphics primitive does not contain all the information needed to draw a particular graphic. A server resource called a *graphics context* (GC) contains values for variables that apply to each graphics primitive. The appearance of everything that is drawn *by a program* is controlled by the GC that is specified with each graphics primitive. (The border and background of a window are not affected or controlled by the GC—they are controlled by window attributes, and are drawn *by the server*.) What is drawn into a pixmap is also controlled by the GC used in the drawing to the pixmap and, again, possibly with a different GC, if the pixmap is copied into a window. To draw, you must first create a GC and set its values, then specify that GC as an argument in the graphics primitive.

There are two performance-related reasons X was designed to use GCs. First, they reduce the traffic between Xlib and the server because the GC information is held in the server and needs to be sent only once before the first graphics request. Each subsequent primitive that specifies the same GC will use the same values. When a few settings of the GC need to be changed, only the selected few need to be sent, not the entire GC. Second, you can create several GCs and then simply specify which GC you want applied to each graphics request. This has important performance benefits on servers that are capable of caching multiple GCs in their display hardware.

The GC also allows for more convenient programming, since to provide the same flexibility without the GC, you would need to specify an absurd number of arguments every time you called a graphics primitive.

A few more words are needed regarding the distinction between the roles of the graphics primitive and the GC. You can think of a graphics primitive as specifying the general shape to be drawn, while the GC specifies how to draw it. For example, a primitive that draws a filled rectangle specifies the top-left corner of the rectangle in the drawable and its dimensions, while the GC specifies its color or the pattern applied to it (among other things). Note that both the graphics primitive and the GC play a role in selecting exactly which pixels are drawn. For example, the graphics primitive specifies the start and end points for lines (including unfilled arcs, rectangles, and polygons), while the GC specifies the width of the line and the shape of the joints and ends of the lines. Other components of the GC affect pixel selection with other graphics primitives. For all primitives, the GC includes a clip mask that you can use to restrict which pixels are drawn.

To predict the effect of particular GC settings on a particular graphics primitive, it is useful to visualize the drawing process in a number of stages, even though in reality the drawing of each bit of each pixel is performed by the server in a single equation.*

1. The first stage is pixel selection. As we just described, pixel selection is specified by the graphics primitive, in some cases along with the `line_width, clip_mask`, and other elements in the GC. The result of the first stage is a bitmap—a single rectangle of bits, with the pixels to be drawn set to one and the pixels not to be drawn set to zero.

2. The second stage applies one or two colors or a pattern to the results of the first stage, resulting in a pixmap which has the same depth (number of bits per pixel) as the drawable.† The output of the second stage is referred to later in this chapter as the *source*.

3. In the third stage, a plane mask may be applied to select which planes of the drawable can be affected by the graphics request. This is done to play tricks with color, such as to draw temporary graphics that can be erased without erasing other things already drawn in a window, as demonstrated in Chapter 7, *Color*. By default, the plane mask is all ones and therefore has no effect on what is drawn.

4. In the fourth stage, the pixel values resulting from stage three can be combined with what is already on the screen using so-called *logical functions*. Most graphics are drawn by simply overwriting the existing graphics using a logical function of `GXcopy`, but there are useful tricks that can be played by using certain other logical functions. One such effect is called *rubber-banding*; the window manager uses this technique to show you the outline of a window you are moving or resizing.

Figure 5-1 illustrates these four stages used in drawing a wide line, and the GC elements that can be used to control each stage. The sections below that describe the various members of the GC are organized according to the stage that they affect. This information is summarized in one of the GC-at-a-glance tables inside the back cover of Volume Two, *Xlib Reference Manual*.

Since we are not yet using any of the tricks that require use of the `plane_mask` or logical `function`, the third and fourth stages in Figure 5-1 use the default values of these GC elements. They therefore do not modify the result of the graphics primitive.

To make this overview complete, it's important to mention that the GC also has the following two features (described more completely in Section 5.6 and Section 5.7):

- The `graphics_exposures` member lets you select `GraphicsExpose` and `No-Expose` events, to indicate whether areas being copied using `XCopyArea()` and `XCopyPlane()` requests are visible or invisible. (This is important because invisible areas cannot be copied, and must be drawn some other way.)

---

*I am indebted to Ollie Jones of PictureTel Corp. for the idea of thinking of the graphics context as affecting several independent stages in drawing, which he calls the "graphics pipeline."

†For `XCopyArea()` this second stage is skipped, since the pixels taken from the source drawable must already have the same depth as the destination drawable.

- The **subwindow_mode** member lets you specify whether subwindows obscure graphics drawn on the parent. The default is **True,** and usually needs changing only for rubber-banding.

Now we will discuss how to create and set the GC, before moving on to details of individual members of the GC.

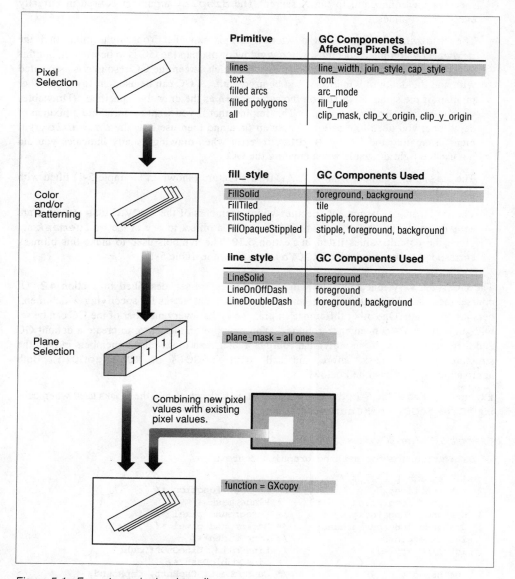

Figure 5-1. Four stages in drawing a line

5.1 Creating and Setting a Graphics Context

Before a GC can be used, you must create it by calling **XCreateGC( )**. **XCreateGC( )** requires only four arguments: *display*, *drawable*, *values*, and *valuemask*.

- The *display* argument (pointer to a **Display** structure) should be familiar by now; it specifies the connection to the X server. The *display* argument is used in virtually every Xlib routine.

- The *drawable* argument is a window or pixmap ID. You might think that the *drawable* argument specifies which window or pixmap the GC is to be used in, but this is not necessarily the case. It really indicates which screen the GC resource is associated with and the depth of windows it can be used with. A GC can be used on any window or pixmap of the same depth and on the same screen as the drawable specified. (Drawables were introduced in Section 2.3.3.) This implies that if you want to draw into a pixmap of depth one, you need to create that pixmap first, and then use it as the *drawable* argument in creating the GC. A **BadMatch** error when drawing usually indicates you did not use the right drawable when creating the GC.

- The *values* argument is an **XGCValues** structure (shown in Example 5-1) filled with the desired settings for the GC.

- The *valuemask* argument specifies which members of the **XGCValues** structure are actually read. The members not represented by a bit set to one in the *valuemask* are given the default values listed in Section 5.10. The symbols used to make this bitmask correspond to the members of **XGCValues** shown in Table 5-1.

The GC is set very much like the window attributes are set, described in Section 4.2. Of course, there is a different structure and there are different masks for specifying which members are to be set. One other difference in practice is that every member of the GC can be set with an individual "convenience routine." You may prefer, therefore, to create a default GC and then modify it with the individual routines rather than to set all the members in both the structure and the mask before you call **XCreateGC( )** or **XChangeGC( )**. Both approaches are demonstrated below.

Example 5-1 and Table 5-1 present the **XGCValues** structure and the masks used when calling **XCreateGC( )** or **XChangeGC( )**.

Example 5-1. The GCValues structure

```
/* Data structure for setting graphics context   */

typedef struct {
        int function;                  /* Logical function */
        unsigned long plane_mask;      /* Plane mask */
        unsigned long foreground;      /* Foreground pixel */
        unsigned long background;      /* Background pixel */
        int line_width;                /* Line width */
        int line_style;                /* LineSolid, LineOnOffDash,
                                        * LineDoubleDash */
        int cap_style;                 /* CapNotLast, CapButt, CapRound,
                                        * CapProjecting */
```

Example 5-1. The GCValues structure (continued)

```
        int join_style;              /* JoinMiter, JoinRound, JoinBevel */
        int fill_style;              /* FillSolid, FillTiled, FillStippled,
                                      * FillOpaqueStippled */
        int fill_rule;               /* EvenOddRule, WindingRule */
        int arc_mode;                /* ArcChord, ArcPieSlice */
        Pixmap tile;                 /* Tile pixmap for tiling operations */
        Pixmap stipple;              /* Pixmap of depth 1 */
        int ts_x_origin;             /* Offset for tile or stipple operations */
        int ts_y_origin;
        Font font;                   /* Font for text operations (except
                                      * XDrawText) */
        int subwindow_mode;          /* ClipByChildren, IncludeInferiors */
        Bool graphics_exposures;     /* Should events be generated on
                                      * XCopyArea, XCopyPlane  */
        int clip_x_origin;           /* Origin for clipping */
        int clip_y_origin;
        Pixmap clip_mask;            /* Bitmap for clipping */
        int dash_offset;             /* Patterned/dashed line information */
        char dashes;
} XGCValues;
```

The meaning and possible values for each member are described in Sections 5.3 through 5.7.

Table 5-1 shows the symbols used to specify which members of the **XGCValues** structure actually contain meaningful values. The *valuemask* is made up of these symbols combined by means of a bitwise OR (|).

Table 5-1. Symbols for Setting the XGCValues Structure

Member	Mask	Set Bit	Default
function	GCFunction	0	GXcopy
plane_mask	GCPlaneMask	1	all 1's
foreground	GCForeground	2	0
background	GCBackground	3	1
line_width	GCLineWidth	4	0
line_style	GCLineStyle	5	LineSolid
cap_style	GCCapStyle	6	CapButt
join_style	GCJoinStyle	7	JoinMiter
fill_style	GCFillStyle	8	FillSolid
fill_rule	GCFillRule	9	EvenOddRule
arc_mode	GCArcMode	22	ArcPieSlice
tile	GCTile	10	pixmap filled with foreground pixel
stipple	GCStipple	11	pixmap filled with 1's
ts_x_origin	GCTileStipXOrigin	12	0
ts_y_origin	GCTileStipYOrigin	13	0
font	GCFont	14	(implementation dependent)
subwindow_mode	GCSubwindowMode	15	ClipByChildren
graphics_exposures	GCGraphicsExposures	16	True

Table 5-1. Symbols for Setting the XGCValues Structure (continued)

Member	Mask	Set Bit	Default
clip_x_origin	GCClipXOrigin	17	0
clip_y_origin	GCClipYOrigin	18	0
clip_mask	GCClipMask	19	None
dash_offset	GCDashOffset	20	0
dashes	GCDashList	21	4 (i.e., the list [4, 4])

Table 5-1 lists the default values for each element of the GC. A useful quick reference to the graphics context is provided inside the back cover of Volume Two, *Xlib Reference Manual*.

A *valuemask* composed of the symbols shown in Table 5-1 is used in **XChangeGC( )**, **XCopyGC( )**, and **XCreateGC( )**. In **XCopyGC( )**, though, the *valuemask* indicates which members are copied from the source GC to the destination GC, and the rest of the members in the destination are left unchanged. In **XChangeGC( )**, the specified members are changed and the rest are left unchanged.

Example 5-2 shows a simple way to set some of the values for a GC before creating it. This example uses the default values except for the foreground and background pixel values. You must always set at least the foreground component of the GC, and also the background component if it is used in what you intend to draw. This is because the default values for the foreground and background components, zero and one respectively, are not guaranteed to be black and white or even contrasting. (The relationship between pixel values and colors is explained in Chapter 7, *Color*.)

Example 5-2. Example of setting a GC while creating it

```
GC gc;
XGCValues values;
unsigned long valuemask;
        .
        .
/* Open display, create window, etc. */
        .
        .
values.foreground = BlackPixel(display,screen_num);
values.background = WhitePixel(display,screen_num);
gc = XCreateGC(display, RootWindow(display, screen_num),
        (GCForeground | GCBackground), &values);
/* Now you can use gc in drawing routines */
```

In Example 5-2, the foreground pixel value is set to the value returned by the **Black-Pixel( )** macro. This will result in a color of black if the default colormap is installed (more on this in Chapter 7, *Color*). To obtain a pixel value that represents any color other than black or white, you will need to allocate the color as described in Chapter 7.

Convenience functions are also available to change most elements of a GC after it is created. These functions are listed in Sections 5.3 through 5.7, which describe each GC element in detail. Example 5-3 performs the same functions as Example 5-2 but by creating a default GC and then modifying the contents with convenience functions.

Example 5-3. Example of setting default GC then changing it

```
GC gc;
        .
        .
        .
/* Open display, create window, etc. */
        .
        .
        .
gc = XCreateGC(display, RootWindow(display, screen_num), 0, NULL);
XSetForeground(display, gc, BlackPixel(display,screen_num));
XSetBackground(display, gc, WhitePixel(display,screen_num));

/* Now you can use gc in drawing routines */
```

NOTE

You may wonder which of these two ways is more efficient, setting the `XGCValues` and `valuemask`, or calling the convenience functions. Actually, there is not much difference, since in both cases, the individual requests to change the same GC are packaged into a single protocol request before being sent to the server. This optimization is implemented by Xlib. The method you should choose is mainly a matter of personal preference.

Also note that Xlib provides the function `XFlushGC()` to defeat Xlib's caching of GC changes by sending them to the server immediately instead of waiting until the GC is needed. `XFlushGC()` is used mainly in extensions that have drawing requests which otherwise would not trigger Xlib's cache.

5.2 Switching Between Graphics Contexts

One purpose of the GC is to store information about how to interpret graphics requests so that the same information does not have to be sent with every request. Another useful feature of the GC concept is that you can create several GCs with the different characteristics you need and then switch between them. Example 5-4 demonstrates how this is done. It creates two slightly different GCs with swapped foreground and background pixel values.

Example 5-4. Example of switching graphics contexts

```
GC gc1, gc2;
XGCValues values;
unsigned long valuemask;
        .
        .
        .
/* Open display, create window, etc. */
```

Example 5-4. Example of switching graphics contexts (continued)

```
values.foreground = BlackPixel(display,screen_num);
values.background = WhitePixel(display,screen_num);

gc1 = XCreateGC(display, RootWindow(display, screen_num),
    (GCForeground | GCBackground), &values);

values.foreground = WhitePixel(display,screen_num);
values.background = BlackPixel(display,screen_num);

gc2 = XCreateGC(display, RootWindow(display, screen_num),
    (GCForeground | GCBackground), &values);

/* Now you can use either gc in drawing routines, thereby
 * quickly swapping the foreground and background colors */
```

Whether it is faster to switch between GCs or to modify a few values of a single GC depends on the particular server implementation. On some types of display hardware, several or many GCs can be cached. On these servers, it is faster to switch between GCs than to change members of them. On servers that do not cache or that cache only one GC, it is faster to change one or two elements of the GC than to switch between two slightly different GCs. There is no way for the application to tell which of these two server types is in use. Therefore, accepted practice is to compromise by creating a small number of GCs (more on this in Section 5.9).

Now that you know how to create, set, and modify the GC, and how to set up multiple GCs, we can go into more detail about each element of the GC. The following sections describe each member of the graphics context, grouped according to the how they affect the drawing process: Pixel Selection, Coloring and Patterning, and Graphics Tricks.

5.3 Controlling Pixel Selection

As previously described, pixel selection can be thought of as the first of four stages in the drawing process. The pixels drawn are selected by a combination of the graphics primitive and various members of the graphics context. This section describes those GC elements.

5.3.1 Line Characteristics

Six of the graphics context components are line characteristics. These components obviously affect the graphics primitives that draw lines, but they also affect those that draw unfilled rectangles, arcs, and polygons. Here are the six line characteristics:

line_width   Specifies the width of the line in pixels. Zero means to draw using the
                server's fastest algorithm with a line width of one pixel, with some
                loss of accuracy.

line_style   Specifies whether the line is solid in foreground, dashed in foreground,
                or alternating foreground and background. Possible values are **Line-**
                Solid, **LineOnOffDash**, or **LineDoubleDash**.

cap_style	Controls the appearance of the ends of a line and in some cases the ends of dashes in a line. Possible values are `CapButt`, `CapNotLast`, `CapProjecting`, and `CapRound`.
join_style	Controls the appearance of joints between consecutive lines drawn within a single graphics primitive. Possible values are `JoinBevel`, `JoinMiter`, and `JoinRound`.
dashes	Specifies a pattern of dash lengths for custom-designed dashed lines. (Used only if the `line_style` is `LineOnOffDash` or `LineDoubleDash`.)
dash_offset	Specifies the starting point of the dash pattern for custom-designed dashed lines. (Used only if the `line_style` is `LineOnOffDash` or `LineDoubleDash`.)

The `line_width`, `line_style`, `cap_style`, and `join_style` components can be set using `XSetLineAttributes()`, while `dashes` and `dash_offset` can be set with `XSetDashes()`. Now we'll describe each of these line characteristics in more detail, followed by an example that sets them.

5.3.1.1 Line Width

The `line_width` member of `XGCValues` is measured in pixels. The line width can be set with `XSetLineAttributes()`.

A `line_width` greater than or equal to 1 is considered a *wide* line, and the value 0 is a special case, considered a *thin* line. Wide and thin lines often use different drawing algorithms. The thin line is intended to be a fast algorithm for drawing a line of width 1 but may not be as uniform as a wide line between different servers.

Wide lines are drawn centered on the path described by the graphics request. A wide line drawn from [x1,y1] to [x2,y2] always draws the same pixels as a wide line drawn from [x2,y2] to [x1,y1], not counting cap and join styles. This is not necessarily the case for thin lines.

Unless otherwise specified by the join or cap style, the bounding box of a wide line with endpoints [x1,y1], [x2,y2] and width *w* is a rectangle with vertices at the following real coordinates:

Lower Left:	[x1-(w*sin(θ)/2), y1+(w*cos(θ)/2)]
Upper Right:	[x1+(w*sin(θ)/2), y1-(w*cos(θ)/2)]
Lower Left:	[x2-(w*sin(θ)/2), y2+(w*cos(θ)/2)]
Lower Right:	[x2+(w*sin(θ)/2), y2-(w*cos(θ)/2)]

where θ is the angle of the line measured from horizontal.

A pixel is drawn if the center of the pixel is fully inside the bounding box (which is viewed as having infinitely thin edges). If the center of the pixel is exactly on the bounding box, it is part of the line only if the interior of the box is immediately to the pixel's right. Pixels with centers on a horizontal edge are part of the line only if the interior of the box is immediately below the pixel.

Thin lines (`line_width == 0`) are one-pixel-wide lines drawn using an unspecified, device-dependent fast algorithm. The set of points comprising thin lines will not be affected by clipping.

A wide line of width 1 and a thin line with `line_width` 0 drawn between the same two points may not be exactly alike. Because of their different drawing algorithms, thin lines may not mix well with wide lines, aesthetically speaking. For precise and uniform results across all displays, use a `line_width` of 1 rather than 0. If speed is the goal, use a `line_width` of 0.

5.3.1.2 Line Style

The `line_style` member of **XGCValues** defines which sections of a line are drawn and in which pixel value, as shown in Figure 5-2. The line style can be set with **XSetLine-Attributes()**. The actual length of each dash and gap is set by the **dashes** member of XGCValues, described in Section 5.3.1.5. The constants used to set `line_style` are as follows:

LineSolid   Specifies that the full path of the line is drawn using the foreground pixel value.

LineOnOffDash   Specifies that only the dashes are drawn, with the foreground pixel value, and `cap_style` applied to the ends of each dash (except that `CapNotLast` is treated as `CapButt` for dash ends).

LineDoubleDash   Specifies that the full path of the line is drawn, dashes with the foreground pixel value, gaps with the background pixel values, and `CapButt` style always used where dashes and gaps meet.

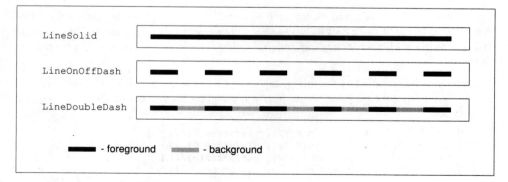

Figure 5-2. The line styles

5.3.1.3 Cap Style

The `cap_style` member of `XGCValues` defines how the endpoints of lines are drawn, as shown in Figure 5-3. The cap style can be set with `XSetLineAttributes()`. The constants used to set `cap_style` are as follows:

CapNotLast	Is equivalent to `CapButt`, except that for a `line_width` of 0 or 1, the final endpoint is not drawn. If specified with `line_style` `LineOnOffDash` or `LineDoubleDash`, the ends of the dashes or where even and odd dashes meet are treated as `CapButt`.
CapButt	Specifies that lines will be square at the endpoint with no projection beyond. The end is perpendicular to the slope of the line.
CapRound	Specifies that lines will be terminated by a circular arc with the diameter equal to the `line_width`, centered on the endpoint (equivalent to `CapButt` for `line_width` of 0 or 1).
CapProjecting	Specifies that lines will be square at the end but with the path continuing beyond the endpoint for a distance equal to half the `line_width` (equivalent to `CapButt` for `line_width` of 0 or 1).

5.3.1.4 Join Style

The `join_style` member of `XGCValues` defines how corners are drawn for wide lines drawn within a single graphics primitive, as shown in Figures 5-4 and 5-5. The join style can be set with `XSetLineAttributes()`. The constants used to set `join_style` are as follows:

JoinMiter	Specifies that the outer edges of the two lines should extend to meet at an angle. If the angle between the two lines is less than 11 degrees, `JoinBevel` is used.
JoinRound	Specifies that lines should be joined by a circular arc with diameter equal to the `line_width`, centered on the join point.
JoinBevel	Specifies `CapButt` endpoint styles, with the triangular notch filled.

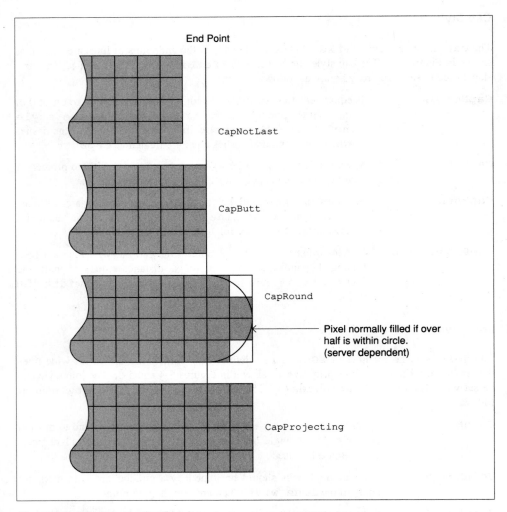

Figure 5-3. The line cap (end) styles

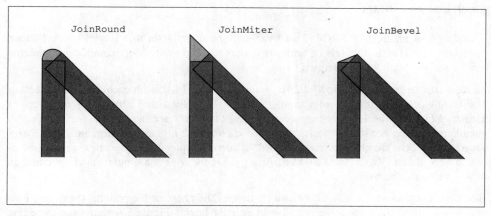

Figure 5-4. The line join styles

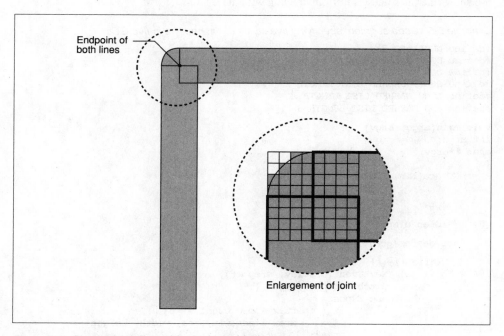

Figure 5-5. Detail of JoinRound for 8-pixel-wide lines

5.3.1.5 Dash List and Offset

The `dashes` member of `XGCValues` can only be directly set to a single, nonzero value specifying the length in pixels of both the dashes and the gaps. More complicated patterns can be set only with `XSetDashes()`.

In `XSetDashes()`, the *dash_list* argument is a real list, with each value representing the length of a single dash or gap in the line. The initial and alternating members of *dash_list* are the length of the *even* dashes; the others are the *odd* dashes (gaps). All members must be nonzero. The length of the *dash_list* is also an argument to `XSet-Dashes()`. The `dashes` element of `XGCValues` is equivalent to specifying a two-member *dash_list* [N, N] in `XSetDashes()`, where *N* is the single value specified in `XGCValues.dashes`.

The `dash_offset` for `XSetDashes()` defines the phase of the pattern, specifying how many pixels into the pattern the line should actually begin. Figure 5-6 shows the same line drawn with and without offset to demonstrate its effect.

Example 5-5 shows a code segment that creates and sets the line dashes of five GCs. Figure 5-6 shows the lines that result from drawing with these GCs.

Example 5-5. Code segment specifying five styles of dashed line in five GCs

```
#define NUMLINES 5
#define DOTTED_LIST_LENGTH 2
#define DOT_DASHED_LIST_LENGTH 4
#define SHORT_DASHED_LIST_LENGTH 2
#define LONG_DASHED_LIST_LENGTH 2
#define ODD_DASHED_LIST_LENGTH 3

void main(argc, argv)
int argc;
char **argv;
{
    GC gca[NUMLINES];
        .
        .
        .
    /* Open display, create windows, etc. */

    set_dashes(gca);

        while (1)  {
                XNextEvent(display, &report);
                switch  (report.type) {
                case Expose:
                        if (report.xexpose.count == 0)
                                draw_lines(win, gca, width, height);
                        break;
        .
        .
        .
}

set_dashes(gca)
GC gca[ ];
{
```

```
     XGCValues gcv;
     int i;
     static int dash_list_length[ ] = {
           DOTTED_LIST_LENGTH,
           DOT_DASHED_LIST_LENGTH,
           SHORT_DASHED_LIST_LENGTH,
           LONG_DASHED_LIST_LENGTH,
           ODD_DASHED_LIST_LENGTH
     };

     /* Must be at least one element in each list */
     static unsigned char dotted[DOTTED_LIST_LENGTH] =
              {3, 1};
     static unsigned char dot_dashed[DOT_DASHED_LIST_LENGTH] =
              {3, 4, 3, 1};
     static unsigned char short_dashed[SHORT_DASHED_LIST_LENGTH] =
              {4, 4};
     static unsigned char long_dashed[LONG_DASHED_LIST_LENGTH] =
              {4, 7};
     static unsigned char odd_dashed[ODD_DASHED_LIST_LENGTH] =
              {1, 2, 3};

     static unsigned char *dash_list[ ] = {
           dotted,
           dot_dashed,
           short_dashed,
           long_dashed,
           odd_dashed,
     };

     int dash_offset = 0;

     /* Open display, create window, etc. */

     gcv.line_style = LineOnOffDash;
     for (i = 0 ; i < NUMLINES; i++) {
           gca[i] = XCreateGC(display, RootWindow(display, screen_num),
                    GCLineStyle, &gcv);
           XSetDashes(display, gca[i], dash_offset, dash_list[i],
                    dash_list_length[i]);
     }
}

draw_lines(win, gca, window_width, window_height)
Window win;
GC gca[ ];
unsigned int window_width, window_height;
{
     int i;
     for (i=0;i < NUMLINES; i++) {
           XDrawLine(display, win, gca[i],
                    window_width/4, 40 + (10 * i),
                    3 * (window_width/4), 40 + (10 * i));
     }

}
```

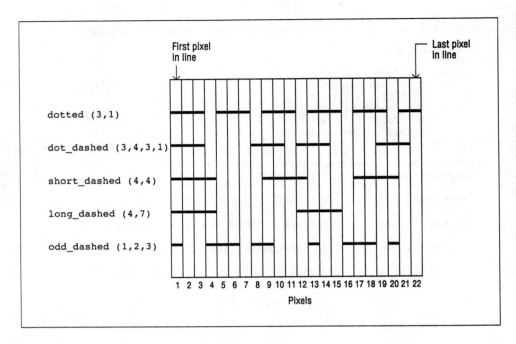

Figure 5-6. Lines drawn with GCs set in Example 5-5

5.3.1.6 Example of Setting Line Characteristics

Example 5-6 demonstrates how to set the line characteristics with **XSetLine-Attributes()**. This routine and **XSetDashes()** (which sets dashes, demonstrated in Example 5-5) are the only ways to set line characteristics, other than with **XCreateGC()** or **XChangeGC()**.

Example 5-6. Setting line characteristics in a GC

```
set_line_attributes(gc)
GC gc;
{
    unsigned int line_width = 3;    /* 0 would be fast line of width 1 */
    int line_style = LineSolid;     /* If LineOnOffDash or LineDoubleDash,
                                     * must set dashes */
    int cap_style = CapRound;       /* else CapNotLast, CapButt, or
                                     * CapProjecting */
    int join_style = JoinRound;     /* else JoinMiter or JoinBevel */

    XSetLineAttributes(display, gc, line_width, line_style,
            cap_style, join_style);
}
```

5.3.2 The Font

The `font` member of a GC specifies which font will be used in text-drawing graphics primitives that use this GC, and can be set with `XSetFont()`. If the specified font has not been loaded by this client, a graphics primitive that tries to draw text will not fail; it just will not draw. Therefore, you should make sure you load the font.

The X server actually loads a requested font into memory only when `XLoadFont()` or `XLoadQueryFont()` is called and if the specified font has not already been loaded by another client. A font is unloaded when the last program using the font exits or unloads it. Duplicate copies of a font are never stored in the server.

There are several ways to deal with fonts. Most programs will use `XLoadQueryFont()` to load a font and get information about the dimensions of each character. `XLoadQueryFont()` returns a pointer to an `XFontStruct`. The font in the GC can then be set to `XFontStruct.fid`. (See Chapter 6, *Drawing Graphics and Text*, for details.)

The default font is always loaded, but it is not the same on all servers. Section 6.2.2 describes how a program can find out about the default font on the particular server it is connected to.

5.3.3 Fill Rule

The `fill_rule` member of `XGCValues` defines which pixels are drawn for paths given in `XFillPolygon()` requests. The *fill_rule* is also an argument to `XPolygonRegion()`, which is described in Section 6.3. The `fill_rule` in the GC is set with `XSetFillRule()`. The `fill_rule` may be `EvenOddRule` (the default in the GC) or `WindingRule`.

As shown in Figure 5-7, `EvenOddRule` means that if areas overlap an odd number of times, they are not drawn. Technically, it specifies that a point is drawn if an infinite ray with the point as origin crosses the path an odd number of times.

`WindingRule`, also shown in Figure 5-7, means that overlapping areas are always filled, regardless of how many times they overlap. Technically, this rule specifies that a point is inside the filled area if an infinite ray with the point as origin crosses an unequal number of clockwise- and counterclockwise-directed path segments.

Since polygons are drawn as a series of points connected by lines, the order of the points determines the direction of each line. A clockwise-directed path segment is one which crosses the ray from left to right as observed from the point. A counterclockwise-directed segment is one which crosses the ray from right to left as observed from the point. The case where a directed line segment is coincident with the ray is uninteresting, because you can simply choose a different ray that is not coincident with a segment.

All calculations are performed on infinitely small points, so that if any point within a pixel is considered inside, the entire pixel is drawn. Pixels with centers exactly on vertical boundaries are considered inside only if the filled area is to the right. On horizontal boundaries, the pixel is considered inside only if the filled area is below the pixel.

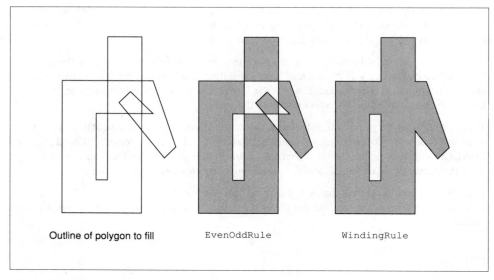

Figure 5-7. fill_rule constants for filling closed polygons

5.3.4 Arc Mode (for Filling)

The **arc_mode** member of **XGCValues** controls filling of arcs drawn with **XFillArc** and **XFillArcs()**. The **arc_mode** is set with **XSetArcMode()**.

An arc is specified for **XFillArc** or **XFillArcs()** as follows:

- The arc is bounded by a rectangle whose center is the center of the arc.

- The position of the upper-left corner of the rectangle is relative to the origin of the destination drawable.

- Two angles indicate the starting and stopping position of the arc. These are measured in sixty-fourths of a degree starting from the three-o'clock position, with positive angles indicating counterclockwise measurement.

The meanings of the arc specifications are demonstrated in Figure 6-1.

The **arc_mode** can be either **ArcPieSlice** or **ArcChord**. Figure 5-8 demonstrates the two modes. For **ArcChord**, the arc and the single line segment joining the endpoints of the arc create a closed figure to fill. For **ArcPieSlice**, the arc and the two line segments joining the endpoints of the arc with the center point create a closed figure to fill.

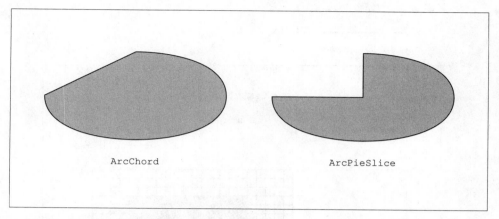

Figure 5-8. arc_mode constants for filling arcs

5.3.5 Clip Mask

Clipping allows you to limit the effect of graphics requests to a particular area or to particular pixels of the window or pixmap. The `clip_mask` member of **XGCValues** is a bitmap that indicates which pixels of the destination drawable are to be affected by graphics requests. By default, all pixels in the destination drawable are affected.

Pixels not represented by a set bit in the clip mask will not be drawn. The `clip_mask` can be set with **XSetClipMask()**, **XSetClipRectangles()**, or **XSetRegion()**. **XSetClipMask()** sets a clip mask composed of an arbitrary set of bits. **XSetClipRectangles()** specifies an array of rectangles that will collectively be used as a clip mask. **XSetRegion()** is another way to set the clip mask to a set of rectangles, sometimes more convenient than **XSetClipRectangles()**. **XUnionRectWithRegion()** can be used to add the rectangle from an **Expose** event into a region. Then **XSetRegion()** sets the GC to clip output to those areas. This is useful for redrawing only the areas that have been exposed. See Example 3-15, which uses this technique. Figure 5-9 shows a rectangular `clip_mask`, which could be set with **XSetClipMask()**, **XSetClipRectangles()**, or **XSetRegion()**.

If the `clip_mask` is set manually with **XSetClipMask()** or while creating the GC, a pixmap of depth 1 must be used. Then the only pixels drawn are those for which the `clip_mask` has a set bit. This pixmap must have the same root as the GC, or a **BadMatch** error will be generated.

The clip origin, which places the `clip_mask` relative to the destination drawable, is specified by two other members of the GC structure: `clip_x_origin` and `clip_y_origin`. Figure 5-9 shows how these coordinates specify the upper-left corner of the clip mask relative to the upper-left corner of the destination drawable specified in the graphics request. The origin of the `clip_mask` can be set with **XSetClipOrigin()**. The gray area in the figure represents the data to be drawn. The rectangle filled with unshaded squares represents the clip mask, which has all bits set to one. The lighter gray at the bottom shows the area outside the clip mask; this data will not be drawn.

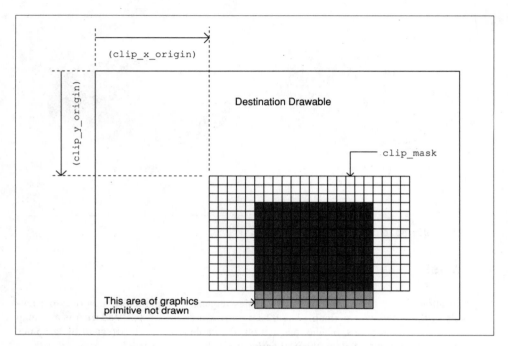

Figure 5-9. Use of clip origin to locate the clip_mask relative to drawable

5.4 Controlling Coloring and Patterning

The first stage of the drawing process (pixel selection) results in a bitmap with bits set to one indicating the pixels to be drawn. However, a window on a color display (or a pixmap to be copied to a color display) must have multiple bits per pixel to represent colors. The second stage of the drawing process colors the pixels.

There are four ways of coloring the pixels, controlled by the **fill_style** member of the GC. One of them uses a single color, and the other three apply patterns in different ways. You can pattern anything you can draw, including text, although lines of width 0 are not patterned.

We will begin by discussing the simple case, drawing with only the foreground color using **fill_style** of **FillSolid**. Then, to understand the effect of the patterning values for the **fill_style**, we must digress into a short description of tiles and stipples, followed by a discussion of the three styles of patterning.

5.4.1 Drawing in Foreground Only

Basic drawing is done using the `foreground` member of the GC. The `foreground` specifies the pixel value to be applied to the pixels selected by the graphics primitive, when the `fill_style` is `FillSolid`.* The uses of the background color are restricted and are described in Section 5.4.5. You can set the `foreground` with `XSetForeground()`.

Figure 5-10 shows the use of the `foreground` pixel value when drawing a character with `XDrawString()`. We will contrast this later with a string drawn using `XDrawImage-String()`, which will also draw the bounding box with the `background` pixel value.

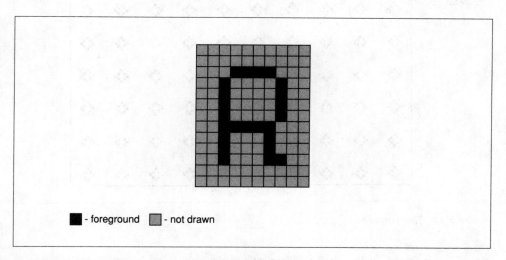

- foreground   - not drawn

Figure 5-10. Use of foreground in XDrawString() character

Now we move on to describe patterning. If you are familiar with tiles and stipples, you can skip Sections 5.4.2 and 5.4.3 and jump to Section 5.4.4.

5.4.2 Tiles

A tile is a pixmap used to pattern the pixels selected by the first stage of the drawing process. The `tile` member of the GC can be set with `XSetTile()`.

---

*For practical purposes, you can loosely think of a pixel value as the "color" in which an object will be drawn, though it applies to both color and monochrome systems. Even on a color system, the actual color resulting from the specified foreground or background pixel value will depend on the plane mask and logical function, as well as the red, green, and blue values stored in the colormap entry to which the resulting value points! Later references in this chapter to drawing in the "foreground color" should be interpreted in this light.

Tiles are so named because they are laid out next to each other in an array like bathroom tile. The origin of the first tile is specified with `ts_x_origin` and `ts_y_origin`, which are relative to the origin of the destination drawable. These members of the GC are set with `XSetTSOrigin()`. Only pixels specified by set bits in the first stage bitmap are tiled. Figure 5-11 shows how tiles are used to pattern an area. Instead of being filled with a solid color (or shade of gray), the area is filled with the tile pattern.

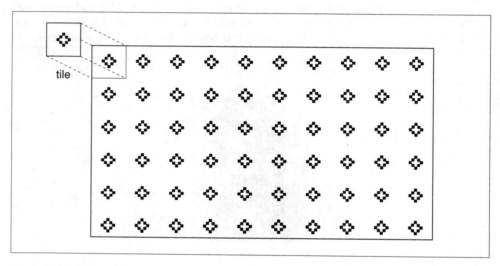

Figure 5-11. Tiling an area

Creating a tile is described in Section 6.1.5. The tile pixmap must be created on the same root window and have the same depth as the destination drawable. If these conditions are not satisfied, a `BadMatch` error is generated. If a pixmap is used simultaneously in a graphics request both as a destination and as a tile, the results are not defined.

Note that on monochrome displays, tiles are often used to simulate different levels of gray. For example, a checkerboard tile of black and white dots will appear gray on the screen. With 4 × 4 tile pixmaps with different arrangements of black and white dots, it is possible to develop several distinguishable levels of gray.

5.4.3 Stipples

Stippling is similar to tiling, except that a stipple is a pixmap of depth 1, not of the depth of the drawable. The pixel values used to draw the pattern are the `foreground` and `background` in the GC.

Just like tiles, stipples are laid out starting from the position specified with `ts_x_origin` and `ts_y_origin`, which are relative to the origin of the destination drawable.

Creating a pixmap of depth one to be used as a stipple is described in Section 6.1.5. The stipple pixmap must be created on the same root window and have the same depth as the destination drawable. If these conditions are not satisfied, a **BadMatch** error is generated. If a pixmap is used simultaneously in a graphics request both as a destination and as a stipple, the results are not defined.

The **stipple** member of the GC may be changed with **XSetStipple()**. If both the **stipple** and **tile** members of the GC are set, the **fill_style** determines which is used. Both cannot be used in a single graphics request.

5.4.4 Fill Style

We have demonstrated the simplest case, drawing using the foreground only with **fill_style** of **FillSolid**. Now that you know about tiles and stipples, we can describe the values for the **fill_style** that cause patterning. The **fill_style** member of **XGCValues** controls whether the source graphics are drawn with a solid color, a tile, or one of the two techniques using a stipple. The **fill_style** member of the GC may be changed with **XSetFillStyle()**.

Remember that only the bits that are set to one in the first stage bitmap are affected by coloring or patterning. The **fill_style** affects all line, text, and fill requests except lines drawn with **line_width** zero. Possible values are:

FillSolid   Specifies that graphics should be drawn using the **foreground** pixel value and in some cases also the **background** pixel value.

FillTiled   Specifies that graphics should be drawn using the **tile** pixmap.

FillStippled   Specifies that graphics should be drawn using the **foreground** pixel value masked by **stipple**. In other words, bits set in the source and **stipple** are drawn in the **foreground** pixel value.

FillOpaqueStippled
                    Specifies that graphics should be drawn using **stipple**, using the **foreground** pixel value for set bits in stipple and the **background** pixel value for unset bits in stipple.

When the depth of the drawable is one, there is no difference between tiling with **fill_style** of **FillTiled** and stippling with **fill_style** of **FillOpaque-Stippled**.

Figure 5-12 demonstrates the four fill styles demonstrated on small pixmaps. Odd dashes (numbering starting from zero) in dotted lines are a special case. For the gaps (odd dashes) in lines with **line_style** of **LineDoubleDash**, **FillSolid** means to draw the gaps in the **background** pixel value, and **FillStippled** means to draw in the **background** pixel value masked by **stipple**. With a **line_style** of **LineDoubleDash**, **Fill-Tiled** and **FillStippled** have the effect of wiping out the odd dashes, so that the line looks like **LineOnOffDash** with the specified fill style.

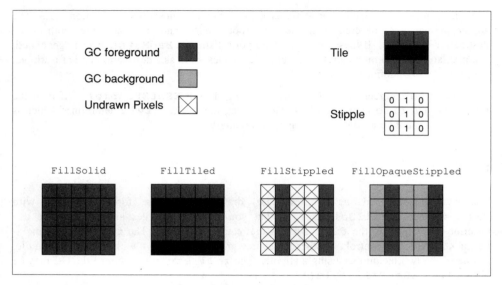

Figure 5-12. fill_style demonstrated on small pixmaps

5.4.5 Drawing in Foreground and Background

The **background** is used for unset bits in the first stage output in just four situations: when using **XDrawImageString()** (see Section 6.2.5), using **XCopyPlane()** (see Section 6.1.6), drawing with **line_style** of **LineDoubleDash** (see Section 5.3.1.2), and with any primitive when the **fill_style** is **FillOpaqueStippled** (see Section 5.4.4).

Figure 5-13 shows the use of the **foreground** and **background** values when drawing a character with **XDrawImageString()**. This primitive draws both the character and its bounding box. The character itself is drawn in the foreground pixel value; the remainder of the pixels in the bounding box are drawn with the background pixel value. The **background** member of the GC is set with **XSetBackground()**.

5.4.5.1 Tile and Stipple Sizes

A pixmap of any size can be used for tiling or stippling, but on some types of hardware, particular tile or stipple sizes run much faster than arbitrary sizes. **XQueryBestSize()** returns the closest tile or stipple size to the one you specify and also the largest allowable cursor. **XQueryBestTile()** and **XQueryBestStipple()** perform the same functions, but only for tiles and stipples, respectively.

Section 6.1.5 explains how to create a tile or stipple.

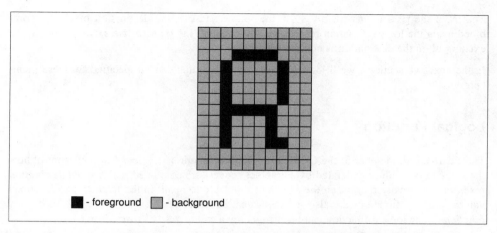

- foreground   - background

Figure 5-13. Use of foreground and background in XDrawImageString() character

5.5 Controlling Graphics Tricks

The GC provides a flexible way to control exactly which planes are affected by graphics requests and how the source and old destination pixel values are used to compute the new destination pixel values. These features are needed only for playing certain tricks like rubber-banding, and nondestructively overlaying graphics. We will demonstrate these techniques later in the book (in Chapters 14 and 7 respectively), but describe the corresponding GC components here.

Example 5-7 shows the types of the logical operation and plane mask components of the GC.

Example 5-7. Members of XGCValues that control combining of source and destination pixels

```
int function;              /* Logical function */
unsigned long plane_mask;  /* Plane mask */
```

The source (result of stage 2 of the drawing process) and existing destination pixels are combined by performing a logical function on the corresponding bits for each pixel. The `plane_mask` restricts the operation to a subset of planes, so that some bits in the source may be excluded from the computation. The `clip_mask` restricts the operation to a subset of the pixels, likewise eliminating some pixels from the result.

The source, destination, and `plane_mask` are combined using the algorithm shown below to yield the new destination pixel values. For each bit in each pixel that has been selected and colored in the first two drawing stages, the following expression defines whether that bit is set in the destination drawable:

```
((src FUNC dst) AND plane_mask) OR (dst AND (NOT plane_mask))
```

That is, if the `plane_mask` bit is set, the source and existing destination pixels are combined using the logical function represented by FUNC. If the `plane_mask` bit is not set, the existing bit in the destination is not changed.

In the next two sections, we'll look at the actual values that can be specified for these members.

5.5.1 Logical Function

The `function` member of the GC selects a logical function. *Logical functions* control how the *source* pixel values generated by a graphics request are combined with the *old destination* pixel values already present on the screen or drawable to result in the *final destination* pixel values. Logical functions are also sometimes called *raster operations*, *raster ops*, or *display functions*. The logical function can be changed by a call to `XSetFunction()`.

The source is the output of a graphics primitive or an area of the screen or drawable (for an `XCopyArea()`); the destination is the area of the drawable or window that is to receive the output. The 16 logical functions defined in *<X11/X.h>* are shown in Table 5-2.

Table 5-2. Logical Functions in the GC

Logical Function	Hex Code	Definition
GXclear	0x0	0
GXand	0x1	src AND dst
GXandReverse	0x2	src AND (NOT dst)
GXcopy	0x3	src
GXandInverted	0x4	(NOT src) AND dst
GXnoop	0x5	dst
GXxor	0x6	src XOR dst
GXor	0x7	src OR dst
GXnor	0x8	(NOT src) AND (NOT dst)
GXequiv	0x9	(NOT src) XOR dst
GXinvert	0xa	(NOT dst)
GXorReverse	0xb	src OR (NOT dst)
GXcopyInverted	0xc	(NOT src)
GXorInverted	0xd	(NOT src) OR dst
GXnand	0xe	(NOT src) OR (NOT dst)
GXset	0xf	1

Figures 5-14a, 5-14b, and 5-14c illustrate the effect of three logical functions on a single pixel of an eight-plane screen given a particular set of source and destination pixel values.

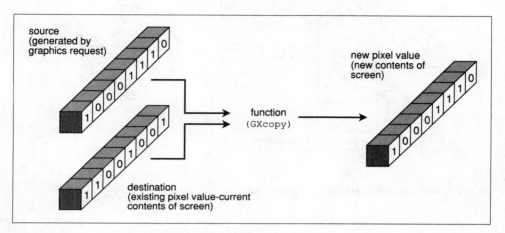

Figure 5-14a. The effect of logical function GXcopy

GXcopy, the default logical function, is the most frequently used because it copies without reference to the existing destination pixels, with predictable effects on both monochrome and color displays. **GXxor** and **GXinvert** are also used quite frequently. Rarely, programs may use other functions in concert with particular planes of a color display. Here is some more detail on the most frequently used logical functions:

GXcopy   Ignores the bits already in the destination drawable. It is used for both monochrome and color.

GXinvert   Ignores the source and inverts the old destination. This logical function is used to change black to white and vice versa when modifying only one plane. This can be used for highlighting on monochrome or color screens, but is not as good as **GXxor** on color screens.

GXxor   Combines the source and existing bits in such a way that, if the operation is repeated, the drawable is returned to its condition just before the two operations. It is important that these two operations occur without intervening manipulation of the selected bits (for windows, the server should be grabbed but for a very short time).* Otherwise, the second XOR operation will not leave the drawable unchanged. **GXxor** has these properties on both monochrome and color screens.

---

*When the server is grabbed, the client that grabbed it has sole control over the server and the screen. All other clients are put on hold; the server saves up events queued for them and does not change the screen on their behalf until the server grab is released. The server is grabbed and released with **XGrabServer()** and **XUngrabServer()**, but this should be done only when really necessary.

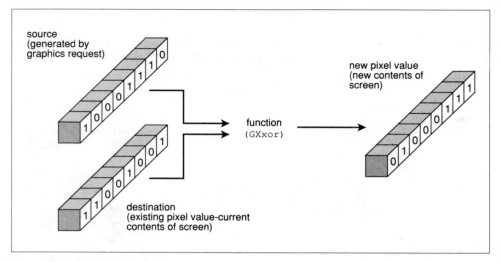

Figure 5-14b. The effect of logical function GXxor

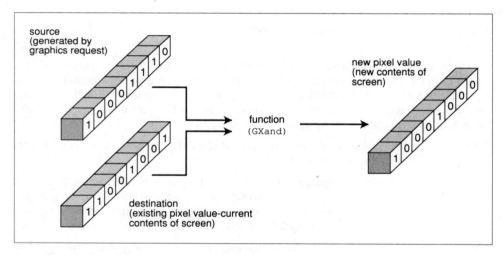

Figure 5-14c. The effect of logical function GXand

5.5.2 Plane Mask

The **plane_mask** member of **XGCValues** determines which planes of the destination drawable are modified. By default, all planes are modified. The **plane_mask** can be changed by a call to **XSetPlaneMask()**.

Destination planes represented by a bit set to 1 in the **plane_mask** can be changed by the graphics primitive, and the other planes cannot. The defined constant **AllPlanes()** provides a **plane_mask** with all bits set, which can be used when every plane is to be affected (this is also the default). A `plane_mask` of 0 cancels the effect of the graphics primitive. A `plane_mask` with only 1 bit set is useful for highlighting on both color and monochrome displays. Other tricks using the `plane_mask` are described in Chapter 7, *Color*. The macro `DisplayPlanes()` returns the number of planes available on the screen. However, the depth of the window is the upper limit on the number of meaningful bits in the `plane_mask`. Figure 5-17 illustrates the effect of the `plane_mask`.

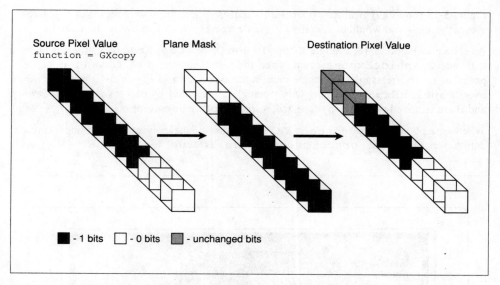

Figure 5-15. The effect of the plane_mask on a 12-plane display

5.6 Graphics Exposure

When using `XCopyArea()` and `XCopyPlane()` to copy data from one drawable to another, it is possible that certain portions of the source region will be obscured, unmapped, or otherwise unavailable. If this is the case, it may be desirable to generate an event to signal the client that one or more areas in the destination window could not be copied to and should be redrawn some other way.

The `graphics_exposures` flag in the GC specifies whether or not events should be generated in such a case. There are actually two event types that can be generated if `graphics_exposures` is set to `True`:

* One or more `GraphicsExpose` events are sent when a destination region cannot be completely drawn because the source region was obscured, unmapped, or otherwise unavailable.

- A single **NoExpose** event occurs when the specified source region is completely available.

These event types are not selected by **XSelectInput()** or in the **event_mask** attribute; setting **graphics_exposures** to **True** is the only way to select them. The **graphics_exposures** member of the GC can be set with **XSetGraphicsExposures()**.

Figure 5-18 shows a typical **XCopyArea()** request where the source region is obscured. It shows the areas that would be specified in the **GraphicsExpose** events generated.

As shown in Figure 5-18, a single **XCopyPlane()** or **XCopyArea()** can result in more than one **GraphicsExpose** event, since the resulting area to be redrawn may be composed of several rectangles. A copy such as the one shown in Figure 5-18 would generate two **GraphicsExpose** events. One rectangle is specified by each event. If windows A and B are removed and the copy repeated, a single **NoExpose** event is generated.

When **graphics_exposures** is **False**, neither of these events is sent under any circumstances. By default, **graphics_exposures** is **True**.

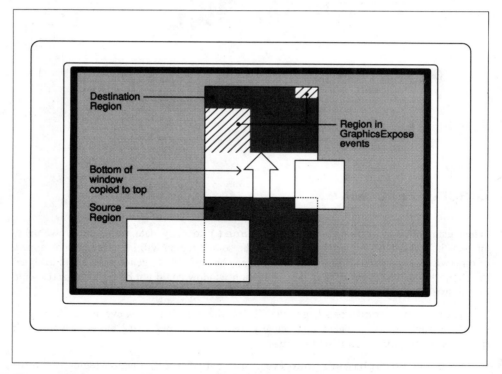

Figure 5-16. Copying a partially unavailable area

5.7 Subwindow Mode

The `subwindow_mode` member of `XGCValues` controls whether subwindows obscure their parent for purposes of drawing on the parent. This member is set with `XSet-SubwindowMode()`.

The value `ClipByChildren` sets the default condition, in which drawing into the area of a window obscured by its visible children produces no effect.

If the `subwindow_mode` is set to `IncludeInferiors`, drawing appears through visible children even when they have opaque backgrounds. The use of `IncludeInferiors` on a window of depth 1 with mapped inferiors of differing depth is not illegal, but the results are not defined in standard Xlib.

One familiar use of `IncludeInferiors` is the window manager's "rubber banding" of window outlines while they are being moved or resized. The outline is drawn on the root window with the GC set to `IncludeInferiors`.

5.8 Sharing GCs Between Clients

Despite the fact that a GC is a server resource and theoretically shareable, separate clients should not attempt to share GCs, because of the way GCs are implemented.

5.9 GCs and Server Efficiency

Some servers can cache a limited number of GCs in their display hardware. These systems achieve highest performance when the number of GCs created by an application is less than the number that can be cached at one time. Furthermore, each GC takes up some amount of server memory. Therefore, it is a general principle that an application should create as few GCs as reasonably possible.

However, this should not be taken to extremes. For example, all applications could be written to use only one GC, changing it frequently every time different characteristics are needed. But this defeats two of the purposes of the GC, which are to reduce network traffic and simplify programming. There are also performance costs when GCs are changed too often.

Deciding how many GCs to create and when to change them is a trade-off between the benefits of a more efficient server against the benefits of reduced network traffic and simpler programming. The designers of X still think that using a small number of GCs is, overall, the best approach.

5.10 Querying the Graphics Context

When you call a number of the GC convenience routines, such as **XSetForeground()** and **XSetLineAttributes()**, you might expect each to generate a separate protocol request to change the GC. But this is not what happens. Xlib saves up the changes in an internal structure and makes a single request to the server just before the GC is actually used by a drawing request.

The type **GC** is a pointer to this internal structure. All Xlib routines use a pointer to this internal structure, not a integer ID, as we have previously implied. However, this fact does not impact how you write Xlib code at all. In practice, a pointer to an opaque structure and an integer ID such as a window ID are treated exactly the same.

In R4, the **XGetGCValues()** function has been added to allow clients to read Xlib's cache of the fields in each GC. This can save an application from having to maintain its own cache of GC values, when it needs to change the GC in several different places in ways that depend on the current contents.

Note that **XGetGCValues()** is not a true round-trip query to the server—there is no protocol request that actually asks the server for these values. This has good and bad consequences. The good part is that **XGetGCValues()** is fast because it is not subject to network delays. The bad side is that the values in Xlib's cache do not include the default values for certain of the GC members. The **tile**, **stipple**, and **font** fields contain invalid IDs when **XGetGCValues()** is called on a default GC. Therefore, even though there is actually a default font that is always loaded on a server, you cannot use **XGetGCValues()** to find out its ID. To get information about the default font, pass the default GC to **XQueryFont()** and it will get information about the default font. Neither is there any obvious reason for needing the IDs of the tile and stipple in the default GC.

Also note that the **clip_mask** and **dashes** members of the GC cannot be queried.

5.11 The Default GC Versus Default Values of a GC

The server creates one GC, called the default GC, when it starts up. This GC is returned by the **XDefaultGC()** and the **DefaultGC()** macro. It contains foreground and background colors that are guaranteed contrasting (but not necessarily black and white), and it contains a default font that is guaranteed to be loaded, but is not necessarily the same font on all servers. The values in the default GC must not be changed.

The default GC can be used in simple applications. But it is not very useful since all applications should provide user customization of fonts and colors, and few can avoid the need to modify other GC components as well.

When you create a GC of your own, its default values are slightly different from the values of the default GC. Its foreground and background values are 0 and 1, respectively, so they are not necessarily black and white or contrasting. That's why you must always set foreground and background when you create a GC. Also, the default font is implementation dependent, and it may not be loaded. Therefore, you must always load the font before attempting to draw with it.

Table 5-3 shows the default values for all members of a graphics context you create.

Table 5-3. The Default Values of a Graphics Context

Component	Value
function	GXcopy
plane_mask	all 1's
foreground	0
background	1
line_width	0
line_style	LineSolid
cap_style	CapButt
join_style	JoinMiter
fill_style	FillSolid
fill_rule	EvenOddRule
arc_mode	ArcPieSlice
tile	Pixmap filled with foreground pixel
stipple	Pixmap filled with 1's
ts_x_origin	0
ts_y_origin	0
font	(Implementation dependent)
subwindow_mode	ClipByChildren
graphics_exposures	True
clip_x_origin	0
clip_y_origin	0
clip_mask	None
dash_offset	0
dashes	4 (i.e., the list [4, 4])

A useful quick reference to the graphics context is provided inside the back cover of Volume Two, *Xlib Reference Manual*.

6

Drawing Graphics and Text

This chapter describes the routines used to draw lines, geometrical figures, and text. It also discusses the use of the pixmaps, images, and regions. You should be familiar with the use of the graphics context before attempting to use these routines.

In This Chapter:

6

Drawing Graphics and Text

Drawing with computers is a little like drawing by hand. Holding the pencil is not hard, but getting anything recognizable to appear on the page is a different matter. Similarly, drawing with X is quite easy, but designing what to draw and where can be a challenge. We can do little more in this chapter than tell you how to hold the pencil; the rest is up to you.

This chapter describes various techniques that have to do with drawing: drawing lines, rectangles, and arcs; using bitmaps; placing and drawing text; using regions; creating and using cursors; and using images.

The `draw_text` and `draw_graphics` routines called in the *basicwin* program in Chapter 3, *Basic Window Program*, are used as examples in this chapter. Also described here are various versions of the `draw_box` routine, which is called in the simple window manager *winman* described in Chapter 16, *Window Management*.

Note that, before you draw anything, you must set up a graphics context to specify, at minimum, the foreground and background pixel values for drawing and the font if you are drawing text. For monochrome applications, you should set these values using the `Black-Pixel()` and `WhitePixel()` macros described in Chapter 3, *Basic Window Program*. For color applications, you should use one of the color allocation routines described in Chapter 7, *Color*. While the default foreground and background values in a GC *may* work on some servers, they are hardcoded (0 and 1) and should *not* be relied upon by any client, since they will give inconsistent results on color displays.

6.1 Drawing

The X drawing primitives are easy-to-use routines capable of drawing points, connected lines (polylines), disconnected lines (disjoint polylines), rectangles, and circles, ellipses, or arcs. Separate primitives are provided that fill rectangles, polygons, circles, ellipses, and arcs.

These primitives select the source pixels that will be operated on according to the graphics context. The GC is described in Chapter 5, *The Graphics Context*. The most common error generated while drawing is `BadMatch`. If you get this error, it means the drawable and the GC specified in the drawing call are not the same depth. The safest way to prevent this is to always create the drawable first, and then use the drawable as an argument when creating the GC that will be used to draw into it.

XDrawPoint() requires only the coordinates of the point to be drawn. **XDraw-Points()** requires a pointer to an array of coordinates for the points, the number of points, and a mode flag which controls whether the coordinates are interpreted relative to the origin of the drawable or relative to the previous point drawn.

XDrawLine() is similar to **XDrawPoint()** but requires two points, a beginning and an end. **XDrawLines()** works just like **XDrawPoints()** but draws lines between consecutive points in the list. If the first and last points coincide, the lines will be joined properly according to the **join_style** in the GC.

XDrawSegments() draws lines that are not necessarily connected end to end. It requires an array of pairs of endpoints. There is no mode flag for **XDrawSegments()**, so the coordinates are always relative to the origin of the drawable. If the end point of one segment and the beginning of the next coincide, the lines will be joined according to the **join_style** in the GC. The remaining end points will be drawn according to the **cap_style** in the GC.

XDrawRectangle() draws the outline of a rectangle when given the upper-left corner and the height and width. **XDrawRectangles()** draws multiple rectangles from an array of corner coordinates and dimensions. The actual width and height of a rectangle is one pixel larger than the dimensions specified, according to the X protocol, as shown in Figure 6-2. These actual dimensions maintain consistency with the definition of a filled rectangle or a clipping region, which are exactly the size specified. The corners of rectangles are drawn according to the **join_style** in the GC.

XDrawArc() is similar to **XDrawRectangle()**, except that it draws an arc that fits inside the rectangle. This function can draw circles and ellipses (or parts thereof) whose axes are parallel to the window coordinates. An elliptical arc occurs if the rectangle is not a square. The extent of the arc is specified by two angles: the first is the starting angle relative to the three-o'clock position, and the second is the angle relative to the starting position. The angles are signed integers in sixty-fourths of a degree (0 to 360 * 64 is a complete circle), with positive values drawing the arc counterclockwise. This scale factor is required so that angles can be specified more accurately than allowed by integral values between 0 and 360 degrees. Figure 6-1 demonstrates the arguments needed for **XDrawArc()**.

X Version 11 also supports the **XDraw()** and **XDrawFilled()** routines that were available in X Version 10, though the performance of these is low. These routines are described in Appendix B, *X10 Compatibility*.

Xlib does not provide routines for drawing Bezier or cubic spline curves.

6.1.1 The Request Size Limit

One caveat of all the Xlib routines that draw multiple objects is that there is a maximum number of objects that can be drawn with a single call, and this number varies according to the server your application is connected to. In Release 4, this affects the calls **XDraw-Arcs()**, **XDrawLines()**, **XDrawPoints()**, **XDrawRectangles()**, **XDraw-Segments()**, **XDrawText()**, **XDrawText16()**, **XFillArcs()**, **XFill-Rectangles()**, and **XFillPolygon()**. In Release 5 and later, it affects only **XDrawArcs()**, **XDrawLines()**, **XDrawText()**, **XDrawText16()**, and

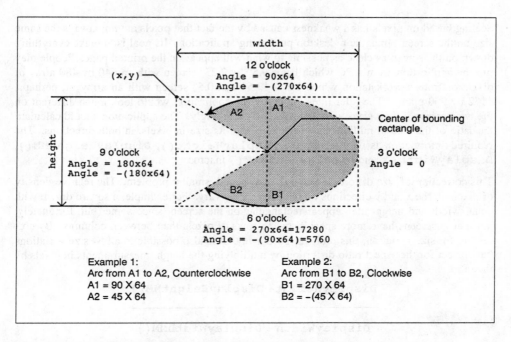

Figure 6-1. Angle measurement for XDrawArc or XDrawArcs()

XFillPolygon () because the other calls are divided into multiple requests. (This cannot be done for **XDrawArcs()** or **XDrawLines()** because this would disturb the server's joining of the lines, and it cannot be done for **XFillPolygon** because it would change the filled area.)

To determine how many objects you can draw in a single call, you find out your server's maximum request size using **XMaxRequestSize()**. Subtract 3, and this is the maximum number of points you can draw in a single **XDrawPoints()** request. You can draw one-half this many lines, segments, or rectangles, and one-third this many arcs. You can specify **XMaxRequestSize()** minus four points in **XFillPolygon**.

For **XDrawText()**, **XDrawText16()**, **XwcDrawText()**, and **XmbDrawText()**, which draw a series of strings as will be described later, the maximum number is based on the number and length of these strings.

6.1.2 Scaling Graphics

All drawing measurements in X are made in pixels. The positions you specify are relative to the origin (upper-left corner inside border) of the window specified in the drawing request. The width and height of a rectangle or bounding box for an arc are also specified in pixels.

Scaling based on pixels has a weakness caused by the fact that pixels are not always the same size on the screen. Imagine a desktop publishing application. Its goal is to make everything drawn on the screen as close as possible to what will appear on the printed page. People may run the application from a PC which has a 9.5" by 7.25" screen with an 640 by 480 array of pixels or from a workstation which has a 13.5" by 10.5" screen with an array of, perhaps, 1152 by 900 pixels. The ruler lines drawn by the application would look much different on the two screens if their sizes were not adjusted accordingly. The application should calculate the ratio of the size in millimeters of the screen to its size in pixels, in both directions. The required information is returned by the **DisplayHeight( )**, **DisplayHeightMM( )**, **DisplayWidth( )**, and **DisplayWidthMM( )** macros.

This correction of size distortion also solves a second, smaller problem. The relative density of pixels in the x and y directions on the screen may vary. For example, a square drawn with equal width and height may appear rectangular on the screen, since some (but, fortunately, not many) screens have more space between rows of pixels than between columns. By correcting for size variation, this problem goes away. It is also possible to allow size variations but correct for the aspect ratio distortion by multiplying the height measurements in pixels by the ratio:

$$\frac{\text{DisplayHeight} + \text{DisplayHeightMM( )}}{\text{DisplayWidth} + \text{DisplayWidthMM( )}}$$

or by multiplying the width measurements in pixels by the inverse of this ratio. Do not multiply both the width and height measurements.

6.1.3 Example of Drawing Graphics

All drawing routines are used in essentially the same way:

- First, create and set the graphics context.

- Then calculate the dimensions and placement of what you want to draw.

- Finally, do the actual drawing.

Example 6-1 shows a routine named **draw_graphics** that places and draws a rectangle. As you can tell from the brevity of the routine, most of the trouble goes into setting the GC properly and positioning the item to be drawn. The actual drawing is very simple.

This routine is called from the *basicwin* program described in Chapter 3, *Basic Window Program*. By the time it is called, we have already done many things. The display is opened, windows and resources created (including the GC), and window manager hints set. Most importantly, **draw_graphics** is called only in response to **Expose** events. It is used to draw the window for the first time and to redraw the contents of areas exposed later.

Example 6-1. The draw_graphics routine

```
draw_graphics(win, gc, window_width, window_height)
Window win;
```

Example 6-1. The draw_graphics routine (continued)

```
GC gc;
unsigned int window_width, window_height;
{
        int x, y;
        unsigned int width, height;

        height = window_height/2;
        width = 3 * window_width/4;
        x = window_width/2 - width/2;   /* Center */
        y = window_height/2 - height/2;
        XDrawRectangle(display, win, gc, x, y, width, height);
}
```

The calling routine gets the `window_width` and `window_height` arguments from
`ConfigureNotify` events because the window being drawn into is a top-level window
which might get resized by the window manager. Routines to draw into descendents of the
top-level window may also require size arguments if the sizes of the windows will be
adjusted in response to a resized top-level window.

6.1.4 Filling

The `XFillArc()`, `XFillArcs()`, `XFillPolygon()`, `XFillRectangle()`, and
`XFillRectangles()` commands act much like the drawing routines described at the
start of Section 6.1 except that they fill an area instead of drawing the outline.

Surprisingly, the filling and drawing versions of the rectangle routines do not draw the same
outline if given the same arguments. The routine that fills a rectangle draws an outline one
pixel shorter in width and height than the routine that just draws the outline, as shown in Figure 6-2. It is easy to adjust the arguments for the rectangle calls so that one draws the outline
and another fills a completely different set of interior pixels. Simply add 1 to *x* and *y* and
subtract 1 from *width* and *height*.

The `XFillPolygon()` routine is somewhat different from the other filling routines, since
there is no directly analogous routine that draws a polygon with lines (though `XDraw-`
`Lines()` can be used to draw a polygon). Like the other routines, `XFillPolygon()`
uses an array of points to specify the nodes to be connected, but it connects the first and last
points to form a closed figure and then fills the resulting shape. The `shape` flag (which can
be one of the symbols `Complex`, `Convex`, or `Nonconvex`) is a hint that may enable the
server to improve the performance of the filling operation. The *mode* argument indicates
whether the coordinates of the vertices are interpreted relative to the origin of the drawable
or relative to the previous point.

The `fill_rule` member of the GC controls how complex, self-intersecting polygons are
filled. The `WindingRule` setting of the `fill_rule` specifies that overlapping areas of a
polygon drawn in a single call are filled. With `EvenOddRule`, areas overlapping an odd
number of times are not filled. See Section 5.3.3 for more information.

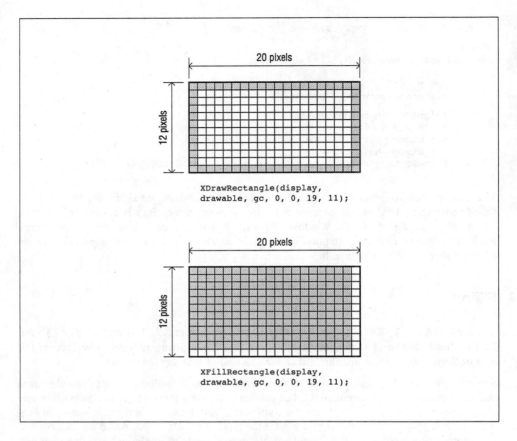

Figure 6-2. The pixels affected by XFillRectangle() vs. XDrawRectangle() with the same arguments

6.1.5 Creating Bitmaps, Pixmaps, Tiles, and Stipples

Bitmaps, tiles, and stipples are all forms of pixmaps, all of type **Pixmap**. Applications often need to create pixmaps for icon patterns, cursors, and tiles.

The data used to create a pixmap for any purpose can be included in a program at compile time or read in at run time. In both methods, you must have a bitmap file created with **XWriteBitmapFile()** or the *bitmap* application.

In the first method, you use an **#include** statement to read the bitmap file at run time and then call **XCreateBitmapFromData()** or **XCreatePixmapFromBitmapData()** if you want a pixmap with depth for a window background or a tile.

In the second method, you create a single-plane **Pixmap** with **XCreatePixmap()** and call **XReadBitmapFile()** to fill the **Pixmap** with the data from the file. Then if you want a pixmap with depth for the background of a window or for a tile, you can create

In the second method, you create a single-plane `Pixmap` with `XCreatePixmap()` and call `XReadBitmapFile()` to fill the `Pixmap` with the data from the file. Then if you want a pixmap with depth for the background of a window or for a tile, you can create another pixmap of the desired depth and call `XCopyPlane()` to copy the bitmap into the pixmap. Normally, an application would choose reading the data from a file if the user needs to be able to change the bitmap between invocations of the client.

`XWriteBitmapFile()` can be used to write the contents of a bitmap into a file conforming to X Version 11 bitmap file format.

Example 6-2 shows some bitmap data in standard X11 bitmap file format and two subroutines, one that creates a stipple from included data and the other that reads the bitmap data from a file.

Example 6-2. Creating a stipple from included data and from data read from a file

```
#define icon_bitmap_width 40
#define icon_bitmap_height 40
static char icon_bitmap_bits[ ] = {
    0xc3, 0xc3, 0x7f, 0x00, 0x78, 0x00, 0x00, 0x00, 0x00, 0xc0, 0x00, 0x00,
    0x00, 0x00, 0x80, 0x38, 0x00, 0x40, 0x00, 0x80, 0x24, 0x00, 0x00, 0x00,
      .
      .
      .

    0x0c, 0x30, 0x18, 0x00, 0x84, 0x04, 0x60, 0x0e, 0x00, 0xdc, 0x02, 0x80,
    0x03, 0x00, 0x70, 0x00, 0x00, 0x00, 0x00, 0x00};

void main(argc, argv)
int argc;
char **argv;
{
      .
      .
      .

    Pixmap stipple;
    unsigned int stip_width, stip_height;
    char *filename = "bitmaps/icon_bitmap";

    if (create_included_stipple(&stipple, &stip_width,
            &stip_height) == False)
        fprintf(stderr, "basic: couldn't create included bitmap\n");
    printf("stipple is %dx%d\n", stip_width, stip_height);

    if (create_read_stipple(&stipple, filename, &stip_width,
            &stip_height) ! = BitmapSuccess)
        fprintf(stderr, "basic: can't read bitmap\n");
    printf("stipple is %dx%d\n", stip_width, stip_height);

      .
      .
      .

}
create_included_stipple(stip, width, height)
Pixmap *stip;                    /* Returned created stipple */
unsigned int *width, *height;   /* Returned */
{
    if ((*stip = XCreateBitmapFromData(display,
```

```
                RootWindow(display, screen_num), icon_bitmap_bits,
                icon_bitmap_width, icon_bitmap_height))
                == False)
        return(False);
    *width = name_width;
    *height = name_height;
    return(True);
}

create_read_stipple(stip, filename, width, height)
Pixmap *stip;                    /* Returned created stipple */
char *filename;
unsigned int *width, *height;   /* Returned */
{
    int value;
    int x_hot, y_hot;           /* Don't care about these unless for
                                 * cursor */

    value = XReadBitmapFile(display, RootWindow(display, screen_num),
            filename, width, height, stip, &x_hot, &y_hot);
    if (value == BitmapFileInvalid)
        fprintf(stderr, "Filename %s contains invalid bitmap data\n",
                filename);
    else if (value == BitmapOpenFailed)
        fprintf(stderr, "Filename %s could not be opened\n",
                filename);
    else if (value == BitmapNoMemory)
        fprintf(stderr, "Not enough memory to allocate pixmap\n");
    return(value);
    /* Returns BitmapSuccess if everything worked */
}
```

To create a pixmap with depth from included data, you can substitute **XCreatePixmap-FromBitmapData()** for **XCreateBitmapFromData()** in the example above. However, to create a pixmap with depth from data read from a file, you must create a bitmap with **XReadBitmapFile()** as shown above, then create a pixmap with depth using **XCreatePixmap()**, then copy from the bitmap to the pixmap using **XCopyPlane()**.

6.1.6 Copying and Clearing Areas

XClearWindow() clears an entire window. If the window has a **background_pixmap** attribute, then the window is redrawn with this tile. If the window has **background_pixmap** or **background_pixel** attribute **None**, then the contents of the window are not changed. No exposure events are generated by **XClearWindow()**, since the usual intent of this command is to clear the window, not to refresh the old contents (which would be the normal response to an exposure event). Conversely, **XClearWindow()** is not needed to clear a window before redrawing it due to an **Expose** event, because the server automatically draws the exposed area with the background pixel value or pixmap.

`XClearArea()` is like `XClearWindow()` but acts on a particular area within a window defined by the call's *x*, *y*, *height*, and *width* arguments. If the *height* or *width* argument is 0, then some special rules take effect that clear an area to the right and/or the bottom of the window, as shown in Figure 6-3.

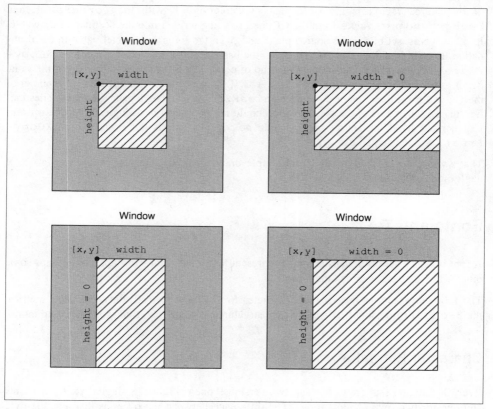

Figure 6-3. XClearArea() — area cleared with various width and height arguments

If the *width* argument is 0, the left edge of the cleared area is *x* and the right edge is the right border of the window. If the *height* is 0, the top is *y* and the bottom is the bottom of the window. If both *height* and *width* are 0, then the area between *x* and *y* and the bottom and right sides of the window are cleared. The *exposures* argument indicates whether an **Expose** event is generated on the cleared area.

`XCopyArea()` is used for many purposes, including copying off-screen pixmaps to the screen and copying one screen area to another. You need to specify the source and destination drawables, the upper-left corner of the source and destination locations, and the width and height of the area. Note that the source and destination drawables must have the same depth, or an error occurs.

Areas of the source that are not visible, not preserved in the backing store, or outside the boundaries of the source drawable are not copied. If the destination has a background tile attribute other than **None**, the destination areas corresponding to the uncopyable areas of the source are filled or tiled according to the background attributes.

The operation of **XCopyPlane()** is quite different from **XCopyArea()**. A single plane of the source region is given "depth" by "coloring" it with the **foreground** and **background** pixel values from the GC, before being written into the destination drawable. In other words, set bits in the source plane are given the foreground pixel value in the destination drawable, while unset bits are given the background pixel value. Therefore, **XCopy-Plane()** is useful for translating a pixmap of depth 1 (a bitmap) into a pixmap of the same depth as a window where it can be displayed. If the **graphics_exposures** member of the GC is **True**, then one or more **GraphicsExpose** events are generated on the destination region when part of the source region could not be copied or a single **NoExpose** event is generated if all the source region could be copied. This is the case for both **XCopy-Area()** and **XCopyPlane()** requests.

That's about all there is to say about simple drawing, filling, copying, and clearing. Now we'll move on to drawing text.

6.2 Fonts and Text

A font in X is a set of bitmaps and may represent text, a set of cursor shapes, or perhaps some other set of shapes for some other purpose.

The following sections describe the character format, how to load fonts, character metrics, the **XFontStruct** and **XCharStruct** structures, placing text, font properties, and more.

6.2.1 Character Format

Every X function that draws text has two versions: one that handles single-byte (8-bit) fonts and one for two-byte (16-bit) fonts. The difference between these two is that a single-byte font is limited to 256 characters, while a two-byte font may have up to 256 rows each with 256 characters, a total of 65,536 characters. Large numbers of characters are necessary for Oriental languages.

On many servers, only single-byte fonts can be used with the routines whose names do not end in 16 and only two-byte fonts may be used with the routines that do end in 16. However, some servers may handle either type in either routine. At the moment, there is only one two-byte font on the standard X distribution, the Kanji font used by the *kterm* program, a terminal emulator for Japanese.

6.2.2 Loading Fonts

A font must be loaded before being used. If one or more clients are using the same font, they share the same copy in the server, but each must request that the font be loaded, if only to get the font ID. The available fonts are stored in a database that is accessible with the **XList-Fonts()** and **XListFontsWithInfo()** commands.

XListFonts() lists the fonts that match the specified pattern (with wildcards) that are available on the current server. The list of font names generated by **XListFonts()** can be freed when no longer needed using **XFreeFontNames()**. See the next section for how to specify font names.

Once the desired font name is found, it can be used as a string in **XLoadFont()**. Some fonts, such as "fixed" and "9x15," are almost always available and should not require a search through the list of fonts. The **XLoadFont()** command loads a font and returns the font ID, which is used in all subsequent references to that font. The font ID is used in **XSetFont()** to associate the font with a GC to be used in drawing text. **XLoadFont()** returns a value that must be checked to make sure the loading succeeded.

If the font is constant width, then it is ready for use as soon as it is loaded. If the font is proportionally spaced and your program needs to calculate the extent of many strings in the same font, then you may want to get the table of the extents of the font characters and perform this calculation locally in order to save repeated round-trip requests to the server. This information is stored in an **XFontStruct** (described in Section 6.2.4.2), which is filled by calling the **XQueryFont()** routine. Both the **XLoadFont()** and **XQueryFont()** operations may be done together with **XLoadQueryFont()**.

If the font ID passed to the **XQueryFont()** routines is of type **GContext**, the information about the font associated with the specified GC is returned. This is how you get information about the default font, which is always loaded. Pass the value returned by

```
XGContextFromGC(DefaultGC(display, screen_num))
```

to **XQueryFont()**.

The **load_font** routine shown in Example 6-3 is called in the *basicwin* program described in Chapter 3, *Basic Window Program*. It loads a font and gets the font information structure for later use in the routines that actually draw the text.

Example 6-3. The load_font routine

```
load_font(font_info)
XFontStruct **font_info;
{
    char *fontname = "9x15";

    /* Access font */
    if ((*font_info = XLoadQueryFont(display,fontname)) == NULL)
    {
        (void) fprintf( stderr, "Basic: Cannot open 9x15 font\n");
        exit( -1 );
    }
}
```

In a more general client, the font name should be an argument to **load_font**, and provision should be made to read it from the command line or resource database.

XListFontsWithInfo( ) returns a list of the loaded fonts matching a font name (with wildcards) and returns the information structure associated with each loaded font. The information returned is identical to that returned by **XQueryFont( )** except that per-character metrics are not returned. Only the maximum metrics over the entire font are returned. If **XFontStruct.min_byte1** and **XFontStruct.max_byte1** are 0, the font is a single-byte font.

XFreeFontInfo( ) should be used to free the font information structure when the font is no longer needed but before the font is unloaded using **XUnloadFont( )**. **XFreeFont( )** combines **XFreeFontInfo( )** and **XUnloadFont( )**.

6.2.3 Font Naming

Your application should allow font names to be specified by the user using resources. However, you do need to specify default fonts. Font naming is defined by the X Logical Font Description convention, known as XLFD. The complete XLFD is presented in Volume Zero, *X Protocol Reference Manual*. However, the basics are covered in Appendix A, *Specifying Fonts*.

6.2.4 Character Metrics

Before going on to the structures that specify characters and fonts, we should go over some terminology. The measurements shown in Figure 6-4 are some of the *font metrics* that are the measurements in pixels that describe both a font as a whole and each character in the font. The names shown for the metrics are members of the font information structures.

Notice that the origin is not at the upper-left corner of each character, as in most of the rest of X. The origin of each character is on the *baseline*, which is a row of pixels somewhere near the lower middle of a line of text. This part of X has been written to conform closely to the existing standards for fonts provided by companies like Adobe.

Notice that two structures are mentioned in Figure 6-4, **XFontStruct** and **XCharStruct**. **XFontStruct** holds information about the entire font, while **XCharStruct** (itself the type of several members of **XFontStruct**) holds information about a single character. These two structures have some common member names, but their meanings are different.

There is a difference between the font **ascent** and **descent** members in **XFontStruct** and the **ascent** and **descent** members in each individual **XCharStruct**. The former specifies the largest of each measurement in any character in the font, and the latter specifies the measurements of single characters.

6.2.4.1 The XCharStruct Structure

One `XCharStruct` structure contains the metrics of a single character in a font. `XChar-Struct` is shown in Example 6-4. Refer to Figure 6-4 for the meaning of each of its members.

Example 6-4. The XCharStruct structure

```
/* Per character font metric information */
typedef struct {
    short lbearing;             /* Origin to left edge of character */
    short rbearing;             /* Origin to right edge of character */
    short width;                /* Advance to next char's origin */
    short ascent;               /* Baseline to top edge of character */
    short descent;              /* Baseline to bottom edge of
                                 * character */

    unsigned short attributes;  /* Per char flags (not predefined) */
} XCharStruct;
```

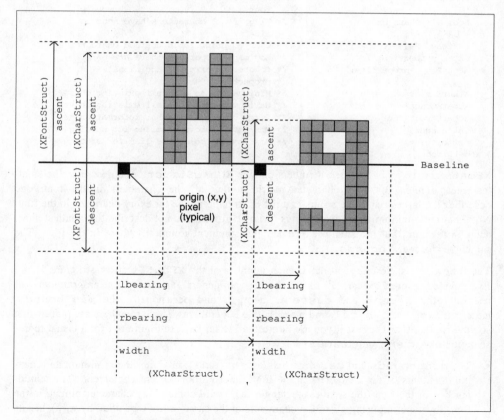

Figure 6-4. The metrics of two characters

The **attributes** member is for font-specific information. It does not have any standard use or meaning.

6.2.4.2 The XFontStruct Structure

Example 6-5 shows the **XFontStruct** structure. This structure contains information about the font as a whole.

Example 6-5. The XFontStruct structure

```
typedef struct {
    XExtData *ext_data;             /* Hook for extension to hang data */
    Font fid;                       /* Font ID for this font */
    unsigned direction;             /* Direction the font is painted */
    unsigned min_char_or_byte2;     /* First character */
    unsigned max_char_or_byte2;     /* Last character */
    unsigned min_byte1;             /* First row that exists (for two-byte
                                     * fonts) */
    unsigned max_byte1;             /* Last row that exists (for two-byte
                                     * fonts) */
    Bool all_chars_exist;           /* Flag if all characters have nonzero
                                     * size */
    unsigned default_char;          /* Char to print for undefined character */
    int n_properties;               /* How many properties there are */
    XFontProp *properties;          /* Pointer to array of additional
                                     * properties*/
    XCharStruct min_bounds;         /* Minimum bounds over all existing char*/
    XCharStruct max_bounds;         /* Maximum bounds over all existing char*/
    XCharStruct *per_char;          /* first_char to last_char information */
    int ascent;                     /* Max extent above baseline for spacing */
    int descent;                    /* Max descent below baseline for spacing */
} XFontStruct;
```

XFontStruct includes three members of type **XCharStruct**: one describes the smallest measurement for each character metric among all the characters in the font; one describes the largest; and one points to a list of structures, one for every character in the font. Note that the minimum character metrics (**min_bounds**) do not describe the smallest character in the font, but the smallest of every measurement found anywhere in the font. The same goes for **max_bounds**.

The following list describes in detail each member of the **XFontStruct** structure. Only font developers need to learn all these members. In general, an application programmer will use only the **ascent** and **descent** members and occasionally the **min_bounds**, **max_bounds**, **min_byte1**, and **max_byte1** members. These members are placed first so you can just scan the rest if you are interested. Refer back to Figure 6-4 for a visual representation of **ascent** and **descent**.

* The **min_bounds** and **max_bounds** are structures containing the minimum and maximum extents of the characters in the font, ignoring nonexistent characters. The bounding box of the font (the smallest rectangle that could contain any character bitmap in the font), by superimposing all of the characters at the same origin (specified by **x, y**), has its upper-left coordinate at:

    [x + min_bounds.lbearing, y - max_bounds.ascent]

The bounding box's width is:

```
max_bounds.rbearing - min_bounds.lbearing
```

Its height is:

```
max_bounds.ascent + max_bounds.descent
```

- `ascent` is the logical extent of the font above the baseline and is used for determining line spacing. Specific character bitmaps may extend beyond this ascent.

- `descent` is the logical extent of the font below the baseline and is used for determining line spacing. Specific character bitmaps may extend beyond this descent. If the baseline is at absolute y coordinate y, then the logical extent of the font is between the y coordinates (`y-XFontStruct.ascent`) and (`y+XFontStruct.descent-1`), inclusive.

- `direction` can be either `FontLeftToRight` or `FontRightToLeft`. This member is a hint about whether most `XCharStruct` members have a positive (`FontLeftToRight`) or a negative (`FontRightToLeft`) character-width metric, indicating the preferred direction of drawing the font.

- `min_byte1` and `max_byte1` are both 0 for single-byte fonts, since the second byte is not used. These members can be tested to see if a font is single- or two-byte. If single-byte, `min_char_or_byte2` specifies the index of the first member of the `per_char` array and `max_char_or_byte2` specifies the index of the last member.

  `min_byte1` and `max_byte1` represent the first and last rows that exist in the font. There may be up to 256 rows in a font, but no normal font is likely to need all 256 rows (256 * 256 characters). For two-byte fonts, both `min_char_or_byte2` and `max_char_or_byte2` will be less than 256, and the two-byte character index values corresponding to `per_char` array member N (counting from 0) are:

$byte1 = N/D$ `min_byte1`	`/* Row offset */`
$byte2 = N\%D$ `min_char_or_byte2`	`/* Column offset */`

  where:

D	=	number of characters per row (`max_char_or_byte2` - `min_char_or_byte2` + 1)
/	=	integer division
%	=	integer modulus

- If the `per_char` pointer is NULL, then all glyphs (characters in the font) between the first and last character, inclusive, have the same extent and other information, as given by both `min_bounds` and `max_bounds`.

- If `all_chars_exist` is True, then all characters in the `per_char` array have nonzero bounding boxes.

- `default_char` specifies the index that will be used when an undefined or nonexistent index is used. `default_char` is a single-byte character. For a font using two-byte matrix format, `default_char` has `byte1` in the most significant byte and `byte2` in the least significant byte. If `default_char` itself specifies an undefined or

Drawing

nonexistent character, then no printing is performed for undefined or nonexistent index values.

The **XFontProp** member of **XFontStruct** is provided to allow additional properties (over and above the predefined properties) to be associated with a font. See Section 6.2.9 for a description of predefined and additional font properties.

6.2.5 Positioning of Text

All the routines that draw text require the same basic techniques for positioning text on the screen.

Let's consider a string drawn with **XDrawImageString()**. **XDrawImageString()** draws the entire rectangle described by the **max_bounds** of the font, with the character drawn in the **foreground** pixel value and the rest drawn in the **background** pixel value (both from the GC). Figure 6-5 demonstrates the drawing of three strings. The origin of the baseline of each text line is specified in the **XDrawImageString()** call. The offset of the first line of text in Figure 6-5 is (**20 + ascent**). Subsequent lines are placed (**ascent + descent**) below the origin of the first line. For routines other than **XDrawImageString()***,† these coordinates still position the background rectangle even though that rectangle is not filled.

- If you want the upper-left corner of the background rectangle to be at pixel coordinate (**x,y**), then pass (**x, y+ascent**) as the baseline origin coordinates to the text drawing routines, where **ascent** is the font ascent as given in **XFontStruct**.

- If you want the lower-left corner of the background rectangle to be at pixel coordinate (**x,y**), then pass (**x, y−descent+1**) as the baseline origin coordinates to the text routines, where **descent** is the font descent as given in **XFontStruct**.

It is important to find out how wide a given string is going to be in the chosen font. This width must be smaller than the width of the drawable if you want to be able to read the end of the text!

Listed below are several routines that return either a string width or its extent (both width and height). Both types of routines return the width of the specified string in pixels. The routines that return an extent also provide vertical size information in the form of ascent and descent measurements for the particular string in question and for the font as a whole.

XTextWidth() and **XTextWidth16()**
   Return the width in pixels of a string in a particular font.

---

†The * (wildcard) notation is used occasionally in this manual to indicate a number of events or routines with similar names. In this case, there are two functions, **XDrawImageString()** and **XDrawImageString16()**, which differ only slightly in name, features, and arguments, as described in Section 6.2.1. Instead of always listing them both, we may use the wildcard notation.

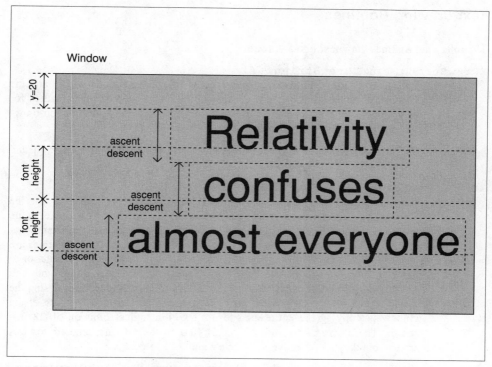

Figure 6-5. The vertical positioning of strings

XTextExtents() and **XTextExtents16()**

>Return string and font metrics, which include the width and height of the bounding box containing the string in the specified font. Use these routines if making repeated calls with the same **XFontStruct**.

XQueryTextExtents() and **XQueryTextExtents16()**

>Perform the same function as **XTextExtents()** and **XTextExtents16()**, but they query the server instead of requiring a filled **XFontStruct** and performing the computation locally. Use these routines if you only need to calculate metrics once (or so) for a given font.

To position text vertically using the returned extents, normally you should use the font **ascent** and **descent** (rather than the string **ascent** and **descent**) if you will be drawing other strings that you want lined up. If you are seriously pressed for space, it is possible to save a few pixel rows with certain strings by using the string **ascent** and **descent** measurements.

Whether you center, left justify, or right justify text is completely up to you. The only crucial test is to see that there is enough room for the height and width of the string at the chosen position.

6.2.6 Text-drawing Routines

The following routines draw text into a drawable:

`XDrawString()` and `XDrawString16()`
> Draw a string into a drawable. They require only the string, its length, and the position of the baseline origin. The font in the GC is used both as a source for the graphics operation and as a clip mask, so that pixels in the destination drawable that are not in each font character are not drawn.
>
> The internationalized versions of these functions are **XmbDrawString()** and **XwcDrawString()** (new in R5).

`XDrawImageString()` and `XDrawImageString16()`
> Act just like `XDrawString()` and `XDrawString16()` except that the bounding box around the text string is filled with the **background** pixel value defined in the GC. This avoids annoying flicker on many screens in clients that do a lot of redrawing, such as editors and terminal emulators. These routines are very useful when you need to be able to highlight the text for selections or to indicate that a menu choice has been made, because the foreground and background of the GC can be swapped to redraw the text highlighted. Using the other text routines to do this requires changing the background attribute of the window or copying the entire area to itself with a logical function of **GXinvert**. The **function** and **fill_style** in the GC are ignored for this request, but they are effectively **GXcopy** and **FillSolid**.
>
> The internationalized versions of these functions are **XmbDrawImageString()** and **XwcDrawImageString()** (new in R5).

`XDrawText()` and `XDrawText16()`
> Can draw one or more strings to the screen using one **XTextItem** structure for each string. Each structure contains the string of text to be drawn, specifies what font to use, and provides a horizontal offset (the **delta** member) from the end of the last item of text. A font member other than **None** causes the font to be stored in the specified GC; otherwise, the font in that GC is used.
>
> Accented or overstruck characters can be drawn in this manner. These functions can also be used to draw complex arrangements of text in one call instead of having to call `XDrawString()` several times, changing the position, text, and font in between each call.
>
> The internationalized versions of these functions are **XmbDrawText()** and **XwcDrawText()** (new in R5).

Example 6-6 displays the **XTextItem** structures used by `XDrawText()` and `XDrawText16()`.

Example 6-6. The XTextItem and XChar2b structures

```
typedef struct {
    char *chars;            /* Pointer to string */
    int nchars;             /* Number of characters */
    int delta;              /* Delta between strings */
    Font font;              /* Font to print it in, None don't change */
} XTextItem;

typedef struct {
    XChar2b *chars;         /* Two-byte characters */
    int nchars;             /* Number of characters */
    int delta;              /* Delta between strings */
    Font font;              /* Font to print it in, None don't change */
} XTextItem16;

typedef struct {           /* Normal 16-bit characters are two bytes */
    unsigned char byte1;
    unsigned char byte2;
} XChar2b;
```

The `font` member of **XTextItem** specifies the font to be used to draw the string in the `chars` member and is stored in the GC for use in subsequent text requests.

The `delta` member specifies a change in horizontal position before the string is drawn. The delta is always added to the character origin and is not dependent on the draw direction of the font. For example, if `x = 40`, `y = 20`, and `items[0].delta = 8`, then the string specified by `items[0].chars` would be drawn starting at `x = 48`, `y = 20`. If `items[0].chars` pointed to two characters with a combined width of 16 pixels, the next delta, `items[1].delta`, would begin at `x = 64`. The next text item would begin at the end of this delta. The `delta` member can also be used to backspace for overstriking characters.

6.2.7 The draw_text Routine

Example 6-7 shows the **draw_text** routine, called from the *basicwin* program described in Chapter 3, *Basic Window Program*. **draw_text** draws three strings in different locations in the window. It demonstrates how to calculate the vertical position of a string using the font ascent.

Example 6-7. The draw_text routine

```
draw_text(win, gc, font_info, win_width, win_height)
Window win;
GC gc;
XFontStruct *font_info;
unsigned int win_width, win_height;
{
    char *string1 = "Hi! I'm a window, who are you?";
    char *string2 = "To terminate program, press any key";
    char *string3 = "or button while in this window.";
    char *string4 = "Screen Dimensions:";
    int len1, len2, len3, len4;
    int width1, width2, width3;
```

Example 6-7. The draw_text routine (continued)

```
    char cd_height[ 50 ], cd_width[ 50 ], cd_depth[ 50 ];
    int font_height;
    int initial_y_offset, x_offset;

    /* Need length for both XTextWidth and XDrawString */
    len1 = strlen(string1);
    len2 = strlen(string2);
    len3 = strlen(string3);

    /* Get string widths for centering */
    width1 = XTextWidth(font_info, string1, len1);
    width2 = XTextWidth(font_info, string2, len2);
    width3 = XTextWidth(font_info, string3, len3);

    /* Output text, centered on each line */
    font_height = font_info->ascent + font_info->descent;

    /* Output text, centered on each line */
    XDrawString(display, win, gc, (win_width - width1)/2,
            font_height, string1, len1);
    XDrawString(display, win, gc, (win_width - width2)/2,
            (int)(win_height - (2 * font_height)),
            string2, len2);
    XDrawString(display, win, gc, (win_width - width3)/2,
            (int)(win_height - font_height),
            string3, len3);

    /* Copy numbers into string variables */
    (void) sprintf(cd_height, " Height — %d pixels",
            DisplayHeight(display,screen_num));
    (void) sprintf(cd_width, " Width  — %d pixels",
            DisplayWidth(display,screen_num));
    (void) sprintf(cd_depth, " Depth — %d plane(s)",
            DefaultDepth(display, screen_num));

    /* Reuse these for same purpose */
    len4 = strlen(string4);
    len1 = strlen(cd_height);
    len2 = strlen(cd_width);
    len3 = strlen(cd_depth);

    /* To center strings vertically, we place the first string
     * so that the top of it is two font_heights above the center
     * of the window; since the baseline of the string is what
     * we need to locate for XDrawString and the baseline is
     * one font_info->ascent below the top of the character,
     * the final offset of the origin up from the center of
     * the window is one font_height + one descent */

    initial_y_offset = win_height/2 - font_height -
            font_info->descent;

    x_offset = (int) win_width/4;

    XDrawString(display, win, gc, x_offset, (int) initial_y_offset,
            string4,len4);

    XDrawString(display, win, gc, x_offset, (int) initial_y_offset +
            font_height,cd_height,len1);
    XDrawString(display, win, gc, x_offset, (int) initial_y_offset +
            2 * font_height,cd_width,len2);
```

Example 6-7. The draw_text routine (continued)

```
XDrawString(display, win, gc, x_offset, (int) initial_y_offset +
            3 * font_height,cd_depth,len3);
}
```

Note that this routine may be called repeatedly in response to **Expose** events. That is why the font is loaded, a GC is created, and its font member is set to the loaded font in separate routines before the event loop. The font information structure (containing the font ID) and GC resource ID are passed to `draw_text` as arguments.

6.2.8 Vertical Text and Rotated Text

Xlib provides routines that draw horizontal strings, but not vertical ones. If you want to draw strings vertically that read normally, you need to use a separate text drawing call for each character. You use a baseline with the same x coordinate but a different y coordinate for each character.

Drawing strings vertically that read sideways is even more of a problem. The core X protocol and font server provides no way to rotate text, and the XLFD provides no way to name such font variations.* One possibility is to use fonts that have their characters sideways. There is only one of these in the distribution from MIT, called *rot-s16*.

Hewlett Packard has developed enhancements to the R5 font server that support rotated and anamorphically scaled text. They come in the form of patches to the source code for the font server in MIT's X distribution. These patches have been donated to the X Consortium so they are freely available for ftp on *export.lcs.mit.edu*. See *The X Resource*, Issue 3, Summer 1992, for a complete description.

6.2.9 Font Properties

Font properties give detailed information about a font, usually for use only in desktop publishing applications. A font is not guaranteed to have any properties. When possible, fonts should have at least the properties represented by the atoms listed in Table 6-1. These atoms are defined in *<X11/Xatom.h>*. `XGetFontProperty()` returns the value of a property given the atom for that property. In the descriptions in Table 6-1, the data associated with a property is referred to with the same name as the property, but in mixed case. For example, the property atom `XA_SUPERSCRIPT_X` contains a value that is referred to as `SuperscriptX` in the description.

Applications that make heavy use of proportionally spaced text may use these properties to space various characters properly.

For a further description of font properties and associated conventions, see Appendix M, *Logical Font Description Conventions*, of Volume Zero, *X Protocol Reference Manual* (as of the second printing).

---

*Some vendors supply a Display PostScript extension that supports scaled and rotated text.

Table 6-1. Font Properties

Property Name	Type	Description
XA_MIN_SPACE	unsigned int	The minimum interword spacing.
XA_NORM_SPACE	unsigned int	The normal interword spacing.
XA_MAX_SPACE	unsigned int	The maximum interword spacing.
XA_END_SPACE	unsigned int	The additional spacing at the end of sentences.
XA_SUPERSCRIPT_X	int	Offset (in pixels) from the character origin where superscripts should begin. If the origin is at [x,y], then superscripts should begin at: [x + SuperscriptX, y - SuperscriptY]
XA_SUPERSCRIPT_Y	int	Offset (in pixels) from the character origin where superscripts should begin. If the origin is at [x,y], then superscripts should begin at: [x + SuperscriptX, y - SuperscriptY]
XA_SUBSCRIPT_X	int	Offset (in pixels) from the character where subscripts should begin. If the origin is at [x,y], then subscripts should begin at: [x + SubscriptX, y + SubscriptY]
XA_SUBSCRIPT_Y	int	Offset (in pixels) from the character where subscripts should begin. If the origin is at [x,y], then subscripts should begin at: [x + SubscriptX, y + SubscriptY]
XA_UNDERLINE_ POSITION	int	Y offset (in pixels) from the baseline to the top of an underline. If the baseline is y-coordinate y, then the top of the underline is at: [y + UnderlinePosition]
XA_UNDERLINE_ THICKNESS	unsigned int	Thickness in pixels of an underline.

Table 6-1. Font Properties (continued)

Property Name	Type	Description
XA_STRIKEOUT_ ASCENT	int	Vertical extents (in pixels) for boxing or voiding characters. If the baseline is at y-coordinate y, then the top of the strikeout box is at: [y - StrikeoutAscent] and the height of the box is: [StrikeoutAscent + StrikeoutDescent]
XA_STRIKEOUT_ DESCENT	int	Vertical extents (in pixels) for boxing or voiding characters. If the baseline is at y-coordinate y, then the top of the strikeout box is at: [y - StrikeoutAscent] and the height of the box is: [StrikeoutAscent + StrikeoutDescent]
XA_ITALIC_ANGLE	int	The angle of the dominant staffs of characters in the font, in degrees scaled by 64, relative to the three-o'clock position from the character origin, with positive indicating counterclockwise motion (as in XDrawArc).
XA_X_HEIGHT	int	"1 ex" as in TeX, but expressed in units of pixels. Often the height of lowercase *x*.
XA_QUAD_WIDTH	int	"1 em" as in TeX, but expressed in units of pixels. The width of an *m* in the current font and point size.
XA_CAP_HEIGHT	int	Y offset from the baseline to the top of the capital letters, ignoring accents, in pixels. If the baseline is at y-coordinate y, then the top of the capitals is at: (y - CAP_HEIGHT)
XA_WEIGHT	unsigned	The weight or boldness of the font, expressed as a value between 0 and 1000.
XA_POINT_SIZE	unsigned	The point size, expressed in tenths of a point, of this font at the ideal resolution. There are 72.27 points to the inch.
XA_RESOLUTION	unsigned	The number of pixels per point, expressed in hundredths, at which this font was created.

It is also possible for fonts to have properties not in this predefined list. If there are such properties, they will be stored in a list of **XFontProp** structures in the **XFontStruct** for the font. Example 6-8 shows the **XFontProp** structure. The documentation for each font must describe these additional properties if they are defined.

Example 6-8. The additional font property structure

```
/* Additional properties to allow arbitrary information with fonts */
typedef struct {
    Atom name;
    unsigned long card32;
} XFontProp;
```

6.2.10 Setting the Font Path

XFreeFontPath( ), **XGetFontPath( )**, and **XSetFontPath( )** are available to get or set the current search path for fonts. These functions are very rarely needed, but you should know that they exist. Their purpose is to allow for additional directories of fonts besides the default, which is */usr/lib/X11/fonts* on UNIX-based systems. The font path is common to all clients of the server, so it should be modified with care. If the directory that contains the standard fonts is removed from the path, neither any client nor the server can access fonts.

In Release 5, font servers need to be added to the font path so the X server can access them.

6.3 Regions

An X *region* is an arbitrary set of pixels on the screen. But usually a region is either a rectangular area, several overlapping or adjacent rectangular areas, or a general polygon. Regions are chiefly used to set the **clip_mask** member of the GC. **XSetRegion( )** sets the **clip_mask** to a region so that output will occur only within the region. Using **XSetRegion( )** is a lot easier than defining a single-plane pixmap with the desired size and shape and then using that bitmap to set the **clip_mask** with **XSetClipMask( )**, and it is more flexible than the **clip_mask** you can set with **XSetClipRectangles( )**.

The most common use of setting the **clip_mask** to a region is to combine the rectangle from each of multiple contiguous **Expose** events on a single window into a single region and clip the redrawing to that region. This provides a performance improvement in some situations. See Section 3.2.13.1 for more information and an example.

A region has an x and y offset, which is used internally when making calculations with regions (offsets for all regions have a common origin). The offset has an effect if the region is used as a **clip_mask**. When making a graphics request with the **clip_mask** of the GC set with **XSetRegion( )**, the offset of the region is added to **clip_x_origin** and **clip_y_origin** to determine the placement of the region relative to the destination drawable.

Regions can be created with **XCreateRegion()** or **XPolygonRegion()**. **XCreateRegion()** creates an empty region to which rectangles can be added with **XUnionRectWithRegion()** and various other functions that perform mathematical operations on regions. **XCreateRegion()** and **XPolygonRegion()** return a pointer to the opaque type **Region**, whose definition a program does not need to know. Just the pointer is used to refer to the region. **XPolygonRegion()** creates a region of the same shape as **XDrawLines()** would draw given the same arguments (except that **XPolygonRegion()** does not require a drawable or a GC and therefore interprets the lines as thin lines). It specifies a list of points and has a flag that indicates whether areas overlapping an odd number of times should be included or not included in the region (just like the **fill_rule** in the GC).

Each region is implemented as a group of nonoverlapping rectangles. Therefore, performance will be best if the regions you use have sides parallel to the coordinate axes. Nonetheless, nonrectangular regions can be created with **XPolygonRegion()**.

A region is destroyed with **XDestroyRegion()**. The best way to clear a region is to destroy it and create a new one.

XClipBox() returns the size and position of the smallest rectangle that completely encloses the given region. This function returns an **XRectangle** structure that contains the coordinates of the upper-left corner and the width and height of the rectangle enclosing a region.

6.3.1 Moving and Resizing Regions

XOffsetRegion() changes the offset of the specified region by the number of pixels specified by its arguments *dx* and *dy*. **XShrinkRegion()** reduces the size of the given region by the number of pixels specified by *dx* and *dy*, with positive values indicating that the region is to be increased in size. **XShrinkRegion()** also modifies the offset of the region to keep the center of the region near its original position.

6.3.2 Computations with Regions

Several functions are available to combine two regions in various ways. Each function takes three regions as arguments: two operands and a region in which to place the result.

XIntersectRegion()	Computes the intersection (overlapping area) of two regions.
XUnionRegion()	Computes the union (total of both areas) of two regions.
XSubtractRegion()	Subtracts two regions. The result is the region listed first minus the intersection of the two regions.
XXorRegion()	Computes the difference between the union and the intersection of two regions.

`XUnionRectWithRegion()` Computes the union of a rectangle and region and sets the region to the result.

6.3.3 Returning Region Information

This group of region functions makes logical determinations about regions. All of these routines return nonzero if their conditions are satisfied.

`XEmptyRegion()` Determines whether there is any area in the specified region.

`XEqualRegion()` Determines whether two regions have the same offset, size, and shape.

`XPointInRegion()` Determines whether a specified point resides in a region.

`XRectInRegion()` Determines whether a rectangle specified by *x*, *y*, *width*, and *height* occurs completely inside, completely outside, or overlapping a given region. It returns `RectangleIn` if the rectangle is completely inside the region, `RectanglePart` if the rectangle overlaps the edge of a region, and `RectangleOut` if the rectangle and the region are nonintersecting.

6.4 Images

Xlib provides an image structure that is capable of storing all the data corresponding to a screen area or pixmap. The major difference between an image and a pixmap is that an image is a structure on the client side, so its contents can be manipulated directly by the client, instead of solely through X protocol requests. Xlib provides the routines **XGet-Image()** and **XPutImage()** that use the X protocol to transfer the contents of a window or pixmap into an image structure and to write the contents of an image structure back into a window or pixmap.

Xlib provides a few minimal routines for manipulating image structures, including routines to create and initialize an empty image structure, destroy an image structure, get a pixel, set a pixel, extract a subimage of an image, and add a constant value to all pixels in an image. These routines can be relatively slow, because they change the byte- and bit-order of the image before performing the operation and then change it back before placing it back in the image. However, in some implementations of Xlib, optimized versions of these routines will automatically be used when the byte- and bit-order used by the server happens to be the same as that used by the machine running the client. This should be quite fast but is not always available.

The image-processing routines provided by Xlib are minimal—they do not provide a complete image manipulation package. However, the image structure does contain all the information necessary to implement a complete package. An application can implement its own routines to manipulate the image data directly. However, this code is difficult to write in a portable and efficient fashion because of the large number of data formats that are possible.*

---

*Anyone thinking of trying to write their own routines to manipulate images should get access to the Xlib code that manipulates images. This code will make you think again.

`XGetImage()` returns data that uses the byte- and bit-order of the server. The application will need to swap this into the native byte- and bit-order before doing image processing. `XPutImage()` takes care of swapping it back before sending it to the server, so that the application need not convert the data back to the server-native byte- and bit-order. However, `XPutImage()` does not convert images of different depths.

The `XImage` data structure is shown in Example 6-9.

Example 6-9. The XImage structure

```
struct _XImage {
    int width, height;              /* Size of image */
    int xoffset;                    /* Number of pixels offset in
                                     * x direction */
    int format;                     /* XYBitmap, XYPixmap, ZPixmap */
    char *data;                     /* Pointer to image data */
    int byte_order;                 /* Data byte order, LSBFirst,
                                     * MSBFirst */
    int bitmap_unit;                /* Quantity of scan line 8, 16, 32 */
    int bitmap_bit_order;           /* LSBFirst, MSBFirst */
    int bitmap_pad;                 /* 8, 16, 32 either XY or Z format */
    int depth;                      /* Depth of image */
    int bytes_per_line;             /* Accelerator to next line */
    int bits_per_pixel;             /* Bits per pixel (ZPixmap format) */
    unsigned long red_mask;         /* Bits in z arrangement */
    unsigned long green_mask;
    unsigned long blue_mask;
    char *obdata;                   /* Hook for the object routines to
                                     * hang on */
    struct funcs {                  /* Image manipulation routines */
        struct _XImage *(*create_image)();
        int (*destroy_image)();
        unsigned long (*get_pixel)();
        int (*put_pixel)();
        struct _XImage *(*sub_image)();
        int (*add_pixel)();
    } f;
} XImage;
```

The function pointers in the image object allow Xlib implementors to replace MIT's generic functions with functions optimized for the byte- and bit-order used in the machine that is running Xlib.

- The `height`, `width`, and `xoffset` are set when an image is created. The offset is used to align an image to even-addressable boundaries.

- The `format` member may be `XYBitmap`, `XYPixmap`, or `ZPixmap`.

  In `XYBitmap`, the bitmap is represented in scan line order, with each scan line made up of multiples of the `bitmap_unit` and padded with meaningless bits. Within each `bitmap_unit`, the bit order depends on `bitmap_bit_order`.

  In `XYPixmap`, each plane is represented as a bitmap, and the planes appear in most significant to least significant bit order, with no padding between planes.

  In `ZPixmap`, the pixels (instead of bits) are listed in scan line order. Each pixel has `bits_per_pixel` bits, and the bits in the pixel that are allocated to red, green, and blue for `DirectColor` and `TrueColor` are specified by `red_mask`, `blue_mask`, and `green_mask`. See Chapter 7, *Color*, for more information on these masks. At the end of each scan line, a pad is used as for `XYBitmap`.

- The `byte_order` is the data byte order, either `LSBFirst` or `MSBFirst`. The `bitmap_bit_order` is the bit order within each byte, again either `LSBFirst` or `MSBFirst`. The `bitmap_unit` specifies how many bits make up a unit of image data (usually the same as the word size), and it can be `8`, `16`, or `32`. Together, these members determine the exact arrangement of bits in memory. Figure 6-6 shows the effect of the various `byte_order` and `bit_order` combinations assuming a `bitmap_unit` of `16`. VAXes and 80*86 systems use `byte_order` of `LSBFirst`, while 68000-family systems use `MSBFirst`. Note that with these three variables alone there are 12 different data formats. The `ImageByteOrder()` and `BitmapBitOrder()` macros return which byte order and bit order is used by the server.

- The `bitmap_pad` member can be `8`, `16`, or `32`, and it specifies the quantum of the scan line. In other words, the start of one scan line and the start of the next are separated by an integer multiple of this number.

- The `depth` of an image is assigned as the image is created. The depth of a window from which image data is read must match this depth.

- The `bytes_per_line` member specifies how many bytes make up a scan line.

- The `bits_per_pixel` member is for `ZPixmap` images only. This member of the `XImage` structure must match the member of the same name in the `ScreenFormat` structure (itself a member of `Display`).

- The `red_mask`, `green_mask`, and `blue_mask` members are for `ZPixmap` only and specify the number of bits in the pixel that are allocated to red, green, and blue. This implies that the visual is `DirectColor` or `TrueColor`. See Chapter 7 for more information.

6.4.1 Manipulating Images

These are the available functions that operate on images:

`XCreateImage()`   Allocates memory for an `XImage` structure and sets various members. Note that it uses the server's data format, which is often not appropriate. The byte- and bit-order fields should usually be changed directly to the client-native format. However, then the call `_XInitImageFuncPtrs(image)` should be issued to reset the mapping to the appropriate versions of the functions for manipulating the image. This call is supposed to be private to Xlib and, therefore, should be watched for changes in later releases, but this is currently the accepted method.

```
Pixel#  0    1    2    3    4    5    6    7    8    9   10   11   12   13   14   15
-------------------------------------------------------------------------------
byte_order = LSBFirst, bitmap_bit_order = LSBFirst
byte    0                                            1
bit     0    1    2    3    4    5    6    7    8    9   10   11   12   13   14   15

byte_order = LSBFirst, bitmap_bit_order = MSBFirst
byte    0                                            1
bit     7    6    5    4    3    2    1    0   15   14   13   12   11   10    9    8

byte_order = MSBFirst, bitmap_bit_order = LSBFirst
byte    0                                            1
bit     8    9   10   11   12   13   14   15    0    1    2    3    4    5    6    7

byte_order = MSBFirst, bitmap_bit_order = MSBFirst
byte    0                                            1
bit    15   14   13   12   11   10    9    8    7    6    5    4    3    2    1    0
```

Figure 6-6. Bit and byte order possibilities for images when bitmap_unit = 16

XGetImage()	Fills an **XImage** structure with data corresponding to a visible area of the screen or a pixmap.
XPutImage()	Dumps an **XImage** structure with data into an area of a window or a pixmap.
XDestroyImage()	Frees the data field in an image structure if the image structure was allocated in the application. If the image was created using **XCreateImage()**, **XGetImage()**, or **XGetSubImage()**, **XDestroyImage()** frees both the data and the image structure. Note that if the image data is stored in static memory in the application, it cannot be freed—to free an image created with **XCreate-Image()** that has statically allocated data, you must set **NULL** into the **data** field before calling **XDestroyImage()**.
XGetPixel()	Gets a single pixel value specified by an x,y location from an image.
XPutPixel()	Puts a single pixel value into an image in a specified location.
XAddPixel()	Increments each pixel in a pixmap by a constant value.
XSubImage()	Creates a new image that is a subset of an existing image. It executes **XCreateImage()** and then performs multiple executions of **XGetPixel()** and **XPutPixel()**, so it may be slow.
XGetSubImage()	Creates an image from a subsection of a drawable.

Functions to read and write images to and from disk files have not yet been defined by the X Consortium.

Example 6-10 demonstrates the use of images. See Volume Two, *Xlib Reference Manual*, for more information on the image-handling functions.

6.4.2 Examples Using Images

Images are one of the areas of X that has not yet been extensively used. Therefore, there are few examples available that use images to their potential.

The unique feature of images is that all the data is stored and is directly accessible in Xlib, rather than in the server like **Pixmap** and **Window** resources. Since images completely represent a screen area, you can do anything you want to any of the pixel values in the image. Applications like image processing and machine vision would probably use images.

Example 6-10 shows a routine using images. This routine reads an image from the screen, manipulates it, and puts a reflected version of the contents in a new window of the same size. It uses **XGetImage( )**, **XPutImage( )**, and **XPutPixel( )**.

Example 6-10. Example using images — reflect_window

```
/* Window and newwindow must have the same size and depth,
 * and window must be visible */
reflect_window (window, newwindow, gc, width, height)
Window window, newwindow;
GC gc;
unsigned int width, height;
{
XImage *xi;
unsigned long pixelvalue1, pixelvalue2;
int y;
int left_x, right_x;

xi = XGetImage(display, window, 0,0, width, height, AllPlanes,
        XYPixmap);
printf("calculating reflection -- this may take awhile...\n");

for (left_x=0 ; left_x<width/2 ; left_x++)
    {
        for (y=0 ; y<height ; y++)
            {
                pixelvalue1 = XGetPixel(xi, left_x, y);
                right_x = width - left_x;
                if (left_x != right_x)
                    {
                        pixelvalue2 = XGetPixel(xi, right_x, y);
                        XPutPixel(xi, left_x, y, pixelvalue2);
                    }
                XPutPixel(xi, right_x, y, pixelvalue1);
            }
    }
printf("putting image\n");
XPutImage(display, newwindow, gc, xi, 0, 0, 0, 0, width, height);
}
```

With sufficient understanding of the format of image data, this routine could be rewritten without **XGetPixel( )** and **XPutPixel( )**, which would speed it up substantially. However, there would have to be separate code for the many different image formats to make the code as portable as the version shown.

6.5 Cursors

The cursor is different from other types of output to the screen since it is transient, passing over the screen without permanently changing it. The cursor is drawn where the pointer is pointing and removed as soon as the pointer moves.

Each window can have a different cursor defined in its window attributes (using **XDefine-Cursor()**). Whenever the pointer is in a visible window, the cursor is set to the cursor defined for that window. If no cursor was defined for that window, the cursor will be the one that was defined for the parent window unless otherwise specified in the attributes.

From X's perspective, a cursor consists of a cursor shape, mask, foreground and background colors, and hotspot (defined in a moment):

- The cursor bitmap determines the shape of the cursor.

- The mask bitmap determines the pixels on the screen that will be modified by the cursor.

- The pixel values determine the foreground color (the 1 bits in the cursor bitmap) and the background color (the 0 bits in the cursor bitmap).

- The *hotspot* defines the point on the cursor that will be reported when a pointer event occurs. The hotspot is the actual tracking position—for example, the center for a crosshair cursor or the point of an arrow.

There usually are limitations imposed by the hardware on cursors as to size, shape, and whether a mask is implemented. **XQueryBestCursor()** is used to find out what sizes are possible.

You need to create a **Cursor** resource to call **XDefineCursor()**. Read on for a description of the various ways to create cursors.

6.5.1 The Standard Cursor Font

Many popular cursor shapes are provided in the standard cursor font, *<X11/cursorfont.h>*. Each of these cursor shapes can be turned into a **Cursor** resource using **XCreateFont-Cursor()**. Example 6-11 demonstrates this process.

The cursor font is shown in Appendix I, *The Cursor Font*, of Volume Two, *Xlib Reference Manual*, and on the reference page for **XCreateFontCursor()** in Volume Two. Each of these cursors uses two characters in the cursor font, only one of which is shown. One determines the shape of the cursor, and the other is a mask which selects which pixels on the screen are disturbed by the cursor. The mask for each standard cursor is very similar to the shape for that cursor but one pixel wider in all directions. This means that when the cursor is black and over a black background, this one pixel outline of the cursor will appear in white around the cursor, making the cursor visible over any background.

Example 6-11. Creating a Cursor from the standard cursor font

```
#include <X11/cursorfont.h>
int cursor_shape = XC_arrow;
Window window;
Cursor cursor;
cursor = XCreateFontCursor(display, cursor_shape);
XDefineCursor(display, window, cursor);
/* Now cursor will appear when pointer is in window */
```

If your client is operating on a color screen and it allows the user to specify window background colors, it may also allow the user to specify cursor colors, since this could improve contrast between the window background and cursor. These pixel values may be specified in the calls to **XCreateGlyphCursor( )** and **XCreatePixmapCursor( )**, or **XRecolorCursor( )** may be called for an existing cursor.

XCreateGlyphCursor( ) allows you to do the same thing as is done with the standard cursors but using font characters you specify from any font. The hotspot of these cursors and those created by **XCreateFontCursor( )** is the origin of each font character (just as if it were text). Usually the hotspot is placed in a logical location, but it is not possible to determine where the hotspot is from within the program or to change its location.

XCreatePixmapCursor( ) allows you to create a cursor from shape and mask pixmaps and foreground and background pixel values, with an explicit hotspot. **XQueryBest-Cursor( )** should be called to determine the allowed cursor sizes before preparing the pixmaps.

You can free the cursor with **XFreeCursor( )** right after the **XDefineCursor( )** call if no further explicit references to it are made.

6.5.2 Creating a Pixmap Cursor

If no cursor in the standard cursor font meets your needs, you can design one of your own. It should be 16 by 16 pixels since some servers may not be able to handle other sizes efficiently. You can design the shape of the cursor with any bitmap editing tool such as the *bitmap* program. You will also have to design a mask. To see the purpose of the mask, move the cursor on your X screen over various backgrounds (highlight some text if necessary to get a different background). The mask provides an outline around the cursor so that the cursor is visible over any background. Therefore, the design of the mask is typically similar to the cursor shape but simpler and more dense. The outline of the mask usually extends one pixel more in every direction than the cursor shape. Figure 6-7 shows a shape and its corresponding mask, as an example of their relationship.

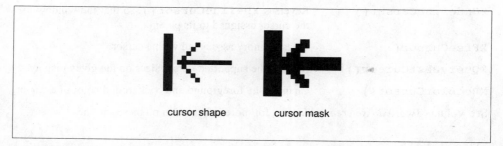

cursor shape   cursor mask

Figure 6-7. A cursor shape pixmap and corresponding mask

Example 6-12 demonstrates the code for creating your own cursor.

Example 6-12. Creating a Pixmap Cursor

```
#include "bill"       /* shape bits */
#include "mask"       /* mask bits */

Pixmap shape, mask;
XColor magenta_def, bviolet_def;

/* shape and mask are single plane pixmaps */
shape = XCreatePixmapFromBitmapData(display, root_window,
        bill_bits, bill_width, bill_height, 1, 0, 1 );
mask = XCreatePixmapFromBitmapData(display, root_window,
        mask_bits, mask_width, mask_height, 1, 0, 1 );

XParseColor(display, colormap, "magenta", &magenta_def );
XParseColor(display, colormap, "BlueViolet", &bviolet_def );

/* colors are applied when making the cursor, not when making
 * the shape and mask pixmaps */
cursor = XCreatePixmapCursor(display, shape, mask, &magenta_def,
        &bviolet_def, bill_x_hot, bill_y_hot );

XDefineCursor(display, window, cursor);
```

6.5.3 Loading and Changing Cursors

The following routines are used to manipulate cursors:

XCreateFontCursor()   Creates a cursor from the font of standard cursors. This is the easiest way to create a cursor.

XCreateGlyphCursor()   Creates a cursor from a font character (glyph) and a mask.

XCreatePixmapCursor()   Creates a cursor from pixmap data.

XDefineCursor()   Associates a cursor with a window, so that the specified cursor is displayed in the window whenever the pointer is in the window.

XUndefineCursor()	Reverses XDefineCursor(), so that the window uses the cursor assigned to its parent.
XFreeCursor()	Frees memory associated with a cursor.
XQueryBestCursor()	Returns the supported cursor sizes on the given display.
XRecolorCursor()	Changes the foreground and background color of a cursor.

See Volume Two, *Xlib Reference Manual*, for more information on these routines.

7

Color

This chapter describes how to use color in your programs. Color handling in X can be more complex than in other graphics systems because of the need for portability to many different types of displays. Certain advanced topics in color handling are still poorly defined in the X standard. This chapter starts with the basics, which everyone working with color should read, and gradually moves to more advanced topics, including R5 device-independent color. Pick and choose from the later sections as appropriate.

In This Chapter:

7
Color

A typical X application allows the user to specify colors for the background and border of each of its windows, colors for the cursor, and foreground and background colors to be set in GCs for drawing text and graphics. More complex applications (such as Computer Aided Design (CAD) applications) might use color to distinguish physical or logical layers. Still more complex applications, such as in imaging, might use fine gradations of color to represent real-world data. Yet in discussing the background and border window attributes and how to set the foreground and background members of the GC, we have spoken only of pixel values.

How are these pixel values translated to colors? And how must an X client manage color if it is to run successfully on the wide variety of screen hardware available in the X environment?

Because X must support a wide variety of systems with differing screen hardware, the Xlib color-handling mechanisms are fairly complex. Even programmers who have previously written color graphics applications will find there are some new concepts to learn.

This chapter starts out by describing the different types of screens that an X application may run on and the mechanisms Xlib provides for determining the screen type. It then describes the simplest color-allocation mechanisms, which could be used by applications whose principal use of color is for decoration. It proceeds to discuss more complex color applications and concludes with a section on writing applications that will be portable across different types of color and monochrome screens.

7.1 Basic Color Terms and Concepts

Most color screens on the market today are based on the RGB color model. Each pixel on the screen is actually made up of three phosphors: one red, one green, and one blue. Each of these three phosphors is sensitive to a separate electron beam. When all three phosphors are fully illuminated, the pixel appears white to the human eye. When all three are dark, the pixel appears black. When the illumination of each primary color varies, the three phosphors generate an additive color that might seem surprising. For example, equal portions of red and green, with no admixture of blue, make yellow. Most people are more familiar with subtractive color mixing, used in paints, where red, yellow, and blue are the three primary colors from which all other colors (except white and shades of gray) can be made.

Color

You, no doubt, know that a color screen uses multiple bits per pixel (also referred to as multiple planes) to specify colors. A *colormap* is used to translate each pixel's value into the visible colors you see on the screen.

A colormap is no more than a lookup table stored in the server. Any given pixel value is used as an index into this table—for example, a pixel value of 16 will select the sixteenth element, or *colorcell*.

On the most common type of color system, each colorcell contains separate 16-bit intensity values for each of the three primary colors.

As shown in Figure 7-1, a pixel value uniquely identifies a particular colorcell. Each pixel value in the visible portions of a window is continuously read out of screen memory and looked up in the colormap. The RGB values in the specified colorcell control the intensity of the three primary colors and thus determine the color that is displayed at that point on the screen.

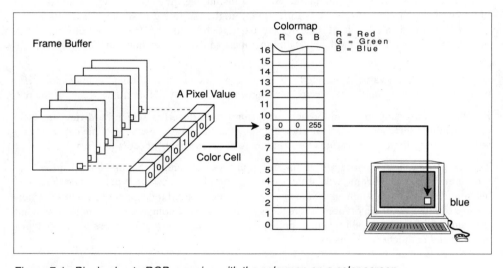

Figure 7-1. Pixel value to RGB mapping with the colormap on a color screen

The range of colors possible on the screen is a function of the number of bits available in the colormap for RGB specification. If eight bits is available for each primary, then the range of possible colors is 256^3 (about 16 million colors).

However, the number of different colors that can be displayed on the screen at any one time is a function of the number of planes. A 4-plane system could index 2^4 colorcells (16 distinct colors); an 8-plane system could index 2^8 colorcells (256 distinct colors); and a 24-plane system could index 2^{24} colorcells (over 16 million distinct colors).

A client attempting to use color does not *specify* a pixel value and the color to be put in that cell in order to draw in a given color. Instead, it requests access to a colorcell in a colormap (managed by the server) and is *returned* a pixel value. This is called *allocating* a color.

When a client allocates a color, it asks the server, "Which colorcell can I use?" and the server responds by saying, "You can use the colorcell specified by this pixel value." There are three basic functions that allocate colors, which are described in detail and demonstrated in later sections in this chapter.

7.2 Color Naming and Specification

The following sections describe the various ways to specify what color you want. In programs that use color only for decoration, the programmer simply chooses default colors, and allows the user to override them with resources.

7.2.1 The Server-side Color Name Database

In order to simplify color specification and to promote sharing of colors, the X server provides a color database that translates string color names into RGB values. Mainly this is a user convenience, since it is easy to specify "yellow" than to figure out the RGB values for yellow. But it also encourages colorcell sharing. As described above, sharing of colorcells can happen only if two clients allocate a read-only cell with the exact same RGB values. If both clients allocate a color specified by one of the 300-odd string names, there is a much better chance of them selecting the exact same RGB values and thereby sharing a cell than if they use one of the 2^{48} possible combinations of RGB values.

Because of differences in screen hardware, the same RGB values may generate quite different colors on different hardware. Therefore, server implementors were intended to change the RGB values corresponding to each color name to make sure that the appropriate color appears on their screen. This is called *gamma correction*. By using names from this database, you are more sure of getting a color close to the one you request. If the server implementor has not provided a gamma-corrected color database, there is no way a program can tell exactly what color is being displayed even when it knows the RGB values. This problem is solved with the X Color Management System, or Xcms, which was introduced in Release 5. Xcms provides a client-side color database, and supports device-independent color specification. In R5, color name strings are looked up first with the client-side color database, and if not found then on the server database.

It is also important to note that the color names are not specified by the X11 protocol or Xlib. Therefore, server implementors may change them, but more often, they will simply add to the list. (Note that some servers allow users to customize this file. For more information, see Volume Three, *X Window System User's Guide*.)

Table 7-1 shows some of the color names and corresponding RGB values in the default color database. The complete R4 database is extensive and is shown in Appendix D, *The Color Database*, of Volume Two, *Xlib Reference Manual*. The text version of this database in the standard distribution on a UNIX-based system is in the file */usr/lib/X11/rgb.txt*. The server reads a compiled version of it.

The color names in the color database are strings in which each character uses the ISO Latin-1 encoding. The ISO (International Standards Organization) Latin-1 encoding is used by virtually all workstations manufacturers. What this means is that the first 127 character codes correspond to 7-bit ASCII and are the normal English characters that appear on U.S. keyboards. But ISO characters are 8-bit, and the characters from 128 to 255 are used for characters with accents and other variations, necessary for other Western languages.

Server vendors should be able to supply a color database file for each foreign language. The RGB values would be the same, but the names would be different. In the English file, the entry for green is encoded with the ISO character codes 103 (g), 114 (r), 101 (e), 101 (e), 110 (n). In German, the same entry would be for *grün*, encoded with the ISO codes 103 (g), 114 (r), 252 (ü), 110 (n). In a workstation configured for German, there will be an easy way to type *ü*.

Note that keysyms also use the ISO Latin-1 standard, as shown in Chapter 8, *Events*.

Table 7-1. Sample from the Server-side Color Database*

English Words	Red	Green	Blue
aquamarine	112	219	147
black	0	0	0
blue	0	0	255
blue violet	159	95	159
brown	165	42	42
cadet blue	95	159	159
coral	255	127	0
cornflower blue	66	66	111
cyan	0	255	255
light gray	168	168	168
light grey	168	168	168
light steel blue	143	143	188
lime green	50	204	50
magenta	255	0	255
maroon	142	35	107
medium aquamarine	50	204	153

Also defined are the color names "gray0" through "gray100", spelled with an "e" or an "a". "gray0" is black and "gray100" is white. See Appendix D, *The Color Database*, of Volume Two, *Xlib Reference Manual*, for a listing of the complete sample database.

7.2.2 Xcms Color Specification

In X11R5, a new string syntax is supported. It allows you to specify colors using device-independent color spaces or using RGB values. We'll show you the form of these specifications here, then return to an explanation of the color spaces in Section 7.9.

A device-dependent RGB value is represented as follows:

RGB:*<red>*/*<green>*/*<blue>*

where *<red>*, *<green>*, and *<blue>* are each between 1 and 4 hexadecimal digits. Different primaries may be specified with different numbers of digits. If fewer than 4 digits are specified, they do not simply represent the most significant bits of the value; instead they represent a fraction of the maximum value. So the single digit 0xA does not mean 0xA000, but 10/15ths of 0xFFFF, or 0xAAAA.

X11R5 supports an additional device-dependent color space, called RGBi, in which each red, green, and blue integer *value* is replaced with a floating-point *intensity* between 0.0 and 1.0. In this model, the range of possible color values are simply mapped onto the real numbers between zero and one. So, for example, 0.5 always represents half intensity of a color. Note that these values represent the physical intensity of a color, which is not linearly proportional to the perceptual intensity of that color. A color specification for RGBi has the following form:

RGBi:*<red>*/*<green>*/*<blue>*

where *<red>*, *<green>*, and *<blue>* are floating-point numbers between 0.0 and 1.0, inclusive.

Device-independent color specifications follow the same syntax—a color space name followed by a colon and slash-separated color space values. The following forms are recognized:

CIEXYZ:*<X>*/*<Y>*/*<Z>*
CIEuvY:*<u>*/*<v>*/*<Y>*
CIExyY:*<x>*/*<y>*/*<Y>*
CIELab:*<L>*/*<a>*/*<b>*
CIELuv:*<L>*/*<u>*/*<v>*
TekHVC:*<H>*/*<V>*/*<C>*

CIEXYZ and the each of the other five strings listed here are the names of color spaces, most of them international standards. Each of the values in these device-independent color spaces is a floating-point number. Note that different color spaces have different ranges of legal values for each parameter. For example, the u parameter of the CIEuvY color space must have a value between 0.0 and approximately 0.6, while the H parameter of the TekHVC color space represents an angle and thus varies between 0.0 and 360.0. Also, the valid values for one parameter often depend on the values of the others. In general, you will need to be familiar with the colorimetric theory behind a particular color space before attempting to specify colors in that space.

Example 7-1 shows this new style of color specification used in a resource file. Notice that color space names are case-insensitive.

Example 7-1. Specifying device-independent colors from a resource file

```
*Background: TekHVC:72.0/50.0/44.0
*Command.background: CIELab:75.0/.38/.71
*quit_button.background: rgbi:1.0/0.0/0.0
```

7.2.3 The Client-side Color Name Database

Support for device-independent colors in X11R5 is, by design, kept entirely on the client side. The X protocol and the X server still use device-dependent RGB colors exclusively, so it is not possible to use the new device-independent color specifications in the color name database read by the server. Because it is sometimes useful to give symbolic names to device-independent colors, X11R5 supports a client-side color database that maps names to device-independent or device-dependent color specifications.

Note that while X11R5 supports such a color database, the MIT release does not provide one, other than as an example to system administrators or users who want to define one of their own. The client-side color database should be thought of as a place for site-specific customizations, and useful, if non-standard, shortcuts for naming colors in user resource files. In particular, since the contents of the database are not standardized, application defaults files should not rely on any particular colors to be in the database.

X clients (on most UNIX systems) look for the client-side database in the file */usr/lib/X11/Xcms.txt* by default, but the MIT sample implementation allows a different file to be specified with the XCMSDB environment variable. The format of the database is implementation-dependent. Example 7-2 shows an example database in the format supported by the MIT distribution.

Example 7-2. Example entries from a client color database

```
XCMS_COLORDB_START 0.1
device red      RGBi:1.0/0/0
device blue     RGB:00/00/ff
navy blue       CIEXYZ:0.0671/0.0337/0.3130
gray0           CIELab:0.0/0.0/0.0
gray50          CIELuv:50.0/0.0/0.0
grey100         TekHVC:0.0/100.0/0.0
rouge           red
roja            rouge
XCMS_COLORDB_END
```

Note that any device-dependent or device-independent color format may be used, and that color *aliases* are allowed to provide alternate names for colors defined elsewhere in the client database or even in the server database. Color names may contain spaces, and the tab character is used to separate color names from color specifications. The first and last lines shown in the example are required before the first and after the last entry of the database. Any text before the first line shown in the example is treated as a comment. Comments may not appear elsewhere in the file.

When the functions XAllocNamedColor( ), XLookupColor( ), XParseColor( ), XStoreNamedColor( ), or their device-independent Xcms analogs are passed a color string, they first attempt to parse it as a new-style specification for one of the supported color spaces. If this fails, they attempt to look up the color in the client-side color name database. If both approaches fail, they fall back on the pre-X11R5 behavior and attempt to parse the string in the old-style numeric format or pass the string to the X server to be looked up in the server database. Because the new X11R5 formats are supported by the pre-X11R5 Xlib functions, all X Toolkit widgets and type converters will work correctly with device-independent color specifications without change.

7.2.4 Hexadecimal Color Specification

It is also possible to specify colors using a hexadecimal string, although this is discouraged as of Release 5.

The hexadecimal form of color specification is necessary in R4 for the user to be able to specify an exact color, not just the rough approximation allowed by an string name. The hexadecimal specification must be in one of the following formats:

#RGB	(*4 bits each of red, green, and blue*)
#RRGGBB	(*8 bits each of red, green, and blue*)
#RRRGGGBBB	(*12 bits each of red, green, and blue*)
#RRRRGGGGBBBB	(*16 bits each of red, green, and blue*)

Each of the letters represents a hexadecimal digit. In the shorter formats, the specified values are interpreted as the most significant bits of a 16-bit value. For example, #3a7 and #3000a0007000 are equivalent.

Use of hexadecimal color specifications does not preclude colorcell sharing, since the user could specify the same hexadecimal value for the color for two or more clients. However, it probably tends to make sharing less likely, since a window manager might allocate all the colors in the color database as read-only cells, and then any client that uses hexadecimal specifications will probably be allocating a separate cell instead of sharing.

7.3 Differences in Display Hardware

The description of color mapping given in the previous section was actually somewhat oversimplified. There are significant differences in how the colormap is used on mid-range color screens, monochrome and gray-scale screens, and high performance color screens. Color handling in X was designed to work with any of these hardware types.

7.3.1 Mid-range Color Displays

The most common type of color screen has between four and eight planes and uses the color-map indexing technique described above. This type of screen is so widespread because it provides a flexible color system while being moderately priced. The mapping of pixel values to colorcells, with arbitrary RGB values stored in each colorcell, allows a very large range of possible colors, even though a more limited number can be shown on the screen at any one time.

Mid-range color screens usually have only one hardware colormap. In other words, the pixel values in all the windows on the screen are mapped to colors using the same colormap. On most of these systems, however, the color in any colorcell in the hardware colormap can be individually changed, and therefore, the entire colormap can be replaced with a new set of values. X provides the concept of the *virtual colormap*, so that more than one set of color-cells can be maintained, even though only one of them can be in use at a time. Virtual color-maps are swapped in and out of the hardware colormap by the window manager. This makes it possible for an application that has special color needs to create its own virtual colormap, which the window manager will load into the hardware colormap when that application is in use. However, since only one hardware colormap is available and all applications share it, when any one application creates a new virtual colormap and the window manager installs it, all other applications will screen in false colors, since the pixel values they use now point to cells in the other client's colormap. This is acceptable, since the window manager always installs the correct colormap for the application in use, but it is obviously not ideal. On high performance systems, described below, this problem is solved by having multiple hardware colormaps.

7.3.2 Monochrome and Gray Scale

Monochrome (black and white) screens have only a single plane of screen memory. Each pixel is made up of a single phosphor, which can be either on or off.

Gray-scale screens are sometimes used for publishing applications, since pixels made up of a single phosphor are smaller than those made up of three phosphors and the resolution is, therefore, better. As shown in Figure 7-2, a gray-scale screen works by looking up the intensity of the pixel in the colormap, which, for this screen type, contains only a single value. This controls the intensity of a single electron beam. Gray scale can be simulated on a color screen by making the red, green, and blue values equal in a given colorcell to determine the brightness of gray pixels on the screen.

A gray-scale screen might have a read-only colormap, so that the gray levels in each cell could not be changed. A monochrome screen is an example of this type; it is a single-plane screen with a two-element read-only colormap.

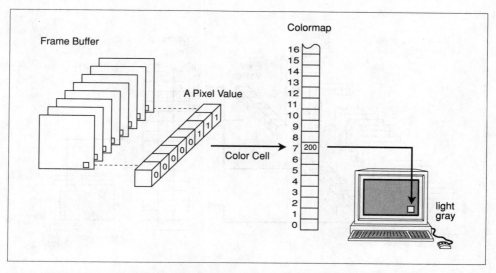

Figure 7-2. Pixel value to RGB mapping — gray scale and monochrome screens

7.3.3 High Performance Color Displays

As memory has become cheaper and applications more advanced, workstations with 24 planes and more have become more common. With 24 bits per pixel, it is possible to screen every discernible color at the same time. This makes it possible to do smooth shading and other applications that use a large number of closely spaced colors.

The problem with having so many planes is that a colormap of the style used in mid-range color screens would be impossibly large: it would contain over 16 million entries. Instead, the available bits per pixel are broken down into three separate colormap indices, one for each primary color, as shown in Figure 7-3. This approach still allows the full range of colors to be generated but makes the job of loading the colormap much more manageable. This scheme requires three primary colormaps of only 256 entries each to specify all 16 million colors on a 24-plane system.

In high performance screens, having a read-only colormap makes just as much sense as having it read/write, because nearly every color imaginable can be simultaneously available. With a read-only colormap, there is a fixed relationship between the pixel values used to select a color and the actual RGB values generated. This makes possible applications that want to calculate pixel values directly instead of having to calculate colors and then determine which pixel value represents that color, as is necessary when the colormap is read/write.

In reality, most screens in this class let you use the color resources in either fashion, using virtual colormaps. There can be one read-only virtual colormap and one read/write virtual colormap. However, unlike on mid-range color screen hardware, most high performance color systems have multiple hardware colormaps, so that both virtual colormaps can be installed and used at the same time. In fact, on many of these systems, each window can have its own virtual colormap installed in the hardware at the same time.

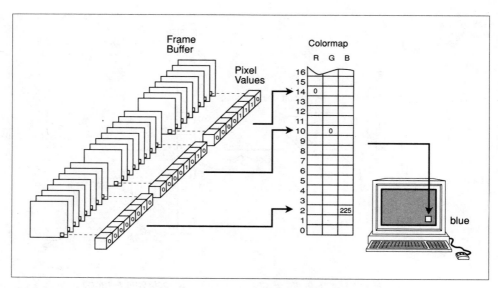

Figure 7-3. Pixel value to RGB mapping — high performance color screens

7.3.4 How X Describes Color Support with Visuals

A *visual* describes the characteristics of a virtual colormap that has been or can be created for use on a particular screen. As used by Xlib, a visual is actually a pointer to a structure (of type `Visual`) containing information about one way of using a particular screen. A visual must be specified when creating a colormap or a window, and the same visual must be used in creating a window as is used to create the colormap to be used in that window.

Most windows inherit their parent's visual, and windows will often share the root window's visual, which is known as the default visual. The default visual describes, naturally, the default colormap. If you create all your windows with `XCreateSimpleWindow()`, you will be using the default visual and colormap.

The `Visual` structure is intended to be opaque; programs are not supposed to access its contents. This is so that Xlib implementors can change the structure without breaking existing clients. The procedure used to avoid accessing its members is not all that cumbersome but is just beginning to come into use by application writers. Up to this point, most programmers have broken this rule. We will show you only the correct method here, since it adds only a few lines to the application.

Even more existing applications have avoided visuals altogether and used only the `DefaultDepth()` or `DisplayPlanes()` macros to attempt to determine whether the screen is monochrome or color. However, this does not work in general, because it does not distinguish between gray-scale screens and color screens (both have more than one plane). The only way to make this distinction is to get information about visuals.

Remember that a visual is only one way to use color on a particular screen. There may be a list of supported visuals on a screen, with each visual describing a different depth and write-ability of the colormap. On a color system, there may be both monochrome and color visuals available.

The correct method to get information about the visuals supported on a particular screen is to use `XMatchVisualInfo()` or `XGetVisualInfo()`. These functions return `XVisualInfo` structures that contain information about the available visuals and are public so their fields can be safely accessed.

The `class` member of `XVisualInfo` contains a constant specifying one of six different visual classes,* corresponding to the basic ways of using a screen: `DirectColor`, `GrayScale`, `PseudoColor`, `StaticColor`, `StaticGray`, or `TrueColor`.

As summarized in Table 7-2, the visual classes distinguish between color or monochrome, whether the colormap is read/write or read-only, and whether a pixel value provides a single index to the colormap or is decomposed into separate indices for red, green, and blue values.

Table 7-2. Comparison of Visual Classes

Colormap Type	Read/Write	Read-only
Monochrome/Gray	GrayScale	StaticGray
Single Index for RG&B	PseudoColor	StaticColor
Decomposed Index for RG&B	DirectColor	TrueColor

There may be more than one way of using color on a particular screen, and therefore, there may be more than one supported visual. This is usually true of high-end workstations. There are ways to search through the available visuals to select the one that most closely meets the needs of your application, as will be described later. Several visuals of the same class may be provided but at different depths. On high performance screens, it is possible to create the colormap as read/write or as read-only. Both methods have certain advantages and would be used for different applications. There would be a separate visual for each of these ways of using the screen hardware. One of these visuals would be `TrueColor` class and the other `DirectColor` class. Some 24-plane screens allow the screen to be treated as two separate 12-plane `PseudoColor` visuals. (This allows for "double-buffering," a technique useful for animation, or for storing distance data to simplify hidden line and plane calculations in 3-D applications.) In fact, on some advanced workstations, you can use a different visual in each window.

Figure 7-4 schematically represents the visual classes that can theoretically be supported by each type of screen hardware. A screen that supports the `DirectColor` class can theoretically support any of the six visual classes. A screen that supports the `PseudoColor` visual class can support `GrayScale`, `PseudoColor`, `StaticColor`, or `StaticGray`

---

*Do not confuse *visual* class with *window* class. While both are represented in certain structures as the `class` member and both are set when a window is created and cannot be changed, they are quite different. The window class is `InputOutput` or `InputOnly`. The visual class is only part of the overall visual, which is the way color is represented for a window.

visual classes. A screen that supports the `GrayScale` visual class can also support `StaticGray` visual classes. The three types of screen with read-only colormaps can only support visuals of their own class. But remember that just because a certain visual class can theoretically be supported by a certain screen hardware does not mean that the server implementors will decide to support that class.

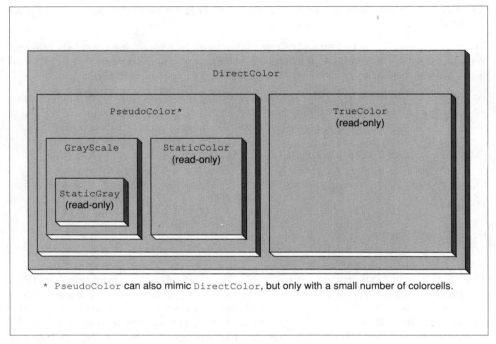

Figure 7-4. Hierarchy of visual classes

7.3.5 Shareability vs. Changeability

Notice that `DirectColor`, `GrayScale`, and `PseudoColor` visuals have changeable colormaps, but `StaticColor`, `StaticGray`, and `TrueColor` have immutable colormaps. Within the changeable colormaps, it is possible to have two types of colorcells: read-only and read/write. The color in a read-only cell is set once by one client and from then on can be shared by any client but not changed. A read/write cell can have its color changed at any time by the client that allocated it but cannot be shared by other clients. In immutable colormaps, you are limited to only read-only cells.

One advantage of immutable colormaps is that all the cells are read-only and can be shared between clients, so all the cells are available to every client. Immutable colormaps also make it possible to calculate pixel values from the colors desired without querying the server, since the mapping between pixel values and colors is predictable. This technique is necessary for smooth shading and 3-D rendering algorithms. As you will see, this is usually not possible with changeable colormaps. The disadvantages of immutable colormaps are that there may not be the exact color you desire (if there are a small number of planes) and you cannot allocate read/write cells, so you cannot change a colorcell to change the color of existing pixels on the screen. To change a color, you have to redraw the graphics with a new pixel value.

In general, the advantage of changeable colormaps is that you can have both private read/write cells and shareable read-only cells. That is why **PseudoColor** and **Direct-Color** are the most useful visuals, when a screen supports them. **PseudoColor** and **DirectColor** allow you to decide whether your client really needs read/write cells or whether it can use read-only cells. Read-only usage is preferred, since these cells can be shared by all clients, which means that the colormap is less likely to run out of free cells.

Try not to confuse the writeability of colormaps with the writeability of colorcells. A colorcell in a read/write colormap can be allocated read/write or read-only. A colorcell in a read-only colormap can only be allocated read-only. A changeable colormap could be made entirely read-only if the window manager or any other client allocates all available colorcells read-only.

The advantages of read/write colorcells, available only in changeable colormaps, are that your program can select exactly the color you want (as long as it is physically possible on the screen) and you can change the color at will, which instantly changes the visible color of everything drawn with that pixel value if the colormap is currently installed. Although any other client can also change the values in a read/write cell, it is a convention that only the client that allocated the cell should change its contents. You *own* that pixel value. Since most clients cannot be satisfied with having no control over their displayed colors, this pixel value is not shareable. That means that if several clients that use read/write colorcells are running, all the colorcells might be used. Then some client will be forced to create its own colormap, with the negative consequences described in Section 7.10.

7.4 Allocating Shared Colors

Since free colorcells can quickly become a scarce resource when clients store private color values, simple clients that mainly use color for decoration are encouraged always to allocate read-only colors, so that these colorcells can be shared by other clients that allocate the same colors read-only.

The returned pixel value can be used to set the **background_pixel** or **border_pixel** attribute of a window or to set the **foreground** or **background** member of a GC, which are used by drawing requests. (See Chapter 4, *Window Attributes*, and Chapter 5, *The Graphics Context*, for more information.)

Read-only colorcells can be allocated with the following routines:

XAllocColor()   Returns the index of the colorcell (a pixel value) that contains the RGB values that are requested or that contains the closest RGB values physically possible on the screen.

	XcmsAllocColor() is the same except that colors are specified using Xcms syntax.
XAllocNamedColor()	Returns the index of the colorcell that contains the RGB values associated with a specified color name from the string color name database or the closest RGB values physically possible on the screen. In R5, XAllocNamedColor() accepts strings in Xcms syntax. XcmsAllocNamedColor() is almost the same except with a different style of arguments. XcmsAllocNamedColor() also is capable of returning a symbol describing the format found in the specified string.

By convention, clients allow the user to specify colors on the command line or in the resource database using a color name. When the RGB values are chosen from the color database by specifying color name strings, sharing of read-only colorcells is much more likely than if colors are specified as raw RGB values or using hexadecimal specifications.

XParseColor() parses a color name string or a hexadecimal color specification string and returns RGB values. It can be used with XAllocColor() or the routines that allocate read/write cells, which will be described later. For color names, it gets the RGB values from the server's color database just like XAllocNamedColor(). You may have noticed that XAllocNamedColor() is very similar to the combination of XParseColor() and XAllocColor(). The difference is slight: XAllocNamedColor() can interpret color names but not hexadecimal specifications—but hexadecimal specifications are rarely made by users anyway. The two-routine combination is more often used because it allows you to separately report errors in parsing the color specified and allocating the colorcell.

Using XQueryColor() and XQueryColors() you can find out what RGB values are in each colorcell. But there is no way to determine whether a given cell is read-only or read/write. The only way to tell how many cells are currently unallocated is to allocate N colors using XAllocColorCells(), using the maximum possible N initially, then reduce N until it succeeds (not recommended). A binary search is a faster way to find N.

A request to allocate a color may fail because there are no free colormap cells and, for read-only colorcells, because no existing colorcell contains the closest color possible on the hardware to the exact color requested. Applications must allocate colors by trial and error. The routines that allocate colorcells all have Status return values. If the call to allocate colorcells returns False, the client may modify the arguments and try again. If repeated attempts fail, the client can settle with BlackPixel and WhitePixel() or, if these colors are inadequate, create a new virtual colormap. An application with picky color needs that cannot be satisfied can simply report to the user that its color needs cannot be met and exit.

Note that XAllocColor() works somewhat differently on dynamic visuals (such as PseudoColor) than it does on static visuals (like StaticColor). On dynamic visuals, it fails if it is unable to allocate the exact RGB values requested (i.e., if there are no free cells and no cells already allocated with the exact RGB values requested). On static visuals, it returns the cell with the closest RGB values. The algorithm used to determine "closest" is server-dependent. The moral of this is that a program must be prepared for XAllocColor() to fail.

7.4.1 The XColor Structure

Both **XAllocColor( )** and **XAllocNamedColor( )** (as well as other functions that manipulate colorcells) take as an argument an **XColor** structure. This structure is used to specify the desired RGB values, as well as to return the pixel value.

The **XColor** structure is shown in Example 7-3. The information it contains closely matches the information in each cell of the colormap.

Example 7-3. The XColor structure

```
typedef struct {
    unsigned long pixel;                /* Pixel value */
    unsigned short red, green, blue;    /* RGB values */
    char flags;                         /* DoRed,  DoGreen,  and/or
                                         * DoBlue */
    char pad;                           /* Unused; pads structure
                                         * to even word boundary */
} XColor;
```

In **XAllocColor( )** and **XAllocNamedColor( )**, the **pixel** member returns the pixel value that will be used to set the foreground or background pixel value in the GC or window attributes. In **XStoreColor( )** and **XQueryColor( )**, which you will see later, the **pixel** member indicates which cell in the colormap is having its color set (read/write cells only) or is having its RGB values queried.

The **red**, **green**, and **blue** members are 16-bit values. Full brightness in a color is a value of 65535, half brightness is 32767, and off is 0. (The server automatically scales these values if the hardware colormap includes fewer bits for RGB values.)

The **flags** member of the **XColor** structure is a bitwise OR of the symbols **DoRed**, **DoGreen**, and **DoBlue**. These flags are used to specify which of the red, green, and blue values should be read while changing the RGB values in a read/write colorcell. How these are used is demonstrated in Example 7-7.

7.4.2 Code to Allocate Read-only Colors

As we have said, applications that have basic color needs should allocate read-only, shareable color cells. Example 7-4 shows code to allocate a color specified using a name from the color name database. In this case, we have simply hardcoded the color name strings. In a real application, you would hardcode the default color but allow user specification of the string, as is done in *basecalc*, described in Chapter 14, *A Complete Application*.

This routine uses **XMatchVisualInfo( )** to determine whether color is supported on the screen. If any of the four color visual classes are supported, it proceeds to attempt to allocate read-only colors. Whenever anything fails or if color is not supported, the routine uses black and white. For some applications, this could be modified to allocate levels of gray on GrayScale visual class screens.

Color

The code for all the examples in this chapter is in the example source in the directory /basicwin/color/. This example is called basic.ro.

Example 7-4. Allocating read-only colorcells

```
#include <X11/Xlib.h>
#include <X11/Xutil.h>
#include <X11/Xos.h>
#include <stdio.h>

extern Display *display;
extern int screen_num;
extern Screen *screen_ptr;
extern unsigned long foreground_pixel, background_pixel,
        border_pixel;
extern char *progname;

#define MAX_COLORS 3

/* This is just so we can print the visual class intelligibly */
static char *visual_class[ ] = {
    "StaticGray",
    "GrayScale",
    "StaticColor",
    "PseudoColor",
    "TrueColor",
    "DirectColor"
};

get_colors()
{
    int default_depth;
    Visual *default_visual;
    static char *name[ ] = {"Red", "Yellow", "Green"};
    XColor exact_def;
    Colormap default_cmap;
    int ncolors = 0;
    int colors[MAX_COLORS];
    int i = 5;
    XVisualInfo visual_info;

    /* Try to allocate colors for PseudoColor, TrueColor,
     * DirectColor, and StaticColor; use black and white
     * for StaticGray and GrayScale */

    default_depth = DefaultDepth(display, screen_num);
    default_visual = DefaultVisual(display, screen_num);
    default_cmap   = DefaultColormap(display, screen_num);
    if (default_depth == 1) {
        /* Must be StaticGray, use black and white */
        border_pixel = BlackPixel(display, screen_num);
        background_pixel = WhitePixel(display, screen_num);
        foreground_pixel = BlackPixel(display, screen_num);
        return(0);
    }

    while (!XMatchVisualInfo(display, screen_num, default_depth,
            /* visual class */i--, &visual_info))
        ;
    printf("%s: found a %s class visual at default depth.\n",
```

Example 7-4. Allocating read-only colorcells (continued)

```
                    progname, visual_class[++i]);

    if (i < StaticColor) { /* Color visual classes are 2 to 5 */
        /* No color visual available at default depth;
         * some applications might call XMatchVisualInfo
         * here to try for a GrayScale visual if they
         * can use gray to advantage, before giving up
         * and using black and white */
        border_pixel = BlackPixel(display, screen_num);
        background_pixel = WhitePixel(display, screen_num);
        foreground_pixel = BlackPixel(display, screen_num);
        return(0);
    }

    /* Otherwise, got a color visual at default depth */

    /* The visual we found is not necessarily the default
     * visual, and therefore it is not necessarily the one
     * we used to create our window; however, we now know
     * for sure that color is supported, so the following
     * code will work (or fail in a controlled way) */
    /* Let's check just out of curiosity: */
    if (visual_info.visual != default_visual)
    {
        printf("%s: %s class visual at default depth\n",
                    progname, visual_class[i]);
        printf("is not default visual! Continuing anyway...\n");
    }

    for (i = 0; i < MAX_COLORS; i++) {
        printf("allocating %s\n", name[i]);
        if (!XParseColor (display, default_cmap, name[i],
                    &exact_def)) {
            fprintf(stderr, "%s: color name %s not in database",
                        progname, name[i]);
            exit(0);
        }
        printf("The RGB values from the database are %d, %d, %d\n",
                    exact_def.red, exact_def.green, exact_def.blue);
        if (!XAllocColor(display, default_cmap, &exact_def)) {
            fprintf(stderr, "%s: can't allocate color:\n",
                        progname);
            fprintf(stderr, "All colorcells allocated and\n");
            fprintf(stderr, "no matching cell found.\n");
            exit(0);
        }
        printf("The RGB values actually allocated are %d, %d, %d\n",
                    exact_def.red, exact_def.green,
                    exact_def.blue);
        colors[i] = exact_def.pixel;
        ncolors++;
    }
    printf("%s: allocated %d read-only color cells\n",
            progname, ncolors);

    border_pixel = colors[0];
    background_pixel = colors[1];
```

Example 7-4. Allocating read-only colorcells (continued)

```
        foreground_pixel = colors[2];
        return(1);
}
```

This code begins by setting variables to the default depth, visual, and colormap for later use. If the default depth is one, then the application is displaying on a monochrome screen, and black and white are returned. Then the code calls **XMatchVisualInfo()** in a loop to look for a color visual at the default depth—it is called up to four times, until a color visual is found. If none is found, it again returns black and white, since this screen must support only a **GrayScale** visual (at this depth, anyway). Some applications may wish to allocate grays in this branch. The rest of the code loops through the list of color names to be allocated, looks them up in the color database, and then allocates them. If either the lookup stage or the allocation stage fails for any color, the routine prints an error and exits. It could instead simply fall back on black and white again; your choice.

As noted in the code, the visual found might not necessarily be the default visual. This does not always matter, because if any color visual is available, it is a good bet that the default visual is also color, and so colors can be allocated without doing any further research. With **XMatchVisualInfo()**, it is difficult to develop an algorithm that is guaranteed to find the default visual. This is much easier with **XGetVisualInfo()**, which returns a list of available visual structures that match a set of criteria you specify. If you pass no criteria, it simply returns the entire list of available visuals. You can then search through the list matching the **visual** member of the **XVisualInfo** structures to the default visual. This will be demonstrated in Section 7.6.

The **XParseColor()** call specifies a color name, and the RGB values corresponding to that name are returned from the color database in the passed **XColor** structure. This structure is then passed to **XAllocColor()**, and the pixel value allocated is returned in the **pixel** field of the structure.

The same calls would be used to parse a hexadecimal color string. Pink could be specified in the call to **XParseColor()** as "#bc8f8f" instead of "pink". But, as we have said before, color names are preferred, because there is a better chance that they will specify a color already allocated or later to be allocated by another client.

It is also possible to specify the desired RGB values explicitly. This is good for default colors because it saves a call to **XParseColor()**, but on the other hand, you might not get a consistent color on all systems because you are bypassing the gamma correction implemented through the color database. Simply declare an **XColor** structure and set its **red**, **green**, and **blue** members to the desired RGB values. Of course, these values can be specified as integers, hexadecimal values, or any other way that the C language allows. Then pass this structure to **XAllocColor()**. But remember, as we have said, it is better to use color names when allocating read-only colorcells than to use any of these explicit RGB values.

7.4.3 Highlighting in Two Colors

It is easy to highlight graphics on a monochrome system. The simplest way is to set the GC to the GXxor logical function and draw your graphics once to draw them and again to undraw them. You must grab the server between the drawing and undrawing so that no other client changes the same pixels in between (by, for example, covering part of the area with another window). On a monochrome system, this always changes white to black and black to white if you set the foreground in the GC to 1 (setting it to BlackPixel() or White-Pixel() is not guaranteed to work on all systems, because either may be 0).

When drawing in BlackPixel() and WhitePixel() on a color system, the color drawn by the GXxor operation is random if BlackPixel() or WhitePixel() are used for the foreground pixel value in the GC. This is because there is no restriction on which pixel value BlackPixel() and WhitePixel() can be on a server—they are not necessarily 1 and 0 and not necessarily different by just one bit. For example, the pixel value drawn if the foreground pixel value in the GC is BlackPixel() and the pixel value on the screen is WhitePixel() is BlackPixel() XOR WhitePixel(), which, unless BlackPixel() and WhitePixel() are different by only one bit, is a third pixel value not allocated by this client. The colorcell identified by this pixel value might contain black, in which case the operation would not change the screen.

The solution to this problem, which works on monochrome and color systems, is to set the foreground pixel value in the GC used in drawing with GXxor to the exclusive OR of BlackPixel() and WhitePixel() or by setting the logical function to GXinvert and using a plane mask which is the exclusive OR of WhitePixel() and Black-Pixel(). All applications that highlight graphics drawn in BlackPixel() and WhitePixel() on a color system should use one of these two methods. The following example illustrates how this works using two arbitrarily chosen pixel values (which could be BlackPixel() and WhitePixel() or could be any two colors).

Let's assume that we draw in two pixel values, which we will call color1 and color2. The pixel values for these could be:

```
color1 = 11111111111111110000000000000000
color2 = 00000000111111111111111100000000
```

The pixel value we will use to draw is generated by taking the exclusive OR of color1 and color2:

```
color1 XOR color2 = 11111111000000001111111100000000
```

Now we set the foreground in the GC to this pixel value and the function in the GC to GXxor and draw. This changes existing pixels that contained color1 to color2 and existing pixels that were color2 to color1.

```
foreground =              11111111000000001111111100000000
existing pixel (color1) = 11111111111111110000000000000000
resulting pixel (color2) = 00000000111111111111111100000000
```

The other way to do this is to set the plane_mask in the GC to (color1 ^ color2) and then use a logical function of GXinvert. This is equally effective.

7.4.4 Choosing Default Colors

A client that uses color should allow the user to specify the colors either on the command line or in the resource database, or both. The resource manager (described in Chapter 13, *Managing User Preferences*) can be used to merge these preferences with the defaults of the program. However, the client needs to have reasonable default colors in case the user does not specify any preferences.

Follow these guidelines for your application's default colors:*

* Use string color names for read-only colorcells if possible, since this maximizes the chance of sharing cells.

* Use colors with large contributions from two or all three primary colors—they light the screen more brightly.

* Avoid shades of pure blue—the human eye is relatively insensitive to and unable to focus on images made of pure blue light. Mix blue shades with white (white contains equal parts of all three primary colors).

* Remember that some users are color blind. Do not use the same intensity of green and red for "safe" and "danger"—use colors with differing intensity.

7.5 Allocating Private Colors

In colormaps of the PseudoColor or DirectColor visual classes, a client can allocate read/write cells. Read/write colorcells should be allocated when:

* The application draws something whose color must be changed dynamically without redrawing it. For example, in a color mixing program, the palette must be drawn in colors that change frequently. If this were done with read-only colors, cells would have to be allocated and freed frequently and the palette area redrawn with each new color. However, with read/write colorcells, the steps of allocation and color setting are separate, so that the color of an already allocated cell can be changed at will. Anything drawn using the pixel value of this colorcell will change color immediately when the RGB values in the colorcell are changed.

* The application needs to overlay graphics on top of other graphics in such a way that the overlayed graphics can be erased without disturbing the underlying graphics. For example, in a Computer Aided Design (CAD) package for chip design, it is often useful to overlay the various layers of a chip in different colors on the screen. When one of the layers is removed, you want to avoid having to redraw all the underlying layers. How to do this by allocating read/write cells will be described.

* The system has a huge colormap, and the application needs to set a large number of colorcells. The calls for manipulating read/write colorcells allow you to manipulate

---

*Courtesy Oliver Jones, Apollo Computer.

multiple cells per call, whereas with read-only cells, you are limited to one cell per call.

Note that read/write colorcell allocation never works on **TrueColor** or **StaticColor** visuals. Therefore, on systems that only support these visuals, an application that uses read/write colorcells cannot work. Read/write colorcells should only be used when really needed.

XAllocColorCells() allocates read/write colorcells. At its simplest, it allows you to allocate read/write cells so you can change the RGB values dynamically.

But to simply allocate just a few cells, you set the *ncolors* argument to the number of colorcells desired and *nplanes* to 0, and all the pixel values you need will be returned in the *pixels* array. The real reason for the *nplanes* and *plane_masks* arguments will become clear in Section 7.5.2. The RGB values of the allocated cells are set with **XStore-Color()**, **XStoreColors()**, or **XStoreNamedColor()**.

XAllocColorPlanes(), on the other hand, is only used when you want to be able to vary a primary color component of graphics already drawn without redrawing them. It allocates read/write cells, so that a preset number of bits are reserved for each primary color. Primarily for **DirectColor**, it also allows you to simulate a small **DirectColor** colormap on a **PseudoColor** visual but uses up colorcells quickly. It treats the colormap as three separate lookup tables, allocating *ncolors* $* 2^{nreds}$ entries in the red lookup table, *ncolors* $* 2^{ngreens}$ entries in the green lookup table, and *ncolors* $* 2^{nblues}$ entries in the blue lookup table.

The following routines are used to actually store colors into read/write colorcells once they are allocated:

XStoreColor()	Changes the read/write colormap cell corresponding to the specified pixel value to the hardware color that most closely matches the RGB values specified.* The flags **DoRed**, **Do-Green**, and **DoBlue** in the **XColor** structure indicate which primary colors in the cell are to be changed. **Xcms-StoreColor()** is similar but allows you to specify the color string in Xcms syntax.
XStoreColors()	Like **XStoreColor()**, except it does multiple cells per call. Changes the read/write colormap cell corresponding to the specified pixel value to the hardware color that most closely matches the RGB values specified. The flags **DoRed**, **DoGreen**, and **DoBlue** in each **XColor** structure indicate which primary colors in each cell are to be changed. **Xcms-StoreColors()** is similar but allows you to specify color strings in Xcms syntax.
XStoreNamedColor()	Performs the same function as **StoreColor()**, except that it stores the RGB values associated with a string color name

---

*Even when storing explicit RGB values, you may not get the precise color you specify. For example, if the hardware colormap supports only four bits of intensity in each primary and you specify eight-bit values, the server will scale the values you provide to the closest possible equivalent on the hardware.

in the RGB database. This call would be useful for loading a private colormap with each of the default named colors. No Xcms equivalent, since this function accepts Xcms syntax (in R5 and later).

7.5.1 Allocating Read/Write Colorcells for Dynamic Colors

As described above, the simplest use of read/write colors is to allocate colorcells whose colors can by changed at any time. Example 7-5 is analogous to the code just shown to allocate read-only colors, except that it allocates read/write colors instead. Note that it calls XAllocColorCells() with the *ncolors* argument set to the number of colorcells desired and *nplanes* set to zero.

Example 7-5. Allocating read/write colorcells for dynamic colors

```
#include <X11/Xlib.h>
#include <X11/Xutil.h>
#include <X11/Xos.h>
#include <stdio.h>

extern Display *display;
extern int screen_num;
extern unsigned long foreground_pixel, background_pixel,
        border_pixel;

#define MAX_COLORS 3

get_colors()
{
    int default_depth;
    Visual *default_visual;
    static char *name[ ] = {"Red", "Yellow", "Green"};
    XColor exact_defs[ MAX_COLORS ];
    Colormap default_cmap;
    int ncolors = MAX_COLORS;
    int plane_masks[ 1 ];
    int colors[ MAX_COLORS ];
    int i;
    XVisualInfo visual_info;
    int class;

    class = PseudoColor;
    default_depth = DefaultDepth(display, screen_num);
    default_visual = DefaultVisual(display, screen_num);
    default_cmap   = DefaultColormap(display, screen_num);
    if (default_depth == 1) {
        /* Must be StaticGray, use black and white */
        border_pixel = BlackPixel(display, screen_num);
        background_pixel = WhitePixel(display, screen_num);
        foreground_pixel = BlackPixel(display, screen_num);
        return(0);
    }

    if (!XMatchVisualInfo(display, screen_num, default_depth,
            PseudoColor, &visual_info)) {
        if (!XMatchVisualInfo(display, screen_num, default_depth,
```

```
                    DirectColor, &visual_info)) {
        /* No PseudoColor visual available at default_depth;
         * some applications might try for a GrayScale
         * visual here if they can use gray to advantage,
         * before giving up and using black and white */
        border_pixel = BlackPixel(display, screen_num);
        background_pixel = WhitePixel(display, screen_num);
        foreground_pixel = BlackPixel(display, screen_num);
        return(0);
    }
}

/* Got PseudoColor or DirectColor visual at default_depth */

/* The visual we found is not necessarily the default
 * visual, and therefore it is not necessarily the one
 * we used to create our window; however, we now know
 * for sure that color is supported, so the following
 * code will work (or fail in a controlled way) */

/* Allocate as many cells as we can */
ncolors = MAX_COLORS;
while (1) {
    if (XAllocColorCells (display, default_cmap, False,
            plane_masks, /* nplanes */0, colors, ncolors))
        break;
    ncolors--;
    if (ncolors == 0)
        fprintf(stderr, "basic: couldn't allocate read/write \
                colors\n");
    exit(0);
}

printf("basic: allocated %d read/write color cells\n", ncolors);

for (i = 0; i < ncolors; i++) {
    if (!XParseColor (display, default_cmap, name[i],
            &exact_defs[i])) {
        fprintf(stderr, "basic: color name %s not in database",
                name[i]);
        exit(0);
    }

    /* Set pixel value in struct to the allocated one */
    exact_defs[i].pixel = colors[i];
    exact_defs[i].flags = DoRed | DoGreen | DoBlue;
}

/* This sets the color of read/write cell */
XStoreColors (display, default_cmap, exact_defs, ncolors);
border_pixel = colors[0];
background_pixel = colors[1];
foreground_pixel = colors[2];
}
```

The `main` that calls this `get_colors` function, shown in Example 7-6 contains an `XQueryColor()` call that gets the current RGB values in the colorcell (necessary because `main` and `get_colors` are in separate source files and the RGB values used in `get_colors` are not global variables) and an `XStoreColor()` call that changes the color of what is drawn in the foreground pixel value every time you press a button in the window. In the example source, this application is in the directory *basicwin/color/* and is called *basic.rw*.

Example 7-6. Main of basic.rw — changing colors of dynamic colorcells

```
       .
       .
       .

void main(argc, argv)
int argc;
char **argv;
{
        .
        .
        .

     XColor color;
     unsigned short red, green, blue;
        .
        .

     /* Open display, etc. */

     color.pixel = foreground_pixel;
     XQueryColor(display, DefaultColormap(display, screen_num),
              &color);
     printf("red is %d, green is %d, blue is %d\n", color.red,
              color.green, color.blue);

     while (1)  {
         XNextEvent(display, &report);
         switch  (report.type) {
            .
            .
            .

         case ButtonPress:
             color.red += 5000;
             color.green -= 5000;
             color.blue += 3000;
             printf("red is %d, green is %d, blue is %d\n",
                     color.red,
             color.green, color.blue);
             XStoreColor(display, DefaultColormap(display,
                     screen_num), &color);
             break;
            .
            .
            .

     }
}
```

7.5.2 Allocating Read/Write Colorcells for Overlays

`XAllocColorCells()` has another use: it allows you to nondestructively overlay one set of graphics over another. The underlying graphics will not be visible where the overlay is drawn, but they can be refreshed by simply setting or clearing one or more complete planes in the drawable. This technique can improve the performance of a client by reducing the amount of complicated graphics that have to be redrawn. It can be useful for highlighting graphics for selection. However, as noted earlier, read/write colorcells can only be allocated in `PseudoColor` and `DirectColor` visuals, so any application that attempts to use this technique should also provide a fallback technique for use on other visuals or in case of failure.

The trick that allows drawing without destroying what is already drawn relies on the fact that we can draw in one plane of the drawable, changing the pixel values and therefore the color, without changing any other plane. This is possible using the `plane_mask` component of the GC. It is these other planes that contain the information about the drawing that was already there. The disadvantage of this approach is that we have to allocate more colorcells than we would normally need. Some of the colorcells will need to be loaded with duplicate RGB values. Because of this waste of colorcells, this technique should be used only when the graphics being preserved are slow for the client or the server to redraw.

To illustrate this trick, we are going to draw in one color (the foreground in the GC), set the `background_pixel` attribute of the window to a second color, and then draw something temporary over the top with a third color.* To do this, we need to allocate four colorcells with `XAllocColorCells()`. The pixel values allocated will look something like this:

Color	Important Bits	Remaining bits
foreground:	----0--0------------------------	*all other bits don't matter*
background:	----0--1------------------------	*all other bits don't matter*
highlight1:	----1--0------------------------	*all other bits don't matter*
highlight2:	----1--1------------------------	*all other bits don't matter*

The bits indicated could have been any bits, but it is significant that only two bits distinguish the four pixel values. The first pixel value is used for the foreground, and the second for the background. We draw overlays in the third or fourth pixel value. Since we do not want to erase what was drawn in the foreground and background pixel values, we use a plane mask to restrict the drawing of the highlighting pixel value to a single plane, the one where bits in the highlighting pixel values are set to 1. When this entire plane (indicated by the 1 in pixel values `highlight1` and `highlight2`) is cleared, anything drawn in `highlight1` or `highlight2` disappears, and anything that was drawn in the foreground or background

---

*Note that the background of a window is redrawn by the server when **Expose** events occur, but this does not effect the process of drawing and removing overlays, because no **Expose** event will be triggered in this process. In other words, even though the background color is set as a window attribute and drawn by the server, the response to other graphics drawn on top is the same as if the background were drawn by the application. The background counts as a color that must be preserved.

will reappear.* The color in the colorcell indicated by `highlight2` must be the same as the color of colorcell `highlight1` so that the same highlighting color appears regardless of the bit already in the drawable that distinguishes the foreground and background pixel values.

`XAllocColorCells()` does not return these four pixel values directly. Instead it returns the arrays *colors* and *plane_masks* that are more convenient for actually using the overlays than a single array of pixel values. (Each of these arrays has the number of members that was specified in the *ncolors* and *nplanes* arguments.) Both arrays consist of unsigned long values like pixel values. One array contains the plane masks of the overlay planes, and the other contains the pixel values that can be used for drawing independent of the overlay planes. Here are the values returned in each array after we call `XAlloc-ColorCells()` with *ncolors* = 2 and *nplanes* = 1. These values are then used to generate the pixel values shown above.

Array Members		Important Bits	Remaining Bits
colors[0]	=	----0--0-------------------------	*other bits don't matter*
colors[1]	=	----0--1-------------------------	
plane_masks[0]	=	----1----------------------------	*all other bits 0*

The two members of the *colors* array are used for the foreground and background. Pixel values `highlight1` and `highlight2` are composed by combining with a bitwise OR each item in the *colors* array with each item in the *plane_masks* array. In this case, `highlight1` is (*colors*[0] | *plane_masks*[0]). The `plane_mask` in the GC used when highlighting should be set to the OR of the members of *plane_masks* used to make the highlighting pixel value. In this simplest case, highlighting should be done with the `plane_mask` in the GC set to *plane_masks*[0].

Note that `highlight2`, generated with (*colors*[1] | *plane_masks*[0]), can be useful. As mentioned earlier, `highlight2` can be used interchangeably with `highlight1`, as long as the `plane_mask` in the GC is set to *plane_masks*[0]. But `highlight2` has another use. With a GC that does not have its `plane_mask` set to *plane_masks*[0] (the GC used for drawing with the foreground or background), this fourth pixel value can be used for drawing in the highlighting color while wiping out the underlying graphics, so that when the highlight is removed, the background color appears regardless of the contents of the drawable before the highlighting.

We have been hinting at the fact that this overlay technique can be used with more than two colors and more than one plane. *ncolors* specifies the number of colors than can be drawn and preserved while drawing in the overlays. *nplanes* specifies how many separate one-color overlays you may have or how many bits of color are available in a single overlay. The pixel values in the *colors* array are the ones that will be preserved through overlays. By ORing together each *colors* with any combination of *plane_masks*, you get the pixel values that are used for drawing the overlays. Note, however, that the plane mask of the GC

---

* To clear an entire plane, set the `plane_mask` of a GC to the desired plane, and then fill the entire drawable using `XFillRectangle()`.

used for the overlaying must be the OR of the same combination of members of the *plane_masks* array as were used to generate the pixel value.

The total number of pixel values (colorcells) allocated by **XAllocColorCells()** is $ncolors * 2^{nplanes}$. Note that the more planes you try to allocate, the less likely this request is to succeed, particularly on **PseudoColor** visuals. Therefore, if you are trying for multiple overlays or one multicolor overlay, this will probably work reliably only on **DirectColor** visuals, so make sure you have a backup plan for more common systems. In most cases, the underlying graphics can be redrawn if the overlays that would preserve them cannot be allocated. It is also possible to use backing store (which can save selective planes) or to manage your own off-screen pixmaps for use in fast redrawing of complicated graphics.

XAllocColorCells() takes a *contig* argument that specifies whether the planes returned in *plane_masks* must be contiguous. The *contig* argument is normally set to **False**, specifying that the allocated planes need not be contiguous, because then the chances of success of the **XAllocColorCells()** call are greater. There are more likely to be a number of noncontiguous planes available than the same number of contiguous planes. The *contig* argument may have to be set to **True** for imaging applications that want to be able to perform mathematical operations on the pixel values. It is easier to perform operations by shifting bits with contiguous planes than to achieve the same effect with random planes.

Each plane mask has one bit for **GrayScale** and **PseudoColor** or three bits for **DirectColor** or **TrueColor**, and none of the masks have bits in common.

Example 7-7 demonstrates allocating the read/write cells for a single overlay plane. It implements the overlay scheme described above. If this overlay plan fails, it allocates three colors so that a highlight can still be implemented even though the underlying graphics will have to be redrawn. If the color allocation fails completely, it uses black and white, which can be highlighted using the **GXxor** logical function to invert the color, as described in Section 7.4.3.

Example 7-7. Using XAllocColorCells() to allocate read/write colorcells for overlay plane

```
#include <X11/Xlib.h>
#include <X11/Xutil.h>
#include <X11/Xos.h>
#include <stdio.h>

extern Display *display;
extern int screen_num;
extern unsigned long foreground, background_pixel, overlay_pixel_1,
        overlay_pixel_2;
extern unsigned long overlay_plane_mask;

#define MAX_COLORS 2
#define MAX_PLANES 1
#define MAX_CELLS 4          /* MAX_COLORS * 2 ^ MAX_PLANES */
#define CANNOT_OVERLAY 0
#define CAN_OVERLAY 1

int
get_colors()
{
```

```
int default_depth;
static char *name[ ] = {"Red", "Yellow", "Green", "Green"};
XColor exact_defs[MAX_CELLS];
Colormap default_cmap;
int ncolors = 4;
int plane_masks[MAX_PLANES];
int colors[MAX_COLORS];
int i;
XVisualInfo visual_info;
int class;

default_depth = DefaultDepth(display, screen_num);
default_cmap  = DefaultColormap(display, screen_num);
if (default_depth == 1) {
    /* Must be StaticGray, use black and white */
    background_pixel = WhitePixel(display, screen_num);
    foreground = BlackPixel(display, screen_num);
    printf("using black and white\n");
    return(CANNOT_OVERLAY);
}

if (!XMatchVisualInfo(display, screen_num, default_depth,
        PseudoColor, &visual_info)) {
    if (!XMatchVisualInfo(display, screen_num, default_depth,
            DirectColor, &visual_info)) {
        /* No PseudoColor or TrueColor visual available at
         * default_depth; some applications might try for a
         * GrayScale visual here if they can use gray to
         * advantage, before giving up and using black and white */
        background_pixel = WhitePixel(display, screen_num);
        foreground = BlackPixel(display, screen_num);
        printf("using black and white\n");
        return(CANNOT_OVERLAY);
    }
}

/* Got PseudoColor or TrueColor visual at default depth */

/* The visual we found is not necessarily the default visual, and
 * therefore it is not necessarily the one we used to create our
 * window; however, we now know for sure that color is supported,
 * so the following code will work (or fail in a controlled way) */

if (XAllocColorCells (display, default_cmap, False, plane_masks,
        1, colors, 2) == 0) {
    /* Can't get enough read/write cells to overlay;
     * try at least to get three colors */
    if (XAllocColorCells (display, default_cmap, False,
            plane_masks, 0, colors, 3) == 0) {
        /* Can't even get that; give up and use black and white */
            background_pixel = WhitePixel(display,
                                    screen_num);
            foreground = BlackPixel(display, screen_num);
        printf("using black and white\n");
        return(CANNOT_OVERLAY);
    }
    else
```

```
            ncolors = 3;
    }

    /* Allocated three or four colorcells successfully, now set their
     * colors -- three and four are set to the same RGB values */
    for (i = 0; i < ncolors; i++)
    {
        if (!XParseColor (display, default_cmap, name[i],
                &exact_defs[i])) {
            fprintf(stderr, "basic: color name %s not in database",
                    name[i]);
            exit(0);
        }
        /* This needed before calling XStoreColors */
        exact_defs[i].flags = DoRed | DoGreen | DoBlue;
    }
    printf("got RGB values\n");

    /* Set pixel value in struct to the allocated ones */
    exact_defs[0].pixel = colors[0];
    exact_defs[1].pixel = colors[1];
    exact_defs[2].pixel = colors[0] | plane_masks[0];
    exact_defs[3].pixel = colors[1] | plane_masks[0];

    /* This sets the color of the read/write cells */
    XStoreColors (display, default_cmap, exact_defs, ncolors);
    printf("stored colors\n");

    background_pixel = exact_defs[0].pixel;
    foreground = exact_defs[1].pixel;
    if (ncolors == 4) {
        overlay_pixel_1 = exact_defs[2].pixel;
        overlay_pixel_2 = exact_defs[3].pixel;
        overlay_plane_mask = plane_masks[0];
        printf("set can\n");
        return(CAN_OVERLAY);
    }
    else {
        /* This must be used as a normal color, not overlay */
        overlay_pixel_1 = exact_defs[2].pixel;
        printf("set can't\n");
        return(CANNOT_OVERLAY);
    }
}
```

The technique used for overlay planes can be used to implement a form of double buffering. Double buffering is a technique common used in animation, where drawing is done in an invisible buffer which is then made visible by a quick operation. While the first buffer is visible, a second invisible buffer is drawn into. When the second buffer is drawn, it is made visible and the first buffer invisible. This technique allows animation to appear smoothly without the person seeing the individual drawing operations that were necessary to draw the pictures.

Implementing this is just like overlays: one buffer is the overlay, and the other is what we have previously considered static graphics. The only change in double buffering is that you draw into the invisible buffer by using pixel values that do not change the visible colors in the visible buffer. Then you use `XFillRectangle()` to set or clear all pixels in the plane or planes that distinguish between the visible and invisible buffers. The price of doing this is that you have much fewer colors in each picture. For example, on an 8-plane system, you can only use 16 colors since you have two buffers of 4 bits each. (Also note that there is a double-buffering extension in progress in the X Consortium.)

7.5.3 Using XAllocColorPlanes()

`XAllocColorPlanes()` also allocates read/write colorcells but in a different way than `XAllocColorCells()`. `XAllocColorPlanes()` is used when you want to be able to change the amount of a primary color in graphics without having to redraw them. In other words, perhaps you are looking at an image and would like to increase the redness of it. The best way to do this is to increase the amount of red in every pixel value. `XAllocColor-Planes()` would be the way to allocate colors to allow this. It is rarely used except in imaging applications and 3-D graphics and will rarely work except on 24-plane workstations with a `DirectColor` visual.

Note that for applications like a paint mixing program, in which you have three bars for the three primary colors and a palette that shows the mixed color, you would not use `XAlloc-ColorPlanes()`. The correct way to implement this is to allocate a single read/write color for the palette and to change it dynamically. (If the primary colors are displayed, they should be allocated using read-only colors.)

The piece of code shown in Example 7-8 is similar to Example 7-7 but it uses `XAlloc-ColorPlanes()`. It is somewhat sketchy, because real applications that use `XAlloc-ColorPlanes()` are complicated.

After allocating colors with `XAllocColorPlanes()`, you can then use `XStore-Colors()` to set the colors. When *nred, ngreen*, and *nblue* are each **8**, only one call to `XAllocColorPlanes()` and one call to `XStoreColors()` are necessary to allocate and set all 16 million colors of an entire 24-plane colormap.

Example 7-8. Using XAllocColorPlanes() to allocate colorcells for DirectColor

```
#define PIXELS 256

Display *display;
int screen_num;
int contig = False;              /* Noncontiguous planes */
unsigned long pixels[PIXELS];    /* Return of pixel values */

/* Number of independent pixel values allocate */
unsigned int ncolors = PIXELS;

/* Need PIXELS * 2 ^ maxplanes defs, where maxplanes
 * is the largest of nred, ngreen, and nblue */
XColor defs[2048];

/* Number of planes to allocate for each primary */
```

```
unsigned int nreds = 3, ngreens = 3, nblues = 2;

/* Returned masks, which bits of pixel value for each primary */
unsigned long red_mask, green_mask, blue_mask;

Colormap colormap;
Status status;

/* Open display, etc. */
/* Get or create large DirectColor colormap */

while (status = XAllocColorPlanes(display, colormap,
         contig, pixels, ncolors, nreds, ngreens, nblues,
         &red_mask, &green_mask, &blue_mask) == 0) {
    /* Make contig False if it was True; reduce value of
     * ncolors; reduce value of nreds, ngreens, and/or
     * nblues; or try allocating new map; break when
     * you give up */
    break;
}
if (status == 0) {
    fprintf(stderr, "%s: couldn't allocate requested colorcells",
             argv[0]);
    exit(-1);
}

/* Define desired colors in defs */

while (status = XStoreColors(display, colormap, defs,
         ncolors) == 0) {
    fprintf(stderr, "%s: can't store colors", argv[0]);
    /* Try to fix problem here, exit or break */
    exit(-1);
}

/* Draw your shaded stuff! */
```

7.6 Getting Complete Visual Information

As mentioned earlier, some systems define more than one visual. The default visual might
not be the most appropriate for your application. Moreover, the visual found using the technique described in Section 7.4.2 using **XMatchVisualInfo()** is fine for applications
with routine color needs but is not necessarily the best. As you may recall, **XMatch-
VisualInfo()** returns a single visual arbitrarily selected from the list that matches the
passed visual class and depth. The most thorough method is to get a complete list of visual
information for every available visual, using **XGetVisualInfo()**, and then choose from
these.

XGetVisualInfo() returns a list of visual structures that match the attributes specified
by template and mask arguments. The template is an **XVisualInfo** structure with members set to the required values, and the mask indicates which members are matched with the

list of available visuals. By passing an empty template structure, you can get a complete list of **XVisualInfo** structures.

7.6.1 The XVisualInfo Structure

The **XVisualInfo** structure returns information about the available visuals. It is used both to select a visual type from those available and as a source of information while using a particular visual.

The **XVisualInfo** structure is shown in Example 7-9.

Example 7-9. The XVisualInfo structure

```
typedef struct {
    Visual *visual;
    VisualID visualid;
    int screen_num;
    unsigned int depth;
    int class;
    unsigned long red_mask;
    unsigned long green_mask;
    unsigned long blue_mask;
    int colormap_size;      /* Same as map_entries member of Visual */
    int bits_per_rgb;
} XVisualInfo;
```

The **visual** member is a pointer to the internal **Visual** structure. This pointer is used as the *visual* argument of **XCreateWindow()** and **XCreateColormap()**.

The **visualid** member is not normally needed by applications.

As discussed earlier, the **class** member specifies whether the screen is to be considered color or monochrome and changeable or immutable. The **class** member can be one of the constants **DirectColor**, **GrayScale**, **PseudoColor**, **StaticColor**, **Static-Gray**, or **TrueColor**.

The **red_mask**, **green_mask**, and **blue_mask** members are used only for the **DirectColor** and **TrueColor** visual classes, where there is a separate map for each primary color. They define which bits of the pixel value index into the colormap for each primary color. Each mask has one contiguous set of bits, with no bits in common with the other masks. These values are zero for monochrome and most four- to eight-plane color systems.

The **colormap_size** member of the structure tells you how many different pixel values are valid with this visual. For a monochrome screen, this value is two. For the default visual of an eight-plane color system, this value is typically 254 or 256 (two colors are often reserved for the cursor). For **DirectColor** and **TrueColor**, **colormap_size** will be the number of cells for the biggest individual pixel subfield. The **colormap_size** member is the same as the **map_entries** member of the visual structure.

The **bits_per_rgb** member specifies how many bits in each of the red, green, and blue values in a colorcell are used to drive the RGB gun in the screen. For a monochrome screen, this value is one. For the default visual of an eight-plane color system, this value is typically eight. The pixel subfields (the red, green, and blue values in each colorcell) are 16-bit unsigned short values, but only the highest **bits_per_rgb** bits are used to drive the RGB gun in the screen. This number corresponds the number of bits of resolution in the Digital to Analog Converter (DAC) in the screen hardware.

7.6.2 Example of Choosing a Visual

Example 7-10 shows a routine that uses **XGetVisualInfo()** to get all the visuals of depth 8 on the current screen, as defined by the X server, and then creates a colormap and window.

Example 7-10. Code to match visuals

```
#include <X11/Xlib.h>
#include <X11/Xutil.h>

visual()
{
Display *display;
Colormap colormap;
Window window;
XSetWindowAttributes attributes;
unsigned long valuemask;
int screen_num;
    .
    .
    .
XVisualInfo vTemplate;    /* Template of the visual we want */
XVisualInfo *visualList;  /* List of XVisualInfo structs that
                           * match */
int visualsMatched;       /* Number of visuals that match */
    .
    .
    .

/* Set up the XVisualInfo template so that it returns a list
 * of all the visuals of depth 8 defined on the current screen
 * by the X server */
vTemplate.screen = screen_num;
vTemplate.depth = 8;
visualList = XGetVisualInfo (display, VisualScreenMask |
        VisualDepthMask, &vTemplate, &visualsMatched);
if ( visualsMatched == 0 )
    fatalError ("No matching visuals\n");

/* Create a colormap for a window using the first of the
 * visuals in the list of XVisualInfo structs returned by
 * XGetVisualInfo */
colormap = XCreateColormap (display, RootWindow(display, screen_num),
    visualList[0].visual, AllocNone);

/* Must specify colormap attribute if using nondefault visual */
attributes.colormap = colormap;
valuemask |= CWColormap;
    .
    .
```

Example 7-10. Code to match visuals (continued)

```
        .
window = XCreateWindow (display, RootWindow(display, screen_num),
    x, y, width, height, border_width, vTemplate.depth,
    InputOutput, visualList[ 0 ].visual, valuemask, &attributes);
XSetWindowColormap(display, window, colormap);

/* All done with visual information; free it */

XFree(visualList);
        .
        .
        .
} /* End routine */
```

Notice that the list of **XVisualInfo** structures is freed with **XFree( )** after use.

7.7 The GrayScale Visual

On a gray-scale workstation or a **GrayScale** visual on a color workstation, a color application should still work correctly. The only problem might be that when colors are allocated,
the closest physically possible colors (returned by **XAllocColor( )**) will result in shades
of gray that provide insufficient contrast. The best way to avoid this is to explicitly check for
the **StaticGray** visual. For true bulletproof operation, it is a good idea to check any user-
specified colors to make sure they contrast.

The color names "gray0" through "gray100", spelled with an "e" or an "a", can be used with
XParseColor( ) to get RGB values for various grays.

You should set the red, green, and blue values to be equal. Some servers only use one of the
values, and others combine all three according to the NTSC standard that makes color televi-
sion signals work on black-and-white televisions:

```
intensity = (.30 * red) + (.59 * green) + (.11 * blue)
```

MIT's implementations use a least-squares algorithm that determines the closest RGB values
in the (gray) colormap to the RGB values specified. Exactly what algorithm is used is up to
the server implementor.

7.8 Standard Colormaps

A *standard colormap* is one in which the mapping between pixel values and colors is predictable. The purpose of standard colormaps is to encourage sharing of entire colormaps (not
just individual cells) between applications that have too demanding color needs to be able to
allocate read-only colors out of the default colormaps.

X defines a set of properties that contain information describing commonly used colormaps.
An application reads these properties by calling **XGetRGBColormaps( )**. This call
returns an **XStandardColormap** structure that contains enough information so that the

application can calculate the colors in every colormap cell (or a certain range within the colormap). This structure may also include the ID of a colormap matching this description that was created by the window manager or another client. The X distribution from MIT includes a standard client, *xstdcmap*, that creates the standard colormaps. The user can arrange for *xstdcmap* to be invoked when the X server starts up, or in the user's *.xsession* or *.xinitrc* file. If this program has not been run, the application can create a new colormap and use the information in the standard colormap properties to allocate and set the colors according to the information in the property. There are functions in the Xmu (miscellaneous utilities) library for allocating standard colormaps.

But how does the sharing work? After creating this colormap, the application (or *xstdcmap*) sets the ID of the created colormap into the `colormap` field of the `XStandard-Colormap` structure and then calls `XSetRGBColormaps()`. This resets the property, so that the next time another client calls `XGetRGBColormaps()`, the `colormap` field of the returned structure will actually contain the ID of the appropriate colormap.

Therefore, although an application must have the code to create, allocate, and set colors in a standard colormap to be robust, in some cases this code will not be executed because some other client will have already done the work. After calling `XGetRGBColormaps()`, if the `colormap` field is zero, the application must create the colormap. Otherwise, the `color-map` field holds the ID of an appropriate colormap.

When an application uses standard colormaps, two (or more) instances of the application can run at the same time without increasing the load on the system caused by creating multiple copies of the same colormap. Applications that do not use standard colormaps will end up creating separate but identical colormaps. The window manager will switch these in and out of the hardware colormap whenever a different instance is in use. Although nothing on the screen will change color because both the colormaps are identical, the server will be performing unnecessary installing and uninstalling, and the extra colormaps will waste server memory.

In some cases, the window manager or even the server will create one or more standard colormaps. This does not change how applications work at all. Applications do not care whether it was the window manager, the server, or some other client that created a standard colormap.

If your application does not create or use a custom colormap, you can skip this section if pressed for time.

Applications can also use the knowledge about a standard colormap to optimize the process of figuring out which existing pixel values correspond to required colors and which colors must be allocated and set from scratch.

7.8.1 The Standard Colormap Properties

The standard colormap properties contain information about a few commonly used colormaps. However, note that even if an application creates a custom colormap unlike any of these, it should still use the standard property mechanism by creating its own standard colormap structure.

Properties were introduced in Section 2.1.4. For a more complete description of properties, see Section 12.1.

In the call to `XGetRGBColormaps()` you specify one of these atoms like `XA_RGB_BEST_MAP` (or, if necessary, one unique to your application).

The following list names the atoms and describes the colormap associated with each one:

`XA_RGB_DEFAULT_MAP`
> This property defines part of the system default colormap. This colormap may be initially completely unallocated, or it may contain a selection of read-only colorcells with the RGB values from the color database and a few unallocated cells for use by applications that need read/write cells. A typical allocation of the `XA_RGB_DEFAULT_MAP` on eight-plane screens is all the colors produced from any combination of six reds, six greens, and six blues. This gives 216 uniformly distributed colors and leaves 40 for other programs or for special purpose colors for text, borders, and so on. A typical allocation for the `XA_RGB_DEFAULT_MAP` on 24-plane screens is 64 reds, 64 greens, and 64 blues. This gives about one million uniformly distributed colors (64 intensities of 4096 different hues) and leaves lots of colorcells available for other purposes.

`XA_RGB_BEST_MAP`
> This property defines the "best" RGB colormap available on the screen. Of course, this is a subjective evaluation. Many image-processing and 3-D programs need to use all available colormap cells and to distribute as many perceptually distinct colors as possible over those cells. In this case, there may be more green values available than red and more green or red than blue.
>
> On an eight-plane `DirectColor` visual, `XA_RGB_BEST_MAP` is usually a 3/3/2 allocation. On a 24-plane `DirectColor` visual, `XA_RGB_BEST_MAP` is usually an 8/8/8 allocation. On other screens, `XA_RGB_BEST_MAP` is purely up to the implementor of the server.

`XA_RGB_RED_MAP, XA_RGB_GREEN_MAP, XA_RGB_BLUE_MAP`
> These properties define all-red, all-green, and all-blue colormaps, respectively. These maps are used by programs that make color-separated images. For example, a user might generate a full color image on an eight-plane screen by rendering an image once with high color resolution in red, once with green, and once with blue and exposing a single frame in a camera with three images.

`XA_RGB_GRAY_MAP`
> This property describes the "best" gray-scale colormap available on the screen.

7.8.2 The XStandardColormap Structure

As described above, an application that wants to use a standard colormap must get the structure that contains the specification for the colormap using `XGetRGBColormaps()`. Some servers and window managers, particularly on high performance workstations, create some or all of the standard colormaps when they initialize. If the desired colormap has already been created, it is returned in the `colormap` member of the `XStandardColormap` structure shown in Example 7-11. If the colormap does not yet exist, the `colormap` member will be zero. In that case, the application can create a colormap and allocate entries to match the specification in the members of `XStandardColormap`, then call `XSet-RGBColormaps()` to allow other clients to share this colormap.

Example 7-11. The XStandardColormap structure

```
typedef struct _XStandardColormap {
    Colormap colormap;
    unsigned long red_max, green_max, blue_max;
    unsigned long red_mult, green_mult, blue_mult;
    unsigned long base_pixel;
    VisualID visualid;          /* Added in R4:  ICCCM version 1 */
    XID killid;                 /* Added in R4:  ICCCM version 1 */
} XStandardColormap;
```

The members of the `XStandardColormap` structure are as follows:

- The `colormap` member is the ID of a colormap created by the `XCreate-Colormap()` function or the default colormap. This ID can be used to install a virtual colormap into the hardware colormap.

- The `red_max`, `green_max`, and `blue_max` fields give the maximum red, green, and blue values, respectively. A typical allocation that provides = 216 read-only, shareable colors in a `PseudoColor` colormap on a standard eight-plane workstation is `red_max` = 5, `green_max` = 5, and `blue_max` = 5. This leaves 40 cells available for special colors and private, nonshareable purposes. On a 24-plane workstation, there would be eight bits available for each color in a `TrueColor` visual, which would allow 256 shades of each primary color. In this case, `red_max` = 255, `green_max` = 255, and `blue_max` = 255. This map would include = 16.38 million total colors.

- The `red_mult`, `green_mult`, and `blue_mult` fields scale each pixel subfield into the proper range in the 16-bit RGB value in the colorcell with the range 0 to 65535. The red pixel subfield is moved `red_mult` bits toward the most significant bit of the pixel value.

  For a 3/3/2 `DirectColor` allocation (eight reds, eight greens, four blues), `red_mult` might be 32, `green_mult` might be 4, and `blue_mult` might be 1 (as shown in Figure 7-5). These effectively move the red value into the most significant bits of the RGB value in the colorcell, the green into the middle, and the blue into the least significant bits. This arrangement is arbitrary but useful. For a six-colors-each allocation, which must be `PseudoColor` since the planes cannot be evenly allocated to separate primaries, `red_mult` might be 36, `green_mult` might be 6, and `blue_mult` might be 1.

- The `base_pixel` field gives the base value that is added to the pixel value calculated from the RGB values and scale factors. Usually the `base_pixel` is obtained from a call to the `XAllocColorPlanes()` function.

- The `visualid` field is the ID of a server resource associated with each visual, of type `VisualID`. You will need this ID only if you intend to use standard colormaps. This field was added in R4 because only with this information can standard colormaps be used with other than the default visual. Prior to R4, standard colormaps were not in wide use, partly because they could only be used with the default visual.

• The `killid` field returns a number that is used if the application needs to free the colormap for some reason. If `killid` is greater than one, then the resources should be freed by calling `XKillClient()` with the `killid` field as the argument. If `killid` is one, then the resources should be freed by calling `XFreeColormap()` with the `colormap` field as the argument. If `killid` is zero, then no attempt should be made to free the resources.

`GrayScale` colormaps should be used just like color visuals in every way. For example, all three color fields in the `XStandardColormap` should be used. The standard client *xstdcmap* currently creates `GrayScale` standard colormaps using the NTSC color-to-mono mapping algorithm described earlier.

7.8.3 The 3/3/2 Standard Colormap

Now let's look at a typical standard colormap. The following example describes the 3/3/2 `DirectColor` standard colormap used on eight-plane screens. Three planes are used for red, three planes for green, and two planes for blue. This 3/3/2 allocation allows values in the range of:

```
red     0-7    thus    red_max    =  7
green   0-7            green_max  =  7
blue    0-3            blue_max   =  3
```

To obtain the pixel value, these RGB values must be shifted to their corresponding planes. If the red value is contained in the three most significant planes or bits, the green values in the three next most significant planes or bits, and the blue value in the two least significant planes or bits, then the pixel can be constructed as shown in Figure 7-5.

In a `DirectColor` system like this, the multiples are equal to 2^n, where n is their lowest plane or bit position. If the red, green, and blue were stored in a different order, the multiples would not be 32, 4, 1 but would still be calculated from the above description and formula. The 3/3/2 standard colormap allocation is fairly standard.

7.8.4 Creating and Using a Standard Colormap

Two members were added to the `XStandardColormap` structure in Release 4 to comply with the ICCCM (interclient communication conventions, described in Chapter 12). Because of this, there are two different sets of routines that manage standard colormaps, one for use with R3 (and earlier) and the other for use with R4 (and later). The now-outdated R3 routines are `XGetStandardColormap()` and `XSetStandardColormap()`; the R4 routines are `XGetRGBColormaps()` and `XSetRGBColormaps()`. The reason for the plural form of the R4 routine `XGetRGBColormaps()` is that it returns a list of colormaps; it also has a *count* argument not present in the R3 routine. According to the ICCCM, only queries of the `XA_RGB_DEFAULT_MAP` standard colormap can return more than one structure.

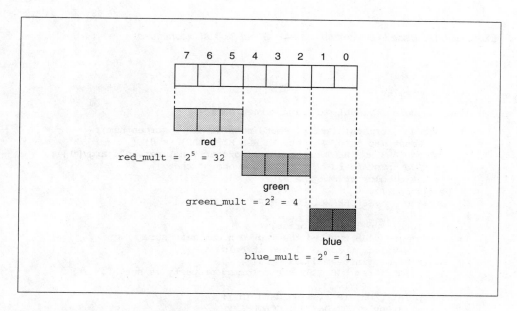

Figure 7-5. Shifting pixel subfields into pixel value

Example 7-12 gets information about the XA_RGB_BEST_MAP standard colormap, creates it if no other client already has, calculates pixel values from it, and sets the colormap window attribute of the window. This example gives up and falls back on read-only colorcell allocation if the standard colormap property is not defined by the server or if creating a colormap returns the default colormap (which happens on systems with an immutable hardware colormap). Also look at the code for *xstdcmap* for a more complete example.

Example 7-12. Code to create and use XA_RGB_BEST_MAP

```
        .
        .
        .
#define USE_DEFAULT_COLORMAP 1
#define USE_STANDARD_COLORMAP 0

void main(argc, argv)
int argc;
char **argv;
{
    XStandardColormap *best_map_info;
    XColor *exact_defs;
    XSetWindowAttributes attrib;
    unsigned long attribmask;
    int i, j, k, l;
    int ncells;
    XVisualInfo *vlist, vinfo_template, *v;
    int num_vis;
    int count;
    Visual *visual;
    int strategy = USE_STANDARD_COLORMAP;
```

Example 7-12. Code to create and use XA_RGB_BEST_MAP (continued)

```
        .
        .
        .
/* Open display */

visual = DefaultVisual(display, screen_num);

if (XGetRGBColormaps(display, RootWindow(display, screen_num),
        &best_map_info, &count, XA_RGB_BEST_MAP) == 0) {
    printf("%s: RGB_BEST_MAP colormap property not set.\n", argv[ 0 ]);
    /* Give up standard colormaps; use one of the
     * basic color strategies */
    get_colors();
    strategy = USE_DEFAULT_COLORMAP;
}
else if (best_map_info->colormap) {
    /* Someone else created the map we need; make sure
     * it's valid, then we'll use it below */
    if (best_map_info->red_max == 0) {
        printf("%s: RGB_BEST_MAP colormap property is set\n",
                argv[ 0 ]);
        printf("but is missing data.\n");
        strategy = USE_DEFAULT_COLORMAP;
    }
    else {
        printf("stnd colormap ID: %d\n", best_map_info->colormap);
        attrib.colormap = best_map_info->colormap;
    }
}
else if (best_map_info->visualid == 0) {
    printf("%s: Standard colormap property is set\n", argv[ 0 ]);
    printf("but is missing data.");
    /* Some systems define the properties but don't
     * place any data in them; this is a server bug,
     * but we'll check for it anyway */
    /* Fall back on a basic color strategy */
    strategy = USE_DEFAULT_COLORMAP;
}
else {
    /* Got information, but the described colormap
     * has not been created yet; create it and
     * allocate all cells read/write */

    /* XCreateColormap requires a visual argument
     * (pointer to a Visual structure); however, the
     * XStandardColormap structure returns a VisualID,
     * which might not be the default visual;
     * Converting between these two is painful */
    vlist = XGetVisualInfo(display, VisualNoMask,
            &vinfo_template, &num_vis);
    for (v = vlist; v < vlist + num_vis; v++) {
        if (v->visualid == best_map_info->visualid) {
            visual = v->visual;
            break;
        }
    }

    best_map_info->colormap = XCreateColormap(display,
```

Example 7-12. Code to create and use XA_RGB_BEST_MAP (continued)

```
                RootWindow(display, screen_num), visual, AllocAll);
        if (best_map_info->colormap ==
                DefaultColormap(display, screen_num)) {
            printf("%s: hardware colormap is immutable:\n",
                    argv[ 0 ]);
            printf("cannot create new colormap.\n");
        }

        attrib.colormap = best_map_info->colormap;

        ncells = best_map_info->base_pixel +
                ((best_map_info->red_max + 1) *
                (best_map_info->green_max + 1) *
                (best_map_info->blue_max + 1));

        exact_defs = (XColor *) calloc(sizeof(XColor), ncells);

        /* Permute the levels of red, green, and blue */
        l = best_map_info->base_pixel;
        for (i = 0; i < best_map_info->blue_max; i++) {
            for (j = 0; j < best_map_info->blue_max; j++) {
                for (k = 0; k < best_map_info->blue_max; k++) {
                    exact_defs[l].red = 0xFFFF * k /
                            best_map_info->red_max;
                    exact_defs[l].green = 0xFFFF * j /
                            best_map_info->green_max;
                    exact_defs[l].blue = 0xFFFF * i /
                            best_map_info->blue_max;
                l++;
                }
            }
        }

        XStoreColors (display, best_map_info->colormap, exact_defs, ncells);

        /* If to be used in a window not created with the
         * default visual, must create the window first and
         * use instead of RootWindow in this call; here we
         * assume the default visual */

        XSetRGBColormaps(display, RootWindow(display, screen_num),
                &best_map_info, count, XA_RGB_BEST_MAP);
    }

    if (strategy == USE_STANDARD_COLORMAP) {
        /* We must not have called get_colors above,
         * must be using standard colormaps strategy */

        /* Note that we act like we have already allocated pixel
         * pixel values, even though actually another client did */
        background_pixel = best_map_info->base_pixel +
            (best_map_info->red_max * best_map_info->red_mult) +
            (best_map_info->green_max * best_map_info->green_mult) +
            (best_map_info->blue_max * best_map_info->blue_mult);

        attribmask = CWBackPixel | CWColormap;

        foreground_pixel = (best_map_info->green_max *
            best_map_info->green_mult / 2) +
            best_map_info->base_pixel;
```

Example 7-12. Code to create and use XA_RGB_BEST_MAP (continued)

```
        border_pixel = (best_map_info->blue_max *
            best_map_info->blue_mult / 2) +
            best_map_info->base_pixel;
    }

    /* Create opaque window */
    win = XCreateWindow(display, RootWindow(display,screen_num), x,
            y, width, height, borderwidth, DefaultDepth(display, screen_num),
            InputOutput, visual, attribmask, &attrib);
    .
    .
    .
}
```

This code begins by reading the `XA_RGB_BEST_MAP` property using the `XGet-`
`RGBColormaps()` call. The name `XGetRGBColormaps()` suggests that the function
returns a description of multiple colormaps—but this is true only for
`XA_RGB_DEFAULT_MAP`. If this call succeeds, the property is defined and its contents have
been placed in the `best_map_info` structure. Since any other, perhaps buggy, client
might have set this property (like your own application while you are debugging it), it is a
good idea not to trust its contents any more than necessary. (Properties set on the root window remain defined even after the client that set them has exited.) The code checks to make
sure that the fields contain reasonable values before using them.

If the `colormap` field of `best_map_info` is nonzero, it should be the ID of a standard
colormap that another client has created. Your application can immediately proceed to use
the pixel values in this colormap as though your application had already allocated them read-
only, even though in reality some other client allocated them read/write.

On the other hand, if the `colormap` field is zero, your application needs to create, allocate,
and set the values of the standard colormap itself. You allocate the cells read/write, because
this allows you to explicitly set the RGB values of each pixel value. Even though you allocate the cells read/write, you should use them as if they were read-only, so that other applications can share them after you reset the `XA_RGB_BEST_MAP` property to include the new
colormap ID. As this suggests, a read/write cell, even though described earlier as being private and changeable by that one client, can be public if all the applications agree not to
change its RGB values.

The algorithm used to store RGB values into the cells in the colormap is somewhat arbitrary.
Conventions for it will probably be adopted by the X Consortium when there is more interest
in standard colormaps. Any algorithm is good enough to allow two instances of the same
application to share a colormap. But for two different applications to share the colormap,
each must know exactly what RGB values the other would place in the colormap if the other
were run before the colormap was created.

The `XGetVisualInfo()` call is described in Section 7.6.

If you pass `AllocAll` to `XCreateColormap()`, you do not need to make an `XAlloc-ColorCells()` call to allocate all the cells read/write. However, you can use `AllocAll` only if you intend the entire colormap to be read-only to all clients. Some clients want a few cells preserved to be rewriteable for dynamically changing colors. If yours is that way, you must use `AllocNone` and then call `XAllocColorCells()` once to create the standard portion of the colormap and again to allocate the cells your application will treat as private.

Once the colormap window attribute of a window is set, the window manager will take care of installing the colormap. When there is only one hardware colormap, the window manager usually installs an application's colormap when that application contains the pointer (for real-estate type window managers) or is given the keyboard focus (for click-to-type style window managers).

When a window manager creates a standard colormap, it can use a slightly different technique to make sure that the standard colormap remains defined even after the window manager exits. Assuming that it has already checked to see whether some other client has created a standard colormap and none has, it performs the following sequence of steps:

- Create a new connection to the same server.

- Determine the color capabilities of the screen. Choose a visual.

- Create a colormap (not required for `XA_RGB_DEFAULT_MAP`).

- Call `XAllocColorPlanes()` or `XAllocColorCells()` to allocate cells in the colormap (if did not use `AllocAll` flag when creating the colormap).

- Call `XStoreColors()` to store appropriate color values in the colormap.

- Fill in the descriptive fields in the `XStandardColormap` structure, including the ID of the created colormap.

- Call `XSetRGBColormaps()` to set the property on the root window. The `killid` field should be set to the colormap ID.

- Use `XSetCloseDownMode()` to make the resource permanent.

- Close the new connection to the server.

7.8.5 RGB-to-Pixel Conversion

The standard colormaps such as `XA_RGB_BEST_MAP` are useful when you want to calculate pixel values from RGB values.

Consider a 3-D display program that draws a smoothly shaded sphere. At each pixel in the image of the sphere, the program computes the intensity and color of light reflected to the viewer. The result of each computation is a triple of red, green, and blue coefficients in the range 0.0 to 1.0. To draw the sphere, the program needs a colormap that provides a large range of uniformly distributed colors. The colormap must be arranged so that the program can convert its RGB triples into pixel values very quickly, because drawing the entire sphere will require many such conversions. An example of one such calculation is shown in

Example 7-13. Example 7-12 demonstrated how to do this for integral RGB values.

Example 7-13. Calculating pixel values from floating point RGB values

```
XStandardColormap best_map_info;
float red, green, blue;
unsigned long pixelvalue;

pixelvalue = best_map_info.base_pixel +
    ((unsigned long)(0.5 + (red * best_map_info.red_max)) *
        best_map_info.red_mult) +
    ((unsigned long)(0.5 + (green * best_map_info.green_max)) *
        best_map_info.green_mult) +
    ((unsigned long)(0.5 + (blue * best_map_info.blue_max)) *
        best_map_info.blue_mult);
```

For gray scale colormaps, only the **colormap**, **red_max**, **red_mult**, and **base_pixel** fields of the **XStandardColormap** structure are defined. The other fields are ignored. Pixel values for a **StaticGray** or **GrayScale** visual must be in the range:

    base_pixel <= pixel_value < (red_max * red_mult) + base_pixel

To compute a gray pixel value, use the following expression:

    pixel_value = gray * red_mult + base_pixel;

where:

gray	=	the gray value you desire (0 to red_max)
red_mult	=	value from XStandardColormap structure
base_pixel	=	value from XStandardColormap structure

7.9 Device-independent Color and Xcms

As already described, the X server supports a color name database in order to translate textual color names into intensity values for the red, green, and blue primaries. This is a convenience for users and a simple attempt at device-independent color—if server vendors tune the database to the particular displays they support, then applications that use the standard named colors can be confident that those colors will appear the same across all displays.

In practice, however, the color database has not been tuned for most displays. Furthermore, there are a growing number of visualization and other applications that use color and shading to display data and convey information rather than simply as decoration. These applications need the ability to precisely specify device-independent colors and often to divide a range of colors into perceptually equal intervals. A small number of hand-tuned named colors in a database is simply not adequate. X11R5 addresses these needs with Xcms, the X Color Management System, which was developed primarily by Tektronix for the X Consortium.

Xcms includes:

*   A new standard textual representation for device-independent color strings.

- Modifications to several existing Xlib functions to support this new standard representation.

- The provision for a database that maps color names to device-independent color specifications. This database is read by Xlib rather than by the X server.

- The Xcms API—a new set of Xlib functions that allow the allocation of device-independent colors and provide extremely precise control over conversions between device-independent color representations. Several of these functions are device-independent analogs to the device-dependent X11R4 color allocation and lookup functions.

- The X Device Color Characterization Conventions (XDCCC), a standard format for new root window properties that contains the information about the physical characteristics of the screen necessary to support the conversion of device-independent color specifications into device-dependent values. X11R5 provides a new client, *xcmsdb*, to set the values of these properties. The XDCCC is part of the ICCCM (Inter-Client Communication Conventions Manual), which is described in Chapter 12.

Xcms involves no changes to the X protocol or the X server. So, for example, an R5 Xcms application can successfully connect to an R4 X server.

7.9.1 The Fundamentals of Color Representation

Colorimetry is an involved science, and this book can only scratch its surface. This section documents the most useful and commonly used Xcms functions, but because a complete understanding of Xcms requires a deeper introduction to colorimetry than is presented here, some of the more obscure functions will be glossed over and left undocumented. Volume Two, *Xlib Reference Manual* contains man pages for all the Xcms functions, but not all of them are described here.

Until Release 5, X provided only an RGB system for describing colors. In this scheme, the color of a pixel is described by three numbers which represent the intensity of the electrical signal sent to the electron guns that excite the red, green, and blue phosphors in a monitor. This model is simple from the standpoint of a systems programmer because it is so closely tied to the physical hardware. Unfortunately, our eyes do not perceive color proportionally to the voltage applied to the electron guns, so equal voltage changes over a range of red, green, or blue intensities do not produce an equal perceptual change. At low intensities, a change of many voltage steps may be required before any perceptual difference is produced. In addition, selecting a desired color by additive mixing of each of the primaries is not as simple as it sounds. Fine-tuning a color by this method is essentially a process of trial and error. The RGB color model is a device-dependent color model because it is tied directly to the physical characteristics of a given screen—the electrical response of the electron guns, the precise composition of the phosphors used, and so on. If the same RGB color specification is displayed on two different monitors, the resulting colors will be noticeably different.

By definition, a device-independent color specification will result in identical displayed colors regardless of the device that is used. The device-independent color representations supported by X11R5 are all based on an international standard color representation model known informally as CIEXYZ. In CIEXYZ and related color spaces, a color is described by the value of three coordinates (as is the case with RGB), and the color space itself is commonly referred to by the names of its coordinates. X11R5 supports the CIEXYZ color space, related spaces known as CIExyY, CIExyY, CIEuvY, CIELuv, CIELab, and a color space designed by Tektronix known as TekHVC. The interpretation of the coordinates of all but the last of these spaces is not particularly intuitive and requires some knowledge of colorimetry. These spaces will not be described here; instead all discussion and examples in this chapter will use the TekHVC color space. This is a perceptually uniform color space designed to be intuitive. It is mathematically related to the CIE spaces, but is easier to describe and to understand. In this model, a color is characterized by Hue, Value, and Chroma. The Hue of a color is what distinguishes it from colors of other color families—the blues are of different hues from the greens, for example. Value describes the lightness or darkness of a color, and Chroma describes the saturation or "vibrancy" of a color. The range of possible values for these three coordinates define the HVC "color solid." It is an irregular solid defined in cylindrical coordinates with Hue as the angle, Chroma the radius, and Value the z-coordinate of a point. The model is designed to make it intuitive to find a desired color. Because the space is perceptually uniform, uniform increments in the value of any of the coordinates of a color result in uniform perceptual differences in displayed colors. Figure 7-6 shows a diagram of the TekHVC "color solid," and a "hue leaf," the cross section of the solid for a single Hue.

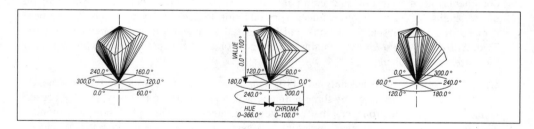

Figure 7-6. Three views of the TekHVC color solid

In the TekHVC space, Hues near 0.0 are reds, Hues near 60.0 are oranges and yellows, Hues near 120.0 are greens, Hues near 180.0 are blue-greens, Hues near 240.0 are blues, and Hues near 300.0 are violets. Because the Hue coordinate is an angle, the reds near 0.0 "wrap around" to Hues near 360.0. At any given Hue, the legal values of Value and Chroma define an approximately triangular area, sometimes called a *hue leaf*. For example, for the red Hues around 10.0, colors with Chromas near 0.0 are almost grey, and as the Chroma increases, the range of legal Values decreases, and the colors redden, passing through various reddish-brown shades, until around the maximum Chroma (near 90.0) there are only a few legal Values (near 50.0), and the colors are all bright "sports car" red. At the same Hue of 10.0, a

Chroma of 55.0 and the minimum legal Value (near 30.0), the color is a deep maroon, and it lightens as the Value increases until at the maximum Value (near 65.0) it is a salmon pink.*

Any color that is visible to the human eye can be described by three coordinates in a device-independent color space, but no given device can display all possible colors. Stated in another way, all colors visible to the human eye lie within the TekHVC color solid, but the colors that can be generated by any particular device lie within some subset of that solid. Each monitor type has a *device gamut* which is the set of colors it can display. When a color is requested that is outside of the gamut for a device, some form of *gamut compression* must be used to map the requested color into a displayable color in a sensible way. When an Xcms function attempts to convert a device-independent color that is outside of the device gamut to a device-dependent color, Xlib automatically performs gamut compression on that color, and the function returns a special value that indicates that compression occurred.

7.9.2 Screen Characterization and the XDCCC

In order for Xcms to convert from device-independent color used by X clients to the device-dependent colors used by the X server, it must know the characteristics of the screen or screens connected to the server. What is needed is a 3 × 3 matrix to convert between the CIEXYZ and RGBi color spaces, and a lookup table to convert from RGBi intensities to RGB integer values. The X server stores this data in properties of the root window of each screen so that the Xcms functions have access to it without the necessity of extending the X Protocol. The names and formats of these root window properties are specified in the X Device Color Characterization Conventions (or XDCCC) which has been added to the *Inter-Client Communication Conventions Manual* (or ICCCM).

X11R5 provides a new client, *xcmsdb*, which reads screen characterization data from a file and sets the data on the appropriate properties. System administrators may configure *xdm* to automatically invoke *xcmsdb* for every screen of a display, or users who make use of device-independent color may invoke it themselves. The source code for *xcmsdb* in the MIT distribution includes two sample screen characterization data files, but the distribution does not attempt to provide data for all possible screen types. If screen characterization data is not specified on root window properties, Xlib will fall back on default data. This means that you can experiment with the new Xcms features, but because the default data will almost certainly not match your display, the colors you see will not actually be the device-independent colors you request. Vendors may make screen characterization data available in the contributed section of the X11R5 release, but even these will not get you truly device-independent color: the physical characteristics of a monitor change as it ages, so for accurate color reproduction, you will have to have your monitor calibrated.

---

*A good way to become familiar with the TekHVC color space is to use the TekColor Editor from Tektronix. It allows a user to interactively and graphically select TekHVC colors. It is not part of the MIT X11R5 distribution, but is available for anonymous ftp from the host *ftp.x.org* in the file *contrib/xtici.tar.Z*. See the Preface for information on how to get files from the Internet.

7.9.3 The Xcms Programming Interface

The Xcms programming interface is part of Xlib and contains many new functions and a number of new datatypes, all of which begin with the prefix "Xcms" (X Color Management System). Some of these new functions are close analogs to the pre-X11R5 color functions that allocate cells in colormaps and that store and query colors in colormap cells. Where the existing Xlib functions operate on an XColor structure, the analogous Xcms colormap functions operate on an XcmsColor structure that allows colors to be specified in a device-independent fashion. These are the functions that will be most frequently used by programmers.

There is a group of Xcms functions used to manipulate an Xcms datatype known as a "color conversion context" or CCC. In X11R5, every colormap has an associated CCC which contains attributes that control the details of the conversion of colors from one color space to another. Default CCCs are automatically handled by Xcms, and many programmers will never have to use them explicitly. The theory behind color conversions is complicated, and so only the simplest and most useful of the CCC functions are documented here.

Xcms also provides a number of functions to query the boundaries of the device gamut. This means that programmers can ensure that allocated colors will be displayable (without gamut compression) on a given screen. Or it means that programmers can query the most vibrant shade of a color displayable on a particular device. The gamut-querying functions that operate with the TekHVC color model are fully documented in this book. Because other color spaces have not been described in any detail in this chapter, those gamut-querying functions that operate in color spaces other than TekHVC are not documented here.

Finally, Xcms provides functions that allow the extension of Xcms by adding new color spaces and support for new types of display devices. These functions are not documented here.

Note that Xcms functions require significantly more computation than their device-dependent analogs. In particular, they require trigonometric and other floating-point operations. In the MIT distribution, the standard math library is not used. Instead, the floating-point operations are implemented in Xlib directly. Because these functions cannot take advantage of floating-point hardware and do not have the efficiency of a highly optimized math library, they are relatively slow. As a result, adding Xcms functions to a program can add noticeable delays, particularly when gamut compression occurs. You can force the Xcms functions to use the standard math library by editing the macros defined in *mit/lib/X/Xcmsint.h* and rebuilding Xlib.

7.9.3.1 Color and Colormap Functions

Xcms provides the following functions for setting or querying colormap cells. They are close analogs to pre-X11R5 color allocation functions, but use the **XcmsColor** structure to specify device-independent colors rather than the **XColor** structure, which can only specify RGB colors. These functions are fully documented in Volume Two, *Xlib Reference Manual*.

XcmsAllocColor()

> Allocates a read-only color cell with the specified color. Returns the color specification of the color actually allocated (i.e., the closest color the hardware could support). Analogous to **XAllocColor()**, but with an additional argument that specifies the desired color space for the return value. If the requested color is outside of the gamut of the screen, gamut compression is performed.

XcmsAllocNamedColor()

> Allocates a read-only color cell with the color specified in the passed color string. Returns the exact color specification for the color string, as well as the color specification and pixel value for the color actually allocated. If the requested color is outside of the gamut of the screen, gamut compression is performed. Analogous to **XAllocNamedColor()**, but with an additional argument that specifies the desired color space of the return values. Any color string that can be allocated by **XcmsAllocNamedColor()** can also be allocated by **XAllocNamedColor()**. The difference is only that the Xcms function returns a device-independent specification of the color.

XcmsLookupColor()

> Converts a color string into an **XcmsColor** specification, but does not store that color in a color map. Returns the exact color specification of the color string as well as the closest color that could actually be produced on the screen. If the requested color is outside the gamut of the screen, gamut compression is performed. Analogous to **XLookupColor()**, but with an additional argument that specifies the desired color space for the return values. Any color string that can be looked up by **XcmsLookupColor()** can also be looked up by **XLookupColor()**. The difference is only that the Xcms function returns a device-independent specification of the color.

XcmsQueryColor()

> Given a pixel value, returns the color of that pixel in the given colormap. Analogous to **XQueryColor()**, but with an additional argument that specifies which color space the queried color should be represented in.

XcmsQueryColors()

> Returns the colors associated with a set of pixels in a given colormap. Analogous to **XQueryColors()**, but with an additional argument that specifies the desired color space for the returned colors.

XcmsStoreColor()

> Sets the color of a read/write color cell in the specified colormap. Analogous to **XStoreColor()**, but has a return value that indicates whether the conversion from device-independent color specification to RGB values was successful. If the requested color is outside the gamut of the screen, gamut compression is performed.

XcmsStoreColors()

Sets the colors of multiple read/write color cells in the specified colormap. Analogous to **XStoreColors()**, but has return values that indicate whether the conversions from device-independent specifications to RGB values were successful. If any of the requested colors are outside the gamut of the screen, gamut compression is performed.

The **XcmsColor** structure is the device-independent analog to the **XColor** structure, and is used by all of the Xcms functions described above. It contains a pixel value, a format value which specifies the device-dependent or device-independent color space used to describe the color, and a union of structures that specify the parameters for each of the supported formats. The structure is shown in Example 7-14.

Example 7-14. The XcmsColor structure

```
typedef struct {
    union {
        XcmsRGB RGB;
        XcmsRGBi RGBi;
        XcmsCIEXYZ CIEXYZ;
        XcmsCIEuvY CIEuvY;
        XcmsCIExyY CIExyY;
        XcmsCIELab CIELab;
        XcmsCIELuv CIELuv;
        XcmsTekHVC TekHVC;
        XcmsPad Pad;
    } spec;                       /* the color specification    */
    unsigned long pixel;          /* pixel value (as needed)    */
    XcmsColorFormat format;       /* the specification format   */
} XcmsColor;
```

The legal values for the format field are: **XcmsUndefinedFormat**, **XcmsCIEXYZ-Format**, **XcmsCIEuvYFormat**, **XcmsCIExyYFormat**, **XcmsCIELabFormat**, **XcmsCIELuvFormat**, **XcmsTekHVCFormat**, **XcmsRGBFormat**, and **XcmsRGBi-Format**. The RGB substructure within the union **spec** consists of three unsigned 16-bit integers. All the other color space structures consist of three doubles, and the **XcmsPad** structure reserves four doubles for possible extensions. Example 7-15 shows these structures.

Example 7-15. Selected XcmsColor sub-structures

```
typedef unsigned int XcmsColorFormat;    /* Color Space Format ID */
typedef double XcmsFloat;

typedef struct {                  /* Device RGB */
    unsigned short red;           /* scaled from 0x0000 to 0xffff */
    unsigned short green;         /* scaled from 0x0000 to 0xffff */
    unsigned short blue;          /* scaled from 0x0000 to 0xffff */
} XcmsRGB;

typedef struct {                  /* RGB intensity */
    XcmsFloat red;                /* 0.0 - 1.0 */
    XcmsFloat green;              /* 0.0 - 1.0 */
    XcmsFloat blue;              /* 0.0 - 1.0 */
} XcmsRGBi;
```

Example 7-15. Selected XcmsColor sub-structures (continued)

```
                        .          /* structures for other color spaces omitted */
                        .

typedef struct {                   /* TekHVC */
    XcmsFloat H;                   /* 0.0 - 360.0 */
    XcmsFloat V;                   /* 0.0 - 100.0 */
    XcmsFloat C;                   /* 0.0 - 100.0 */
} XcmsTekHVC;

typedef struct {                   /* 4 doubles of pad */
    XcmsFloat pad0;                /* for use by Xcms extensions */
    XcmsFloat pad1;
    XcmsFloat pad2;
    XcmsFloat pad3;
} XcmsPad;
```

Example 7-16 shows a procedure that uses the TekHVC color space and **XcmsAlloc-
Color()** to allocate a number of colors with a given Hue and Chroma, and with perceptually uniform steps between a given maximum and a given minimum Value.

Example 7-16. Allocating device-independent colors

```
/*
 * This procedure allocates n colors with the given Hue and Chroma, and
 * with Values equally spaced between minv and maxv.  The pixels values
 * are returned in the passed array of pixels, which is assumed to be
 * large enough to hold them.  Returns XcmsFailure if one of the calls
 * to XcmsAllocColor returned XcmsFailure, otherwise XcmsSuccess.
 */
Status AllocShades(dpy, cmap, hue, chroma, minv, maxv, pixels, n)
Display *dpy;
Colormap cmap;
double hue, chroma, minv, maxv;
long *pixels;              /* RETURN */
int n;
{
    XcmsColor color;
    double value, deltav;
    int i;

    if (n > 1) deltav = (maxv - minv)/(n-1);
    else deltav = (maxv-minv);

    color.format = XcmsTekHVCFormat;
    color.spec.TekHVC.H = hue;
    color.spec.TekHVC.C = chroma;
    for(i = 0; i < n; i++) {
        color.spec.TekHVC.V = minv + i*deltav;
        if (XcmsAllocColor(dpy, cmap, &color, XcmsTekHVCFormat) == XcmsFailure)
            return XcmsFailure;
        pixels[i] = color.pixel;
    }
    return XcmsSuccess;
}
```

Color

Example 7-16 has one serious weakness: no checking is performed to ensure that the minimum and maximum Values passed to the procedure are valid. This is particularly important because the range of valid Values depends on both Hue and Chroma. If either of the specified Values is outside the boundaries of the TekHVC color space, or outside the gamut of the device being used, gamut compression will occur on the allocated colors. Later in this section, we develop a refinement to this example that allocates shades, all of which are within the gamut of the device.

7.9.3.2 Color Conversion

In X11R5, each colormap has a *color conversion context* automatically associated with it. A color conversion context, or CCC, is an opaque structure of type **XcmsCCC**. It contains the attributes that control the details of color conversion from one color space to another. These attributes include the procedure that is called to perform gamut compression when a device-independent color specification is outside the range of displayable colors for a particular device.

Xlib contains functions to create and destroy CCCs, set and get CCC attribute values, and associate a CCC with a colormap. Because the colorimetric theory behind these CCC attributes is beyond the scope of this chapter, these functions will not be described here. Many programmers will never have to use CCCs at all. Others may use CCCs, but will never use anything but the default CCC. This section describes the CCC functions that are useful to this second category of programmer.

Because every colormap has a CCC associated with it, all of the Xcms functions described so far have had an implicit CCC argument. The functions that will be described in the next section, however, do not require a colormap argument but are passed a CCC directly. For these functions, you may obtain the CCC of a colormap with the function **Xcms-CCCOfColormap( )**, or you may obtain the default CCC of a screen with **Xcms-DefaultCCC( )**.

The color conversion context controls the details of color conversions performed by other Xcms functions. It can also be used to control the explicit conversion of colors with the function **XcmsConvertColors( )**. This function takes a CCC as an argument, along with an array of **XcmsColor** structures and converts those colors to a single specified target format.

The functions **XcmsCCCOfColormap( )**, **XcmsDefaultCCC( )**, and **XcmsConvert-Colors( )** are documented in the reference section of this book. The remaining CCC functions are listed in Table 7-3. For information on these functions and an explanation of the CCC attributes, see Volume Two, *Xlib Reference Manual* or *The X Color Management System*.

Table 7-3. Other Color Conversion Context Functions

XcmsClientWhitePointOfCCC	XcmsScreenWhitePointOfCCC
XcmsCreateCCC	XcmsSetCCCOfColormap
XcmsDisplayOfCCC	XcmsSetCompressionProc
XcmsFreeCCC	XcmsSetWhiteAdjustProc
XcmsScreenNumberOfCCC	XcmsSetWhitePoint

7.9.3.3 Gamut-querying Functions

To make full use of a screen's color capability, some applications will want to explicitly query the gamut of a screen. Even programs that are not concerned with the precise boundaries of a screen's gamut may need to query the boundaries of an irregular color space to ensure that requested color specifications are legal for that space. In the TekHVC space, for example, the maximum value of Chroma varies with Hue, and the maximum and minimum legal Value varies with both Hue and Chroma. The functions described here can be used to verify that requested colors are legal for the color space, are within the device gamut, and can therefore be displayed as requested, without gamut compression.

The functions XcmsQueryBlack(), XcmsQueryWhite(), XcmsQueryRed(), XcmsQueryGreen(), and XcmsQueryBlue() return the device-independent color specification, in the desired format, of pure black, white, red, green, and blue. That is, they convert from the device-dependent colors RGBi:0.0/0.0/0.0, RGBi:1.0/1.0/1.0, RGBi:1.0/0.0/0.0, RGBi:0.0/1.0/0.0, and RGBi:0.0/0.0/1.0 to the specified color space. These functions are fully documented in the reference section at the end of this book.

The following functions are used to query the screen gamut in terms of the TekHVC color space:

XcmsTekHVCQueryMaxC()
> Determines the maximum displayable Chroma for a given Hue and Value.

XcmsTekHVCQueryMaxV()
> Determines the maximum displayable Value for a given Hue and Chroma.

XcmsTekHVCQueryMinV()
> Determines the minimum displayable Value for a given Hue and Chroma.

XcmsTekHVCQueryMaxVC()
> For a given Hue, determines the maximum displayable Chroma and the Value at which that Chroma is reached.

XcmsTekHVCQueryMaxVSamples()
> For a given Hue, partitions the displayable values of Chroma into a specified number of sampling intervals and determines the maximum value for each interval. This can be used to plot the boundaries of a screen's gamut at a given Hue.

These functions are fully documented in Volume Two, *Xlib Reference Manual*. Similar query functions exist for the CIELab and CIELuv color spaces, and are listed in Table 7-4. Because CIELab and CIELuv are analogous but less intuitive than the TekHVC space, those functions are not documented here. See Volume Two, *Xlib Reference Manual* or *The X Color Management System* for complete information.

Table 7-4. Gamut-querying Functions for the CIELab and CIELuv Color Spaces

CIELab Queries	CIELuv Queries
XcmsCIELabQueryMaxC	XcmsCIELuvQueryMaxC
XcmsCIELabQueryMaxL	XcmsCIELuvQueryMaxL
XcmsCIELabQueryMaxLC	XcmsCIELuvQueryMaxLC
XcmsCIELabQueryMinL	XcmsCIELuvQueryMinL

Example 7-17 is a refinement to Example 7-16. It queries the screen's gamut to determine the minimum and maximum displayable Values for the given Hue and Chroma and allocates a specified number of colors spaced at perceptually equal intervals between that minimum and maximum. If the specified Hue and Chroma are within the screen's gamut, this function will only allocate colors that do not require gamut compression.

Example 7-17. Querying the screen gamut and allocating colors

```
/*
 * This routine allocates n shades of the color with specified Hue and
 * Chroma.  The shades will be at perceptually equal intervals between
 * the minimum and maximum Values of the device gamut for the given Hue
 * and Chroma.
 */
Status AllocShades(dpy, cmap, hue, chroma, pixels, n)
Display *dpy;
Colormap cmap;
double hue, chroma;
long *pixels;          /* RETURN */
int n;
{
    XcmsColor color;
    XcmsCCC ccc;
    int i;
    double minv, maxv;
    double deltav;

    ccc = XcmsCCCOfColormap(dpy, cmap);

    if (XcmsTekHVCQueryMinV(ccc, hue, chroma, &color) == XcmsFailure)
        return XcmsFailure;
    else
        minv = color.spec.TekHVC.V;

    if (XcmsTekHVCQueryMaxV(ccc, hue, chroma, &color) == XcmsFailure)
        return XcmsFailure;
    else
        maxv = color.spec.TekHVC.V;
```

```
    if (n > 1) deltav = (maxv - minv)/(n-1);
    else deltav = maxv - minv;

    for(i=0; i < n; i++) {
        color.format = XcmsTekHVCFormat;
        color.spec.TekHVC.H = hue;
        color.spec.TekHVC.C = chroma;
        color.spec.TekHVC.V = minv + i*deltav;
        if (XcmsAllocColor(dpy, cmap, &color, XcmsRGBFormat) == XcmsFailure)
            return XcmsFailure;
        pixels[i] = color.pixel;
    }
    return XcmsSuccess;
}
```

7.10 Creating and Installing Colormaps

In discussing colormaps earlier in this chapter, we mentioned that there are hardware color-maps and virtual colormaps, but we did not discuss the ramifications of this fact.

A hardware colormap is a physical register from which the screen hardware reads the RGB intensity values that generate the colors on the screen. Most workstations have only one hardware colormap, in which case all windows on the screen are interpreted using the same colormap. Some high performance workstations have multiple hardware colormaps, in which case separate windows may have their own independent hardware colormaps.

If the hardware colormap cannot be changed, it is termed *immutable*. Monochrome systems normally have an immutable colormap, since it does little good to swap the two entries or make them both black or white. Some low-cost color systems and some X terminals have immutable hardware colormaps. The **StaticColor**, **StaticGray**, and **TrueColor** visuals are the only visuals that can possibly work on systems that have immutable hardware colormaps. In immutable colormaps, no client can allocate private colorcells and all RGB values are preset. On these systems, **XCreateColormap()** succeeds, but it just gives you another copy of the default colormap (or one of the default colormaps if there are multiple immutable colormaps). The application should check for this when creating colormaps.

On most color workstations, you can write new values into the hardware colormap or color-maps to change that mapping. These hardware colormaps are termed *changeable*. The **DirectColor**, **GrayScale**, and **PseudoColor** visuals are available only on systems that have changeable colormaps.

X manages multiple colormaps by keeping *virtual colormaps* in memory and installing them as instructed by the window manager. *Installing* a colormap is the process of moving a vir-tual colormap into the hardware colormap. Only installed colormaps are used to determine the colors appearing on the screen. When there is only one hardware colormap and a new virtual colormap is installed, the virtual colormap that was previously installed becomes *uninstalled*.

Up to this point in this chapter, we have been allocating colors out of the default colormap, which is created and installed when the server starts up. On the most common color workstations, with four to eight planes, it is quite easy for clients that require precise colors to allocate all the available colorcells. Virtual colormaps are a response to this problem. When a client cannot get the colorcells it needs from the installed colormap, it can create a new virtual one. The window manager will then install this virtual colormap when this application is in use.

When a virtual colormap is installed and there is only one hardware colormap, all the clients that used the old colormap will be displayed in false colors, since the pixel values in their windows will be interpreted according to the new colormap.

When an application creates a virtual colormap, it must set the colormap window attribute of its top-level window so that the window manager can find out what colormap to install. By default, this attribute indicates the default colormap. If its subwindows use different colormaps from the main window, there is a property that can be set to tell this to the window manager, as described in Chapter 12, *Interclient Communication*.

It is a hard rule that an application should never install its own colormaps. This is required by the current conventions described in Chapter 12.

By now you should be getting the idea that it is much better to arrange to share the default colormap with the other applications than to try to create one of your own. The only time when you should really need to create a special colormap is when you are doing smooth shading or similar applications that need many strangely distributed colors. On the other hand, creating a virtual colormap might be the only way to make your application that has demanding color needs work on a system that provides only a **PseudoColor** visual. On systems with multiple hardware colormaps, you can create your own colormap and have it installed without affecting other applications. You can use **XListInstalled-Colormaps()** to get information about how many colormaps are installed into the hardware.

7.10.1 Functions for Manipulating Colormaps

The following functions should be used by applications only if they need a special purpose colormap:

XCreateColormap() Creates a virtual colormap resource, either with no allocated entries or with all allocated read/write, that matches the passed visual. If no entries are allocated, they can be allocated either as read/write or as read-only cells. If all entries are allocated read/write, the colormap is completely private and just needs its colors set with **XStoreColors()**.

XFreeColormap() Uninstalls the specified virtual colormap and frees the resources associated with the colormap. Applications are allowed to use this. Sends a **ColormapNotify** event to any windows that were using the colormap.

```
XListInstalledColormaps()
```
> Lists the installed colormaps.

```
XCopyColormapAndFree()
```
> Moves all the client's existing colormap entries to a new colormap and frees those entries of the old colormap. This is used when colorcell allocation fails and some cells have already been allocated. It saves needing to create a colormap and start from the beginning allocating colors. For applications with special color needs that can't make do, they can call **XCopyColormapAndFree()**, set their colormap window attribute, and continue allocating colors in the new colormap where they left off.

`XSetWindowColormap()` Sets the colormap window attribute of a window.

The following functions are use by the window manager to install and uninstall colormaps:

`XInstallColormap()` A function only to be used by window managers to install a colormap. Any window using that colormap ID as its colormap attribute receives a **ColormapNotify** event.

`XUninstallColormap()` A function only to be used by window managers to uninstall a colormap. Removes a virtual colormap from the set of installed hardware colormaps. On systems with only one hardware colormap, the default colormap is reinstalled. Sends **ColormapNotify** event to windows that are using the specified map.

7.10.2 The ColormapNotify Event

ColormapNotify events notify an application when the colormap specified in the colormap attribute for a particular window has been installed, uninstalled, or freed or when the attribute itself has been changed. The former is used by applications, and the latter (attribute changes) by window managers.

If your application wants to know when your colormap is installed or uninstalled, it should watch for these events and act accordingly. To receive **ColormapNotify** events, pass **ColormapChangeMask** (ORed with the other masks you need) to **XSelectInput()**. Example 7-18 shows the **XColormapEvent** structure.

Example 7-18. The ColormapEvent structure

```
typedef struct {
    int type;
    unsigned long serial;    /* # of last request processed by server */
    Bool send_event;         /* True if this came from SendEvent
                              * request */
    Display *display;        /* Display the event was read from */
    Window window;
    Colormap colormap;       /* Colormap or None */
```

Example 7-18. The ColormapEvent structure (continued)

```
    Bool new;
    int state;                    /* ColormapInstalled, ColormapUninstalled */
} XColormapEvent;
```

Here is a brief explanation of each member of the **XColormapEvent** structure:

window
: The window for which this event was selected, whose colormap attribute was changed or whose colormap specified in that attribute was installed, uninstalled, or freed.

colormap
: The colormap associated with the window, either a colormap ID or the constant **None**. It will be **None** only if this event was in response to an **XFreeColormap()** call.

new
: **True** when the colormap attribute has been changed, or **False** when the colormap is installed or uninstalled.

state
: Either **ColormapInstalled** or **ColormapUninstalled**; it indicates whether the colormap is installed or uninstalled.

XFreeColormap(), **XInstallColormap()**, and **XUninstallColormap()** generate this event for windows that have their colormap attribute set to the colormap that was affected. **XSetWindowColormap()** and **XChangeWindowAttributes()** can also generate this event. From the information in the structure, you can tell which of these calls generated the event and what the current status of the colormap is. See Chapter 12, *Interclient Communication*, in this manual and Appendix L, *Interclient Communication Conventions*, of Volume Zero, *X Protocol Reference Manual* (as of the second printing) for an additional description of the conventions regarding colormaps.

7.10.3 The Required Colormap List

The X protocol specifies that each server can specify a required list of colormaps, which affects what happens when other colormaps are installed or uninstalled. Here is what the protocol specification says about the required list (translated into Xlib terms):

> At any time, there is a subset of the installed maps, viewed as an ordered list, called the required list. The length of the required list is at most **min_maps**, where **min_maps** is a member of the **Display** structure. The required list is maintained as follows. When a colormap is an explicit argument to **XInstallColormap()**, it is added to the head of the list, and the list is truncated at the tail if necessary to keep the length of the list to at most **min_maps**. When a colormap is an explicit argument to **XUninstallColormap()** and it is in the required list, it is removed from the list. A colormap is not added to the required list when it is installed implicitly by the server, and the server cannot implicitly uninstall a colormap that is in the required list.

In less precise words, the **min_maps** most recently installed maps are guaranteed to be installed. This number will often be one; clients needing multiple colormaps should beware.

7.11 Miscellaneous Color-handling Functions

The following miscellaneous functions provide additional ways to use the color database, to find out the RGB values in a colormap cell, and to free cells that are no longer needed:

XLookupColor()   Looks up a string color name in the color database and returns separate color structures containing the exact RGB values specified in the database for that name and the closest RGB values available on the hardware. This function does not look at any cells in the colormap, even though it has a *colormap* argument! This argument specifies which screen the color should be looked up on, which is relevant only if each screen has a different color characterization or color database. The difference between XLookupColor() and XParseColor() is that XParseColor() accepts the hexadecimal color specification (which XLookupColor() does not), while XLookupColor() returns the closest colors available on the hardware (which XParseColor() does not). XLookupColor() might be useful for making sure that user-specified colors are contrasting. There is also an Xcms version, XcmsLookupColor(), that is analogous to XLookupColor() except with different arguments and the Xcms version returns a device-independent color specification.

XQueryColor()   Fills an XColor structure with the RGB values corresponding to the colormap cell indicated by a pixel value. Also sets the flags member of the structure to (DoRed | DoGreen | DoBlue). The Xcms version, XcmsQueryColor(), translates the current RGB values in the colormap cell into a device-independent specification.

XQueryColors()   Fills multiple XColor structures with the RGB values and flags corresponding to the colormap cells indicated by a pixel values. Also sets each flags member to (DoRed | DoGreen | DoBlue). The Xcms version, XcmsQueryColors(), translates the current RGB values in the colormap cells into device-independent specifications.

XFreeColors()   Frees the colormap cells associated with the given pixel values and/or frees the given planes. Since all the colorcells an application allocates are freed when the application exits, this routine is needed only when an application is finished with cells before it exits. Freeing a read/write colorcell makes that cell available to other applications. Freeing a read-only cell may make the cell unallocated, but only if no other application is sharing that cell.

8

Events

This chapter is another must-read. Events are central to X. The fundamental framework for handling events was given in Chapter 3, but this chapter gives much more detail, both on selecting events for a window and on handling them when they arrive. It discusses each of the masks used to select events; for a description of the event structures themselves, see Appendix E.

In This Chapter:

8
Events

An event, to quote the Oxford English Dictionary, is an "incident of importance" or a "consequence, result, or outcome." This definition holds for X. An event reports some device activity or is generated as a side effect of an Xlib routine.

From a programmer's point of view, an event reports:

- Something that your program needs to know about, such as user input or information available from other clients.

- Something your program is doing that other clients need to know about, such as making text available for pasting to another client.

- Something the window manager needs to know, such as a request by your program for a change to the layout of the screen by mapping a window.

Programming with events is quite different from traditional methods of programming for input. You cannot simply wait for a user to type something and expect nothing else to happen in the meantime. Other programs are running concurrently and sharing the same system resources including the screen. They can affect your program. What happens if another window is placed over yours in the middle of the instruction your user is typing? The program must be able to listen to several types of events at once and jump back and forth when acting on them. Events imply a philosophy that the program should respond to the user's actions, not the other way around. Events make this type of programming straightforward.

Events occur asynchronously and get queued for each client that requested them. It is possible for more than one client to get copies of the same event. Usually a program handles each one in turn and performs the appropriate action before reading the next one. But there is usually no way for a program to predict in what order it will find the events on the queue.

This chapter covers events in detail, going further than the introduction to events in Chapter 2, *X Concepts*. Here we discuss the event union and structure types, the selection and propagation of events, how each event type is usually used, how events are received and handled in a program, and how they are sent by one client to another.

After you have read and understood this chapter, see Chapter 9, *The Keyboard and Pointer*, which demonstrates how to use events to handle the user's input, and Appendix E, *Event Reference*, which describes all the event types in a reference format.

8.1 Overview of Event Handling

There are three important steps in a program's handling of events. First, the program selects the events it wants for each window. Then it maps the windows. Finally, it provides an event loop which reads events from the event queue as they occur.

This process is quite simple, the only complication being the variety of events that may occur, each perhaps having a different meaning when it occurs in a different window. You have to know every circumstance in which a particular event is generated and make sure that your program does the right thing with it. But you will not need to understand the details of every event in order to begin using the most important ones.

The easiest way to select events is to call **XSelectInput()** for each window that you want to receive events. You can also set the **event_mask** attribute directly with **XChangeWindowAttributes()** or **XCreateWindow()**. You specify a mask which specifies which event types you want, combining any number of the event mask symbols with the bitwise OR operator (|).

You must make sure that every window that is to receive events appears on the screen after the events are selected for that window but before the event loop begins. Otherwise, the client will miss the first **Expose** event that triggers the drawing of the window's contents. For top-level windows, the client might also miss the **ConfigureNotify** event that reports the size of the window granted by the window manager. For a window to appear on the screen, it must be mapped and all its ancestors must be mapped. It is permissible to map all the windows except the top-level ones at any time, but the mapping of children of the root window must be done between the **XSelectInput()** call and the routine that gets events for the event loop.

A simple event loop was shown in Chapter 3, *Basic Window Program*. The only difference between this loop and the loops in real clients is in the number of different event types handled and the complexity of each branch.

Even though selection of events must be done first, we are going to start by describing how to handle events once you have them, because there are fewer details involved. We will return to the exact procedure for selecting events and the meaning of each event mask symbol in Section 8.3.

8.2 Event Processing

This section describes what an event type is and what an event structure contains, reviews how the event queue stores events and how a program reads events from it, and summarizes all the routines that can be used to get events.

8.2.1 The Event Structures

An event is implemented as a packet of information stored in a structure. The simplest event structure is shown in Example 8-1.

Example 8-1. The XAnyEvent structure

```
typedef struct {
        int type;               /* The type of event */
        unsigned long serial;   /* # of last request processed by server */
        Bool send_event;        /* True if sent from a SendEvent request */
        Display *display;       /* Display the event was read from */
        Window window;          /* Window that receives event */
} XAnyEvent;
```

There are 30 different event structures. Virtually all of them have the members shown in the `XAnyEvent` structure. Most of the event structures also contain various additional members that provide useful information for clients. The first member of every event structure, `type`, indicates the type of event. We will come back to the type in Section 8.2.2. The `serial` member identifies the last protocol request processed by the server, for use in debugging. The `send_event` flag indicates whether this event was sent from the server (`False`) or from another client (`True`). Other clients can send events with `XSend-Event()`, as described in Section 8.4.

Many of the event structures also have a `display` member or a `root` member or both. The `display` member identifies the connection to the server that this event came from. (Some applications connect with more than one server.) The `root` member indicates the screen on which the event occurred (a server may control more than one screen). Most programs only use a single screen and therefore do not need to worry about the `root` member. The `display` member can be useful for passing the display variable into routines by simply passing a pointer to the event structure.

Most event structures also have a `window` member, which indicates the window that selected and received the event. This is the window where the event arrives if it is a keyboard or pointer event and has propagated through the hierarchy, as described in Section 8.3.2. One event type may have two different meanings to a client, depending on which window the event appears in.

8.2.2 Event Types and XEvent Union

All the event structures are padded when necessary to be the same size. The `XEvent` union contains all the event structures, as shown in Example 8-2.* The first member of the `XEvent` union is the type of event. Each event structure within the `XEvent` union also begins with the type of event. A client determines the type of event by looking at the `type` member of `XEvent`. Then the client branches to specific code for that event type. After the initial determination of the event type, only the event structure containing the specific information for each event type should be used in each branch. For example, assuming you have

---

*See a C language tutorial or reference manual if you are unfamiliar with unions.

declared an **XEvent** variable called **report**, the **report.xexpose** structure should be used within the branch for **Expose** events. This lets you use the fields unique to the **Expose** event structure.

The value of **type** is any one of the constants listed in the center column of Table 8-3, presented later in this chapter. After determining the event type, you know which event structure from the **XEvent** union contains specific information about the event. You can then use the appropriate event structure name, such as **xkey**, to access the specific information unique to that event structure. The event structure name is also shown on each event reference page in Appendix E, *Event Reference*.

Example 8-2. The XEvent union

```
typedef union _XEvent {
     int type;          /* Must not be changed; first member */
     XAnyEvent xany;
     XKeyEvent xkey;
     XButtonEvent xbutton;
     XMotionEvent xmotion;
     XCrossingEvent xcrossing;
     XFocusChangeEvent xfocus;
     XKeymapEvent xkeymap;
     XExposeEvent xexpose;
     XNoExposeEvent xnoexpose;
     XGraphicsExposeEvent xgraphicsexpose;
     XVisibilityEvent xvisibility;
     XCreateWindowEvent xcreatewindow;
     XDestroyWindowEvent xdestroywindow;
     XUnmapEvent xunmap;
     XMapEvent xmap;
     XMappingEvent xmapping;
     XMapRequestEvent xmaprequest;
     XReparentEvent xreparent;
     XConfigureEvent xconfigure;
     XGravityEvent xgravity;
     XResizeRequestEvent xresizerequest;
     XConfigureRequestEvent xconfigurerequest;
     XCirculateEvent xcirculate;
     XCirculateRequestEvent xcirculaterequest;
     XPropertyEvent xproperty;
     XSelectionClearEvent xselectionclear;
     XSelectionRequestEvent xselectionrequest;
     XSelectionEvent xselection;
     XColormapEvent xcolormap;
     XClientMessageEvent xclient;
} XEvent;
```

8.2.3 Xlib's Event Queue

The event structures are placed on an event queue in the order they occur, so that the program can read them and act accordingly. As shown in Figure 8-1, the server maintains one event queue, on which all events are placed, and distributes events to the Xlib in each client. The events in the server's queue are periodically transferred over the network to the Xlib queues. Two clients can receive copies of the same events if they each select them.

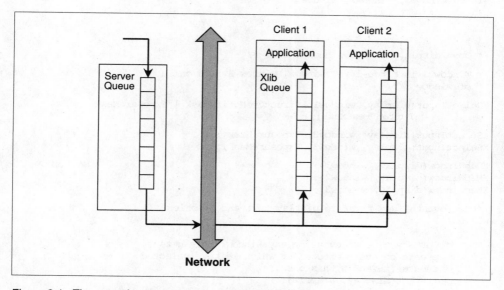

Figure 8-1. The server's event queue and client's event queue

The client sets up an event-receiving loop to handle the events that arrive on its event queue. There are several routines a client can use to get events. They differ in how many windows they monitor, how many types of events they look for, and whether they wait for events to appear before returning. For a description of the event-getting routines, see Section 8.2.6.

8.2.4 Writing the Event Loop

In *basicwin* (the example program in Chapter 3, *Basic Window Program*), you have already seen the structure of the code you should write to handle events. In a more complex application, the code for each event type will simply be divided according to the values in the members in each event structure. Usually, the next branch after the event type will test the window in which the event occurred.

The branch for **Expose** events in Example 8-3 demonstrates how an event might be handled when there are several windows involved. The example also notes when each of the selected events—and the events that may be delivered without your selecting them—should be handled within your event loop. Depending on your application, other events might need to be handled as well.

Notice how the specific event structure names such as **xexpose** are used to access information in the event structures.

Example 8-3. An event-handling loop

```
XEvent report;
Window window1, window2, window3;
     .
     .
     .

/* Open display, create windows, etc. */

/* Window 1 is a top-level window, window 2 is a child
 * of window 1 */

XSelectInput(display, window1, StructureNotifyMask | ExposureMask
        | ButtonPressMask);

XSelectInput(display, window2, ExposureMask);
XSelectInput(display, window3, ExposureMask);

XMapWindow(display, window1);
XMapWindow(display, window2);
XMapWindow(display, window3);

/* Get events, use first to display text and graphics */
while (1)
{
    /* Get any type of event on any window; this gets
     * events on every window for which we have selected
     * events (three in this case) */
    XNextEvent(display, &report);

    switch (report.type)  {
    case Expose:
        printf("got an Expose event\n");
        /* Redraw contents of windows; note that we can't
         * use switch because window IDs are not constant */
        if (report.xexpose.window == window1)
            /* Redraw window 1 */;
        else if (report.xexpose.window == window2)
            /* Redraw window 2 */;
        else (report.xexpose.window == window3)
            /* Redraw window 3 */;
        break;
    case ButtonPress:
        printf("got a ButtonPress event\n");
        /* Respond to buttonpress, probably depending on
         * which window is reported in report.xbutton.window */
        break;
    case ConfigureNotify:
        printf("got a ConfigureNotify event\n");
        /* Window was resized, moved, or restacked or border
         * width was changed; reset application variables
         * so Expose branch will scale graphics properly */
        break;
```

Example 8-3. An event-handling loop (continued)

```
        case MappingNotify:
            printf("got a MappingNotify event\n");
            /* Keyboard or Pointer mapping was changed by another
             * client; if keyboard, should call XRefreshKeyboardMapping,
             * unless keyboard events are not used */
            break;
        case ClientMessage:
            printf("got a ClientMessage event\n");
            /* Primarily used for transferring selection data,
             * also might be used in a private interclient
             * protocol; otherwise, not needed in event loop */
            break;
        case SelectionClear:
            printf("got a SelectionClear event\n");
            /* If this application previously called
             * XSetSelectionOwner, it may get this event;
             * otherwise, you don't need it in your
             * event loop */
            break;
        case SelectionNotify:
            printf("got a SelectionNotify event\n");
            /* If this application calls XConvertSelection,
             * it will get this event; otherwise, you don't
             * need it in your event loop */
            break;
        case SelectionRequest:
            printf("got a SelectionRequest event\n");
            /* If this application previously called
             * XSetSelectionOwner, it may get this event;
             * otherwise, you don't need it in your
             * event loop */
            break;
        case GraphicsExpose:
            /* Fall through into NoExpose */
        case NoExpose:
            printf("got a GraphicsExpose or NoExpose event\n");
            /* If this application calls XCopyArea or XCopyPlane
             * and the graphics_exposures member of the GC is
             * True and the source is a window, these events may
             * be generated; handle GraphicsExpose like Expose */
        default:
            printf("Event being thrown away\n");
            /* All *Notify events except ConfigureNotify will
             * be thrown away; they are not needed by most
             * applications but are sent because ConfigureNotify
             * can't be selected independently */
            break;
    }   /* End switch on event type */
}  /* End while (1) */
```

The **XNextEvent()** routine gets the next event on the queue for our client or waits until one appears before returning. There are many other routines that get events of particular types, in particular windows, with or without waiting for the event to appear. These routines are described in Section 8.2.6.

Events

The first member of the **XEvent** report contains the type of event. This information is used in a "switch" statement to branch according to the event type. Once the type is known, the specific event structure is known, and its contents can be accessed. For example, the width of the exposed area in the window is contained in the **XExposeEvent** structure as **report.xexpose.width**, where **report** is the **XEvent** variable, **xexpose** is the member of the **XEvent** union, and **width** is a member of the **XExposeEvent** structure type.

8.2.5 Printing the Event Type

We recommend that you print the event type and perhaps other event information in each branch of the event loop while you are in the application debugging stage. Be very careful that the loop handles all the events that can occur and that the Xlib routine you choose to get events is capable of getting all the events you need. If your program hangs and cannot be interrupted with CTRL-C, it is probably waiting for an event that you did not select. For example, you may have called **XMaskEvent()** with a mask of **ButtonReleaseMask** but you did not select **ButtonReleaseMask** in the **XSelectEvent()** call. The event-getting routines do not check to make sure you have selected the events you are requesting.

Instead of printing the event type as a number which you then have to interpret using the *<X11/X.h>* include file, you can have your program print the real name of the event. Example 8-4 creates an include file containing an array of strings spelling out the event type names. Example 8-5 then prints the correct event name.

Example 8-4. An include file for printing the event type — eventnames.h

```
static char *event_names[ ] = {
        "",
        "",
        "KeyPress",
        "KeyRelease",
        "ButtonPress",
        "ButtonRelease",
        "MotionNotify",
        "EnterNotify",
        "LeaveNotify",
        "FocusIn",
        "FocusOut",
        "KeymapNotify",
        "Expose",
        "GraphicsExpose",
        "NoExpose",
        "VisibilityNotify",
        "CreateNotify",
        "DestroyNotify",
        "UnmapNotify",
        "MapNotify",
        "MapRequest",
        "ReparentNotify",
        "ConfigureNotify",
        "ConfigureRequest",
```

```
    "GravityNotify",
    "ResizeRequest",
    "CirculateNotify",
    "CirculateRequest",
    "PropertyNotify",
    "SelectionClear",
    "SelectionRequest",
    "SelectionNotify",
    "ColormapNotify",
    "ClientMessage",
    "MappingNotify"
};
```

Note that *eventnames.h* is not a standard include file but one we have written for the purpose of printing the event type more legibly. You could use a similar method to identify windows, but since their IDs are not constants, you would need to load the array dynamically after you have created the windows.

Example 8-5 demonstrates printing an event using the include file shown in Example 8-4.

Example 8-5. Printing the event type

```
#ifdef DEBUG
#include "eventnames.h"
#endif

XEvent event;
XNextEvent(display, &event);

#ifdef DEBUG
fprintf(stderr, "winman: got a %s event\n", event_name[event.type]);
#endif
```

8.2.6 Routines that Get Events

There are several functions that get event structures from the queue. They differ in the following respects:

- The number of windows they monitor (whether they inspect the **window** member).

- Whether they look for particular event types.

- Whether the event is removed from the queue when it is read.

- Whether a routine you write is used to determine whether the event should be returned.

- Whether Xlib waits until an event meeting the criteria arrives or immediately returns a success or failure code.

- Whether the connection to the server is flushed to see if any more events become available.

Events

The following is a list of the event-handling routines and their differences. In all of these routines, you pass a pointer to an **XEvent** structure to be filled.

XNextEvent( )   Gets the next event of any type on any window. This function flushes the request buffer if Xlib's queue does not contain an event and waits for an event to arrive from the server connection.

XMaskEvent( )   Gets the next event matching the specified mask on any window. This function flushes the request buffer if Xlib's queue does not contain a matching event and waits for a matching event to arrive from the server connection.

XCheckMaskEvent( )   Behaves like **XMaskEvent( )** but immediately returns **False** if there is no matching event in Xlib's queue and none could be read from the server connection after flushing the request buffer. Returns **True** if a matching event was found.

XWindowEvent( )   Gets the next event matching both the specified mask and the specified window. This function flushes the request buffer if Xlib's queue does not contain a matching event and waits for a matching event to arrive from the server connection.

XCheckWindowEvent( )   Behaves like **XWindowEvent** but immediately returns **False** if there is no matching event in Xlib's queue and none could be read from the server connection after flushing the request buffer. Returns **True** if a matching event was found.

XIfEvent( )   Looks for an event on the queue that matches the conditions set by a user-supplied predicate procedure. This function flushes the request buffer if Xlib's queue does not contain a matching event and waits for a matching event to arrive from the server connection.

XCheckIfEvent( )   Behaves like **XIfEvent( )** but immediately returns **False** if there is no matching event in Xlib's queue and none could be read from the server connection after flushing the request buffer. Returns **True** if a matching event was found.

XPeekEvent( )   Gets the next event of any type from any window without removing the event from the queue. This function flushes the request buffer if Xlib's queue is empty and waits for an event to arrive from the server connection.

XPeekIfEvent( )   Gets the next event that matches the specified predicate procedure, without removing the event from the queue. This function flushes the request buffer if Xlib's queue does not contain a matching event and waits for a matching event to arrive from the server connection.

| XCheckTypedEvent() | Searches the queue from the oldest event for the desired event type, without discarding all those searched that do not match. If no matching event is found in Xlib's queue, this function flushes the request buffer and returns **False**. |

| XCheckTypedWindowEvent() | |
| | Searches the queue from the oldest event for the desired window and event type, without discarding those searched that do not match. If no matching event is found in Xlib's queue, this function flushes the request buffer and returns **False**. |

| XEventsQueued() | Returns the number of events on the queue but has three modes that specify what else is done. All three modes count the events already in Xlib's queue and return if there are any. **QueuedAlready** returns even if there are not any events in the queue. **QueuedAfterFlush** flushes the request buffer and attempts to read more events from the connection before returning. **QueuedAfterReading** attempts to read more events from the connection without flushing the buffer. |

| XPending() | Returns the number of events on the queue. If there are none, it flushes the request buffer and tries another count. This is identical to **XEventsQueued()** with mode **QueuedAfterFlush**. |

| XPutBackEvent() | Puts an event you supply back on Xlib's queue, so that it will be the next to be received by **XNextEvent()**. |

| XGetMotionEvents() | Gets all the motion events that occurred on the specified window in a specified time period. Motion history buffers were implemented for the first time in the R5 sample servers from MIT. An application should check to see if **XDisplayMotionBufferSize(display) == 0**, which indicates that motion history buffer is not supported. |

| XQLength() | Returns the number of events on the queue, without flushing the request buffer. |

Note that the functions that have mask arguments do not return non-maskable events (MappingNotify, Selection events, and ClientMessage).

You may notice that there are two broad categories of routines that get input: those that wait for a matching event and those that do not wait. The latter may be used in porting applications that use the "polling" style of programming, which checks to see if input has arrived at regular intervals by continuously calling a "polling" function in a loop. Given the choice, however, it is much better to use the routines that wait for events as much as possible, since this technique does not waste processor cycles. This is true event-*driven* programming.

Table 8-1 organizes the event-receiving functions according to whether they wait for events if none are present on Xlib's queue.

Table 8-1. Event-getting Routines

Event Specifications	Desired Result		
	Wait if necessary	Return **False** immediately if none queued	Leave in queue (may wait)
Any event	XNextEvent	n/a	XPeekEvent
With predicate	XIfEvent	XCheckIfEvent	XPeekIfEvent
For window	XWindowEvent	XCheckWindowEvent	n/a
For event mask	XMaskEvent	XCheckMaskEvent	n/a
For type	n/a	XCheckTypedEvent	n/a
For window and type	n/a	XCheckTypedWindow-Event	n/a

Note that most of the routines apparently missing from Xlib according to Table 8-1 can be simulated with other routines and fairly simple code. The hole on the top row can be filled by calling **XCheckMaskEvent()** with a mask set to all 1's. For the four routines missing in the last column, you can write a predicate procedure and call **XPeekIfEvent()**. An example predicate procedure is shown in Example 8-6. The two routines missing in the first column can also be replaced with a predicate procedure and **XIfEvent()**.

The event-getting routines with **Check** in their names are useful for programs that need to poll for input to handle interrupts. To illustrate the handling of interrupts, let's say you have a routine in a program that performs a complex, lengthy calculation like a Fourier transform. You want to be able to abort the calculation midway. Therefore, you need to be able to check the keyboard to see if a CTRL-C or other interrupt character has been typed. You also might want to provide for exposure events during the long wait, though you might be able to get away without this provision. This would be a good application for **XCheckTyped-Event()** or **XCheckTypedWindowEvent()**, since these routines poll without waiting if no events can be read. When an event does arrive, you can decide from the type or window whether to bother processing it.

8.2.7 Predicate Procedures

The routines **XCheckIfEvent()**, **XIfEvent()**, and **XPeekIfEvent()** allow you to supply a procedure that returns **True** or **False** depending on some characteristic of the event. You would use one of these routines if you have a matching algorithm that is compli-cated or simply to enable you to clear up the code by putting some of the event processing in a separate routine.

Your predicate procedure is called with the same arguments as the event-getting routine (except for the predicate procedure pointer, of course). Example 8-6 shows a predicate pro-cedure and the **XIfEvent()** call that uses it. This code would normally use **XNext-Event()**, but we have substituted **XIfEvent()** so that we can filter out button events on buttons other than button 1. This predicate procedure returns **True** for all events except the undesirable button events.

Example 8-6. A predicate procedure and XIfEvent() call

```
void main(argc, argv)
int argc;
char **argv;
{
        .
        .
        .

        Bool predproc();
        static char *stuff = "do this or that";
        .
        .
        .

        XSelectInput(display, wint, ExposureMask | ButtonPressMask
                | ButtonReleaseMask | ButtonMotionMask
                | PointerMotionHintMask);
        .
        .
        .

        while (1)  {
                XIfEvent(display, &report, predproc, stuff);
                switch (report.type) {
        /* Note that no code here for eliminating button
         * events on other buttons, because only button
         * one events are returned by XIfEvent */
                case ButtonPress:
                        points[index].x = report.xbutton.x;
                        points[index].y = report.xbutton.y;
                        break;
                case ButtonRelease:
                        index++;
                        points[index].x = report.xbutton.x;
                        points[index].y = report.xbutton.y;
                        break;
                        .
                        .
                        .

                }
        }
}
Bool predproc(display, event, arg)
Display *display;
XEvent *event;
char *arg;
{
        printf("The arg is %s\n", arg);
        switch (event->type) {
                case Expose:
                case MotionNotify:
                case ConfigureNotify:
                case KeyPress:
                        return(True);
                        break;
                case ButtonPress:
                case ButtonRelease:
                        if (event->xbutton.button == Button1)
```

Example 8-6. A predicate procedure and XIfEvent() call (continued)

```
                                return(True);
                    else
                                return(False);
                    break;
                default:
        }
}
```

8.3 Selecting Events

For each window, a client must select which event types it wants placed in its queue when they occur in that window. This is normally done with **XSelectInput()**, which sets the **event_mask** attribute of a window. The client need not select events on all of its windows, only those in which it wants to see the events that occur.

To select event types for a window, pass an **event_mask** as an argument to **XSelect-Input()** or set the **event_mask** member of the **XSetWindowAttributes** structure and call **XChangeWindowAttributes()** or **XCreateWindow()**. (For more information on the **XSetWindowAttributes** structure, see Section 4.1.)

The **event_mask** is formed by combining the event mask symbols listed in the first column of Table 8-2 with the bitwise OR operator (|). Each mask symbol sets a bit in the **event_mask**.

Table 8-2 also describes briefly the circumstances under which you would want to specify each symbol. You will need to read about each mask in Section 8.3.3; see the examples using the events in Chapter 9, *The Keyboard and Pointer*, and throughout this manual; and look at the event structures in Appendix E, *Event Reference*, before you will really understand when to use each of these symbols.

Table 8-2. Event Mask Definitions

Event Mask Symbol	Circumstances
NoEventMask	No events
KeyPressMask	Keyboard down events
KeyReleaseMask	Keyboard up events
ButtonPressMask	Pointer button down events
ButtonReleaseMask	Pointer button up events
EnterWindowMask	Pointer window entry events
LeaveWindowMask	Pointer window leave events
PointerMotionMask	All pointer motion events
PointerMotionHintMask	Fewer pointer motion events
Button1MotionMask	Pointer motion while button 1 down
Button2MotionMask	Pointer motion while button 2 down
Button3MotionMask	Pointer motion while button 3 down

Table 8-2. Event Mask Definitions (continued)

Event Mask Symbol	Circumstances
Button4MotionMask	Pointer motion while button 4 down
Button5MotionMask	Pointer motion while button 5 down
ButtonMotionMask	Pointer motion while any button down
KeymapStateMask	Any keyboard state change on EnterNotify, LeaveNotify, FocusIn or FocusOut
ExposureMask	Any exposure (except GraphicsExpose and NoExpose)
VisibilityChangeMask	Any change in visibility
StructureNotifyMask	Any change in window configuration.
ResizeRedirectMask	Redirect resize of this window
SubstructureNotifyMask	Notify about reconfiguration of children
SubstructureRedirectMask	Redirect reconfiguration of children
FocusChangeMask	Any change in keyboard focus
PropertyChangeMask	Any change in property
ColormapChangeMask	Any change in colormap
OwnerGrabButtonMask	Modifies handling of pointer events

The do_not_propagate_mask window attribute is formed in the same way as event_mask but can only be set with XChangeWindowAttributes() or XCreateWindow(). Its function is described in Section 8.3.2.

Example 8-7 shows how to set the event_mask and call XSelectInput().

Example 8-7. An example of selecting input

```
Display display;
Window window;
unsigned long event_mask;
    .
    .
    .
/* Must open display, create window, etc. */

/* Select key events */
event_mask = ExposureMask | KeyPressMask | KeyReleaseMask;
XSelectInput(display, window, event_mask);

/* Map window after selecting */

/* Get events */
```

In Example 8-7, events are selected *before* the window is mapped. This sequence is important, since otherwise the window will not receive the first Expose event that occurs after a new window is mapped and it will not know when to redraw the window. You will remember from *basicwin* that an Expose event signifies that a window has become visible and needs to be redrawn. Every Expose event, including the first, should trigger the drawing of the window's contents.

Events

Also, note that you cannot add to the selected events by calling `XSelectInput()` with a single additional mask. You must specify all the desired event masks every time you call it.

8.3.1 Correspondence Between Event Masks and Events

Each event mask symbol indicates that a certain type of event or group of event types should be queued when they occur. For example, when used alone as an *event_mask* argument to `XSelectInput()`, a `KeyPressMask` symbol indicates that only `KeyPress` events are desired. A `FocusChangeMask` symbol, on the other hand, indicates an interest in two types of events: `FocusIn` and `FocusOut`.

On the other hand, there is more than one event mask symbol for `MotionNotify` events; the different masks specify the conditions under which pointer motion events are desired. For example, if both `Button1MotionMask` and `Button3MotionMask` symbols are combined to form an *event_mask* argument to `XSelectInput()`, only one event type is requested: `MotionNotify` events. However, this event type will be queued only if the pointer moves while the first or third button (or both) is held down.

Table 8-3 lists each event mask, its associated event types, and the associated structure definition. The structures for each event type are described in Appendix E, *Event Reference*.

Table 8-3. Event Masks, Event Types, and Event Structures

Event Mask	Event Type	Structure
KeyPressMask	KeyPress	XKeyPressedEvent
KeyReleaseMask	KeyRelease	XKeyReleasedEvent
ButtonPressMask	ButtonPress	XButtonPressedEvent
ButtonReleaseMask	ButtonRelease	XButtonReleasedEvent
OwnerGrabButtonMask	n/a	n/a
KeymapStateMask	KeymapNotify	XKeymapEvent
PointerMotionMask PointerMotionHintMask ButtonMotionMask Button1MotionMask Button2MotionMask Button3MotionMask Button4MotionMask Button5MotionMask	MotionNotify	XPointerMovedEvent
EnterWindowMask	EnterNotify	XEnterWindowEvent
LeaveWindowMask	LeaveNotify	XLeaveWindowEvent
FocusChangeMask	FocusIn FocusOut	XFocusInEvent XFocusOutEvent
ExposureMask	Expose	XExposeEvent

Table 8-3. Event Masks, Event Types, and Event Structures (continued)

Event Mask	Event Type	Structure
(Selected in GC by graphics_expose member)	GraphicsExpose NoExpose	XGraphicsExposeEvent XNoExposeEvent
ColormapChangeMask	ColormapNotify	XColormapEvent
PropertyChangeMask	PropertyNotify	XPropertyEvent
VisibilityChangeMask	VisibilityNotify	XVisibilityEvent
ResizeRedirectMask	ResizeRequest	XResizeRequestEvent
StructureNotifyMask	CirculateNotify ConfigureNotify DestroyNotify GravityNotify MapNotify ReparentNotify UnmapNotify	XCirculateEvent XConfigureEvent XDestroyWindowEvent XGravityEvent XMapEvent XReparentEvent XUnmapEvent
SubstructureNotifyMask	CirculateNotify ConfigureNotify CreateNotify DestroyNotify GravityNotify MapNotify ReparentNotify UnmapNotify	XCirculateEvent XConfigureEvent XCreateWindowEvent XDestroyWindowEvent XGravityEvent XMapEvent XReparentEvent XUnmapEvent
SubstructureRedirectMask	CirculateRequest ConfigureRequest MapRequest	XCirculateRequestEvent XConfigureRequestEvent XMapRequestEvent
(Always selected)	MappingNotify	XMappingEvent
(Always selected)	ClientMessage	XClientMessageEvent
(Always selected)	SelectionClear	XSetSelectClearEvent
(Always selected)	SelectionNotify	XSelectionEvent
(Always selected)	SelectionRequest	XSelectionRequestEvent

There is no event mask for several of the event types listed at the end of this table, because the X server or another client can send them to any client without them being selected. For example, MappingNotify indicates that the keyboard mapping (see Section 9.1.2.3) or pointer mapping has changed. This event is reported to all clients by the server when any client changes those mappings. The selection events are a means of interclient communication, where one client announces with an event that it has a selection of text or graphics available for pasting, and another client responds with an event specifying in what format it would like the information. Similarly, **ClientMessage** events are always selected because they are sent from one client directly to another using the **XSendEvent()** routine.

Also note that **SubstructureNotifyMask** and **StructureNotifyMask** select the same event types but on different windows. The former selects the events when they occur in any *child* of the window specified in the call to **XSelectEvent()**, and the latter only when they occur in the window specified. (These are perhaps the two least often used masks.)

8.3.2 Propagation of Device Events

The fifth member in almost every event structure, **window**, contains the ID of the window in which the event appears to have occurred. This is called the *event window*. For **Button-Press**, **ButtonRelease**, **KeyPress**, **KeyRelease**, and **MotionNotify** events, the event window is not necessarily the window in which the event originally happened, which is called the *source window*.

Which window is reported in the event on the queue depends on the results of propagation up through the window hierarchy and is controlled by the **event_mask** and **do_not_propagate_mask** window attributes.

The source window is the *lowest* visible window in the hierarchy that encloses the pointer when the device event occurs. It is also the *smallest* visible window enclosing the pointer. The **window** member of the event in the queue (the event window) will be the source window only if the **event_mask** attribute (set with **XSelectInput()**) of the source window selected the event's type.

If the event was not selected for the source window, then the event is sent to the parent and so on until the event arrives at an ancestor window that has selected the right event type. The ID of this window is then placed in the **window** member of the event structure and that structure is placed on the queue for this client. Once a window that has selected the event is found, the event no longer propagates. If no window selected the event anywhere in the hierarchy up to and including the root window, the server never sends the event.

The **do_not_propagate_mask** window attribute also gets involved in this process. When an event arrives at a window but finds it has not been selected, the **do_not_propagate_mask** determines whether the event will be sent to ancestor windows. By default, all events that can propagate do. If the mask for the event type that occurred is included in the **do_not_propagate_mask**, the event is never sent.

Figures 8-4a, 8-4b, and 8-4c demonstrate the propagation of an event through the hierarchy, given three different **event_mask** and **do_not_propagate** attribute settings.

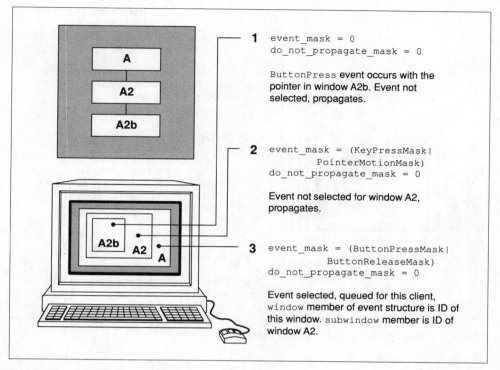

1 `event_mask = 0`
`do_not_propagate_mask = 0`

`ButtonPress` **event occurs with the pointer in window A2b. Event not selected, propagates.**

2 `event_mask = (KeyPressMask|`
`         PointerMotionMask)`
`do_not_propagate_mask = 0`

Event not selected for window A2, propagates.

3 `event_mask = (ButtonPressMask|`
`         ButtonReleaseMask)`
`do_not_propagate_mask = 0`

Event selected, queued for this client, `window` **member of event structure is ID of this window.** `subwindow` **member is ID of window A2.**

Figure 8-2a. One possible selection scheme

The `do_not_propagate_mask` is rarely used. However, here is one scenario in which setting the `do_not_propagate_mask` attribute would be useful. Consider an application with two windows, a parent and a child. The program lets the user draw in the child by moving the pointer while holding down a pointer button. However, like *basicwin*, the application exits on a **ButtonPress** event in the parent window. Since **ButtonPress** events are not selected in the child window, they will be propagated to the parent and will cause the application to exit. But a **ButtonPress** is necessary because we want the drawing in the child window to occur only when a button is held. By setting the `do_not_propagate_mask` attribute of the child window to **ButtonPressMask**, this problem is solved.

Events

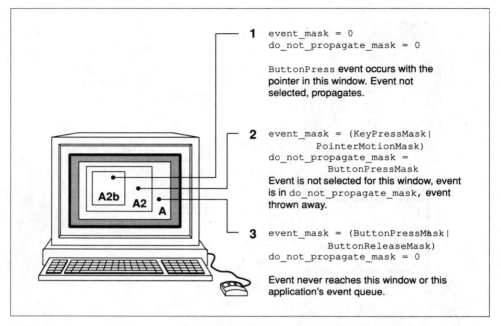

Figure 8-2b. Another possible selection scheme

Here's an example of where event propagation requires care in selecting events. Imagine a program that creates one large window and a small subwindow. The large window takes `ButtonPress` events to exit, and the small subwindow draws dots whenever the pointer is moved with a button held down. If you select `ButtonPressMask` alone for the parent, and `ButtonMotionMask` alone for the child, it does not work! The reason is that when the `ButtonPress` occurs, it propagates to the parent, and initiates a grab of all pointer events. (This is an automatic grab, discussed in the next section, not the result of an `XGrabButton()` or `XGrabPointer()` call). Since the parent did not select motion events, no `MotionNotify` events are received by the program. The moral of the story is that if a parent (or any ancestor) selects `ButtonPress` events, then its children must also select `ButtonPress` events in order for the children to get any other type of pointer events (including `MotionNotify`, `EnterNotify`, `LeaveNotify`).

NOTE

For brevity, we need conventions for describing the distribution of events. We'll say that an event is *sent* to a window when it is generated in that window either because of device action or as a side effect to an Xlib routine. A window *receives* an event sent to it only if the window has selected that event type or if the event type is always selected. Only when a window *receives* an event is it placed on the queue for that client.

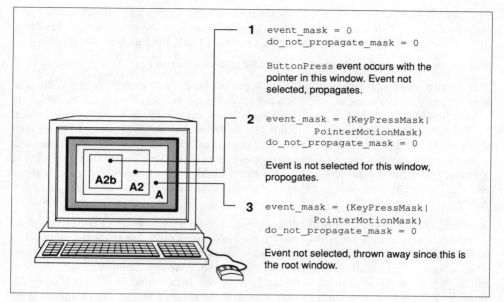

```
1   event_mask = 0
    do_not_propagate_mask = 0

    ButtonPress event occurs with the
    pointer in this window. Event not
    selected, propagates.

2   event_mask = (KeyPressMask|
              PointerMotionMask)
    do_not_propagate_mask = 0

    Event is not selected for this window,
    propogates.

3   event_mask = (KeyPressMask|
              PointerMotionMask)
    do_not_propagate_mask = 0

    Event not selected, thrown away since this is
    the root window.
```

Figure 8-2c. Yet another possible selection scheme

Another convention is helpful in describing the selection of events. We will say that "the window has selected that event type" rather than the more cumbersome "the program has called **XSelectInput()**, specifying the window and the mask that selects that event type."

We have described the way device events propagate normally. But two other actions can modify this operation: changing the keyboard focus window or grabbing the keyboard or pointer. Not only do these change the distribution of normal events, they create new events as side effects. We'll just introduce these here and return to them in Chapter 9, *The Keyboard and Pointer*.

8.3.2.1 The Keyboard Focus Window

The keyboard focus window affects the distribution of **KeyPress** and **KeyRelease** events. Normally, the window manager allows the user to specify which window, if any, should be the keyboard focus. Only the focus window and its descendants receive keyboard input, and within them, event propagation occurs normally. Events occurring outside the focus window are delivered to the focus window. By default, the focus window is the root and keyboard events are normally distributed to all windows on the screen, since all the windows on a screen are descendants of the root.

The keyboard focus is set to a window with **XSetInputFocus()**. The focus window must be viewable.* If it is not viewable or later becomes not viewable, the focus reverts to another window specified in the **XSetInputFocus()** call, the *revert_to* window.

The current focus window can be read with **XGetInputFocus()**.

FocusOut events are delivered to the old focus window, and **FocusIn** events to the window which receives the focus. Windows in between these two windows in the hierarchy are said to be virtually crossed and receive focus change events depending on the relationship and direction of transfer between the origin and destination windows. Some or all of the windows between the window containing the pointer at the time of the focus change and that window's root can also receive focus change events. By checking the **detail** member of **FocusIn** and **FocusOut** events, a client can tell which of its windows can receive input. See Chapter 9, *The Keyboard and Pointer*, for more information about tracking the keyboard focus.

Applications should set the keyboard focus to one of their own windows only when absolutely necessary, because this will prevent other clients from receiving keyboard events. It is permissible for clients to set the focus window when the mouse enters their top-level window, as long as they set it back to the root window when the pointer leaves again. A client might want to do this to send all keyboard input to one of its subwindows. See Chapter 12, *Interclient Communication*, for more information about what a client should do regarding the keyboard focus.

8.3.2.2 Keyboard and Pointer Grabbing

The keyboard and/or the pointer can be grabbed when their input should not be allowed to be interrupted by other clients. As the name implies, grabbing prevents other clients from receiving input and, therefore, can be antisocial. It should not be done unless absolutely necessary. Grabbing the pointer is particularly troublesome, because there is no event to announce to other clients that this has happened. See Appendix L, *Interclient Communication Conventions*, of Volume Zero, *X Protocol Reference Manual* (as of the second printing).

In general, grabbing is an advanced topic that you do not need to understand in detail until you find a reason to use it. But there are two exceptions to this rule. You do need to know what will happen when other clients grab, so that your client can prepare for it. Secondly, an automatic grab takes place between **ButtonPress** and **ButtonRelease** events if your client has selected both. You must understand grabbing to understand the implications of this automatic grab.

An *active grab* causes pointer and keyboard events to be sent to the grabbing window regardless of the current position of the pointer. Active grabs are invoked directly by calling **XGrabPointer()** and **XGrabKeyboard()**. A *passive grab* (invoked by calling **XGrabKey()** or **XGrabButton()**) causes an active grab to begin when a certain key or button combination is pressed. Passive grabs are useful in implementing menus.

---

*For a window to be viewable, it must be mapped and all its ancestors must be mapped, but it may be obscured.

When you grab a device, you have the option of confining the pointer to any window within the grabbing client and of controlling the further processing of both keyboard and pointer events.

Grabbing the keyboard effectively selects all keyboard events, whether you selected them previously or not. Grabbing the keyboard also causes `FocusIn` and `FocusOut` events to be sent to the old and new focus windows, but they must be selected by each window to be received. In the call to grab the pointer, however, you specify what types of pointer, button, and enter/leave events you want.

Grabs take precedence over the keyboard focus window. Grabs of the keyboard generated `FocusIn` and `FocusOut` events, so that if your client selects these, it can determine whether or not it can get keyboard events. Pointer grabbing is more problematic, since no event notifies other clients when one client has grabbed it. However, pointer grabs are almost always temporary.

For more on keyboard and pointer grabbing, see Section 9.4. For a description of server grabbing, which is a different topic though still related to events, see Chapter 16, *Window Management*.

8.3.3   Event Masks

This section describes the event masks and the events they select. After reading this section, you should have a good idea of what types of events exist, what they are for, how to select them, and when to use them. Chapter 9, *The Keyboard and Pointer*, and the sections listed in Table 8-5 provide practical examples and describe the use of some of the more commonly used events in more detail. Appendix E, *Event Reference*, provides a complete reference to each event type.

8.3.3.1   KeyPressMask and KeyReleaseMask

`KeyPress` and `KeyRelease` events report when a keyboard key has been pressed or released. Most, but not all, servers are capable of generating `KeyRelease` events. Shift, Control, and other modifier keys generate events just like the main keyboard.

The `KeyPress` and `KeyRelease` events provide a keycode that identifies the key, but the keycodes are server-dependent and should not be used to interpret the event. Instead you can use `XLookupString()` to translate the keycode into a portable symbol called a keysym, which represents the symbol on the cap of the key, and into an ASCII character string. Both the mapping between keycodes and keysyms and the mapping between keysyms and ASCII strings can be modified.

In `XLookupString()`, the main routine used for interpreting `KeyPress` and `KeyRelease` events, there is a provision for a special Compose key which is available on some keyboards, so that multikey sequences, usually used to type characters for languages other than English, can be entered and translated into the appropriate keysym. The Compose key feature, however, is not implemented in the versions of Xlib provided by MIT.

The events selected by `KeyPressMask` and `KeyReleaseMask` are used in the examples in Section 9.1.1.

8.3.3.2 ButtonPressMask, ButtonReleaseMask, and OwnerGrabButtonMask

`ButtonPress` and `ButtonRelease` events occur when the pointer buttons are pressed. There are generally between three and five buttons on the pointer, and the event structure specifies not only the button that caused the event but also the current state of all the pointer buttons and the modifier keys on the keyboard. The mapping between the bits in the button mask and the physical buttons can be changed with `XSetPointerMapping()` and read with `XGetPointerMapping()` and is global to the server.

The pointer is automatically grabbed between the `ButtonPress` and `ButtonRelease` events on behalf of the client for whose window the `ButtonPress` was selected. This way, you always expect to receive button events in pairs since the release will be sent to your client regardless of the position of the pointer at that time. Only one client can select button events on any one window at one time, due to the grab that automatically takes place.

The `OwnerGrabButtonMask` does not select any event by itself, but it controls the distribution of button events to your client during the automatic grab between the `ButtonPress` and `ButtonRelease` (and during any grab your client might make). If it is selected, the automatic grab has the same effect as an `XGrabButton()` call with the *owner_events* argument set to `True`, so that the `ButtonRelease` event is sent to whichever of the client's windows the pointer is in. If the `ButtonRelease` occurs outside the client's windows or if `OwnerGrabButtonMask` is not selected, all events will be sent only to the window where the `ButtonPress` occurred. Current wisdom suggests that you should always select `OwnerGrabButtonMask` with `ButtonPressMask`.

The events selected by `ButtonPressMask` and `ButtonReleaseMask` are discussed in Section 9.2.2 and demonstrated in Examples 9-9, 16-1, and 16-6.

8.3.3.3 The Pointer Motion Masks

There are eight pointer motion masks: `PointerMotionMask`, `PointerMotion-HintMask`, `ButtonMotionMask`, `Button1MotionMask`, `Button2Motion-Mask`, `Button3MotionMask`, `Button4MotionMask`, and `Button5MotionMask`. Up to five pointer buttons are supported, even though most mice have only three buttons and some have only one.

- `PointerMotionMask` selects motion events that occur when any or none of the pointer buttons are pressed. Each event includes the position of the pointer within the event window and the position relative to the origin of the root window. All motion events contain a mask that gives the current status of the modifier keys and pointer buttons and the current server time. `MotionNotify` events occur in large numbers while the pointer is moving steadily. Therefore, this mask is selected alone only by clients that require a complete record of pointer position, such as painting programs.

- `PointerMotionHintMask` is used in concert with other pointer motion masks to reduce the number of events generated. By itself, it does not select any events.

`PointerMotionHintMask` specifies that the server should send only one `Motion-Notify` event when the pointer moves, until a key or button state changes, the pointer leaves the window, or the client calls `XQueryPointer()` or `XGetMotionEvents()`. The idea is that instead of processing hundreds of pointer motion events, the client gets only one event per movement and then queries the pointer position or examines the motion history buffer (the latter may not exist on some servers) for the current position. This approach is suitable for clients that need the pointer position at particular times but that do not need all the intermediate positions. Even though each query for the pointer position is a round-trip request, the performance of this approach is better than that of selecting all the events with `PointerMotionMask` alone, because of the reduced network traffic.

- `ButtonMotionMask` selects any pointer motion events that occur when at least one button is pressed.

- `Button1MotionMask`, `Button2MotionMask`, `Button3MotionMask`, `Button4MotionMask`, and `Button5MotionMask` select pointer motion events that occur when the specified button is pressed. If two or more of these masks are used, events with any combination of the specified buttons (except both released) will be selected.

Handling the events selected by these masks is described in Section 9.2.1 and demonstrated in three examples in that section.

8.3.3.4 FocusChangeMask

`FocusIn` and `FocusOut` events occur when the keyboard focus window is changed. A window that selects `FocusChangeMask` receives a `FocusOut` event if it was the old focus window or is in the same branch of the hierarchy as the old focus window. It receives a `FocusIn` event if it is the new focus window or is in the same branch of the hierarchy as the new focus window. The `detail` member in the event tells the relationship of the window to the new or old focus window. With this information, it is possible to tell whether the window can receive keyboard input. You can read the details of what events are delivered in Appendix E, *Event Reference*.

`EnterNotify`, `LeaveNotify`, `FocusIn`, and `FocusOut` events are often used together to track whether the pointer is in a window and whether the client has the keyboard focus. If the focus is the root, `EnterNotify` and `LeaveNotify` events are used. With any other focus, the `FocusIn` and `FocusOut` events take precedence.

`FocusIn` and `FocusOut` events are described and used in Section 9.3.

8.3.3.5 EnterWindowMask and LeaveWindowMask

`EnterNotify` and `LeaveNotify` events are typically used to inform a client that the pointer just entered or just left one of its windows. If the client receives a `LeaveNotify` event in its top-level window, the client will not be receiving any more key, button, or motion events until it gets an `EnterNotify` event, unless it is the keyboard focus window or has grabbed the keyboard or pointer.

An `EnterNotify` event is also generated when a window is mapped over the current position of the pointer, and a `LeaveNotify` is generated when a window containing the pointer is unmapped.

`EnterNotify` and `LeaveNotify` events are described and used in Section 9.3.

8.3.3.6 KeymapStateMask

A `KeymapNotify` event notifies the client about the keyboard state when the pointer or keyboard focus enters a window. The keyboard state is represented (in the event structure) by 32 bytes of data called a *keyboard vector*, with one bit for each keyboard key. The number of a bit in the vector for a particular key is the same as the key's keycode. This vector is the same as the vector returned by `XQueryKeymap()`.

This event type, if it is selected, always follows immediately after an `EnterNotify` or `FocusIn` event. It allows a client to find out which keys were pressed when the pointer or the keyboard focus entered the window. Since the state of the modifier keys is already reported in `EnterNotify` and `FocusIn` events, the `KeymapNotify` event is only useful for reporting the state of other keys.

`KeymapState` events are not used in the examples in this manual, because they are rarely needed. For more information about them, see Appendix E, *Event Reference*.

8.3.3.7 ExposureMask

An `Expose` event tells a client which window or area within a window has just become visible. The usual response is to redraw the contents of the area or of the entire window, if that is easier and comparably fast. Figure 8-3 shows a typical window hierarchy before and after window *C* is lowered. Two `Expose` events are sent to window *A* specifying areas *E1* and *E2*, and one `Expose` event is sent to window *B* specifying area *E3*.

The handling of `Expose` events is fully described and demonstrated in Section 3.2.13.1.

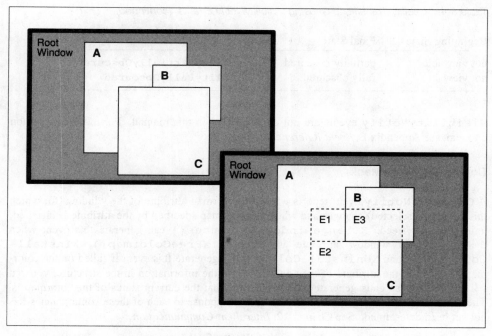

Figure 8-3. Expose events generated by lowering of window C

8.3.3.8 VisibilityChangeMask

A `VisibilityNotify` event is sent when a window makes any change in visibility, as shown in Table 8-4, except when the window becomes not viewable. (Becoming not viewable means that the window or one of its ancestors was unmapped, which generates an `UnmapNotify` event.) This event might be used by a client that must be completely visible in order to be useful.

The symbol returned in the `state` flag of the event is shown in the third column of the table.

Table 8-4. Visibility Transitions Causing VisibilityNotify Events

Beginning State	Final State	`state` Flag
unobscured	partially obscured	`VisibilityPartiallyObscured`
unobscured	fully obscured	`VisibilityFullyObscured`
partially obscured	unobscured	`VisibilityUnobscured`
partially obscured	fully obscured	`VisibilityFullyObscured`
fully obscured	unobscured	`VisibilityUnobscured`
fully obscured	partially obscured	`VisibilityPartiallyObscured`
not viewable	unobscured	`VisibilityUnobscured`

Table 8-4. Visibility Transitions Causing VisibilityNotify Events (continued)

Beginning State	Final State	`state` Flag
not viewable	partially obscured	`VisibilityPartiallyObscured`
not viewable	fully obscured	`VisibilityFullyObscured`

`VisibilityNotify` events are not demonstrated in this manual. For more information on them, see Appendix E, *Event Reference*.

8.3.3.9 ColormapChangeMask

A `ColormapNotify` event reports when the colormap attribute of the window (for which this mask was selected) changes and when the colormap specified by the attribute is installed, uninstalled, or freed. `XChangeWindowAttributes()` can generate this event when the `colormap` window attribute is changed. `XFreeColormap()`, `XInstall-Colormap()`, and `XUninstallColormap()` generate this event if called on the colormap specified in the attribute of the window. From the information in the structure, you can tell which of these calls generated the event and what the current status of the colormap is. The conventions for what the client should do in response to each of these contingencies has not yet been determined. See Chapter 12, *Interclient Communication*.

`ColormapNotify` events are discussed in Section 7.10.2.

8.3.3.10 PropertyChangeMask

A `PropertyNotify` event indicates that a property of a certain window was changed or deleted. This event is generated when `XChangeProperty()`, `XDeleteProperty()`, or `XRotateWindowProperties()` is called or when `XGetWindowProperty()` is called with certain arguments. Beyond its normal purpose, this event can be used to get the current server time. This is done by appending zero-length data to a property using `XChangeProperty()`, which generates a `PropertyNotify` event containing the time.

The uses of `PropertyNotify` events are described in Chapter 12.

8.3.3.11 StructureNotifyMask and SubstructureNotifyMask

`StructureNotifyMask` selects a group of event types that report when the state of a window has changed. This includes the window's configuration (size, position, border width, stacking order), whether it was destroyed, whether it was moved due to its `win_gravity` window attribute, whether it was mapped or unmapped, and whether it was reparented.

`SubstructureNotifyMask` selects the same events plus one that indicates that a window has been created; it monitors all the *subwindows* of the window specified in the `XSelectInput()` call that used this mask. Only `SubstructureNotifyMask` selects `CreateNotify` events, because the window does not exist beforehand, and therefore, no ID exists to use in a call to `XSelectInput()` using `StructureNotify-Mask`.

Applications often select `StructureNotifyMask` to be notified that they have been manipulated by the window manager or some other client, so that they can act accordingly.

The following list describes the events selected by `StructureNotifyMask` and `SubstructureNotifyMask`:

- A `CirculateNotify` event reports a call to change the stacking order and includes whether the final position is on top or on bottom. This event is generated by `XCirculateSubwindows()`, `XCirculateSubwindowsDown()`, or `XCirculateSubwindowsUp()`.

- A `ConfigureNotify` event reports changes to a window's configuration, including its size, position, border width, and stacking order. This event is generated by `XConfigureWindow()`, `XLowerWindow()`, `XMapRaised()`, `XMove-ResizeWindow()`, `XMoveWindow()`, `XRaiseWindow()`, `XResize-Window()`, `XRestackWindows()`, and `XSetWindowBorderWidth()`.

- A `CreateNotify` event reports that a new window has been created with either `XCreateSimpleWindow()` or `XCreateWindow()`.

- A `DestroyNotify` event reports that a window has been destroyed with `XDestroyWindow()` or `XDestroySubwindows()`. When a window is destroyed, this event is delivered to all subwindows of the window before it is delivered to the window itself, unless the subwindows are in another client's save-set (see Chapter 16, *Window Management*, for a description of save-sets).

- A `GravityNotify` event reports when a window is moved because its parent was resized and had its window gravity attribute set.

- A `MapNotify` event reports when a window is mapped. This event is generated by `XMapWindow()`, `XMapRaised()`, and `XMapSubwindows()`.

- A `ReparentNotify` event reports when a client successfully reparents a window (see Chapter 16 for a description of window reparenting).

- An `UnmapNotify` event reports when a mapped window is unmapped. This event also indicates whether the unmapping of a child window was due to the fact that the parent window was resized and the child had a window gravity attribute of `UnmapGravity`.

The `ConfigureNotify` event is used in the *basicwin* application described in Chapter 3, *Basic Window Program*. The rest of these events are used in a similar fashion by applications that need detailed knowledge of their state.

Events

8.3.3.12 SubstructureRedirectMask

The three event types selected by SubstructureRedirectMask—Circulate-Request, ConfigureRequest, and MapRequest—can be used by a client (virtually always the window manager) to intercept and cancel window-configuration-changing requests made by other clients to change the window configuration. Only one client at a time can select SubstructureRedirectMask on a particular window. Normally, SubstructureRedirectMask is selected on the root window to allow the window manager to intercept layout-changing requests for the top-level windows of each application. When these events are selected, the Xlib requests noted in the paragraphs below do not perform their usual function but instead simply generate these events. The window manager is then able to modify the requests according to its layout policy before repeating the requests itself with its modified arguments.

These events differ from CirculateNotify, ConfigureNotify, and MapNotify in that the *Request events* deliver the parameters of the request before the requests are carried out and indicate that the original request has been cancelled. The *Notify requests indicate the final outcome of such requests, unhindered.

Each of the event structures associated with the following event types includes an override_redirect member, which is either True or False. If it is True, the window manager should ignore the event, since this indicates that the client has set the override_redirect attribute to indicate that this is a temporary window. (For more information, see Section 16.2.)

* CirculateRequest events report when an Xlib function, such as XCirculate-Subwindows(), XCirculateSubwindowsDown(), XCirculate-SubwindowsUp(), or XRestackWindows() is called to change the stacking order of a group of children.

* ConfigureRequest events report when an Xlib function, such as XConfigure-Window(), XLowerWindow(), XMoveResizeWindow(), XMoveWindow(), XRaiseWindow(), XResizeWindow(), or XSetWindowBorderWidth() is called to resize, move, restack, or change the border width of a window.

* MapRequest events report when XMapWindow() or XMapSubwindows() is called to map a window.

The uses of the event types selected by SubstructureRedirectMask are described in Chapter 16, *Window Management*.

---

*The wildcard (*) notation is used occasionally in this manual to indicate a number of events or routines with similar names. In this case, *Request means all event types whose symbols end in Request.

8.3.3.13 ResizeRedirectMask

The `ResizeRequest` event is generated when some other client (usually the window manager) attempts to resize the window on which `ResizeRedirectMask` is selected. `XConfigureWindow()`, `XMoveResizeWindow()`, and `XResizeWindow()` generate this event. Only one client can select `ResizeRedirectMask` at a time on a particular window.

This event includes the *requested* size. The final size may be adjusted by the window manager and can be found from the resulting `ConfigureNotify` event or, if the window is visible, from the `Expose` event.

A client might wish to select this mask if it has only one acceptable size. Then when any client attempted to resize the window, the request would be sent as an event and can be safely ignored. However, if some client (say, the window manager) has selected `SubstructureRedirectMask` for the parent of the window on which `ResizeRedirectMask` was selected, the substructure redirect takes precedence. Therefore, this usually will not work. `ResizeRedirectMask` is not very useful, given that most window managers select `SubstructureRedirectMask`.

8.3.3.14 Automatically Selected Events

Seven types of events can be sent to your program even if you do not explicitly select them. Your client must handle or throw away `MappingNotify` events regardless of whether the client reads the keyboard. All the others are generated in response to your own actions (either by the server or by other clients), and therefore, you should know that you are going to get them. Example 8-3 described when each of these events should be present in your event loop.

- `MappingNotify` events are caused by `XChangeKeyboardMapping()`, `XSetModifierMapping()`, and `XSetPointerMapping()` calls that set the pointer button, keyboard key, and keyboard modifier key mappings. Since these mappings are global to the server, each client must call the correct function to refresh its knowledge of the mappings.

  If the changed mapping is of the keyboard, a receiving client should call `XRefreshKeyboardMapping()`, which updates a client's knowledge of the server's mapping between keycodes and keysyms.

  If the changed mapping is of the pointer, the client can call `XGetPointerMapping()` to update its knowledge. Most current clients do not do this, however, because it is assumed that the button mappings were intentionally changed by the user. That means that the client should not attempt to adjust its operation so that the buttons have their old meanings.

- `ClientMessage` events are sent as a result of a call to `XSendEvent()` by a client to a particular window. They contain data described by an `Atom`. These events are normally used to transfer selection data. The `send_event` member of the event structure will always be set.

- SelectionClear, SelectionNotify, and SelectionRequest events are used to communicate back and forth between two applications that are transferring information. This process is described in Section 12.4.

- GraphicsExpose and NoExpose events are selected not by an event mask but by the graphics_exposures member of the GC. One or the other of them (or both) is generated by each XCopyArea() or XCopyPlane() request when the GC specified for the request has this member set to True. Otherwise, the events are not generated. The GraphicsExpose event indicates that a source area could not be completely copied into a destination because the source was partially or fully obscured. The No-Expose event indicates that the copy was not affected by an obscured source. More than one GraphicsExpose event can be generated by a single XCopyArea() or XCopyPlane() request, depending on the number and position of the obscuring windows, but only one NoExpose is possible as a result of a single copy. Graphics-Expose events are often handled just like Expose events.

8.4 Sending Events

The XSendEvent() function may be used to send a ClientMessage event or any other event type to a particular window, to the current keyboard focus window, or to the window in which the pointer is located. Sending events is necessary in selection processing, as described in Section 12.4. It may also be useful for designing test procedures for your input handling or for making demonstration programs that simulate user input.

The send_event member of each event structure indicates the origin of the event. If True, it was sent from another client rather from the server. Note that, unless this flag is explicitly checked, events from the server and from other clients will appear the same to your application.

8.5 Where to Find More on Each Event

All event types are described in reference format in Appendix E, *Event Reference*. The information on each page includes the event structure definition, description of each event structure member, XEvent union name, how to select the event, when it is generated, and notes on its use. Table 8-5 shows other places in this manual where you can find information about using certain event types.

Table 8-5. Where Events are Described Further

Event Type	Section
KeyPress KeyRelease	Section 9.1.1.1
ButtonPress ButtonRelease	Section 9.2.2
KeymapNotify	Section 9.3.1
MotionNotify	Section 9.2.1
EnterNotify LeaveNotify	Section 9.3
FocusIn FocusOut	Section 9.3
Expose	Section 3.2.13.1
GraphicsExpose NoExpose	Section 5.6
ColormapNotify	Section 7.10.2
PropertyNotify	Section 12.1
ConfigureNotify	Section 3.2.16
CirculateRequest ConfigureRequest MapRequest	Section 16.2
MappingNotify	Section 9.1.2.3
SelectionClear	Section 12.4*
SelectionNotify	Section 12.4*
SelectionRequest	Section 12.4*

*Also in Appendix L, *Interclient Communication Conventions*, of Volume Zero, *X Protocol Reference Manual* (as of the second printing).

9

The Keyboard and Pointer

This chapter not only describes how to handle keyboard and pointer events but also describes many other topics related to these two input devices. In particular, it discusses X's use of keysyms as portable symbols for character encoding, keyboard remapping, keyboard and pointer "grabs," and keyboard and pointer preferences. Internationalized keyboard input is described in Chapter 11.

In This Chapter:

9
The Keyboard and Pointer

In Chapter 3, *Basic Window Program*, we showed you quite thoroughly how to deal with **Expose** events. But all we did with pointer and keyboard events was to exit the program. As you can guess, there can be more to it than that. This chapter describes and demonstrates the handling of keyboard and pointer events, describes keyboard and pointer mapping, and describes how to set keyboard preferences. Internationalized keyboard input is described in Chapter 11, *Internationalized Text Input*, although it depends on many concepts described in this chapter.

9.1 The Keyboard

The keyboard is an area like color, where X clients have to be made portable across systems with different physical characteristics. In the case of the keyboard, these variations are in two areas: whether the keyboard provides **KeyPress** and **KeyRelease** events or just **KeyPress** events, and the symbols on the caps of the keys.

Almost all serious workstations provide both **KeyPress** and **KeyRelease** events. Some personal computers, however, may not. Therefore, avoid depending on **KeyRelease** events if you want your client to be portable to the lowest classes of machines.

The second problem is adjusting for variations in the keys available on each keyboard and the codes they generate. We'll start explaining how this problem is solved by describing the contents of a key event.

KeyPress and **KeyRelease** events are stored in **XKeyEvent** structures, shown in Example 9-1. Each key event contains the **keycode** of the key that was pressed and **state**, a mask which indicates which modifier keys and pointer buttons were being held down just before the event. A *modifier key* is a key like Shift or Control that can modify the meaning of a key event. In addition to their effect on the processing of other keys, the modifier keys also generate key events with unique keycodes.

Example 9-1. The XKeyEvent structure

```
typedef struct {
    int type;                      /* Of event */
    unsigned long serial;          /* Last request processed by server */
    Bool send_event;               /* True if from a SendEvent request */
```

Keyboard/Pointer

Example 9-1. The XKeyEvent structure (continued)

```
        Display *display;               /* Server connection */
        Window window;                  /* "event" window reported in */
        Window root;                    /* Root window event occurred on */
        Window subwindow;               /* Child window */
        Time time;                      /* Milliseconds */
        int x, y;                       /* Coordinates in event window */
        int x_root, y_root;             /* Coordinates relative to root */
        unsigned int state;             /* Key or button mask */
        unsigned int keycode;           /* Detail */
        Bool same_screen;               /* Same screen flag */
} XKeyEvent;
typedef XKeyEvent XKeyPressedEvent;
typedef XKeyEvent XKeyReleasedEvent;
```

The **keycode** member of **XKeyEvent** is a number between 8 and 255. The keycode is the same regardless of whether a key is pressed or released. The keycode for each physical key never changes on a particular server, but the key with the same symbol on it on different brands of equipment may generate different keycodes. For portability reasons and because the keycode by itself without the state of the modifier keys does not provide enough information to interpret an event, clients cannot use keycodes by themselves to determine the meaning of key events.

Instead of using the keycode alone, X clients call **XLookupString( )** to translate the key event into a keysym. A *keysym* is a defined constant that corresponds to the meaning of a key event. For example, the translation of the keycode generated by the "a" key on any system would be **XK_a** if no other keys were being held and **XK_A** if the Shift key were being held or if Shift Lock was in effect (all keysyms begin with **XK_**). The translation of the keycode for the Return key (which is labeled Enter or just with an arrow on some keyboards) would be **XK_Return**. The Enter key on the keypad, if any, would have the keysym **XK_KP_Enter**. Example 9-2 shows some keysym definitions. All keysyms are defined in *<X11/keysymdef.h>*.

Example 9-2. Some sample keysym definitions

```
#define XK_BackSpace        0xFF08    /* Back space, back char,... */
#define XK_Left             0xFF51    /* Move left, left arrow */
#define XK_Undo             0xFF65    /* Undo, oops */
#define XK_Num_Lock         0xFF7F
#define XK_KP_Multiply      0xFFAA
#define XK_Shift_L          0xFFE1    /* Left shift */
#define XK_space            0x020     /* Space */
#define XK_numbersign       0x023     /* # */
#define XK_3                0x033
#define XK_question         0x03f     /* "?" */
#define XK_A                0x041
#define XK_e                0x065
```

XLookupString( ) also provides an ASCII string that corresponds to the keysym or NULL if there is no associated string. By default, all the keys that have ASCII values will have that value as their string. For example, **XK_A** would have the string "A", **XK_ampersand** would have the string "&", and **XK_4** would have the string "4". **XK_Return**, **XK_Escape**, and **XK_Delete** have ASCII values, but they are not printable.

XK_Shift_L (the Shift key on the left side of the keyboard) would not normally have an associated string.

The ASCII value for a particular keysym as returned by XLookupString() can be changed by the client using XRebindKeysym(), and it can be a string of any length, not just a single character. Even though keysyms like XK_F1 (the F1 key) have no default ASCII mapping, they can be given strings. This mapping would apply only to the client that calls XRebindKeysym().

With these introductory comments, we'll move right to the examples that handle keyboard input. Then we'll return to discuss keysyms in more detail and the various keyboard mappings and how they can be changed.

9.1.1 Simple Keyboard Input

Example 9-3 shows the framework of the code for translating a keyboard event into both a keysym and an ASCII string. You will need the keysym to determine what the keystroke means, and the ASCII string if the keystroke is a printable character. If the keystroke is printable, the program would append the ASCII interpretation of the key event to the end of the result string (and display it). If the keystroke is a modifier key being pressed, the event can normally be ignored, since the modifier status of events on other keys is already dealt with by XLookupString(). But XK_Delete or XK_Backspace would indicate that a character should be removed from the string.

The function keys are not initially mapped to ASCII strings and can be ignored, but if the client allows the user to map them to an arbitrary string, it should treat them like any other printable character.

You may notice in Example 9-3 that XLookupString() returns something called an XComposeStatus. Some keyboards provide a Compose key, which is used to type characters not found on the keyboard keys. Its purpose is to make it possible to type characters from other languages without disturbing the normal operation of the keyboard. As it usually works, you press the Compose key followed by some other key to generate characters like é. A table is usually provided which tells you which keys correspond to each foreign character. Processing of multikey sequences using the Compose key is now supported as an input method through the Release 5 internationalization features. So the XComposeStatus argument of XLookupString() is now just a dummy.

Example 9-3. Translating a key event to keysym and ASCII

```
Display *display;
XEvent event;
char buffer[20];
int bufsize = 20;
KeySym key;
XComposeStatus compose;
int charcount;
    .
    .
    /*  Open display, create window, select, map */
```

Example 9-3. Translating a key event to keysym and ASCII (continued)

```
XNextEvent(display, &event);
switch( event.type ) {
        .
        .
        .
case KeyPress:
        charcount = XLookupString(&event, buffer, bufsize, &keysym,
                &compose);
        /* Branch according to keysym, then use buffer
         * if the key is printable */
        break;
case MappingNotify:
        XRefreshKeyboardMapping(&event);
        break;
}
```

Keysyms for accented vowels, tildes, and most combinations found in Western languages are provided in the LATIN1 set. If you want to display an accented *e*, for example, the keysym is **XK_eacute**. If the desired character is not present in the desired font, the client can prepare two or more text items for **XDrawText()** for displaying the desired overstrike character and use the **delta** member to move the second character back over the first. **XDrawText()** is capable of drawing in a different font for each text item, in case the desired accent is in a separate font from the desired character.

9.1.1.1 Getting a String — A Dialog Box

Let's say you are porting a nonevent-driven program to X, and you have a routine called **get_string** that gets an ASCII string from the user. It gets the entire string before returning. But under X, the user might stop typing midway through, pop some other window on top to check some bit of information, then pop the original application back on top. That means you need to handle exposure in the middle of the input string, which, in turn, means you need a function that remembers the string's state so that it can be redrawn in the **get_string** routine. You also have to be prepared in case the keyboard gets remapped by some other client. Suddenly your tiny subroutine to get a string now must be integrated into the event loop.

Example 9-4 is a modification to the *basicwin* program described in Chapter 3, *Basic Window Program*, that puts up a pop-up dialog box. If the user presses a button in the *basicwin* window, the application puts up a dialog box, which the user can type into until a carriage return is typed. All the printable characters except Tab are supported, and Delete or Backspace operate as would be expected. The code allows the user to type the string while also handling the other events that might occur. This is done by placing the code for popping up the dialog in the branch for **ButtonPress** events, placing the code to redraw the dialog string in the branch for **Expose** events, and placing the code to process key events in the branch for **KeyPress** events.

Example 9-4. Implementing a dialog box

```
/* Other include files */
#include <X11/keysym.h>

/* Other defined constants */
#define MAX_POPUP_STRING_LENGTH 40
#define MAX_MAPPED_STRING_LENGTH 10

/* Global variables display and screen */

void main(argc, argv)
int argc;
char **argv;
{
    /* Declarations from basicwin */
    .
    .
    .

    /* The following are for pop-up window */
    static Window pop_win;
    char buffer[MAX_MAPPED_STRING_LENGTH];
    int bufsize=MAX_MAPPED_STRING_LENGTH;
    int start_x, start_y;
    KeySym keysym;
    XComposeStatus compose;
    int count;
    unsigned int pop_width, pop_height;
    char string[MAX_POPUP_STRING_LENGTH];
    int popped = False;
    int length;

    /* Create main window (win) and select its events */
    .
    .
    .

    XMapWindow(display, win);

    /* Get events, use first to display text and graphics */
    while (1)  {
        XNextEvent(display, &report);
        switch  (report.type) {
        case Expose:
            if (report.xexpose.window == pop_win) {
                /* If pop_win is nonzero, it has been created,
                 * and window in Expose is never zero */
                if (popped)
                    XDrawString(display, pop_win, gc, start_x,
                            start_y, string, strlen(string));
            }
            else {  /* It's the main window */
                /* Refresh main window as in basicwin */
            }
            break;
        case ConfigureNotify:
            /* Same as in basicwin */
            .
            .
```

Example 9-4. Implementing a dialog box (continued)

```
        .
        break;
   case ButtonPress:
        /* Put up pop-up window, create if necessary */
        if (!pop_win) {  /* Create it and pop it */
   /* Determine pop-up box size from font information */
   pop_width = MAX_POPUP_STRING_LENGTH *
           font_info->max_bounds.width + 4;
   pop_height = font_info->max_bounds.ascent +
           font_info->max_bounds.descent + 4;
   pop_win = XCreateSimpleWindow(display, win, x, y,
           pop_width, pop_height, border_width,
           BlackPixel(display, screen),
           WhitePixel(display, screen));
   /* Calculate starting position of string in window */
   start_x = 2;
   start_y = font_info->max_bounds.ascent + 2;
   XSelectInput(display, pop_win, ExposureMask | KeyPressMask);
        }
        /* If window is already mapped, no problem */
        XMapWindow(display, pop_win);
        popped = True;
        break;
   case KeyPress:
        if (report.xkey.window == win) {
            /* Key on main window indicates exit */
            XUnloadFont(display, font_info->fid);
            XFreeGC(display, gc);
            XCloseDisplay(display);
            exit(1);
        }
        else {
            /* Get characters until you encounter a
             * carriage return; deal with backspaces, etc. */
            count = XLookupString(&report, buffer, bufsize,
                    &keysym, &compose);
                    buffer[count] = NULL;  /* add NULL terminator */
            /* Now do the right thing with as many
             * keysyms as possible */
            if ((keysym == XK_Return) || (keysym == XK_KP_Enter)
                    || (keysym == XK_Linefeed)) {
                XUnmapWindow(display, pop_win);
                popped = False;
                printf("string is %s\n", string);
                break;
            }
            else if (((keysym >= XK_KP_Space)
                    && (keysym <= XK_KP_9))
                    || ((keysym >= XK_space)
                    && (keysym <= XK_asciitilde))) {
                if ((strlen(string) + strlen (buffer)) >=
                    MAX_POPUP_STRING_LENGTH)
                    XBell(display, 100);
                else
                    strcat(string, buffer);
            }
```

Example 9-4. Implementing a dialog box (continued)

```
                    else if ((keysym >= XK_Shift_L)
                            && (keysym <= XK_Hyper_R))
                        ;/* Do nothing because it's a modifier key */
                    else if ((keysym >= XK_F1)
                            && (keysym <= XK_F35))
                        if (buffer == NULL)
                            printf("Unmapped function key\n");
                        else if ((strlen(string) + strlen (buffer)) >=
                                MAX_POPUP_STRING_LENGTH)
                                XBell(display, 100);
                        else
                            strcat(string, buffer);

                    else if ((keysym == XK_BackSpace) ||
                            (keysym == XK_Delete)) {
                        if ((length = strlen(string)) > 0) {
                            string[length - 1] = NULL;
                            XClearWindow(display, pop_win);
                        }
                        else
                            XBell(display, 100);
                    }
                    else {
                        printf("keysym %s is not handled\n",
                                XKeysymToString(keysym));
                        XBell(display, 100);
                    }
                    XDrawString(display, pop_win, gc, start_x,
                            start_y, string, strlen(string));
                    break;
                }
        case MappingNotify:
                XRefreshKeyboardMapping(&report);
                break;
        default:
                /* All events selected by StructureNotifyMask
                 * except ConfigureNotify are thrown away here,
                 * since nothing is done with them */
                break;
        } /* End switch */
    } /* End while */
}
```

Example 9-4 takes advantage of the fact that the keysyms are constants arranged in groups with consecutive values. By looking for any keysym in a given range, you do not need to specify every keysym you intend to match.

Notice that the program uses keysyms to match all the keystrokes and then does different things depending on whether the keysym is a normal key, a modifier key, a function key, a delete key, or an enter key. If the key is printable, it copies the ASCII values returned by `XLookupString()` into the result string. Note that the result string is not NULL terminated.

Keyboard/Pointer

This program does have some weaknesses.* One of them is that it redraws the entire string instead of just the character being changed. Secondly, using `XTextItem` structures for each character and calling `XDrawText()` instead of `XDrawString()` would support Tab characters and functions keys mapped to strings. Since a tab has to be expanded into a number of spaces before being drawn and function keys may be mapped to arbitrary strings, it is difficult to properly implement them with the approach we have used in Example 9-4.

9.1.2 The Keyboard Mappings

As we have said, there are several translations that take place between the pressing of a key and its interpretation within a program. The first, the mapping between physical keys and keycodes, is server-dependent and cannot be modified. A client cannot determine anything about this first mapping, and it is just a fact that certain physical keys generate certain keycodes. The second mapping, keycodes to keysyms, can be modified by clients but is server-wide, so it usually is not modified. The specification of which keycodes are considered modifiers is also part of the second level of mapping, because it affects the mapping of keycodes to keysyms. The third mapping, from keysyms to strings, is local to a client. This is the mapping with which a client can allow the user to map the function keys to strings for convenience of typing.

We are going to describe the mapping between keysyms and strings first, because this is the mapping that applications are most likely to change. Following that, we'll describe what you need to know about the keycode-to-keysym mapping and modifier mapping to write normal applications. These mappings are normally only changed by clients run from the user's startup script that do nothing else, because they change the keyboard mapping for all applications.

After that, Sections 9.1.3.1 and 9.1.3.2 are optional reading. They describe the background and development of keysyms and how to write special purpose programs to change the server-wide mapping of keycodes to keysyms and the modifier mapping. These techniques are not needed in normal applications.

9.1.2.1 Keysyms to Strings

The default mapping of keysyms to ASCII is defined by the server. The ASCII representation of the keys on the main keyboard are the ASCII codes for the single characters on the caps of the keys. Keysyms that do not have ASCII representations, such as the function keys, initially have mappings to NULL, but they can sometimes be mapped to strings, as we'll describe. However, the modifier keys on some machines cannot be mapped to strings at all.

---

*We could say we left it this way because it is simpler, and it is, but that is not why we wrote it this way. We did not realize the other way would be better until the program was already done. We will leave it as an exercise for you to modify it as described!

Any client in which the user is expected to type a large amount of text should support remapping of the function keys to strings. **XRebindKeysym( )** is the only function that can change this string, the one returned by **XLookupString( )**. The string can be any length. This change affects only the client that calls **XRebindKeysym( )**.

Example 9-5 is a short code sample that demonstrates how to remap function keys to strings. It binds the string "STOP" to Shift-F1 and "ABORT" to CTRL-Shift-F1. Since keyboards may have two Shift and two Control keys, one on each side, the process has to be done for both. Mapping the function keys combined with modifiers will not work on all servers. (On the Sun sample server, this code results in STOP being generated when F1 is pressed with any modifiers and ABORT never being generated.) However, mapping of unmodified function keys should work on all servers.

Example 9-5. Mapping keys to strings
```
#include <X11/keysym.h>
        .
        .
        .
Display *display;

KeySym modlist[2];              /* Array of modifier keysyms */
unsigned int string_length;
unsigned int list_length;
        .
        .
        .
/* Open display */
        .
        .
        .
/* Map Shift-F1 to "STOP"   */
string_length = 4;
list_length = 1;
modlist[0] = XK_Shift_R;  /* Do right shift key */
XRebindKeysym(display, XK_F1, modlist, list_length, "STOP",
        string_length);
modlist[0] = XK_Shift_L;  /* Do left shift key */
XRebindKeysym(display, XK_F1, modlist, list_length, "STOP",
        string_length);

/* Map CTRL-Shift-F1 to "ABORT"   */
string_length = 5;
list_length = 2;

/* Both right pressed */
modlist[0] = XK_Shift_R; modlist[1] = XK_Control_R;
XRebindKeysym(display, XK_F1, modlist, list_length, "ABORT",
        string_length);

/* Left Shift, Right Control */
modlist[0] = XK_Shift_L; modlist[1] = XK_Control_R;
XRebindKeysym(display, XK_F1, modlist, list_length, "ABORT",
        string_length);

/* Right Shift, Left Control */
modlist[0] = XK_Shift_R; modlist[1] = XK_Control_L;
XRebindKeysym(display, XK_F1, modlist, list_length, "ABORT",
        string_length);

/* Both left pressed */
```

Keyboard/Pointer

Example 9-5. Mapping keys to strings (continued)

```
modlist[0] = XK_Shift_L; modlist[1] = XK_Control_L;
XRebindKeysym(display, XK_F1, modlist, list_length, "ABORT",
        string_length);
```

`XLookupString()` currently uses a linear search to find the keysym corresponding to each key event, and each call to `XRebindKeysym()` causes `XLookupString()` to run somewhat slower. This problem is exacerbated if you want a function key (or any other key) to generate the same string with any combination of modifier keys, since this requires 15 or more calls to `XRebindKeysym()`.

9.1.2.2 The Modifier Keys

A keysym represents the meaning of a certain combination of a key and modifier keys such as Shift and Control. For example, `XK_A` represents the letter "a" pressed while the Shift key is held down or while Shift Lock is on. As in this example, the keysym depends on what modifier key is being held.

Although Shift is present on all keyboards and Control on most, the remaining modifier keys are not standardized. There may be Meta, Hyper, Super, Left, Right, or Alternate keys. X, however, has a fixed set of logical modifiers, listed in the first column of Table 9-1. Each of these logical modifier symbols corresponds to a bit in the `state` member of the `XKeyEvent` structure. On each keyboard, there is a mapping between the physical modifier keys and these logical modifiers. Table 9-1 also shows the keysyms of the keys that are by default mapped to the logical modifiers on a Sun-3 system and the corresponding keycodes for that system. You can use the *xmodmap* command without arguments to find out the default modifier mapping on any system.

Table 9-1. Logical Modifiers and a Typical Modifier Key Mapping

Logical Modifier	Default Keycodes of Modifier Keys (Sun-3)	Modifier Keysym (Sun-3)
`ShiftMask`	(0x6a), (0x75)	`XK_Shift_L`, `XK_Shift_R`
`ShiftLockMask`	(0x7e)	`XK_Caps_Lock`
`ControlMask`	(0x53)	`XK_Control_L`
`Mod1Mask`	(0x7f), (0x81)	`XK_Meta_L`, `XK_Meta_R`
`Mod2Mask`	(unmapped)	
`Mod3Mask`	(unmapped)	
`Mod4Mask`	(unmapped)	
`Mod5Mask`	(unmapped)	

Each keycode may have a list of keysyms, one for every logical modifier. Each list, of varying length, conveys the set of meanings for the key with each of the modifier keys pressed. This array of keysyms for each keycode is initially defined by the server. In most cases, only two keysyms are defined for the keys that represent single printable characters and only one for the rest.

9.1.2.3 Keycodes to Keysyms

Clients can change the mapping of keycodes to keysyms (with `XChangeKeyboard-Mapping()`), but they rarely do because this mapping is global to the server. This change would affect every client operating on the server. Every client would receive a `Mapping-Notify` event (regardless of whether they selected it or whether they actually use keyboard input) and must then get a new keysym table from the server with `XRefreshKeyboard-Mapping()`. (This table is stored in the `Display` structure and is used by `XLookup-String()` and the other routines that return keysyms.) `XRefreshKeyboard-Mapping()` works by erasing the copy of the keyboard and/or modifier mappings that are present in the `Display` structure (the `keysyms` and `modifiermap` members). The next time that an Xlib call is made that requires either of these mappings, a request is made to the server, the new mappings are transferred to Xlib, and the pointers in the `Display` structure are reset to the new mapping data. Subsequent calls to access this data use the `Display` structure instead of querying the server.

One of few applications that might change the mapping between keycodes and keysyms would be an application that converted between QWERTY and DVORAK keyboard layout. These are the nicknames for two different layouts for the alphabetic characters on English language keyboards. The QWERTY keyboard in common use was originally designed to be slow enough so that mechanical typesetting machine operators would not be able to type fast enough to jam their machines. The DVORAK keyboard, on the other hand, was designed to place the most common letters in the English language under the home row of keys and is much faster.

Let's say a user wanted to use the DVORAK layout instead of the default, which is QWERTY. This application would not even need to create a window, but it would change the mapping of keycodes to keysyms with `XChangeKeyboardMapping()`. The user could then move the keycaps around on the keyboard or label them somehow. Except for calling `XRefreshKeyboardMapping()`, other applications would operate as usual. From then on, while the server was running, all applications would work properly with the DVORAK layout.

9.1.3 Background on Keysyms

Keysyms are a concept developed especially for X. It may help you to understand them better to read about how they were designed. But this is optional reading, and you can skip to Section 9.2 if you do not plan to write programs that change the mapping of keycodes to keysyms.

The keysyms are defined in two include files, *<X11/keysym.h>* and *<X11/keysymdef.h>*. Together these files define several sets of keysyms for different languages and purposes. There are sets for Latin, Greek, Cyrillic, Arabic, and so on, intended to allow for internationalization of programs. There are also sets for publishing and technical purposes, because these fields have their own "languages." *<X11/keysym.h>* defines which character sets are active, and *<X11/keysymdef.h>* defines the symbols in all the sets. Only *<X11/keysym.h>* needs to be included in an application because it includes *<X11/keysymdef.h>*.

By default, the enabled sets of defined keysyms include the ISO Latin character sets (1-4), a set of Greek characters, and a set of miscellaneous symbols common on keyboards (Return, Help, Tab, and so on). These are sufficient for making an application work in any Western language. Symbols for Katakana, Arabic, Cyrillic, Technical, Special, Publishing, APL, and Hebrew character sets are defined in *<X11/keysymdef.h>* but are not enabled in *<X11/keysym.h>* and may not be available on all servers. This is because some C compilers have a limit to the number of allowable defined symbols.

Many of the keysym sets share keysyms with sets earlier in the *<X11/keysymdef.h>* include file. For example, there is only one **XK_space** keysym because a space is common to all languages. **XK_space** is in LATIN1 so that it is always available. The LATIN2 and LATIN3 sets are quite short because they share most of their symbols with the previous sets.

9.1.3.1 The Design of Keysyms

English language keyboards tend to be quite standard in the alphanumeric keys, but they differ radically in the miscellaneous function keys. Many function keys are left over from early timesharing days or are designed for a specific application. Keyboard layouts from large manufacturers tend to have lots of keys for every conceivable purpose, whereas small workstation manufacturers often have keys that are solely for support of some unique function.

There are two ways of thinking about how to define keysyms given such a situation: the *Engraving* approach and the *Common* approach.

The Engraving approach is to create a keysym for every unique key engraving. This is effectively taking the union of all key engravings on all keyboards. For example, some keyboards label function keys across the top as F1 through F*n*, others label them as PF1 through PF*n*. These would be different keys under the Engraving approach. Likewise, Lock would differ from Shift Lock, which is different from the up-arrow symbol that has the effect of changing lower case to upper case. There are lots of other aliases such as Del, DEL, Delete, Remove, and so forth. The Engraving approach makes it easy to decide if a new entry should be added to the keysym set: if it does not exactly match an existing one, then a new one is created. One estimate is that there would be on the order of 300 to 500 miscellaneous keysyms using this approach, not counting foreign translations and variations.

The Common approach tries to capture all of the keys present on a number of common keyboards, folding likely aliases into the same keysym. For example, Del, DEL, and Delete are all merged into a single keysym. Vendors would be expected to augment the keysym set (using the vendor-specific encoding space) to include all of their unique keys that were not included in the standard set. Each vendor decides which of its keys map into the standard keysyms. It is more difficult to implement this approach, since a judgement is required whether a sufficient set of keyboards implement an engraving to justify making it a keysym in the standard set and which engravings should be merged into a single keysym. Under this scheme, there are an estimated 100 to 150 keysyms for an English language keyboard.

While neither scheme is perfect, the Common approach has been selected because it makes it easier to write a portable application. Having the Delete functionality merged into a single keysym allows an application to implement a deletion function and expect reasonable bindings on a wide set of workstations. Under the Common approach, application writers are still free to look for and interpret vendor-specific keysyms, but because they are in an extended set, application developers should be more conscious that they are writing applications in a nonportable fashion.

9.1.3.2 Conventions for Keysym Meaning

For each keycode, the server defines a list of keysyms, corresponding to the key pressed while various modifier keys are being held. There are conventions for the meanings of the first two keysyms in the list. The first keysym in the list for a particular key should be construed as the symbol corresponding to a `KeyPress` when no modifier keys are down. The second keysym in the list, if present, usually should be construed as the symbol when the Shift or Shift Lock modifier keys are down. However, if there is only one keysym for a particular keycode, if it is alphabetic, and if case distinction is relevant for it, then the appropriate case should be based on the Shift and Lock modifiers. For example, if the single keysym is an uppercase *A*, you have to use the `state` member of `XKeyEvent` to determine if the Shift key is held. `XLookupString()` should translate the event into the correct ASCII string anyway.

X does not suggest an interpretation of the keysyms beyond the first two and does not define any spatial geometry of the symbols on the key by their order in the keysym list. This is because the list of modifier keys varies widely between keyboards. However, when programming, it should be safe to assume that the third member in the keysym list would correspond to the key pressed with the next most common modifier available on the keyboard, which might be Control.

For keyboards with both left-side and right-side modifier keys (for example, Shift keys on each side that generate different keycodes), the bit in the `state` member in the event structure defines the OR of the keys. If electronically distinguishable, these keys can have separate keycodes and up/down events generated and your program can track their individual states manually.

9.1.4 Changing the Server-wide Keyboard Mappings

Both the keycode-to-keysym mapping and the modifier mapping affect all clients when they are changed by any client. That is why normal applications will not change them. Special purpose programs, however, can be written to change these mappings, usually to be run from a user's startup script. These sections describe how to write such programs. If you do not plan to write one, you can skip ahead to Section 9.1.5.

9.1.4.1 Changing the Keycode-to-Keysym Mapping

XChangeKeyboardMapping() changes the current mapping of the specified range of keycodes to keysyms.

Example 9-6 shows a simple program called *mapkey* that changes the keyboard mapping for all the applications running on the server. This application takes pairs of arguments that are keysyms and maps the keycode associated with the first keysym to the second keysym. In other words, you could use it to map the F1 key to be Escape and Home to be a Control key on the right side of the keyboard by typing the following:

```
$  mapkey F1 Escape Home Control_R
```

Use mapkey with care, because it is easy to disable a server by remapping an alphanumeric key. Such a remapping cannot be reversed except by restarting the server.

Example 9-6. An application for server-wide keymapping

```
#include <stdio.h>
#include <X11/Xlib.h>
#include <X11/Xutil.h>
#include <X11/Xatom.h>
#include <X11/keysym.h>

main(argc, argv)
int argc;
char **argv;
{
        KeySym old, new;
        int old_code;
        Display *display;

        if (!(display = XOpenDisplay(""))) {
                fprintf(stderr,"Cannot open display '%s'\n",
                            XDisplayName(""));
                exit(1);
        }
        argv++, argc--;

        if (argc & 0x1) {
                fprintf(stderr,"Usage:  Keysymfrom Keysymto Keysymfrom \
                            Keysymto ...\n");
                exit(1);
        }
        while (argc > 1) {
                old = XStringToKeysym(*argv++);
                new = XStringToKeysym(*argv++);
                argc--, argc--;
                old_code = XKeysymToKeycode(display, old);
                XChangeKeyboardMapping(display, old_code, 1, &new, 1);
        }
        XFlush(display);
        XCloseDisplay(display);
        exit(0);
}
```

The application in Example 9-6 could be rewritten on a larger scale to change a keyboard from QWERTY to DVORAK layout as described in Section 9.1.2.3. Since the keycodes are server-dependent, the QWERTY-to-DVORAK conversion program would not be portable between machines unless it used `XGetKeyboardMapping()` to get the current mapping of keycodes to keysyms and then remapped them.

`XGetKeyboardMapping()` returns an array of keysyms that represent the current mapping of the specified range of keycodes.

9.1.4.2 Changing Modifier Mapping

X allows you to control which physical keys are considered modifier keys. Normal applications will not do this. The modifier mapping might be changed for a left-handed user if, by default, there was only one Control key on the left side of the keyboard and the user preferred to have a Control key on the right side. In that case, a conveniently placed key on the right side could be mapped to a logical Control key. Like keycode-to-keysym remapping, this would typically be done by a special purpose application run from the user's startup script.

While modifier keys generate `KeyPress` and `KeyRelease` events like other keys, modifier keys are the only keys reported in the `state` member of every key, button, motion, or border crossing event structure. The `state` member is a mask that indicates which logical modifiers were pressed when the event occurred. Each bit in `state` is represented by a constant such as `ControlMask`. `state` is used by `XLookupString()` to generate the correct keysym from a key event. Note that the `state` member of events other than key, button, motion, and border crossing events does not have the meaning described here.

`XInsertModifiermapEntry()` and `XDeleteModifiermapEntry()` provide the easiest ways by far to add or delete a few keycodes for a modifier.

Using `XInsertModifiermapEntry()` and `XDeleteModifiermapEntry()` is straightforward. You get the current modifier mapping stored in an `XModifierKeymap` structure with a call to `XGetModifierMapping()`. You specify this structure, a keycode, and one of the eight modifier symbols as the three arguments to `XInsertModifiermapEntry()` or `XDeleteModifiermapEntry()`. Both routines return a new `XModifierKeymap` structure suitable for calling `XSetModifierMapping()`. You should add or delete all the keycodes you intend to change before calling `XSetModifierMapping()`.

You should not need to understand how the modifiers are stored to use the procedure described above for adding or deleting keycodes.

`XSetModifierMapping()` is the routine that actually changes the mapping. As such, it is when calling `XSetModifierMapping()` that any errors appear, even though they are usually caused by an invalid `XModifierKeymap` structure that was set earlier.

These are the requirements for the **XModifierKeymap** structure specified to **XSet-ModifierMapping()**:

- Zero keycodes are ignored.

- No keycode may appear twice anywhere in the map (otherwise, a **BadValue** error is generated).

- All nonzero keycodes must be in the range specified by **min_keycode** and **max_keycode** in the **Display** structure (else a **BadValue** error).

- A server can impose restrictions on how modifiers can be changed. For example, certain keys may not generate up transitions in hardware or multiple modifier keys may not be supported. If a restriction is violated, then the status reply is **MappingFailed**, and none of the modifiers are changed.

If the new keycodes specified for a modifier differ from those currently defined and any (current or new) keys for that modifier are in the down state, then the status reply is **Mapping-Busy**, and none of the modifiers are changed.

XSetModifierMapping() generates a **MappingNotify** event on a **Mapping-Success** status.

When finished mapping the keyboard, you can free the **XModifierKeymap** structures by calling **XFreeModifiermap()**.

9.1.5 Other Keyboard-handling Routines

Several routines in addition to **XLookupString()** provide ways to translate key events. None of these routines are commonly needed in applications.

You might think that **XKeysymToString()** and **XStringToKeysym()** describe the mapping between keysyms and strings, but they don't. **XKeysymToString()** does not return the same string as is placed in the *buffer* argument of **XLookupString()**, when **XKeysymToString()** is given the keysym that **XLookupString()** returns. **XKeysymToString()** changes the symbol form of a keysym (**XK_Return**), which is a number, into a string form of the symbol ("Return"), and **XStringToKeysym()** does the reverse. **XKeysymToString()(XK_F1)** would return "F1" regardless of what string is currently mapping to the F1 key. Only **XLookupString()** returns the string mapped to a particular keysym with **XRebindKeysym()**.

XKeycodeToKeysym() and **XKeysymToKeycode()** make the mapping between single keycodes and keysyms more accessible. (**XLookupKeysym()** actually takes a key event, extracts the keycode, and calls **XKeycodeToKeysym()**.) For **XKeycode-ToKeysym()** and **XLookupKeysym()**, you must specify which keysym you want from the list for the keycode, with the *index* argument. Remember that the list of keysyms for each keycode represents the key with various combinations of modifier keys pressed. The meaning of the keysym list beyond the first two (unmodified, Shift or Shift Lock) is not defined. Therefore, the *index* values of 0 and 1 are the most commonly used.

9.2 The Pointer

The pointer generates events as it moves, as it crosses window borders, and as its buttons are pressed. It provides position information that can define a path in the two-dimensional space of the screen, tell you which window the pointer is in and allow the user to "point and click," generating input without using the keyboard. In fact, the pointer is the most unique feature of a window system.

This section describes how to track the pointer and how to handle the pointer buttons. Border crossing events are discussed in Section 9.3, because they must be handled in concert with keyboard focus change events.

9.2.1 Tracking Pointer Motion

There are three ways of handling pointer motion events:

- Getting all motion events. The program simply receives and processes every motion event. This option is suitable for applications that require all movements to be reported, no matter how small. Since many motion events are generated and reporting the processing of the events may lag behind the pointer, this approach is not suitable for applications that require the most current information about pointer position.

- Getting hints and querying pointer position. This method greatly reduces the number of motion events sent but requires that `XQueryPointer()` be called to get the current pointer position. This option is suitable for applications that require only the final position of the mouse after each movement.

- Reading the motion history buffer. After checking that the buffer exists, call `XGet-MotionEvents()` when you want the array of events occurring between two specified times. This option is not available on all servers, but it is suitable for detailed pointer position reporting. Its advantage over getting all motion events is that the list of pointer positions in the motion history buffer can be used for undoing or responding to exposure events in drawing applications.

Let's look at each of these methods in detail.

9.2.1.1 Getting All Motion Events

The most obvious way to handle motion events is to get all motion events. The only complication is that you must keep the processing of each event to a minimum so that the feedback loop to the user is reasonably fast.

Example 9-7 shows another modification to *basicwin*, the program described in Chapter 3, *Basic Window Program*. It creates a child window of the top-level window of the application and allows the user to draw into it by moving the pointer with any button held down.

Example 9-7. Getting all motion events

```
/* Global declarations of display and screen */
    .
    .
    .

#define BUF_SIZE 2000
void main(argc, argv)
int argc;
char **argv;
{
    /* Declarations from basicwin */
        .
        .
        .

    Window wint;
    int xpositions[BUF_SIZE], ypositions[BUF_SIZE];
    int i;
    int count = 0;
    Bool buffer_filled = False;

    /* Open display and create window win */
        .
        .
        .

    wint = XCreateSimpleWindow(display, win, 20, 20, 50, 50,
            border_width, BlackPixel(display, screen),
            WhitePixel(display,screen));

    XSelectInput(display, wint, ExposureMask | PointerMotionMask);

    XMapWindow(display, wint);
        .
        .
        .

    /* Select events for and map win */
    while (1)  {
        XNextEvent(display, &report);
        switch  (report.type) {
        case MotionNotify:
            printf("got a motion event\n");
            xpositions[count] = report.xmotion.x;
            ypositions[count] = report.xmotion.y;
            XDrawPoint(display, wint, gc,
                    report.xmotion.x, report.xmotion.y);
            /* The following implements a fast ring buffer
             * when count reaches buffer size */
            if (count <= BUF_SIZE)
                count++;
            else {
                count = 0;
                buffer_filled = True;
            }
            break;
        case Expose:
            printf("got expose event\n");
```

Example 9-7. Getting all motion events (continued)

```
                if (report.xexpose.count != 0)
                        break;
                if (report.xexpose.window == wint) {
                        /* This redraws the right number of points;
                         * if the ring buffer is not yet filled,
                         * it draws count points; otherwise, it
                         * draws all the points */
                        for (i=0 ; i < (buffer_filled ?
                                BUF_SIZE : count) ; i++)
                                XDrawPoint(display, wint, gc, xpositions[i],
                                        ypositions[i]);
                }
                else {
                        if (window_size == SMALL)
                                TooSmall(win, gc, font_info);
                        else {
                                /* Place text in window */
                                draw_text(win, gc, font_info, width, height);

                                /* Place graphics in window */
                                draw_graphics(win, gc, width, height);
                        }
                }
                break;
                /* Other event types handled same as basicwin */
                        .
                        .
                        .
        } /* End switch */
    } /* End while */
}
```

The program keeps a record of the points drawn so that they can be redrawn in case of an **Expose** event. The event record is a ring buffer so that the latest **BUF_SIZE** pointer positions are always maintained.

The program requires that one or more of the pointer buttons must be held down while drawing. (Most drawing applications require a button to be held, because otherwise it is impossible to move the pointer into a different application without drawing a trail of points to the edge of the window.) Therefore, drawing applications normally select **ButtonMotion-Mask**.

It would be quite easy to extend this program by giving each button a different meaning. Drawing with button 1 could mean drawing in black, button 2 could mean drawing in white, and button 3 could mean toggling the previous state of the drawn pixels. The only change necessary to implement this would be code that changes the foreground pixel value and logical operation in a GC or creates three GCs with these variations. The routine would determine which button was pressed from the **state** member of the event structure and determine what to do if more than one button was pressed.

9.2.1.2 Using Pointer Motion Hints

If you do not need a record of every point the pointer has passed through but only its current position, using motion hints is the most efficient method of handling pointer motion events. This method could be used for dragging in menus or scrollbars, in a window manager when it moves the outlines of windows, or in a drawing application in a line drawing mode. We'll demonstrate the technique in a line drawing application.

To use this method, select `PointerMotionHintMask` in addition to the specific event masks you desire. `PointerMotionHintMask` is a modifier; it does not select events by itself.

Example 9-8 demonstrates how to read pointer events with `PointerMotionHintMask` selected. The code shown in the example draws lines between the series of points the user specifies with button clicks. The `ButtonPress` event indicates the beginning of a line, `MotionNotify` events allow the application to draw a temporary line to the current pointer position, and `ButtonRelease` events indicate that the line should be drawn permanently between the points indicated by the `ButtonPress` and `ButtonRelease` events.

Example 9-8. Using pointer motion hints

```
/* Declare global variables display and screen */
     .
     .
     .

void main(argc, argv)
int argc;
char **argv;
{
     /* Declarations from basicwin */
        .
        .
        .

     int root_x, root_y;
     Window root, child;
     unsigned int keys_buttons;
     Window wint;
     XPoint points[ BUF_SIZE ];
     int index = 1;
     int pos_x, pos_y;
     int prev_x, prev_y;
     GC gcx;

     wint = XCreateSimpleWindow(display, win, 20, 20, 50, 50,
                border_width, BlackPixel(display, screen),
                WhitePixel(display,screen));

     XSelectInput(display, wint, ExposureMask | ButtonPressMask
                | ButtonReleaseMask | ButtonMotionMask
                | PointerMotionHintMask);

     gcx = XCreateGC(display, win, 0, NULL);
     XSetFunction(display, gcx, GXxor);
     XSetForeground(display, gcx, BlackPixel(display, screen));
```

Example 9-8. Using pointer motion hints (continued)

```
     XMapWindow(display, wint);
     while (1)   {
         XNextEvent(display, &report);
         switch  (report.type) {
         case ButtonPress:
              points[index].x = report.xbutton.x;
              points[index].y = report.xbutton.y;
              break;
         case ButtonRelease:
              index++;
              points[index].x = report.xbutton.x;
              points[index].y = report.xbutton.y;
              break;
         case MotionNotify:
              printf("got a motion event\n");
              while (XCheckMaskEvent(display,
                     ButtonMotionMask, &report));
              if (!XQueryPointer(display, report.xmotion.window,
                     &root, &child, &root_x, &root_y,
                     &pos_x, &pos_y, &keys_buttons))
                  /* Pointer is on other screen */
                  break;

              /* Undraw previous line, only if not first */
              if (index != 1)
                  XDrawLine(display, wint, gcx, points[index].x,
                           points[index].y, prev_x, prev_y);

              /* Draw current line */
              XDrawLine(display, wint, gcx, points[index].x,
                        points[index].y, pos_x, pos_y);
              prev_x = pos_x;
              prev_y = pos_y;
              break;
         case Expose:
              printf("got expose event\n");

              if (report.xexpose.window == wint) {
                  while (XCheckTypedWindowEvent(display,
                          wint, Expose, &report));
                  XSetFunction(display, gcx, GXcopy);
                  XDrawLines(display, wint, gcx, points,
                          index, CoordModeOrigin);
                  XSetFunction(display, gcx, GXxor);
              }
              else {
                  /* Same code as basicwin */
              }
              break;
         } /* End switch */
     } /* End while */
}
```

In some applications, you do not need to track pointer motion events to know where the pointer is at particular times. The pointer position is given in **ButtonPress**, **Button-Release**, **KeyPress**, **KeyRelease**, **EnterNotify**, and **LeaveNotify** events. You can use any of these events to locate objects in a window.

9.2.1.3 Motion History

If the motion history buffer exists on the server (**XDisplayMotionBufferSize()** (**display**) > 0), all selected motion events are placed in a list of **XTimeCoord** structures. There is no macro for accessing this member of the **display** structure. You specify the desired range of times to **XGetMotionEvents()**, and it returns a pointer to a list of **XTimeCoord** structures, representing all the pointer positions during the range of times. The reported pointer positions may be in finer detail than would be reported by **Motion-Notify** events.

In the MIT sample distribution of Xlib, motion history buffers were first implemented in Release 5. In any case, they are not a required part of a server implementation. Therefore, an application that uses motion history should also support the all-motion-events approach for use on servers that do not have the buffer.

The **XTimeCoord** structure is shown in Example 9-9.

Example 9-9. The XTimeCoord structure

```
typedef struct _XTimeCoord {
     short x,y;  /* Position relative to root window */
     Time time;
} XTimeCoord;
```

Example 9-11 shows another version of the program used to demonstrate getting all motion events.

Example 9-10. Reading the motion history buffer

```
/* Global declarations of display and screen */
     .
     .
     .
#define BUF_SIZE 2000

void main(argc, argv)
int argc;
char **argv;
{
     /* Declarations from basicwin */
          .
          .
          .

     Window wint;
     int xpositions[ BUF_SIZE ], ypositions[ BUF_SIZE ];
     int i;
     int count = 0;
     Bool buffer_filled = False;
```

Example 9-10. Reading the motion history buffer (continued)

```
/* Open display and create window win */
    .
    .
    .

if (XDisplayMotionBufferSize(display) <= 0)
    {
    printf("%s: motion history buffer not provided on server",
            argv(0));
    exit(-1);   /* Or use all events method instead */
    }
wint = XCreateSimpleWindow(display, win, 20, 20, 50, 50,
        border_width, BlackPixel(display, screen),
        WhitePixel(display,screen));

XSelectInput(display, wint, ExposureMask | ButtonMotionMask
        | PointerMotionHintMask);

XMapWindow(display, wint);
    .
    .
    .

/* Select events for and map win */

while (1)  {
    XNextEvent(display, &report);
    switch  (report.type) {
    case MotionNotify:
            printf("got a motion event\n");
        while (XCheckTypedEvent(display, MotionNotify, &report));
        start = prevtime;
        stop = report.xmotion.time;
        xytimelist = XGetMotionEvents(display, window, start,
                stop, &nevents);
        for (i=0;i<nevents;i++)
            XDrawPoint(display, window, gc, xytimelist[i]->x,
                    xytimelist[i]->y);
        break;
    case Expose:
        printf("got expose event\n");
        if (report.xexpose.window == wint) {
            while (XCheckTypedWindowEvent(display,
                    wint, Expose, &report));
            xytimelist = XGetMotionEvents(display, window,
                    0, CurrentTime, &nevents);
            for (i=0 ; i < nevents ; i++)
                XDrawPoint(display, window, gc, xytimelist[i]->x,
                        xytimelist[i]->y);
        }
        else {
            while (XCheckTypedWindowEvent(display,
                    win, Expose, &report));
            if (window_size == SMALL)
                TooSmall(win, gc, font_info);
            else {
                /* Place text in window */
```

Keyboard/Pointer

Example 9-10. Reading the motion history buffer (continued)

```
                          draw_text(win, gc, font_info, width, height);

                          /* Place graphics in window */
                          draw_graphics(win, gc, width, height);
                      }
                  }
                  break;
             /* Other event types handled same as basicwin */
               .
               .
               .
          } /* End switch */
      } /* End while */
}
```

9.2.2 Handling Pointer Button Events

The examples of tracking pointer motion in Section 9.2.1 use the buttons to some extent, but they do not tell you the whole story. There is the subject of automatic button grabs, and there are issues involved in making each button perform a different function. Let's tackle grabs first.

When a pointer button is pressed, an active grab is triggered automatically (as described in Section 8.3.2.2, an active grab means that all button events before the matching **Button-Release** event on the same button always goes to the same application, or sometimes the same window, as the **ButtonPress**). The automatic grab does not take place if an active grab already exists or a passive grab on the present key and button combination exists for some higher level window in the hierarchy than the window in which the **ButtonPress** occurred.

The **OwnerGrabButtonMask** that you can specify in calls to **XSelectInput()** controls the distribution of the **ButtonRelease** event (and any other pointer events that occur between the **ButtonPress** and **ButtonRelease**). If **OwnerGrabButton-Mask** is selected, the **ButtonRelease** event will be sent to whichever window in the application the pointer is in when the event occurs. If the pointer is outside the application or if **OwnerGrabButtonMask** is not selected, the event is sent to the window in which the **ButtonPress** occurred.

OwnerGrabButtonMask should be selected when an application wants to know in which window **ButtonRelease** events occur. This information is useful when you require that both the **ButtonPress** and the matching **ButtonRelease** events occur in the same window in order for an operation to be executed. In practice, it does not hurt to select **OwnerGrabButtonMask** even if you do not need the response it provides. If you do not select **OwnerGrabButtonMask**, any changes you try to make to the event mask of the grabbing window before the **ButtonRelease** will not take effect.

The automatic grabs affect only the window to which button events are sent. To be more precise, they affect the value of the **window** member in the button event structures in the application's event queue. And for the event to be placed on the queue in the first place, it must have been selected on the window specified in the `window` member.

Now let's talk about distinguishing which pointer button was pressed. Two members of the `XButtonEvent` structure contain information about the button state. The `button` member specifies the button that changed state to trigger the event. The `state` member gives the state of all the buttons and modifier keys just before the event. You will need the state member only if you require that certain key or button combinations be pressed to trigger an operation.

Especially if you require that the same button must be pressed and released in a certain window, be sure to account for the case where, for example, button 1 is pressed, then buttons 2 and 3 are pressed and released (perhaps repeatedly) or pressed and held, before button 1 is again released. You must be careful if you structure your code as shown in Example 9-11 to handle `ButtonPress` and `ButtonRelease` events in pairs.* There is no case for `ButtonRelease` in the example. Instead the code for `ButtonPress` looks for the matching `ButtonRelease` event. The matching `ButtonRelease` might not be the next button event, so intervening events must be dealt with. This problem appears only if you are trying to distinguish the button that was pressed.

Example 9-11. Accepting button events in pairs

```
case ButtonPress:
    /* Draw pane in white on black */
    paint_pane(event.xbutton.window, panes, gc, rgc,
            font_info, BLACK);

    /* Keep track of which button was pressed */
    button = event.xbutton.button;

    /* Keep track of which window press occurred in */
    inverted_pane = event.xbutton.window;

    /* Get the matching ButtonRelease on same button */
    while (1) {
        /* Get rid of presses on other buttons */
        while (XCheckTypedEvent(display, ButtonPress,
                &event));
        /* Wait for release; if on correct button, exit */
        XMaskEvent(display, ButtonReleaseMask, &event);
        if (event.xbutton.button == button)
            break;
    }

    /* All events are sent to the grabbing window
     * regardless of whether this is True or False,
     * because owner_events only affects the
     * distribution of events when the pointer is
     * within this application's windows; we don't
     * expect it to be for a window manager */
    owner_events = True;

    /* We don't want pointer or keyboard events
     * frozen in the server */
```

---

*This code is an excerpt from *winman*, the simple window manager described in Chapter 16, *Window Management*.

Example 9-11. Accepting button events in pairs (continued)

```
        pointer_mode = GrabModeAsync;
        keyboard_mode = GrabModeAsync;

        /* We don't want to confine the cursor */
        confine_to = None;

        GrabPointer(display, menuwin, owner_events,
                    ButtonPressMask | ButtonReleaseMask,
                    pointer_mode, keyboard_mode,
                    confine_to, hand_cursor, CurrentTime);

        /* If press and release occurred in same window,
         * do command; if not, do nothing */
        if (inverted_pane == event.xbutton.window)
                {
                /* Convert window ID to window array index  */
                for (winindex = 0; inverted_pane !=
                        panes[winindex]; winindex++)
                    ;
                switch (winindex)
                    {
                case 0:
                    raise_lower(display, screen,
                            RAISE);
                    break;
                .
                .
                .
                case 9: /* Exit */
                    XSetInputFocus(display,
                        RootWindow(display,screen),
                        RevertToPointerRoot,
                        CurrentTime);
                    /* Turn all icons back into windows */
                    /* Must clear focus highlights */
                    XClearWindow(display, RootWindow(display, screen));
                    /* Need to change focus border width back here */

                    XFlush(display);
                    XCloseDisplay(display);
                    exit(1);
                default:
                    (void) fprintf(stderr,
                            "Something went wrong\n");
                    break;
                    } /* End switch */
                } /* End if */

        /* Invert back here (logical function is GXcopy) */
        paint_pane(event.xexpose.window, panes, gc, rgc,
                font_info, WHITE);

        inverted_pane = NONE;
        draw_focus_frame();
        XUngrabPointer(display, CurrentTime);
        XFlush(display);
        break;
case DestroyNotify:
```

Example 9-11. Accepting button events in pairs (continued)

.
.
.

9.2.3 Changing the Pointer Button Mapping

Some applications may allow the user to modify the mapping between the physical pointer buttons and the logical buttons that are reported when a button is pressed. In other words, if physical button 1 were mapped to logical button 3, then when either button 3 or button 1 were pressed, it would appear to all applications that only button 3 was pressed.

There are five logical buttons, but the number of physical buttons may range from one up to and perhaps greater than five. Mapping the pointer buttons might be done, for example, to simulate buttons 4 and 5 on a system with a three-button mouse. However, while physical buttons 1 and 2 were mapped to logical 4 and 5, no buttons would be mapped to logical 1 and 2. Therefore, there would have to be a way of toggling between the modes, perhaps using a function key.

The mapping of pointer buttons is analogous to the mapping between keycodes and keysyms in that it is global to the server and affects all clients. However, since the translation of a pointer event takes place in the server, unlike key event processing routines that use information stored in Xlib whenever possible, no routine is necessary to update the pointer mapping like `XRefreshKeyboardMapping()` updates the keyboard mapping.

`XGetPointerMapping()` returns the current mapping between physical and logical pointer buttons. `XSetPointerMapping()` sets this mapping.

9.2.4 Moving the Pointer

The `XWarpPointer()` routine moves the pointer to a relative or global position. Its use should be minimized and constrained to particular predictable circumstances, because it often confuses the user.

`XWarpPointer()` has various features for moving only in certain situations. See the reference page in Volume Two, *Xlib Reference Manual*, for details.

Warping the pointer generates `MotionNotify` and border crossing events just as if the user moved the pointer.

Keyboard/Pointer

9.3 Border Crossing and Keyboard Focus Change Events

LeaveNotify and EnterNotify events are generated when the pointer crosses a window border. If the window manager is of the real-estate-driven variety (as is *uwm*), you might be tempted to assume that a LeaveNotify event indicates that the window will not receive keyboard input until it receives a matching EnterNotify. However, this assumption is not true if the user has been allowed to set a keyboard focus window. It is also not true if the window manager is of the listener variety (see Chapters 1, 12, and 16). Ideally, you should be prepared to deal with either type of window manager.

Pointer input can only be delivered to a window when the pointer is inside the window (unless the window grabs the pointer). Therefore, an application that depends on pointer input can expect to be idle when the pointer leaves the window and to be active again when the pointer enters. Notice that keyboard input can be diverted with the keyboard focus or grabs, while pointer input can only be diverted by grabs.

FocusIn and FocusOut events occur when the keyboard focus window changes (when some client calls XSetInputFocus()). By using focus events together with the border crossing events, an application should be able to determine whether or not it can get keyboard input. If it cannot get keyboard input, it may change its behavior somewhat. If it polls for keyboard input to allow for interrupts, it can stop polling. If it normally highlights a window when the pointer enters it, it should not do so if the keyboard focus is not the root window.

In general, to determine if it will get keyboard input, an application should first check FocusIn and FocusOut events. If the focus window is the root window, then the application should check LeaveNotify and EnterNotify to see if keyboard events are possible.

Additional focus change and border crossing events are generated when the origin and destination of the focus or pointer crossing do not have a parent-child relationship. These events are called *virtual crossing* events. See Appendix E, *Event Reference*, for a description of when these events are generated and how to distinguish them from normal crossing events.

Example 9-12 shows the code that would be used to monitor whether the application will receive keyboard input. When keyboard_active is True in this code, the application could highlight its main window.

Example 9-12. Monitoring whether keyboard input will be available

```
Bool keyboard_active;
Bool focus;

/* Open display, create window, select input */

/* Select input before setting keyboard focus, if application does */

while (1)  {
    XNextEvent(display, &report);
    switch  (report.type) {
        .
        .
        .
```

```
        case EnterNotify:
             printf("enter\n");
             /* Make sure focus is an ancestor */
             (report.xcrossing.focus) ?
                          (keyboard_active = True)
                          : (keyboard_active = False);
             break;
        case LeaveNotify:
             printf("leave\n");
             /* We get input only if we have the focus */
             (focus) ? (keyboard_active = True)
                          : (keyboard_active = False);
             break;
        case FocusIn:
             /* We get keyboard input for sure */
             printf("focus in\n");
             focus = True;
             keyboard_active = True;
             break;
        case FocusOut:
             /* We lost focus, get no keyboard input */
             printf("focus out\n");
             focus = False;
             keyboard_active = False;
             break;

             .
             .
             .

        }
} /* End while */
```

Example 9-12 could be used as a basis for code that highlights a portion of an application when it can get keyboard input. It would be in *active* mode when the **keyboard_active** flag is **True**. When an **EnterNotify** event is received, the **focus** member of the event structure is checked to see that the focus window is an ancestor of the window in question. If so, **keyboard_active** is **True**. When a **LeaveNotify** event is received, **keyboard_active** is **True** only if the application has the focus. On **FocusIn** events, **keyboard_active** is **True**, and a flag (**focus**) is set to indicate whether the keyboard will be active after **LeaveNotify** events.

9.3.1 The KeymapNotify Event

The **KeymapNotify** event, when selected, always follows on the queue immediately after a **FocusIn** or **EnterNotify** event. Its purpose is to allow the application to easily determine which combination of keys were pressed when the focus was transferred to the window or the pointer entered it. The **KeymapNotify** event contains a keyboard *vector*, which is a 32-element array of type **char**, in which each bit represents a key. For a given key, its keycode is its position in the keyboard vector.

The XQueryKeymap() function also returns this keyboard vector. Keyboard vectors are always independent of all the keyboard mapping and reading functions, since the bits in the vector correspond to keycodes that cannot be changed. This way of reading the keyboard is just like reading the pointer buttons. It can be useful for applications that treat the keyboard not as characters but, for example, as piano keys or drum pads.

Since XQueryKeymap() makes a routine trip request, reading the keyboard this way could not achieve the same performance when operating over a network as the same program implemented using events.

9.4 Grabbing the Keyboard and Pointer

There are times when a program might want to bypass the normal keyboard or pointer event propagation path in order to get input independent of the position of the pointer. This is the purpose of grabbing the keyboard and pointer. There are routines to grab the keyboard (XGrabKeyboard()) or the pointer (XGrabPointer()), or to arrange that they become grabbed when a certain combination of keys and/or buttons is pressed (XGrab-Button(), XGrabKey()). There are corresponding calls to ungrab (XUngrab-Button(), XUngrabKey(), XUngrabKeyboard(), XUngrabPointer()), and there is one call to change the characteristics of a pointer grab (XChangeActive-PointerGrab()).

One of the most common situations where grabbing takes place is with button events. Most applications want both a ButtonPress and a ButtonRelease, so that they can compare the two positions. Since this is such a common desire, the server *automatically* grabs the pointer between the ButtonPress and ButtonRelease if both are selected, so that you do not have to make an explicit grab.

One reason for grabbing a device is so that you can handle a series of events contiguously without fear of intervening events. But when you grab a device, no other application can receive input from that device. Therefore, it is something to do only when absolutely necessary.

The routines that grab take several arguments that tailor the input response in these ways:

- When the pointer is grabbed, the cursor may be confined to any window (the *confine_to* argument).

- The distribution of events to windows within the application can be modified by the *owner_events* argument. If *owner_events* is True, then the grabbed events will be sent to the window within the application that the pointer indicates. If *owner_events* is False or the pointer is outside the applications, then the events are always sent only to window specified by *window*.

- A window called the *grab_window* is specified. All events that occur outside the calling application's windows are reported to the grab window. All events within the application's windows will be sent to the grab window if the *owner_events* argument is False, or they will be reported normally within the application (to the window indicated by the pointer or propagating from that window if it did not select the event) if *owner_events* is `True`.

- For events that occur outside the calling application's windows, and events that occur inside when *owner_events* is `False`, the *event_mask* argument specifies which types of events are selected for the grab window. This *event_mask* overrules the existing *event_mask* for the grab window unless *owner_events* is `True`.

- Event processing for either keyboard or pointer events or both may be halted altogether during the grab until a releasing `XAllowEvents()` call is invoked by setting the *pointer_mode* or *keyboard_mode* arguments to `GrabModeSync`.

- The *cursor* argument specifies a particular `Cursor` to be displayed while the grab is active. This cursor indicates to the user that input is going to the grabbing window, since the cursor will not change when moved across the screen as it normally would.

- Grabbing calls may specify a time when the grab should take place (the *time* argument).

You can change several of the conditions of an active pointer grab, namely the *event_mask*, *cursor*, and *time*, using `XChangeActivePointerGrab()`.

`XGrabKey()` and `XGrabButton()` arrange for a grab to take place when a certain combination of keys or buttons is pressed. After one of these routines is called, a passive grab is said to be in effect, until the specified keys and buttons are pressed. At that time, the grab is active and is indistinguishable from a grab generated by a call to `XGrabKeyboard()` or `XGrabPointer()`. After a passive grab, an active pointer grab will take effect when the following four conditions are met:

- The specified button is pressed when an optional set of modifier keyboard keys is pressed and no other keys or buttons are pressed.

- The pointer is contained in the grab window specified in the grabbing call.

- The cursor-confining window (specified in the *confine_to* argument of `XGrab-Pointer()` or `XGrabButton()`) must be visible, if one is specified.

- These conditions are not satisfied by any ancestor.

Grabbing the keyboard is similar to setting the keyboard focus window, but grabbing is more flexible, since there are more arguments to modify the effect. Focus changes and keyboard grabs and ungrabs all generate the same `FocusIn` and `FocusOut` events.

If pointer grabs and ungrabs cause the pointer to move in or out of a window, they generate `EnterNotify` and `LeaveNotify` events.

The `XAllowEvents()` routine is used only when the *pointer_mode* or *keyboard_mode* in previous grabbing calls were set to `GrabModeSync`. Under these conditions, the server queues any events that occur (but does not send them to the Xlib event queues for each application), and the keyboard or pointer is considered "frozen." `XAllow-Events()` releases the events that are queued in the server for the frozen device. After the call, the device is still frozen, and the server again queues any events that occur on that device until the next `XAllowEvents()` or `Ungrab*` call. In effect, `XAllow-`

`Events()` allows events to come in a batch through the network to the event queues for each application in Xlib.

The pointer modes have no effect on the processing of keyboard events and vice versa.

Both a pointer grab and a keyboard grab may be active at the same time by the same or different clients. If a device is frozen on behalf of either grab, no event processing is performed for the device. It is possible for a single device to be frozen by both grabs. In this case, the freeze must be released on behalf of both grabs before events can again be processed.

9.4.1 Implementing Type-ahead for Information Entry

Normally, the keyboard input focus, which is the window to which all keyboard input is sent, is controlled by the window manager. However, the window manager only gives the keyboard input focus to top-level windows. So essentially the window manager gives the keyboard focus to one application at a time.

Order entry applications need to move the keyboard focus from subwindow to subwindow within the application. Many of them interpret the Tab key as a command to move to the next information entry field. To do this reliably while allowing type-ahead, they must use the keyboard focus in combination with grabs. Here's why, as written by Wayne Dyksen of Purdue University.* It begins with a little more about synchronous and asynchronous grabs, which you need to understand to follow the rest.

As "raw" events occur on devices, the Server processes them and sends them to clients. For example, given a raw event, the Server must determine to which window the event is to be sent; that is, the Server must determine the value of the **window** member of the event structure. The parameters `pointer_mode` and `keyboard_mode` arguments of `XGrab-Button()`, `XGrabPointer()`, `XGrabKey()`, and `XGrabKeyboard()` control the processing of raw events during a grab; they can have either of the values `GrabMode-Async` or `GrabModeSync`.

If the value `GrabModeAsync` is used, then event processing for the grabbed device is asynchronous, as usual. That is, the Server processes and sends all grabbed events to the grabbing client as soon as they occur. Note that all ungrabbed events (e.g., **Expose**) are processed and sent normally.

If `GrabModeSync` is used, then, when the grab occurs, the Server records raw device events in an internal queue, but it temporarily stops processing and sending them to the grabbing client. The Server resumes raw event processing when the grabbing client sends either an `XAllowEvents()` request or an ungrab request.

Using `GrabModeSync` is often referred to as *freezing* the keyboard or pointer. This term is the source of some confusion since using `GrabModeSync` does *not* freeze (lockup) the pointer or keyboard themselves in any intuitive sense. One would guess that if the pointer or keyboard were "frozen," then using them would have no effect. In fact, use of the pointer

---

*This is an excerpt of the paper "Controlling Event Delivery with Grabs and Keyboard Focus," by Wayne Dyksen, that appeared in *The X Resource*, Issue 2.

and keyboard during a freeze continues to generate raw events which are recorded (but not processed or sent) by the Server. For example, the pointer cursor continues to move on the screen. Using `GrabModeSync` does *not* freeze the physical pointer or keyboard themselves, but rather it freezes the raw pointer or keyboard *events* at the Server. The raw events (not the devices) are eventually *thawed* (processed and sent) when the freezing client sends either an `XAllowEvents()` request or an ungrab request.

Consider the simplified forms fill-in application illustrated in Figure 9-1. Recall that the user gets from one blank to the next (from one window to the next) by using a special key (say Next). Each blank in the form is implemented by a separate X window. The client changes the keyboard input focus (via `XSetInputFocus()`) to the next blank (window) each time it receives a Next `KeyPress` event.

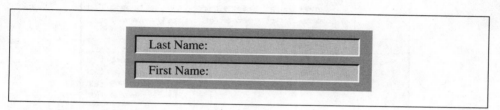

Figure 9-1. Simplified forms fill-in application

Suppose first that a client were to attempt to implement this forms fill-in application by having the "form" window (the parent of the blanks) *asynchronously* grab the Next key. When the form window receives a Next `KeyPress` event, it issues an `XSetInputFocus()` request, changing the keyboard input focus to the next blank.

Consider the possible scenario of events when a user types "D-y-k-s-e-n-Next-W-a-y-n-e," as illustrated in Figure 9-2. Each Snapshot shows the events and requests in queues at a moment in time; events as they are first generated ("Raw Events"), events as the server determines the window to which they should be delivered ("Cooked Events"), and requests made by the client in response to the arrival of these events. "Raw Events" are physical device events which the Server has queued and must process; for example, "s —> ?" indicates that the "s" key has been pressed and that the Server must decide to which window the `KeyPress` event is to be sent. "Cooked Events" are events which the Server has processed and is about to dispatch; for example, "D —> Last" indicates that the "D" key has been pressed and that the event is to be sent to the "Last Name" window. "Requests" are requests which have come from the client in response to events; for example, "D —> Last" indicates that the client has requested the Server to draw a "D" in the "Last Name" window.

Consider now what might happen if a user were to type "D-y-k-s-e-n-Next-W-a-y-n-e." When the event "Next —> Form" illustrated in Snapshot 2 is received by the "Form" window, the client issues the request "Focus —> First" shown in Snapshot 3. Unfortunately, while the client is processing the Next `KeyPress` event, the Server is asynchronously processing further keyboard events. Thus, until the Server actually receives and processes the "Focus —> First" request, it continues to dispatch `KeyPress` events to the "Last Name" window. This is illustrated in Snapshot 3 where the Server is dispatching "W-a-y" to the "Last Name" window. Since the events "W-a-y" are sent to the "Last Name" window, the

Contiguous Snapshots of the Server Queues			
Snapshot	**Raw Events**	**Cooked Events**	**Requests**
1	D ⟶ ? y ⟶ ? k ⟶ ?		
2	s ⟶ ? e ⟶ ? n ⟶ ? Next ⟶ ? W ⟶ ? a ⟶ ? y ⟶ ?	D ⟶ Last y ⟶ Last k ⟶ Last	
3	W ⟶ ? a ⟶ ? y ⟶ ? n ⟶ ? e ⟶ ?	s ⟶ Last e ⟶ Last n ⟶ Last Next ⟶ Form	Draw D ⟶ Last Draw y ⟶ Last Draw k ⟶ Last
4	n ⟶ ? e ⟶ ?	W ⟶ Last a ⟶ Last y ⟶ Last	Draw s ⟶ Last Draw e ⟶ Last Draw n ⟶ Last Set Focus ⟶ First
5		n ⟶ First e ⟶ First	Draw W ⟶ Last Draw a ⟶ Last Draw y ⟶ Last
6			Draw n ⟶ First Draw e ⟶ First

Figure 9-2. Possible scenario of events using an asynchronous key grab

client issues the requests shown in Snapshot 4 to draw "W-a-y" in the "Last Name" window. Eventually, the Server does receive and process the "Focus —> First" request. Snapshot 4 and 5 show "n-e" being sent to and drawn in the "First Name" window. The above scenario produces the incorrect result illustrated in Figure 9-3.

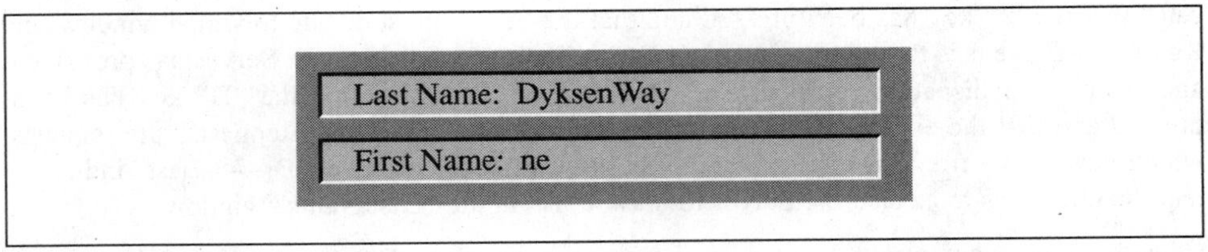

Last Name: DyksenWay

First Name: ne

Figure 9-3. Possible incorrect forms fill-in result using an asynchronous key grab

Note that the actual forms fill-in result using an asynchronous grab varies depending on the time between KeyPress events. In fact, the form would produce the correct result if a user were to type "D-y-k-s-e-n-Next" followed by a sufficiently long pause followed by "W-a-y-n-e."

Consider again the above example, only this time suppose that the client *synchronously* grabs the Next key (before any key events are processed). The sequence of events that occur in response to the user typing "D-y-k-s-e-n-Next-W-a-y-n-e" is illustrated in Figure 9-4.

Contiguous Snapshots of the Server Queues			
Snapshot	Raw Events	Cooked Events	Requests
1	D ⟶ ? y ⟶ ? k ⟶ ?		
2	s ⟶ ? e ⟶ ? n ⟶ ? Next ⟶ ? W ⟶ ? a ⟶ ?	D ⟶ Last y ⟶ Last k ⟶ Last	
3	W ⟶ ? a ⟶ ? y ⟶ ? n ⟶ ? e ⟶ ?	s ⟶ Last e ⟶ Last n ⟶ Last Next ⟶ Form	Draw D ⟶ Last Draw y ⟶ Last Draw k ⟶ Last
4	W ⟶ ? a ⟶ ? y ⟶ ? n ⟶ ? e ⟶ ?		Draw s ⟶ Last Draw e ⟶ Last Draw n ⟶ Last Set Focus ⟶ First Allow Keyboard Events
5	n ⟶ ? e ⟶ ?	W ⟶ Last a ⟶ Last y ⟶ Last	
6		n ⟶ First e ⟶ First	Draw W ⟶ Last Draw a ⟶ Last Draw y ⟶ Last
7			Draw n ⟶ First Draw e ⟶ First

Figure 9-4. Scenario of events using a synchronous key grab

As soon as the Server sees the raw Next `KeyPress` event, it initiates a synchronous grab. Snapshot 3 shows that the Server is continuing to record raw `KeyPress` events, but it has stopped "cooking" them. The `KeyPress` events "W-a-y-n-e" have accumulated in the Server's "Raw Events" queue. After receiving the Next `KeyPress` event, the client sends a request to the Server to change the focus to the "First Name" window ("Focus —> First") followed by a request to start cooking events ("Allow Events"). Because of the synchronous grab, the client knows that the Server receives and processes the "Focus —> First" request before it processes the raw event "W —> ?." The desired result is illustrated in Figure 9-5.

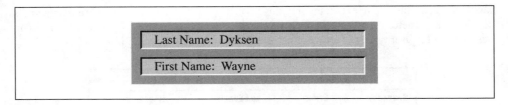

Figure 9-5. Correct forms fill-in result using a synchronous key grab

To summarize, the solution to this form of type-ahead problem is to use **GrabModeSync** as the **keyboard_mode** argument of the passive grab on the Tab key. Then call **XAllow-Events()** in response the arrival of the Tab key event that signals the change in windows. This synchronizes the change of keyboard focus from one window to another and assures that the events go to the intended window.

9.5 Keyboard Preferences

Xlib provides routines to control beep pitch and volume, key click, Shift-Lock mode, mouse acceleration, keyboard lights and keyboard auto-repeat. Not all servers will actually be able to control all of these parameters.

There are five routines that deal with the keyboard and pointer preferences. **XGet-KeyboardControl()** and **XChangeKeyboardControl()** are the primary routines for getting or setting all these preferences at once. **XAutoRepeatOff()** and **XAuto-RepeatOn()** set the global keyboard auto-repeat status but are not able to control the auto-repeat of individual keys as **XChangeKeyboardControl()** can.

9.5.1 Setting Keyboard Preferences

XChangeKeyboardControl() uses the standard X method of changing internal structure members. The *values* argument to **XChangeKeyboardControl()** specifies the structure containing the desired values; the *value_mask* argument specifies which members in the structure specified in *values* should replace the current settings. See the reference page for **XChangeKeyboardControl()** in Volume Two, *Xlib Reference Manual*, for a list of the mask symbols.

Example 9-13 shows the **XKeyboardControl()** structure.

Example 9-13. The XKeyboardControl() structure

```
typedef struct {
    int key_click_percent;
    int bell_percent;
    int bell_pitch;
    int bell_duration;
    int led;
    int led_mode;               /* LedModeOn or LedModeOff */
```

Example 9-13. The XKeyboardControl() structure (continued)

```
    int key;
    int auto_repeat_mode;        /* AutoRepeatModeOff, AutoRepeatModeOn,
                                  * AutoRepeatModeDefault */
} XKeyboardControl;
```

The following list describes each member of the **XKeyboardControl()** structure:

* **key_click_percent** sets the volume for key clicks between 0 (off) and 100 (loud), inclusive.

* **bell_percent** sets the base volume for the bell (or beep) between 0 (off) and 100 (loud), inclusive.

* **bell_pitch** sets the pitch (specified in Hz) of the bell.

* **bell_duration** sets the duration (specified in milliseconds) of the bell.

* **led_mode** controls whether the keyboard LEDs are to be used. If **led** is not specified and **led_mode** is **LedModeOn**, the states of all the lights are changed. If **led_mode** is **LedModeOff**, then the states of the lights are not changed. If **led** is specified, the light specified in **led** is turned on if **led_mode** is **LedModeOn** or turned off if **led_mode** is **LedModeOff**.

* **led** is a number between 1 and 32, inclusive, which specifies which light is turned on or off, depending on **led_mode**.

* **auto_repeat_mode** specifies how to handle auto-repeat when a key is held down. If only **auto_repeat_mode** is specified, then the global auto-repeat mode for the entire keyboard is changed, without affecting the per-key settings. If the **auto_repeat_mode** is **AutoRepeatModeOn**, the keys that are set to auto-repeat will do so. If it is set to **AutoRepeatModeOff**, no keys will repeat. If it is set to **AutoRepeatModeDefault**, all the keys or the specified key will operate in the default mode for the server. Normally the default mode is for all nonmodal keys to repeat (everything except Shift Lock and similar keys). The **auto_repeat_mode** can also be set using the **XAutoRepeatOff()** and **XAutoRepeatOn()** routines. None of the other members of the **XKeyboardControl()** structure have convenience routines for setting them.

* **key** specifies the keycode of a key whose auto-repeat status will be changed to the setting specified by **auto_repeat_mode**. If this value is specified, **auto_repeat_mode** affects only the key specified in **key**. This is the only way to change the mode of a single key.

Setting any of **bell_duration**, **bell_percent**, **bell_pitch**, or **key_click_percent** to –1 restores the default value for that member.

The initial state of many of these parameters may be determined by command line arguments to the X server. On systems that operate only under the X Window System, the server is executed automatically by *xdm* during the boot procedure, and the defaults may have been modified in one of the *xdm* configuration files.

Keyboard/Pointer

Table 9-2 shows the ranges for each member when no command line arguments are specified for the server. The defaults when these values are not set are server-dependent.

Table 9-2. Keyboard Preference Settings — Ranges

Parameter	Range
`key_click_percent`	0 to 100
`bell_percent`	0 to 100
`bell_pitch`	hertz (20 to 20K)
`bell_duration`	milliseconds
`led`	1 to 32
`led_mode`	`LedModeOff`, `LedModeOn`
`key`	8 to 255
`auto_repeat_mode`	`AutoRepeatModeDefault`, `AutoRepeatModeOff`, `AutoRepeatModeOn`

9.5.2 Getting Keyboard Preferences

To obtain the current state of the user preferences, use **XGetKeyboardControl()**. This routine returns an **XKeyboardState()** structure, as shown in Example 9-14.

Example 9-14. The XKeyboardState() structure

```
typedef struct {
    int key_click_percent;
    int bell_percent;
    unsigned int bell_pitch, bell_duration;
    unsigned long led_mask;
    int global_auto_repeat;
    char auto_repeats[32];
} XKeyboardState;
```

Except for **led_mask**, **global_auto_repeat**, and **auto_repeats**, these members have the same range of possible values listed in Table 9-2.

The **led_mask** member is not directly analogous to any member of **XKeyboard-Control()**. Each bit set to 1 in **led_mask** indicates a lit LED. The least significant bit of **led_mask** corresponds to LED one.

The **global_auto_repeat** member is either **AutoRepeatModeOff** or **Auto-RepeatModeOn**. It reports the state of the parameter set by the **auto_repeat_mode** member of **XKeyboardControl()**.

The **auto_repeats** member is a key vector like the one in **KeymapNotify** events and returned by **XQueryKeymap()**. Each bit set to 1 in **auto_repeats** indicates that auto-repeat is enabled for the corresponding key. The vector is represented as 32 bytes. Byte *N* (from 0) contains the bits for keycodes *8N* to *8N+7*, with the least significant bit in the byte representing keycode *8N*. Every key on the keyboard is represented by a bit in the vector.

9.6 Pointer Preferences

`XChangePointerControl()` sets the parameters that control pointer acceleration, and `XGetPointerControl()` gets them. *Pointer acceleration* is a feature that allows the user to move the cursor more quickly across the screen. If pointer acceleration is active, when the pointer moves more than a certain *threshold* amount in a single movement, the cursor will move a *multiple* of the amount the physical pointer moved. The effect of acceleration is that you can have detailed control over the pointer for fine work and, by flicking the wrist, you can also move quickly to the far reaches of the screen.

`XChangePointerControl()` takes three arguments (in addition to the ubiquitous *display*): *accel_numerator*, *accel_denominator*, and *threshold*.

The *accel_numerator* and *accel_denominator* arguments make up a fraction that determines the multiple used to determine how many pixels to move the cursor based on how much the physical pointer moved. The *threshold* argument specifies how many pixels the physical pointer must have moved for acceleration to take effect.

9.7 X Input Extension

As of Release 5, the X Input extension is now a standard way to get input from devices other than keyboard and mouse (such as trackballs and tablets), or from multiple such devices. However, not many servers currently support the extension. For more information on the X Input extension, see *The X Resource*, Issue 4, or the forthcoming volume *Extensions and Utilities*.

10

Internationalization

There are several good reasons to internationalize your applications, including sales to foreign markets and simple courtesy to users who would prefer to run those applications in different languages. Because internationalization involves some confusing concepts, the topic is divided into two chapters. If there is any chance, however, that you will someday have to port your applications to run in a different country or language, you should at least be familiar with the concepts and techniques introduced in these chapters. If you know what is involved in internationalization, you can avoid writing applications that will be difficult to internationalize later on.

In This Chapter:

10
Internationalization

An internationalized application is one that runs, without changes to the binary, in any given "locale." Among other things, this means that a program must display all text in the user's language, accept input of all text in that same language, and display times, dates, and numbers in the user's accustomed format.

The internationalization of terminal-based programs is a problem that has been satisfactorily solved where terminals exist that can display and accept input for a particular language. The ANSI-C library contains mechanisms for this terminal-based internationalization, and R5 internationalization is based on these mechanisms. This chapter begins with a detailed overview of the goals, concepts, and techniques of internationalization, starting with ANSI-C internationalization and progressing to the new R5 internationalization features. After the overview, each section covers an individual topic in X internationalization. Internationalized text input with R5 is a large subject and is given its own chapter following this one.

Internationalization is implemented with a separate set of functions for handling keyboard input and drawing text, that are new in Release 5. All the input and drawing techniques shown in previous chapters continue to work, but they do not support internationalization. So it is up to you which set of functions to use depending on your needs.

Also note that the internationalization features of R5 are not self contained, and therefore may not work on all systems. If you do not have the ANSI-C internationalization features, you may be able to make do with alternatives provided by Xlib and by contributed libraries, but these have not been thoroughly tested and you may encounter difficulties. In ANSI-C internationalization, the C library reads a "localization database" customized for each locale. Many systems (systems sold in the U.S., at least) support ANSI-C internationalization, but do not ship databases for any but a default locale.*

---

*If you have a system like this and are building X from the MIT distribution, and would like to experiment with X internationalization, add **–DX_LOCALE** to the **StandardDefines** definition in the *.cf* file for your system (in the directory *mit/config/*) before you build the release. This variable should allow X internationalization to work without the ANSI-C locale databases. It will not, of course, make ANSI-C internationalization itself work. If your system does not have any of the ANSI-C internationalization support, and in particular does not define the type **wchar_t** (a "wide character" used for text in some locales), you will also need to add **–DX_WCHAR** to the **Standard-Defines** variable. Finally, your programs should include the file *<X11/Xlocale.h>* instead of the standard *<locale.h>* and be compiled with **–DX_LOCALE**; this will replace the ANSI-C **setlocale** with an X version of the function.

One more warning and disclaimer is required. These internationalization features are new in Release 5, and therefore there is no experience in their use. So the coverage in this book probably does not yet answer every question you might have, nor present a foolproof procedure for writing an internationalized application. We hope to add more practical instructions once we know better what to tell you.

A final point of terminology: the word "internationalization" contains 20 letters. In the MIT X documentation and elsewhere, you may find it abbreviated as *i18n*—the letter "i" followed by 18 letters and the letter "n."

10.1 An Overview of Internationalization

If you are a native English speaker, particularly an American, you may never have thought much about what is required for the internationalization of programs for the simple reason that all the programs you use already speak your language. There are four general areas that require attention when writing an internationalized application:

- An internationalized application must display all text in the user's native or preferred language. This includes prompts, error messages, and text displayed by buttons, menus, and other widgets. The obvious approach to this sort of internationalization is to remove all strings that will be displayed from the source code of the application and put them instead in a file that will be read in when the application starts up. Then it is a relatively simple matter to translate the file of strings to other languages and have the application read the appropriate one at startup. Many X applications that use the X resource manager to provide an app-defaults file are already internationalized in this way, though some still have non-internationalized error messages. Another approach to the internationalization of strings is the message catalog facility defined by the *X/Open Portability Guide, Issue 3* (often known as XPG3).* The three functions `catopen`, `catgets`, and `catclose`, provide a simple mechanism for retrieving numbered strings from a plain text file. These functions are available on some systems, but are not part of any formal standard, and are not universally available.

An internationalized application must display times, dates, numbers, etc. in the format that the user is accustomed to. Where an American user sees a date in the form *month/day/year*, an English user should see *day/month/year*, and a German user should see *day.month.year*. And where an American user sees the number 1,234.56, a French user should see 1.234,56. The definition of "alphabetical order" is a similar customary usage that varies from country to country. In Spain, for example, the string "ch" is treated as a single letter that comes after "c." So while the strings "Chile" and "Colombia" are in alphabetical order for an American user, they are out of order for a Spanish user. These and related problems of local customs are resolved with the ANSI-C `set-locale` mechanism. Calling this function causes the ANSI-C library to read a database of localization information. Other functions in the C library (such as `printf` for displaying numbers and `strcoll` for comparing strings) use the information in this

---

*X/Open is an influential international group working to encourage computer inter-operability. It is not related to the X Consortium or the X Window System.

database so that they can behave correctly in the current locale. The R5 internationalization mechanisms are built upon this `setlocale` mechanism. It is described in more detail in the next section.

- An internationalized program must be capable of displaying all the characters used in the user's language, and must allow the user to generate all these characters as input. For terminal-based applications, this can be thought of as a hardware issue: a French user's terminal must be capable of displaying the accented characters used in French, and there must be some way to generate those characters from the keyboard. With X and bit-mapped displays, character display is not a problem—simply a matter of finding the required font or fonts. For languages like Chinese, fonts with many characters are required, but X supports 16-bit fonts, which is large enough for almost all languages. Keyboard input for Chinese and other ideographic Asian languages is another matter, however. When there are more characters in a language than there are keys on a keyboard, some sort of "input method" is required for converting multiple keystrokes into a single character. Ideographic languages require complex input methods, and often there is more than one standard method for a language. An internationalized application must support any input method chosen by the user. R5 provides this capability; it is described in Chapter 11, *Internationalized Text Input*.

- An internationalized program must operate regardless of the encoding of characters in the user's language. A program (or operating system) that ignores or truncates the eightth bit of every character won't work in Europe, because the accented characters used in many European languages are represented with numbers greater than 127. An application that assumes that every character is 8 bits long won't work in Japan where there are many thousands of ideographic characters. Furthermore, common Japanese usage intermixes 16-bit Japanese characters with 8-bit Latin characters, so it is not even safe to assume that characters are of a uniform width. When internationalizing an application, two areas of particular difficulty are string manipulation (how, for example, can you iterate through the characters of a string when those characters have differing widths) and text input and output. (How, for example, do you display a Japanese string that contains characters from different fonts?)

One approach to the encoding problem is to side-step it by defining a universal encoding used everywhere. The Latin-1 encoding is suitable for English and most western European languages, and this shared encoding dramatically simplifies the problem of porting applications to work in many European countries. But this approach does not work outside of Europe, and while ANSI-C provides some rudimentary internationalized string manipulation functions, it leaves issues of text input and output to the terminal hardware or terminal driver software. It is here that R5 makes its real contribution to internationalization—in an extension to the `setlocale` model, an internationalized X application reads a localization file at startup that contains information about the text encoding used in the locale. This information allows X to correctly parse strings into characters and figure out how to display them. There are a number of issues surrounding character encoding in internationalized applications, and it is possible to explore them in full and confusing detail. In practice, though, most of the string encoding details are hidden by the operating system, or with X internationalization, by Xlib. Section 10.1.2 explains some of the basics of text encoding in more detail.

When thinking about applications that run in other languages, it is important to recognize the distinction between an internationalized application and a multilingual application. A text editor that works in any given locale is internationalized; a mail reading program that labels its push buttons with text in the language of the locale is internationalized, but if it also allows a user to compose mail in a second language and include excerpts from a message in a third language, then it is multilingual. The requirements and problems of multilingual applications are not yet well understood, and the X Consortium made a considered decision that R5 would support internationalized applications but not explicitly support multilingual ones.

The following sections continue this introduction to internationalization with a description of the ANSI-C `setlocale` mechanism and a further discussion of character encoding and text representation issues.

10.1.1 Internationalization with ANSI-C

Clearly it is not feasible to write an application that has special case code for the formatting customs of every country in the world. A simpler approach is to use a library that reads a customizing database at startup time. This database would contain the currency symbol, the decimal separator symbol, abbreviations for the days of the weeks and names of the months in the local language, the collation sequence of the alphabet, etc. This is the approach taken by the ANSI-C library. The process of writing an application that is flexible enough to use the values from this database is called internationalization, and the process of creating the runtime database for a locale is called *localization*.

The first step in any internationalized application is to establish the locale—to cause the localization database to be read in. This is done with the C library function `setlocale`. It takes two arguments: a locale category and the locale name. The locale name specifies the database that should be used to localize the program, and the locale category specifies which behaviors (for example, the collation sequence of the alphabet or the formatting of times and dates) of the program should be changed. `setlocale` will most often be used as shown below:

```
setlocale(LC_ALL, "");
```

Passing the empty string as the locale name will cause `setlocale` to get the name of the locale from the operating system environment variable named **LANG**. This allows the application writer to leave the choice of locale to the end user of the application. There is no standard format for locale names, but they often have the form:

language[*_territory*[*.codeset*]]

So the locale "Fr" might be used in France, while "En_GB" might specify English as used in Great Britain, and "En_US" English as used in the U.S. The *codeset* field can be used to specify the encoding (i.e., the mapping between numbers and characters) to be used for all strings in the application when there is not a single default encoding used for the language in the territory. The locale "ja_JP.ujis" is an example—"ujis" is the name of one of the encodings in common use for Japanese. The name of the default locale is simply "C." This locale is familiar to American computer users and all C programmers. Finally, note that the return value of `setlocale` is a `char *`. It returns the name of the locale that was just set, or if it is passed a locale name of NULL (not the same as " "), it will return the name of the current locale.

The category LC_ALL instructs `setlocale` to set all internationalization behavior defined by ANSI-C to operate in the given locale. The locale may also be specified for each category individually. The standard categories (other, non-standard, categories may also be defined) and the aspects of program behavior that they control are listed below:

LC_COLLATE

> This category defines the collation sequence used by the ANSI-C library functions `strcoll` and `strxfrm` which are used to order strings alphabetically.

LC_CTYPE

> This category defines the behavior of the character classification and case conversion macros (such as `isspace` and `tolower`) defined in the header file *<ctype.h>*. Different languages will have different classifications for characters. Not all characters have uppercase equivalents, for example, and characters with codes between 128 and 255 which are non-printing in ASCII are important alphabetic characters in many European languages.

LC_MONETARY

> This category does not affect the behavior of any C library functions. The problem of formatting monetary quantities was deemed too intricate for any standard library function, so the library simply provides a way for an application to look up any of the localized parameters it needs to do its own formatting of monetary quantities. The ANSI-C function `localeconv` returns a pointer to a structure of type `lconv` that contains the parameters (such as decimal separator, currency symbol, and flags that indicate whether the currency symbol should appear before or after positive and negative quantities, etc.) needed for numeric and monetary formatting in the current locale.

LC_NUMERIC

> This category affects the decimal separator used by `printf` (and its variants), `scanf` (and its variants), `gcvt` (and related functions), `strtod`, and `atof`. It also affects the values in the `lconv` structure returned by `localeconv`.

LC_TIME

> This category affects the behavior of the time and date formatting functions `strftime` and `strptime`. It defines such things as the names of the days of the week and their standard abbreviations in the language of the locale.

If you use `setlocale` and the new C library functions mentioned above (and carefully avoid the use of the old C functions that they replace), you will be well on your way to an internationalized application. For more information on `setlocale` and the functions it affects, see the documentation supplied by your vendor (a UNIX system should have reference pages for these functions). The *POSIX Programmer's Guide* by Donald Lewine, published by O'Reilly & Associates, may also be useful—it has a chapter on ANSI-C internationalization and a complete reference section of ANSI-C and POSIX (IEEE standard UNIX) functions.

10.1.2 Text Representation in an Internationalized Application

Think for a minute about the fundamentals of text representation by computer. Remember that characters displayed by your computer are represented by numbers. The correspondence between numbers and characters (on most American computers) is defined by the ASCII (American Standard Code for Information Interchange) encoding. There is nothing special about ASCII except that it is one of the most firmly established standards of the computer world. Text composed in one encoding (ASCII, for example) and displayed in another (perhaps EBCDIC, still used by IBM mainframes) will be nonsense because the number-to-character mappings of the encodings are not the same.

We've been using the term encoding rather loosely. Before we consider text representation any further, some definitions are appropriate. A *character* is an abstract element of text, distinct from a *font glyph*, which is the actual image that gets displayed. A *character set* is simply a set of characters; there are no numbers associated with those characters. We are all familiar with the character set used by ASCII. The Latin-1 character set used by many Western European Latin-based languages is an extension of ASCII that contains the accented characters required by many of those languages. An encoding is any numeric representation of the characters in a character set. The term *codeset* is sometimes used as a synonym for encoding. A *charset* (not the same as a character set) is an encoding in which all characters have the same number of bits. ASCII is a 7-bit encoding, for example, and is therefore a charset. Figure 10-1 diagrams the relationship between character sets, charsets, fonts, and font glyphs.

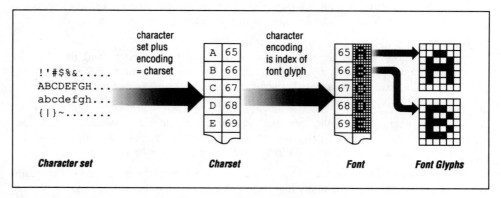

Figure 10-1. Character sets, encodings, charsets, fonts, and glyphs

The last two fields of an X font name specify a charset. By definition, the index of a font glyph in the font is the same as the encoding of the corresponding character in that charset. When the encoding of a locale is a charset, this obviously simplifies matters a great deal: text in the locale can be displayed using glyphs from a single font, and the character encoding can be used directly as the index of the corresponding font glyph.

Not all languages can be represented with a single charset, however. Japanese text, for example, commonly requires Japanese ideographic characters, Japanese phonetic characters, and Latin characters. Each of these character sets has its own standard fixed-width encoding, and is therefore a charset. Note, however, that the ideographic charset is 16-bits wide while the phonetic and Latin charsets are 8-bits wide. Full Japanese text display requires a font for each charset, and Japanese text representation requires a "super-encoding" that combines each of the component encodings. There are, in fact, several encodings commonly used for Japanese text. What they have in common is the use of "shift sequences" to indicate which charset the following character belongs to.

It is crucial to the concept of a locale that each locale has a single well-defined encoding. Many languages have only a single standardized encoding. If a language can be encoded in more than one standard way, each encoding defines a locale of its own, and the name of the encoding is part of the name of the locale.

10.1.2.1 ISO8859-1 and Other Encodings

If you examine the names of the X fonts on your system (using `xlsfonts`) you will probably find that most of them have the charset "iso8859-1." This charset is sometimes called "Latin-1" and was designed to be suitable for use by most Western European languages (Greek being a notable exception). The character set of ISO8859-1 comprises all the ASCII characters plus a wide variety of accented and special characters. (You can take a look at the characters using the `xfd` program.) Because there are fewer than 256 characters in the set, ISO8859-1 can use a state-independent 8-bit encoding. This means that all characters are 8 bits long, and there are no special shift sequences that modify the interpretation of characters. Because there are not any shift sequences, it is possible to use the encoding of all Latin-1 characters directly as font indices.

ISO8859-1 contains a superset of the ASCII characters. Every character in the ASCII character set has the same encoding in Latin-1 as it does in ASCII. (But Latin-1 does not define any control characters such as linefeed, backspace or the bell character.) Because it is an 8-bit encoding, Latin-1 strings can be represented using the usual C null-terminated array of `char`. Because the characters are a uniform 8 bits and because strings do not contain embedded shift states, it is possible to use Latin-1 strings with the standard C string manipulation routines (`strlen`, `strcat`, etc.) In conjunction with the ANSI-C internationalization facilities, the careful design of ISO8859-1 means that most programs originally written for ASCII use can easily be ported for use in most Western European countries.

But it is not so simple once we try to go beyond Western Europe and Latin-based alphabets. Japanese text, for example, commonly uses (at least within the computer industry) words written in the Latin alphabet along with phonetic characters from the *katakana* and *hiragana* alphabets and ideographic *kanji* characters. Each of these types of text has its own charset (8- or 16-bit), but they must be combined into a single encoding for Japanese text. This is done with shift sequences, bytes embedded in the running text which control the character set in which the following character will be interpreted. It is possible to use "locking shifts" which modify the interpretation of the next and subsequent characters, but this scheme is infrequently used because it makes strings of text very difficult to manipulate.

Compound Text is another text representation that is used in X applications. Compound Text strings identify their encoding using embedded escape sequences (they can also have multiple sub-strings with multiple encodings) and are therefore locale-independent. The Compound Text representation was standardized as part of X11R4 for use as a text interchange format for interclient communication. It is often used to encode text properties and for the transfer of text via selections, and is not intended for text representation internal to an application. There are new R5 routines that convert X property values to and from the Compound Text representation. Note that Compound Text is not the same thing as the Compound Strings used by the Motif widget set.

10.1.2.2 Multi-byte Strings and Wide-character Strings

Strings in encodings that contain shift sequences and characters with non-uniform width can be stored in standard NULL-terminated arrays of characters, but can be difficult to work with in this form: the number of characters in a string cannot be assumed to be equal to the number of bytes, and it is not possible to iterate through the characters in a string by simply incrementing a pointer. On the other hand, strings of `char` are usefully passed to standard functions like `strcat` and `strcpy`, and assuming a terminal that understands the encoding, functions like `printf` work correctly with these strings.

As an alternative to these multi-byte strings, ANSI-C defines a wide-character type, `wchar_t`, in which each character has a fixed size and occupies one array element in the string. (The `wchar_t` is 2 bytes on some systems, 4 bytes on others, and may be 1 byte on systems that support nothing but the default C locale.) ANSI-C defines functions to convert between multi-byte and wide-character strings: `mblen`, `mbstowcs`, `mbtowc`, `wcstombs`, and `wctomb`.* As you can see here, and as you will see with the R5 internationalized text input and output functions, "multi-byte" is commonly abbreviated "mb" in function names, and "wide character" is abbreviated "wc." Multi-byte strings are usually more compact than wide-character strings, but wide-character strings are easier to work with. Note that ANSI-C does not provide wide-character string manipulation functions. There is, however, a contributed library of wide character functions that is shipped with the MIT R5 release; see the directory *contrib/lib/Xwchar*.

In an internationalized application, you must take care to handle all strings properly. Unfortunately the ANSI-C library does not provide adequate functions or conventions for sophisticated internationalized text manipulation. Note, though, that many applications can do internationalized text input and output without performing any manipulations on that text. The following list gives a few guidelines for handling internationalized strings:

- Multi-byte strings are null-terminated. There is no single convention for the termination of wide character strings, but strings passed to `wcstombs` are null-terminated. As was the case before R5, X text output and input functions take and return strings with a count of the characters they contain.

- If an encoding is state-dependent (i.e., if it uses locking shifts) multi-byte strings are assumed to begin in the default shift state of the encoding. There is no convention for the

---

*If your C library does not define these functions, you can try the library contributed with R5 in *contrib/lib/Xwchar*.

shift state at the end of a string, so when concatenating two strings, the first may need to be reset to the default shift state in order to guarantee correct interpretation of the second. In practice, state-dependent encodings are rarely used.

- None of the C library string-handling functions work with wide-character strings.

- The following C string-handling functions may be safely used with multi-byte strings (in a state-independent encoding): `strcat`, `strcmp`, `strcpy`, `strlen`, `strncmp`. Note that the string comparison routines are only useful to check for byte-for-byte equality. To compare strings for sorting, use `strcoll`.

- Multi-byte strings can be written to file or output streams. Assuming a terminal that operates in the current locale, printing a multi-byte string to `stdout` or `stderr` will cause the correct text to be displayed.

- Multi-byte strings can be read from files or from the `stdin` input stream. If the file is encoded in the current locale, or the terminal operates in the locale, then the strings that are read will be meaningful.

10.1.3 Internationalization Using X

The techniques of internationalization described so far have had little to do with X, and they have been sufficient only to internationalize a terminal-based application. X applications draw text directly into their windows and get input directly from keyboard events. When an application must use multi-byte strings in an encoding that contains shift sequences and non-uniform width characters, deciding which characters to draw can be tricky, and when a language contains far more characters than fit on a keyboard, interpreting KeyPress events becomes difficult. Additionally, X clients often communicate with other clients. Because internationalized clients can run in different locales an internationalized interclient communication method is required. Also, X clients make heavy use of resource files and databases, and will need a mechanism for the correct localization of resources. The internationalization of R5 is based on the ANSI-C locale model, but the function `setlocale` is not sufficient for locale management in an X application. Two new functions are defined which are used along with `setlocale` when an X application starts up. Finally, all these new internationalization features of Xlib will require some changes to the Xt architecture as well.

The sections below cover these topics as follows:

- Section 10.2 describes the X locale management functions.

- Section 10.3 describes internationalized text output with R5.

- Section 10.4 describes string encoding changes in various Xlib functions.

- Section 10.5 describes interclient communication using internationalized properties and interlocale string conversions.

- Section 10.6 describes the localization of resource databases.

- Section 10.7 describes changes to the X Toolkit to support internationalization.

Chapter 11, *Internationalized Text Input*, covers the lengthy topic of internationalized text input.

10.2 Locale Management in X

An internationalized X application begins in the same way as a ANSI-C terminal-based internationalized program: with a call to `setlocale`. An X program, however, generally goes two steps further.

Immediately after calling `setlocale`, an application should call `XSupportsLocale()` to determine if the Xlib implementation supports the current locale. This function takes no arguments and return a `Bool`. If this function returns `False`, an application will typically print a "Locale not supported" message and exit.

After verifying that the locale is supported, an application should call `XSetLocaleModifiers()`. A "locale modifier" can be thought of as an extension to the name of a locale; it specifies more information about the desired localized behavior of an application. R5 as shipped by MIT recognizes one locale modifier, used to specify the input method (see Chapter 10, *Internationalization*) to be used for internationalized text input for the locale.

`XSetLocaleModifiers()` allows the programmer to specify a list of modifiers (usually none) which will be concatenated with a list of user-specified modifiers from an operating system environment variable (XMODIFIERS in POSIX). The strings passed to `XSetLocaleModifiers()` and set in the XMODIFIERS environment variable are a series of concatenated "@*category=value*" strings. Thus to specify that the "Xwnmo" input method should be used by an application, a user might set the XMODIFIERS as follows:

```
setenv XMODIFIERS @im=_XWNMO
```

Example 10-1 shows code that uses `setlocale` and the two functions described here to correctly establish its locale.

Example 10-1. Establishing the locale of an X application

```
#include <stdio.h>
#include <X11/Xlib.h>
/*
 * include <locale.h> or the non-standard X substitutes
 * depending on the X_LOCALE compilation flag
 */
#include <X11/Xlocale.h>

main(argc, argv)
int argc;
char *argv[ ];
{
    char *program_name = argv[ 0 ];

    /*
     * The error messages in this program are all in English.
     * In a truly internationalized program, they would not be
     * hardcoded; they would be looked up in a database of some sort.
     */

    if (setlocale(LC_ALL, "") == NULL) {
        (void) fprintf(stderr, "%s: cannot set locale.\n", program_name);
        exit(1);
    }
```

Example 10-1. Establishing the locale of an X application (continued)

```
if (!XSupportsLocale()) {
    (void) fprintf(stderr, "%s: X does not support locale
                program_name, setlocale(LC_ALL, NULL));
    exit(1);
}

if (XSetLocaleModifiers("") == NULL) {
    (void) fprintf(stderr, "%s: Warning: cannot set locale modifiers.\n",
                program_name);
}
    .
    .
    .
}
```

Not all systems support the `setlocale` function, but X can be built for these systems by defining the `X_LOCALE` compilation flag. When writing programs in an environment that does not have `setlocale`, include the header file *<X11/Xlocale.h>*. If this file is compiled with `X_LOCALE` defined, it defines `setlocale` as a macro for an Xlib-internal function. Otherwise, it simply includes the standard header *<locale.h>* to get the correct declaration of the real *setlocale*.

10.3 Internationalized Text Output in X

Before R5, the Xlib drawing routines made the fundamental assumption that the encoding of a character was equal to the index of the character's glyph in the font. As explained in Section 10.1.2, this is a useful and valid assumption when text in a language can be most naturally encoded as an 8- or 16-bit wide charset. Unfortunately, it is not valid in many important cases.

R5 bases its new text output routines on a new Xlib abstraction, the **XFontSet**. An **XFontSet** is bound to the locale in which it is created, and contains all the fonts needed to display text in that locale, or all the independent charsets used in the encoding of that locale. Technical Japanese text, for example, often mixes Latin with Japanese characters, so for a Japanese locale, fonts might be required with the charsets jisx0208.1983-0 for Kanji ideographic characters, jisx0201.1976-0 for Kana phonetic characters, and iso8859-1 for Latin characters.

Drawing internationalized text in R5 is conceptually very similar to drawing text in X11R4—there are routines that allow you to query font metrics, measure strings, and draw strings. The new R5 functions use an **XFontSet** rather than an **XFontStruct** or a font specified in a graphics context. The drawing and measuring routines interpret text in the encoding of the locale of the fontset, and correctly map wide or multi-byte characters to the corresponding font glyph (or glyphs).

10.3.1 Creating and Manipulating Fontsets

A fontset is created with a call to **XCreateFontSet()**. This function checks the current setting of the locale to determine which charsets are required for the locale, and uses a supplied *base font name list* to load a set of fonts that supply those charsets. A base font name list can be a single wildcarded font name that specifies little more than the desired size of the fonts, or it can be a (comma separated) list of partially wildcarded font names, or it can even be a list of fully-specified names. Note of course that if a fully-specified base font name list is used, it will only work for one particular locale. Generally you will want to use a very generic base font name, and allow the end user to override it (to choose individual typefaces that look good together, for example) with application resources.

XCreateFontSet() returns a list of the charsets for which no font could be found, and a default string that will be drawn in place of characters from the missing charset or charsets. The list of missing charsets should be freed with a call to **XFreeStringList()**. The returned default string should not be freed by the programmer. Example 10-2 shows how to create an **XFontSet**.

Example 10-2. Creating an XFontSet

```
XFontSet fontset;
char **missing_charsets;
int num_missing_charsets = 0;
char *default_string;
int i;
        .
        .
        .
fontset = XCreateFontSet(dpy,
                "-misc-fixed-*-*-*-*-*-130-75-75-*-*-*-*",
                &missing_charsets, &num_missing_charsets,
                &default_string);
/*
 * if there are charsets for which no fonts can
 * be found, print a warning message.
 */
if (num_missing_charsets > 0) {
    (void)fprintf(stderr, "%s: The following charsets are missing:\n",
                program_name);
    for(i=0; i < num_missing_charsets; i++)
        (void)fprintf(stderr, "%s:    %s\n", program_name,
                missing_charsets[i]);
    (void)fprintf(stderr, "%s: The string
                program_name, default_string);
    (void)fprintf(stderr, "%s: of any characters from those sets.\n",
                program_name);
    XFreeStringList(missing_charsets);
}
        .
        .
        .
```

If you use a very generic base font name list, be aware that **XCreateFontSet( )** may have to search through a large number of font names in order to find fonts of the appropriate charset. Also, when using an R5 X server, try to specify a base font name that will not require scaling. For example, many of the Japanese fonts shipped with the MIT distribution are defined at odd point sizes (11, 13, 15, etc.) instead of the even sizes more commonly used for Latin-1 fonts. If your base font name list specifies a 14-point font, the X server or font server may have to scale thousands of ideographic characters, causing a significant delay in your application; the server may even freeze up while the scaling is performed. See Chapter 6 and Appendix A for more information about font scaling.

The following routines also use or operate on font sets:

XFreeFontSet( )
> Frees an **XFontSet** and all information associated with it.

XFontsOfFontSet( )
> Returns the list of **XFontStruct**s and font names associated with an **XFontSet**.

XBaseFontNameListOfFontSet( )
> Returns a string containing the comma-separated base font name list for the given **FontSet**.

XLocaleOfFontSet( )
> Returns the name of the locale of the specified **XFontSet**.

Complete documentation for these (and all functions described in this chapter) can be found in the reference section of this book.

10.3.2 Querying Fontset Metrics

Because the **XFontSet** is an opaque structure, it is not possible to read font metrics directly from an **XFontSet** as is done with an **XFontStruct**. Instead, R5 defines the function **XExtentsOfFontSet( )** which takes an **XFontSet** as its sole argument and returns a pointer to a structure of type **XFontSetExtents**. This structure is shown in Example 10-3.

Example 10-3. The XFontSetExtents() structure

```
typedef struct {
    XRectangle max_ink_extents;         /* over all drawable characters */
    XRectangle max_logical_extents;     /* over all drawable characters */
} XFontSetExtents;
```

Each **XRectangle** specifies, as usual, the upper left-hand corner of a rectangle, and a positive width and height. The **max_ink_extents** rectangle specifies the bounding box around the actual glyph image of all characters in all fonts of the font set. The **max_logical_extents** rectangle describes the bounding box for all characters in all fonts of the font set that encloses the character ink plus intercharacter and interline spacing. For the layout of running text, the logical extents will be more useful. Note that these rectangles do not simply describe the biggest character in the font set, but describe a bounding box that will enclose all characters in the font set; a box big enough to accommodate the largest descent, the largest ascent, and so on. The `XFontSetExtents()` structure returned by `XExtentsOfFontSet()` is private to Xlib and should not be modified or freed by the application.

10.3.3 Context Dependencies in Displayed Text

In some text, such as Arabic script, there is not a one-to-one mapping between characters and font glyphs—the glyph used to display a character depends on the position of the character in the string. In other languages, a sequence of characters may map to a single glyph or a single character may map to multiple glyphs. In cases like this, it is not possible to assume that the width of a string is the sum of the widths of its component characters, and it may not be possible to insert or delete a character from a displayed string without redrawing the surrounding characters. The only safe assumption is that context dependencies do not extend beyond whitespace in a string. An example of context dependencies in the English language is the use of ligatures in typeset text—the substitution of the special glyphs "fl" and "fi" for the character sequences "fl" and "fi." This is an artificial example though, and for practical purposes, no Latin-based language has context dependencies.

The function `XContextDependentDrawing()` returns `True` if the locale associated with a font set includes context dependencies in text drawing. An internationalized application could use this function to check if it can take the various shortcuts allowed in non-context dependent locales. If `XSupportsLocale()` returns `True`, then any context dependencies in the text of a locale are correctly handled by the text-measuring and text-displaying routines described below.

There is another, more difficult, kind of context dependency in languages such as Hebrew and Arabic which are drawn right-to-left except for numbers which are drawn left-to-right. In this case it is not valid to assume that characters that are adjacent in a string will be adjacent when displayed. R5 does not make any provisions for handling this sort of text with mixed drawing directions.

10.3.4 Measuring Strings

R5 provides internationalized versions of `XTextWidth()` and `XTextExtents()`. They require an `XFontSet` and either a multi-byte or wide-character string. They are described below:

`Xmb/XwcTextEscapement()`*
    Return the number of pixels the given string would require in the x dimension if drawn.

---

*In this and following sections, functions that operate on multi-byte (mb) strings and the equivalent functions that operate on wide characters (wc) will often be grouped together and named with this `Xmb/Xwc` syntax. For `Xmb` functions, the *text* argument is of type `char *`, and the *length* argument gives the number of bytes in the string, which may not be the number of characters. In `Xwc` functions, the *text* argument is of type `wchar_t *`, and the *length* argument specifies the number of wide characters in the string, which is not the same as the number of bytes.

`Xmb/XwcTextExtents()`
> Return the text escapement as the value of the function, and also return a bounding box for all the ink in the string, and a bounding box for all the ink plus intercharacter and interline spacing.*

The term "escapement" is used instead of "width" to emphasize that `Xmb/XwcText-Escapement()` returns a positive value whether text is drawn left-to-right or right-to-left. This differs from `XTextWidth()` which returns a negative width for strings drawn right-to-left.

There is another pair of text extent functions that are useful when there are context dependencies in the displayed text. `Xmb/XwcTextPerCharExtents()` return the escapement and extents of a string as the above functions do, but also return the ink extents and the logical extents of each character in the string. These extents are measured relative to the drawing origin of the string, not the origin of the particular glyph. Note that these extents are returned for each character of the string, not for each font glyph displayed. If a sequence of characters map to a single glyph, each of those characters will have identical extent rectangles. Similarly if a single character requires several font glyphs to display, its extents will be the combined extents of those glyphs. The dimensions of the rectangle are independent of the drawing direction of the character.†

Example 10-4 in the next section shows a use of `XmbTextExtents()` and `XmbTextPerCharExtents()`.

10.3.5 Drawing Internationalized Text

R5 provides internationalized wide-character and multi-byte versions of `XDrawString()`, `XDrawImageString()`, and `XDrawText()`. They are listed below:

`Xmb/XwcDrawString()`
> Draw the specified string. The foreground pixels of each font glyph are drawn, but the background pixels of each glyph are not.

`Xmb/XwcDrawImageString()`
> Draw the specified string. Both the foreground and background pixels of each glyph are drawn.

`Xmb/XwcDrawText()`
> Draw text with complex spacing or font set changes. These routines draw text described in an array of `XmbTextItem` or `XwcTextItem` structures. These structures are shown in Example 10-4.

---

*The public release R5 version of the Xsi implementation had some serious bugs. However, later patches from the X Consortium fixed many of them. You should make an effort to get a patched version before attempting to use Xsi.
†As this book goes to press, there are two major bugs in the Xsi implementation of `Xmb/XwcTextPerChar-Extents()`. First, the returned per-character metrics are not relative to the drawing origin—the logical extents rectangles all have an x-coordinate of 0. Second, these functions do not allow a programmer to pass NULL for bounding boxes or arrays of bounding boxes that are not of interest—a dummy pointer to valid memory must always be passed.

These functions are passed a graphics context and a font set, and draw with fonts from the font set rather than the font of the GC. For this reason, they may modify the font value of the GC. Other than the font, they use the same GC elements as their pre-R5 text-drawing analogs. When using these functions, remember that context dependencies may mean that it is not valid to draw or modify displayed strings a single character at a time.

Example 10-4. The XmbTextItem() and XwcTextItem() structures

```
typedef struct {
    char        *chars;         /* pointer to string */
    int         nchars;         /* number of bytes in string */
    int         delta;          /* pixel delta between strings */
    XFontSet    font_set;       /* fonts, None means don't change */
} XmbTextItem;

typedef struct {
    wchar_t     *chars;         /* pointer to wide char string */
    int         nchars;         /* number of wide characters */
    int         delta;          /* pixel delta between strings */
    XFontSet    font_set;       /* fonts, None means don't change */
} XwcTextItem;
```

Example 10-5 shows the use of **XwcDrawImageString()**.

Example 10-5. Centering and drawing a multi-byte string

```
#include <X11/Xlib.h>
/*
 * This function draws a specified multi-byte string centered in
 * a specified region of a window.
 */
void DrawCenteredMbString(dpy, w, fontset, gc,
                          str, num_bytes, x, y, width, height)
Display *dpy;
Window w;
XFontSet fontset;
GC gc;
char *str;
int num_bytes;
int x, y, width, height;
{
    XRectangle boundingbox;
    XRectangle dummy;
    int originx, originy;

    /*
     * Figure out how big the string will be.
     * We should be able to pass NULL instead of &dummy, but
     * XmbTextExtents is buggy in the Xsi implementation.
     * Also, it should return the escapement of the string, but doesn't.
     */
    (void) XmbTextExtents(fontset, str, num_bytes,
                          &dummy, &boundingbox);
    /*
     * The string we want to center may be drawn left-to-right,
     * right-to-left, or some of both, so computing the
     * drawing origin is a little tricky.  The bounding box's x
```

Example 10-5. Centering and drawing a multi-byte string (continued)

```
     * and y coordinates are the upper left hand corner and are
     * relative to the drawing origin.
     * if boundingbox.x is 0, the string is pure left-to-right.
     * If it is equal to -boundingbox.width then the string is pure
     * right-to-left, but it may not be either of these, so what
     * we've got to do is choose the origin so that the bounding box
     * is centered in the window without assuming that the origin is
     * at one end or another of the string.
     */
    originx = x + (width - boundingbox.width)/2 - boundingbox.x;
    originy = y + (height - boundingbox.height)/2 - boundingbox.y;

    /*
     * now draw the string
     */
    XmbDrawImageString(dpy, w, fontset, gc,
                       originx, originy,
                       str, num_bytes);
}
```

10.4 String Encoding Changes for Internationalization

Perhaps the most fundamental concern of internationalization is the encoding of strings. So far we've considered text drawing and string input, and have used multi-byte or wide-character strings in the encoding of the locale. Because X is a networked window system, however, an X client must communicate with the X server, usually with a window manager, sometimes with a session manager, and often with other clients through the X selection mechanism (which is used to implement copy-and-paste). When we allow the internationalization of X programs, we must confront the issues of communication between clients that use different locales, and of communication between an internationalized client and a "locale-neutral" X server. Furthermore we must make decisions about the encodings of any other strings used in the X and Xt specifications.

Some of the issues that must be considered are the appropriate encoding for color and font names passed to the X server, the encoding of bitmap files, the encoding of strings selected in one client and copied to another, and the encoding of resource values and names. When making decisions on questions like these, the designers of X internationalization had several choices. They could specify that particular strings were:

- In the encoding of the locale.

- In the COMPOUND_TEXT encoding, in which each string is encoded along with the name of its encoding.

- In the STRING encoding, which is Latin-1 plus the newline and tab control characters.

- In ASCII, which as the encoding of the C language, is actually fairly portable.

- In an implementation-dependent encoding.

- Not in any encoding, and are simply interpreted as a sequence of bytes.

Compound text is an encoding designed to represent text from any locale. As such it is well suited to be a standard string format for clients that communicate using string properties. It does not, however, address the problem of converting strings from one locale to another, and often this is simply not possible. In most cases it is not meaningful to select text from an application running in one locale and paste it into an application running in a different one. This is the realm of multilingual applications which are not addressed by R5.

Note that the above list refers to the COMPOUND_TEXT and STRING encodings. These capitalized names refer to the Atom names used in the ICCCM to specify the type of a "Property." The ICCCM also specifies a selection conversion target Atom, TEXT, which simply means a string in whatever encoding is convenient for the selection owner.

Sometimes the best choice of encodings is ASCII. It may seem unfair to non-English locales that the ASCII encoding should be singled out for special treatment, but for strings that are to be shared between X client and X server (such as Display, Property, and font and color names) some standard encoding must be specified. Because ASCII is widespread and is the usual encoding for C programming, it is a natural choice. In many cases, though, it is not the specific ASCII encoding that is important, but the fact that there is some common encoding for all the characters used by ASCII. R5 never actually refers to ASCII. Instead, it defines the *X Portable Character Set* as a set of basic characters that must exist in all locales supported by Xlib. Those characters are:

```
a..z A..Z 0..9
!"#$%&'()*+,-./:;<=>?@[\\]^_`{|}~
<space>, <tab>, and <newline>
```

R5 also defines the *Host Portable Character Encoding* as the encoding for that character set. The encoding itself is not defined; the only requirement is that the same encoding is used for all locales on a given host machine. A string in the Host Portable Character Encoding is understood to contain only characters from the X Portable Character Set. Finally, the *Latin Portable Character Encoding* is the characters of the X Portable Character Set encoded as a subset of the Latin-1 encoding. (Latin-1 is itself a superset of ASCII.) Note that if an X client running on one host has a different portable encoding than an X server running on a different host, then translation from one encoding to the other will be required (for color names, font names, etc.) and would be done by the Xlib communication layer. In practice, however, it is likely that all systems will simply use an encoding which is a superset of ASCII, (with the possible exception of mainframes that use EBCDIC) and therefore all characters in the X Portable Character Set will share a single, standard (ASCII) encoding. Appendix K of Volume Two, *Xlib Reference Manual* summarizes all the encodings.

String-encoding issues arise throughout Xlib, and particularly so for functions that involve X properties and resource databases. The internationalization of client-to-window-manager and client-to-client communication via properties is described in 10.5 below and the internationalization of X resource databases is discussed in 10.6. Here we itemize the remaining changes to the Xlib specification that involve string encodings. Table 10-1 lists Xlib functions and the encodings of the strings that are passed in and out of them. These are not so much changes to the Xlib specification as clarifications of it to make the encodings explicit.

Table 10-1. String Encodings Used by Various Xlib Functions

Function	String Encoding
XDrawImageString() XDrawString() XQueryTextExtents() XTextExtents() XTextWidth() XTextItem structure XChar2b structure	No encoding; "characters" are treated as glyph indexes into the font, independent of locale.
XServerVendor() ServerVendor() macro	If the X server uses the Latin Portable Character Encoding, this function will return a string in the Host Portable Character Encoding; otherwise the encoding is implementation-dependent.
XOpenDisplay() XDisplayName() DisplayName() macro XDisplayString() DisplayString() macro	Display names in the Host Portable Character Encoding are supported; additional encodings are implementation dependent.
XAllocNamedColor() XLookupColor() XStoreNamedColor() XParseColor()	Color names in the Host Portable Character Encoding are supported; Xlib implementations may support additional encodings, and may look up color names in locale-specific databases before passing them to the server.
XLoadFont() XLoadQueryFont()	Font names in the Host Portable Character Encoding are supported; implementations may support additional encodings.
XListFonts() XListFontsWithInfo()	Font patterns in the Host Portable Character Encoding are supported; implementations may support additional encodings. Returned strings are in the Host Portable Character Encoding if the server returns strings in the Latin Portable Character Encoding; otherwise the encoding is implementation-dependent.
XSetFontPath() XGetFontPath()	The encoding and interpretation of the font path is implementation-dependent.
XParseGeometry() XGeometry() XWMGeometry()	Geometry strings in the Host Portable Character Encoding are supported; implementations may support additional encodings.

Table 10-1. String Encodings Used by Various Xlib Functions (continued)

Function	String Encoding
XInternAtom()	Atom names in the Host Portable Character Encoding are supported; implementations may support additional encodings.
XGetAtomName()	The returned atom name is in the Host Portable Character Encoding if the server returns a value in the Latin Portable Character Encoding.
XStringToKeysym()	Keysym names in the Host Portable Character Encoding are supported; implementations may support additional encodings.
XKeysymToString()	The returned string is in the Host Portable Character Encoding.
XInitExtension() XQueryExtension()	Extension names in the Host Portable Character Encoding are supported; implementations may support additional encodings.
XListExtensions()	The returned strings are in the Host Portable Character Encoding if the server returns strings in the Latin Portable Character Encoding.
XReadBitmapFile()	The bitmap file is parsed in the encoding of the current locale.
XWriteBitmapFile()	The file is written in the encoding of the current locale.
XFetchBytes() XFetchBuffer() XStoreBytes() XStoreBuffer()	No encoding; data in cut buffers is treated as uninterpreted bytes.
XGetErrorDatabase- Text()	Name and message arguments in the Host Portable Character Encoding are supported; implementations may support additional encodings. The *default_string* argument is encoded in the current locale, and the returned text is also in encoded in the current locale.
XGetErrorText()	The returned text is in the current locale.

Table 10-1. String Encodings Used by Various Xlib Functions (continued)

Function	String Encoding
XSetWMProperties( ) XSetStandard- Properties( ) XStoreName( ) XSetIconName( ) XSetCommandP( ) XSetClassHint( )	Strings in the Host Portable Character Encoding are supported; implementations may support additional encodings. The strings are set as the values of a property of type STRING.
Function	String Encoding
XFetchName( ) XGetIconName( ) XGetCommand( ) XGetClassHint( )	Returned strings are in the Host Portable Character Encoding if the data returned by the server is in the Latin Portable Character Encoding.

10.5 Internationalized Interclient Communication

You'll need to understand non-internationalized interclient communication before reading this; see Chapter 12.

When writing an internationalized application it is not safe to assume that all interclient communication with text properties will be done with Latin-1 or ASCII strings. R5 provides some new functions that do not make this assumption. The first is a convenience routine for communication with window managers. **XmbSetWMProperties( )** is a function very similar to **XSetWMProperties( )**, except that the *window_name* and *icon_name* arguments are multi-byte strings (rather than **XTextProperty** pointers) in the encoding of the locale. If these strings can be converted to the STRING encoding (Latin-1 plus newline and tab), then their corresponding WM_NAME and WM_ICON_NAME properties are created with type STRING. If this conversion cannot be performed, the strings are converted to Compound Text (this conversion can always be done, by the definition of Compound Text), and the properties are created with type COMPOUND_TEXT. Note that there is no wide-character version of this function.

Since X properties have a single contiguous block of data as their value, they cannot directly represent types such as **char ****. But sometimes such a complex type must be represented (imagine a text editor setting a property to a set of disjoint selected strings). To allow this, X11R4 defined the **XTextProperty** structure (shown in Example 10-6) and the functions **XStringListToTextProperty( )** and **XTextPropertyToStringList( )**.

Example 10-6. The XTextProperty structure

```
typedef struct {
        unsigned char *value;    /* property data */
```

Example 10-6. The XTextProperty structure (continued)

```
        Atom encoding;             /* type of property */
        int format;                /* 8, 16, or 32 */
        unsigned long nitems;      /* number of items in value */
} XTextProperty;
```

These functions assume input strings are in Latin-1 and always create properties of type STRING, which is not correct behavior in internationalized applications. So R5 provides the new functions **Xmb/XwcTextListToTextProperty()** and **Xmb/XwcText-PropertyToTextList()** which operate correctly with localized strings, converting between text encoded in the locale and STRING or COMPOUND_TEXT types. The **Xmb/wc-TextListToTextProperty()** functions take a new argument of type **XICCEncodingStyle**, which is shown in Example 10-7.

Example 10-7. The XICCEncodingStyle type

```
typedef enum {
        XStringStyle,              /* STRING */
        XCompoundTextStyle,        /* COMPOUND_TEXT */
        XTextStyle,                /* text in owner's encoding (current locale) */
        XStdICCTextStyle           /* STRING, else COMPOUND_TEXT */
} XICCEncodingStyle;
```

The *style* argument to these functions specifies how the text is to be converted. The possible values have the following meanings:

- **XStringStyle** specifies that the text should be converted to the STRING encoding, and the encoding field of the returned **XTextProperty** should be set to the Atom STRING. Note that text cannot always be converted to this type without loss of data—only characters that are in the Latin-1 character set will be convertible.

- **XCompoundTextStyle** specifies that the text should be converted to the Compound Text encoding and the encoding field of the returned **XTextProperty** should be set to the Atom COMPOUND_TEXT.

- **XTextStyle** specifies that the text should be left unconverted in the encoding of the current locale. The encoding field of the returned **XTextProperty** structure is set to an Atom which names that encoding.

- **XStdICCTextStyle** specifies that the text should be converted to STRING if that conversion is possible and otherwise it should be converted to Compound Text. The encoding field of the returned **XTextProperty** will be set to the Atom STRING or COMPOUND_TEXT depending on which conversion was performed.

The returned **XTextProperty** is suitable to pass to **XSetTextProperty()**.

The other two routines, **Xmb/XwcTextPropertyToTextList()**, perform the conversion in the opposite direction. They are passed an **XTextProperty** (obtained with a call to **XGetTextProperty()**, perhaps) and return an array of pointers to **char *** or an array of pointers to **wchar_t ***. These routines do not require an argument of type **XICCEncodingStyle**; they always convert from the encoding of the property to the encoding of the current locale if such a conversion is possible. The application is responsible for freeing the memory allocated by these functions. To free the array of multi-byte strings (and the strings themselves) returned by **XmbTextPropertyToTextList()** use **XFreeStringList()**, which is a pre-R5 function. To free the array of wide-character strings (and the strings themselves) allocated by **XwcTextPropertyToTextList()** use the new function **XwcFreeStringList()**.

These four functions return an integer. The possible values and their meanings are as follows:

Success
: The conversion is completely successful; all characters were converted.

XNoMemory
: There was not enough memory available to perform the conversion.

XLocaleNotSupported
: The current locale is not supported. By definition, no conversions are possible to or from the encoding of an unsupported locale. This error code will never be returned if **XSupportsLocale()** has returned **True** for the current locale.

XConverterNotFound
: No converter could be found between the encoding of the text property and the current locale. There is always a converter for converting between **STRING** and **COMPOUND_TEXT** and encoding of the current locale (if that locale is supported, of course), so **Xmb/wcTextListToTextProperty()** never returns this error code, and **Xmb/XwcTextPropertyToTextList()** will never return it if the text property is in the **STRING** or **COMPOUND_TEXT** encodings.

any value > 0
: There were unconvertible characters in the string, and the return value indicates how many. Even when the current locale is supported, and an appropriate converter is found, it is by no means guaranteed that all the characters of the string can be converted. If two locales use the same character set but simply encode those characters differently, then strings will be fully convertible between the locales. But imagine trying to convert from French text to ASCII—any accented characters would be unconvertible because they simply do not exist in the ASCII character set. When converting between languages as dissimilar as Arabic and Korean, for example, there will be no convertible characters.* Note that the return value **Success** has a value of 0, and the other return values, **XNoMemory**, **XLocaleNotSupported**, and **XConverterNotFound** all have negative values. Therefore any positive return value indicates unconvertible characters.

Table 10-2 shows the possible results of the conversions performed by **Xmb/XwcTextListToTextProperty()** and **Xmb/XwcTextPropertyToTextList()**.

---

*If Korean is the current (supported) locale, and the Arabic text has been "wrapped" into a Compound Text encoding, a converter will exist between Compound Text and the current locale, but no meaningful conversion will be performed. Until the advent of multilingual applications (or specialized applications using a special Korean/Arabic locale) such a conversion attempt (triggered by a user's copy-and-paste actions, for example) will not be meaningful, and should be ignored or produce an error message.

Xmb/XwcTextListToTextProperty()		
XICCEncodingStyle	Converter found?	Characters convertible?
XStringStyle	yes	maybe
XCompoundTextStyle	yes	yes
XTextStyle	yes	yes
XStdICCStyle	yes	yes
Xmb/XwcTextPropertyToTextList()		
Encoding of property	Converter found?	Characters convertible?
same as current locale	yes	yes
STRING	yes	maybe
COMPOUND_TEXT	yes	maybe
other locale	maybe	maybe

When there are unconvertible characters in a string, the conversion functions substitute a locale-dependent default string (encoded in the current locale). The value of the default string may be queried with **XDefaultString()**, and may be the empty string (" "). There is no way to set the value of the default string. The default string is independent of the default string used by the R5 text-drawing routines when an **XFontSet** does not contain all the characters needed to represent text in a locale.

10.6 Localization of Resource Databases

We've seen that X resources are a useful way to allow the localization of strings—rather than hardcoding its strings, an X client can look them all up by name from a locale-dependent resource file. The twist here is that although resource values can be localized, and may contain text in the encoding of the locale, resource *names* must still be hardcoded into the application. As you might expect, R5 specifies that resource names in the Host Portable Character Encoding are always supported, and that any other encodings are implementation-dependent. What this means is that a Chinese user who wishes to customize the behavior of an application written by a Japanese programmer will have to specify values for resources that are named using Latin characters in the X Portable Character Set. Those resource names may be English phonetic representations of Japanese words which are mnemonic to the Japanese programmer, but which are meaningless to the Chinese (or American) user. This situation is unfortunate but there is no way around it within the scope of the X Resource Manager mechanisms. If resource names are to be localized, they would have to be looked up in a database as well, and then we would need hardcoded names for the names. Another approach would be to use resource numbers in place of resource names. These remain constant across all locales, but where a resource name is mnemonic to the original programmer, at least, a resource number would be mnemonic to no one.

When a resource file or string are parsed into an **XrmDatabase( )**, that parsing is done in the current locale, and the database is bound to that locale even if the current locale changes. We can speak of the "locale of the database" in the same way that we speak of the "locale of the **XFontSet**." To determine the locale of a database, call **XrmLocale-OfDatabase( )**.

The internationalization of resources requires additions to the Xlib specification to make explicit the encoding and interpretation of the strings that are passed in and out of the **Xrm** functions. Table 10-3 lists the resource manager functions that have been respecified.

Table 10-3. String Encoding and Locale Changes to Xrm Functions

Function	String Encoding and Locale Changes
XrmStringToQuark( ) XrmStringToQuarkList( ) XrmStringToBinding- QuarkList( )	Quark names in the Host Portable Character Encoding are supported; implementations may support additional encodings.
XrmQuarkToString( )	No specified encoding; the returned string is equal byte-for-byte to the string originally passed to one of the string-to-quark routines.
XrmGetFileDatabase( )	The file is parsed in the current locale.
XrmGetStringDatabase( )	The string is parsed in the current locale.
XrmPutLineResource( )	The line is parsed in the locale of the database. The resource name part of the line and the colon are in the Host Portable Character Encoding or some implementation-dependent encoding.
XrmPutFileDatabase( )	The resource file is written in the locale of the database. Resource names in the Host Portable Character Encoding, and resource values in the encoding of the locale of the database are supported; implementations may support additional encodings.
XrmPutResource( )	Resource specifiers and types in the Host Portable Character Encoding are supported; implementations may support additional encodings. The resource value is stored as uninterpreted bytes.
XrmQPutResource( )	The resource value is stored as uninterpreted bytes.
XrmPutStringResource( )	Resource specifiers in the Host Portable Character Encoding are supported; implementations may support additional encodings. The resource value is stored as uninterpreted bytes. The resource type is set to the quark for the string "String" encoded in the Host Portable Character Encoding.

Function	String Encoding and Locale Changes
`XrmQPutStringResource()`	The resource value is stored as uninterpreted bytes. The resource type is set to the quark for the string "String" encoded in the Host Portable Character Encoding.
`XrmGetResource()`	Resource names and classes in the Host Portable Character Encoding are supported; implementations may support additional encodings.
`XrmMergeDatabases()`	The database values and types are merged as uninterpreted bytes regardless of the locales of the databases. The locale of the target database is not changed.
`XResourceManagerString()`	The **RESOURCE_MANAGER** property is converted from **STRING** encoding to the encoding of the current locale in the same way that XmbTextPropertyToTextString performs conversions.
`XrmParseCommand()`	The option strings in the **XrmOptionDescList** are compared byte-for-byte with the characters in **argv**, independent of locale. The name argument and the resource specifier strings in the **XrmOptionDescList** are in the Host Portable Character Encoding or in an additional implementation-dependent encoding. The resource values are stored in the database as uninterpreted bytes, and all database entries are created with their type set to the quark for the string "String" in the Host Portable Character Encoding.
`XGetDefault()`	The use of this function is discouraged.

10.7 Summary: Writing an Internationalized Application

This chapter has covered a lot of tricky material. The following guidelines summarize the requirements for ANSI-C and R5-based internationalization:

- Set the locale desired by the user by calling `setlocale` with the empty string (" ") as the locale name argument. Verify that the locale is supported by Xlib with `XSupportsLocale()`. Set the X locale modifiers as desired by the user by passing the empty string to `XSetLocaleModifiers()`. In an X Toolkit application, use `XtSetLanguageProc` to register a procedure to set the locale. The default language procedure (which is not actually registered by default) performs all of the above functions.

- Use ANSI-C functions such as `strcoll` and `strftime` which make use of the current setting of the locale. Avoid the superseded functions that do not.

- Place all strings which will be displayed by the application in an X resource file. Use X Resource Manager functions in the application to look those strings up.

- Do not assume that the strings your application handles have a uniform state-independent encoding. Treat them as multi-byte strings or convert them to wide-character strings.

- Create an `XFontSet` for the locale and use it with the new R5 text output functions to measure and display multi-byte and wide-character strings.

- Use `XmbSetWMProperties()` to set the essential properties for communication with the window manager.

- Use the new R5 property routines to convert from or to the encoding of the current locale when setting or reading text properties.

- Pay attention to the encoding of strings such as Atom and Display names, font and color names, resource names, and resource values specifications.

- Use the new X input method mechanisms to get correctly encoded multi-byte and wide-character input. Chapter 11 explains how to do this.

11

Internationalized Text Input

Converting user keystrokes into text in the encoding of the locale is perhaps the most difficult task in internationalization. This chapter is a continuation of the last, and assumes knowledge of the basics of internationalization covered in that chapter. The first two sections provide an overview of the internationalized text input model used by R5, and are valuable to any programmer writing internationalized applications. The remaining sections describe the new Xlib functions and datatypes for internationalized text input, and are quite detailed. Programmers who will be writing output-only applications or who will be using toolkits or widgets with internationalized text input capabilities built in can skip these sections.

In This Chapter:

11
Internationalized Text Input

In an internationalized program, you can't assume any particular mapping between keystrokes and input characters. An internationalized program must run in any locale on a single workstation, using a single keyboard. The mapping between keystrokes and Japanese characters is very different (and more complex) than the mapping between keystrokes and Latin characters, for example. When there are more characters in the codeset of a locale than there are keys on a keyboard, some sort of *input method* is required for mapping between multiple keystrokes and input characters. R5 supports the internationalization of keyboard input with the new abstractions *X Input Method* (**XIM**) and *X Input Context* (**XIC**) and the new functions, `XmbLookupString()` and `XwcLookupString()`, which return a string in the encoding of the locale. Because internationalized text input is a complex topic, we begin with a discussion of the important issues of internationalized text input in Section 11.1 and an overview of the X input method architecture in Section 11.2. The remaining sections explain the individual topics required in order to implement internationalized text input.

Before beginning with internationalized text input, bear in mind that input methods are a technology that has previously been used only in *ad hoc* ways for specific languages. Driven by industry demand, it has very quickly advanced from research topic to X Consortium standard, and now must operate correctly in any locale. It is a difficult problem and R5 does not provide a complete solution. One frustration is the ambiguity, in places, of the XIM specification, which defines how an input method interacts with an Xlib application. This book attempts to resolve those ambiguities in reasonable ways, but in practice, much remains "implementation defined," and internationalized programs may have to be tailored to operate correctly with a few particular target input methods. None of the input methods that are shipped with R5 are part of the core distribution, and none are fully robust or well documented (not in English, at least). The XIM designers envision that their internationalized text input mechanism will be incorporated within toolkits and Xt widgets, and thus will be hidden from most programmers. Until these widgets are available, however, performing truly internationalized text input may be a difficult task.

R5 as shipped from MIT contains two separate implementations of the input method internationalization facilities. The "Xsi" implementation is the default on all but Sony machines, which use the "Ximp" implementation. Each implementation defines its own protocol for communication between Xlib and input methods (which are implemented as Separate processes). Ximp and Xsi each come with contributed input methods which are not compatible with each other. Steps are now going on within the X Consortium to standardize on one of these implementations, so you should enquire about the status of that effort before putting significant effort into a product using one of these implementations.

11.1 Issues of Internationalized Text Input

Think for a moment about how we use a keyboard to enter text into a computer. There are not enough keys on a standard keyboard for all the lowercase and uppercase letters used in English as well as the number and punctuation characters, so we use a shift key to effectively double the number of characters we can enter.

But for many European languages, this technique is not sufficient. The most common accented characters may appear directly on a keyboard (the é, è, and ç in French, for example) but this still leaves a variety of other characters that cannot be entered with any single shifted or unshifted keystroke. French typewriters have a key that will produce an umlaut or a caret, without advancing the carriage, so to produce a û, for example, you would strike the caret key followed by the "u" key. In computer systems, a variety of methods have been developed for entering these accented characters. Often they involve a Compose key (found on many DEC keyboards) or any "dead key" which, does not send a code when struck but places the keyboard into a special compose mode (sometimes indicated by a light on the keyboard) in which one or more of the following keystrokes are combined into a single character. If this sort of input method is implemented in the keyboard hardware or in the operating system software, then it behaves transparently to the programmer who can simply read characters, assured that the user will have some way of entering any text desired.

As with internationalized text output, it is with the Asian ideographic languages that things become complicated. Japanese and Korean both have phonetic alphabets that are small enough to physically map onto a keyboard. It is sometimes adequate to leave text in this phonetic alphabet, but usually the user will want the final text to be in the full ideographic language. Input methods for these languages commonly have the user type the phonetic symbols for a particular word or words and signal somehow when this composition or pre-editing is finished. The input method then looks up that string of phonetic characters in a dictionary and converts it to the equivalent character or characters in the ideographic system. Sometimes there will be more than one character with a given phonetic representation, in which case the user will have to select between them.

These methods are obviously more complex than European compose methods. They are modal, and must display a lot of state information. It is not enough to have a keyboard light that tells users that they are composing an ideographic character; the computer must display the phonetic characters as the user types them, allow the user to edit them, and then when the user is done, compose them into an ideographic character or characters. The conversion from phonetic to ideographic characters requires a large dictionary, and finally, as noted above, the input method may have to display a menu or popup dialog box so the user can choose among ideograms with the same phonetic representation.

Because input methods can be so large and complex, and because they vary so much from locale to locale, it does not make sense to link every application with a generic input method which is somehow localized at application startup. Instead, an *input manager* is usually run as a separate process that communicates with the X server and with the application. At application startup, the setting of the locale or the "im" locale modifier determines to which input manager the application establishes a connection. R5 provides new routines and datatypes in Xlib which support this sort of internationalized text input. The next section provides an overview of the Xlib architecture for internationalized text input.

11.2 Overview of the X Input Method Architecture

The sections below present an overview of the concepts, datatypes, and functions used in R5 to support input methods. An understanding of material presented here will make the implementation details presented in later sections easier to follow.

11.2.1 Input Methods and Input Servers

An internationalized X application gets user text input by communicating with an input method. At application startup, the application is localized by opening the particular input method appropriate for the locale. Often, opening an input method causes Xlib to establish a connection to another process known as the "input manager" or "input server." The input manager can provide input method service to multiple X clients that use the same locale. Sometimes an input manager will connect to a third process, the translation server, which performs dictionary lookup and translation from pre-edit text (often phonetic) to composed text (often ideographic). The details of input method architecture are of course implementation dependent. Simple input methods, for example, can be implemented directly in Xlib, without need of other processes. The default Xsi implementation shipped with the MIT distribution does just this for European compose methods that do not require any dictionary lookup or graphical feedback. Figure 11-1 diagrams several possible connections between a client and its input method.

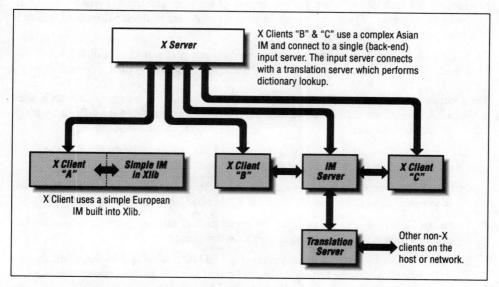

Figure 11-1. Possible input method architectures

The XIM architecture was designed to support two models of input method, known as front-end and back-end methods. A *front-end input method* intercepts events from the X server before they reach the application. A *back-end method* filters events from the application, before the application has processed them. Because internationalized programs must support either model of input method, the distinction is of little importance to the programmer. It is discussed in the XIM specification, however, and you may run across it in other discussions of input methods.

Recall the distinction between internationalized and multilingual applications. There is nothing to prevent an application from opening multiple input methods for multiple locales, but internationalized applications will generally operate only in a single locale and will therefore only need a single input method.

11.2.2 User Interaction with an Input Method

In order for a complex input method to provide feedback or otherwise interact with the user, it must have regions of the screen that it can draw text or bitmaps into. The X Input Method specification defines three of these areas:

- The *Status* area is an output-only window in which the input method can display information about its internal state. It can be thought of as a logical extension of the keyboard mode indicators, such as the Caps Lock indicator. The client generally provides this area to the input method, but the input method is solely responsible for its contents.

- The *Preedit* area is the region for the display of the intermediate text typed while composing a character. The client generally provides this area to the input method, which is responsible for its contents.

- The *Auxiliary* area is a transient window used for any popup menus or dialog boxes that are needed by the input method. This area is managed entirely by the input method.

The location and use of the Preedit and Status areas depend on the interaction style used between the application and the input method. Four interaction styles are defined by the X Input Method specification.

- In the *root-window* pre-editing style, the input method displays data outside of the application in a window that is a child of the root window.

- In the *off-the-spot* pre-editing style, the input method displays pre-edit data in a fixed location of the application window, often in a "message line" near the bottom.

- In the *over-the-spot* pre-editing style, the input method displays pre-edit data a window of its own which is placed over the current insertion point.

- In the *on-the-spot* pre-editing style, the input method directs the application to display the pre-edit data. When using this style, the application can display the pre-edit text in a way that matches the display of the already composed text.

The client must choose an interaction style from a list of styles supported by the input method, and must provide the Preedit and Status areas as required by that style. Additionally, in the case of on-the-spot pre-editing, the client must supply callbacks that the input method can call to control the pre-edit process.

11.2.3 The X Input Method

An application that wishes to use an input method must first call **XOpenIM()**. This function establishes a connection to the input method appropriate for the current locale, and returns an opaque handle of type **XIM**. Opening an input method is conceptually similar to opening a display, and the **XIM** returned is analogous to the **Display *** returned by **XOpenDisplay()**. An input method is bound to the particular locale that was in effect when it was created, even if this locale is subsequently changed. **XOpenIM()** and related functions are documented in Section 11.4.1.

11.2.4 The X Input Context

Just as the X server can display multiple windows for a single client, an input method can maintain multiple *input contexts* for an application. The function **XCreateIC()** creates a new input context in an input method. The function returns an opaque handle of type **XIC**. Like the **Window** or **GC** types, **XIC** has a number of attributes which can be set. These attributes control the interaction style for input done under that context, the regions to be used for the Preedit and Status areas, the **XFontSet** with which the text should be drawn, and so on. **XCreateIC()** and related routines to set and get the values of input context attributes are documented in Section 11.5.2.

A text editor that supported multiple editing windows within a single top-level window could choose to create one IC for each editing window, or to share only one IC among all such windows. In the first case, each window would have different Preedit and Status areas, and each could be in a different intermediate state of pre-editing. In the second case, there would be a single Preedit and a single Status area shared by all editing windows, and the application would probably reset the state of the IC each time the input focus moved from one window to another.

11.2.5 Input Context Focus Management

Because there is only one keyboard associated with an X display, X allows only one window to have the input focus at a time. For the same reason, only one input context (per application) can have the focus at a time. The function **XSetICFocus()** causes key events to be directed to a particular IC. It should be called at least once by every application that uses input contexts. In addition, the application should set the **FocusWindow** attribute of the IC to the window in which the key events will occur.

If an application has multiple text entry windows using multiple input contexts, that application will have to call **XSetICFocus()** every time the input focus changes. An application that shares a single IC among multiple text entry windows will have to set the **FocusWindow** attribute of that IC each time the focus changes. Note that focus changes can be changes of the focus window known to the X server, or they can be application-internal focus changes, controlled by event redirection as is done in Xt and other toolkits.

11.2.6 Preedit and Status Area Geometry Management

Depending on interaction style, an input method may require screen space to display pre-edit and status information. The application is responsible for providing these areas, but except for the on-the-spot interaction style, the input method will handle all output to them. When an input method requires screen space, the application should query its desired size and attempt to honor it. Note however that the input method must make do with whatever area it is given. This geometry management and geometry negotiation is handled through attributes of each input context and with a "geometry callback" function. These are described in Sections 11.7 and 11.8.1.

11.2.7 Preedit and Status Callbacks

When using the on-the-spot interaction style, the IM will request the application to display pre-edit and status information for it. This is more complicated for the application, but because the application has finer control over the positioning of the information, it allows the appearance of a seamless interface with the IM. The IM makes requests of the application through a series of callback functions specified as attributes of the IC. The prototypes and responsibilities of these functions will be described in Section 11.8.

11.2.8 Getting Composed Input

When the application gets a **KeyPress** event, it should use that event in a call to **Xmb-LookupString()** or **XwcLookupString()**. These functions are analogs of **XLookupString()**, but return multi-byte or wide-character strings in the codeset of the locale, where **XLookupString()** can only return Latin-1 strings. Because it may take multiple keystrokes to enter a single character of text, these functions may return a status code that indicates that no composed input is ready.

Some input methods intercept keyboard events before the application has a chance to see them. If this is the case, they will send a synthetic **KeyPress** event with a keycode of 0 when there is composed input that should be looked up by the application.

11.2.9 Filtering Events

In order for an input method to perform pre-editing of input, it must have access to all **Key-Press** events. These events are passed to it through one of the internationalized **Lookup-String** functions. All but the most simple input methods, however, need access to other events as well. An IM that displays graphical feedback to the user will have to receive expose events, and an IM that displays a menu of homonyms, for example, will need to receive mouse motion and button events. **XFilterEvent()** provides the hook that makes this possible. This function must be called from within an application's event loop before each new event is processed. If the IM has registered a (Xlib-internal) filter for that event, **XFilterEvent()** invokes the filter and the IM has a chance to examine the event. If the IM is interested in the event, **XFilterEvent()** will return **True**, and the application should not dispatch the event any further. Notice that an IM can use **XFilterEvent()** to filter KeyPress events before the application can call one of the **LookupString** functions, but this is not the primary purpose of the function.

It is not safe to assume that the IM will only need events that the application currently receives, so the IM places an event mask for events in which it is interested in an attribute of each IC. The application is responsible for requesting to receive those events in the window of the IC.

1.2.10 The Big Picture

With the above explanations in mind, we can now consider the saga of a keystroke as it is processed through an internationalized application. Figure 11-2 diagrams the path a character follows between being typed on the keyboard and being displayed on the screen in an internationalized application.

1. When the user strikes a key on the keyboard, the keyboard sends a hardware-specific keycode to the X server.

2. The X server sends an event to the client or clients that have expressed interest in keystroke events for the window that had focus when the keystroke occurred.

3. The keystroke event will be received in the client's event loop by a call to **XNext-Event()**.

4. The event is immediately passed to **XFilterEvent()** to give the input method the opportunity to use it. Generally, the input method will not filter a **KeyPress** event.

5. Back in the application, if **XFilterEvent()** returns **True**, then the application will discard the event and wait for the next one.

6. Otherwise, the application will go ahead and process the event. For every **KeyPress** event, the application will call **XmbLookupString()** or **XwcLookupString()**.

7. The input method now processes the keystroke: it adds a new character to its pre-edit text and updates the display in the Preedit and Status areas of the application. If the keystroke is a control character such as Delete, the input method may modify the pre-edit text.

8. If the keystroke indicates that the user is done pre-editing and wishes to compose the pre-edited text, the input method does any necessary translation and the result becomes the return value of **Xmb/XwcLookupString()**. In most applications, this returned string will be immediately echoed in the window with a call to one of the internationalized text drawing functions. If the keystroke merely adds to the pre-edit text, then the

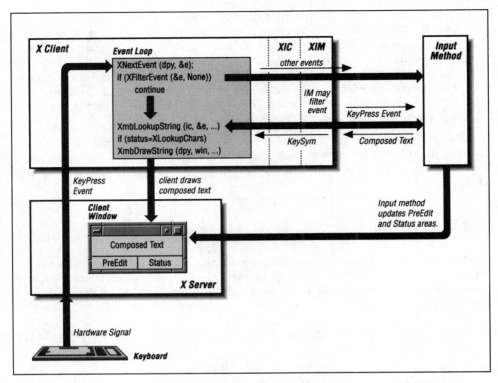

Figure 11-2. How a keystroke becomes a displayed character in an internationalized application

status value returned by **Xmb/wcLookupString()** indicates that there is no composed text ready.

The above sections have presented an overview of the XIM architecture. The sections below describe how to write programs with input methods and input contexts. They explain how to implement each of the steps in the "big picture" above.

11.3 XIM Programming Interface

The input method programming interface departs in some ways from the style established by the rest of Xlib. Functions that set, modify, or query the attributes of an **XIM** or **XIC** have a variable-length argument list interface, similar to the interface of the X Toolkit **XtVaSet-Values** function, for example. Attributes are specified by a null-terminated list of name/value pairs. Names are null-terminated character strings (of type **char ***), and values are of type **XPointer**, which is a new Xlib generic pointer type, like **XtPointer**, which replaces the non-standard **caddr_t**. There are predefined symbols for all of the **XIM** and **XIC** attribute names. These are named similarly to X Toolkit resource names: they are prefixed with **XN** (not **XtN**) and words in the name are separated by capitalization rather than underscores. They differ from the Xt convention in that the first letter after the **XN** prefix *is* capitalized. Example 11-1 shows this naming convention and the varargs interface used in C code. There is only a single defined **XIM** attribute, which is explained in Section 11.4.2. There are a number of **XIC** attributes, which are explained in Section 11.6.

Example 11-1. The XIM varargs interface and attribute naming conventions

```
status = XSetICValues(ic, XNFocusWindow, w,
                      XNGeometryCallback, HandleIMGeometry,
                      NULL);
```

The **XNPreeditAttributes** and **XNStatusAttributes** attributes of an input context have a number of sub-attributes. In order to set or query these values, the programmer must specify a nested argument list of type **XVaNestedList ***. A value of this type is created with a call to the function **XVaCreateNestedList()**. This function takes a dummy integer argument (as required by ANSI-C) followed by a null-terminated variable length list of name/value pairs. **XVaCreateNestedList()** can be conveniently called from within an argument list to another function, as is shown in Example 11-2.

Example 11-2. A nested call to XVaCreateNestedList()

```
XVaNestedList nlist;
ic = XCreateIC(im, XNInputStyle, XIMPreeditPosition | XIMStatusNothing,
               XNPreeditAttributes, nlist = XCreateVaNestedList(
                   0,  /* dummy argument */
                   XNSpotLocation, cursor_location,
                   XNFontSet, font_set,
                   NULL),
               XNFocusWindow, focus_window,
               NULL);
XFree(nlist);
```

Nested argument lists can also be used to specify top-level attributes. To do this, use the special name **XNVaNestedList** which will cause the contents of the following nested list to be logically inserted into the argument list at the current position.

Note that **XVaCreateNestedList()** allocates memory for the list it returns, which must be freed with a call to **XFree()**. Also note that if any of the values in the list are pointer types, the data pointed to must remain valid for the lifetime of the list.

The designers of the XIM specification chose this varargs-and-named-attributes interface over the more familiar structure-and-flags interface used by **XChangeWindow-Attributes()** and **XChangeGC()**, for example, because they felt it provided "more flexibility." The perceived flexibility to the programmer is probably a matter of personal taste, but the varargs interface certainly provides more flexibility for future extensions—new attributes and vendor- or IM-specific attributes can easily be added without destroying binary compatibility.

11.4 XIM Functions

An **XIM** is an opaque structure that serves as a handle to the input method. Because input methods are generally implemented as separate processes, we generally talk about "opening," not "creating," an input method. In this respect, an **XIM** can be thought of as analogous to a **Display ***. The sections below explain how to open and close a connection to an input method, and how to query the values of input method attributes.

11.4.1 Opening and Closing an Input Method

A connection to an input method is opened with a call to **XOpenIM()**. This function takes as arguments the Display, an **XrmDatabase()**, and a resource name and resource class of type **char ***. The database is used by the input method to look up resources private to it. The resource name and class are used as resource name and class prefixes by the input method when looking up resources for input contexts. In an Xt program, the database created when the display is initialized can be used. In Xlib programs, the programmer will have to explicitly build the database, or simply pass an empty one.

XOpenIM() also uses the current locale and locale modifiers as implicit arguments. The locale determines the default input method that **XOpenIM()** will connect to, as well as the encoding of the strings which will be returned by **Xmb/XwcLookupString()**. The locale is bound to an input method when it is open—the locale that was in effect when the input method was opened will be used by all input contexts of that input method regardless of the current locale when they are created.

The locale determines a default input method to be opened by **XOpenIM()**, but it cannot be assumed that only one input method will be available in each locale. Therefore X defines a locale modifier named "im" which can be used to override the default input method of the locale. The programmer should call **XSetLocaleModifiers()** to set all X locale modifiers ("im" is currently the only one). The user can specify a desired input method by setting the (UNIX) environment variable **XMODIFIERS** to a string of the form "@im=*input method name.*"

When an input method will no longer be used, it may be closed with a call to **XCloseIM()**.

Example 11-3 shows how to establish the locale and open a connection to the input method for that locale.

Example 11-3. Establishing the locale and opening an XIM

```
#include <stdio.h>
#include <X11/Xlib.h>
/*
 * include <locale.h> or the non-standard X substitutes
 * depending on the X_LOCALE compilation flag
 */
#include <X11/Xlocale.h>

main(argc, argv)
int argc;
```

Example 11-3. Establishing the locale and opening an XIM (continued)

```
char *argv[ ];
{
    Display *dpy;
    XIM im;
    char *program_name = argv[0];

    /*
     * The error messages in this program are all in English.
     * In a truly internationalized program, they would not
     * be hardcoded; they would be looked up in a database of
     * some sort.
     */

    if (setlocale(LC_ALL, "") == NULL) {
        (void) fprintf(stderr, "%s: cannot set locale.\n",program_name);
        exit(1);
    }

    if ((dpy = XOpenDisplay(NULL)) == NULL) {
        (void) fprintf(stderr, "%s: cannot open Display.\n", program_name);
        exit(1);
    }

    if (!XSupportsLocale()) {
        (void) fprintf(stderr, "%s: X does not support locale
                        program_name, setlocale(LC_ALL, NULL));
        exit(1);
    }

    if (XSetLocaleModifiers("") == NULL) {
        (void) fprintf(stderr, "%s: Warning: cannot set locale modifiers.\n",
                        program_name);
    }

    /*
     * Connect to an input method.
     * In this example, we don't pass a resource database
     */
    if ((im = XOpenIM(dpy, NULL, NULL, NULL)) == NULL) {
        (void)fprintf(stderr, "%s: Couldn't open input method\n",
                        program_name);
        exit(1);
    }
        .
        .
        .
```

11.4.2 Querying Input Method Values

The function XGetIMValues() is used to query attributes of the input method. At this point, there is only one defined attribute, named XNQueryInputStyle. This is a read-only attribute that specifies the interaction styles supported by the input method. When an input context is created, one of the interaction styles from this list must be specified. Because the one attribute currently defined for input methods is read-only, there is no XSet-IMValues procedure.

To get the list of supported interaction styles, call **XGetIMValues()** passing the IM, the name **XNQueryInputStyle**, and the address of a variable of type **XIMStyles ***. The **XIMStyles** structure is shown in Example 11-4.

Example 11-4. The XIMStyles structure

```
typedef unsigned long XIMStyle;

typedef struct {
    unsigned short count_styles;
    XIMStyle *supported_styles;
} XIMStyles;
```

The call to **XGetIMValues()** will return a pointer to a **XIMStyles** structure which contains a list of supported styles and the number of styles in the list. The client is responsible for freeing the **XIMStyles** structure when done with it.

Each **XIMStyle** in the list of supported styles is an **unsigned long** in which various bit flags describing the style are set. The valid flags and their meanings are described below:

XIMPreeditCallbacks
> The client must provide pre-edit callback procedures so that the input method can cooperate with the application to perform on-the-spot pre-editing.

XIMPreeditPosition
> The client must provide the location of the insertion cursor so that the input method can do over-the-spot pre-editing.

XIMPreeditArea
> The client must provide geometry management of an area in which the input method can do off-the-spot pre-editing.

XIMPreeditNothing
> The input method can perform root window pre-editing with no geometry management provided by the client.

XIMPreeditNone
> The input method does not do any pre-editing, or does not display any pre-edit data.

XIMStatusCallbacks
> The client must provide status callback procedures so that the input method can request the application to display status data when needed.

XIMStatusArea
> The client must provide geometry management of an area in which the input method can display status values.

XIMStatusNothing
> The input method can display status information in the root window with no geometry management provided by the client.

XIMStatusNone
> The input method does not display any status information.

When examining the `supported_styles` list, you may assume that each `XIMStyle` will have only one `XIMPreedit` flag and one `XIMStatus` flag set.* Example 11-5 in Section 11.5.2 shows how to query the supported styles of an input method.

11.5 XIC Functions

An input context is to an input method almost as a Window is to a Display. Each independent internationalized text input stream requires an IC, and the attributes of an IC define the behavior and appearance of the IM for that input stream. The sections below describe how to choose an input style for an IC, how to create and destroy an IC, how to set and get the attribute values of an IC, how to reset an IC, and how to set focus to an IC. The attributes of an IC are documented in Section 11.6.

11.5.1 Choosing an Interaction Style

The input or interaction style to be used by an input context must be specified when the input context is created. The style chosen must be one of those supported by the input method, and must also be supported by the client. The simplest of applications may choose to provide only minimal interaction with the input method, and may support only the `XIMPreedit-Nothing` and `XIMStatusNothing` interaction styles, forcing the input method to display its information in the root window. More complicated applications will probably support at least `XIMPreeditArea` and `XIMStatusArea` styles, as well as the "do nothing" styles. Generally, the right choice of interaction style is the most complicated (and therefore most user-friendly) style supported both by the application and the input method. An application may also choose to provide a resource so that the user can specify a desired style. Note that the choice of Preedit interaction style must be made independently of the Status style.

Section 11.4.2 lists the possible interaction styles, and explains how to query an input method for supported styles. Example 11-5 shows how to select Preedit and Status interactions styles and create an IC to use those styles.

11.5.2 Creating and Destroying Input Contexts

An `XIC` is created with a call to `XCreateIC()` and destroyed with a call to `XDestroy-IC()`. `XCreateIC()` takes an `XIM` as its first argument followed by a `NULL`-terminated variable-length argument list of attribute name/attribute value pairs. The IC is created in the locale of the IM, regardless of the current locale. The names of the IC attributes and their meanings are described in Section 11.6. Note that the `XNInputStyle` and `XNFontSet` attributes must be specified when an input context is created, and depending on the input

---

*The XIM spec places no restrictions on how many flags may be set in an `XIMStyle`, but it does not assign any meaning to a style which has multiple `XIMPreedit` or `XIMStatus` flags.

style, `XNSpotLocation` and all of the callback attributes may also have to be specified at creation time. The `XNClientWindow` attribute need not be specified when the IC is created, but must be specified before any input is done with the IC. Example 11-5 shows how to choose an interaction style and create an IC.

Example 11-5. Choosing an interaction style and creating an IC

```
#include <stdio.h>
#include <X11/Xlib.h>
#include <X11/Xlocale.h>

main(argc, argv)
int argc;
char *argv[ ];
{
    Display *dpy;
    Window win;
    XFontSet fontset;
    XIM im;
    XIC ic;
    XIMStyles *im_supported_styles;
    XIMStyle app_supported_styles;
    XIMStyle style;
    XIMStyle best_style;
    XVaNestedList list;
    char *program_name = argv[ 0 ];
    int i;
        .
        .
        .

    /* figure out which styles the IM can support */
    XGetIMValues(im, XNQueryInputStyle, &im_supported_styles, NULL);

    /* set flags for the styles our application can support */
    app_supported_styles = XIMPreeditNone | XIMPreeditNothing | XIMPreeditArea;
    app_supported_styles |= XIMStatusNone | XIMStatusNothing | XIMStatusArea;

    /*
     * now look at each of the IM supported styles, and
     * chose the "best" one that we can support.
     */
    best_style = 0;
    for(i=0; i < im_supported_styles->count_styles; i++) {
        style = im_supported_styles->supported_styles[i];
        if ((style & app_supported_styles) == style) /* if we can handle it */
            best_style = ChooseBetterStyle(style, best_style);
    }

    /* if we couldn't support any of them, print an error and exit */
    if (best_style == 0) {
        (void)fprintf(stderr, "%s: application and program do not share a\n",
                program_name);
        (void)fprintf(stderr, "%s: commonly supported interaction style.\n",
                program_name);
        exit(1);
    }

    XFree(im_supported_styles);
```

```
        /*
         * Now go create an IC using the style we chose.
         * Also set the window and fontset attributes now.
         */
        list = XVaCreateNestedList(0, XNFontSet, fontset, NULL);
        ic = XCreateIC(im, XNInputStyle, best_style,
                        XNClientWindow, win,
                        XNPreeditAttributes, list,
                        XNStatusAttributes, list,
                        NULL);
        XFree(list);
        if (ic == NULL) {
            (void) fprintf(stderr, "Couldn't create input context\n");
            exit(1);
        }
            .
            .
            .
}


/*
 * This function chooses the "more desirable" of two input styles.  The
 * style with the more complicated Preedit style is returned, and if the
 * styles have the same Preedit styles, then the style with the more
 * complicated Status style is returned.  There is no "official" way to
 * order interaction styles; this one seems reasonable, though.
 * This is a long procedure for a simple heuristic.
 */
XIMStyle ChooseBetterStyle(style1,style2)
XIMStyle style1, style2;
{
    XIMStyle s,t;
    XIMStyle preedit = XIMPreeditArea | XIMPreeditCallbacks |
        XIMPreeditPosition | XIMPreeditNothing | XIMPreeditNone;
    XIMStyle status = XIMStatusArea | XIMStatusCallbacks |
        XIMStatusNothing | XIMStatusNone;

    if (style1 == 0) return style2;
    if (style2 == 0) return style1;
    if ((style1 & (preedit | status)) == (style2 & (preedit | status)))
        return style1;

    s = style1 & preedit;
    t = style2 & preedit;
    if (s != t) {
        if (s | t | XIMPreeditCallbacks)
            return (s == XIMPreeditCallbacks)?style1:style2;
        else if (s | t | XIMPreeditPosition)
            return (s == XIMPreeditPosition)?style1:style2;
        else if (s | t | XIMPreeditArea)
            return (s == XIMPreeditArea)?style1:style2;
        else if (s | t | XIMPreeditNothing)
            return (s == XIMPreeditNothing)?style1:style2;
    }
    else { /* if preedit flags are the same, compare status flags */
        s = style1 & status;
        t = style2 & status;
```

Example 11-5. Choosing an interaction style and creating an IC (continued)

```
        if (s | t | XIMStatusCallbacks)
            return (s == XIMStatusCallbacks)?style1:style2;
        else if (s | t | XIMStatusArea)
            return (s == XIMStatusArea)?style1:style2;
        else if (s | t | XIMStatusNothing)
            return (s == XIMStatusNothing)?style1:style2;
    }
}
```

11.5.3 Querying and Modifying an XIC

Attributes of an **XIC** can be set with a call to **XSetICValues()** and can be queried with a call to **XGetICValues()**. Both functions take an **XIC** as their first argument, followed by a **NULL**-terminated variable-length argument list of attribute name/attribute value pairs. The names, types, and usage of the attributes are explained in Section 11.6. Note that some of the attributes are read-only, some must be specified when the IC is created, and others must be specified once and may not be changed once specified.*

The value arguments passed to **XGetICValues()** must be valid pointers to locations in which to store the requested attribute values. **XGetICValues()** will allocate memory for the storage of some of these attributes, and this memory must be freed by the client with a call to **XFree()**.†

To query the values of Preedit and Status sub-attributes, create a nested list of name/value pairs, where the values are pointers to storage and pass this nested list as the value of the **XNPreeditAttributes** or **XNStatusAttributes** attributes. You cannot query the value of all sub-attributes by passing a **XVaNestedList *** as the value of **XNPreedit-Attributes** or **XNStatusAttributes**—**XGetICValues()** does not build and return a nested list of sub-attributes

---

*Some attributes, such as **XNGeometryCallback** and **XNArea**, have values that are pointer types. The spec does not say whether the values pointed to by these attributes are copied. It appears that the Xsi implementation (the default) does make a copy of all these attribute values, with the exception of the **XNResourceName** and **XNResourceClass** attributes, which are strings and not of fixed length.

†The R5 spec is self-contradictory about which attributes will have memory allocated for them. It says, "Each argument value (following a name) must point to a location where the value is to be stored. **XGetICValues()** allocates memory to store the values, and client [sic] is responsible for freeing each value by calling **XFree()**." The first sentence indicates that the program provides memory for the attribute value. The second indicates that the program provides memory for a pointer to the attribute value. The Xsi implementation (the default) takes the first approach, and the Ximp implementation takes the second. So, for example, to query the value of the **XNFocus-Window** attribute, you would pass the address of a **Window** to **XGetICValues()** if using the Xsi implementation, but the address of a **Window *** if using the Ximp implementation. In the second case, the returned **Window** * value points to allocated memory which must be freed. When querying attributes like **XNResourceName** and **XNGeometryCallback**, which have values that are pointer types, it is not clear what types should be passed in the query, nor is it clear whether the returned pointer points to a copy of the value which must be freed, or to the value itself which must not be freed. As a programmer, your best bet is to avoid the use of **XGetICValues()**, except when necessary for the **XNFilterEvents** and **XNAreaNeeded** attributes.

Both `XSetICValues()` and `XGetICValues()` return a `char *` which is `NULL` if no errors occurred, or points to the name of the first attribute that could not be set or queried.

11.5.4 Resetting an Input Context

If text input is interrupted while pre-editing is in progress, the input context may be left in a non-initial internal state. To reset the state of an `XIC`, call `XmbResetIC()` or `Xwc-ResetIC`. Both reset the IC to its initial state and discard any pending input. Both functions may return the current pre-edit string, but it is implementation dependent how and whether they do this. The only difference between these functions is in the type of string they return. The returned string, if any, should be freed by the client with `XFree()`.

11.5.5 Setting Input Context Focus

When the focus window of an input context receives the application input focus, the application should call `XSetICFocus()` on that IC. Use `XUnsetICFocus()` when the focus window of an IC loses focus, or simply call `XSetICFocus()` on the IC of the new focus window. This will allow the input method to perform internal housekeeping and display special graphics (such as a highlighted border) in the Pre-Edit and Status windows of the IC that has the focus.

If you are using a single IC to handle input across several windows, and the input focus shifts from one of these windows to another, then the IC's `XNFocusWindow` attribute should be changed, you needn't call `XSetICFocus()`. Depending upon your user interface, you may also want to reset the IC when focus changes like this.

11.5.6 Input Context Utility Functions

The following utility functions are sometimes useful when using input methods and input contexts:

`XIMOfIC()`   Returns the IM associated with a given IC.

`XDisplayOfIM()` Returns the Display associated with a given IM.

`XLocaleOfIM()` Returns the locale associated with a given IM. The returned string is owned by Xlib and should not be freed by the client. It will be freed by Xlib when the IM is closed.*

---

*The R5 spec does not state whether the client should free this string, nor when it will be freed by Xlib.

11.6 Input Context Attributes

The behavior of an input method for a particular stream of input is controlled by the attributes of the input context of that stream. There is an attribute, for example, that specifies the interaction style (which must be one of the styles supported by the IM), there are attributes that specify the pre-edit callbacks to be called by the input method when over-the-spot interaction is being used, and there are attributes that specify the foreground and background pixels and colormap for the IM to use when drawing in its Preedit area.

Some attributes are used for communication in the other direction. One is used by the input method to tell the client which types of X events it requires, and another is used by the input method to request a new size for its Preedit and Status areas. Most attributes may be freely modified, but note that some must be set when the IC is created, others must be set exactly once, and others still are read-only and must never be set.

The attributes are listed below. Most attributes provide default values, but recall that some must be specified, either when the IC is created or at some later time before it is used.

11.6.1 XNInputStyle

The `XNInputStyle` attribute specifies the interaction style to be used by the input method for this input context. It is of type `XIMStyle`. It must be one of the supported styles queried from the input method with `XGetIMValues()`. This attribute must be specified when the IC is created. It may be queried but not changed.

11.6.2 XNClientWindow

The `XNClientWindow` attribute specifies the window in which the input method will display its Preedit and Status areas. It is of type `Window`. All geometry values for those areas are specified relative to this window. This attribute must be specified (with `XCreateIC()` or `XSetICValues()`) before any input is done, and once set may not be changed.

11.6.3 XNFocusWindow

If a single IC is used to handle multiple input streams within a single client window (as in a multi-buffer text editor that displays several paned editing windows and provides pre-editing in a message line at the bottom of the client window), the `XNFocusWindow` attribute (of type `Window`) is used to specify which sub-window currently has the focus. The input method may select events on this window, send synthetic events to it, set or change properties on it, or grab the keyboard within it. If not specified, this attribute will default to the value of `XNClientWindow`. If this attribute is specified, it should generally be a child of the client window. The value of `XNFocusWindow` may be changed freely.

11.6.4 XNResourceName and XNResourceClass

The `XNResourceName` and `XNResourceClass` attributes are null-terminated strings which completely specify the resource name and class used to obtain resources for the client window. If the input method allows per-IC customization using X resources, those resources will be looked up using the name and class hierarchies specified by `XNResourceName` and `XNResourceClass`. If your application is named "iedit" with class name "Iedit," and the client window is a widget named "itext" of class "IText" and it is within a top-level manager widget named "main" of class "Form," then the `XNResourceName` attribute should be set to "iedit.main.itext," and the `XNResourceClass` attribute should be set to "IEdit.Form.IText." If these attributes are not set, the input method will not be able to look up resource values for the IC in its resource database. Both attributes may be set at any time, but because resource lookup is generally done only when an IC is created, they will only be useful if specified to `XCreateIC()`. The specification does not say whether or not the values of these strings are copied. To be safe, the strings passed as values of `XNResourceName` and `XNResourceClass` should not be freed or modified until the IC is destroyed or new values are provided for those attributes.

11.6.5 XNGeometryCallback

The `XNGeometryCallback` attribute, of type `XIMCallback *`, specifies a procedure which an input method may call to request a different size for it's Preedit or Status areas. Because the client is never obliged to meet IM geometry requests, specifying this attribute is optional.

11.6.6 XNFilterEvents

The `XNFilterEvents` attribute is used by the input method to notify the client of the X events it needs to receive. It is an event mask, a long integer of the format passed to `XSelectInput()`. The client must query this resource before any input is done and augment the event mask for the `XNClientWindow` with it. This attribute is read-only and should never be set.

11.6.7 XNPreeditAttributes and XNStatusAttributes

Each of these attributes specifies a list of sub-attributes that control the position, behavior, and appearance of the Preedit and Status areas of the IC. They have type `XVaNestedList` and should be created with a call to `XVaCreateNestedList()`. Most of these attributes are used by the input method for both the Preedit and the Status areas. They are ignored, of course, for `XIMPreeditNone` and `XIMStatusNone` interaction styles. All of these attributes except the callbacks are ignored for interaction styles `XIMPreeditCallbacks` and `XIMStatusCallbacks`. They are described individually below.

11.6.7.1 XNArea

The `XNArea` attribute is a pointer to an **XRectangle**. If the interaction style is `XIMPreeditArea` or `XIMStatusArea`, then the rectangle defines the region of the client window in which pre-editing and status display is to take place. An input method may create sub-windows of the client window that conform to this geometry. If the pre-edit interaction style is `XIMPreeditPosition` instead of **XIMPreeditArea**, then this attribute specifies a clipping region in the focus window of the IC to be used in conjunction with the `XNSpotLocation` attribute to implement over-the-spot pre-editing. This attribute must be specified if any of the above interaction styles are in use. For all other pre-edit and status interaction styles, this attribute is ignored.

11.6.7.2 XNAreaNeeded

The `XNAreaNeeded` attribute is also a pointer to an **XRectangle**. It is used for geometry negotiation between client and input method for the **XIMPreeditArea** and `XIMStatusArea` interaction styles, and is ignored for all other styles. The client may provide a hint to the input method about the area it is likely to get by setting a non-zero width or height in this attribute (the x and y values are ignored). The client may query the input method's preferred size for those areas by reading the value of this attribute. A well-behaved input method will not request a size larger than any hints it has received. Note that neither step is required—the client can always set any size it desires with the **XNArea** attribute. See Section 11.7 for more details on geometry negotiation.

11.6.7.3 XNSpotLocation

The `XNSpotLocation` attribute is a pointer to **XPoint**. It is used when the Preedit interaction style is `XIMPreeditPosition` and is ignored for all Status interaction styles and all other Preedit interaction styles. The value of this attribute should be set to the position (in the focus window) at which the next character would be drawn. The input method will use this point and the clipping region specified in **XNAreaNeeded** to implement over-the-spot pre-editing in a sub-window of the focus window. Each time a newly-composed character is drawn or the text modified in any way, the value of this attribute should be changed to reflect the new value of the "spot." When the interaction style is `XIMPreeditPosition`, this attribute must be specified when the IC is created.

11.6.7.4 XNColormap

The `XNColormap` attribute specifies the colormap which the input method should use for any windows it creates itself. It is of type `Colormap`. If the colormap is unspecified, the input method will provide a default.

11.6.7.5 XNStdColormap

The `XNStdColormap` attribute provides an alternate method of specifying the colormap to be used by the input method. It is of type `Atom`, and should be set to a value appropriate for a call to `XGetStandardColormap()`. If both this attribute and the `XNColormap` attribute are passed in a call to `XSetICValues()`, it is implementation-dependent which will take precedence.

11.6.7.6 XNForeground

The `XNForeground` attribute specifies the foreground pixel value to be used by the input method. It is of type `unsigned long`.

11.6.7.7 XNBackground

The `XNBackground` attribute specifies the background pixel value to be used by the input method. It is of type `unsigned long`.

11.6.7.8 XNBackgroundPixmap

The `XNBackgroundPixmap` attribute specifies a pixmap to be used as the background of the Preedit or Status window created by the input method. It is of type `Pixmap`.

11.6.7.9 XNFontSet

The `XNFontSet` attribute specifies a fontset to be used by the input method for text drawing in the Preedit or Status window. It is of type `XFontSet`. The locale of the specified fontset must match the locale of the input method. This attribute must be specified when the IC is created.

11.6.7.10 XNLineSpacing

The `XNLineSpacing` attribute specifies the line spacing* to be used by the input method when displaying multi-line text. It is of type `int`.

---

*The R5 spec simply says "line spacing" and does not specify whether the value should be a baseline-to-baseline spacing or just interline spacing. A baseline-to-baseline spacing was probably the intent, but it will be safest to leave this attribute unspecified and use the IM default.

11.6.7.11 XNCursor

The `XNCursor` attribute specifies the mouse cursor to be used in the Preedit or Status windows. It is of type `Cursor`.

11.6.7.12 Preedit and Status Callbacks

There are seven callback attributes, four of which must be specified for `XIMPreedit-Callbacks` interaction style, and three of which must be specified for `XIMStatus-Callbacks` interaction style. Each callback attribute is of type `XIMCallback *`. This type, the callback prototypes, and requirements will be explained in Section 11.8. If the `XIMPreeditCallbacks` or `XIMStatusCallbacks` interaction styles are in use, the appropriate callbacks must be specified when the IC is created. The callback attributes are the following:

- `XNPreeditStartCallback`, called when pre-editing starts. It gives the client the opportunity to provide feedback to the user, to rearrange characters in the window to make room for pre-editing, etc.

- `XNPreeditDoneCallback`, called when a character is composed and pre-editing stops. It gives the client the opportunity to provide feedback to the user, close up any space opened for pre-editing, etc.

- `XNPreeditDrawCallback`, called when the input method wants the client to draw characters in the window.

- `XNPreeditCaretCallback`, called when the input method wants the client to move the text-insertion cursor (which for some applications may have the shape of a caret).

- `XNStatusStartCallback`, called when the input context gets the focus. It gives the client the chance to provide user feedback.

- `XNStatusDoneCallback`, called when the input context loses focus (or is destroyed). It gives the client the chance to provide user feedback.

- `XNStatusDrawCallback`, called when the input method wants the client to draw text or a bitmap into the status area.

11.7 Negotiating Preedit and Status Area Geometries

For the `XIMPreeditArea` and `XIMStatusArea` interaction styles, the input method needs an area of the application window in which it can create a sub-window and perform its necessary pre-editing and display status information. The application is responsible for providing these areas to the input method (with the `XNArea` sub-attribute) and the input method must accept whatever area it is given.

The simplest applications may simply force the input method to use some pre-defined area, but slightly more flexible applications will want to query the input method for its desired size. To allow this, a protocol for geometry negotiation between application and input method has been defined. The protocol uses the **XNAreaNeeded** sub-attribute of an input context in two distinct ways: when the application sets this attribute with a non-zero width and/or height, the input method interprets these as hints about the size that will eventually be assigned to it by the client. When the application queries the value of the **XNAreaNeeded** attribute, it is returned the input method's preferred size which it may choose to honor when setting the size in the **XNArea** attribute.

An example best demonstrates the use of this protocol: Suppose an internationalized client wants to place the pre-edit area across the bottom of its application window. This means that the width of the area is constrained to be the width of the window, but the height of the area is not constrained. So the application specifies the width of the **XNAreaNeeded** attribute to be the width of the window and leaves the height of the attribute set to 0. Now the input method may use this information to re-compute its desired size. If it would have liked a one line pre-edit area 500 pixels wide, for example, and has just received a hint that it will not get an area wider than 350 pixels, it might choose to request a pre-edit area that is two lines high. Now when the application queries the **XNAreaNeeded** attribute it will get the input method's new desired size. If an application has no constraints for the input method, it can omit the first step and simply read from **XNAreaNeeded**.

This negotiation protocol is not reserved for application startup; it may take place at any time. Note that if the application changes the **XNFocusWindow** attribute of an IC or the **XNFontSet** or **XNLineSpacing** sub-attributes of the pre-edit or status areas, the input method will probably have a new desired size for those areas, and the application should redo the geometry negotiation process. When the application's window is resized, the application will probably want to place the pre-edit and status areas at a new location, and may also have new constraints on their size. The application should set its size constraints in **XNArea-Needed** even if those constraints have not changed since the last time geometry was negotiated.* Example 11-6 shows a procedure that handles the geometry negotiation process. It was designed to be called from an application's event loop when the main window is resized.

Example 11-6. Negotiating Preedit and Status area geometries

```
#include <X11/Xlib.h>

/*
 * This procedure sets the application's size constraints and returns
 * the IM's preferred size for either the Preedit or Status areas,
 * depending on the value of the name argument.  The area argument is
 * used to pass the constraints and to return the preferred size.
 */
void GetPreferredGeometry(ic, name, area)
XIC ic;
char *name;             /* XNPreeditAttributes or XNStatusAttributes */
XRectangle *area;       /* in: constraints;  out: IM preferred size */
{
    XVaNestedList list;

    list = XVaCreateNestedList(0, XNAreaNeeded, area, NULL);
    /* set the constraints */
    XSetICValues(ic, name, list, NULL);
```

_____
*The R5 spec makes no statement about the duration of the validity of the application's constraints.

Example 11-6. Negotiating Preedit and Status area geometries (continued)

```
    /* query the preferred size */
    XGetICValues(ic, name, list, NULL);
    XFree(list);
}
/*
 * This procedure sets the geometry of either the Preedit or Status
 * Areas, depending on the value of the name argument.
 */
void SetGeometry(ic, name, area)
XIC ic;
char *name;             /* XNPreeditAttributes or XNStatusAttributes */
XRectangle *area;       /* the actual area to set */
{
    XVaNestedList list;

    list = XVaCreateNestedList(0, XNArea, area, NULL);
    XSetICValues(ic, name, list, NULL);
    XFree(list);
}
/*
 * Called when the window is resized.  If the interaction style
 * uses the Preedit or Status areas, then their size needs to
 * be re-negotiated.  This procedure places both the Preedit and
 * Status areas at the bottom of the window, and constrains the
 * Preedit area to occupy no more than 4/5ths of the window width
 * on the right hand side of the window, and constrains the Status
 * area to occupy no more than 1/5th of the window on the left.
 * It does not constrain the height of these areas at all.
 */
void NegotiateICGeometry(ic, event, style, preedit_area, status_area)
XIC ic;
XEvent *event;
XIMStyle style;
XRectangle *preedit_area, *status_area;
{
    if ((preedit_area != NULL) && (style & XIMPreeditArea)) {
        preedit_area->width = event->xconfigure.width*4/5;
        preedit_area->height = 0;
        GetPreferredGeometry(ic, XNPreeditAttributes, preedit_area);
        preedit_area->x = event->xconfigure.width - preedit_area->width;
        preedit_area->y = event->xconfigure.height - preedit_area->height;
        SetGeometry(ic, XNPreeditAttributes, preedit_area);
    }
    if ((status_area != NULL) && (style & XIMStatusArea)) {
        status_area->width = event->xconfigure.width/5;
        status_area->height = 0;
        GetPreferredGeometry(ic, XNStatusAttributes, status_area);
        status_area->x = 0;
        status_area->y = event->xconfigure.height - status_area->height;
        SetGeometry(ic, XNStatusAttributes, status_area);
    }
}
```

Finally, an application may choose to provide a callback procedure that will be called by the input method to request a new size for its pre-edit or status areas. This callback may be triggered by changes to attributes such as **XNFontSet** as described above, or may be triggered directly by the user's interactions with the input method (an input method could provide "resize handles" on its pre-edit area, for example). If an application provides a geometry callback, it should attempt to honor any resize requests made by the input method. (An input method might choose whether or not to display "resize handles" on its pre-edit area depending on the presence or absence of such a callback.) The prototype geometry callback is described in Section 11.8.1.

11.8 Geometry, Preedit, and Status Callbacks

An application interacting with an input method using the **XIMPreeditArea** and/or **XIMStatusArea** styles may optionally provide a callback to be called when the input method would like to renegotiate the size of its pre-edit or status areas. An application using the **XIMPreeditCallbacks** style must provide a suite of pre-edit callback routines that allow the input method and application to cooperate and provide pre-editing that appears to be an integral part of the application itself. Similarly, an application using the **XIMStatusCallbacks** must provide a suite of callbacks for the display of status information.

Each callback attribute is of type **XIMCallback**, which is shown in Example 11-7.

Example 11-7. The XIMCallback structure

```
typedef void (*XIMProc)();

typedef struct {
    XPointer client_data;
    XIMProc callback;
} XIMCallback;
```

If you have used X Toolkit callbacks, you will be familiar with the use of the `client_data` field. This is untyped data registered with the callback and passed to the callback every time it is invoked. When a single callback procedure is registered on several different callback attributes, the `client_data` can serve in a `switch` statement to determine how the callback should behave. It is also often used to pass data to the callback (such as a window ID or a widget pointer), which the callback would otherwise not have access to. The type of *client_data* is **XPointer**, which is a new Xlib generic pointer type, like **XtPointer**.

Most of the callback procedures have the prototype shown in Example 11-8.

Example 11-8. A prototype XIM callback procedure

```
void CallbackPrototype(ic, client_data, call_data)
    XIC ic;
    XPointer client_data;
    XPointer call_data;
```

The **XIC** passed to the callback procedure will be the input context that caused the callback to be invoked. The *client_data* argument will be the untyped data registered with the callback as described above. It is up to the callback to know the actual type of this data and cast it as appropriate before use. The *call_data* argument is data passed by the input method to the callback; it is the data required by the callback to perform whatever action the input method needs done. Each callback passes a different type in this argument. Note that the Xlib header files do not actually define **CallbackPrototype**, only the type **XIMProc** shown in the previous example. Since the definition of the **XIMProc** type does not have a prototype, callback procedures may be written with any desired types for *client_data* and *call_data*.

11.8.1 The Geometry Callback

The geometry callback (**XNGeometryCallback**) is triggered when the input method would like to renegotiate the geometry of its pre-edit or status areas. It is not passed any data in its *call_data* argument. Note that this callback does not indicate whether the input method wants renegotiation of the pre-edit area or the status area or both. If the application and the input method are interacting through both **XIMPreeditArea** and **XIMStatus-Area** styles, then the application should renegotiate the geometry of both areas. The geometry negotiation process is described in Section 11.7.

11.8.2 The PreeditStartCallback and the PreeditEndCallback

The **XNPreeditStartCallback** and **XNPreeditEndCallback** are called when the input method begins and ends pre-editing. They give the application the opportunity to do any necessary internal setup or cleanup and provide graphical feedback to the user that the application is entering or leaving pre-edit mode. Both callbacks are passed **NULL** as their *call_data* values. **XNPreeditStartCallback** will not be called twice for the same IC without an intervening call to **XNPreeditEndCallback**.

The **XNPreeditStartCallback** has one additional requirement. It must return an **int** (and therefore does not satisfy the general callback prototype given above) to the input method which indicates the maximum number of bytes the application is able to handle in the pre-edit string. If this callback returns a positive value, the input method should not expect the application to be able to successfully display pre-edit strings any longer than that value. If the callback returns the value -1, it indicates that the application can handle pre-edit strings of any length.

11.8.3 The PreeditDrawCallback

This callback is called when the input method wants the application to insert, delete, or replace text in the pre-edit string. It is also used by the input method to request that some characters or substrings be highlighted (to indicate a selected region of the pre-edit string, for example). The callback is expected to display the pre-edit text to the user and will have to maintain an internal pre-edit string. The pre-edit text will likely appear within the running text of the application, but cursor and character positions referred to in this callback are all relative to the beginning of the pre-edit string. The **XNPreeditDrawCallback** is passed *call_data* of type **XIMPreeditDrawCallbackStruct**, which is shown in Example 11-9.

Example 11-9. The XIMPreeditDrawCallbackStruct

```
typedef unsigned long XIMFeedback;

#define XIMReverse      1L
#define XIMUnderline    (1L<<1)
#define XIMHighlight    (1L<<2)
#define XIMPrimary      (1L<<3)
#define XIMSecondary    (1L<<4)
#define XIMTertiary     (1L<<5)

typedef struct _XIMText {
    unsigned short length;
    XIMFeedback *feedback;
    Bool encoding_is_wchar;
    union {
        char * multi_byte;
        wchar_t * wide_char;
    } string;
} XIMText;

typedef struct _XIMPreeditDrawCallbackStruct {
    int caret;
    int chg_first;
    int chg_length;
    XIMText text;
} XIMPreeditDrawCallbackStruct ;
```

The **XNPreeditDrawCallback** must do the following:

- If **chg_length** is positive, then the application must delete the characters in the pre-edit string between **chg_first** and **chg_first + chg_length−1** inclusive.* Note that manipulations of the pre-edit string are always done on the basis of character positions, so it will generally be most useful to store the pre-edit string in wide-character format.

- If the **text** field is non-NULL, and **text.string** is non-NULL, the application must insert that string at the position specified by **chg_first**. A position of 0 indicates that the string should be inserted before the first character of the pre-edit string, a position of 1 indicates that the string should be inserted before the second character of the pre-edit string, and so on. If **text.encoding_is_wchar** is TRUE then the string to be inserted is the wide-character string **text.string.wide_char** which is **text.length** characters long. If FALSE, then the string to be inserted is the multi-byte string **text.string.multi_byte**, which is also **text.length** characters (not bytes) long. Since there is no way to request that the IM use either wide-character or multi-byte strings, your application will have to be prepared to handle either case. When

---

*The R5 spec says, "Characters starting from chg_first to chg_first+chg_length must be deleted."

passed a multi-byte string, it will probably be easiest to convert it to a wide-character string and operate on it in that representation.

- If there is a string to be inserted, and `text.feedback` is not NULL then `text.feedback` is an array of `XIMFeedback` with `text.length` elements. Each character of the string to be inserted must be drawn with the "feedback style" indicated by the corresponding element of the `text.feedback` array. If the array element is 0 then no special highlighting of the character needs to be done. Otherwise the character must be highlighted in one of the following ways:

  - `XIMReverse` means the character should be drawn with foreground and background colors reversed.

  - `XIMUnderline` means that a line should be drawn along the character's baseline.

  - `XIMHighlight` means that the character should be drawn highlighted in some style other than the styles used for `XIMReverse` and `XIMUnderline`.*

  - `XIMPrimary` means that the character should be drawn in some application defined highlighting style which is not the same as the style used for `XIMSecondary`.

  - `XIMSecondary` means that the character should be drawn in some application defined highlighting style which is not the same as the style used for `XIMPrimary`.

  - `XIMTertiary` means that the character should be drawn in some application defined highlighting style.

- If `text.feedback` is not NULL, but `text.string` is NULL, then no string needs to be inserted, but the characters between *chg_first* and *chg_first* + *text.length-1* inclusive should be redrawn with the highlight style indicated by *text.feedback*.

- After any insertions and deletions have been performed, the text insertion cursor (called the "caret" in the XIM spec) should be moved to the position specified in the *caret* field. If the position is 0, the cursor should be positioned so that new text will be inserted before the first character of the pre-edit string. If it is 1, the cursor should be positioned so that new text will be inserted before the second character of the pre-edit string, and so on.

11.8.4 The PreeditCaretCallback

This callback is called by the input method when it wants the application to move the current position of the text insertion cursor or to change the way the cursor is displayed. It is called with *call_data* of type `XIMPreeditCaretCallbackStruct` which is shown in Example 11-10.

---

*The R5 spec says nothing about the `XIMHighlight` style.

Example 11-10. The XIMPreeditCaretCallbackStruct

```
typedef enum {
    XIMForwardChar, XIMBackwardChar,
    XIMForwardWord, XIMBackwardWord,
    XIMCaretUp, XIMCaretDown,
    XIMNextLine, XIMPreviousLine,
    XIMLineStart, XIMLineEnd,
    XIMAbsolutePosition,
    XIMDontChange,
} XIMCaretDirection;

typedef enum {
    XIMIsInvisible,
    XIMIsPrimary,
    XIMIsSecondary,
} XIMCaretStyle;

typedef struct _XIMPreeditCaretCallbackStruct {
    int position;
    XIMCaretDirection direction;
    XIMCaretStyle style;
} XIMPreeditCaretCallbackStruct;
```

The `XNPreeditCaretCallback` is required to move the cursor as specified in the `direction` field, display it in the style specified in the `style` field, and return the new character position of the cursor by setting the value of the `position` field. The position field must be set by the callback because in some cases the input method will not be able to compute it itself. This is the case when the cursor is moved down a line, for example—the new character position of the cursor will depend on the number of characters in each line, which is a figure known to the application but not to the input method. Note that to correctly implement this callback, the application will have to remember the position of the insertion cursor at all times, and this position will have to be updated by both the `XNPreeditDraw-Callback` and the `XNPreeditCaretCallback`.

The possible values of the `direction` field and their meanings are listed below. Note that in no case should the insertion cursor be moved to a position before the beginning or after the end of the pre-edit string.*

- `XIMForwardChar` means move the cursor forward one character.

- `XIMBackwardChar` means move the cursor backwards one character.

- `XIMForwardWord` means move the cursor forward one word. It is up to the application to decide what constitutes a "word" in a pre-edit string. In many locales, a word will be delimited by characters for which `isspace` returns `True`.

- `XIMBackwardWord` means move the cursor backwards one word.

- `XIMCaretUp` means move the cursor up one line, keeping its position in the line constant if possible.

---

*The R5 spec does not say what an application should do if a cursor motion request would take the cursor beyond the pre-edit text. You should probably leave the cursor where it is or move it to one end of the text. In either case simply return the new or unchanged position.

- **XIMCaretDown** means move the cursor down one line, keeping its position in the line constant if possible.

- **XIMPreviousLine** means move the cursor to the beginning of the previous line of pre-edit text.

- **XIMNextLine** means move the cursor to the beginning of the next line of pre-edit text.

- **XIMLineStart** means move the cursor to the beginning of the line it is currently on.

- **XIMLineEnd** means move the cursor to the end of the line it is currently on.

- **XIMAbsolutePosition** means move the cursor to the absolute character position specified in the **position** field of the **XIMPreeditCallbacksStruct**. If the position is 0, the cursor should be positioned so that new text will be inserted before the first character of the pre-edit string. If it is 1, the cursor should be positioned so that new text will be inserted before the second character of the pre-edit string, and so on.

- **XIMDontChange** means that the cursor position should not be changed. The current position of the cursor must still be returned in the **position** field, however.

The **XNPreeditCaretCallback** can also be called to request that the insertion cursor become hidden or be drawn in a different style. Different cursor appearances may be used by the input method to indicate different pre-editing modes, insert versus overwrite mode, for example. The possible values of the **style** field and their meanings are as follows:

- **XIMIsInvisible** means that the insertion cursor should not be displayed.

- **XIMIsPrimary** means that the insertion cursor should be displayed in its primary or normal style. The particular style used is up to the application.

- **XIMIsSecondary** means that the insertion cursor should be displayed in its secondary or special style. The particular style used is up to the application.

Note that there is no provision for the handling of mouse clicks (for example, to move the position of the insertion cursor in the pre-edit text) in this interaction style. Since the input method does not know how the pre-edit text is displayed, it cannot interpret mouse clicks over the text, and there is no specified way for the IM to request the application to convert pixel locations to character positions. Furthermore, the application cannot handle mouse clicks on the pre-edit text because it has no way of changing the internal insertion position of the IM. Note that some input methods will allow mouse clicks and drags while pre-editing in the **XIMPreeditPosition** and **XIMPreeditArea** interaction styles; in this case these styles may actually provide a more consistent user interface than the **XIMPreedit-Callbacks** style.

11.8.5 The StatusStartCallback and the StatusDoneCallback

These callbacks are called when an IC gains focus or loses focus (possibly by being destroyed). They give the application the chance to set up or clean up any internal structures for handling status display, and allow the application to provide graphical feedback of the new

IC focus state to the user. Both are passed **NULL** *call_data* and neither has any required actions.

11.8.6 The StatusDrawCallback

The input method invokes the **XNStatusDrawCallback** when it wants the application to display a string or a bitmap in the status area. The callback procedure is passed *call_data* of type **XIMStatusDrawCallbackStruct**, which is shown in Example 11-11.

Example 11-11. The XIMStatusDrawCallbackStruct

```
typedef enum {XIMTextType, XIMBitmapType} XIMStatusDataType;

typedef struct _XIMStatusDrawCallbackStruct {
    XIMStatusDataType type;
    union {
        XIMText text;
        Pixmap  bitmap;
    } data;
} XIMStatusDrawCallbackStruct ;
```

If the **type** field is **XIMTextType**, then the callback must display the text described by **data.text** in the status area of the IC. The **XIMText** type is also used by the **XNPreeditDrawCallback**, and is shown and explained in Section 11.8.3. The text may be in multi-byte or wide-character form, so the application must be able to handle either case. Recall that the **length** field of the **XIMText** structure gives the number of characters of text, even when the text is in multi-byte form. The length in bytes of a multi-byte string is required for a call to **XmbDrawImageString()**, so when text is passed in multi-byte form, the application will have to use **strlen** to determine its length before displaying it.

If the **type** field is **XIMBitmapType**, then the callback must display the 1-bit deep **Pixmap data.bitmap**.* Notice that the callback does not return the width or height of the pixmap, so these must be obtained with a call to **XGetGeometry()** before the pixmap is displayed.

The **XIMStatusCallbacks** interaction style does not allow for any communication between the application and the input method about the maximum size of the status area. Since it can always be passed data to display that is larger than the area it has allocated, the **XNStatusDrawCallback** must be prepared either to clip or provide scrolling for the strings and pixmaps it is passed, or to attempt to enlarge the status area. Resizing the status area requires the main application window to be made larger or other windows to be rearranged or resized. The **XIMStatusCallbacks** interaction style can be useful for an application designed to be used with a single input method which calls the **XNStatusDrawCallback** with well specified values. In general, however, when you don't know what sort of data your application will be asked to display (or the meaning of that data), you won't be able to do anything beyond displaying the data in some rectangular region of your

---

*The R5 spec does not say anything about the depth of this **Pixmap**.

application, which amounts to the same thing as the **XIMStatusArea** interaction style. So in these cases it may make more sense to use **XIMStatusArea** if the input method supports it.

11.9 Filtering Events

An input method needs to receive X events other than keystrokes. It must receive expose events when its Preedit or Status areas need refreshing, it needs mouse button events if it is to support full-featured editing of pre-edit text, and it needs mouse motion events if it implements popup menus. The input method needs to get first crack at these events, but will not always be able to intercept them directly from the server, so the application is responsible for passing all events to the input method before processing them itself. This is done with the function **XFilterEvent()**. It should be called from the event loop of all internationalized applications, generally right after **XNextEvent()**. **XFilterEvent()** takes two arguments, the event to filter, and the window to which the event is directed. If the application (or a toolkit used by the application) performs event redirection, this window may not be the same as the window in which the event occurred. If the window argument is **None**, the window of the event will be used. An application cannot know in advance which events the IM will need to filter; it must pass all events to **XFilterEvent()**. If **XFilter-Event()** returns **True**, it filtered the event the application should dispatch the event no further.

Remember that an input method may be interested in different types of events than the application is. If the application is to pass events to the input method through **XFilter-Event()**, the application must have registered interest in receiving those events with **XSelectInput()**. The **XNFilterEvents** input context attribute contains a mask of events that the input method is interested in receiving, and all clients should read this attribute and use it when selecting events. Example 11-12 shows code that does this and an event loop that uses **XFilterEvent()**.

Example 11-12. Selecting events for an IM and using XFilterEvent() in an event loop

```
long im_event_mask;
     .
     .
     .
XGetICValues(ic, XNFilterEvents, &im_event_mask, NULL);
XSelectInput(dpy, win, ExposureMask | KeyPressMask
             | StructureNotifyMask | im_event_mask);

for(;;) {
    XEvent e;

    XNextEvent(dpy, &e);
    if (XFilterEvent(&e, None)) continue;
    switch (e.type) {
        .
        .    /* dispatch the event here */
        .
    }
}
```

The R5 X Toolkit Intrinsics have been modified to make appropriate use of `XFilter-Event()` in the function `XtDispatchEvent()` called from `XtAppMainLoop()`.

11.10 Getting Composed Text

Prior to R5, `XLookupString()` was used to convert the keycode returned in a KeyPress event into a KeySym and further into a character string that could be passed to the X text drawing functions. Unfortunately, this function only works for the Latin-1 charset. To support internationalization in a limited way, there were alternate `LookupString` functions in the Xmu library: `XmuLookupLatin2()`, `XmuLookupJISX0201()`, `XmuLookup-Greek()`, etc. In R5, these have been superseded by `XmbLookupString()` and `Xwc-LookupString()`. These functions are identical except in the type of string they return: the Xmb version returns a multi-byte string of `char`, and Xwc version returns a wide-character string of `wchar_t`. In both cases the string will be encoded as appropriate for the locale of the IC.*

Whenever a `KeyPress` event is delivered to an application that is performing internationalized text input, the application should use that event in a call to `XmbLookupString()` or `XwcLookupString()`. (Note that `KeyRelease` events should not be passed to these functions—they will result in undefined behavior.) The application should not expect that each call to `Xmb/XwcLookupString()` will return a string. Depending on the complexity of the input method in use, a user may type many keystrokes before any composed input is ready for the application. Neither should the application expect that `Xmb/XwcLookup-String()` will return a single character at a time—in some input methods a user may type a phrase, a sentence, or more before hitting the key that triggers the conversion from pre-edit to composed text.

`XmbLookupString()` and `XwcLookupString()` take as arguments the IC for which input is to be looked up (which is usually the IC with the focus), the X event that triggered the call, a buffer to return the multi-byte or wide-character string in, a pointer to a location to return a keysym, and a pointer to a location to return a status value. The value returned by both functions is an integer which specifies the number of bytes in the returned multi-byte string or the number of `wchar_t` in the returned wide-character string. There are five status values that these functions return, each of which may require separate processing:

- `XLookupNone` means that the input method does not have any composed input ready to pass to the application, and the application need not do any further processing on the current key event. When this status value is returned, the return value of the function will be 0.

- `XLookupKeySym` means that a keysym, but no string, has been returned. This likely means that the user has struck a special key of some sort (a function key, an arrow key,

---

*There were bugs in the public R5 version of the Xsi implementation of `XwcLookupString()`. It is supposed to return as its value the number of characters in the returned string, but appears, at least in some cases, to return the number of bytes instead.

Delete, etc.). The application should handle the keysym as appropriate. Because no string is returned, the return value of the function is 0. Be careful to capitalize the constant **XLookupKeySym** correctly; Xlib also defines the function **XLookupKeysym( )**.

- **XLookupChars** means that a string, but no keysym, has been returned. The multi-byte or wide-character string is encoded in the codeset of the locale of the IC and is placed in the buffer passed to the function. The return value of the function is the length of the multi-byte string in bytes or the length of the wide-character string in wide characters.

- **XLookupBoth** means that both a string and a keysym are returned. This may indicate that a single keystroke has passed through the input method without any pre-editing, as is common in European input methods, for example. The return value of the function is the length of the string, as described for **XLookupChars** above.

- **XBufferOverflow** means that the string to be returned will not fit in the provided buffer. The return value of the function is the required size of the buffer (in bytes or wide characters), and nothing is returned in the string buffers. The input string remains in the IC, waiting to be looked up. The application should allocate a buffer of the required size and look up the string, or should display an error message and flush the pending input with a call to **XmbResetIC( )** or **XwcResetIC**. If this return status is ignored, the large input string will remain pending and block any further input on that IC.

Some input method architectures allow the input method to intercept events from the X server before the application ever sees them. If these input methods remove all **KeyPress** events from the input stream, then the application will never be triggered to call **Xmb/wc-LookupString( )**. If this is the case, the input method will send a synthetic **KeyPress** event to the application when it has composed input ready for lookup. By convention, the keycode in this synthetic event should be 0. Note, though, that these are architectural details and do not affect the structure of an internationalized applications.

Example 11-13 shows code that uses **XwcLookupString( )** and handles each of the possible return status values.

Example 11-13. Looking up internationalized input

```
XEvent event;
int len;
int buf_len = 10;
wchar_t *buffer = (wchar_t *)malloc(buf_len * sizeof(wchar_t));
KeySym keysym;
Status status;

while(1) {
    XNextEvent(dpy, &event);
    if (XFilterEvent(&event, None))
      continue;

    switch (event.type) {
    case Expose:
        Redraw();
        break;
    case KeyPress:
        len = XwcLookupString(ic, &event, buffer, buf_len,
                        &keysym, &status);
```

Example 11-13. Looking up internationalized input (continued)

```
        if (status == XBufferOverflow) {
            buf_len = len;
            buffer = (wchar_t *)realloc(buffer, buf_len*sizeof(wchar_t));
            len = XwcLookupString(ic, &event, buffer, buf_len,
                                  &keysym, &status);
        }
        switch (status) {
        case XLookupNone:
            break;
        case XLookupKeySym:
        case XLookupBoth:
            /* Handle backspacing */
            if ((keysym == XK_Delete) || (keysym == XK_BackSpace)) {
                Backspace();
                break;
            }
            if (status == XLookupKeySym) break;
        case XLookupChars:
            Insert(buffer, len);
            break;
        }
        break;
    }
}
```

11.11 XIM Programming Checklist

The following list provides useful guidelines when writing an Xlib or Xt application or Xt widget that uses the R5 internationalized input mechanisms. It is followed by an example Xlib program that performs simple internationalized text input and implements most of the steps in the list.

- Set the locale with **setlocale**. Use a locale name from a resource, or specify the empty string (" "). In an Xt application do this from the special callback procedure registered with **XtSetLanguageProc()**.

- Verify that X supports the locale with **XSupportsLocale()**.

- Set the locale modifiers (i.e., the name of the input method to use) from a resource or with the empty string.

- If you want your input method to be customizable with resources, create a database or get a handle to an already created one. In an Xt application, use **XtDatabase()**.

- Open a connection to the IM of the locale with **XOpenIM()**. Pass a resource database and the name and class the IM should use for looking up its resources in that database. Verify that the IM is successfully opened. If you are writing a widget, you can assume that a valid **XIM** will be passed as a resource, and skip this step.

- Query the IM for its supported interaction styles. Choose one that your application can support based on the value of user-specified resources, or upon some criteria for which will provide the best user interface for your application. In a widget, this should be in the `initialize` method.

- Create an `XFontSet` for use by the IC. The base font name list for the `XFontSet` should be obtained from a resource. In an Xt application, you should use the constant `XtDefaultFontSet` as the default value for this resource. If you are writing a widget, you can assume that a valid `XFontSet` will be passed as a resource.

- Create a `Window` for use by the IC. If you are programming with Xt, create a widget. If you are writing your own widget, the window will be created for you by the `realize` method.

- Create an IC with `XCreateIC()`, specifying the interaction style you choose, the `XNEditWindow`, and the `XNFontSet` sub-attribute for both the Preedit and Status Areas. If you are using the `XIMPreeditPosition` style, you must also specify the `XNAreaNeeded` attribute, and if you are using `XIMPreeditCallbacks` or `XIMStatusCallbacks` styles, you must specify values for all the applicable callback attributes. You may also specify any other attributes at this point. If you are writing a widget, create the IC in the `initialize` method, but specify the window in the `realize` method. In a widget, you should provide widget resources which control the setting of IC attributes like `XNLineSpacing` and `XNCursor`.

- Query the value of the `XNFilterEvents` attribute of the IC and augment the event mask for your window with those events. If you are writing an Xt program, call `XtAdd-EventHandler` for the event mask with a no-op procedure. If you are writing a widget, call `XtAddEventHandler()` in the same way from the `realize` method.

- If you have selected the `XIMPreeditArea` or the `XIMStatusArea` interaction styles, negotiate a geometry for either or both of those areas using the `XNAreaNeeded` attribute of the IC. Set the geometry you decide on in the `XNArea` attribute. If you are writing a widget, begin the negotiation in the `initialize` method, and set the `XNArea` attribute when the window is created in the `realize` method. Renegotiate geometry whenever your application window changes size.

- If you have selected the `XIMPreeditPosition` interaction style, set the initial location of your insertion cursor in the `XNSpotLocation` attribute, and a region within which pre-editing is allowed in the `XNArea` resource. If you are writing a widget, do this in the `resize` method. In a widget, you may want to implement the Preedit and Status areas as sub-widgets.

- For a simple application that does no focus management, set the focus to your IC with `XSetICFocus()`. For more complicated applications, you should set and unset IC focus when you receive `FocusIn` and `FocusOut` events, or whenever your application-internal or toolkit focus changes. In an Xt program or widget, you can use an event handler or a translation and action to track focus changes.

- Use `XFilterEvent()` in your event loop before dispatching an event. If it returns `True`, discard the event and wait for another. In Xt programs, this is handled for you by `XtDispatchEvent()` in `XtAppMainLoop()`.

- When `XFilterEvent()` returns an unfiltered `KeyPress` event, use `Xmb/wc-LookupString()` to convert it to a KeySym or a string in the encoding of the locale.

In Xt programs or widgets, use an event handler or a translation and action to get these events.

- Echo the newly input characters with **Xmb/wcDrawString()** or one of the other R5 text drawing functions.

- If you are using the **XIMPreeditPosition** interaction style, update the values of the **XNSpotLocation** and **XNArea** attributes of the IC each time you move the insertion cursor.

- If your application supports the **XIMPreeditArea** or **XIMStatusArea** interaction styles, optionally write a **GeometryCallback** procedure to handle requests from the IM to change the size of those areas. If you are writing a composite widget, the **GeometryCallback** and the **geometry_manager** method may be able to share code.

- If your application supports the **XIMPreeditCallbacks** or **XIMStatus-Callbacks** interaction styles, write the required callback procedures to support those styles.

Example 11-14 is the complete code of a program that performs simple internationalized text input. Many of the examples in this chapter and the last are fragments of this program.*

Example 11-14. Performing internationalized text input: a complete program

```
/*
 * This program demonstrates some of the R5 internationalized text
 * input functions.  It creates a very simple window, connects to an
 * input method, and displays composed text obtained by calling
 * XwcLookupString.  It backspaces when it receives the Backspace or
 * Delete keysyms.
 *
 * Note that this program contains a work-around for a bug
 * in the Xsi implementation of XwcLookupString.  If you are using
 * the Ximp implementation, or if the bug has been fixed in your Xlib,
```

---

*To run this program successfully, you must have an input method running. Because there are no input methods as part of the core R5 distribution, this may be difficult. If your Xlib uses the Xsi implementation of the R5 internationalization features, you can use the input method in *contrib/im/Xsi*. In order to run this program, I had to do the following:

- Build everything in *contrib/im/Xsi*.

- Install everything in *contrib/im/Xsi*. This involved installing a number of files under */usr/local/lib/wnn*, and adding a new user "wnn" to the */etc/passwd* file.

- Start the "translation server" *contrib/im/Xsi/Wnn/jserver/jserver*.

- Start the "input manager" *contrib/im/Xsi/Xwnmo/xwnmo* which was also installed in */usr/bin/X11*.

- Set the **XMODIFIERS** environment variable to "@im=_XWNMO."

- Set the **LANG** environment variable to something appropriate, ja_JP.ujis, for example.

With these steps accomplished, I was able to run the program and type Latin characters, but I was never able to figure out how to actually make use of the input method to input Japanese. Since the Xsi input method is contributed software, it may have been updated since this program was written, and the above list may no longer be correct.

```
 * you will need to undo the workaround.  See the comment below, near
 * the call to XwcLookupString.
 *
 * This program has not been tested with the Ximp implementation.
 */

#include <stdio.h>
#include <malloc.h>
#include <X11/Xlib.h>
#include <X11/keysym.h>
/*
 * include <locale.h> or the non-standard X substitutes
 * depending on the X_LOCALE compilation flag
 */
#include <X11/Xlocale.h>

/*
 * This function chooses the "more desirable" of two input styles.  The
 * style with the more complicated Preedit style is returned, and if the
 * styles have the same Preedit styles, then the style with the more
 * complicated Status style is returned.  There is no "official" way to
 * order interaction styles.  This one makes the most sense to me.
 * This is a long procedure for a simple heuristic.
 */
XIMStyle ChooseBetterStyle(style1,style2)
XIMStyle style1, style2;
{
    XIMStyle s,t;
    XIMStyle preedit = XIMPreeditArea | XIMPreeditCallbacks |
        XIMPreeditPosition | XIMPreeditNothing | XIMPreeditNone;
    XIMStyle status = XIMStatusArea | XIMStatusCallbacks |
        XIMStatusNothing | XIMStatusNone;

    if (style1 == 0) return style2;
    if (style2 == 0) return style1;
    if ((style1 & (preedit | status)) == (style2 & (preedit | status)))
        return style1;

    s = style1 & preedit;
    t = style2 & preedit;
    if (s != t) {
        if (s | t | XIMPreeditCallbacks)
            return (s == XIMPreeditCallbacks)?style1:style2;
        else if (s | t | XIMPreeditPosition)
            return (s == XIMPreeditPosition)?style1:style2;
        else if (s | t | XIMPreeditArea)
            return (s == XIMPreeditArea)?style1:style2;
        else if (s | t | XIMPreeditNothing)
            return (s == XIMPreeditNothing)?style1:style2;
    }
    else { /* if preedit flags are the same, compare status flags */
        s = style1 & status;
        t = style2 & status;
        if (s | t | XIMStatusCallbacks)
            return (s == XIMStatusCallbacks)?style1:style2;
        else if (s | t | XIMStatusArea)
            return (s == XIMStatusArea)?style1:style2;
        else if (s | t | XIMStatusNothing)
```

```
            return (s == XIMStatusNothing)?style1:style2;
    }
}
void GetPreferredGeometry(ic, name, area)
XIC ic;
char *name;
XRectangle *area;
{
    XVaNestedList list;
    XRectangle *area2;

    list = XVaCreateNestedList(0, XNAreaNeeded, area, NULL);
    XSetICValues(ic, name, list, NULL)
    XFree(list);
    list = XVaCreateNestedList(0, XNAreaNeeded, &area2, NULL);
    XGetICValues(ic, name, list, NULL);
    XFree(list);

    *area = *area2;
    XFree(area2);
}

void SetGeometry(ic, name, area)
XIC ic;
char *name;              /* XNPreEditAttributes or XNStatusAttributes */
XRectangle *area;        /* the actual area to set */
{
    XVaNestedList list;

    list = XVaCreateNestedList(0, XNArea, area, NULL);
    XSetICValues(ic, name, list, NULL);
    XFree(list);
}

main(argc, argv)
int argc;
char *argv[];
{
    Display *dpy;
    int screen;
    Window win;
    GC gc;
    XGCValues gcv;
    XEvent event;
    XFontSet fontset;
    XIM im;
    XIC ic;
    XIMStyles *im_supported_styles;
    XIMStyle app_supported_styles;
    XIMStyle style;
    XIMStyle best_style;
    XVaNestedList list;
    long im_event_mask;
    XRectangle preedit_area;
    XRectangle status_area;
    char *program_name = argv[0];
    char **missing_charsets;
    int num_missing_charsets = 0;
```

```
char *default_string;
wchar_t string[ 200 ];
int str_len = 0;
int i;

/*
 * The error messages in this program are all in English.
 * In a truly internationalized program, they would not
 * be hardcoded; they would be looked up in a database of
 * some sort.
 */
if (setlocale(LC_ALL, "") == NULL) {
    (void) fprintf(stderr, "%s: cannot set locale.\n",program_name);
    exit(1);
}

if ((dpy = XOpenDisplay(NULL)) == NULL) {
    (void) fprintf(stderr, "%s: cannot open Display.\n", program_name);
    exit(1);
}

if (!XSupportsLocale()) {
    (void) fprintf(stderr, "%s: X does not support locale
                    program_name, setlocale(LC_ALL, NULL));
    exit(1);
}

if (XSetLocaleModifiers("") == NULL) {
    (void) fprintf(stderr, "%s: Warning: cannot set locale modifiers.\n",
                    argv[ 0 ]);
}

/*
 * Create the fontset.
 */
fontset = XCreateFontSet(dpy,
                    "-adobe-helvetica-*-r-*-*-*-120-*-*-*-*-*-*,\
                    -misc-fixed-*-r-*-*-*-130-*-*-*-*-*-*",
                    &missing_charsets, &num_missing_charsets,
                    &default_string);

/*
 * if there are charsets for which no fonts can
 * be found, print a warning message.
 */
if (num_missing_charsets > 0) {
    (void)fprintf(stderr, "%s: The following charsets are missing:\n",
                    program_name);
    for(i=0; i < num_missing_charsets; i++)
        (void)fprintf(stderr, "%s:     %s\n", program_name,
                    missing_charsets[i]);
    XFreeStringList(missing_charsets);

    (void)fprintf(stderr, "%s: The string
                    program_name, default_string);
    (void)fprintf(stderr, "%s: of any characters from those sets.\n",
                    program_name);
}
```

```
    screen = DefaultScreen(dpy);

    win = XCreateSimpleWindow(dpy, RootWindow(dpy, screen), 0, 0, 400, 100,
                              2, WhitePixel(dpy,screen),BlackPixel(dpy,screen));

    gc = XCreateGC(dpy,win,0,&gcv);
    XSetForeground(dpy,gc,WhitePixel(dpy,screen));
    XSetBackground(dpy,gc,BlackPixel(dpy,screen));

    /* Connect to an input method.  */
    /* In this example, we don't pass a resource database */
    if ((im = XOpenIM(dpy, NULL, NULL, NULL)) == NULL) {
        (void)fprintf(stderr, "Couldn't open input method\n");
        exit(1);
    }

    /* set flags for the styles our application can support */
    app_supported_styles = XIMPreeditNone | XIMPreeditNothing | XIMPreeditArea;
    app_supported_styles |= XIMStatusNone | XIMStatusNothing | XIMStatusArea;

    /* figure out which styles the IM can support */
    XGetIMValues(im, XNQueryInputStyle, &im_supported_styles, NULL);

    /*
     * now look at each of the IM supported styles, and
     * chose the "best" one that we can support.
     */
    best_style = 0;
    for(i=0; i < im_supported_styles->count_styles; i++) {
        style = im_supported_styles->supported_styles[i];
        if ((style & app_supported_styles) == style) /* if we can handle it */
            best_style = ChooseBetterStyle(style, best_style);
    }

    /* if we couldn't support any of them, print an error and exit */
    if (best_style == 0) {
        (void)fprintf(stderr, "%s: application and program do not share a\n",
                      argv[0]);
        (void)fprintf(stderr, "%s: commonly supported interaction style.\n",
                      argv[0]);
        exit(1);
    }

    XFree(im_supported_styles);

    /*
     * Now go create an IC using the style we chose.
     * Also set the window and fontset attributes now.
     */
    list = XVaCreateNestedList(0,XNFontSet,fontset,NULL);
    ic = XCreateIC(im,
                   XNInputStyle, best_style,
                   XNClientWindow, win,
                   XNPreeditAttributes, list,
                   XNStatusAttributes, list,
                   NULL);
    XFree(list);
    if (ic == NULL) {
        (void) fprintf(stderr, "Couldn't create input context\n");
```

```
        exit(1);
    }

    XGetICValues(ic, XNFilterEvents, &im_event_mask, NULL);
    XSelectInput(dpy,win, ExposureMask | KeyPressMask
                    | StructureNotifyMask | im_event_mask);

    XSetICFocus(ic);

    XMapWindow(dpy,win);

    while(1) {
        int buf_len = 10;
        wchar_t *buffer = (wchar_t *)malloc(buf_len * sizeof(wchar_t));
        int len;
        KeySym keysym;
        Status status;
        Bool redraw = False;

        XNextEvent(dpy, &event);
        if (XFilterEvent(&event, None))
            continue;

        switch (event.type) {
        case Expose:
            /* draw the string at a hard-coded location */
            if (event.xexpose.count == 0)
                XwcDrawString(dpy, win, fontset, gc, 10, 50, string, str_len);
            break;
        case KeyPress:
            len = XwcLookupString(ic, &event, buffer, buf_len,
                                    &keysym, &status);
            /*
             * Workaround:  the Xsi implementation of XwcLookupString
             * returns a length that is 4 times too big.  If this bug
             * does not exist in your version of Xlib, remove the
             * following line, and the similar line below.
             */
            len = len / 4;

            if (status == XBufferOverflow) {
                buf_len = len;
                buffer = (wchar_t *)realloc((char *)buffer,
                                            buf_len * sizeof(wchar_t));
                len = XwcLookupString(ic, &event, buffer, buf_len,
                                        &keysym, &status);
                /* Workaround */
                len = len / 4;
            }

            redraw = False;

            switch (status) {
            case XLookupNone:
                break;
            case XLookupKeySym:
            case XLookupBoth:
                /* Handle backspacing, and <Return> to exit */
                if ((keysym == XK_Delete) || (keysym == XK_BackSpace)) {
                    if (str_len > 0) str_len--;
```

```
                    redraw = True;
                    break;
                }
                if (keysym == XK_Return) exit(0);
                if (status == XLookupKeySym) break;
            case XLookupChars:
                for(i=0; i < len; i++)
                    string[str_len++] = buffer[i];
                redraw = True;
                break;
            }

            /* do a very simple-minded redraw, if needed */
            if (redraw) {
                XClearWindow(dpy, win);
                XwcDrawString(dpy, win, fontset, gc, 10, 50, string, str_len);
            }
            break;
        case ConfigureNotify:
            /*
             * When the window is resized, we should re-negotiate the
             * geometry of the Preedit and Status area, if they are used
             * in the interaction style.
             */
            if (best_style & XIMPreeditArea) {
                preedit_area.width = event.xconfigure.width*4/5;
                preedit_area.height = 0;
                GetPreferredGeometry(ic, XNPreeditAttributes, &preedit_area);
                preedit_area.x = event.xconfigure.width - preedit_area.width;
                preedit_area.y = event.xconfigure.height - preedit_area.height;
                SetGeometry(ic, XNPreeditAttributes, &preedit_area);
            }
            if (best_style & XIMStatusArea) {
                status_area.width = event.xconfigure.width/5;
                status_area.height = 0;
                GetPreferredGeometry(ic, XNStatusAttributes, &status_area);
                status_area.x = 0;
                status_area.y = event.xconfigure.height - status_area.height;
                SetGeometry(ic, XNStatusAttributes, &status_area);
            }
            break;
        }
    }
}
```

12

Interclient Communication

As a multi-window environment, X must support a mechanism for communication between applications. There are three: properties, selections, and cut buffers, all of which are described in this chapter. The special case of communication between an application and the window manager is also covered here. Internationalized interclient communication is described in Section sintcom. Standard conventions for additional aspects of interclient communication are covered in Appendix L of Volume Zero, X Protocol Reference Manual.

In This Chapter:

12
Interclient Communication

Communication is necessary to make sure that all applications running under X cooperate properly with the window manager and share the system resources politely. Communication also allows applications to interchange data. Most applications in an integrated computing environment should have the ability to transfer data to and accept data from other applications.

Communication between clients takes place through *properties*. Sometimes properties are set directly by one application and read by another. This is the case with most communication between the window manager and the clients.

There is also a simple but limited means of communication through properties called *cut buffers*. But the preferred and most powerful method of general communication between clients is called *selections*. Selections actually establish a dialog between the two applications, not just a one-way communication. Both cut buffers and selections are ways of using properties for communication.

Successful communication depends on conventions for the meanings of the data communicated through properties and selections. The conventions in this area were established initially in Release 4, with the adoption as an X Consortium standard of the *Inter-Client Communication Conventions Manual* (ICCCM), which is reprinted in Appendix L, *Interclient Communication Conventions*, of Volume Zero, *X Protocol Reference Manual* (as of the second printing). The current version of the ICCCM is version 1.

Several R3 routines are now obsolete because of new routines added to Xlib in R4. This edition describes only the currently valid interfaces. The outdated routines formerly used by applications are `XSetStandardProperties()`, `XSetWMHints()`, `XSetZoomHints()`, `XSetNormalHints()`, `XStoreName()` and `XSetIconName()`.

12.1 Properties and Atoms

Properties allow you to associate arbitrary information with windows, usually to make that data available to the window manager or other applications. Properties are stored in the server.

Each property has a unique integer ID, called an atom. An atom is just a nickname for a property, so that arbitrary length property name strings do not have to be transferred back and forth between Xlib and the server. The atom is assigned by the server and will remain defined in the server even after the client that defined it terminates. The atoms for the pre-defined properties are constants defined in *<X11/Xatom.h>*; all of them begin with the prefix **XA_**. This naming convention avoids name clashes with user-defined symbols.

A property is uniquely identified by an atom and a window. Therefore, there may be one property on each window identified by a given atom. In other words, there can be a **XA_WM_NAME** property on each and every window, even though by convention this property is only set or read on the top-level windows of each application. A property on a window takes up space only once it is set.

Each property also has a name, which is an ASCII string. For the predefined properties, the name is never used in code. That is why we have chosen for this manual to refer to all pre-defined properties by their atoms. But for properties defined by convention between related clients (not predefined), the property name string is used so that the applications can determine the correct atom for the property. The first client to call **XInternAtom( )** with the property name string as an argument gets a new atom. Subsequent clients that call **XInternAtom( )** with the same string will get the same atom. After each client has called **XInternAtom( )**, they use the atom rather than the string to refer to the property. They use this process because for properties defined by clients, the actual number used for an atom may differ between invocations of the server.

Once created, an atom remains defined in the server even after the client that created it has exited. A server remembers all atoms that were ever defined since the server started up. This means that one client can refer to an atom first interned by another client even if that other client has already exited.

Each property has a type, which itself is a property. There are several predefined properties for use as some of the more often needed types.

The data associated with a property can be stored as an array of 8-bit quantities, 16-bit quantities, or 32-bit quantities only. Properties can contain structures or raw data, but if one is to contain a structure of complex type, it must be encoded into one of the three byte formats by the program before being sent to the server and decoded when read from the server. The pre-defined property types have been carefully designed to match one of the data formats so that encoding and decoding are not necessary.

Properties remain set until the window to which they are attached is destroyed, which happens automatically when the client that created the window exits. However, properties set on the root window remain defined even after the client that set them has exited, since the root window is never destroyed.

There are 68 predefined properties for window manager communication, selections, standard colormaps, and font specifications. The properties used for window manager communication and selections are described in this chapter. The standard colormap properties are described in Chapter 7, *Color*, and the font properties are described in Chapter 6, *Drawing Graphics and Text*.

Properties are set with `XChangeProperty()` and read with `XGetWindow-Property()`. Whenever `XChangeProperty()` is called, a `PropertyNotify` event is generated.

12.2 The Compound Text Encoding

An X Consortium standard defines a format for text properties that support multiple character sets, such as multi-lingual text. It is called the Compound Text Encoding. As of late 1992, the Compound Text Encoding specification is printed in Volume Zero, *X Protocol Reference Manual*.

The format is based on ISO standards for encoding and combining character sets. Compound Text is intended to be used in three main contexts: inter-client communication using selections; window properties (e.g., window manager hints); and resources (e.g., as defined in Xlib and the Xt Intrinsics). All of the standard routines for setting window manager hints that set text properties support the compound text encoding. If you are only concerned with your program operating in English on a system where the window manager also uses English, these routines are easy to use.

The target type for selections in the Compound Text encoding is COMPOUND_TEXT.

12.3 Communicating with the Window Manager

To permit window managers to perform their role of mediating the competing demands for screen space and colormaps, the clients being managed must adhere to certain conventions. These conventions specify things that clients must do, things they should or can do if desired, and things that they must not do. The most basic thing clients are expected to do is to set certain properties so that the window manager has information on which to base its decisions.

It is a fundamental principle of client-window manager communication that a general client should not care which window manager is running or, indeed, if one is running at all. The choice of window manager is up to the user or perhaps the system administrator, not the client.

The fact that window managers need information about the clients they are managing and yet that window managers vary and might not be running lead to the concept of the hint. A *hint* is a suggestion to the window manager about a preference of the application made by setting a property. Xlib makes this easy by providing routines that conveniently set the right properties. The window manager is encouraged to honor as many of the hints as possible, but it is not required to honor any of them. Therefore, the application must not depend on its hints being honored; it must be capable of operating when any of its hints are ignored or denied.*

In general, the object of the X11 design is that clients should, as far as possible, do exactly what they would do in the absence of a window manager, except for:

- Hinting to the window manager about the screen space and colormaps they would like to use.

- Cooperating with the window manager by accepting the resources they are allocated, even if not those requested.

- Being prepared for hardware-limited resource allocations to change at any time. The client can select events that will announce these changes.

Note that these procedures are not required for the virtually unlimited X resources such as windows or cursors.

Clients create one or more windows that are children of the root window. All these windows are known as top-level windows. It is these windows that the window manager controls, and it is also these windows on which the application sets window manager hint properties.

12.3.1 Standard Properties for Window Manager

Once the client has created one or more top-level windows but before it maps them, it must place properties on those windows to help the window manager manage them effectively. The following sections describe each property that must or should be set and how to set it.

It is important to remember that the version 1 conventions are the accepted X Consortium standard and will continue to be valid in R5 and later; there will be additions but not incompatible changes.

Some of the properties that a client sets for the window manager are mandatory (the *standard properties*), and some are optional. **XSetWMProperties()** which was introduced and used in *basicwin* in Chapter 3, *Basic Window Program*, sets all the required properties. The purpose of **XSetWMProperties()** is to provide a simple interface for the programmer who wants to code an application quickly. Other functions are provided to communicate more optional information to the window manager.

In order to work well with most window managers, every program should call **XSetWMProperties()** for each top-level window. These provide the window manager with the following information:

- Name of the application for titlebar.

- Name string for the icon.

- Command and arguments used to invoke the program.

---

*Applications that create their own colormap are the only ones that will not be able to run without a window manager if they honor the conventions, because the window manager is responsible for installing the colormap.

- Icon pixmap and mask or window.

- Preferred initial icon position.

- Size hints for window in normal state.

- Startup state (normal or iconified).

- Keyboard focus model used by the application.

- Window group; for applications with multiple top-level windows, this describes which window is the main window for iconifying.

The window manager, not Xlib, chooses its own default response when any of these properties are not set. Also, they are only hints. A window manager determines what to do with this information and is allowed to ignore it. They will, of course, be ignored if no window manager is running.

The following sections describe the properties set by the client that indicate its preferences to the window manager. Table 12-1 shows all the predefined properties that clients can set and the section in this chapter where they are described.

Table 12-1. The Window Manager Hints Property Atoms

Property	Property Type	C Type	Description	See
For window manager:				
XA_WM_CLASS	XA_STRING	XClassHint	Application class and name for resource database lookup.	Section 12.3.1.5
XA_WM_HINTS	XA_WM_HINTS	XWMHints	Additional hints set by client for use by window manager.	Section 12.3.1
XA_WM_ICON_NAME	"TEXT"	XTextProperty	Name to be used in icon.	Section 12.3.1.2
XA_WM_NAME	"TEXT"	XTextProperty	Application name.	Section 12.3.1.1
XA_WM_NORMAL_HINTS	XA_WM_SIZE_HINTS	XSizeHints	Size hints for window in normal state (not iconified or zoomed).	Section 12.3.1.3
XA_WM_TRANSIENT_FOR_HINT	XA_STRING	char *	Tells window manager which window is the real main window with which a temporary window is associated.	Section 12.3.1.4.6

Table 12-1. The Window Manager Hints Property Atoms (continued)

Property	Property Type	C Type	Description	See
`XA_WM_ZOOM_HINTS`	`XA_WM_SIZE_HINTS`	`XSizeHints`	Size hints for zoomed window.	Section 12.3.1.3
For session manager:				
`WM_CLIENT_MACHINE`	`"TEXT"`	`XText-Property`	The name of machine running the client, as seen from the machine running the server.	Section 12.3.1
`XA_WM_COMMAND`	`"TEXT"`	`XTextPro-perty`	Command and arguments, separated by ASCII 0's, used to invoke application.	Section 12.3.2.1

In addition to the functions mentioned above that set all of the standard properties, Xlib also provides separate functions for setting and getting each property. These are referenced in the sections below describing each property. See the relevant pages in Volume Two, *Xlib Reference Manual*, for full details on each function. Applications set these properties and never read them, and the window manager gets them but never sets them. Therefore, if you are writing an application, you will only use the routines that set these properties.

12.3.1.1 Application Name – XA_WM_NAME

The `XA_WM_NAME` property is a string that the client wishes displayed in association with the window (for example, in a window titlebar).

Window managers are expected to make an effort to display this information; simply ignoring `XA_WM_NAME` is not acceptable window manager behavior. Clients can assume that at least the first part of this string is visible to the user, unless the user has made an explicit decision to make it invisible by placing the headline off-screen or covering it by other windows. But `XA_WM_NAME` should not be used for application-critical information nor to announce changes of application state that require timely user response. The expected uses are:

- To permit the user to identify one of a number of instances of the same client.

- To provide the user with noncritical state information.

Even window managers that support headline bars will place some limit on the length of string that can be visible; brevity here is important.

`XSetWMName()` and `XGetWMName()` set and get the `XA_WM_NAME` property. These interfaces support the use of the Compound Text Encoding.

12.3.1.2 Icon Name – XA_WM_ICON_NAME

The `XA_WM_ICON_NAME` property is a string that the client wishes displayed in association with its icon window when the client is iconified (for example, an icon label). In other respects, it is similar to `XA_WM_NAME`. Fewer characters will normally be visible in `XA_WM_ICON_NAME` than `XA_WM_NAME`, for obvious geometric reasons.

If an icon pixmap has been specified in the standard properties or `XA_WM_HINTS`, it may be displayed in the icon in addition to or instead of the icon name. `XSetWMIconName()` and `XGetWMIconName()` set the `XA_WM_NAME` property.

12.3.1.3 Window Size Hints – XA_WM_NORMAL_HINTS

An application must tell the window manager its geometry preferences for each of its top-level windows before mapping them.* These hints specify not only the preferred initial size (and sometimes position) of the window but also the preferred increments of sizes and aspect ratios the window manager should respect when allowing the user to resize the application. (The aspect ratio is the ratio of the width of the application to its height.)

`XSetWMProperties()` normally sets the `XA_WM_NORMAL_HINTS` property for a window in normal state. `XSetWMNormalHints()` is also available if for some reason `XSet-WMProperties()` is not suitable.

The `XA_WM_NORMAL_HINTS` property is an `XSizeHints` structure, shown in Example 12-1.

Example 12-1. The XSizeHints structure

```
typedef struct {
        long flags;                          /* Marks defined members in
                                              * structure */
        int x, y;                            /* Obsolete */
        int width, height;                   /* Obsolete */
        int min_width, min_height;
        int max_width, max_height;
        int width_inc, height_inc;
        struct {
                int x;                       /* Numerator */
                int y;                       /* Denominator */
        } min_aspect, max_aspect;
        int base_width, base_height;
        int win_gravity;
} XSizeHints;
```

• The `x`, `y`, `width`, and `height` members describe a desired position and size for the window. The coordinate system for `x` and `y` is the root window, irrespective of any reparenting that may have occurred. These fields are obsolete, because the window manager will use the initial size and position of the window when mapped to get this information. (The window manager *redirects* the application's mapping request to itself, so that

---

*The pop-up menu is the only type of top-level window that does not need to have `XA_WM_NORMAL_HINTS` set for it. Instead, the `override_redirect` window attribute should be set to `True`.

the window manager can inspect the position and size of the window set by the application, and perhaps change them, before mapping the window.)

- The `min_width` and `min_height` members specify the minimum size that the window can be for the application to be useful. Most window managers will not allow the user to resize the application smaller than this size. The `base_width` and `base_height` fields if set are used instead of `min_width` and `min_height`. If they are not set, `min_width` and `min_height` are used.

- The `max_width` and `max_height` members specify the maximum useful size.

- The `width_inc` and `height_inc` members define an arithmetic progression of sizes, from the minimum size to the maximum size, into which the window prefers to be resized. For example, *xterm* prefers size increments matching the dimensions of the font being used.

  The following algorithm should be used by the window manager to calculate the displayed size of the top-level window. `i` and `j` are nonnegative integer loop variables within the window manager that would be incremented until a size that matches the window manager's window management policy is reached.

  ```
  width = base_width + (i * width_inc)
  height = base_height + (j * height_inc)
  ```

  (When `base_width` and `base_height` are not set, `min_width` and `min_height` are used instead of `base_width` and `base_height`.) Window managers will use `i` and `j` instead of `width` and `height` in reporting window sizes to users. Similarly, applications should interpret the command line or user default geometry using `width_inc` and `height_inc` pixels instead of single pixels as the unit. *xterm*, for example, interprets size specifications in terms of multiples of the font dimensions, not in pixels. A default *xterm* window has 80 columns and 24 rows of characters. To create an *xterm* window with more rows, you can use the command:

  ```
  spike% xterm —geometry 80x40
  ```

- The `min_aspect` and `max_aspect` members specify the desired range of ratios of width to height for the window and are each expressed as a ratio of the `x` and `y` members of `min_aspect` and `max_aspect`. (The ratio `x / y` in `min_aspect` or `max_aspect` is the minimum or maximum value for `width / height`.)

- The `base_width` and `base_height` fields if set are used instead of `min_width` and `min_height`. If they are not set, `min_width` and `min_height` are used.

- The `win_gravity` field controls how the window's initial position will be interpreted by the window manager. By default, this hint is `NorthWestGravity`, which means that the position of the window when mapped by the application is used by the window manager as the position of the northwest corner (top-left) of the window. The other values for this field are `CenterGravity`, `EastGravity`, `NorthEastGravity`, `NorthGravity`, `SouthEastGravity`, `SouthGravity`, `SouthWestGravity`, and `WestGravity`. If the hint is set to `CenterGravity`, the window manager will place the center of the window where the origin of the window was when the application mapped it.

- The `flags` member of `XSizeHints` indicates which members in the structure contain important information. The constants in Table 12-2 can be combined with bitwise OR to set `flags`. The `USPosition` and `USSize` flags indicate that the user specified the desired values, while `PPosition` and `PSize` indicate that the program determined the values. This distinction is important since it supports the power structure—the user overrides the window manager, and the window manager overrides the program in decisions about window layout. The window manager can override the program's choice of window location or geometry when `PPosition` or `PSize`, respectively, are set, but the user's choices should override the window manager's choice when `USPosition` or `USSize` are set.

Table 12-2. The XSizeHints Flags

Flag	Description
USPosition	User-specified x, y
USSize	User-specified width, height
PPosition	Program-specified position
PSize	Program-specified size
PMinSize	Program-specified minimum size
PMaxSize	Program-specified maximum size
PResizeInc	Program-specified resize increments
PAspect	Program-specified min and max aspect ratios
PBaseSize	Program-specified base size
PWinGravity	Program-specified window gravity
PAllHints	Program-specified all hints

`XSetWMSizeHints()` is only useful if an application and a window manager agree on a private protocol that defines a new type of size hint atom beyond the one defined by the version 1 conventions or if a new type of size hint is added in later conventions.

`XAllocSizeHints()` allocates an `XSizeHints` structure and zeros all the fields. This function should be used so that new fields can be added in later releases while maintaining binary compatibility of applications written with earlier releases. In other words, using this function avoids compiling in the size of this structure, which may change. You declare only a pointer to this structure and then set it by calling `XAllocSizeHints()`. `XAllocSizeHints()` is used in the example program in Chapter 3.

`XGetWMNormalHints()` is normally used by the window manager to read the hints.

12.3.1.4 Additional Window Manager Hints – XA_WM_HINTS

The hints stored in the XA_WM_HINTS property provide an assortment of information to the window manager. Setting this property is required according to the ICCCM. Normally this is done by calling XSetWMProperties(). The XA_WM_HINTS property includes:

- Whether the program sets the keyboard focus window independently or only when assigned by the window manager.

- Whether the program desires to begin life as a window or as an icon.

- A window to be used by the window manager as an icon, or a pixmap and mask to be used by the window manager to draw on an icon window it creates.

- The initial position of the icon.

This property is normally set by the client with XSetWMProperties(). You should use the new XAllocWMHints() function to allocate an XWMHints structure, then set its fields, and then call XSetWMProperties(). An example doing this is shown in Chapter 3. The XWMHints structure is shown in Example 12-2.

Example 12-2. The XWMHints structure

```
typedef struct {
    long flags;             /* Marks defined members in structure */
    Bool input;             /* Does application need window
                             * manager for keyboard input */
    int initial_state;      /* See below */
    Pixmap icon_pixmap;     /* Pixmap to be used as icon */
    Window icon_window;     /* Window to be used as icon */
    int icon_x, icon_y;     /* Initial position of icon */
    Pixmap icon_mask;       /* Pixmap to be used as mask
                             * for icon_pixmap */
    XID window_group;       /* ID of related window group */
    /* This structure may be extended in the future */
} XWMHints;
```

The following sections describe each member of XWMHints and how it should be set.

12.3.1.4.1 Flags Field.
The client must set the flags field to indicate which members of the XWMHints structure are to be read by the window manager. This is done by combining the symbols shown in Table 12-3 using bitwise OR (|).

Table 12-3. Flags for Window Manager Hints

Member	Flag	Bit
input	InputHint	0
initial_state	StateHint	1
icon_pixmap	IconPixmapHint	2
icon_window	IconWindowHint	3
icon_x, icon_y	IconPositionHint	4

Table 12-3. Flags for Window Manager Hints (continued)

Member	Flag	Bit
icon_mask	IconMaskHint	5
window_group	WindowGroupHint	6
All of the above	AllHints	0-6

.3.1.4.2 Input Field and the Keyboard Focus. The `input` member of `XWMHints` is used to communicate to the window manager the keyboard focus model used by the application.* For the input hint to be read by the window manager, the `InputHint` constant must be specified in the `flags` field of `XWMHints`.

There are four input models:

- **No Input**. The client never expects keyboard input. An example would be *xload* or another output-only client.

- **Passive Input**. The client expects keyboard input but never explicitly sets the keyboard focus. An example would be a simple client with no subwindows, which will accept input in `PointerRoot` mode, or when the window manager sets the keyboard focus to its top-level window (in click-to-type mode).

- **Locally Active Input**. The client expects keyboard input and explicitly sets the keyboard focus but only does so when one of its windows already has the focus.

  An example of a Locally Active style client would be a client with subwindows defining various data entry members. Such an application might use Next and Prev keys to move the keyboard focus between the members, once its top-level window has acquired the focus in pointer-following mode or when the window manager sets the keyboard focus to its top-level window (in click-to-type mode).

- **Globally Active Input**. The client expects keyboard input and explicitly sets the keyboard focus even when the focus is set to a window the client does not own. An example would be a client with a scrollbar that wants to allow users to scroll the window without disturbing the keyboard focus even if it is in some other window. The client wants to acquire the keyboard focus when the user clicks in the scrolled region, but not when the user clicks in the scrollbar itself, and then set the focus back to its original window. Thus, the client wants to prevent the window manager setting the keyboard focus to any of its windows.

---

*To remind you, the keyboard focus is the window to which keyboard events go, sometimes ignoring the pointer position. When the pointer is outside the keyboard focus window, all keyboard events are delivered to that window. When the pointer is inside the keyboard focus window or any of its descendants, keyboard events are delivered to the window containing the pointer.

Clients using the Globally Active and No Input models should set the `input` flag to `False`. Clients using the Passive and Locally Active models must set the `input` flag to `True`.

NOTE

If your application requires keyboard input and you neglect to set the `input` flag to `True`, you application will not get keyboard events under some window managers, such as *olwm*.

Under version 1 conventions, clients that use the Locally Active or Globally Active focus models *must* participate in one of the WM_PROTOCOLS called WM_TAKE_FOCUS, as described in Section 12.3.3.2.

12.3.1.4.3 Initial State Field. The `initial_state` member of `XWMHints` indicates to the window manager whether the application prefers to start off in iconified or normal state. `initial_state` specifies the state the client prefers to be in at the time the top-level window is mapped. The window manager does not reread this property so it is not useful for changing state after a window has been mapped. How to request a change of state is described in Section 12.3.6.1. The `initial_state` flags are shown in Table 12-4.

Table 12-4. Initial State Hint Flags

Flag	Description
`IconicState`	Client wants to be iconified.
`NormalState`	Client wants top-level normal window visible.

When setting the `initial_state` member of `XWMHints`, you must OR the `StateHint` constant set into the `flags` member of `XWMHints` to indicate that the field is to be set.

Even though there is have no flag for an inactive state, a window manager might implement a concept of inactive state in which an infrequently used client's window would be represented as a string in a menu. But this state is invisible to the client, which would see itself merely as being in `IconicState`.

12.3.1.4.4 Icon Hints Fields. Under X, icons are by convention managed by the window manager, except that the client is allowed to provide a variety of pixmap patterns, names, and an icon window among which the window manager may pick and choose. The four members of `XWMHints` shown in Example 12-3 provide this information to the window manager.

Example 12-3. The icon hints elements of the XWMHints structure

```
typedef struct {
        .
        .
        .
    Pixmap icon_pixmap;         /* Pixmap for icon */
    Pixmap icon_mask;           /* Pixmap to be used as mask for
                                 * icon_pixmap */
    Window icon_window;         /* Window to be used as icon */
    int icon_x, icon_y;         /* Initial position of icon */
        .
        .
        .
} XWMHints;
```

`icon_pixmap` is the pattern to be used to distinguish the icon from other clients. This pixmap should be:

- One of the sizes specified in the `XA_WM_ICON_SIZE` property on the root, as described in Section 12.3.4.1.

- One bit deep. The window manager will select, through the resource database, suitable background (for the 0 bits) and foreground (for the 1 bits) colors. These resources can, of course, specify different colors for the icons of different clients.

The `icon_mask` is a one-bit-deep pixmap that determines which pixels in `icon_pixmap` are drawn on the icon window. This allows for icons that appear to be nonrectangular. Some window managers (including *uwm*) use the icon pixmap as a background tile for the icon window, a method which does not allow for the use of a mask.

`icon_window` is a window created but not mapped by the client. Clients that need to know their icon's ID or want to draw more than a simple two-color bitmap on the icon should set this hint. For example, *xbiff* and *xmh* change their icon pixmap when mail arrives, and they need to know their icon's ID to do this. Therefore, they must supply an icon window.

The `icon_window` hint should not be used unless needed. When it is not specified, the window manager creates the icon window itself.

You do not know which of the hints the window manager will honor. With current window managers, you can be confident that if `icon_window` is set, the window it names will be visible. If not, if `icon_pixmap` is set, the pixmap it names is visible. Otherwise, the window's `XA_WM_ICON_NAME` string is visible.

The conventions specify that the window manager must use the specified icon window. Therefore the application can read events from that icon window if desired.

An application that sets an `icon_window` is responsible for redrawing the window in case of `Expose` events. One way to set the icon design to be displayed is to set the background pixmap attribute of the icon window. The advantage of this approach is that there is no need to handle `Expose` events for the icon, because the background is automatically redrawn by the server. The disadvantage is that there is no way to apply a mask to generate a nonrectangular icon.

The icon window:

- Must be an `InputOutput` child of the root window.

- Should be one of the sizes specified in the **XA_WM_ICON_SIZE** property on the root (described in Section 12.3.4.1).

- Must use the default visual and default colormap for the screen in question.

- Should not be mapped, unmapped, or configured by the client.

- Should not have the **override_redirect** window attribute set to **True** (should be left as the default).

The client must not:

- Select **ResizeRedirectMask** on the icon.

- Depend on being able to receive input events via their icon windows, although most window managers will allow some subset of key and button events through.

- Manipulate the borders of their icon windows.

To summarize the client procedures regarding icons:

- Use **XSetWMIconName()** to set a string in **XA_WM_ICON_NAME**. All clients should do this, since it provides a fallback for window managers whose ideas about icons differ widely from those of the client.

- Set a pixmap into the **icon_pixmap** member of the **XA_WM_HINTS** property and possibly another into the **icon_mask** member. The window manager is expected to display the pixmap masked by the mask. The pixmap should be one of the sizes found in the **XA_WM_ICON_SIZE** property on the root. Window managers will normally clip or tile pixmaps which do not match **XA_WM_ICON_SIZE**.

Or:

- Set a window into the **icon_window** member of the **XA_WM_HINTS** property. The window manager is expected to use that window instead of creating its own and to map that window whenever the client is in **IconicState**. In general, the size of the icon window should be one of those specified in **XA_WM_ICON_SIZE** on the root, if that property exists. Window managers may resize icon windows. If the client supplies an icon window, it is responsible for redrawing it when necessary.

12.3.1.4.5   Window Group Field. The **window_group** member of **XWMHints** lets the client specify that it has multiple top-level windows which should be iconified together or managed by the window manager as a group. For example, group leaders may have the full set of decorations and other group members a restricted set.

Applications with only one top-level window need not set this hint.

One of the top-level windows is known as the group leader. The **window_group** member of the hints for each of the other top-level windows should be set to the window ID of the group leader.

The group leader may be a window which exists only for that purpose and may never be mapped. Its `window_group` member should contain its own ID. The properties of the window group leader are those for the group as a whole (for example, the icon to be shown when the entire group is iconified). Every other top-level window may also have its own hints applicable only to itself.

2.3.1.4.6 Transient Window Field. All temporary subwindows of the root, such as pop-up menus and dialog boxes, should use `XSetTransientForHint()` to set the `XA_WM_TRANSIENT_FOR` property to the ID of the top-level window of the application that is creating the temporary window. This allows the window manager to process the temporary window accordingly (perhaps by decorating it differently than if it were a separate application). In particular, window managers will present newly mapped transient windows without requiring any user interaction, even if mapping top-level windows normally does require interaction.

It is important not to confuse `XA_WM_TRANSIENT_FOR` with the `override_redirect` window attribute. The `override_redirect` attribute specifies that the window manager does not get the chance to intercept the mapping request and thus no chance at all to decorate the window. This should be done only on the most temporary of windows, such as menus, or on windows that the programmer wants to be mapped without window manager intervention, such as automated demonstration programs. `XA_WM_TRANSIENT_FOR` should be used when other windows are allowed to be active while the transient window is visible, such as when the pointer is not grabbed while the window is popped up. If other windows must be frozen, use `override_redirect` and grab the pointer while the window is mapped.

Temporary windows that are popped up frequently should also set the `save_under` window attribute so that windows beneath the window may not need to redraw themselves quite so often.

To summarize, clients wishing to pop up a window should do one of three things:

*   They can create and map another normal top-level window, which will get decorated and managed as a separate client by the window manager. See the discussion of window groups in Section 12.3.1.4.5.

*   If the window will be visible for a relatively short time and deserves a somewhat lighter treatment, they can set the `XA_WM_TRANSIENT_FOR` property. They can expect less decoration but should set all the normal window manager properties on the window. An example of an appropriate case would be a dialog box.

*   If the window will be visible for a very short time and should not be decorated at all, the client can set the `override_redirect` window attribute. In general, this should be done only if the pointer is grabbed while the window is mapped. The window manager will never interfere with these windows, which should be used with caution. An example of an appropriate use is a pop-up menu.

12.3.1.5 Application Class Name and Instance Name – XA_WM_CLASS

The XA_WM_CLASS property is a string containing two null-separated fields, res_class and res_name. res_class is meant to be used by the window manager to look up resources applicable to this application in the resource database. The window manager uses res_name for the titlebar of the window.

The application should normally specify res_class as the application name with an initial capital.

If the res_name field is NULL, then the following is used:

a. If "–name NAME" is given on the command line, NAME is used as the instance name.

b. Otherwise, if the environment variable RESOURCE_NAME is set, its value will be used as the instance name.

c. Otherwise, argv[0] stripped of any directory names is used as the instance name.

Note that WM_CLASS strings, being null-terminated, differ from the general conventions that text properties are null-separated. This inconsistency is necessary for backwards compatibility.

An application should look up its own resources in the resource database using XGet–Default() or with the resource manager routines described in Chapter 13, *Managing User Preferences*. If the user defaults are not found under res_name, the application should use res_class.

The XA_WM_CLASS property should only be written once and must be present when the window is mapped; window managers will ignore changes to it while the window is mapped.

The XA_WM_CLASS property contains a structure of type XClassHint. Example 12-4 shows the XClassHint structure.

Example 12-4. The XClassHint structure

```
typedef struct {
    char *res_name;
    char *res_class;
} XClassHint;
```

The XAllocClassHint() function should be used to allocate and zero the XClass-Hint structure. An example of doing this is presented in Chapter 3.

XA_WM_CLASS can be set by the client with XSetClassHint() and read by the window manager with XGetClassHint().

12.3.2 Standard Properties for Session Manager

A session manager is in charge of starting and stopping applications in a controlled manner, so that a session made up of several running applications can be halted and restarted in its original state. This is useful, for example, when the user wants to log out without having to start from scratch when logging back in.

Note that session managers are rare or nonexistent at the present time. Nonetheless, these conventions should be honored because it is only a matter of time before session managers become available. And the session manager does not necessarily need to be a separate client from the window manager. A window manager may have session-management capabilities.

There are two properties that need setting for the benefit of session managers, WM_COMMAND and WM_CLIENT_MACHINE. These supply the command and arguments needed to invoke an application in its current state and the machine on which it should be run. Together they supply enough information to restart the application. These are described in the following sections.

12.3.2.1 Application Command and Arguments

The `XA_WM_COMMAND` property stores the shell command and arguments used to invoke the application, separated by `NULL` characters.

Applications use `XSetCommand()` function to set the command property. Window managers use `XGetCommand()` to read it.

Clients should ensure, by resetting this property as often as necessary, that it always reflects a command that will restart them in their current state.

12.3.2.2 Client Machine

To restart a client, the session manager needs to know not only the command and arguments but also the machine on which the client was running. The application sets the WM_CLIENT_MACHINE property to contain this information, using `XSetWMClient-Machine()`.

This property should be set to a string forming the name of the machine running the client as seen from the machine running the server.

12.3.3 Optional Properties for Window and Session Manager

The client will need to set one or more of the following properties if it uses multiple colormaps, if it takes the keyboard focus, if it has data that must be saved before the session manager kills it, or if it has multiple top-level windows and it would like to survive when the user deletes one of them.

12.3.3.1 Using Created Colormaps – WM_COLORMAP_WINDOWS

An application should never install its own colormap. The window manager needs certain information from the application to be able to install colormaps at the appropriate times. An application that uses colormaps other than the default must do two things to make sure that the window manager knows which colormaps to install for each window:

- Set the `colormap` window attribute of each window that is to use a colormap other than the default.

- Set the WM_COLORMAP_WINDOWS property on the application's top-level window to tell the window manager which windows use colormaps different from the top-level window's colormap. In other words, you do not need to set WM_COLORMAP_WINDOWS unless your application uses more than one colormap.

The top-level window is always assumed to need its colormap installed. Applications set the WM_COLORMAP_WINDOWS property with `XSetWMColormapWindows()`, and the window manager reads it with `XGetWMColormapWindows()`.

12.3.3.2 Window Manager Protocols – WM_PROTOCOLS

Setting the WM_PROTOCOLS property is optional. It is for applications that can benefit from being notified by the window manager or session manager of certain conditions.

The WM_PROTOCOLS property contains a list of atoms, each identifying a communication protocol between the application and the window manager in which the application wants to participate. Atoms can identify both standard protocols and private protocols specific to individual window managers. All the protocols in which a client can volunteer to take part involve the window manager sending the client a `ClientMessage` event. The `message_type` field of the event will be the atom for WM_PROTOCOLS, and the `data` field will contain the atom for one of the protocols listed in Table 12-5.

Table 12-5. Current Standard WM_PROTOCOLS

Protocol	Purpose
WM_TAKE_FOCUS	Assignment of keyboard focus.
WM_SAVE_YOURSELF	Save client state warning.
WM_DELETE_WINDOW	Request to delete top-level window.
More to come . . .	

Note that none of the above properties are represented by predefined atoms. Therefore, you will need to call `XInternAtom()` once for each one that you intend to use.

An application sets the WM_PROTOCOLS property using `XSetWMProtocols()`, and the window or session manager reads it with `XGetWMProtocols()`.

WM_TAKE_FOCUS. Applications that use the Locally Active and Globally Active focus models should specify that they want to participate in this protocol. Under both these focus models, the application explicitly sets the keyboard focus to one of its windows. Any application that does not set the keyboard focus to any of its windows does not need to participate in this protocol.

To applications that specify WM_TAKE_FOCUS, the window manager may send a `Client-Message` event with the atom corresponding to WM_TAKE_FOCUS in their `data[0]` field. If the application wants the keyboard focus, it should respond by calling `XSetInput-Focus()` with its *window* argument set to the window of theirs that last had the keyboard focus or to their default input window and with the *time* argument set to the timestamp in the message. The *revert_to* argument should be set to `RevertToParent`.

A client could receive WM_TAKE_FOCUS when opening from an icon or when the user has clicked outside the top-level window in an area that indicates to the window manager that it should assign the focus (for example, clicking in the headline bar can be used to assign the focus).

The goal of WM_TAKE_FOCUS is to support window managers that want to assign the keyboard focus to a top-level window in such a way that the top-level window can either assign it to one of its subwindows or decline the offer of the focus. A clock, for example, or a text editor with no currently open frames might not want to take focus even though the window manager generally believes that clients should take the keyboard focus after being deiconified or raised.

Clients that call `XSetInputFocus()` must set the *time* argument to the timestamp of the event that caused them to make the attempt. Note that this cannot be a `FocusIn` event, since they do not have timestamps, and that clients may acquire the focus without a corresponding `EnterNotify`. Clients must not use `CurrentTime` in the *time* field.

Clients using the Globally Active model can only use `XSetInputFocus()` to acquire the input focus when they do not already have it on receipt of one of the following events: `ButtonPress`, `ButtonRelease`, passive-grabbed `KeyPress`, and passive-grabbed `KeyRelease`.

In general, clients should avoid using passive-grabbed key events for this purpose except when they are unavoidable (as, for example, a selection tool that establishes a passive grab on the keys that cut, copy, or paste).

Clients that set the input focus should set the *revert_to* argument of the `XSetInput-Focus()` request to the parent of the window that is to be the new focus window. This determines the behavior of the input focus if the window the focus has been set to becomes not viewable. All other settings lead to problems, as described in Appendix L, *Interclient Communication Conventions*, of Volume Zero, *X Protocol Reference Manual* (as of the second printing).

Clients should not give up the input focus of their own volition. They should ignore input that they receive instead.

12.3.3.2.2 WM_SAVE_YOURSELF. This protocol is for applications that would like to be notified before the window or session manager terminates them, so that they can save their state and place themselves in a state from which they can be restarted. Such termination, from the application's perspective, would otherwise bypass all the application's internal safety measures (such as when an editor reminds you to save before exiting).

Applications that express interest in this protocol may receive a **ClientMessage** event the atom for WM_SAVE_YOURSELF in its **data[0]** field.

Clients receiving WM_SAVE_YOURSELF should place themselves in a state from which they can be restarted and should update **XA_WM_COMMAND** (by calling **XSetCommand()**) to be a command that will restart them in this state. The session manager will be waiting for a **PropertyNotify** event on **XA_WM_COMMAND** as a confirmation that the client has saved its state, so that **XA_WM_COMMAND** should be updated (perhaps with a zero-length append) even if its contents are correct. No interactions with the user are permitted during this process.

After receiving the WM_SAVE_YOURSELF message through the event, saving its state, and updating **XA_WM_COMMAND**, the client should not change its state (in the sense of doing anything that would require a change to **XA_WM_COMMAND**) until it receives a mouse or keyboard event. Once it does so, it can assume that the danger is over. The session manager will ensure that these events do not reach clients until the danger is over or until the clients have been killed.

Clients with multiple top-level windows should ensure that only one of their top-level windows has a nonzero-length **XA_WM_COMMAND** property. They should also respond to a WM_SAVE_YOURSELF message by (in this order):

1. Updating the nonzero length **XA_WM_COMMAND** property if necessary.

2. Updating the **XA_WM_COMMAND** property on the window for which they received the WM_SAVE_YOURSELF message if it was not updated in step 1.

12.3.3.2.3 WM_DELETE_WINDOW. This protocol prevents the possibility of an application with multiple top-level windows being terminated unexpectedly by the session manager. It should be selected by applications whose server connection must survive the deletion of some of their top-level windows. Clients which choose not to include WM_DELETE_WINDOW in the WM_PROTOCOLS property will be disconnected from the server if the user asks for one of the client's top-level windows to be deleted.

Once an application has expressed interest in this protocol, if one of the top-level windows is deleted, the application will receive a **ClientMessage** event whose **data[0]** field is the atom for WM_DELETE_WINDOW.

Clients receiving a WM_DELETE_WINDOW message should behave as if the user selected "delete window" from a (hypothetical) menu. They should perform any confirmation dialogue with the user, and if they decide to complete the deletion, either:

- Change the window's state to Withdrawn (as described in Section 12.3.6.1) and release all associated state (backing store, for example), or

- Destroy the window.

If the user aborts the deletion during the confirmation dialogue, the client should continue as if it never received the ClientMessage event that began the dialogue.

If the client aborts a destroy and the user then attempts to delete the window again, the window manager should start the WM_DELETE_WINDOW protocol again. Window managers should not use XDestroyWindow() on a window that has WM_DELETE_WINDOW in its WM_PROTOCOLS property.

Note that the WM_SAVE_YOURSELF and WM_DELETE_WINDOW protocols are orthogonal to each other and may be selected independently.

12.3.4 Properties Set by the Window Manager

The properties described above are those which the client is responsible for maintaining on its top-level windows. This section describes what the client can do with the properties that the window manager sets to give information to the client. There are currently two such properties. XA_WM_ICON_SIZE stores information about the sizes of icons that the window manager prefers. The application should use this information to create an icon pixmap or window of one of the right sizes.

The other property, WM_STATE, stores the current state (normal, iconic, or withdrawn) of the application. This is mostly for communication between the window manager and session manager but may also be used by some applications.

12.3.4.1 XA_WM_ICON_SIZE

The window manager may set the XA_WM_ICON_SIZE property on the root window to specify the icon sizes it allows. Clients should read this property using XGetIconSizes() and provide an icon window or pixmap of an appropriate size as part of the XWMHints described in Section 12.3.1.4.4. This property is an XIconSize structure shown in Example 12-5.

Example 12-5. The XIconSize structure

```
typedef struct {
    int min_width, min_height;
    int max_width, max_height;
    int width_inc, height_inc;
} XIconSize;
```

The `width_inc` and `height_inc` members define an arithmetic progression of sizes, from the minimum size to the maximum size, representing the supported icon sizes. `XGet-IconSizes()` actually returns a list of these structures, in case the window manager needs more than one to specify all of its accepted icon sizes.

Some commercial window managers set this property. Clients should be prepared to create an icon pixmap to fit the hint of each of the standard window managers and can even use the hint to determine which window manager is in operation.

Window managers use `XSetIconSize` to set this property for clients.

`XAllocIconSize()` function should be used to allocate and zero the `XIconSize` structure.

12.3.4.2 WM_STATE

According to the ICCCM adopted as of Release 4, the window manager sets this property on top-level windows. The contents of this property is for communication between window managers and session managers. However, the existence of the property set on a window may be used to identify the top-level windows of other applications, for applications that need this information.

Xlib currently provides no routines for reading or writing this property, but of course, you can use `XChangeProperty()` or `XGetWindowProperty()`.

This property does not have a predefined atom—to read or write this property you will need to call `XInternAtom()` to get the atom for this property.

12.3.5 Text Properties

There are functions to set and read text properties that support encodings suitable for non-Western languages.

You will need to convert strings into `XTextProperty` structures before you can call `XSetWMProperties()`, `XGetWMClientMachine()`, `XGetWMIconName()`, `XGetWMName()`, `XSetWMClientMachine()`, `XSetWMIconName()`, or `XSetWMName()`.

These routines use the `XTextProperty` structure, which contains enough information to read and write the property in any format (8-bit, 16-bit, or 32-bit). The `XTextProperty` structure is shown in Example 12-6.

Example 12-6. The XTextProperty structure

```
typedef struct {
    unsigned char *value;      /* Property data */
    Atom encoding;             /* Type of property */
    int format;                /* 8, 16, or 32 */
    unsigned long nitems;      /* Number of items in value */
} XTextProperty;
```

You need to set the fields in two copies of this structure before calling **XSet-WMProperties()**, in order to set the window name and icon name properties, as was done in *basicwin* in Chapter 3, *Basic Window Program*. There are two ways to do this: one is to set the fields directly one at a time, and the other is to use **XStringListToText-Property()**. The latter is easier and better, because it does not require hardcoding the format or encoding. See Example 3-9 for a demonstration of how to do this.

Four more routines are provided to manipulate the **XTextProperty** structure:

XTextPropertyToStringList()
Creates a list of strings from an **XTextProperty** structure. This is used internally by **XGetCommand()**—it is useful for reading properties composed of multiple strings. This is rarely used in normal application code.

XFreeStringList()
Frees memory allocated by **XTextPropertyToString-List()**.

XSetTextProperty()
Convenience routine for **XChangeProperty()** that sets a property according to the information in an **XText-Property** structure.

XGetTextProperty()
Convenience routine for **XGetWindowProperty()** that reads a property into an **XTextProperty** structure. This helps because **XGetWindowProperty()** is complicated.

12.3.6 Constraints on Client Actions

The window manager is allowed to change the border width, color, or pattern of an application's top-level window's border (usually to indicate which window has the keyboard focus), so this window must be an **InputOutput** window. This also means that the application should not try to use the border to indicate any application state.

The client may receive notification that its window has been reparented, moved, resized, raised, or lowered or that its border width has been changed by selecting **Structure-NotifyMask** on its top-level window. It should not respond to these events by trying to change any of these characteristics, however.

Interclient
Communication

12.3.6.1 Changing Application State

Some applications may need to tell the window manager that they wish to be iconified, deiconified, or taken completely off the screen. There are right and wrong ways to do this.

An application can call **XIconifyWindow()** to have one of its top-level windows iconified. This function sends a **ClientMessage** event to the window manager, telling it to iconify this application. There is no equivalent routine to have the window manager return the application to normal state.

It is also possible to tell the window manager to unmap both the top-level window and its icon. This is done by calling **XWithdrawWindow()**. This is useful because the window manager rereads all the standard properties when the window returns from withdrawn to normal state.*

There is no routine to tell the window manager to change a withdrawn application back into normal state. The technique under version 1 conventions is for client to set the **initial_state** field of the **XWMHints** structure to **NormalState**, then call **XSetWMHints()** to reset this property, and then map the top-level window.

To change from withdrawn state to iconic state, the application should follow the same procedure but set the **initial_state** field to **IconicState**.

To change from iconic state to normal state, the client needs only to map the window—it need not reset the property.

If a client selects **StructureNotifyMask** on the top-level window, it will receive an **UnmapNotify** event when it moves to iconic state and a **MapNotify** when it moves to normal state.

Clients can also select **VisibilityChangeMask** on their top-level or icon windows. They will then receive a **VisibilityNotify** event (with the **state** field set to **VisibilityFullyObscured**) when the window concerned becomes completely obscured even though mapped (and thus perhaps a waste of time to update) and a **VisibilityNotify** event (with **state** field not set to **VisibilityFullyObscured**) when it becomes even partly viewable.

12.3.6.2 Reconfiguring the Top-level Window

Clients can resize, reposition, and restack their top-level windows using **XReconfigureWMWindow()**. This routine is the same as **XConfigureWindow()**, except that it takes care of an error condition possible when running under a reparenting window manager. **XReconfigureWMWindow()** lets you specify a sibling window relative to which your top-level window should be stacked, and this will work even if the window manager has reparented your top-level window so that what once was a sibling is no longer a sibling.

---

*Remember that resetting a property with a complex structure such as **XA_WM_HINTS** or **XA_WM_NORMAL_HINTS** redefines all members in that property. You must reset all fields, even those which you are not changing since the last time you set the property.

Even when the client is not attempting to change the stacking order, the entire reconfigure request is sent by the server to the window manager for approval, and the window manager has the opportunity to honor, modify, or deny the request. The client finds out the window manager's decision through `ConfigureNotify` events.

Most applications do not need to specify or even suggest the position of their top-level windows. However, when doing so, the position the client specifies should be relative to the root window regardless of reparenting.

Client requests to reconfigure the top-level window are interpreted by the window manager in the same manner as the initial window geometry mapped from withdrawn state. There is no guarantee that the window manager will allocate the requested size or location, and clients must be prepared to deal with *any* size and location.

The window manager has several options in deciding how to respond to a request by the application to reconfigure a top-level window:

- Not changing the size or location of the window at all, a client will receive a synthetic `ConfigureNotify` event describing the (unchanged) state of the window. The (x,y) coordinates will be in the root coordinate system, adjusted for the border width the client requested, irrespective of any reparenting that has taken place. The `border_width` will be the border width the client requested. The client will not receive a real `ConfigureNotify`, since no change has actually taken place.

- Moving the window without resizing it, a client will receive a synthetic `Configure-Notify` event following the move describing the new state of the window, whose (x,y) coordinates will be in the root coordinate system adjusted for the border width the client requested. The `border_width` will be the border width the client requested. The client may not receive a real `ConfigureNotify` event describing this change, since the window manager may have reparented the top-level window. If it does receive a real event, the synthetic event will follow the real one.

- Resizing the window (whether or not it is moved), a client which has selected `StructureNotifyMask` will receive a `ConfigureNotify` event. Note that the coordinates in this event are relative to the parent, which may not be the root if the window has been reparented, and will reflect the actual border width of the window, which the window manager may have changed. `XTranslateCoordinates()` can be used to convert the coordinates if required.

The general rule is that coordinates in real `ConfigureNotify` events are in the parent's space, whereas in synthetic events, they are in the root space.

Clients should be aware that their borders may not be visible. Most window managers use reparenting techniques to decorate client's top-level windows with titles, controls, and other details. Ones that do are likely to override the client's attempts to set the border width and set it to zero. Clients should, therefore, not depend on the top-level window's border being visible nor use it to display any critical information. Other window managers will allow the top-level windows' borders to be visible.

Clients should ignore the **above** field of all `ConfigureNotify` events that they receive on their top-level windows, since they cannot be guaranteed to contain useful information.

12.4 Selections

Selections are the primary mechanism X11 defines for clients that want to exchange information with other clients. A selection transfers arbitrary information between two clients. You can think of a selection as a piece of text or graphics that is highlighted in one application and can be pasted into another, though the information transferred can be almost anything. Clients are strongly encouraged to use this mechanism so that there is a uniform procedure in use by all applications.

The user may want to transfer information from an application and, at other times, to the application. Many applications need to be able to assume either role. In particular, clients should not display text in a permanent window without allowing the user to select it and convert it into a string, and any application that requires the user to type extensively should allow the user to paste in text from other applications.

Selections communicate between an *owner* client and a *requestor* client. The owner has the data representing the value of a selection, and the requestor wants it. The selection mechanism provides a way to notify other clients when useful data is placed in a property and to allow the owner of the data to convert it to a type asked for by the requestor.

Note that in the X11 environment, *all* data transferred between clients must go via the server (unless they are running on the same host, but that is a special case). An X11 client can neither assume that another client can open the same files nor communicate directly through IPC channels. The other client may be talking to the server via a completely different networking mechanism (for example, one client might be DECnet and the other TCP/IP). Thus, passing indirect references to data such as file names, hostnames, port numbers, and so on is permitted only if both clients specifically agree.

12.4.1 The Selection Mechanism

Let's look how a typical selection transaction occurs and then go into all the details of how to make it happen. From the user's point of view, it works like this:

1. The user highlights a selection of text or graphics in one application. For example, in *xterm*, selections are highlighted with the foreground and background colors reversed.

2. The user moves the pointer into another application and presses the key or button that indicates that the selection should be pasted. The keys or buttons used for this purpose in all applications probably should be the ones used by *xterm*, since most users use the cutting and pasting feature of *xterm* frequently.

The desired result is that the text or graphics should appear in the application in which it was pasted. Now how do two applications actually make this happen?

The application in which the text or graphics is being selected must first of all figure out what information is being selected and be able to convert it into a format that can be transferred to other applications. If the selection is text (usually the selection is a string) and the selected area is highlighted, by having the user drag the pointer over the area, then this application has to become the owner of a selection atom.

There are two built-in selection atoms: XA_PRIMARY and XA_SECONDARY. Unless the client foresees needing two simultaneous selections, it should use XA_PRIMARY. It calls XSet-SelectionOwner(), specifying the selection atom, any window that it created (this window is used by other applications to identify the owner), and the time. The time used should be from the event that triggered the bid to own the selection (not CurrentTime) because of race conditions that can otherwise occur. If the client does not already own the selection atom, then this call will generate a SelectionClear event for the old owner, telling it to unhighlight the old selection.

Each client that wants to be able to have a selection pasted into it must set aside a key or button combination to indicate that the user wishes to paste in the current selection. In response to the event that occurs when that key or button combination is pressed, the client calls XConvertSelection(). This call specifies which selection the application wants (XA_PRIMARY until other conventions are established), the property to place the data in, the window on which to set this property, and the time. These arguments are quite clear. But the XConvertSelection() call also specifies a target type that the application wants the data in. You need to understand what happens after the XConvertSelection() call to understand the purpose of the target type property.

The server places all the arguments of the XConvertSelection() call into an XSelectionRequestEvent and sends the event to the selection owner. The owner then tries to convert the selection data into the format specified in the target type property. If the selection owner knows how to convert the data into the requested type, it puts the data in the property specified in the event and returns the atom of this property in the property member of a SelectionNotify event. If the selection owner cannot convert the selection into the requested type, it returns None as the property member in the SelectionNotify event. The owner sends this SelectionNotify event using XSendEvent().

When the requestor receives the SelectionNotify event, it either reads the property if it is set, repeats the request with a different target type if the owner returned None, or gives up on pasting data from that selection owner. It could be that the user is trying to do something like paste graphics into a text-only application.

Now you should understand the selection mechanism in general, so let's look at a more tangible example of how it takes place.

12.4.2 An Example of Selection

Let's say a text editor is the owner of the selection XA_PRIMARY. The user is editing a C program and debugging the same C program in another window. The user would like to select a line in the source code and instruct the debugger to stop at that same line without having to type in the line number. Perhaps the debugger would have a button labeled "stop at," which, when pressed, would tell the debugger to request a value for the primary selection. The text editor would allow the user to select text on a line and would be able to convert that selection into a string if it were pasted into another text editor or into a line number if it were pasted into the debugger. Which type the text editor would choose would depend on the target type of the selection request.

Assuming the text editor already uses the selection mechanism to transfer text to other applications, adding the line number capability should be easy. It would simply need to look for a new target type that indicated to it to figure out what line number the selected text is on. It might choose the first line, if more than one line were selected, or simply display an error message telling the user to select a single line.

The debugger application would then make the call shown in Example 12-7.

Example 12-7. Setting the primary selection to a line number

```
Display display;
Atom target;
Window debugger_window;
Time time;
Bool only_if_exists;
Atom data_prop;

/* We create atom for data to be put into */
data_prop = XInternAtom(display, "STOP_LINE_NUM",
         only_if_exists = False);

/* Target type atom must have been created by owner */
target_type = XInternAtom(display, "LINE_NUMBER",
         only_if_exists = True);

if (target_type == None) {
    fprintf(stderr, "%s: selection owner did not create \
            LINE_NUMBER atom", argv[ 0 ]);
    return(False);
}

XConvertSelection(display, XA_PRIMARY, target_type,
        data_prop, debugger_window, time = triggering_event_time)

/* Wait for a SelectionNotify event and, if the property
 * member is the same as data_prop, the conversion went fine;
 * if the property member is None, the conversion failed */
```

The server sends all of the above information in a **SelectionRequest** event to the text editor client (which had previously made itself the owner of the selection with **XSetSelectionOwner()**).

The text editor stores the data in the property specified in the **SelectionRequest** event on **debugger_window**, then sends a **SelectionNotify** event (using **XSendEvent()**) to the requesting application. Upon receiving this event, the debugger reads this property and uses its value to place a break point in the C program.

Now that you have seen a more practical application of selections, we'll move on to a more precise description of each step in the selection transfer process.

12.4.3 Acquiring Selection Ownership

When the user decides to select something in an application, the application needs to become the selection owner. Being the selection owner means that when any other application requests the value of the selection with **XConvertSelection()**, the owner gets the resulting **XSelectionRequest** event. The transfer of selection ownership also makes sure that only one application at a time is attempting to set the properties. The previous application to call **XSetSelectionOwner()**, if it was another application, receives a **SelectionClear** event, which indicates to it that it should clear any area it has highlighted.

Note that if the time in the **XSetSelectionOwner()** request is in the future relative to the server's current time or if it is in the past relative to the last time the selection concerned changed hands, the **XSetSelectionOwner()** request appears to the client to succeed, but ownership is *not* actually transferred. To ensure that ownership has been transferred, a client must perform the sequence shown in Example 12-8.

Example 12-8. Code to ensure transfer of selection ownership

```
XSetSelectionOwner(display, selection_atom, owner, time);
if (XGetSelectionOwner(display, selection_atom) != owner) {
    /* We didn't get the selection */
}
```

If **XGetSelectionOwner()** returns a window ID rather than **None**, then the selection ownership was successfully transferred.

12.4.4 Responsibilities of the Selection Owner

When a requestor wants the value of a selection, the owner receives a **Selection-Request** event. Example 12-9 shows the **XSelectionRequestEvent** structure.

Example 12-9. The XSelectionRequestEvent structure

```
typedef struct {
    int type;
    unsigned long serial;      /* # of last request processed by
                                * server */
    Bool send_event;           /* True if this came from SendEvent
                                * request */
    Display *display;          /* Display the event was read from */
    Window owner;
    Window requestor;
    Atom selection;
    Atom target;
    Atom property;
    Time time;
} XSelectionRequestEvent;
```

The **owner** and the **selection** members will be the values specified in the **XSet-SelectionOwner()** request, and therefore, the selection owner is interested in them only if it owns more than one selection.

The owner should convert the selection into the type specified by the **target** member and set the property specified by the **property** member of the **SelectionRequest** event. Current conventions hold that all properties used to reply to **SelectionRequest** events should be placed on the requestor window. If the data comprising the selection cannot be stored on the requestor window (for example, because the server cannot provide sufficient memory), the owner must refuse the selection request as above.

The owner should also send the requestor a **SelectionNotify** event using **XSend-Event()** with an *event_mask* of 0. The members of the **SelectionNotify** event should be set to the same values received in the **SelectionRequest** event, except that if the selection could not be converted to the requested type, the **property** member should be set to **None**. Example 12-10 shows the **XSelectionEvent** structure which is used for **SelectionNotify** events.

Example 12-10. The XSelectionEvent structure

```
typedef struct {
    int type;
    unsigned long serial;      /* # of last request processed by
                                * server */
    Bool send_event;           /* True if this came from SendEvent
                                * request */
    Display *display;          /* Display the event was read from */
    Window requestor;
    Atom selection;
    Atom target;
    Atom property;             /* Atom or None */
    Time time;
} XSelectionEvent;
```

The **selection**, **target**, and **property** members should be set to the values received in the **SelectionRequest** event. Setting the **property** member to **None** indicates that the conversion requested could not be made.

The data stored in the property must eventually be deleted. According to the current conventions, selection requestors are responsible for deleting the converted properties whose names they receive in **SelectionNotify** events. Owners are responsible for deleting all other properties involved in communicating selections.

A selection owner may need confirmation that the data comprising the selection has actually been transferred. They should express interest in **PropertyNotify** events for the requestor window and wait until the property in the **SelectionNotify** event has been deleted before assuming that the selection data has been transferred.

12.4.5 Giving Up Selection Ownership

When some other client becomes the owner of a particular selection, the previous owner receives a `SelectionClear` event. The **XSelectionClearEvent** structure is shown in Example 12-11.

Example 12-11. The XSelectionClearEvent structure

```
typedef struct {
    int type;
    unsigned long serial;      /* # of last request processed by
                                * server */
    Bool send_event;           /* True if from a SendEvent request */
    Display *display;          /* Display the event was read from */
    Window window;
    Atom selection;
    Time time;
} XSelectionClearEvent;
```

The `time` member is the time at which the ownership changed hands, and the **owner** member is the window the new owner specified in its **XSetSelectionOwner()** request.

If an owner loses ownership while it has a transfer in progress, that is to say before it receives notification that the requestor has received all the data, it must continue to service the ongoing transfer to completion.

To relinquish ownership of a selection voluntarily, a client should execute a **XSetSelectionOwner()** call for that selection atom, with *owner* specified as **None** and *time* specified as **CurrentTime**. Alternatively, the client may destroy the window used as the *owner* argument of the **XSetSelectionOwner()** call, or it may exit. In both cases, the ownership of the selection involved will revert to **None**.

12.4.6 Requesting a Selection

A client wishing to obtain the value of a selection in a particular form issues an **XConvertSelection()** call. The arguments of the call are three atoms, a window, and the time. The first atom is the selection, usually **XA_PRIMARY**. The second atom is the target type, the type in which the requestor wants the data. The conventions will specify a standard list of target type atoms. The third atom specifies the property that the owner should set to the converted data. The window argument is the window on which the property containing the data is to be set. The `time` member should be set to the timestamp on the event triggering the request for the selection value. Note that the requestor of a selection does not need to know the owner of the selection or the window it specified in the **XSetSelectionOwner()** call.

The client that calls **XConvertSelection()** call will get a **SelectionNotify** event sent to it from the selection owner. The *requestor, selection, time,* and *target* arguments of this event will be the same as those on the **XConvertSelection()** request.

If the `property` member is `None`, the conversion has been refused. This can mean that there is no owner for the selection, that the owner does not support the conversion implied by `target`, or that the server did not have sufficient space to accommodate the data.

If the `property` member is not `None`, then that property will exist on the requestor window. The value of the selection can be retrieved from this property using `XGet-WindowProperty()`. When using `XGetWindowProperty()` to retrieve the value of a selection, the *property* argument should be set to the `property` member in the `SelectionNotify` event. The `type` member should be set to `AnyPropertyType`, because the requestor has no way of knowing beforehand what type the selection owner will use.

The property in the `SelectionNotify` should be deleted by invoking `XGetWindow-Property()` with the *delete* argument set to `True`. As discussed above, the owner has no way of knowing when the data has been transferred to the requestor unless the property is removed.

12.4.7 Large Data Transfers

Selections can get large, and this poses two problems:

- Transferring large amounts of data to the server is expensive, and it would be beneficial to be able to reuse the data once it has been sent to answer further `XConvert-Selection()` requests.

- All servers will have limits on the amount of data that can be stored in a single property. Exceeding this limit will result in a `BadAlloc` error on the `XChangeProperty()` call that the selection owner uses to store the data.

The proposed conventions for dealing with these problems are given in Appendix L, *Interclient Communication Conventions*, of Volume Zero, *X Protocol Reference Manual* (as of the second printing).

12.4.8 More on Selection Properties and Types

A given selection has a *type* associated with it. Built-in property types that might apply to selections are `XA_BITMAP`, `XA_CARDINAL`, `XA_INTEGER`, `XA_PIXMAP`, `XA_POINT`, `XA_RECTANGLE`, and `XA_STRING`. Other types that clients could define might be `XA_FILE_NAME` or `XA_PICTURE` (a sequence of graphics primitives to reproduce a picture—the Macintosh uses this type of selection to cut and paste graphics into text applications and vice versa).

It is important to observe that defining a new atom consumes resources in the server, and they are not released until the server reinitializes. Thus, it must be a goal to reduce the need for newly minted atoms.

The selection named by `XA_PRIMARY` is used for all commands which take only a single argument. It is the principal means of communication between clients which use the selection mechanism.

It is suggested that the selection named by XA_SECONDARY be used:

- As the second argument to commands taking two arguments. For example, it might be used when exchanging the primary and secondary selections.

- As a means of obtaining data when there is a primary selection, and the user does not wish to disturb it.

The CLIPBOARD selection can be used to hold deleted data (it has no predefined atom). There is a client called *xclipboard* that will display the contents of the CLIPBOARD, even if the client where the data was selected has already been killed.

12.4.9 Target Atoms

The atom that a requestor supplies as the *target* argument of XConvertSelection() determines the form of the data supplied. The set of such atoms is extensible, but a generally accepted base set of *target* atoms is needed. The set specified in the conventions is shown in Appendix L, *Interclient Communication Conventions*, of Volume Zero, *X Protocol Reference Manual* (as of the second printing). However, some types are already predefined properties, and these can safely be used.

Target properties describe types of data. They contain the C language types of the structures that are used for many of the Xlib functions. The predefined target atoms are shown in Table 12-6.

Table 12-6. Predefined Target Type Atoms

Type Atom	C Language Type
XA_ARC	XArc
XA_POINT	XPoint
XA_ATOM	Atom
XA_RGB_COLOR_MAP	Atom (standard colormap)
XA_BITMAP	Pixmap (of depth 1)
XA_RECTANGLE	XRectangle
XA_CARDINAL	int (dimensionless)
XA_STRING	char *
XA_COLORMAP	Colormap
XA_VISUALID	VisualID
XA_CURSOR	Cursor
XA_WINDOW	Window
XA_DRAWABLE	Drawable
XA_WM_HINTS	XWMHints
XA_FONT	Font
XA_INTEGER	int
XA_WM_SIZE_HINTS	XSizeHints
XA_PIXMAP	Pixmap

The owner should not translate the selection into some arbitrary fallback target type (such as XA_STRING) and return the fallback target to the requestor in the SelectionNotify event, because this might confuse the requestor. The conversion should simply fail. The requestor then has the option of requesting another type. The requestor can supply the target TARGETS to get a list of target types the owner supports.

12.5 Cut Buffers

Cut buffers are provided as a simple but limited method of communication between applications. Cut buffers are particularly good for editors, because they can act like a stack of buffers, recording the history of deletions.

The selection mechanism is superior for many applications, since it allows communication regarding the type of the data transferred. Selections are described in Section 12.4. It is also possible for an application to use both cut buffers and selections.

The cut buffers are eight properties on the root window of screen 0 of a server. The buffers are numbered 0 to 7. Cut buffers rely on a prior agreement between the two clients regarding the format of the data to be placed in the cut buffers. The data that can be placed in a single cut buffer is limited to the maximum size of a single property, which is server-dependent.

Because the cut buffers are properties, it is possible to be notified when they have been written into. PropertyNotify events can assist applications in timing their communication. These are selected with PropertyChangeMask.

The functions that are used to read and write to cut buffers are XFetchBuffer(), XFetchBytes(), XStoreBuffer(), and XStoreBytes(). The routines with Bytes in the name use cut buffer 0 only, while the others may use any of the eight. XRotateBuffers() moves the contents of the eight buffers any number of positions.

The cut buffer properties are named by the predefined atoms XA_CUT_BUFFER0 to XA_CUT_BUFFER7.

The cut buffers can let applications implement a first-in, last-out stack of data. A client using this cut buffer mechanism must initially ensure that all eight buffer properties exist, using XChangeProperty() to append zero-length data to each. A client storing data in the cut buffers (an owner) must first rotate the ring of buffers by +1, using XRotateWindow-Properties to rename XA_CUT_BUFFER0 to XA_CUT_BUFFER1 to .... to XA_CUT_BUFFER7 to XA_CUT_BUFFER0. It must then store the data into XA_CUT_BUFFER0, using XStoreBytes().

A client obtaining data from the cut buffers should use XFetchBytes() to retrieve the contents of XA_CUT_BUFFER0.

A client may, in response to a specific user request, rotate the cut buffers by −1, using XRotateWindowProperties to rename XA_CUT_BUFFER7 to XA_CUT_BUFFER6 .... and so on and XA_CUT_BUFFER0 to XA_CUT_BUFFER7.

Data should be stored to the cut buffers and the ring rotated only when requested by explicit user action. Users depend on their mental model of cut buffer operation and need to be able to identify operations that transfer data to and from the buffers.

Note that there is nothing magic about the properties used by Xlib's cut buffer routines or those routines themselves. If an application needs more buffers, it can intern additional atoms for `CUT_BUFFER8` and so on and write its own equivalent of `XStoreBuffer()` and `XFetchBuffer()` that can write and read these properties.

13

Managing User Preferences

It is a fundamental part of the X philosophy that the user, not the application, should be in control of the way things work. For this reason, applications should allow the user to specify window geometry and many other characteristics both via command line options and in a file that specifies default preferences. This chapter discusses the use of the resource manager, which helps an application to evaluate and merge its own default with user preferences. While the information in this chapter is not essential for X programming, it is essential for writing programs that will work in ways that users will come to expect. For additional information on the resource manager at work, see Chapter 12.

In This Chapter:

13
Managing User Preferences

Applications can and should be made user customizable. Every application should provide command line options for the most important configurable elements of the application, such as colors or patterns for the window border and background, foreground colors for drawing, desired geometry of the application, fonts, and so on. Furthermore, an application should allow users to set all options through the resource database.

A *resource* is a configurable program option (completely different from a server resource, such as a window). There are a set of *resource files* and *resource properties* that may contain settings for program options. When all the resource files and properties are merged into a single database by Xlib, the result is called the *resource database*. Each setting for a resource in any of these files or properties or in the resource database is called a *resource specification*. The routines and database structures used for managing user preferences are collectively referred to as the *resource manager*.

Prior to X11 Release 2, users stored their resource specifications in a file in their home directory called *.Xdefaults*. Additional resource specifications could be stored in a file pointed to by the shell environment variable XENVIRONMENT or in a host-specific file called *.Xdefaults-host*, where **host** is the name of the system where the client is running.

However, experience showed that this approach caused problems for users running clients from multiple machines across the network. A separate *.Xdefaults* file had to be maintained for each machine. For this reason, the *xrdb* program was designed to install the user's preferences in the XA_RESOURCE_MANAGER property on the root window of the current server. In this way, all clients running on the same server share the same user preferences. The old mechanism is still supported for compatibility, but *.Xdefaults* is read only if the XA_RESOURCE_MANAGER property has not be set with *xrdb*. Another advantage of having the user's resource specifications set with *xrdb* is that they are stored in a property instead of a file, and therefore, they can be more easily managed by the session manager (although none of these exist yet), since changing a property from a program is much easier than editing a file from a program.

XGetDefault() provides a simplified interface that applications can use to read options from the resource database. However, there is also a complete set of resource manager routines, which were originally developed for the Xt Toolkit, which can be used to process resources in a more thorough and expandable way. The Xt Toolkit resource manager was merged into Xlib because the task of managing user preferences is common to all X applications. By making the resource manager part of Xlib, the developers ensured that all toolkits layered on Xlib will use the same mechanism, providing users with a consistent interface. In the Xt Toolkit, all objects (called *widgets*) are configurable through the resource database. And as you will see, the object-oriented nature of the Xt Toolkit is also apparent in the resource manager. Even though most Xlib applications are not object-oriented and therefore cannot take full advantage of the capabilities of the resource manager, they can still benefit from using it.

All resource manager routines except **XGetDefault()** have names beginning with *Xrm*, so they are conveniently grouped together in Volume Two, *Xlib Reference Manual*. You must include *<X11/Xresource.h>* to use **XGetDefault()** or the other resource manager functions.

In the following sections, we'll talk about handling user preferences using **XGet-Default()** and using the resource manager routines. We'll also talk about how to use **XParseGeometry()** and **XGeometry**, which parses the standard format for window size and placement preferences (whether specified on the command line or in a resource file or property).

After that, we'll discuss the format of the data in the resource manager database. The rules for specifying preferences are fairly complex, although for most Xlib applications, using them is quite simple.

Finally, we'll talk briefly about some more advanced resource manager routines.

13.1 Using XGetDefault()

XGetDefault() allows a program to determine a value for an option by searching the resource database. In R5 and later, use of **XGetDefault()** is discouraged because it does not read all the current resource files and properties; the low level routines described in Section 13.2 should be used instead.

XGetDefault() reads the resource specifications from the **XA_RESOURCE_MANAGER** property in the server or, if that is not set, the user's *.Xdefaults* file. Next, if there is an XENVIRONMENT environment variable, then the file specified in it is loaded as well. The value returned by **XGetDefault()** for a particular program/option key will be the last match found in this list.

Actually, the **XA_RESOURCE_MANAGER** property is automatically copied from the server into the **Display** structure returned by **XOpenDisplay()**. Therefore, each call to **XGet-Default()** does not really read that property directly but, instead, a local copy of it. Therefore, **XGetDefault()** does not require a round-trip request and is quite fast.

Unfortunately, **XGetDefault()** does not do the whole job of handling program options. **XGetDefault()** does not parse the command line options or read the application-specific resource file. You need to use the other resource manager routines to handle these.

Normally, the command line options are read one at a time, and if a command line argument is present for a particular option, it overrides any value that might be present in the resource database, and therefore **XGetDefault()** does not need to be called. But if no value for a particular option is found, **XGetDefault()** must be called. If **XGetDefault()** returns a non-NULL string, that is the option value, which usually has to be converted into a useful type for the program. If **XGetDefault()** returns **NULL**, your program needs a default value, which it can read from a database file in the *app-defaults* directory using **XrmGet-FileDatabase()** and **XrmGetResource()** or, less desirable but easier, it can hard-code the default values.

The sequence of operation for using **XGetDefault()** is shown in Figure 13-1.

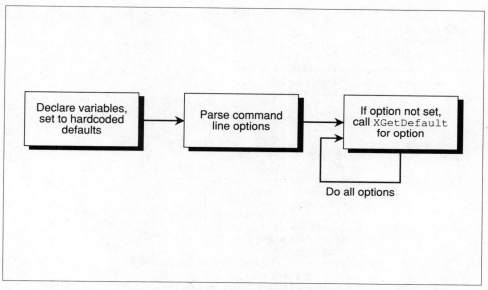

Figure 13-1. Procedure for processing user resource specifications with XGetDefault()

Example 13-1 shows the code for one way to handle program options using **XGet-Default()**. It is taken without modification from the X demo *puzzle.**

Example 13-1. Handling program options with XGetDefault()

```
#define DEFAULT_SPEED           2
int      PuzzleSize = 4;
int      PuzzleWidth=4, PuzzleHeight=4;
char     *ProgName;
int      UsePicture = 0;
int      CreateNewColormap = 0;
char     *PictureFileName;
int      TilesPerSecond;

/* Other global declarations */

main(argc,argv)      /* This is complete */
int argc;
```

---

*Be sure to try the puzzle program using the mandrill face picture (*puzzle –picture mandrill.cm*) on an eight-plane color screen. It is the most visually impressive X application we have seen, and the program is very well written, too.

Example 13-1. Handling program options with XGetDefault() (continued)

```
char *argv[ ];
{
      int i, count;
      char *ServerName, *Geometry;
      char *puzzle_size = NULL;
      char *option;

      ProgName = argv[ 0 ];

      ServerName = "";
      Geometry   = "";
      TilesPerSecond = -1;

      /*******************************/
      /** parse command line options **/
      /*******************************/

      for (i=1; i<argc; i++) {
            char *arg = argv[ i ];

      if (arg[ 0 ] == '-') {
            switch (arg[1 ]) {
                  case 'd':          /* -display host:display */
                        if (++i >= argc) usage ();
                        ServerName = argv[ i ];
                        continue;
                  case 'g':          /* -geometry geom */
                        if (++i >= argc) usage ();
                        Geometry = argv[ i ];
                        continue;
                  case 's':          /* -size WxH or -speed n */
                        if (arg[2 ] == 'i') {
                              if (++i >= argc) usage ();
                              puzzle_size = argv[ i ];
                              continue;
                        } else if (arg[2 ] == 'p') {
                              if (++i >= argc) usage ();
                              TilesPerSecond = atoi (argv[ i ]);
                              continue;
                        } else
                              usage ();
                        break;
                  case 'p':          /* -picture filename */
                        if (++i >= argc) usage ();
                        UsePicture++;
                        PictureFileName = argv[ i ];
                        continue;
                  case 'c':          /* -colormap */
                        CreateNewColormap++;
                        continue;
                  default:
                        usage ();
            }     /* End switch */
      } else
            usage ();
      }     /* End for */

      /* Open display here */
```

Example 13-1. Handling program options with XGetDefault() (continued)

```
     SetupDisplay (ServerName);

     if (!Geometry) {
         Geometry = XGetDefault (display, ProgName, "Geometry");
     }

     if (!puzzle_size) {
         option = XGetDefault (display, ProgName, "Size");
         puzzle_size = option ? option : "4x4";
     }

     if (TilesPerSecond <= 0) {
         option = XGetDefault (display, ProgName, "Speed");
         TilesPerSecond = option ? atoi (option) : DEFAULT_SPEED;
     }

     if (!UsePicture) {
         option = XGetDefault (display, ProgName, "Picture");
         if (option) {
         UsePicture++;
         PictureFileName = option;
         }
     }

     if (!CreateNewColormap) {
         option = XGetDefault (display, ProgName, "Colormap");
         if (option) {
         CreateNewColormap++;
         }
     }

     sscanf (puzzle_size, "%dx%d", &PuzzleWidth, &PuzzleHeight);
     if (PuzzleWidth < 4 || PuzzleHeight < 4) {
         fprintf (stderr, "%s:  Puzzle size must be at least 4x4\n",
                     ProgName);
     exit (1);
     }
     PuzzleSize = min((PuzzleWidth/2)*2,(PuzzleHeight/2)*2);

     Setup (Geometry,argc,argv);
     ProcessInput();
     exit (0);
}
static char *help_message[ ] = {
     "where options include:",
     "     -display host:display     X server to use",
     "     -geometry geom            geometry of puzzle window",
     "     -size WxH                 number of squares in puzzle",
     "     -speed number             tiles to move per second",
     "     -picture filename         image to use for tiles",
     "     -colormap                 create a new colormap",
     NULL
};

usage()
{
     char **cpp;

     fprintf (stderr, "usage:  %s [—options ... ]\n\n", ProgName);
```

Example 13-1. Handling program options with XGetDefault() (continued)

```
    for (cpp = help_message; *cpp; cpp++) {
         fprintf (stderr, "%s\n", *cpp);
    }
    fprintf (stderr, "\n");
    exit (1);
}
```

In Example 13-1, as in most existing applications, the program default values are hardcoded. Ideally, they should be taken from a file so that the code does not have to be recompiled to change them. Example 13-2 shows how this could be added to the code in Example 13-1. Only the processing of a single option is shown.

Example 13-2. Processing geometry option using program resource specifications file

```
}
    XrmDatabase applicationDB;
    char *classname = "puzzle";
    char name[ 255 ];        /* Would be 15 for System V */
    char Geometry[ 20 ];
    char Geostr[ 20 ];
    char *str_type[ 20 ];
    XrmValue value;
    unsigned int border_width;
    unsigned int font_width, font_height;
    int pad_x, pad_y;

    XSizeHints *size_hints;
    int x, y;
    unsigned int width, height;
    int gravity;

    if (!(size_hints = XAllocSizeHints())) {
         fprintf(stderr, "%s: failure allocating memory\n", progname);
         exit(0);
    }

    /* set program's default size hints as demonstrated in Chapter 3 */

    for (i=1; i<argc; i++) {
         char *arg = argv[ i ];
         if (arg[ 0 ] == '-') {
              switch (arg[ 1 ]) {
                   .
                   .
                   .
                   case 'g': /* -geometry geom */
                        if (++i >= argc) usage ();
                        Geometry = argv[ i ];
                        continue;
                   .
                   .
                   .
              }
         }
         else
              usage();
    }
```

Example 13-2. Processing geometry option using program resource specifications file (continued)

```
if (!Geometry) {
     Geometry = XGetDefault (display, ProgName, "Geometry");
}

(void) strcpy(name, "/usr/lib/X11/app-defaults/");
(void) strcat(name, classname);
/* Get application resource specifications file, if any */
if ((applicationDB = XrmGetFileDatabase(name)) == NULL)
     fprintf(stderr, "%s: program default file not found",
             ProgName);

/* Get the program default geometry string regardless of
 * whether it has been specified on command line or in
 * resource database, because those specifications may be
 * partial; we're going to use XGeometry to fill in the gaps */
if (XrmGetResource(applicationDB, "puzzle.geometry",
        "Puzzle.Geometry",
             str_type, &value) == True) {
(void) strncpy(Geostr, value.addr, (int) value.size);
} else {
     fprintf(stderr, "%s: default geometry option not found",
             ProgName);
Geostr[ 0 ] = NULL;
}

XWMGeometry(display, screen_num, Geometry, Geostr,
             (border_width = 0), size_hints,
             (pad_x = 0), (pad_y = 0), &x, &y, &width, &height, &gravity);
/* Now x, y, width, and height are the specs to use when
 * creating the window and nothing has been hardcoded */
```

13.2 Using the Low-level Resource Manager Routines

As you can see, handling program options properly with **XGetDefault()** is not trivial, even though **XGetDefault()** is supposed to be the simple interface to the resource manager. Also, **XGetDefault()** does not read all the resource files and properties that an application should use. It is not any easier to use the low-level resource manager calls, but they do a more thorough job.

For one, there is a single routine that takes care of parsing the command line and loading the values found there into the resource database. Secondly, there are several more resource files that **XGetDefault()** does not read but that an application really should. You can mechanize the whole process of handling program options by turning every set of options into a database, merging them into a single database, and then extracting the correct values. The resulting code is easier to expand or modify than code that uses **XGetDefault()**.

First, let's describe the additional resource files that we will handle with the low-level resource manager routines.

13.2.1 Resource Files and Merging

All applications need fallback settings for all configurable options in case the user does not set these options. Instead of hardcoding these as defined constants, they can be placed in another resource file. Then if they need to be changed by the application writer, only the resource file needs editing, and the application does not need to be recompiled. Another advantage of this approach is that it allows all fixed text in the application to be specified in resource files instead of in the code, and this makes it easier to convert an application to a foreign language. The application-specific resource specifications can also be stored in a file in the directory */usr/lib/X11/app-defaults*. (Each file should have the same name as the application itself, except with the first letter capitalized, unless the application name begins with an X, in which case the first two letters can be capitalized.)

The other additional resource files add flexibility; each is intended to be set by either the user, the application writer, or the system administrator. More are for foreign language conversion. The user will only be expected to use the *.Xdefaults* file or the property set by the *xrdb* utility. The complete set of resource files and properties and the order in which they are merged as of R4 as follows:

- *Classname* file in the *app-defaults* directory.

- *Classname* file in the directory specified by the XUSERFILESEARCHPATH or XAPPLRESDIR environment variables.

- Property set using *xrdb*, accessible through the `XResourceManagerString()` macro or, if that is empty, the *.Xdefaults* file in the user's home directory.

- File specified by the XENVIRONMENT environment variable or, if not set, the *.Xdefaults-hostname* file in the user's home directory.

- Command line arguments.

The order in which the various options are merged is important. A value for an option in the user's resource specifications should override the program's default for that option, but a value on the command line would override both the program's and the user's default value.

In R5 and later, the order of merging defined by the Xt Intrinsics sets the standard in this area now that `XGetDefault()` is not recommended. For complete information on the order of merging done by Xt, see Chapter 6 in the *Programmer's Supplement for Release 5* or Volume Four, *X Toolkit Intrinsics Programming Manual*.

13.2.2 Including Files in a Resource File

The Xrm functions that read resources from files, `XrmGetFileDatabase()` and `XrmCombineFileDatabase()` (new in R5), recognize a line of the form:

```
#include "filename"
```

as a command to include the named file at that point. The directory of the included file is interpreted relative to the directory of the file in which the include statement occurred. Included files may themselves contain `#include` directives, and there is no specified limit to the depth of this nesting. Note that the C syntax `#include <filename>` is not supported; neither Xlib nor Xt defines a search path for included files.

The ability to include files is useful when producing a special app-defaults file for use on a color screen, for example, you can simply include the monochrome app-defaults file and then set or override the color resources as you desire. This technique is particularly useful when producing app-defaults files for use with the customization resource defined by the Xt Intrinsics. Example 13-3 shows a hypothetical color resource file for the "xmail" application.

Example 13-3. The resource file

```
! include the basic (monochrome) defaults
#include "XMail"

! and augment them with color
*Background: tan
*Foreground: navy blue
*Command*Foreground: red
*to*Background: grey
*subject*Background: grey
```

Do not confuse this file inclusion syntax with the `#include`, `#ifdef`, etc. syntax provided by the program *xrdb*. That program invokes the C preprocessor to provide C include, macro, and conditional processing. The include functionality described here is provided directly by Xlib.

13.2.3 Resource Properties

`XResourceManagerString()`, returns the contents of the RESOURCE_MANAGER property on the root window of the default screen of the display. This property contains the user's resource customizations in string form, and is usually set with the program *xrdb*. The contents of this property should be merged in when creating the resource database to be used by an application. Until R5 this single RESOURCE_MANAGER property contained resources for all screens of a display, and there was no way for a user to specify different resources for different screens (for example, color vs. monochrome).

In R5, *xrdb* can set resources in the SCREEN_RESOURCES property on the root window of each screen of a display. Now the specifications in the SCREEN_RESOURCES property should be used to override the screen-independent RESOURCE_MANAGER specifications. The resource database that is created in this way is the database of the screen, rather than the database of the display. If the same application is executed on different screens of a display, or if a single application creates top-level windows on more than one screen of a display, a resource database will be created for each screen, and the application instances or top-level windows will find resources in them that are appropriate for that screen.

Two new functions support screen-dependent resources and resource databases. The contents of the SCREEN_RESOURCES property on the root window of a screen are returned by the function `XScreenResourceString()`.

The client *xrdb* has been rewritten for R5 to handle the new screen-specific properties. Any load, merge, or query operation can now be performed on the global RESOURCE_MANAGER property, a specific screen property, all screen properties, or all screen properties plus the global property. This last option is the default and "does the right thing"—the input file is processed through the C preprocessor once for each screen, and resource specifications that would appear in all of the per-screen properties are placed in the global property and removed from the screen-specific properties. With this new system, a defaults file which uses #ifdef COLOR to separate color from monochrome resource specifications can be used to correctly set the values of the screen-dependent and screen-independent properties for a two-screen monochrome-and-color display. An application can then be run on either screen and find the correct user defaults for that screen. Example 13-4 shows a user default file that takes advantage of the *xrdb* functionality to set different defaults on color and monochrome screens.

Example 13-4. A user defaults file for color and monochrome screens

```
! generic, non-color resources
*Font: -*-courier-medium-r-*-*-*-180-75-75-*-*-iso8859-1
xclock.geometry: -0+0

#ifdef COLOR
! resources for color screens here
*Background: grey
*Foreground: navy blue
XTerm*Foreground: maroon
#else
! resources for monochrome screens here
XTerm*reverseVideo: true
#endif
```

13.2.4 The Low Level Xrm Routines

The basic routines that every application that processes resources this way will include:

XrmInitialize()   Initializes the resource manager database. Must be called before any other routines.

XrmParseCommand()   Parses command line options into a data structure compatible with other resource manager routines. Various styles of command line options (with or without arguments and with various styles of arguments) are supported.

XrmGetFileDatabase()   Reads a resource file and stores the data in a resource manager database structure. This routine can be used to read the *.Xdefaults* file, the *app-defaults/** file, and the file (if any) pointed to by the XENVIRONMENT environment variable.

XrmGetStringDatabase()   Reads preferences from a string. This routine can be used to read resource specifications from the copy of the

	XA_RESOURCE_MANAGER property stored in the Display structure.
XrmMergeDatabases()	Merges databases created with other routines into a single combined database. This routine is used to combine the separate resource databases created with the functions described immediately above. The order in which the various databases are merged determines which databases take precedence.
XrmGetResource()	Extract a resource definition from the database so that it can be used to set program variables.

Several new functions were added to Xlib in R5 to support changes in the Xt Intrinsics. Some Xlib applications may find these useful:

XrmSetDatabase()	Associates a resource database with a display. This function is useful in applications that manipulate multiple displays or multiple databases. New in R5.
XrmGetDatabase()	Queries the database of a display. This function is useful in applications that manipulate multiple displays or multiple databases. New in R5.
XrmLocaleOfDatabase()	Returns the locale of a resource database (for internationalization). New in R5.
XrmCombineDatabase()	Merge the contents of two resource databases stored in memory. New in R5. This is more flexible than XrmMergeDatabases().
XrmCombineFileDatabase()	
	Merge the contents of two databases read from files. New in R5. This is more flexible than XrmMergeDatabases().
XrmEnumerateDatabase()	Calls a user-supplied procedure once for each entry in a resource database that matches any completion of a specified partial name and class list. The enumeration can be performed a single level below these name and class prefixes, or for all levels below. New in R5.

The sequence of operations for a typical R4 application is shown in Figure 13-2. For the R5 order of merging resource files and properties, see Volume Four, *X Toolkit Intrinsics Programming Manual*.

Routines that use these functions are shown and described in Chapter 14, *A Complete Application*.

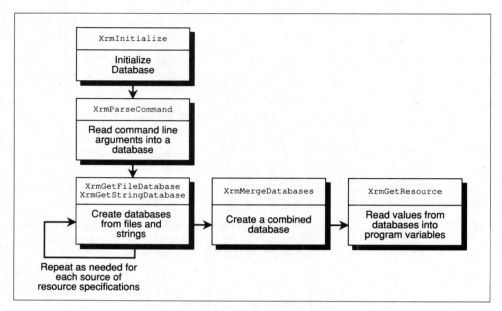

Figure 13-2. R4 Procedure for processing resource specifications with resource manager functions

13.3 Standard Geometry

One of the preferences that must be handled by clients is the preferred size and placement of a window or icon. By convention, rather than having the user specify various elements of the size and placement with separate options, clients accept a single *standard geometry string*, which has the following format:

*<width>*x*<height>*{+-}*<xoffset>*{+-}*<yoffset>*

Items enclosed in <> are integers, and items enclosed in {} are a set from which one item is allowed. The *xoffset* and *yoffset* values are optional. They determine the position of the window or icon—for the top-level window, they are, by convention, interpreted relative to the origin of the root window. The convention is that if the sign of *xoffset* or *yoffset* is positive, they specify that the offset is measured from the top or left edge of the application window to the top or left edge of the screen. If the sign of *xoffset* or *yoffset* is negative, they specify that the offset is measured from the bottom or right edge of the application window to the bottom or right edge of the screen.

After being read in from the command line or from a preference file, this string can be separated into separate x, y, width, and height values with XParseGeometry(). See Chapter 14 for an example that uses XParseGeometry().

In addition, there is a function called **XWMGeometry()** that can be used to parse a partial geometry specification from the user. **XWMGeometry()** takes a geometry string specified (presumably) by the user, which might not be complete, and the set of size hints that define the programs desired geometry. If the user-specified string specifies an element of the geometry, that value is used; otherwise, the corresponding value from program's default geometry string is used. The resulting values are used to set the window manager hints.

XWMGeometry returns a **win_gravity** value. After calling **XWMGeometry**, the application should pass this value on to **XSetWMProperties()**, as described in Section 4.3.4. The values returned can be **NorthEastGravity**, **NorthWestGravity**, **South-EastGravity** or **SouthWestGravity**.

These functions should not be confused with **XGetGeometry()**, which gets from the server the current geometry string, border width, depth, and root window of the specified window.

13.4 Resource Specification and Matching

A resource specification consists of an optional name of a client, followed by one or more predefined variables that indicate the preference to set, followed by a colon, optional white space, and the actual value of the preference.*

The format of these preference strings is most easily seen by looking at a resource database file, such as the one shown in Example 13-5.

Example 13-5. A simple resource database file

```
*font:                  fixed
.borderWidth:           2

xterm.scrollBar:        on
xterm.title:            xterm
xterm.windowName:       xterm
xterm.boldFont:         8x13
xterm.curses:           off
xterm.internalBorder:   2
xterm.iconStartup:      off
xterm.jumpScroll:       on
xterm.reverseWrap:      true
xterm.saveLines:        700
xterm.visualBell:       off
```

The options which begin with a period apply to all programs unless overruled by a program-specific entry with the same resource name. The last element between a period or asterisk and the colon is the resource name.

---

*Thanks to Jim Fulton of the X Consortium for providing an explanation of the resource manager on the *comp.window.x* network news group, from which portions of this section are excerpted.

This simple example demonstrates the rules as commonly practiced in Xlib applications. However, there are a number of additional rules that come into play in more complex, object-oriented applications, such as those written with the Xt Toolkit. Preferences may apply only to a particular subwindow within an application. For example, the *xmh* mail handler allows the user to set preferences for multiple levels of windows. These levels can be specified explicitly or by using a wildcard syntax denoted by the asterisk.

As a result, you should think of the syntax for preference specifications, not as:

> *client.keyword: value*

but as:

> *object ... subobject ... resourcename: value*

where the hierarchy of objects and subobjects not only usually corresponds to major structures within an application (such as windows, panels, menus, scrollbars, and so on) but also can be a class of such objects.

Individual elements in the hierarchy of objects and subobjects are called *components*. Component names can be either *instance names* or *class names*. By convention, instance names always begin with a lowercase letter, while class names always begin with an uppercase letter. Instances and classes are concepts in object-oriented programming, not normally used in Xlib programming. For a detailed description of instance and classes and how they appear in resource specifications, see Volume Four, *X Toolkit Intrinsics Programming Manual*.

Both instance and class names may include either uppercase or lowercase letters anywhere but in the starting position; in fact, for clarity, a component name is often made up of multiple words concatenated without spaces, with an initial capital serving as the word delimiter. For example, `buttonBox` might be the instance name for a window containing command buttons, while `ButtonBox` would be the corresponding class name.

For example, consider a hypothetical mail-reading program called *xmail*, which is similar to the current *xmh* application.* As shown in Figure 13-3, *xmail* is designed in such a manner that it uses a complex window hierarchy, all the way down to individual command buttons which are small subwindows. If each window is properly assigned a name and class, it becomes easy for the user to specify attributes of any portion of the application.

The top-level window is called `xmail`. It contains a series of vertically-stacked windows (panes), one of which contains all the command buttons controlling the program's functions. This control pane is named `toc` (table of contents). One of the command buttons is used to incorporate (fetch) new mail.

This button needs the following resources:

- Label string
- Font
- Foreground color

---

*We do not discuss the actual *xmh* application, even though it does use an object-oriented approach, because speaking hypothetically gives us greater freedom to set up illustrative examples.

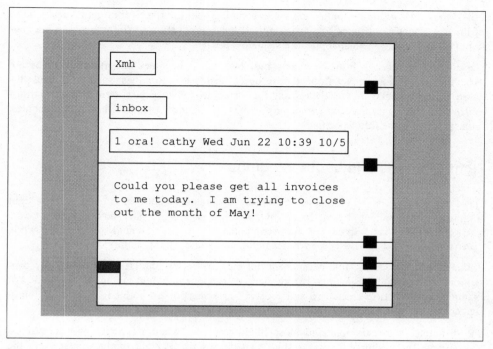

Figure 13-3. The hypothetical xmail display

- Background color
- Foreground color for its highlighted state
- Background color for its highlighted state

A full instance name specifying the background color of the include button might be:

```
xmail.toc.includeButton.backgroundColor
```

Defining class names allows the user to set resource values more freely. The pane containing the buttons could be of class **ButtonBox**, and the buttons themselves are all of class **CommandButton**. Therefore, the background of all the buttons could be identified with:

```
Xmail.ButtonBox.CommandButton.BackgroundColor
```

The user could do something like this:

```
Xmail.ButtonBox.CommandButton.BackgroundColor:  blue
xmail.toc.includeButton.backgroundColor:        red
```

which would make all command buttons blue except the one instance specified (**include-Button**), which would be red.

It might not be immediately apparent how you could use a class for the name of the application itself. However, consider the emacs family of text editors. Microemacs and GNU emacs could both be considered members of the class **Emacs**. Or assume that you were using a toolkit to build a group of applications with a similar user interface. It might be desirable to let the user specify attributes for features of all these applications. You might define a general class of vertically paned applications called **Vpane**.

The distinction between instance names and class names becomes important when you are retrieving an option value from the resource database. Routines such as **XrmGet-Resource()** that retrieve data from the database must specify two separate strings (*retrieval keys*)—one made up completely of instance names, and the other of class names. Both strings must be fully specified.

13.4.1 Tight Bindings and Loose Bindings

The components in a resource specification can be bound together in two ways: by a tight binding (a dot, `.`) or by a loose binding (an asterisk, `*`). Thus, **xmail.toc.background** has three name components tightly bound together, while **Vpane*Command.foreground** uses both a loose and a tight binding.

Bindings can precede the first component but may not follow the last component. By convention, if no binding is specified before the first component, a tight binding is assumed. For example, **xmail.background** and **.xmail.background** both begin with tight bindings before the **xmail**, while ***xmail.background** begins with a loose binding.

The difference between tight and loose bindings comes when a function like **XrmGet-Resource()** is comparing two resource specifications. A tight binding means that the components on either side of the binding must be sequential. A loose binding is a sort of wildcard, meaning that there may be unspecified components between the two components that are loosely bound together. For example, **xmail.toc.background** would match **xmail*background** and ***background**, but not **xmail.background** or **background**.

Because loose bindings are flexible, they are very useful for defining resource specifications. They allow resource specifications to match many specific applications and will still match if the applications are slightly changed (for example, if an extra level is inserted into the hierarchy.)

A resource specification used to store data into the database can use both loose and tight bindings. This allows the user to specify a data value which can match many different retrieval keys. In contrast, retrieval keys from the database can use only tight bindings. You can only look up one item in the database at a time.

Remember also that a resource specification can mix name and class components, while the retrieval keys are a pair of specifications without values, one consisting purely of name (first character lowercase) components and one consisting purely of class (first character uppercase) components.

13.4.2 Wildcarding Resource Component Names

In R5 and later, resource databases allow the character **?** to be used to wildcard a single component (name or class) in a resource specification. Thus the specification:

```
xmail.?.?.Background: antique white
```

sets the background color for all widgets (and only those widgets) that are grandchildren of the top-level window of the application **xmail**. And the specification:

```
xmail.?.?*Background: brick red
```

sets the background color of the grandchildren of the top-level window and all of their descendants. It does not set the background color for the child of the top-level window or for any popup windows. These kinds of specifications simply cannot be done without the **?** wildcard; sometimes the ***** wildcard does not provide the necessary fine-grained control. To set the background of all the grandchildren of an application window without the **?** wildcard, it would be necessary to specify the background for each grandchild individually.

There is one obvious restriction on the use of the **?** wildcard: it cannot be used as the final component in a resource specification—you can wildcard widget names, but not the resource name itself. Also, remember that the wildcard **?** (like the wildcard *****) means a different thing in a resource file than it does on a UNIX command line.

The **?** wildcard is convenient in cases like those above, but it has more subtle uses that have to do with its precedence with respect to the ***** wildcard. First, note the important distinctions between the **?** and the ***** wildcards: a **?** wildcards a single component name or class and falls between two periods (unless it is the first component in a specification), while the ***** indicates a "loose binding" (in the terminology of the resource manager) and falls between two component names or classes. A **?** does not specify the name or class of a resource component, but does at least specify the existence of a component. The ***** on the other hand only specifies that zero or more components have been omitted from the resource.

Recall that in order to look up the value of a resource, an application must provide a fully specified resource name, i.e., the name and class of each resource component. The returned value will be from the resource in the database that most closely matches the full resource specification provided by the application. To determine which resource matches best, the full resource specification is scanned from left to right, one component at a time. When there is more than one possible match for a component name, the following rules are applied: As these rules are applied, component by component, entries in the resource database are eliminated until there are none remaining or until there is a single matching entry remaining after the last component has been checked. These rules are not new with R5; they have simply been updated to accommodate the new **?** wildcard.

With these rules of precedence in mind, consider what happens when users specify a line like ***Background: grey** in their personal resource files. They would like to set the background of all widgets in all applications to grey, but if the app-defaults file for the application "xmail" has a specification of the form ***Dialog*Background: peach**, the background of the dialog boxes in the xmail application will be peach-colored, because this second specification is more specific. So if they really don't like those peach dialog boxes, (pre-R5) users will have to add a line like **XMail*Background: grey** to their personal resource files, and will have to add similar lines for any other applications that specify colors like "xmail" does. The reason this line works is rule 1 above: at the first level of the resource specification, "XMail" is a closer match than *.

This brings us to the specific reason that the ? wildcard was introduced: any resource specification that "specifies" an application name with a ? takes precedence over a specification that elides the application name with a *, no matter how specific the *rest* of that specification is. So in R5, the frustrated users mentioned above could add the single line:

```
?*Background: grey
```

to their personal resource files and achieve the desired result. The sequence ? * is odd-looking, but correct. The ? replaces a component name, and the * is resource binding, like a dot (.).

The solution described above relies, of course, on the assumption that no app-defaults files will specify an application name in a more specific way than the user's ?. If the "xmail" app-defaults file contained one of the following lines:

```
xmail*Dialog*Background: peach
XMail*Background: maroon
```

then the user would be forced to explicitly override them, and the ? wildcard would not help. To allow for easy customization, programmers should write app-defaults files that do not use the name or class of the application, except in certain critical resources that the user should not be able to trivially or accidentally override. The standard R5 clients have app-defaults files written in this way.

13.4.3 The –name Option

If you set up your resource specifications to use the class name for a program instead of an instance name, users can then list instance resources under an arbitrary name that they specify with the *-name* option to a program. For example, if *xterm* were set up this way, with the following resources defined:

```
XTerm*Font:              6x10
smallxterm*Font:         3x5
smallxterm*Geometry:     80x10
bigxterm*Font:           9x15
bigxterm*Geometry:       80x55
```

the user could use the following commands to create *xterm*s of different sizes:

```
xterm &                  (create a normal xterm)
xterm –name smallxterm   (create a small xterm)
xterm –name bigxterm     (create a big xterm)
```

13.4.4 Storage/Access Rules

As described in Section 13.2, Xlib merges the various sources of resource databases into a single database when an application starts up. When your application requests a value for a particular parameter from the resource database, using `XrmGetResource()`, this is called a *query*. The query takes completely specified instance and class names that we will call *retrieval keys*, and selects the most closely matching resource specifications from the database. The magic of the resource manager is that it always returns a single value even if multiple entries in the database match the retrieval keys. The algorithm for determining which resource database entry best matches a given query is the heart of the resource manager.

The resource manager compares component by component, matching a component from the resource specification against both the corresponding component from the instance retrieval key and the corresponding component from the class retrieval key. If the resource specification component matches either retrieval key component, then that component is considered to match. For example, the resource specification `xmail.toc.Foreground` matches the instance retrieval key `xmail.toc.foreground` and the class retrieval key `Vpane.Box.Foreground`.

Because the resource manager allows loose bindings (wildcards) and mixing names and classes in the resource specification, it is possible for many resource specifications to match a single instance/class retrieval key pair. To solve this problem, the resource manager uses the following precedence rules to determine which is the best match (and only the value from that match will be returned). To determine which of two resource specifications takes precedence, each level (and each binding) of the two resource specifications is compared, starting from the colon and working from right to left. Each of the rules is applied at each level, before moving to the next level, until only one resource specification remains. The precedence rules starting from the highest precedence are as follows:

1. A resource that matches the current component by name, by class, or with the `?` wildcard takes precedence over an resource that omits the current component by using a `*`.

    ```
    *topLevel.quit.background:          and
    *topLevel.Command.background:       and
    *topLevel.?.background:             take precedence over
    *topLevel*background:
    ```

2. A resource that matches the current component by name takes precedence over a resource that matches it by class, and both take precedence over a resource that matches it with the `?` wildcard.

    ```
    *quit.background:          takes precedence over
    *Command.background:       takes precedence over
    *?.background:
    ```

3. A resource in which the current component is preceded by a dot (`.`) takes precedence over a resource in which the current component is preceded by a `*`.

    ```
    *box.background:           takes precedence over
    *box*background:
    ```

Situations where both rule 2 and rule 3 apply often cause confusion. In these cases, remember that rule 2 takes precedence since it occurs earlier in the list above. Here is an example:

```
*box*background:            takes precedence over
*box.Background:
```

As an example of applying these rules, assume the following user preference specifications:

```
xmail*background:                        red
*command.font:                           8x13
*command.background:                     blue
*Command.Foreground:                     green
xmail.toc*Command.activeForeground:      black
xmail.toc.border:                        3
```

A query for the name:

```
xmail.toc.messageFunctions.include.activeForeground
```

and class:

```
Vpane.Box.SubBox.Command.Foreground
```

would match **xmail.toc*Command.activeForeground** and return "black." However, it also matches ***Command.Foreground** but with lower preference, so it would not return "green."

The programmer should think carefully when deciding which classes to use. For example, many text applications have some notion of background, foreground, border, pointer, and cursor or marker color. Usually the background is set to one color, and all of the other attributes are set to another, so that they may be seen on a monochrome display. To allow users of color displays to set any or all of them, the colors might be organized into classes as follows:

Table 13-1. Setting Classes

Instance	Class
background	Background
foreground	Foreground
borderColor	Foreground
pointerColor	Foreground
cursorColor	Foreground

Then to configure the application to run in "monochrome" mode but using two colors, the user would have to use only two specifications:

```
obj*Background:  blue
obj*Foreground:  red
```

Then if the user decided to make the cursor yellow but have the pointer and the border remain the same as the foreground, you would need only one new resource specification:

```
obj*cursorColor: yellow
```

All the resource manager rules for matching and precedence are explained in more detail in Volume Four, *X Toolkit Intrinsics Programming Manual*.

13.4.5 Resource Manager Values and Representation Types

The resource manager stores character strings in a structure called an `XrmValue`. Physically, database values consist of a size and an address. The size is specified in machine-dependent units, while the address is a machine-dependent pointer to the character string in uninterpreted machine memory.

The declaration of the `XrmValue` is shown in Example 13-6.

Example 13-6. The XrmValue structure

```
typedef struct {
    unsigned int size;
    caddr_t addr;
} XrmValue, *XrmValuePtr;
```

In addition, a representation type is stored along with each value in the data structure. The corresponding representation type is returned along with the data value when the database is accessed. The type provides a way to distinguish between different representations of the same information. For example, a color may be specified by a color name ("red") or be coded in a hexadecimal string ("#4f6c84"), by a pixel value, or by RGB values. Representation types are user-defined character strings describing the way the data is represented. You specify them when you store data, and you interpret them when you access data. Previous releases of X contained programs to perform automatic type conversion. These converter routines and types were found to be insufficiently general and were removed from Xlib. However, similar conversion functions are now being implemented in the X Toolkit.

You create representation types from simple character strings by using the macro `Xrm-StringToRepresentation`. For example:

```
XrmStringToRepresentation("RGB_value")
```

might be used if the data to be stored was a color represented as an RGB value. Certain functions let you store data without specifying a representation type. These functions always take data in the form of a `char[ ]` and automatically assign it the representation type `String`. The type `XrmRepresentation` is internally represented as an `XrmQuark`, since it is an ID for a string. (See Section 13.5.6 for details.)

13.5 Other Resource Manager Routines

The resource manager includes a number of other routines that will be of limited use to most application developers. They are discussed briefly here for the sake of completeness.

13.5.1 Putting Resources into the Database

While all most applications will need to do is to merge various sources of user preferences into a database and then read individual values, routines also exist for putting explicit resource values into the database or writing out the database into a file. For example, the *xrdb* program allows a user to write out the current contents of the resource manager database into a file. An application could allow users to modify the application resource specifications file and would then need those routines.

Routines for putting resources include:

`XrmPutResource()`	Stores preference data into a resource database.
`XrmPutLineResource()`	Stores a single line of preference data into a resource database.
`XrmPutStringResource()`	Stores a preference string into a resource database.
`XrmPutFileDatabase()`	Writes a resource database into a file.

The resource manager only frees or overwrites entries when new data is stored into a database with `XrmMergeDatabases()` or `XrmPutResource()` and related routines. A client that does not use these functions should be safe using the addresses to strings returned by routines like `XrmGetResource()`.

13.5.2 Combining the Contents of Databases

The pre-R5 function `XrmMergeDatabases()` combines the contents of a "source" database and a "target" database, using the contents of the source to override the contents of the target. With this function, there is no way to get "augment"-style behavior; i.e., there is no way to combine the two databases so that when source and target contain different values for the same resource specification the value in the target database is left unchanged. The two new functions `XrmCombineDatabase()` and `XrmCombineFileDatabase()` address this problem. They take a source database and a target database, or the name of a resource file and a target database, and also a `Bool` argument which specifies whether the resource from the source database or the file should override values in the target database. Thus the following two function calls are equivalent:

```
XrmMergeDatabases(source, target);
XrmCombineDatabase(source, target, True);
```

Because the contents of resource files are often merged into databases, the function `Xrm-CombineFileDatabase()` was added as a shortcut for a call to `XrmGetFile-`

Database() followed by a call to XrmCombineDatabase(). Note that the new R5 functions use the singular "Database," while XrmMergeDatabases() uses the plural.

These functions were added in R5 because of a required change in the way the X Toolkit builds up its resource database. Prior to R5, that database was built from sources in low-priority to high-priority order, each new source overriding the existing contents of the database, and XrmMergeDatabases() was sufficient for this purpose. But with the advent of the customization resource in R5, it was necessary to build the database in reverse order so that the value of the customization resource could be obtained from any of the other sources before being used to locate the application's app-defaults file. When the order of database creation was reversed, it was necessary to combine databases by augmenting rather than overriding so that the resulting single merged database would be the same. XrmCombine-Database() and XrmCombineFileDatabase() were added for precisely this purpose.

13.5.3 Enumerating Database Entries

Prior to R5 it was possible to query particular resources in a database or write the contents of a database to a file, but there was no way for a program to individually process each entry of a database. XrmEnumerateDatabase() fills this need. This function calls a user-supplied procedure once for each entry in a database that matches any completion of a specified partial name and class list. The enumeration can be performed a single level below these name and class prefixes, or for all levels below. The "callback" procedure invoked by this function returns a Bool and causes the enumeration to terminate by returning True.

The client appres, which previously relied on internal knowledge of the opaque Xrm-Database(), type now uses XrmEnumerateDatabase().

13.5.4 Associating a Resource Database with a Display

It is common practice for Xlib applications (and automatic in Xt applications) to build a resource database for each display that is opened, and it is common to talk about the "database of the display." Before R5, however, there was no standard way to associate a database with a display for later retrieval. In the MIT Xlib implementation, there is a database field in the Display structure, and prior to R5 the X Toolkit used this field even though the Display structure is supposed to be opaque.

In R5, however, there are functions to set and get the database of the display: XrmSet-Database() and XrmGetDatabase(). These are simply utility functions; they provide a public interface to fields in an opaque data structure. No Xlib routines use these functions, but XtDisplayInitialize() sets the database of the display for later use by XtResolvePathname(). Note that Xlib does not provide a way to associate a display with a screen.

13.5.5 Getting the Locale of a Database

As described in Chapter 10, every `XrmDatabase()` is parsed in the current locale and has that locale associated with it. To return the name of the locale of a database, use the new function `XrmLocaleOfDatabase()`.

13.5.6 Quarks

A special data type called a *quark* is used internally by the resource manager to represent strings. They were created to improve the efficiency of the resource manager. The resource manager needs to make many comparisons of strings when it gets data from the database. It must compare, component by component, the name and class specification of the requested resource to each stored key in the database. Quarks are simple identifiers (presently represented as integers) for strings. Thus, instead of comparing strings, the resource manager converts each component of the string into the corresponding quark and compares the quarks instead. This converts lengthy string comparisons into quick numeric comparisons, with the obvious savings in efficiency. The price is the overhead needed to convert back and forth between strings and quarks, but this is a small price for avoiding multiple string comparisons in a large database.

In summary, then, a quark is to a string as an atom is to a property. Quarks, however, are local to the application.

Quarks are implemented using an internal table of strings. The function `XrmString-ToQuark()` returns a pointer to the quark for a given string. Clients that do more than just access their resource specifications once might consider calling `XrmStringToQuark()` for each string and then using the quark form of the routines that get resources.

Prior to R5, the resource manager functions made a copy of all strings when they were registered as quarks. Most strings were widget names, resource names, and resource classes hardcoded into an application's executable, but the copying was required for those few quarks that were created with dynamically-allocated strings. R5 contains a new function, `Xrm-PermStringToQuark()`, which behaves like the existing `XrmStringToQuark()` except that it assumes that the passed string is either a string constant hardcoded into the application or at least is in memory that will not be modified or de-allocated for the lifetime of the application. This assumption means that the string need not be copied, and therefore memory is saved. There is no direct connection between `XrmPermStringToQuark()` and `Xpermalloc()`. Strings in memory allocated with `Xpermalloc()` may be passed to `XrmPermStringToQuark()` as long as they will not be changed during the lifetime of the application.

The following functions convert between strings and quarks:

- `XrmQuarkToString()`
- `XrmStringToBindingQuarkList()`
- `XrmStringToQuark()`
- `XrmPermStringToQuark()`

- `XrmStringToQuarkList()`

- `XrmUniqueQuark()`

The following routines can be used to work directly on quarks rather than strings when retrieving or storing resources:

- `XrmQGetResource()`

- `XrmQGetSearchList()`

- `XrmQGetSearchResource()`

- `XrmQPutResource()`

- `XrmQPutStringResource()`

All of the quark routines are unlikely to be used by application developers. However, they will be of use to toolkit developers. See Volume Two, *Xlib Reference Manual*, for more information.

You will need to use a group of special macros with the routines that handle quarks. They are described in Appendix C, *Macros*, of Volume Two, *Xlib Reference Manual*, and listed below. Unfortunately, they do not follow the normal naming convention for macros, since they begin with *Xrm* (no other macros begin with *X*), possibly because the resource manager used to be part of a separate library.

- `XrmClassToString()`

- `XrmNameToString()`

- `XrmRepresentationToString()`

- `XrmStringToClass()`

- `XrmStringToName()`

- `XrmStringToRepresentation()`

Managing User Preferences

14

A Complete Application

While the simple application in Chapter 3 demonstrated the most important X programming techniques, it was far from a complete application. This chapter describes a calculator program that provides for calculations in several bases. This program has a more robust event loop than the simple application in Chapter 3 and demonstrates the use of the resource manager routines for integrating user preferences.

In This Chapter:

14
A Complete Application

Our basic window program in Chapter 3, *Basic Window Program*, did not do all the things an application normally should do. We should have more complete communication with the window manager, parse the command line, and merge these options with the user's defaults to set up user-preferred colors and miscellaneous options. This chapter describes and demonstrates these techniques with a real application, *basecalc*.

The *basecalc* application is a programmer's calculator that allows integer calculations in binary, octal, decimal, and hexadecimal and conversions between these bases. It is not quite as complicated as *xcalc*, the standard calculator for X, but it demonstrates X techniques just as well. *basecalc* also does base conversions, logical operations, and unsigned arithmetic, which *xcalc* does not.

Only the sections of the program that illustrate X concepts are shown and described in this chapter. The entire program is shown in Appendix D, *The basecalc Application*.

This program has one characteristic that is not strictly correct in the X environment. It has only one allowable size. If the window manager refuses its request for that size or its main window is reduced in size by the user, it should print a message indicating that it cannot operate in that space. Luckily, most window managers honor the application's size hints and refuse to resize the window.

14.1 Description of basecalc

Figure 14-1 shows *basecalc* on the screen. It is a calculator which can perform integer math in decimal, octal, hexadecimal, or binary and can convert values between any of these bases. The calculator may be operated with the pointer by pressing any pointer button on the calculator pads or with the keyboard by typing the same symbols shown on the calculator face.

See the *Preface* for information on how to get the example source code.

The long horizontal window along the top of the calculator is the display, in which the values punched on the calculator and the results are displayed. The digits (0 to 9) and letters (A to F) in the left-hand portion of the calculator keypad are for entering values. The top row of the right-hand portion of the keypad is for base selection. These can be used either to set the

Figure 14-1. The basecalc application on the screen

current base of calculations or to convert a value between bases. Only one of the base indicators is highlighted at a time.

Only valid numbers in the current base are allowed to be entered. Valid pads are black, while invalid ones are light gray. When a pad is triggered by pressing a pointer button, it flashes white, and the operation or value indicated by the pad is executed if the pointer button is released in the same pad. The pad also responds to the pointer entering or leaving the window while a pointer button is pressed.

The calculator also operates from the keyboard. Numbers, letters, and special characters can be typed in (or pasted from another application) to represent all the functions except Clear Entry (CE). The Backspace key also performs this function.

This application runs on any X system, since it uses only the colors black and white. It achieves the appearance of different levels of gray by creating a pattern with differing amounts of black and white. It also provides command line arguments for colors and uses them if the user specifies them and if connected to a color screen.

Here is the list of available functions and how they are used. If you do not plan to be using *basecalc*, skip to Section 14.2, because you will not need to know how to use *basecalc* from the desktop.

All operations work in all bases. You may shift bases at any point in any calculation. The last of any series of consecutive operators pressed will be acted upon.

+, -, *, /	Normal addition, subtraction, multiplication, and division. A number is entered, then one of these operators, then another number, and finally the equal sign, Enter key, or any operator. The result will then be displayed in the window. If the last character entered was an operator, you can continue specifying numbers and operators in alternation.
|, &	AND and OR. Used just like the addition operator. The "|" and "&" symbols on the keyboard trigger this function.
<<, >>	Shift Left and Shift Right. Used just like the addition operator. Enter the number to be shifted, then the ">>" or "<<" pad (or the ">" or "<" keys), and then the number of bits to shift the number, followed by the "=" or Enter key.
^	Exclusive OR. Used just like the addition operator. Sets all bits that are in either number but not both. Available from the caret (^) key.
%	Mod (remainder after division). Used like the addition operator. Available on the percent (%) key.
`	Change sign. This is a unary operator, since it performs its function immediately on the current contents of the display. Its results depend on whether the calculator is in signed or unsigned mode. If in unsigned mode, the result is the unsigned equivalent of a negative number. This function is available from the left single quote key.
~	One's complement. This is a unary operator. It changes all the bits in the value.
CE	Clear Entry. Erases the last value entered. The Backspace key also performs this function.
CD	Clear Digit. Erases the last digit entered.
CA	Clear All. Clears all operator and value registers.
U or S	Unsigned or Signed. Specifies whether all other operations should be performed in signed or unsigned mode.
=	Compute. The Return key also performs this function.

These mathematical operations have nothing to do with X, and how they are implemented is not described here. They are provided so that you can use the program if you have the code and so you can more easily understand the complete code in Appendix D, *The basecalc Application*. In this chapter, we are going to concentrate on the aspects of the program that are standard to X applications. On that note . . .

14.2 Include Files

The include files used in Example 14-1 are the standard ones, except for the few needed to perform system calls to get the user's home directory, current Rubout key, etc. The *<X11/Xresource.h>* file is necessary to use the resource manager.

Example 14-1. basecalc — include files

```
#include <X11/Xlib.h>
#include <X11/Xutil.h>
#include <X11/Xresource.h>
#include <X11/cursorfont.h>

#include <stdio.h>

#ifdef SysV
#include <termio.h>
#else
#include <sgtty.h>
#include <sys/ttychars.h>
#endif SysV

#include <ctype.h>
#include <pwd.h>

/* Global declarations file for this application */
#include "basecalc.h"
```

The constant definitions and global variables declared or defined in *./basecalc.h* are shown above the routines in which they are used in the *basecalc* example program. You can take a look at the entire include file in Appendix D.

14.3 The Main of basecalc

The main is a very short and straightforward outline for the major routines to follow.

Example 14-2. basecalc — the main

```
char myDisplayName[ 256 ];

/* X11 Integer Programmer's Calculator with base conversions */

main (argc, argv)
int argc;
register char *argv[ ];
{
    /* So we can use the resource manager data merging functions */
    XrmInitialize();

    /* Parse command line first so we can open display, store any
     * options in a database */
    parseOpenDisp (&argc, argv);

    /* Get server defaults, program defaults, .Xdefaults;
     * merge them and finally the command line */
    mergeDatabases();
```

Example 14-2. basecalc — the main (continued)

```
      /* Extract values from database and convert to form usable
       * by this program */
      extractOpts ();
      /* Load font, make pixmaps, set up arrays of windows */
      initCalc ();

      /* Get keyboard settings for interrupt, delete, etc. */
      initTty ();

      /* Make a standard cursor */
      makeCursor ();

      /* Set standard properties, create and map windows */
      makeWindows (argc, argv);

      /* Get events */
      takeEvents ();

      /* Bow out gracefully */
      XCloseDisplay(display);
      exit (1);
}
```

`initTty` is not shown in this chapter, but it is included in Appendix D. It simply performs a few system calls to determine which keys are being used for erase, delete, and interrupt.

The following sections describe each routine called in the main. Each section will begin with a brief description of the routine, followed by the declarations from *basecalc.h* that are needed with that routine and then the code.

14.4 Getting User Preferences

This section describes and demonstrates the use of the resource manager in a typical application. For an additional theoretical description of the resource manager, see Chapter 13, *Managing User Preferences*.

14.4.1 User Defaults for basecalc

As described in Chapter 13, the user's default values for options are normally found in the **XA_RESOURCE_MANAGER** property on the root window. That property is normally set by the user with the *xrdb* program. For compatibility, if there is no **XA_RESOURCE_MANAGER** property defined (either because *xrdb* was not run or if the property was removed), your program should assume that the defaults can be found in a file called *.Xdefaults* in the user's home directory.

Note that `XGetDefault()`, described in Chapter 13, only deals with some of this complexity. It does not read the **XA_RESOURCE_MANAGER** property, and it does not merge in the command line arguments. That is why, in this example, we have used a different, more thorough technique, using the native resource manager calls.

Example 14-3 shows a sample resource database file with two options for *basecalc*.

Example 14-3. A sample .Xdefaults file

```
basecalc.base:          2
basecalc.unsigned:      False
```

For a complete description of preference matching rules, see Chapter 13. The `basecalc.base` preference sets the base with which the calculator will start and is here specified as binary (base 2). The `basecalc.unsigned` preference specifies whether the calculator should start up in signed mode or unsigned mode.

14.4.2 Parsing the Command Line

`XrmInitialize()` must be called before any other resource manager function. (It simply sets up a default `XrmRepresentation` type for strings, but that fact does not affect how the resource manager is used in applications.) After that, the first thing to be done is to parse the command line so that we can read the display argument out of it before opening the display. `parseOpenDisp` does this, loading all the command line options that match resources in the option table into a database for later merging with the user's defaults. Take a look at the code in Example 14-4, and then we'll explain it.

Example 14-4. basecalc — the parseOpenDisp routine

```
/* Global variables */
Display *display;
int screen_num;
char myDisplayName[ 256 ];

/* Command line options table; we don't do anything with many
 * of these resources, but the program is ready for expansion
 * to allow variable sizes, fonts, etc. */

#define GEOMETRY        "*geometry"
#define ICONGEOMETRY    "*iconGeometry"
#define UNSIGNED        "*unsigned"
#define BASE            "*base"
#define ICONSTARTUP     "*iconStartup"

static int opTableEntries = 25;
static XrmOptionDescRec opTable[ ] = {
{"-unsigned",       UNSIGNED,           XrmoptionNoArg,     (caddr_t) "off"},
{"-x",              BASE,               XrmoptionNoArg,     (caddr_t) "16"},
{"-hex",            BASE,               XrmoptionNoArg,     (caddr_t) "16"},
{"-dec",            BASE,               XrmoptionNoArg,     (caddr_t) "10"},
{"-oct",            BASE,               XrmoptionNoArg,     (caddr_t) "8"},
{"-binary",         BASE,               XrmoptionNoArg,     (caddr_t) "2"},
{"-geometry",       GEOMETRY,           XrmoptionSepArg,    (caddr_t) NULL},
{"-iconGeometry",   ICON_GEOMETRY,      XrmoptionSepArg,    (caddr_t) NULL},
{"-iconic",         ICONSTARTUP,        XrmoptionNoArg,     (caddr_t) "on"},
{"-background",     "*background",      XrmoptionSepArg,    (caddr_t) NULL},
{"-bg",             "*background",      XrmoptionSepArg,    (caddr_t) NULL},
{"-fg",             "*foreground",      XrmoptionSepArg,    (caddr_t) NULL},
{"-foreground",     "*foreground",      XrmoptionSepArg,    (caddr_t) NULL},
{"-xrm",            NULL,               XrmoptionResArg,    (caddr_t) NULL},
```

Example 14-4. basecalc — the parseOpenDisp routine (continued)

```
{"-display",        ".display",       XrmoptionSepArg,     (caddr_t) NULL},
/* Remainder not currently supported: */
{"-bd",             "*borderColor",   XrmoptionSepArg,     (caddr_t) NULL},
{"-bordercolor",    "*borderColor",   XrmoptionSepArg,     (caddr_t) NULL},
{"-borderwidth",    ".borderWidth",   XrmoptionSepArg,     (caddr_t) NULL},
{"-bw",             ".borderWidth",   XrmoptionSepArg,     (caddr_t) NULL},
{"-fn",             "*font",          XrmoptionSepArg,     (caddr_t) NULL},
{"-font",           "*font",          XrmoptionSepArg,     (caddr_t) NULL},
{"-name",           ".name",          XrmoptionSepArg,     (caddr_t) NULL},
{"-title",          ".title",         XrmoptionSepArg,     (caddr_t) NULL},
};

static XrmDatabase commandlineDB;

/* Get command line options */
parseOpenDisp (argc, argv)
int *argc;
register char *argv[ ];
{
    XrmValue value;
    char *str_type[ 20 ];

    myDisplayName[ 0 ] = '\0';

    XrmParseCommand(&commandlineDB, opTable, opTableEntries, argv[ 0 ],
              argc, argv);

    /* Check for any arguments left */
    if (*argc != 1) Usage();

    /* Get display now, because we need it to get other databases */
    if (XrmGetResource(commandlineDB, "basecalc.display",
              "Basecalc.Display", str_type, &value)== True) {
        (void) strncpy(myDisplayName, value.addr, (int) value.size);
    }

    /* Open display */

    if (!(display = XOpenDisplay(myDisplayName))) {
        (void) fprintf(stderr, "%s: Can't open display '%s'\n",
              argv[ 0 ], XDisplayName(myDisplayName));
        exit(1);
    }

    screen_num = DefaultScreen(display);
    visual = DefaultVisual(display, screen_num);
    colormap = DefaultColormap(display, screen_num);
}
```

The large options table (`opTable`) defines all the command line arguments that **Xrm-ParseCommand()** is going to look for. It describes not only what flag to look for but also the style of each option. Some options are a simple flag, others are a flag followed by a value with no space or with a space, and so on. The options table also specifies what to call each option when searching for it in the database.

Example 14-5 shows the structure that defines the options table.

Example 14-5. XrmOptionDescRec, XrmOptionDescList, and XrmOptionKind declarations

```
typedef struct {
        char *option;                   /* Option specification string in argv */
        char *resourceName;             /* Binding and resource name (without
                                         * application name) */
    XrmOptionKind argKind;              /* Which style of option it is */
        caddr_t value;                  /* Value to provide if XrmoptionNoArg */
} XrmOptionDescRec, *XrmOptionDescList;

typedef enum {
        XrmoptionNoArg,                 /* Value is specified in
                                         * OptionDescRec.value */
        XrmoptionIsArg,                 /* Value is the option string itself */
        XrmoptionStickyArg,             /* Value is chars immediately following
                                         * option */
        XrmoptionSepArg,                /* Value is next argument in argv */
        XrmoptionResArg,                /* Resource and value in next argument
                                         * in argv */
        XrmoptionSkipArg,               /* Ignore this option and next argument
                                         * in argv */
        XrmoptionSkipLine               /* Ignore this option and the rest of
                                         * argv */
} XrmOptionKind;
```

The styles of command line arguments allowed are as follows:

XrmoptionNoArg   If this flag is present, take the value in the **value** member (the last column) of the options table. For example, the *-u* (unsigned) option for the calculator indicates that the value should be **off** and the calculator should begin in unsigned mode.

XrmoptionIsArg   The flag itself indicates something without any additional information. In the case of the calculator, *-x* or *-h* indicates that it should start up in hexadecimal mode.

XrmoptionStickyArg   The value is the characters immediately following the option with no white space intervening. This is not used in the calculator, but it is like the arguments for *uucico*, where *-sventure* means to call system *venture*.

XrmoptionSepArg   The next item after the white space after this flag is the value of the option. For example, the option *-fg blue* would be of this type and would indicate that blue is the value for the resource specified by *-fg*.

XrmoptionResArg   The resource name and its value are the next argument in **argv** after the white space after this flag. For example, the flag might be *-res* and the resource name/value might be **basecalc*background:white**.

XrmoptionSkipArg   Ignore this option and the next argument in **argv**.

XrmoptionSkipLine   Ignore this option and the rest of **argv**.

As `XrmParseCommand()` parses the command line, it removes arguments that it finds in the options table from `argv` and `argc`. Therefore, if `argc` is nonzero after `XrmParse-Command()`, at least one of the command line arguments was illegal. The best thing to do is print both the illegal options (by printing `argv`) and the correct option syntax.

If all the options were correctly parsed, then it is time to extract the display name so that we can connect with the display. We need to connect now because we want to get the user's resource database from the server to merge with the command line arguments we already have. If there was no display specified on the command line, we use **NULL** as usual to connect to the server indicated in the UNIX environment variable DISPLAY. We set the global variable `screen_num` to the default screen number so that we can use it in future macro calls.

It would be possible (and actually preferable) to search the other local databases, namely the *app-defaults/** and *.Xdefaults* files, for a display name before connecting to the display. This was not done in *basecalc* because of an oversight.

14.4.3 Getting the Databases

The `mergeDataBases` routine shown in Example 14-6 reads in options from four sources, merges them together in the proper order, and then merges in the database obtained from the command line. As described in Chapter 13, *Managing User Preferences*, we will use the R4 set of resource files and merging order since it's a lot less complicated than the R5 order defined by the Xt Intrinsics:

- *Classname* file in the *app-defaults* directory.

- *Classname* file in the directory specified by the XUSERFILESEARCHPATH or XAPPLRESDIR environment variables.

- Property set using *xrdb*, accessible through the **XResourceManagerString()** macro or, if that is empty, the *.Xdefaults* file.

- XENVIRONMENT environment variable or, if not set, *.Xdefaults-hostname* file.

- Command line arguments.

Example 14-6 shows the global declarations and the routine. This routine is quite similar to the routine in the Xt Toolkit that performs the same function (that was its origin).

Example 14-6. basecalc — the GetUsersDataBase routine

```
Display *display;
XrmDatabase rDB;      /* For final merged database */

/* Get program's and user's defaults */
mergeDatabases()
{
    XrmDatabase homeDB, serverDB, applicationDB;

    char filenamebuf[ 1024 ];
    char *filename = &filenamebuf[ 0 ];
    char *environment;
```

Example 14-6. basecalc — the GetUsersDataBase routine (continued)

```
    char *classname = "Basecalc";
    char name[ 255 ];

    (void) strcpy(name, "/usr/lib/X11/app-defaults/");
    (void) strcat(name, classname);
    /* Get application defaults file, if any */
    applicationDB = XrmGetFileDatabase(name);
    (void) XrmMergeDatabases(applicationDB, &rDB);

    /* Merge server defaults, created by xrdb, loaded as a
     * property of the root window when the server initializes
     * and loaded into the display structure on XOpenDisplay;
     * if not defined, use .Xdefaults */
    if (XResourceManagerString(display) != NULL) {
        serverDB = XrmGetStringDatabase(XResourceManagerString
                     (display));
    } else {
        /* Open .Xdefaults file and merge into existing database */
        (void) GetHomeDir(filename);
        (void) strcat(filename, "/.Xdefaults");

        serverDB = XrmGetFileDatabase(filename);
    }
    XrmMergeDatabases(serverDB, &rDB);

    /* Open XENVIRONMENT file or, if not defined, the .Xdefaults,
     * and merge into existing database */
    if ((environment = getenv("XENVIRONMENT")) == NULL) {
        int len;
        environment = GetHomeDir(filename);
        (void) strcat(environment, "/.Xdefaults-");
        len = strlen(environment);
        (void) gethostname(environment+len, 1024-len);
    }
    homeDB = XrmGetFileDatabase(environment);
    XrmMergeDatabases(homeDB, &rDB);

    /* Command line takes precedence over everything */
    XrmMergeDatabases(commandlineDB, &rDB);
}
```

XrmGetFileDatabase() reads the application defaults file and loads it into a database, returning a pointer to the database. This database should contain the default values for each configurable variable used in the program. This file should look just like a user preference file, and it should parallel every option in the command line options table. In case this file is unavailable, the application should also have hardcoded defaults for all these values, but it should not have to use them.

Note that Example 14-6 gets the user's database set by *xrdb* from the value returned by the XResourceManagerString() function. This function returns a pointer to a string stored in the Display structure. This string is set by XOpenDisplay() to the value of the XA_RESOURCE_MANAGER property on the root window of screen 0.* This string can easily be translated into a database with XrmGetStringDatabase().

14.4.4 Getting Options from the Database

The extractOpts routine performs the final merging of the defaults database with the command line database and then reads options out of the database and sets program variables appropriately. The program in Example 14-7 does not take advantage of all the options supported in the options table, but it is ready to be expanded to do so.

Example 14-7. basecalc — the extractOpts routine

```
extractOpts()
{
    char *str_type[ 20 ];
    char buffer[ 20 ];
    long flags;
    XrmValue value;
    int x, y, width, height;
    XColor screen_def;

    /* Get geometry */
    if (XrmGetResource(rDB, "basecalc.geometry",
            "Basecalc.Geometry", str_type, &value)== True) {
        (void) strncpy(Geostr, value.addr, (int) value.size);
    } else {
        Geostr[ 0 ] = NULL;
    }

    if (XrmGetResource(rDB, "basecalc.iconGeometry",
            "Basecalc.IconGeometry", str_type, &value)== True) {
        (void) strncpy(iconGeostr, value.addr, (int) value.size);
    } else {
        iconGeostr[ 0 ] = NULL;
    }

    if (XrmGetResource(rDB, "basecalc.unsigned", "Basecalc.Unsigned",
            str_type, &value)== True)
        if (strncmp(value.addr, "False", (int) value.size) == 0)
            Unsigned = False;

    if (XrmGetResource(rDB, "basecalc.base", "Basecalc.Base",
            str_type, &value)== True) {
        (void) strncpy(buffer, value.addr, (int) value.size);
        buffer[ value.size ] = NULL;
        Base = atoi(buffer);
    } else Base = 10;

    if (XrmGetResource(rDB, "basecalc.foreground",
            "Basecalc.Foreground", str_type, &value)== True) {
        (void) strncpy(buffer, value.addr, (int) value.size);
```

_____
*Note that because the XA_RESOURCE_MANAGER property is read by XOpenDisplay(), it is read only once, during application startup. Therefore, any changes to this property after startup will not be reflected in the application. This property (and all the other resource files) is for initial startup information only.

Example 14-7. basecalc — the extractOpts routine (continued)

```
        if (XParseColor(display, colormap, buffer,
                    &screen_def) == 0) {
            (void) fprintf(stderr, "basecalc: fg color \
                    specification %s invalid", buffer);
            foreground = BlackPixel(display, screen_num);
        } else {
            /* Accessing visual is cheating, but in the
             * interests of brevity, we'll do it anyway */
            if ((visual->class == StaticGray) ||
                    (visual->class == GrayScale))
                foreground = BlackPixel(display, screen_num);
            else if (XAllocColor(display, colormap, &screen_def) ==
                    0) {
                foreground = BlackPixel(display, screen_num);
                (void) fprintf(stderr, "basecalc: couldn't allocate \
                        color: %s.\n", buffer);
            }
            else
                foreground = screen_def.pixel;
        }
    } else {
    foreground = BlackPixel(display, screen_num);
}

    if (XrmGetResource(rDB, "basecalc.background",
                "Basecalc.Background", str_type, &value)== True) {
        (void) strncpy(buffer, value.addr, (int) value.size);
        if (XParseColor(display, colormap, buffer,
                    &screen_def) == 0) {
            (void) fprintf(stderr, "basecalc: bg color \
                    specification %s invalid", buffer);
            background = WhitePixel(display, screen_num);
        } else {
            if ((visual->class == StaticGray) ||
                    (visual->class == GrayScale))
                background = WhitePixel(display, screen_num);
            else if (XAllocColor(display, colormap, &screen_def) ==
                    0) {
                background = WhitePixel(display, screen_num);
                (void) fprintf(stderr, "basecalc: couldn't allocate \
                        color: %s.\n", buffer);
            }
            else
                background = screen_def.pixel;
        }
    } else {
    background = WhitePixel(display, screen_num);
}

    /* One last check to make sure the colors are different! */
    if (background == foreground) {
        background = WhitePixel(display, screen_num);
        foreground = BlackPixel(display, screen_num);
    }

    /* Get window geometry information */
    if (Geostr != NULL) {
```

Example 14-7. basecalc — the extractOpts routine (continued)

```
        flags = XParseGeometry(Geostr,
                &x, &y, &width, &height);
    if ((WidthValue|HeightValue) & flags)
        Usage ();
    if (XValue & flags) {
        if (XNegative & flags)
            x = DisplayWidth(display, screen_num) +
                    x - sizehints.width;
        sizehints.flags |= USPosition;
        sizehints.x = x;
    }
    if (YValue & flags) {
        if (YNegative & flags)
            y = DisplayHeight(display, screen_num) +
                    x - sizehints.width;
        sizehints.flags |= USPosition;
        sizehints.y = y;
    }
}

/* Get icon geometry information */
if (iconGeostr != NULL) {
    iconGeostr[0] = '=';
    flags = XParseGeometry(iconGeostr,
            &x, &y, &width, &height);
    if ((WidthValue|HeightValue) & flags)
        Usage ();
    if (XValue & flags) {
        if (XNegative & flags)
            x = DisplayWidth(display, screen_num) +
                    x - iconsizehints.width;
        iconsizehints.flags |= USPosition;
        wmhints.flags |= IconPositionHint;
        wmhints.icon_x = x;
        iconsizehints.x = x;
    }
    if (YValue & flags) {
        if (YNegative & flags)
            y = DisplayHeight(display, screen_num) +
                    x - iconsizehints.width;
        iconsizehints.flags |= USPosition;
        wmhints.flags |= IconPositionHint;
        wmhints.icon_y = y;
        iconsizehints.y = y;
    }
}
}
}
```

The variables that are used to access the data returned from the database are **background**, **Base**, **iconGeostr**, **iconOnly**, **foreground**, **Geostr**, and **Unsigned**. The routine then calls **XrmGetResource()** for each resource, which places the data which resulted from the combination of the command line and the resource database into user-accessible variables. **Geostr** and **iconGeostr** are used to set up the window manager size hints. Later in the code, the variables **background**, **Base**, **foreground**, **iconOnly**, and **Unsigned** will also be used.

Complete Application

The next step is to get the standard geometry strings from the database, parse them, and use these or the defaults to set the window manager hints to match. This program repeats this process for the main window and for the icon. Strictly speaking, it is not necessary to set window manager hints for the icon, and they are not used for that purpose in this program.

`XParseGeometry()` returns a bitmask which indicates which parts of the geometry string were actually set on the command line or in the resource database. There are symbols to indicate each bit in this mask, and they are:

`XValue, YValue`	Position of window or icon.
`WidthValue, HeightValue`	Dimensions of window or icon.
`XNegative, YNegative`	Indicates whether `XValue` or `YValue` is negative.

14.5 Printing a Usage Message

`GetOpts` calls `Usage` when the user tries to specify dimensions for the main window or icon, since this program cannot deal with that complexity.

Example 14-8. basecalc — the Usage routine

```
/* Print message to stderr and exit */
Usage ()
{
    fprintf (stderr,
        "%s: [-iconic] [-unsigned] [-hex|x|dec|oct|binary]\
[-display <display>] [-geometry <geometrystring>]\
[-iconGeometry <icongeometrystring>\n",
        calcName ? calcName : "basecalc");
    exit (1);
}
```

14.6 Initializing the Calculator

The `initCalc` routine in Example 14-9 performs three major functions: it loads the font to be used in all text, creates GCs for foreground and background of the calculator, and then sets the initial pixmaps for all pads. The windows for each pad do not exist yet.

Again, we'll begin with the declarations that are used in the routine.

Example 14-9. basecalc — declarations for initCalc

```
/* Pattern for disabled buttons (Light Gray) */
#define lgray_width 16
#define lgray_height 16
static char lgray_bits[ ] = {
    0x88, 0x88, 0x22, 0x22, 0x88, 0x88, 0x22, 0x22,
    0x88, 0x88, 0x22, 0x22, 0x88, 0x88, 0x22, 0x22,
    0x88, 0x88, 0x22, 0x22, 0x88, 0x88, 0x22, 0x22,
```

Example 14-9. basecalc — declarations for initCalc (continued)

```
    0x88, 0x88, 0x22, 0x22, 0x88, 0x88, 0x22, 0x22};

/* Background pattern for calculator (Dark Gray) */
#define gray_width 16
#define gray_height 16
static char gray_bits[ ] = {
    0xaa, 0xaa, 0x55, 0x55, 0xaa, 0xaa, 0x55, 0x55,
    0xaa, 0xaa, 0x55, 0x55, 0xaa, 0xaa, 0x55, 0x55,
    0xaa, 0xaa, 0x55, 0x55, 0xaa, 0xaa, 0x55, 0x55,
    0xaa, 0xaa, 0x55, 0x55, 0xaa, 0xaa, 0x55, 0x55};

#define    WHITE       0
#define    BLACK       1
#define    DARKGRAY    2
#define    LIGHTGRAY   3

int pressedColor =         WHITE;
int unpressedColor = BLACK;
int disabledColor =  LIGHTGRAY;
int displayColor =         WHITE;

#define NBUTTONS 38

struct windata {
      int   color;     /* Color */
      char  *text;     /* Pointer to the text string */
      int   x;         /* x coordinate of text */
      int   y;         /* y coordinate of text */
      int   value;     /* 0 to 16 for number, symbol for operator */
      int   type; /* Digit, operator, conversion, or special */
} windata[ NBUTTONS ] = {
      { 1, "                                    0 ", 2, 3, 0, WTYP_DISP },

      { 0, "C", 5, 3, 12, WTYP_DIGIT },
      { 0, "D", 5, 3, 13, WTYP_DIGIT },
      { 0, "E", 5, 3, 14, WTYP_DIGIT },
      { 0, "F", 5, 3, 15, WTYP_DIGIT },

      { 0, "8", 5, 3,  8, WTYP_DIGIT },
      { 0, "9", 5, 3,  9, WTYP_DIGIT },
      { 0, "A", 5, 3, 10, WTYP_DIGIT },
      { 0, "B", 5, 3, 11, WTYP_DIGIT },

      { 0, "4", 5, 3, 4, WTYP_DIGIT },
      { 0, "5", 5, 3, 5, WTYP_DIGIT },
      { 0, "6", 5, 3, 6, WTYP_DIGIT },
      { 0, "7", 5, 3, 7, WTYP_DIGIT },

      { 0, "0", 5, 3, 0, WTYP_DIGIT },
      { 0, "1", 5, 3, 1, WTYP_DIGIT },
      { 0, "2", 5, 3, 2, WTYP_DIGIT },
      { 0, "3", 5, 3, 3, WTYP_DIGIT },

      { 0, "CA", 6, 3, OPR_CLRA, WTYP_SPECIAL },
      { 0, "CE", 6, 3, OPR_CLRE, WTYP_SPECIAL },
      { 0, "CD", 6, 3, OPR_CLRD, WTYP_SPECIAL },
      { 0, "=", 17, 2, OPR_ASGN, WTYP_OPERATOR },

      { 0,  "+", 5, 3, OPR_ADD, WTYP_OPERATOR },
      { 0,  "-", 5, 3, OPR_SUB, WTYP_OPERATOR },
      { 0,  "*", 5, 4, OPR_MUL, WTYP_OPERATOR },
```

Example 14-9. basecalc — declarations for initCalc (continued)

```
      { 0,  "/",  5,  3,  OPR_DIV,  WTYP_OPERATOR },
      { 0,  "%",  5,  3,  OPR_MOD,  WTYP_OPERATOR },

      { 0,  "|",  5,  3,  OPR_OR,   WTYP_OPERATOR },
      { 0,  "&",  5,  3,  OPR_AND,  WTYP_OPERATOR },
      { 0,  ">>",1,  3,  OPR_SHR,  WTYP_OPERATOR },
      { 0,  "<<",0,  3,  OPR_SHL,  WTYP_OPERATOR },
      { 0,  "^",  5,  3,  OPR_XOR,  WTYP_OPERATOR },

      { 0,  "HEX", 2,  3,  16,  WTYP_CONVERSION },
      { 0,  "DEC", 2,  3,  10,  WTYP_CONVERSION },
      { 0,  "OCT", 2,  3,   8,  WTYP_CONVERSION },
      { 0,  "BIN", 2,  3,   2,  WTYP_CONVERSION },

      { 0,  "U",  5,  3,  OPR_UNS,  WTYP_SPECIAL },
      { 0,  "/",  5,  3,  OPR_NEG,  WTYP_OPERATOR },
      { 0,  "~",  5,  3,  OPR_NOT,  WTYP_OPERATOR },
};

/* Font for all numbers and text */
char *myFontName =   "8x13";

/* For keeping track of colors */
GC    fgGC;
GC    bgGC;
```

The data in **lgray** and **gray** are for making pixmaps for tiling in various shades of gray. This program is written to operate correctly on any kind of display. If the display is simple monochrome without grays, you can still get gray shades by creating different pixmaps with slightly different ratios of black and white pixels. The light gray pixmap is used for disabled pads, which are not valid in the current base. The dark gray pixmap is used for the background of the calculator. Simple pixel values of **BlackPixel( )** and **White-Pixel( )** are used for valid and selected pads. The symbols **BLACK**, **WHITE**, **DARKGRAY**, and **LIGHTGRAY** are defined to clarify the code. If foreground and background colors are specified on the command line, they will also be used in the pixmaps, and their colors will be mixed.

The **windata** structure provides information about each subwindow on the calculator: the color, text, position relative to the individual pad subwindows, value (digit or symbol), and type of pad. The first window in the list of data is the display window, where the entered values and results are shown. As you can see, the data for all the windows is initialized, except for the color, which is set in **initCalc**. None of these values change during the operation of the program except the color and the value in the display window.

The **type** member of **windata** indicates which of the four major classes of pads the window fits in. These are **WTYP_CONVERSION**, **WTYP_DIGIT**, **WTYP_OPERATOR**, and **WTYP_SPECIAL** and represent digits, operators, conversions (bases), and special keys. The special keys are Clear All (CA), Clear Digit (CD), Clear Entry (CE), and Unsigned (U). Each pad within each type is identified with the **value** member of **windata**. For digits, this is the digit itself, and for operators, conversions, and special keys, it is a symbol representing each key.

Last but not least, `fgGC` and `bgGC` are two GCs which are used to save the colors between which the pads are changed. The pads have to change back and forth between black and white frequently, and having one GC for each reduces the traffic to the server.

Without further ado, Example 14-10 shows the `initCalc` routine.

Example 14-10. basecalc — the initCalc routine

```
/* Initialize calculator options */
initCalc ()
{
    register int win;
    register int found = -1;
    XGCValues values;
    extern char lgray_bits[ ];

    if ((theFont = XLoadQueryFont (display, myFontName)) == NULL) {
        (void) fprintf(stderr, "basecalc: can't open font %s\n",
                myFontName);
        exit(-1);
    }

    /* Make the utility pixmaps */
    grayPixmap = makePixmap(gray_bits, gray_width, gray_height);
    lgrayPixmap = makePixmap(lgray_bits, lgray_width, lgray_height);

    /* Make the utility gc's */
    values.font = theFont->fid;
    values.foreground = foreground;
    fgGC = XCreateGC(display, DefaultRootWindow(display),
            GCForeground|GCFont, &values);
    values.foreground = background;
    values.function = GXcopy;
    bgGC = XCreateGC(display, DefaultRootWindow(display),
            GCForeground|GCFont|GCFunction, &values);

    /* Loop through buttons, setting disabled buttons
     * to Color Light Gray; also, find the window which
     * corresponds to the starting display base; also
     * add ascent to y position of text */
    for (win = 1; win < NBUTTONS; win++) {
        if (windata[win].type == WTYP_CONV &&
                windata[win].value == Base) {
            found = win;
        } else
            if (windata[win].type == WTYP_DIG &&
                    windata[win].value >= Base) {
                windata[win].color = disabledColor;
            } else
            if (windata[win].type == WTYP_SPEC &&
                    windata[win].value == OPR_UNS) {
                if (Unsigned)
                    windata[win].text = "U";
                else
                    windata[win].text = "S";
                windata[win].color = pressedColor;
            }
            else
                windata[win].color = unpressedColor;
```

Example 14-10. basecalc — the initCalc routine (continued)

```
        windata[win].y += theFont->max_bounds.ascent;
    }
    windata[0].y += theFont->max_bounds.ascent;
    if (found >= 0) {
        winBase = found;
        windata[found].color = pressedColor;
    } else {
            (void) fprintf(stderr, "basecalc: can't use base %d\n",
                    Base);
        exit(-1);
    }
    windata[0].color = displayColor;
}
```

The first action in this routine is to load the font. The process of loading and using a font should be familiar to you from the discussion and examples in Chapter 6, *Drawing Graphics and Text*.

The routine then calls **makePixmap** to make pixmaps out of the **lgray** and **gray** data in the include file. This routine calls **XCreatePixmapFromBitmapData()** to convert a single-plane pixmap into a pixmap with depth suitable for tiling. Then **initCalc** creates two GCs, each with a different foreground color. These are used later in **drawButton**.

Now **initCalc** begins a loop through all the window data set up in the array of structures called **windata**. The first operation within the loop is to adjust the position of text in each button according to the font information. Then the pad colors are set according to the **Base** and **Unsigned** variables. These variables have default values (10 and U), but they may have been updated according to the command line or the resource database.

Finally, **initCalc** sets the color of the display window and the current base pad. If the base is not valid, this will not have been caught until now, so the routine prints out a message and exits.

14.7 Making Windows

The **makeWindows** routine creates a cursor, sets up attributes, and creates the main window, all the pad windows, and the display window. It also creates the icon pixmap from data and then uses it as the background attribute for creating the icon window. The icon will be tiled with this pixmap independent of the icon size. Finally, all the standard properties and window manager hints are set.

There is nothing in **makeWindows** that you have not seen in previous examples, so we will not show it here. Look at the code in Appendix D, *The basecalc Application*, if you are interested.

14.8 Selecting Events

`selectEvents` selects events for all the windows of the application.

Example 14-11. basecalc — the selectEvents routine

```
selectEvents ()
{
    int win;

    /* Window behind calculator */
    XSelectInput (display, calcWin, KeyPressMask|KeyReleaseMask);

    /* Where results are drawn */
    XSelectInput (display, dispWin, ExposureMask);

    /* Pad windows */
    for (win = 1; win < NBUTTONS; win++)
        XSelectInput (display, Buttons[win].ID,
            ExposureMask|ButtonPressMask|ButtonReleaseMask|
            EnterWindowMask|LeaveWindowMask);
}
```

The entire calculator window requires key events, because we want to be able to operate the calculator from the keyboard as well as with the pointer.

The display window (`dispWin`) requires exposure events, because it must be able to refresh itself for the usual reasons.

All other windows (pads) require exposure events for refresh, button events for selection, and border crossing events so that the button only needs to be released within a pad to activate the pad. This last feature makes it easier to work quickly with the calculator.

14.9 Processing Events

The routine in Example 14-12 processes events. The top portion of **takeEvents** converts key events to the corresponding button event, and then the bottom sets the colors and flags and draws the button in the new color. Key codes are mapped to ASCII with **XLookup-String()**, and **keyToWin** is called to get the offset into **windata** that is represented by this key. When key events occur, the appropriate pad is flashed.

Example 14-12. basecalc — the takeEvents routine

```
takeEvents ()
{
    XEvent Event;
    register int win;
    register int Pressed = False;
    register int inWindow = False;
    char buffer[10];
    register char *keyChars = buffer;
    register int keyDown = False;
    int i, nbytes;
```

Example 14-12. basecalc — the takeEvents routine (continued)

```
while (1) {
     /* Get event if key not down */
     if (!keyDown)
          XNextEvent (display, &Event);
     else
          Event.type = KeyRelease;

     /* Map keyboard events to window events */
     if (Event.type == KeyPress || Event.type == KeyRelease) {
          nbytes = XLookupString (&Event, buffer,
               sizeof(buffer), NULL, NULL);
          if (Event.type == KeyPress)
               {
               Event.type = ButtonPress;
               keyDown = True;
               }
          else
               {
               for (i=0; i<60000; i++)
                    ; /* Wait */
               Event.type = ButtonRelease;
               }
          if ((Event.xbutton.window =
               keyToWin (keyChars, nbytes)) == None){
               keyDown = False;
               continue;
          }
     }
     for (win=0; win < NBUTTONS; win++)
          if (Buttons[win].ID == Event.xbutton.window)
               break;
     switch (Event.type) {
     case ButtonPress:
          if (windata[win].color == disabledColor)
               break;
          Pressed = win;
          if (!keyDown)
               inWindow = True;
          windata[win].color = pressedColor;
          drawButton (win, 0);
          break;
     case LeaveNotify:
          if (Pressed != win)
               break;
          inWindow = False;
          windata[win].color = unpressedColor;
          drawButton (win, 0);
          break;
     case EnterNotify:
          if (Pressed != win)
               break;
          inWindow = True;
          windata[win].color = pressedColor;
          drawButton (win, 0);
          break;
     case ButtonRelease:
```

Example 14-12. basecalc — the takeEvents routine (continued)

```
                if (windata[win].color == disabledColor ||
                    Pressed != win) {
                       keyDown = False;
                       break;
                }
                Pressed = False;
                windata[win].color = unpressedColor;
                if (keyDown || inWindow)
                       winPressed (win);
                keyDown = False;
                inWindow = False;
                drawButton (win, 0);
                break;
          case Expose:
                drawButton (win, 1);
                break;
          }
          XFlush(display);
     }
}
```

14.10 Drawing a Pad

This routine simply sets colors and draws the text in a pad. Example 14-13 shows the
`drawButton` routine.

Example 14-13. basecalc — the drawButton routine

```
/* Draw a single pad with its text */
drawButton (win, exposeEvent)
register int win;
{
     register char *string;
     register int x, y;
     struct windata *winp;
     char *Measure;
     XSetWindowAttributes attributes;
     unsigned long valuemask;
     GC gc;

     winp = &windata[win];
     x = winp->x;
     y = winp->y;
     string = winp->text;

     switch (windata[win].color) {
     case WHITE:
          gc = fgGC;
          attributes.background_pixel = background;
          attributes.border_pixel = foreground;
          valuemask = CWBackPixel|CWBorderPixel;
          break;
     case BLACK:
```

Example 14-13. basecalc — the drawButton routine (continued)

```
        gc = bgGC;
        attributes.background_pixel = foreground;
        attributes.border_pixel = background;
        valuemask = CWBackPixel|CWBorderPixel;
        break;
    case LIGHTGRAY:
        gc = bgGC;
        attributes.background_pixmap = lgrayPixmap;
        attributes.border_pixel = foreground;
        valuemask = CWBackPixmap|CWBorderPixel;
        break;
    }
    if (!exposeEvent){
        XChangeWindowAttributes(display, Buttons[win].self,
                valuemask, &attributes);
        XClearWindow(display, Buttons[win].self);
    }
    XDrawString (display, Buttons[win].self, gc, x, y, string,
            strlen (string));
    if (win == 0) {
        switch (Base) {
            case 10:
            case 8:
                Measure = Octmeasure;
                break;
            default:
            case 16:
            case  2:
                Measure = Hexmeasure;
                break;
        }
        XDrawString (display, dispWin, gc, 7, 6, Measure, 31);
    }
}
```

14.11 Routines Not Shown

The following is a brief description of all the subroutines of *basecalc* that were not shown in this chapter. All of these can be seen in full in Appendix D, *The basecalc Application*.

convButton   Changes the current base and converts a value, if any.

digitButton   Gets a digit and assigns it to **Value**.

displayVal   Calculates appropriate format string for base.

initTty   Performs system calls to get user's current erase, delete, and interrupt characters.

keyToWin   Translates a keycode as if a pad had been selected.

makePixmap   Makes a pixmap from bitmap data, shown and described in Chapter 6, *Drawing Graphics and Text*.

`operButton`	An operation. Either does it or waits for next value and = .
`printInBase`	Composes the string that should be displayed. Called from `Sprintf`.
`specButton`	Clears a digit, an entry, or all, or toggles unsigned mode.
`Sprintf`	A modified version of `sprintf`, the standard C utility, which does not print in binary. `Sprintf` calls `printInBase`.
`winPressed`	Determines whether pad pressed was a digit, an operator, a conversion, or a special pad.

15

Other Programming Techniques

As its title implies, this chapter discusses a few orphaned techniques that didn't quite fit in anywhere else. This chapter is important if you want to use one of these techniques, but most readers may just want to skim it.

In This Chapter:

15
Other Programming Techniques

This chapter covers a few obscure but occasionally necessary programming techniques. The routines and techniques described here will not be needed in most programs.

The end of the chapter contains information about porting and portability.

15.1 Reading and Writing Properties

Chapter 12, *Interclient Communication*, described many of the usual properties used in communication with the window manager and other clients. Xlib provides convenience routines for reading and writing these properties. But if you establish any other private protocols between two of your applications or between your application and a proprietary window manager, you will need to write your own routines to read and write properties. Example 15-1 is the code for **XFetchName()** that shows how to read a property containing a string.

Example 15-1. Reading a property

```
#include "Xatom.h"

Status XFetchName (dpy, w, name)
    register Display *dpy;
    Window w;
    char **name;
{
    Atom actual_type;
    int actual_format;
    unsigned long nitems;
    unsigned long leftover;
    unsigned char *data = NULL;
    if (XGetWindowProperty(dpy, w, XA_WM_NAME, 0L, (long)BUFSIZ,
            False, XA_STRING, &actual_type, &actual_format,
            &nitems, &leftover, &data) != Success) {
        *name = NULL;
        return (0);
    }
    if ( (actual_type == XA_STRING) && (actual_format == 8) ) {

        /* The data returned by XGetWindowProperty is guaranteed
         * to contain one extra byte that is null terminated to
```

Example 15-1. Reading a property (continued)

```
        * make retrieving string properties easy */

      *name = (char *)data;
      return(1);
      }
   if (data) Xfree ((char *)data);
   *name = NULL;
   return(0);
}
```

Using **XChangeProperty()** is easier than reading a property with **XGetWindow-Property()**, since there are many fewer arguments. Example 15-2 shows the companion function to **XFetchName()**, **XStoreName()**.

Example 15-2. Writing a property

```
XStoreName (dpy, w, name)
   register Display *dpy;
   Window w;
   char *name;
{
   XChangeProperty(dpy, w, XA_WM_NAME, XA_STRING,
         8, PropModeReplace, (unsigned char *)name,
         name ? strlen(name) : 0);
}
```

15.2 Screen Saver

Screen saver routines are provided to control the blanking of the screen when it has been idle for a time. **XSetScreenSaver()** sets the operation of the screen saver, including:

- How long the display remains idle before it is blanked.

- The time between random pattern motions.

- Whether the application prefers screen blanking or not (regardless of whether the screen is capable of it).

- Whether exposures are generated when the screen is restored.

XActivateScreenSaver() and **XResetScreenSaver()** turn the screen saver on and off, respectively, and **XForceScreenSaver()** can turn it on or off according to a flag. **XGetScreenSaver()** returns the current settings of the screen saver.

At this writing, the X Consortium is working on an X extension that will support more advanced screen saving abilities.

15.3 Host Access and Security

Once an application successfully connects to a server, X does not provide any protection from unauthorized access to individual windows, pixmaps, or other resources. If a program succeeds in connecting with a server and finds out a resource ID, it can manipulate or even destroy the resource.

There are several kinds of security that can prevent connections from being made by clients running on other machines. First, to provide a minimal level of protection, connections are only permitted from machines which are listed on a *host access list*. This is adequate on single-user workstations but obviously breaks down on machines running more than one server.

In X11R4, per-user control was added with the **MIT-MAGIC-COOKIE-1 MIT-MAGIC-COOKIE-1** is not too secure, however, because it passes its secret key ("cookie") between client and server without encryption.

X11R5 defines, and the MIT release implements, two new mechanisms that can be used for secure access control. **XDM-AUTHORIZATION-1** is similar to **MIT-MAGIC-COOKIE-1**, but uses DES (Data Encryption Standard) encryption to encrypt the authorization data that is passed between client and server. To compile this authorization scheme, you need an implementation of DES in the file *mit/lib/Xdmcp/Wraphelp.c*. Due to U.S. export regulations, this file may not appear in your distribution. If you do not plan to export the file outside of the U.S., you may legally obtain it over the network from the X Consortium. Ftp to the host *export.lcs.mit.edu* and see the file *pub/R5/xdm-auth/README*. Outside the U.S. you may be able to obtain a compatible version of this file from the directory */pub/X11R5* on the machine *ftp.psy.uq.oz.au* (130.102.32.1). If you have this file, but this security mechanism is not automatically built on your system, you can add the following line to the file *mit/config/site.def* before building X11R5:

    #define HasXdmAuth YES

The other R5 authorization mechanism is named **SUN-DES-1**, and is based on the public key Sun Secure RPC system included with recent version of SunOS. If your system provides this secure RPC system, then the *.cf* file for your system in *mit/config* should define the variable **HasSecureRPC**, which will cause this security mechanism to be automatically built. The forthcoming (late 1992) *X Window System Administrator's Guide* from O'Reilly & Associates explains the issues of X security and these X11R5 security mechanisms in detail.

15.3.1 The Host Access List

The initial access control list is read at startup and reset time. The initial set of hosts allowed to open connections consists of:

- The host the window system is running on.

- On UNIX-based systems, each host listed in the */etc/X?.hosts* file, where *?* indicates the number of the server (the number between : and . in the *display_name* argument to **XOpenDisplay()** that would connect to the server). This file should consist of host names separated by newlines. DECnet nodes must terminate in "::" to distinguish them from Internet hosts.

If a host is not in the access control list when the access control mechanism is enabled and the host attempts to establish a connection, the server refuses the connection.

You can add, get, or remove hosts with **XAddHost( )**, **XAddHosts( )**, **XListHosts( )**, **XRemoveHost( )**, and **XRemoveHosts( )**. All the host access control functions use the **XHostAddress** structure. The members in this structure are:

family   Specifies which address family to use (for example, TCP/IP or DECnet). The family symbols **FamilyInternet**, **FamilyDECnet**, and **Family-Chaos** are defined in *<X11/X.h>*.

length   Specifies the length of the address in bytes.

address   Specifies a pointer to the address.

Example 15-3. The XHostAddress structure

```
typedef struct {
        int family;        /* For example FamilyInternet */
        int length;        /* Length of address, in bytes */
        char *address;     /* Pointer to where to find the bytes */
} XHostAddress;
```

For these functions to execute successfully, the client application must run on the same host as the X server and must have permission in the initial authorization at connection setup before calling these functions.

15.3.2 Enabling and Disabling Access Control

Normally the access control list determines whether a client succeeds in connecting to the server. Sometimes it is more convenient (though less safe) to allow a client or *any* host to have access. In this case, a client running on the same host as the server can call **XDisableAccessControl( )**. Thereafter, the host access list will no longer be used to filter connection requests. To reset the server to its default condition with access control, use **XEnableAccessControl( )**. **XSetAccessControl( )** performs either of these functions according to a flag.

15.4 Getting the Window Hierarchy

XQueryTree() lets you get the IDs of the windows in any portion of the window hierarchy with a single call. This is the only way to find out the IDs of windows created by other clients. XQueryTree() gets the root window ID, the parent window ID, and the list of child window IDs given a window. It also returns the number of children.

One possible use of XQueryTree() is to find out whether your application's top-level window has been reparented by the window manager, and it returns the ID of the new parent.

15.5 Close Down Mode

Normally all resources associated with a client will be destroyed when the connection between the client and the server closes. This can happen without prior warning to either the server or the client when, for example, the network cable is accidentally pulled out of one of the machines or the machine running the server crashes. Therefore, robust applications need a way of recovering from that occurrence. XSetCloseDownMode() helps implement one method of recovery.

Clients in the default DestroyAll close down mode will have all their resources killed when the connection to the server dies. XSetCloseDownMode() can set two other modes, RetainPermanent and RetainTemporary, which allow client resources to live on for a time. A client may want its resources to live on to assist in the process of recovering from a broken connection with the server, usually caused by a network failure. When next run after the problem has been corrected, the application could somehow determine which resources were its own and continue operating where it left off. The "somehow" is the crux of the problem. The only way we can think of to allow the client to find out the IDs of its resources after the client is resurrected is for the client to save all the resource IDs in a file (or perhaps in a property, but this would not survive a server crash) immediately after they are created. Then upon startup, it can read this information and see if the specified resources still exist. If they do, it can skip creating them.

A dying connection between the server and client raises other problems, too. Even if a client's resources are put on life support, there is no longer any "brain" behind them. The user's instructions will go unanswered, and there will be no visible warning on the screen that the client is no longer connected. The window manager or some other program, if running on the same machine as the server, could conceivably detect this situation and print a message. However, this kind of functionality in a window manager has not been demonstrated up to now. Otherwise, the user can only be warned that the connection could die and that this would cause the window to freeze (if the client's resources were preserved; the window would disappear if the close down mode had not been set). The user could then restart the client from an *xterm* window to reactivate the window.

XKillClient() can kill resources that remain alive after the connection closes. It can kill resources associated with a single client by specifying any resource ID associated with that client, or it can kill all resources of all clients that terminated with mode RetainTemporary if given the argument AllTemporary. XKillClient() might be used by the window manager or conceivably by a separate client to save space in the server by cleaning up resources after clients die that have requested that their resources be kept alive. This should not be done unless the user agrees with it, because it could upset an application's attempt to recover from a broken connection with the server.

15.6 Connection Close Operations

When the connection between the X server and a client is closed, either by a call to `XCloseDisplay()` or by an exiting process, the X server performs these automatic operations:

- Disowns all selections made by the program.

- Releases all passive grabs made by the program.

- Performs an `XUngrabPointer()` and `XUngrabKeyboard()` if the client application had actively grabbed the pointer or the keyboard.

- Performs an `XUngrabServer()` if the client had grabbed the server.

- Marks all resources (including colormap entries) allocated by the client application as permanent or temporary, according to whether the close down mode is `Retain-Permanent` or `RetainTemporary` (see Section 15.5).

The X server performs these operations when the close down mode is `DestroyAll`:

- The *save-set* is a list of other client's windows, referred to as save-set windows (see Section 16.4 for a complete description of save-sets). If any window in the client's save-set is an inferior of a window created by the client, the X server reparents the save-set window to the closest ancestor so that the save-set window is not an inferior of a window created by the client.

- Performs an `XMapWindow()` request on the save-set window if the save-set window is unmapped. The X server does this even if the save-set window was not an inferior of a window created by the client.

- Destroys all windows created by the client, after examining each window in the client's save-set.

- Performs the appropriate free request on all nonwindow resources (`Bitmap`, `Colormap`, `Cursor`, `Font`, `GC`, and `Pixmap`) created by the client.

Additional processing occurs when the *last* connection to the X server closes with close down mode `DestroyAll`. The X server:

- Resets its state, as if it had just been started. The X server destroys all lingering resources from clients that have terminated in `RetainPermanent` or `RetainTemporary` mode.

- Deletes all but the predefined atom IDs.

- Deletes all properties on all root windows.

- Resets all device attributes (key click, bell volume, acceleration) and the access control list.

- Restores the standard root tiles, cursors, default pointing device, and default font path.

- Restores the keyboard focus to `PointerRoot`.

15.7 Data Management

Xlib provides two ways to help you manage data within an application: the context manager and association tables. The former saves you the trouble of creating arrays and dynamically allocating memory for data to be used only within your application. The latter is a different way of doing the same thing, maintained for backwards compatibility with X10. We will describe only the context manager. If you are interested in investigating association tables, see Appendix B, *X10 Compatibility*.

15.7.1 The Context Manager

Four routines are provided to let you associate data with a window locally in Xlib, rather than in the server as in properties. The context manager routines store and retrieve untyped data according to the display, a window ID, and an assigned context ID. The display argument to the context manager routine (returned from `XOpenDisplay()`) is used as an additional dimension to the array, not as a pointer to the display structure. No requests to the server are made.

First, you call `XUniqueContext()` to obtain an ID for a particular type of information you want to assign to windows. `XUniqueContext()` just provides a unique integer ID every time you call it (you can also make up your own if you wish). This ID indicates to the application what type of information is stored, but none of the calls require you to specify the data type. Then use `XSaveContext()` to store information into the context manager and `XFindContext()` to read it. If you plan to rewrite a particular piece of data corresponding to a window ID and context ID, it is better in terms of time and space to erase the current entry with `XDeleteContext()` before calling `XSaveContext()` again. `XDelete-Context()` does not make the context ID invalid.

If you have many different pieces of data of the same type, such as an array, that must be associated with each window, you have the option of packing it in a single chunk of data and storing it by context or creating a different context ID for each member of the array. The context ID indicates the *meaning* of the data (how you interpret it), not necessarily the C language type.

15.8 The After Function

Every Xlib function that generates a protocol request calls an *after function* just before it returns. This function is normally **NoOp**, but the program may specify the name of any function using **XSetAfterFunction()**.

15.9 Coordinate Transformation

XTranslateCoordinates() translates coordinates relative to one window into the coordinates relative to a second and determines whether the resulting position relative to the second window is in a subwindow of the second window.

Because the window-based coordinate system is so convenient, this function is rarely needed. Since **XTranslateCoordinates()** makes a round-trip request, it cannot be used heavily to port to X programs that use global coordinates.

15.10 ANSI-C and POSIX Portability

The MIT Release 5 X distribution is compliant with ANSI-C and POSIX standards, and portable across a wide variety of platforms. While the goal of the ANSI-C and POSIX standards is portability, many systems do not implement these standards, or do not implement them fully, so the MIT R5 distribution defines new header files that attempt to mask the differences between systems. The header files are *<X11/Xfuncproto.h>*, *<X11/Xfuncs.h>*, *<X11/Xosdefs.h>*, and *<X11/Xos.h>*. None of these files are part of the official R5 standard, so they may not be shipped with your system. But they can be very useful in writing portable applications, so we have included them with the code from this book, which you can get as described in the *Preface*.*

15.10.1 <X11/Xosdefs.h>

The file *<X11/Xosdefs.h>* defines symbols that describe a system's support for ANSI-C and POSIX. Symbols that describe a system's support for other standards may be added in the future. It defines two new symbols, **X_NOT_STDC_ENV** and **X_NOT_POSIX**, for systems that do not have the ANSI-C and POSIX header files, respectively. When standard header files exist, your code should include them. On systems which do not have them, however, attempting to include them would cause a compilation error. The symbols in *<X11/Xosdefs.h>* allow you to write code that takes the right action in either situation. Note that **X_NOT_STDC_ENV** is different from **__STDC__**, which simply indicates whether or not the compiler supports ANSI-C.

---

*The sections below have been adapted from the X Consortium R5 Release Notes.

An example of using X_NOT_STDC_ENV might be to know when the system declares getenv:

```
#ifndef X_NOT_STDC_ENV
#include <stdlib.h>
#else
extern char *getenv();
#endif
```

It is convention in the R5 code from MIT is to put the standard case first using #ifndef.

Lack of the symbol X_NOT_STDC_ENV does *not* mean that the system has <stdarg.h>. This header file is part of ANSI-C, but the X Consortium found it more useful to check for it separately because many systems have all the ANSI-C files except this one. The symbol __STDC__ is used to control inclusion of this file.

X_NOT_POSIX means the system does not have POSIX.1 header files. Lack of this symbol does *not* mean that the POSIX environment is the default. You may still have to define _POSIX_SOURCE before including the header file to get POSIX definitions.

An example of using X_NOT_POSIX might be to determine what return type would be declared for getuid in <*pwd.h*>:

```
#include <pwd.h>
#ifndef X_NOT_POSIX
    uid_t uid;
#else
    int uid;
    extern int getuid();
#endif
    uid = getuid();
```

Note that both X_NOT_STDC_ENV and X_NOT_POSIX, when declared, state a noncompliance. This was chosen so that porting to a new, standard platform would be easier. Only non-standard platforms need to add themselves to <*X11/Xosdefs.h*> to turn on the appropriate symbols.

Not all systems for which the X Consortium leaves these symbols undefined strictly adhere to the relevant standards. Thus you will sometimes see checks for a specific operating system near a check for one of the *Xosdefs.h* symbols. The X Consortium found it most useful to label systems as conforming even if they had some holes in their compliance. Presumably these holes will become fewer as time goes on.

<*X11/Xosdefs.h*> is automatically included by the header <*X11/Xos.h*>.

5.10.2 <X11/Xos.h>

This header file portably defines some of the most commonly used operating system and C library functions, and masks some of the most common system incompatibilities. It should be used instead of <*string.h*>, <*strings.h*>, <*sys/types.h*>, <*sys/file.h*>, <*fcntl.h*>, <*sys/time.h*>, and <*unistd.h*>. Most of these are POSIX standard header files, but are not yet universal. <*X11/Xos.h*> defines any of the four functions index, rindex, strchr, and

strrchr, which are not defined by the host operating system. It defines **gettimeofday** and **time** as well as all the standard string functions. It also defines the type **caddr_t**, and the constants used by the **open** system call (O_RDONLY, O_RDWR, etc.) and the constants used by the **fcntl** system call (R_OK, W_OK, etc.).

Unfortunately, there is not a header file for declaring **malloc** correctly, and it can be a bit tricky. The MIT R5 distribution uses lines like the following (from *mit/lib/Xt/Alloc.c*) to declare **malloc** and related functions:

```
#ifndef X_NOT_STDC_ENV
#include <stdlib.h>
#else
    char *malloc(), *realloc(), *calloc();
#endif
#if defined(macII) && !defined(__STDC__)
    char *malloc(), *realloc(), *calloc();
#endif /* macII */
```

Note that because **index** may be a macro declared in this header, you should be sure to avoid this identifier in variable and structure field names.

15.10.3 <X11/Xfuncs.h>

This new header file provides definitions for the BSD functions **bcopy**, **bzero**, and **bcmp**. These are not standard functions, but are widely used in the X source code. Including this header file allows them to be used portably.

15.10.4 <X11/Xfuncproto.h>

This file contains definitions for writing function declarations in a way that is portable between ANSI-C compilers that support function prototypes and pre-ANSI-C compilers that do not support or only partially support function prototypes.

For external header files that might get used from C++, you should wrap all of your function declarations like this:

```
_XFUNCPROTOBEGIN...
...function declarations...
_XFUNCPROTOEND...
```

When in doubt, assume that the header file might get used from C++.

A typical function declaration uses **NeedFunctionPrototypes**, like this:

```
extern Atom XInternAtom(
#if NeedFunctionPrototypes
        Display*                /* display */,
        _Xconst char*           /* atom_name */,
        Bool                    /* only_if_exists */
#endif
);
```

If there are const parameters,* use the symbol _Xconst instead, as above. This symbol will be defined only if the compiler supports const parameters. If it is plausible to pass a string constant to a char* parameter, then it is a good idea to declare the parameter with _Xconst, so that literals can be passed in C++.

If there are nested function prototypes, use NeedNestedPrototypes:

```
extern Bool XCheckIfEvent(
#if NeedFunctionPrototypes
        Display*                /* display */,
        XEvent*                 /* event_return */,
        Bool (*) (
#if NeedNestedPrototypes
        Display*                /* display */,
        XEvent*                 /* event */,
        XPointer                /* arg */
#endif
        )                       /* predicate */,
        XPointer                /* arg */
#endif
);
```

If there is a variable argument list, use NeedVarargsPrototypes:

```
extern char *XGetIMValues(
#if NeedVarargsPrototypes
    XIM /* im */, ...
#endif
);
```

If you have parameter types in library functions that will widen (be silently cast to a larger type) in traditional C, then you should use NeedWidePrototypes so that functions compiled with an ANSI-C compiler may be called from code compiled with a traditional C compiler, and vice versa.

```
extern XModifierKeymap *XDeleteModifiermapEntry(
#if NeedFunctionPrototypes
    XModifierKeymap*     /* modmap */,
#if NeedWidePrototypes
    unsigned int         /* keycode_entry */,
#else
    KeyCode              /* keycode_entry */,
#endif
    int                  /* modifier */
#endif
);
```

If you use _Xconst, NeedNestedPrototypes, NeedVarargsPrototypes, or NeedWidePrototypes, then your function implementation also has to have a function prototype. For example:

---

*The const keyword is new in ANSI-C. It indicates that a particular variable or function argument will not be changed. A compiler may be able to perform special optimizations on const parameters.

```
#if NeedFunctionPrototypes
Atom XInternAtom (
    Display *dpy,
    _Xconst char *name,
    Bool onlyIfExists)
#else
Atom XInternAtom (dpy, name, onlyIfExists)
    Display *dpy;
    char *name;
    Bool onlyIfExists;
#endif
{
    ...
}
```

Actually, whenever you use a function prototype in a header file, you should use a function prototype in the implementation, as required by ANSI-C.

15.10.5 Other Symbols

Do not use the names **class**, **new**, or **index** as variables or structure members. The names **class** and **new** are reserved words in C++, and you may find your header files used by a C++ program someday. Depending on the system, **index** can be defined as a macro in *<X11/Xos.h>*; this rules out any other use of that name.

The following system-specific symbols are commonly used in X sources where OS dependencies intrude:

    USG   Based on System V Release 2.
    SYSV   Based on System V Release 3.
    SVR4   System V Release 4.

For other system-specific symbols, look at the **StandardDefines** parameters in the *mit/config/*.cf* files.

15.11 Porting Programs to X

Any program that runs on an ASCII terminal can be run directly under the terminal emulator *xterm*. The only problem is how to deal with changing the size of the window while the application is running. The application may read the termcap definition to determine the original window size. Look at the X application *resize*, which makes changes to TERMCAP. The *resize* reference page (see Volume Three, *X Window System User's Guide*) suggests a couple of C shell aliases for commands to resize *xterm* windows.

If you have a Berkeley 4.3-compatible tty driver, *xterm* sets the tty driver's row and column attributes when its top-level window is resized. *vi* and *more* and several other programs also look at those attributes when figuring out the terminal size. Also, *xterm* will send a SIGWINCH signal to the controlling process, which, if it is *vi* or *more*, will understand this signal and change its own notion of screen size, repainting the window in the process. This is the best way to deal with window resizing under *xterm*.

Graphics programs face a more difficult porting path. They must be rewritten to use the X library. It is a good idea to use a toolkit rather than trying to write completely in Xlib.

Programs written for single-user systems such as PCs will be a little more difficult, since they must be converted to respond to events instead of asking for one type of input at a time. They must also be modified to work in a multitasking environment.

Byte order is another traditionally thorny issue in porting. Byte order refers to the order in which bytes of data are stored in memory. There are actually four ways for two-byte data to be ordered, since the direction of each byte has two variations and the position of the most significant byte is also variable.

For X pixmaps, byte order is defined by the server and clients with different native byte ordering must swap bytes as necessary. For all other parts of the protocol, the byte order is defined by the client and the server swaps bytes as necessary.

15.12 Programming for Multiple X Releases

In R5 and later, Xlib defines the symbol `XlibSpecificationRelease` with the release number as the value (i.e., 5). This can be used to allow an application to successfully compile with more than one release of Xlib (assuming of course it depends only on features present in the releases which it will be compiled). Example 15-4 shows a code segment into which R4, R5 and R6 code could be inserted:

Example 15-4. Using the XlibSpecificationRelease symbol

```
#ifdef XlibSpecificationRelease
    if (XlibSpecificationRelease == 5)
        ;/* R5 */
    else if (XlibSpecificationRelease == 6)
        ;/* R6 */
    else
        ;/* R7 or error */
#elseif
    /* R4 */
#endif
```

15.13 Using Extensions to X

An extension is a set of routines and capabilities that a hardware vendor has provided for use on a particular machine, in addition to the standard X library.

Extensions to X are not second-class citizens, and there should be very little to distinguish the use of an extension from that of the core protocol. The only difference is that the application should check to make sure the extension exists and then query the extension to find out the major opcode, additional event types, and additional error types so that the extension can be integrated properly. If the extensions have been written properly so that they initialize themselves when first called, they should be usable just like other X library functions.

`XListExtensions()` returns a list of all extensions supported by the server. Once the name of the desired extension is known, `XQueryExtension()` should be called to get specific information about the extension. `XFreeExtensionList()` should then be used to free the memory allocated by `XListExtensions()`.

The standard extensions as of this writing are the Shape extension, which supports non-rectangular windows, the X Input extension, which supports input devices other than the single mouse and keyboard normally connected to an X server, and PEX, a 3-D graphics extension. All extensions are optional, however. Only the Shape extension is available in virtually all X servers as of this writing.

16

Window Management

X programs may be expected to cooperate with any one of a number of different window managers. This chapter discusses the design of a simple window manager, not so you will be able to write one but so you will know what to expect from one. As it turns out, some of the techniques used in this program (such as menus) could be adapted for other clients as well. Everyone should at least look through this chapter.

In This Chapter:

16
Window Management

A window manager is a program implemented with Xlib to control the layout of windows on the screen, responding to user requests to move, resize, raise, lower, or iconify windows. The window manager may also enforce a policy for window layout (such as mandating a standard window or icon size and placement) and provide a menu for commonly used shell commands.

This chapter is not primarily for window manager writers, as these are a rare breed. There are several good customizable window managers available, and there is very little reason for users or application writers to want to write their own. Only a few people in the X community are going to be actively involved in writing window managers, and chances are good they will already know all of what is described here. This chapter is presented for two reasons: so that application writers will get a better understanding of how to cooperate with the window manager, and so we can describe and demonstrate the Xlib routines that are provided mainly for the purpose of window management. As it turns out, the examples in this chapter also have elements (such as menus) that could be useful in ordinary applications as well.

We'll begin by describing the features and routines in Xlib that are provided mainly to give window managers the authority they need to control window layout and the flexibility to provide a good user interface. These features include the following:

- Substructure redirection, which allows the window manager to intercept requests to change the screen layout. This enables a window manager to enforce a window layout policy.

- Reparenting, which lets the window manager build a frame or other "decoration" around each top-level window. The frame could possibly contain boxes which could be used to move or resize the window.

- The save-set, which ensures that the windows the window manager iconifies or reparents are returned to their original state if the window manager dies unexpectedly.

Then we'll describe what the window manager can do with the properties set by clients, building on the description of interclient communication presented in Chapter 12, *Interclient Communication*.

Finally, we'll describe a simple window manager program. You should find this program helpful not only in demonstrating window management techniques but also for showing Xlib programming in a more complex setting than *basicwin* in Chapter 3, *Basic Window Program*, or *basecalc* in Chapter 14, *A Complete Application*. You should understand both those programs before tackling this one.

16.1 Layout Policy

A window manager may have a policy on how top-level windows will be placed on the screen.

The standard window managers *uwm* and *twm* do not have a window layout policy, but some existing window managers do. For example, the Siemens RTL Tiled window manager mandates that only temporary pop-up windows can overlap. That policy makes exposure a rare occurrence but makes resizing much more common. A second simpler example is the window manager designed by Stellar Computer for its high performance workstations. The Stellar window manager aligns icons along the top edge of the screen, along with the Stellar logo. Since the window manager creates the icons or is passed their IDs through hints, it can distinguish them from other windows on the screen.

Within its window layout policy, the window manager should honor the window size and position hints returned by `XGetNormalHints()` and `XGetWMHints()` as closely as possible (each application sets these hints). Under *uwm* and *twm*, the user selects the size of a newly created window by moving a flashing outline of a window. The size hints provided by the application determine the minimum dimensions, maximum dimensions, and desired increment for the window size, and these are indicated in the motion of the outline. For example, in both *uwm* and *twm*, the minimum size hints take priority over the user's input, so that the user cannot resize the window smaller than the minimum size.

Applications are free to resize or move the children of their top-level windows as necessary. The window manager has no control over these windows.

16.2 Substructure Redirection

The window manager enforces its window layout policy using substructure redirection. When the window manager selects `SubstructureRedirectMask` on the root window, an attempt by any other client to change the configuration of any child of the root window will fail. Instead an event describing the layout change request will be sent to the window manager. The window manager then reads the event and determines whether to honor the request, modify it, or deny it completely. If it decides to honor the request, it calls the routine that the client called that triggered the event with the same arguments. If it decides to modify the request, it calls the same routine but with modified arguments.

The *structure*, as the term is used here, is the location, size, stacking order, border width, and mapping status of a window. The *substructure* is all these statistics about the children of a particular window. This is the complete set of information about screen layout that the window manager might need in order to implement its policy. *Redirection* means that an event is sent to the client selecting redirection (usually the window manager), and the original structure-changing request is not executed.

The events that are selected by `SubstructureRedirectMask` and the routines that are intercepted are as follows:

- `CirculateRequest` events report when an Xlib function, such as `XCirculate-Subwindows()`, `XCirculateSubwindowsDown()`, `XCirculate-SubwindowsUp()`, or `XRestackWindows()`, is called to change the stacking order of a group of children.

- `ConfigureRequest` events report when an Xlib function, such as `XConfigure-Window()`, `XLowerWindow()`, `XMoveResizeWindow()`, `XMoveWindow()`, `XRaiseWindow()`, `XResizeWindow()`, or `XSetWindowBorderWidth()`, is called to resize, move, restack, or change the border width of a window.

- `MapRequest` events report when `XMapWindow()` or `XMapSubwindows()` is called to map a window.

When `SubstructureRedirectMask` is selected on the root window, the only time that a configuration request on a child of the root window is not intercepted is when the `override_redirect` attribute of that child window has been set to `True`. This is intended for temporary pop-up windows that should not be reparented or affected by the window manager's layout policy.

Only one window manager at a time can select `SubstructureRedirectMask` or `ResizeRedirectMask` on a particular window.

`ResizeRedirectMask` also selects `ConfigureRequest` events when a client has called `XConfigureWindow()`, `XMoveResizeWindow()`, or `XResizeWindow()`. However, if any client has selected `SubstructureRedirectMask` on the parent of the window for which `ResizeRedirectMask` is selected, the `Substructure-RedirectMask` takes precedence.

Substructure redirect allows the window manager to separate the portion of itself that moves and resizes windows from the portion that enforces window policy. While the window reconfiguration section is driven by user events, the policy section can be completely driven from the `*Request` events that signal that the user has proposed a change to the window layout. And since applications will only attempt to resize or move their top-level windows in direct response to a user request, those requests are just as valid as the ones from the window reconfiguration section of the window manager.

16.3 Reparenting

A window manager can decorate windows on the screen with titlebars and place little boxes on the titlebar with which the window can be moved or resized. This is only one possibility, modeled on the user interface on the Macintosh™.

To do this, the window manager creates a child of the root somewhat larger than the top-level window of the application. Then it calls `XReparentWindow()`, specifying the top-level window of the application as *win* and the new parent as *parent*. *win* and all its descendants will then be descendants of *parent*.

In the area where the new parent is visible around the top-level window of the application, the window manager can put anything it wants. This could include text, graphics, and small windows which perform certain functions when a button is clicked in them.

The window manager can decorate all top-level windows, but it will normally ignore windows that are mapped with their `override_redirect` attribute set, since no `*Request` events will be generated for them. The window manager may also decorate differently windows that have set the `XA_WM_TRANSIENT_FOR` property and apply its window layout policy to them. The window manager calls `XGetTransientForHint()` for each window to get this property.

By the way, it is impossible (except by luck) for the window manager to match the colors of the decoration to the colors of the window it is decorating. A window manager cannot find out what colors a window uses for its border or background because these window attributes cannot be queried.

16.3.1 Shadows

Window shadows can be imperfectly implemented by reparenting top-level windows. The shadow would appear to be the same size as the corresponding window but slightly offset diagonally (see Figure 16-1).

What happens if we try to accomplish the following style of background with two windows: one `InputOutput` window slightly larger in both dimensions than the application's top-level window, and one `InputOutput` shadow window the same size as the application window, offset into the corner of the `InputOnly` window?* The larger window would have its `background_pixmap` attribute set to `ParentRelative` so that it looked invisible, and the smaller window would have its background set to black or gray to make the shadow. Figure 16-2 shows how the layers are lined up.

When the window with the shadow is moved around the screen when no other applications are on the screen, the shadow looks good. But when the window is moved over other applications, a strange thing happens. The background of the root window shows itself in the "invisible" corner of the shadow, as shown in Figure 16-3, later in this chapter.

---

*See Section 2.4.3 for a description of the characteristics of `InputOnly` windows.

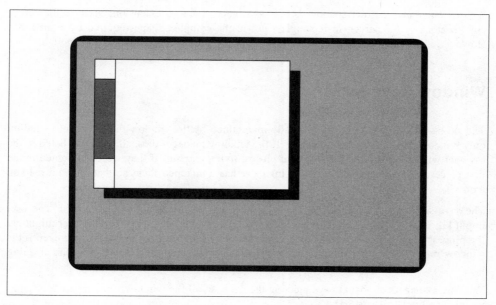

Figure 16-1. Goal of background shadow

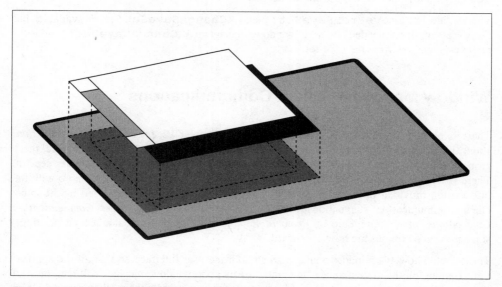

Figure 16-2. Window layering for background shadow

It turns out that a perfect shadow is not possible without an extension, because the server clips regions of the screen in rectangles, not in the complex shape required by a shadow.* However, if the shadow is only two pixels wide, this approach might look good enough.

16.4 Window Save-set

The save-set is a list of windows, usually maintained by the window manager, but including only windows created by other clients. If the window manager dies, all windows listed in the save-set will be reparented back to their closest living ancestor if they were reparented in the first place and mapped if the window manager has unmapped them so that it could map an icon.

The save-set is necessary because the window manager might not exit normally. The user might kill it with CTRL-C if it is running in the foreground, or more likely, the user might get the process number and kill it. Actually, the actions of the save-set are performed even if the window manager exits normally, so less code is needed since the save-set does the cleaning up.

Window managers almost always place in the save-set all the windows they reparent or iconify, using XAddToSaveSet().

Windows are automatically removed from the save-set when they are destroyed. If this were not the case, the window manager would have to monitor DestroyNotify events and explicitly remove the windows from the save-set.

The routines XRemoveFromSaveSet() and XChangeSaveSet() are available, but they are not often needed even in window managers. XChangeSaveSet() adds or removes a window from the save-set.

16.5 Window Manager – Client Communications

There is no point in reiterating all that was said in Chapter 12, *Interclient Communication*, about the properties that applications set for the window manager. As described there, these properties are hints that the window manager may use or ignore as the programmer sees fit. There is a large amount of flexibility and variety in what window managers can do with the information provided in these hints. Its actions are to some extent constrained by the interclient communication conventions described in Appendix L, *Interclient Communication Conventions*, of Volume Zero, *X Protocol Reference Manual* (as of the second printing), since these conventions are now a standard.

These hints allow the window manager to smooth the user interface so that all the applications running on the system appear integrated. Any good window manager will read most, if not all, of the properties described in this section and try to do with them what is most helpful to applications and users..

---

*The Shape extension supports nonrectangular windows.

16.5.1 Reading the Hints

Hints help the window manager conform to the needs of the application while at the same time letting it control window layout and policy. The window manager gets the hints with the routines shown in Table 16-1.

Table 16-1. Window Manager Hints

Hint	Set (by Application)	Get (by Window Manager)
Window Name	XSetWMName()	XGetWMName()
Icon Name	XSetWMIconName()	XGetWMIconName()
Shell Command and Arguments	XSetCommand()	XGetCommand()
Icon Pixmap	XSetWMProperties() or XSetWMNormalHints()	XGetWMNormalHints()
Normal Size Hints	XSetWMNormalHints()	XGetWMNormalHints()
WM Hints	XSetWMHints()	XGetWMHints()
Transient Window	XSetTransientForHint()	XGetTransientForHint()
Class Hint	XSetClassHint()	XGetClassHint()
Client Machine	XSetWMClientMachine()	XGetWMClientMachine()
WM Protocols	XSetWMProtocols()	XGetWMProtocols()

16.5.2 Setting Icon Sizes

The icon size property is the only hint that the window manager should set for applications to read. The window manager may prefer particular sizes of icons to yield a consistent appearance for all icons on the screen. The window manager calls **XSetIconSizes()** (which sets the **XA_WM_ICON_SIZE** property on the root window), indicating the preferred sizes. The icon size hints include maximum and minimum dimensions and size increments. Once standard window managers evolve that set this property (*twm* does not), applications may have one icon pixmap prepared for each standard window manager.

16.5.3 Window Manager Protocols

As described in Section 12.3.3.2, the client can express interest in certain window manager actions by calling **XSetWMProtocols()**, which sets a property. The window manager calls **XSetWMProtocols()** to get the property. Thereafter, the window manager can send the client **ClientMessage** events to notify the client of imminent window manager actions. At this writing, the protocols notify the client of a change in the keyboard focus, an application about to be killed, or a top-level window about to be destroyed. See Section 12.3.3.2 for the current list of window manager protocols, their meanings, and the values to set into the `ClientMessage` event.

16.6 Window Management Functions

The functions described in this section are used primarily by the window manager on top-level windows. Applications can also use them on their top-level windows; conventions for doing so are described in Appendix L, *Interclient Communication Conventions*, of Volume Zero, *X Protocol Reference Manual* (as of the second printing). Applications can use these routines freely on their subwindows.

`XConfigureWindow()` is the most general routine for changing the configuration of a window, namely its size, position, border width, and stacking position.

The routines to move and resize windows are `XMoveWindow()`, `XMoveResize-Window()`, and `XResizeWindow()`. The routine to change the border width of a window is `XSetWindowBorderWidth()`.

Quite a variety of routines are provided to change the stacking order of windows. These operations affect only a single group of siblings. Furthermore, they affect only overlapping siblings. If any of the siblings specified do not overlap, their stacking order is not changed.

`XCirculateSubwindowsDown()`
> Moves the lowest mapped sibling to the top of the stacking order.

`XCirculateSubwindowsUp()`
> Moves the highest mapped sibling to the bottom of the stacking order.

`XCirculateSubwindows()`
> Performs either `XCirculateSubwindowsDown()` or `XCirculate-SubwindowsUp()` according to a flag.

`XRestackWindows()`
> Specifies a list of siblings in the desired stacking order.

`XRaiseWindow()`
> Moves a window to the top of the stacking order among its siblings.

`XMapRaised()`
> Maps a window, placing it on top of the stacking order of its siblings. For a window mapped for the first time, this is equivalent to `XMapWindow()`. But when an already mapped window is unmapped, it retains its stacking order when mapped again with `XMapWindow()`.

`XLowerWindow()`
> Moves a window to the bottom of the stacking order among its siblings.

```
XConfigureWindow()
```
Restacks the window according to a **stack_mode** and relative to a particular sibling. This function is also capable of moving, resizing, and changing the border width of a window.

All these functions have the ability to change the screen layout and therefore can be monitored and intercepted by the window manager. They are also commonly used by the window manager itself to allow the user to change the screen layout.

The **stack_mode** of the **XConfigureWindow()** routine has five possible values: **Above**, **Below**, **BottomIf**, **TopIf**, and **Opposite**. If the window is simultaneously being moved or resized, this calculation is performed with respect to the window's final size and position, not its initial position. If a sibling and a **stack_mode** are specified, the window is restacked as described in Table 16-2.

Table 16-2. Meaning of Stacking Mode with Sibling Specified

Window Stack Mode	Description
Above	Window is placed just above sibling.
Below	Window is placed just below sibling.
TopIf	If sibling obscures window, then window is placed at the top of the stack.
BottomIf	If window obscures sibling, then window is placed at the bottom of the stack.
Opposite	If any sibling occludes window, then window is placed at the top of the stack, else if window occludes any sibling, then window is placed at the bottom of the stack.

If a **stack_mode** is specified but no sibling is specified, the window is restacked as described in Table 16-3.

Table 16-3. Meaning of Stacking Mode without Sibling

Window Stack Mode	Description
Above	Window is placed at the top of the stack.
Below	Window is placed at the bottom of the stack.
TopIf	If any sibling obscures window, then window is placed at the top of the stack.
BottomIf	If window obscures any sibling, then window is placed at the bottom of the stack.
Opposite	If any sibling occludes window, then window is placed at the top of the stack, else if window occludes any sibling, then window is placed at the bottom of the stack.

Another set of routines that are usually only used by the window manager are the ones that grab and ungrab the server. `XGrabServer()` and `XUngrabServer()` are used when a program requires total control of the screen, so that output requests from other programs are queued but not displayed. One application of grabbing is to draw temporary moving objects on the screen, such as the outline of a window being moved. This is called *rubber-banding*. The outline (or grid) is drawn with logical function `GXxor`, which, when drawn twice, leaves the screen as it was initially. If the server were not grabbed in between the first drawing and the second of the same line, some other program might update the same part of the display, resulting in glitches after the second drawing. This server grab also speeds up the rubber-banding, because the server stops performing updates to other windows.

16.7 A Basic Window Manager

This section describes the design of a simple window manager called *winman*. This example window manager should be helpful in several ways. It demonstrates many of the Xlib routines that are intended to be used only by window managers. It also shows what a window manager might do with the properties that applications set and how window managers implement icons. This window manager also demonstrates the use of the save-set to make sure that, if it dies, the windows it has iconified will be restored. It does not, however, demonstrate substructure redirection or reparenting. See the code for *twm* for examples of substructure redirection and reparenting.

The *winman* program also demonstrates some techniques that may be helpful in ordinary applications, such as how to implement a menu using Xlib. (Most applications will ultimately do this with a toolkit.)

If you have the example programs from O'Reilly and Associates, you can compile and run *winman* to see how it works (how to get this code is described in the *Preface*). Be sure to stop or kill any other window managers running before running *winman*. Both *winman* and the other window manager may get confused because they are not designed to cooperate with each other. The following explanations will be easier to follow if you have used the program.

16.7.1 Operation of the Program

The *winman* program creates a menu composed of horizontal bars and places it in the upper-right corner of the screen, as shown in Figure 16-4.

The menu provides a number of basic functions for manipulating windows on the screen:

Raise   Brings a window to the top of the stack, so that it is fully visible.

Lower   Lowers a window to the bottom so that the area formerly hidden is made visible.

Move   Changes the position of a window on the screen, and raises it.

Resize   Changes the size of a window, and raises it.

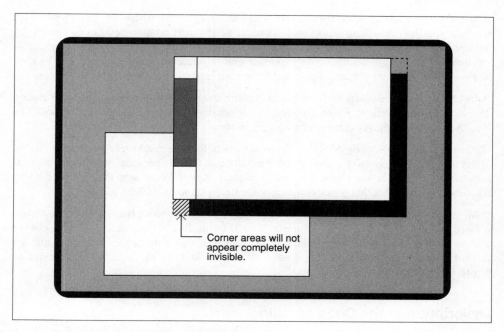

Figure 16-3. Actual effect of shadow attempt

`CirculateDn`	Moves the window on the bottom to the top.
`CirculateUp`	Moves the window on the top to the bottom.
`(De)Iconify`	Turns a window into a small marker window or vice versa.
`Keybrd Focus`	Assigns all keyboard input to the selected window, regardless of the position of the pointer.
`New Xterm`	Creates a new **xterm** window, and places it at the upper-left corner of the screen. You can subsequently move or resize the new window with the Move and Resize functions.
`Exit`	It is good practice for all programs to provide a way to quit. (*uwm* requires the user to look up the process number and kill the process.) Since this window manager is primarily for demonstration purposes, this choice is provided to make it easy to kill the program.

All input for the window manager is supplied through the pointer. A cursor (which tracks the pointer) is assigned to the menu to indicate that input in this area selects a menu item. Choices are made from the menu by pressing a pointer button in the appropriate region of the menu. When a menu choice is made, the menu bar and its label change to inverse video. In other words, everything that was black in the bar changes to white and vice versa (*winman* works in black and white on all systems, even those with color). After the choice is made but before the operation is complete, the pointer is grabbed, so that all pointer input is directed to the menu window independent of the position of the pointer. While the pointer is grabbed, *winman*'s cursor changes to a hand and tracks the pointer anywhere on the screen. This reminds you that the window manager is expecting the next pointer input even though the pointer is no longer on the menu. When the chosen operation is complete, the menu is returned to its initial condition, and the pointer grab is released. If this menu was to be used in a normal application, a passive grab would be used instead of the active one used here.

If CirculateDn, CirculateUp, or New Xterm is chosen, selection of a window is not necessary. The circulation operations act on all overlapping windows that are children of the root. The New Xterm choice simply creates a new *xterm* window.

If Raise, Lower, (De)Iconify or Kybrd Focus is chosen, the user must press a pointer button to select a window. (*winman*'s own menu cannot be iconified, because this would make it impossible to recover the window manager menu.) Kybrd Focus sets the keyboard focus window and highlights that window with a white background behind the window.

If Move or Resize is chosen, the user must press a pointer button on the window to be manipulated, drag the pointer with the button held until the outline of the window is in the chosen size or position, and then release the button. (*winman*'s own menu can be moved but not resized.) A moving outline of the window is used to indicate the intended dimensions or position of the window.

16.7.2 Description of the Code of main

Example 16-1 shows the `main` for the *winman* window manager. The `isIcon` routine that is called in `main` is described in Section 16.7.15 below. The `draw_box` routine, also called in `main`, is described in Section 16.7.13. All the rest of *winman*'s code is described in sections following `main`.

Instead of breaking up the code in little pieces as we have done in earlier examples, this time we'll show you `main` together in one place. By this point in the manual, you should know enough to understand most of this code. Any questions you may have should be answered by the description immediately following the code.

Example 16-1. winman — main C program

```
#include <X11/Xlib.h>
#include <X11/Xutil.h>
#include <X11/Xatom.h>
#include <X11/Xos.h>
#include <X11/cursorfont.h>

#include <stdio.h>
#include <signal.h>

#include "bitmaps/focus_frame_bi"      /* Name must be <= 14 chars
                                        * for sys V compatibility */

/* Include file for printing event types */
#include "eventnames.h"

#define MAX_CHOICE 10
#define DRAW 1
#define ERASE 0
```

Example 16-1. winman — main C program (continued)

```
#define RAISE 1
#define LOWER 0
#define MOVE 1
#define RESIZE 0
#define NONE 100
#define NOTDEFINED 0
#define BLACK  1
#define WHITE  0

Window focus_window;
Window inverted_pane = NONE;

static char *menu_label[ ] =
    {
    "Raise",
    "Lower",
    "Move",
    "Resize",
    "CirculateDn",
    "CirculateUp",
    "(De)Iconify",
    "Kybrd Focus",
    "New Xterm",
    "Exit",
    };


Display *display;
int screen_num;
XFontStruct *font_info;
char icon_name[ 50 ];

main()
{
    Window menuwin;
    Window panes[ MAX_CHOICE ];
    int menu_width, menu_height, x = 0, y = 0, border_width = 4;
    int winindex;
    int cursor_shape;
    Cursor cursor, hand_cursor;
    char *font_name = "9x15";
    int direction, ascent, descent;
    int char_count;
    char *string;
    XCharStruct overall;
    Bool owner_events;
    int pointer_mode;
    int keyboard_mode;
    Window confine_to;
    GC gc, rgc;
    int pane_height;
    Window assoc_win;
    XEvent event;
    unsigned int button;

    if ( (display=XOpenDisplay(NULL)) == NULL ) {
        (void) fprintf( stderr, "winman: cannot connect to \
                X server %s\n", XDisplayName(NULL));
```

Example 16-1. winman — main C program (continued)

```
        exit( -1 );
    }

    screen_num = DefaultScreen(display);

    /* Access font */
    font_info = XLoadQueryFont(display,font_name);

    if (font_info == NULL) {
        (void) fprintf( stderr, "winman: Cannot open font %s\n",
                font_name);
        exit( -1 );
    }

    string = menu_label[ 6 ];
    char_count = strlen(string);

    /* Determine the extent of each menu pane based on
     * the font size */
    XTextExtents(font_info, string, char_count, &direction, &ascent,
            &descent, &overall);

    menu_width = overall.width + 4;
    pane_height = overall.ascent + overall.descent + 4;
    menu_height = pane_height * MAX_CHOICE;

    /* Place the window in upper-right corner*/
    x = DisplayWidth(display,screen_num) - menu_width -
            (2*border_width);
    y = 0;    /* Appears at top */

    /* Create opaque window */
    menuwin = XCreateSimpleWindow(display, RootWindow(display,
            screen_num), x, y, menu_width, menu_height,
            border_width, BlackPixel(display,screen_num),
            WhitePixel(display,screen_num));

    /* Create the choice windows for the text */
    for (winindex = 0; winindex < MAX_CHOICE; winindex++) {
        panes[winindex] = XCreateSimpleWindow(display, menuwin, 0,
                menu_height/MAX_CHOICE*winindex, menu_width,
                pane_height, border_width = 1,
                BlackPixel(display,screen_num),
                WhitePixel(display,screen_num));
        XSelectInput(display, panes[winindex], ButtonPressMask
                | ButtonReleaseMask | ExposureMask);
    }

    XSelectInput(display, RootWindow(display, screen_num),
            SubstructureNotifyMask);

    /* These do not appear until parent (menuwin) is mapped */
    XMapSubwindows(display,menuwin);

    /* Create the cursor for the menu */
    cursor = XCreateFontCursor(display, XC_left_ptr);
    hand_cursor = XCreateFontCursor(display, XC_hand2);

    XDefineCursor(display, menuwin, cursor);

    focus_window = RootWindow(display, screen_num);
```

Example 16-1. winman — main C program (continued)

```
/* Create two graphics contexts for inverting panes (white
 * and black).  We invert the panes by changing the background
 * pixel, clearing the window, and using the GC with the
 * contrasting color to redraw the text.  Another way is using
 * XCopyArea.  The default is to generate GraphicsExpose and
 * NoExpose events to indicate whether the source area was
 * obscured.  Since the logical function is GXinvert, the
 * destination is also the source.  Therefore, if other
 * windows are obscuring parts of the exposed pane, the
 * wrong area will be inverted.  Therefore, we would need
 * to handle GraphicsExpose and NoExpose events.  We'll do
 * it the easier way. */
gc = XCreateGC(display, RootWindow(display, screen_num), 0,
        NULL);
XSetForeground(display, gc, BlackPixel(display, screen_num));
rgc = XCreateGC(display, RootWindow(display, screen_num), 0,
        NULL);
XSetForeground(display, rgc, WhitePixel(display, screen_num));

/* Map the menu window (and its subwindows) to the screen_num */
XMapWindow(display, menuwin);

/* Force child processes to disinherit the TCP file descriptor;
 * this helps the shell command (creating new xterm) forked and
 * executed from the menu to work properly */
if ((fcntl(ConnectionNumber(display), F_SETFD, 1)) == -1)
    fprintf(stderr, "winman: child cannot disinherit TCP fd");

/* Loop getting events on the menu window and icons */
while (1) {
    /* Wait for an event */
    XNextEvent(display, &event);

    /* If expose, draw text in pane if it is pane */
    switch (event.type) {
    case Expose:
        if  (isIcon(event.xexpose.window, event.xexpose.x,
                event.xexpose.y, &assoc_win, icon_name, False))
            XDrawString(display, event.xexpose.window, gc, 2,
                    ascent + 2, icon_name, strlen(icon_name));
        else { /* It's a pane, might be inverted */
            if (inverted_pane == event.xexpose.window)
                paint_pane(event.xexpose.window, panes, gc, rgc,
                    BLACK);
            else
                paint_pane(event.xexpose.window, panes, gc, rgc,
                    WHITE);
        }
        break;
    case ButtonPress:

        paint_pane(event.xbutton.window, panes, gc, rgc, BLACK);

        button = event.xbutton.button;
        inverted_pane = event.xbutton.window;

        /* Get the matching ButtonRelease on same button */
        while (1) {
```

Example 16-1. winman — main C program (continued)

```
        /* Get rid of presses on other buttons */
        while (XCheckTypedEvent(display, ButtonPress,
                &event));
        /* Wait for release; if on correct button, exit */
        XMaskEvent(display, ButtonReleaseMask, &event);
        if (event.xbutton.button == button)
            break;
}

/* All events are sent to the grabbing window
 * regardless of whether this is True or False;
 * owner_events only affects the distribution
 * of events when the pointer is within this
 * application's windows */
owner_events = True;

/* We don't want pointer or keyboard events
 * frozen in the server */
pointer_mode = GrabModeAsync;
keyboard_mode = GrabModeAsync;

/* We don't want to confine the cursor */
confine_to = None;
XGrabPointer(display, menuwin, owner_events,
        ButtonPressMask | ButtonReleaseMask,
        pointer_mode, keyboard_mode,
        confine_to, hand_cursor, CurrentTime);

/* If press and release occurred in same window,
 * do command; if not, do nothing */
if (inverted_pane == event.xbutton.window) {
    /* Convert window ID to window array index  */
    for (winindex = 0; inverted_pane !=
            panes[winindex]; winindex++)
        ;
    switch (winindex) {
    case 0:
        raise_lower(menuwin, RAISE);
        break;
    case 1:
        raise_lower(menuwin, LOWER);
        break;
    case 2:
        move_resize(menuwin, hand_cursor, MOVE);
        break;
    case 3:
        move_resize(menuwin, hand_cursor, RESIZE);
        break;
    case 4:
        circup(menuwin);
        break;
    case 5:
        circdn(menuwin);
        break;
    case 6:
        iconify(menuwin);
        break;
    case 7:
```

Example 16-1. winman — main C program (continued)

```
                    focus_window = focus(menuwin);
                    break;
              case 8:
                    execute("xterm&");
                    break;

              case 9: /* Exit */
                    XSetInputFocus(display,
                            RootWindow(display,screen_num),
                            RevertToPointerRoot,
                            CurrentTime);
                    /* Turn all icons back into windows */
                    /* Must clear focus highlights */
                    XClearWindow(display, RootWindow(display,
                            screen_num));
                    /* Need to change focus border width back here */

                    XFlush(display);
                    XCloseDisplay(display);
                    exit(1);
              default:
                    (void) fprintf(stderr,
                            "Something went wrong\n");
                    break;
            } /* End switch */
        } /* End if */

        /* Invert Back Here (logical function is invert) */
        paint_pane(event.xexpose.window, panes, gc, rgc, WHITE);

        inverted_pane = NONE;
        draw_focus_frame();
        XUngrabPointer(display, CurrentTime);
        XFlush(display);
        break;
    case DestroyNotify:
        /* Window we have iconified has died, remove its
         * icon; don't need to remove window from save-set
         * because that is done automatically */
        removeIcon(event.xdestroywindow.window);
        break;
    case CirculateNotify:
    case ConfigureNotify:
    case UnmapNotify:
        /* All these uncover areas of screen_num */
        draw_focus_frame();
        break;
    case CreateNotify:
    case GravityNotify:
    case MapNotify:
    case ReparentNotify:
        /* Don't need these, but get them anyway since
         * we need DestroyNotify and UnmapNotify */
        break;
    case ButtonRelease:
        /* Throw these way, they are spurious here */
        break;
    case MotionNotify:
```

Example 16-1. winman — main C program (continued)

```
                    /* Throw these way, they are spurious here */
                    break;
                default:
                    fprintf(stderr, "winman: got unexpected %s event.\n",
                            event_names[event.type]);
            } /* End switch */
        } /* End menu loop (while) */
    } /* End main */
```

16.7.3 Window Layering

The first issue that comes up when writing a menu is how to layer the windows that contain each menu item. It would be possible to write a menu that only used one window, placing the text within the window in the right places and highlighting areas when the pointer coordinates in the **ButtonPress** events indicated that an item was chosen. This is a hard way, because it does not take advantage of X's windowing capabilities. It would also be possible to make each menu panel a subwindow of the root window. While this would simplify the event handling and highlighting, we would have to define a cursor for each of the windows. More importantly, the user would have to move all the windows separately if the menu were to be moved, unless we monitored movement of any one of the windows and made the rest follow. There are also other ramifications, including that it would be difficult to identify the menu as a whole to make sure it was not iconified; this would require comparing the IDs in events with the IDs of all the windows. The best solution is a combination of the above approaches.

The menu is created by superimposing ten small **InputOutput** child windows (**defs[ ]**) on one large **InputOutput** parent window (**menuwin**), as shown in Figure 16-5. This has the advantage that there is a single parent window for the window manager, which we can use to locate the panes of the menu and to identify the menu as a whole. You can also assign a cursor to the larger window, and since the smaller windows are its children, the same cursor appears in all of them. This avoids nine cursor assignments.

The nine smaller windows do three other convenient things; their borders make a neat division between areas of the menu, they determine which area of the menu the user chooses, and they define a convenient area to invert from black on white to white on black to indicate which menu choice was made.

16.7.4 Selecting Input

Now that we have decided how to layer the windows to best advantage, it is time to plan what events are going to be needed. The **menuwin** window requires no events, since it is chiefly there to tie together the menu panes. **ButtonPress**, **ButtonRelease**, and **Expose** events are required for the panes, so they can accept a choice and redraw the pane in case anything obscures and then exposes part or all of the menu. **ButtonRelease** events are selected so that we can verify menu choices by making sure the

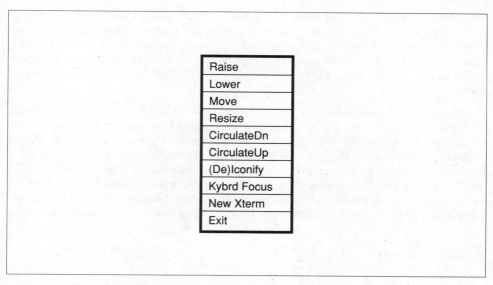

Figure 16-4. The menu created by winman

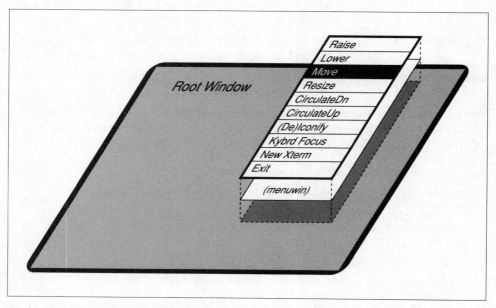

Figure 16-5. Window layering for the menu

ButtonRelease happens in the same window as the **ButtonPress**. Since the pointer is grabbed during the selection of a window on the screen to be manipulated (a window not associated with the window manager), we do not need to select input on any of these windows. However, we need to know when applications that *winman* has iconified have been killed, so that we can remove the icon. This requires selecting **SubstructureNotify-Mask** on the root window.

Some of the other events selected by **SubstructureNotifyMask** also come in handy for triggering the redrawing of the highlighting background drawn around the focus window by *winman*. This background is drawn on the root window and might have to be redrawn whenever a new area of the root window becomes exposed. It has to be redrawn when **CirculateNotify**, **ConfigureNotify**, or **UnmapNotify** events arrive. This could also have been done by selecting **Expose** events on the root window, but since we have already selected these other events and they will be sent from the server to Xlib anyway, it improves performance slightly to use them instead of **Expose** events on the root window.

16.7.5 Handling Input

There are numerous commands available for getting input. The routines used in **main** are **XCheckTypedEvent()**, **XMaskEvent()**, and **XNextEvent()**.

XCheckTypedEvent()   Allows you to choose the types of events to look for, monitors all windows, and does not wait even if no matching event is on the queue.

XMaskEvent()   Allows you to choose which event masks of the events to look for, monitoring all windows. It waits until an event arrives.

XNextEvent()   Used to get any type of event that occurs in any window. It waits until an event arrives.

These routines were described and most of them demonstrated in Chapter 8, *Events*, and Chapter 9, *The Keyboard and Pointer*. But the way they are used in **main** might need some explanation. Consider the excerpt from **main** shown in Example 16-2.

Example 16-2. Using event-getting routines together

```
/* Get the matching ButtonRelease on same button */
while (1) {
    /* Get rid of all presses (on other buttons) */
    while (XCheckTypedEvent(display, ButtonPress,
            &event))
        ;
    /* Wait for release; if on correct button, exit *

    XMaskEvent(display, ButtonReleaseMask, &event);
    if (event.xbutton.button == button) {
        /* Get rid of other releases */
        while (XCheckTypedEvent(display, ButtonRelease,
                &event))
            ;

        break;
```

Example 16-2. Using event-getting routines together (continued)

```
        }
}
```

Here we have already read a **ButtonPress** event and are waiting for a **Button-Release** on the same button. This cannot be done with **XMaskEvent()** alone, because we might get a **ButtonRelease** on a different button first and there is no way to select or get only the button events on a single button (except by writing a predicate procedure as shown in Example 8-6). Therefore, **XMaskEvent()** is called in a loop, and the **button** member in each event must be checked. Furthermore, the **CheckTypedEvent** calls are necessary to make sure that Xlib's queue does not fill up with **ButtonPress** or **Button-Release** events that are not wanted, since the code is really waiting for a particular button release. **XCheckTypedEvent()** is used again in the routine that actually moves or resizes a window to throw away excess **MotionNotify** events.

The **Expose** event processing in **main** redraws *winman*'s menu only when the **count** field in the **Expose** event is zero, thus responding only to the last **Expose** event in a contiguous series on a single window. Remember that any of the menu panes or any icon can receive **Expose** events. We also minimize redrawing by redrawing only the panes that are exposed.

16.7.6 Inverting an Area

There are at least four possible strategies for inverting a menu pane containing text. They are not all equally good.

One is to use **XCopyArea()** to copy the pane to itself using **GXinvert** as the logical function in the GC. This approach is weak because **GXinvert** would not achieve the desired effect on a color system, even though it would work fine on a monochrome system.

The second strategy, adopted in **main**, is to change the background pixel value of the window and change the foreground pixel value in the GC to draw the text in a contrasting color. In *winman*, the colors are black and white, but this approach will work correctly with any two contrasting colors.

The third approach would be to use **XDrawImageString()** to draw the text. **XDrawImageString()** draws a complete rectangle, with the text in the foreground pixel value from the GC and the rest of the rectangle in the background pixel value. If this rectangle were the same size as the menu pane, the entire pane could be inverted in color simply by swapping the foreground and background pixel values in the GC. The one weakness of this approach is that the rectangle drawn by **XDrawImageString()** might not leave as much space around the text as you would like. However, this is a very fast approach, useful in menus and for the selection of text, which works in both monochrome and color.

The fourth approach involves a trick using colors allocated by **XAllocColorCells()**. It is possible to allocate colors so that the two contrasting colors in the drawable are swapped by setting to 1 or 0 all the bits in a plane of the drawable. In this technique, the text does not need drawing at all for highlighting, because the plane on which the text is drawn is not modified by the operation to set or clear the bits in the other plane. You would need to allocate four colorcells, two of which contained the foreground RGB values and two the background. This would not work on a monochrome system, since you could not allocate four colorcells. This technique is described in Section 7.5.2.

16.7.7 Cursors

The `main` creates two cursors: one an arrow for selecting from the menu, and the other a hand for manipulating windows. It uses the call to grab the pointer to change the cursor to the hand. That has the nice side effect that the cursor will automatically change back when the grab is released, so that the `cursor` window attribute does not need to be changed with `XDefineCursor()`.

16.7.8 Grabbing the Pointer

`XGrabPointer()` is called to allow the user to select a window anywhere on the screen to be manipulated. While the pointer is grabbed, all pointer input is sent to the menu. Note that keyboard input is still sent normally to the application the pointer is in.

The arguments of `XGrabPointer()` can be confusing. The *owner_events* argument affects the distribution of events when the pointer is within this application's windows. Therefore, it does not affect our application, because we are using the grab to get input from outside the menu windows. The *pointer_mode* and *keyboard_mode* arguments also do not apply to the job at hand, so they are set to **GrabModeAsync**, which does not affect the processing of events. Their other settings cause events to be held in the server until a releasing `XAllowEvents()` call. Finally, the *confine_to* argument also does not fit our job, because we want the pointer to be able to roam around the screen rather than be confined to a window.

That about wraps up the new techniques used in `main` that have not been used earlier in this manual. Now we'll move on to some of the routines that `main` calls, beginning with `paint_pane`.

16.7.9 Painting the Menu

The `paint_pane` routine in Example 16-3 displays text in a menu pane. It is called when an exposure event occurs on a pane. When the menu is exposed, all of the exposure events are sent contiguously, refreshing each of the panes that was exposed. When the menu is first mapped, the **Expose** events trigger the drawing of all the panes for the first time.

Each call of this routine draws the text in one choice window. The first operation compares the window ID from the event with the IDs in the `panes` array to determine which string from the `menu_label` array to use.

Window backgrounds are automatically redrawn by the server when exposure occurs. But `paint_pane` is not always called in response to **Expose** events; it is also used to invert the pane when a choice is made. Therefore, the request buffer will not necessarily be flushed before the next call to draw the area. Therefore, an `XClearWindow()` call is necessary to redraw the background. (A completely different strategy could have been used. The background could be filled with `XFillRectangle()` instead of using the server.)

Example 16-3. winman — the paint_pane routine

```
static char *menu_label[ ] = {
     "Raise",
     "Lower",
     "Move",
     "Resize",
     "CirculateDn",
     "CirculateUp",
     "(De)Iconify",
     "Kybrd Focus",
     "New Xterm",
     "Exit",
};

paint_pane(window, panes, ngc, rgc, mode)
Window window;
Window panes[ ];
GC ngc, rgc;
int mode;
{
     int win;
     int x = 2, y;
     GC gc;

     if (mode == BLACK) {
          XSetWindowBackground(display, window, BlackPixel(display,
                    screen_num));
          gc = rgc;
     }
     else {
          XSetWindowBackground(display, window, WhitePixel(display,
                    screen_num));
          gc = ngc;
     }
     /* Clearing repaints the background */
     XClearWindow(display, window);

     /* Find out index of window for label text */
     for (win = 0; window != panes[win]; win++)
          ;

     y = font_info->max_bounds.ascent;

     /* The string length is necessary because strings
      * for XDrawString may not be null terminated */
     XDrawString(display, window, gc, x, y, menu_label[win],
             strlen( menu_label[win]));
}
```

16.7.10 Circulating Windows

The `circup` and `circdn` routines are simple, because they have no arguments and they require no user input. They simply take all overlapping top-level windows and move the bottom one to the top or the top one to the bottom.

Example 16-4. winman — the circle up and circle down routines

```
circup(menuwin)
Window menuwin;
{
     XCirculateSubwindowsUp(display, RootWindow(display,screen_num));
     XRaiseWindow(display, menuwin);
}

circdn(menuwin)
Window menuwin;
{
     XCirculateSubwindowsDown(display, RootWindow(display,screen_num));
     XRaiseWindow(display, menuwin);
}
```

16.7.11 Raising and Lowering Windows

The `raise_lower` routine gets a **ButtonPress** event, finds out which window it occurred in, and raises or lowers the window unless it was the root.

The `XQueryPointer()` call is used to get the window ID of the window that the button is pressed in. This call is necessary because the program did not create or select input on the windows that it is going to manipulate.

Example 16-5. winman — the raise and lower routines

```
raise_lower( menuwin, raise_or_lower )
Window menuwin;
Bool raise_or_lower;
{
     XEvent report;
     int root_x,root_y;
     Window child, root;
     int win_x, win_y;
     unsigned int mask;
     unsigned int button;

     /* Wait for ButtonPress, find out which subwindow of root */
     XMaskEvent(display, ButtonPressMask, &report);
     button = report.xbutton.button;
     XQueryPointer(display, RootWindow(display,screen_num), &root,
              &child, &root_x, &root_y, &win_x, &win_y,
              &mask);

     /* If not RootWindow, raise */
     if (child != NULL) {
          if (raise_or_lower == RAISE)
```

Example 16-5. winman — the raise and lower routines (continued)

```
            XRaiseWindow(display, child);
        else
            XLowerWindow(display, child);
        /* Make sure window manager can never be obscured */
        XRaiseWindow(display, menuwin);
    }

    /* Get the matching ButtonRelease on same button */
    while (1)  {
        XMaskEvent(display, ButtonReleaseMask, &report);
        if (report.xbutton.button == button) break;
    }
    /* Throw out any remaining events so we start fresh */
    while (XCheckMaskEvent(display, ButtonReleaseMask |
            ButtonPressMask, &report))
        ;
}
```

16.7.12 Moving and Resizing Windows

The `move_resize` routine shown in Example 16-6 is similar to `raise_lower` but uses the difference in position between a **ButtonPress** and a **ButtonRelease** event to determine the change in position or size of the window. It also uses **MotionNotify** events to draw an outline of the window during the move or resize. During resizing, the upper-left corner of the window stays in place, while the lower-right corner moves the same way the pointer does between the press and the release. The code could be expanded to allow any corner of the window to be resized.

The routine that draws the box for the temporary window outline was described in Chapter 6, *Drawing Graphics and Text*.

If there is an icon associated with the moved window, that icon is not moved. Similarly, if the window moved is an icon, its associated main window is not moved. This is an arbitrary window manager policy decision. Some window managers might legislate a certain relationship between the position of a window and its icon.

Example 16-6. winman — the move and resize routines

```
move_resize(menuwin, hand_cursor, move_or_resize)
Window menuwin;
Cursor hand_cursor;
Bool move_or_resize;
{
        XEvent report;
        XWindowAttributes win_attr;
        int press_x, press_y, release_x, release_y, move_x, move_y;
        static int box_drawn = False;
        int left, right, top, bottom;
        Window root, child;
        Window win_to_configure;
        int win_x, win_y;
        unsigned int mask;
```

Example 16-6. winman — the move and resize routines (continued)

```
unsigned int pressed_button;
XSizeHints size_hints;
Bool min_size, increment;
unsigned int width, height;
int temp_size;
static GC gc;
static int first_time = True;
long user_supplied_mask;

if (first_time) {
    gc = XCreateGC(display, RootWindow(display,screen_num), 0,
            NULL);
    XSetSubwindowMode(display, gc, IncludeInferiors);
    XSetForeground(display, gc, BlackPixel(display, screen_num));
    XSetFunction(display, gc, GXxor);
    first_time = False;
    }

/* Wait for ButtonPress choosing window to configure */
XMaskEvent(display, ButtonPressMask, &report);
pressed_button = report.xbutton.button;

/* Which child of root was press in? */
XQueryPointer(display, RootWindow(display,screen_num), &root,
        &child, &press_x, &press_y, &win_x,
        &win_y, &mask);
win_to_configure = child;

if ((win_to_configure == NULL)  ||
        ((win_to_configure == menuwin)
        && (move_or_resize == RESIZE)))  {
    /* If in RootWindow or resizing menuwin,
     * get release event and get out */
while (XCheckMaskEvent(display, ButtonReleaseMask |
        ButtonPressMask, &report))
    ;
    return;
}

/* Button press was in a valid subwindow of root */

/* Get original position and size of window */
XGetWindowAttributes(display, win_to_configure,
        &win_attr);

/* Get size hints for the window */
XGetWMNormalHints(display, win_to_configure, &size_hints,
        &user_supplied_mask);
if (size_hints.flags && PMinSize)
    min_size = True;
if (size_hints.flags && PResizeInc)
    increment = True;

/* Now we need pointer motion events */
XChangeActivePointerGrab(display, PointerMotionHintMask |
        ButtonMotionMask | ButtonReleaseMask |
        OwnerGrabButtonMask, hand_cursor, CurrentTime);

/* Don't allow other display operations during move
 * because the moving outline drawn with Xor won't
```

Example 16-6. winman — the move and resize routines (continued)

```
    * work properly otherwise */
   XGrabServer(display);

   /* Move outline of window until button release */
   while (1) {
       XNextEvent(display, &report);
       switch (report.type) {
           case ButtonRelease:
               if (report.xbutton.button == pressed_button) {
                   if (box_drawn)
                       /* Undraw box */
                       draw_box(gc, left, top, right, bottom);

                   /* This may seem premature but actually
                    * ButtonRelease indicates that the
                    * rubber-banding is done */
                   XUngrabServer(display);

                   /* Get final window position */
                   XQueryPointer(display, RootWindow(display,
                           screen_num), &root, &child,
                           &release_x, &release_y, &win_x,
                           &win_y, &mask);

                   /* Move or resize window */
                   if (move_or_resize == MOVE)
                       XMoveWindow(display, win_to_configure,
                           win_attr.x + (release_x -
                           press_x), win_attr.y +
                           (release_y - press_y));
                   else
                       XResizeWindow(display, win_to_configure,
                           win_attr.width + (release_x - press_x),
                           win_attr.height + (release_y - press_y));

                   XRaiseWindow(display, win_to_configure);
                   XFlush(display);
                   box_drawn = False;
                   while (XCheckMaskEvent(display,
                           ButtonReleaseMask
                           | ButtonPressMask,
                           &report))
                       ;
                   return;
               }
               break;

           case MotionNotify:
               if (box_drawn == True)
                   /* Undraw box */
                   draw_box(gc, left, top, right, bottom);

               /* Can get rid of all MotionNotify events in
                * queue, since otherwise the round-trip delays
                * caused by XQueryPointer may cause a backlog
                * of MotionNotify events, which will cause
                * additional wasted XQueryPointer calls */
               while (XCheckTypedEvent(display, MotionNotify,
```

Example 16-6. winman — the move and resize routines (continued)

```
                       &report));

               /* Get current mouse position */
               XQueryPointer(display, RootWindow(display,
                       screen_num), &root, &child, &move_x,
                       &move_y, &win_x, &win_y, &mask);

           if (move_or_resize == MOVE) {
               left = move_x - press_x + win_attr.x;
               top = move_y - press_y + win_attr.y;
               right = left + win_attr.width;
               bottom = top + win_attr.height;
           }
           else
               {
               if (move_x < win_attr.x)
                   move_x = 0;
               if (move_y < win_attr.y )
                   move_y = 0;
               left = win_attr.x;
               top = win_attr.y;
               right = left + win_attr.width + move_x
                       - press_x;
               bottom = top + win_attr.height + move_y
                       - press_y;
               /* Must adjust size according to size hints */
               /* Enforce minimum dimensions */
               width = right - left;
               height = bottom - top;

               /* Make sure dimension are increment of
                * width_inc and height_inc and at least
                * min_width and min_height */
               for (temp_size = size_hints.min_width;
                       temp_size < width;
                       temp_size += size_hints.width_inc)
                   ;

               for (temp_size = size_hints.min_height;
                       temp_size < height;
                       temp_size += size_hints.height_inc)
                   ;
               /* Most applications (xterm
                * included) pad their right
                * and bottom dimensions by
                * 2 pixels */
               bottom = top + temp_size + 2;
               right = left + temp_size + 2;
               }

           draw_box(gc, left, top, right, bottom);
           box_drawn = True;
           break;
       default:
           /* StructureNotify events should not appear
            * here because of the ChangeActivePointerGrab
```

Example 16-6. winman — the move and resize routines (continued)

```
                    * call, but they do for some reason; anyway,
                    * it doesn't matter */
                 /* fprintf(stderr, "unexpected event type %s\n",
                    * report.type); */
                    ;
            } /* End switch */
        } /* End outer while */
} /* End move */
```

Figure 16-6 shows an example of the screen during a move operation.

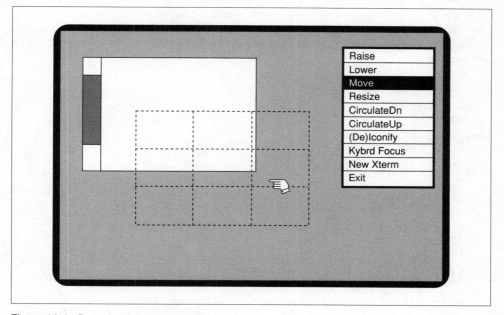

Figure 16-6. Dragging a window outline

The **XChangeActivePointerGrab()** function is used to narrow the types of events that are received. In other terms, it changes the events that are selected for the window for the duration of the grab. This makes it unnecessary to throw away **ButtonPress** events that are used early in the program but not needed in this routine.

The server is grabbed in this example to make sure that no other program displays output on the screen while the box is being dragged. This is necessary because the box is drawn and then undrawn with the same command and GC using the **GXxor** logical function. Graphics drawn twice with Exclusive OR will appear as they started but only if the pixels affected are not changed by any other application in between. If any other client were allowed to draw between the draw and the undraw, the screen might not be returned to normal.

Note that the actual color of the rubber-banded line is unpredictable on a color system, because the pixel value is simply the Exclusive OR of what was already there. If a particular color of rubber-banded line is desired, you will have to use the overlay technique described in Section 7.5.2.

16.7.13 The draw_box Routine

The `draw_box` routine shown in Example 16-7 modifies a GC and draws a box. It raises some interesting issues since it draws on the root window. It is called from the simple window manager program *winman* described in Chapter 16, *Window Management*. Its purpose is to draw an outline of a window during the rubber-banding that shows the user the current size or position of a window being resized or moved. The program also calls this routine to erase the box and to redraw the box to show the current position or size of a window as it is moved.

Example 16-7. The draw_box routine

```
Display *display;
int screen;

draw_box(gc, x, y, width, height)
GC gc;
int x, y,
unsigned int width, height;
{
        /* Set foreground pixel value -- default may be white on white */
        XSetForeground(display, gc, BlackPixel(display,screen));

        /* Drawing on root window -- through all windows */
        XSetSubwindowMode(display, gc, IncludeInferiors);

        /* Logical function is XOR, so that double drawing erases box
         * on both color and monochrome screens */
        XSetFunction(display, gc, GXxor);

        XDrawRectangle(display, RootWindow(display,screen), gc, x, y,
                    width, height);
}
```

This routine uses a couple of tricks that need explanation. Notice that three elements of the GC are changed and that the drawing request draws on the root window. Since the box may be moved anywhere on the screen during a move operation (by the window manager), the box must be drawn on the root window. We set the foreground color to black so that the box will be visible over the default backgrounds of most windows (white). By default, the `subwindow_mode` member is set to `ClipByChildren`, specifying that graphics drawn to a window do not show through child windows. Because we want the entire box to be visible anywhere on the screen, we set the `subwindow_mode` to `IncludeInferiors`.

We are using a logical operation of `GXxor` so that the box can be drawn again to erase itself. This logical operation has the unique feature of returning the pixels to their original state in monochrome or color if the box is drawn twice, as long as none of the pixels were changed between the first and second drawings. To make sure nothing else is drawn in between, the program that calls `draw_box` grabs the server for the brief period of the window manipulation. Avoid grabbing the server unless absolutely necessary.

16.7.14 (De)Iconifying Windows

The `iconify` routine must be able to turn a window into an icon or turn an icon back into a window. It is completely up to the window manager to keep track of the association between windows and icons. Therefore, a substantial portion of *winman*'s code is devoted to maintaining a list of the main windows and their associated icon windows. We will look at the code for the routine that `main` calls, `iconify`, and then delve into the details of implementing icons.

Example 16-8 shows the `iconify` routine that is called in response to the user selecting the (De)Iconify item on *winman*'s menu.

Example 16-8. winman — the iconify routine

```
iconify(menuwin)
Window menuwin;
{
     XEvent report;
     extern Window focus_window;
     Window assoc_win;
     int press_x,press_y;
     Window child;
     Window root;
     int win_x, win_y;
     unsigned int mask;
     unsigned int button;

     /* Wait for ButtonPress, any win */
     XMaskEvent(display, ButtonPressMask, &report);
     button = report.xbutton.button;

     /* Find out which subwindow the mouse was in */
     XQueryPointer(display, RootWindow(display,screen_num), &root,
          &child, &press_x, &press_y, &win_x, &win_y, &mask);

     /* Can't iconify rootwindow or menu window */
     if ((child == NULL) || (child == menuwin))
          {
          /* Wait for ButtonRelease before exiting */
          while (1)  {
               XMaskEvent(display, ButtonReleaseMask, &report);
               if (report.xbutton.button == button) break;
               }
          return;
          }
     /* Returned value of isIcon not used here, but
      * it is elsewhere in the code */
     isIcon(child, press_x, press_y, &assoc_win, icon_name, True);
     /* Window selected is unmapped, whether it is icon
      * or main window; the other is then mapped */
     XUnmapWindow(display, child);
     XMapWindow(display, *assoc_win);
```

Example 16-8. winman — the iconify routine (continued)

```
    /* Wait for ButtonRelease before exiting */
    /* Get the matching ButtonRelease on same button */
    while (1)   {
        XMaskEvent(display, ButtonReleaseMask, &report);
        if (report.xbutton.button == button) break;
    }
    /* Throw out any remaining events so we start fresh
     * for next op */
    while (XCheckMaskEvent(display, ButtonReleaseMask |
            ButtonPressMask, &report))
        ;
}
```

If the window is not an icon, the window is unmapped and an icon window is created and mapped. If the window is an icon, it is unmapped and the associated main window is remapped. The `iconify` routine guards against iconifying the menu, since there is no way in this program to undo that operation.

The `iconify` routine calls the `isIcon` routine. If the window selected is not an icon, `isIcon` creates an icon window, enters it into a linked list, and returns the icon window's ID. If the window selected is an icon, the associated main window's ID is returned. Either way, the window selected is unmapped and the associated window is mapped.

The routines underlying `isIcon` are a simplified version of the icon-handling code from *uwm*. Notice that these routines are in a separate source file, so they must include the standard include files and declare as **extern** the global variables set in *winman.c*.

Example 16-9. winman — the isIcon routine

```
#include <X11/Xlib.h>
#include <X11/Xatom.h>
#include <X11/Xutil.h>
#include <X11/cursorfont.h>

#include <stdio.h>

extern Display *display;
extern int screen_num;

/* For linked list containing window ID, icon ID, and icon_name;
 * own indicates whether winman created the icon window (True)
 * or was passed it through the WMHints (False) */
typedef struct _windowList {
    struct _windowList *next;
    Window window;
    Window icon;
    Bool own;
    char *icon_name;
} WindowListRec, *WindowList;

WindowList Icons = NULL;

Bool isIcon(win, x, y, assoc, icon_name, makeicon)
Window win;
int x, y;
Window *assoc;
```

Example 16-9. winman — the isIcon routine (continued)

```
char *icon_name;
Bool makeicon;
{
      WindowList win_list;
      Window makeIcon();

      /* Go through linked list of window-icon structures */
      for (win_list = Icons; win_list; win_list = win_list->next) {
          if (win == win_list->icon) { /* Win is icon */
              *assoc = win_list->window;
              strcpy(icon_name, win_list->icon_name);
              return(True);
          }
          if (win == win_list->window) { /* Win is main window */
              *assoc = win_list->icon;
              strcpy(icon_name, win_list->icon_name);
              return(False);
          }
      }
      /* Window not in list means icon not created yet; create icon
       * and add main window to save-set in case window manager dies */
          if (makeicon) {
          *assoc = makeIcon(win, x, y, icon_name);
          XAddToSaveSet(display, win);
      }
      return(False);
}
```

The `isIcon` routine looks through the linked list of structures, of which there is one for each top-level window that has ever been iconified.

- If `win` is found in the structures and it is an icon, `isIcon` returns `True`.

- If `win` is found and it is a main window, `isIcon` returns `False`.

- If `win` is not found at all, `isIcon` calls `makeIcon` to create an icon for the window and then calls `XAddToSaveSet()` to add the window to *winman*'s save-set. This code only gets called when an application is being iconified for the first time. Since it is possible that *winman* will get killed before it has a chance to remap the main windows of the applications it has iconified, these windows must be automatically remapped when *winman* dies. That is what the save-set does. (*winman* can be killed by typing CTRL-C in the window it was invoked from if it has been run in the foreground or with the Exit choice from *winman*'s menu.)

16.7.15 Creating the Icons

The `makeIcon` routine called in `isIcon` is used to read the hints that the application has specified for the icon. As you will recall, the window manager has the option of honoring or ignoring these hints. *winman* honors them to the greatest extent possible. It allows an application to specify an icon pixmap or icon window, an icon name, and the icon's position.

If some or all of these hints are not set, *winman* does the best it can. If no icon window is specified, *winman* creates one. If no icon pixmap is specified, *winman* uses a white background and writes the icon name on it in black.

Example 16-10. winman — the makeIcon routine

```
Window makeIcon(window, x, y, icon_name_return)
Window window;                              /* Associated window */
int x, y;                                   /* Current mouse position */
char *icon_name_return;
{
    int icon_x, icon_y;                     /* Icon U. L. X and Y
                                             * coordinates */

    int icon_w, icon_h;                     /* Icon width and height */
    int icon_bdr;                           /* Icon border width */
    int depth;                              /* For XGetGeometry */
    Window root;                            /* For XGetGeometry */
    XSetWindowAttributes icon_attrib;       /* For icon creation */
    unsigned long icon_attrib_mask;
    XWMHints *wmhints;                      /* See if icon position
                                             * provided */

    XWMHints *XGetWMHints();
    Window FinishIcon();
    char *icon_name;

    /* Process window manager hints.  If icon window hint
     * exists, use it directly.  If icon pixmap hint exists,
     * get its size.  Otherwise, get default size.  If icon
     * position hint exists, use it; otherwise, use the
     * position passed (current mouse position). */
    if (wmhints = XGetWMHints(display, window)) {
        if (wmhints->flags&IconWindowHint)
            /* Icon window was passed; use it as is */
            return(finishIcon(window, wmhints->icon_window,
                False, icon_name));
        else if (wmhints->flags&IconPixmapHint)
        {
            /* Pixmap was passed.  Determine size of icon
             * window from pixmap.  Only icon_w and icon_h
             * are significant. */
            if (!XGetGeometry(display, wmhints->icon_pixmap,
                &root, &icon_x, &icon_y,
                &icon_w, &icon_h, &icon_bdr, &depth)) {
                fprintf(stderr, "winman: client passed invalid \
                    icon pixmap." );
                return( NULL );
            }
            else {
                icon_attrib.background_pixmap = wmhints->icon_pixmap;
                icon_attrib_mask = CWBorderPixel|CWBackPixmap;
            }
        }
    /* Else no window or pixmap passed */
    else {
        icon_name = getDefaultIconSize(window, &icon_w, &icon_h);
        icon_attrib_mask = CWBorderPixel | CWBackPixel;
        icon_attrib.background_pixel = (unsigned long)
                WhitePixel(display,screen_num);
```

Example 16-10. winman — the makeIcon routine (continued)

```
        }
    }
    /* Else no hints at all exist */
    else {
        icon_name = getDefaultIconSize(window, &icon_w, &icon_h);
        icon_attrib_mask = CWBorderPixel | CWBackPixel;
    }
    /* Pad sizes */
    icon_w += 2;
    icon_h += 2;

    strcpy(icon_name_return, icon_name);

    /* Set the icon border attributes */
    icon_bdr = 2;
    icon_attrib.border_pixel = (unsigned long)
            BlackPixel(display,screen_num);

    /* If icon position hint exists, get it; this also checks
     * to see if wmhints is NULL, which it will be if WMHints
     * were never set at all */
    if (wmhints && (wmhints->flags&IconPositionHint))
    {
        icon_x = wmhints->icon_x;
        icon_y = wmhints->icon_y;
    }
    else
    {
        /* Put it where the mouse was */
        icon_x = x;
        icon_y = y;
    }

    /* Create the icon window */
    return(finishIcon(window, XCreateWindow(display,
            RootWindow(display, screen_num),
            icon_x, icon_y, icon_w, icon_h,
            icon_bdr, 0, CopyFromParent, CopyFromParent,
            icon_attrib_mask, &icon_attrib),
            True, icon_name));
}
```

6.7.16 Getting the Icon Size

We will show you `getDefaultIconSize` (which calls `getIconName`) and then
`finishIcon`, the two routines called from `makeIcon`. `getDefaultIconSize` and
`getIconName` are shown in Example 16-11.

Example 16-11. winman — the getDefaultIconSize and getIconName routines

```
char *
getDefaultIconSize(window, icon_w, icon_h)
Window window;
int *icon_w, *icon_h;
```

```
{
    /* Determine the size of the icon window */
    char *icon_name;

    icon_name = getIconName(window);

    *icon_h = font_info->ascent + font_info->descent + 4;
    *icon_w = XTextWidth(font_info, icon_name, strlen(icon_name));

    return(icon_name);
}
char *
getIconName(window)
Window window;
{
    char *name;

    if (XGetIconName( display, window, &name )) return( name );

    /* Get program name if set */
    if (XFetchName( display, window, &name )) return( name );

    return( "Icon" );
}
```

The routines in Example 16-11 simply get the icon name and determine a size for the icon from the name, given the font dimensions. If no icon name is available, they use the program name, and if that is not available, they use the string "Icon." However, this should never happen if the applications are written properly.

16.7.17 Updating the Icon List

Now we'll turn to `finishIcon`, which is called from `makeIcon`. `finishIcon` creates and defines a cursor for the icon, selects `Expose` events for it, and updates the linked list of structures to include the new icon and its associated window. (Actually, the cursor should have been created in another routine, because here it is executed every time a new icon is created.)

Example 16-12. winman — the finishIcon routine

```
Window finishIcon(window, icon, own, icon_name)
Window window, icon;
Bool own; /* Whether winman created the icon window */
char *icon_name;
{
    WindowList win_list;
    Cursor manCursor;

    /* If icon window didn't get created, return failure */
    if (icon == NULL) return(NULL);

    /* Use the man cursor whenever the mouse is in the
     * icon window */
    manCursor = XCreateFontCursor(display, XC_man);
```

Example 16-12. winman — the finishIcon routine (continued)

```
        XDefineCursor(display, icon, manCursor);

        /* Select events for the icon window */
        XSelectInput(display, icon, ExposureMask);

        /* Set the event window's icon window to be the new
         * icon window */
        win_list = (WindowList) malloc(sizeof(WindowListRec));
        win_list->window = window;
        win_list->icon = icon;
        win_list->own = own;
        win_list->icon_name = icon_name;
        win_list->next = Icons;
        Icons = win_list;

        return(icon);
}
```

One nice user interface possibility is suggested by the code for `finishIcon`. We could let the user turn an icon back into a main window by pressing some key or button in the icon. To do this, we would select button or key events on the icon and then look for them in one of the event loops in `main`. If button events were chosen, we would need to identify which window the button event appeared in to distinguish between events from the menu and events in the icon, but this would be easy.

16.7.18 Removing Icons

Finally, we need a way to remove icons for applications that have been iconified but exit while the window manager is running. The `main` selects `StructureNotifyMask` to be notified when top-level windows are destroyed and responds by calling `removeIcon`, which is shown in Example 16-13.

Example 16-13. winman — the removeIcon routine

```
removeIcon(window)
Window window;
{
        WindowList win_list, win_list1;

        for (win_list = Icons; win_list; win_list = win_list->next)
            if (win_list->window == window) {
                if (win_list->own)
                    XDestroyWindow(display, win_list->icon);
                break;
            }
        if (win_list) {
            if (win_list==Icons) Icons = Icons->next;
            else
                for (win_list1 = Icons; win_list1->next;
                        win_list1 = win_list1->next)
                    if (win_list1->next == win_list) {
                        win_list1->next = win_list->next;
                        break;
```

Example 16-13. winman — the removeIcon routine (continued)

```
                    };
    }
}
```

Whether *winman* exits graciously (through the Exit choice on the menu) or by being killed, all the main windows it has iconified have already been placed in the save-set, so that they will automatically be mapped. Therefore, no routine to clear the icons is necessary.

16.7.19 Changing Keyboard Focus

Setting the keyboard focus allows the user to stop worrying about whether the pointer is in the window to be typed into. The underlying function here is **XSetInputFocus()**. It causes keyboard input to go to the selected window regardless of the position of the pointer. When the root window is selected, keyboard events are distributed normally according to the position of the pointer (this is the default situation).

winman highlights the focus window by increasing the width of the border and drawing a white outline around the window. This is necessary because it would not be obvious which application had the focus unless the application itself was programmed to indicate when it has the focus. Of course, applying the keyboard focus to a window that does not use keyboard input, like the main window of *xclock*, would cause your input to be just thrown away and the only indication of what is happening would be the highlighting drawn around the focus window.

The **focus** routine in Example 16-14 selects a window much like the **raise_lower** function does. If the subwindow returned by **XQueryPointer()** is NULL, the pointer must be on the root window, and the focus can be set to the ID of the root window. Otherwise we need to find out if the subwindow is an icon. The focus should be on the real window as opposed to the icon, since the icon is controlled by the window manager and does not accept keyboard input for the application.

To change the border width of the new focus window, we need to get the old width with **XGetWindowAttributes()**, and save it so it can be replaced when the focus is changed again.

Example 16-14. winman — the focus routine

```
focus(menuwin)
Window menuwin;
{
    XEvent report;
    int x,y;
    Window child;
    Window root;
    Window assoc_win;
    extern Window focus_window;
    int win_x, win_y;
    unsigned int mask;
    char *icon_name;
    unsigned int button;
```

Example 16-14. winman — the focus routine (continued)

```
    XWindowAttributes win_attr;
    static int old_width;
    static Window old_focus;
    int status;

    /* Wait for ButtonPress, any win */
    XMaskEvent(display, ButtonPressMask, &report);
    button = report.xbutton.button;

    /* Find out which subwindow the mouse was in */

    XQueryPointer(display, RootWindow(display,screen_num), &root,
            &child, &x, &y, &win_x, &win_y, &mask);

    if ((child == NULL) || (isIcon(child, x, y, &assoc_win,
            &icon_name)))
        focus_window = RootWindow(display, screen_num);
    else
        focus_window = child;

    if (focus_window != old_focus)  { /* If focus changed */
        /* If not first time set, set border back */
        if  (old_focus != NULL)
            XSetWindowBorderWidth(display, old_focus, old_width);

        XSetInputFocus(display, focus_window, RevertToPointerRoot,
                CurrentTime);
        if (focus_window != RootWindow(display, screen_num)) {
            /* Get current border width and add one */
            if (!(status = XGetWindowAttributes(display,
                    focus_window, &win_attr)))
                fprintf(stderr, "winman: can't get attributes for \
                    focus window\n");
            XSetWindowBorderWidth(display, focus_window,
                    win_attr.border_width + 1);
            /* Keep record so we can change it back */
            old_width = win_attr.border_width;
        }
    }

    /* Get the matching ButtonRelease on same button */
    while (1)  {
        XMaskEvent(display, ButtonReleaseMask, &report);
        if (report.xbutton.button == button) break;
    }

    old_focus = focus_window;
    return(focus_window);
}
```

16.7.20 Drawing the Focus Frame

The `focus` routine calls **`draw_focus_frame`** to further highlight the focus window. There are several ways to do this, ranging from almost trivial to fairly complex. The easiest way is to change the border width and/or color to indicate which window is the focus. Another way is to draw on the root window behind the focus window. This has a slightly different effect in that no highlight would appear on windows where they did not contact the root window. We do both to be absolutely sure the current focus window is well indicated. The window is highlighted by increasing its border width and by tiling a region underneath the current focus window with a pixmap.

A third and more complicated way is to reparent the focus window into a background frame, as described above in Section 16.3. This would work well if the windows already had been reparented to add a titlebar.

The **`draw_focus_frame`** routine shown in Example 16-15 also demonstrates the two-step process of creating a useful pixmap from the data in an include file generated by the bitmap program. You must create a bitmap from the data before making a pixmap from the bitmap.

Example 16-15. winman — the draw_focus_frame routine

```
draw_focus_frame()
{
    XWindowAttributes win_attr;
    int frame_width = 4;
    Pixmap focus_tile;
    GC gc;
    int foreground = BlackPixel(display, screen_num);
    int background = WhitePixel(display, screen_num);
    extern Window focus_window;
    Bool first_time = True;

    if (first_time) {
        /* Make Bitmap from bitmap data */
        focus_tile = XCreatePixmapFromBitmapData(display,
                RootWindow(display,screen_num),
                focus_frame_bi_bits, focus_frame_bi_width,
                focus_frame_bi_height, foreground,
                background, DefaultDepth(display, screen_num));

        /* Create graphics context */
        gc = XCreateGC(display, RootWindow(display,screen_num), 0,
                NULL);
        XSetFillStyle(display, gc, FillTiled);
        XSetTile(display, gc, focus_tile);
        first_time = False;
    }
    /* Get rid of old frames */
    XClearWindow(display, RootWindow(display,screen_num));

    /* If focus is RootWindow, no frame drawn */
    if (focus_window == RootWindow(display,screen_num)) return;

    /* Get dimensions and position of focus_window*/
```

Example 16-15. winman — the draw_focus_frame routine (continued)

```
    XGetWindowAttributes(display, focus_window, &win_attr);

    XFillRectangle(display, RootWindow(display,screen_num), gc,
        win_attr.x - frame_width, win_attr.y - frame_width,
        win_attr.width + 2 * (win_attr.border_width + frame_width),
        win_attr.height + 2 * (win_attr.border_width + frame_width));
}
```

16.7.21 Executing a Shell Command

The menu item to create a new *xterm* window uses **execute**, which is a routine taken directly from the code for *uwm*. This routine can be used to execute any shell command and, therefore, may come in handy in virtually any application, not just a window manager. Example 16-16 shows the **execute** routine. Obviously, this routine is for UNIX-based systems. Code for other operating systems can be added between preprocessor directives (**#ifdef, #endif**).

Example 16-16. winman — the execute routine

```
#ifdef SYSV
#ifndef hpux
#define vfork() fork()
#endif /* hpux */
#endif /* SYSV */

/* The following procedure is a copy of the implementation of
 * system, modified to reset the handling of SIGINT, SIGQUIT,
 * and SIGHUP before executing */
execute(s)
char *s;
{
    int status, pid, w;
    register int (*istat)(), (*qstat)();

    if ((pid = vfork()) == 0) {
        signal(SIGINT, SIG_DFL);
        signal(SIGQUIT, SIG_DFL);
        signal(SIGHUP, SIG_DFL);
        execl("/bin/sh", "sh", "-c", s, 0);
        _exit(127);
    }
    istat = signal(SIGINT, SIG_IGN);
    qstat = signal(SIGQUIT, SIG_IGN);
    while ((w = wait(&status)) != pid && w != -1)
        ;
    if (w == -1)
        status = -1;
    signal(SIGINT, istat);
    signal(SIGQUIT, qstat);
    return(status);
}
```

There is some code in **main** that helps **execute** do its thing. It makes sure that the new process does not inherit any open files from the parent process, our window manager. Without this call, the child process might affect the operation of the client instead of being completely separate. All routines that execute shell commands should include the code shown in Example 16-17 in the routine that calls **execute**.

Example 16-17. winman — code for assisting execution of shell commands

```
/* Force child processes to disinherit the TCP file.
 * descriptor; this helps the shell command (creating
 * new xterm) forked and executed from the menu to work
 * properly */
if ((fcntl(ConnectionNumber(display), F_SETFD, 1)) == -1)
     fprintf(stderr, "winman: child cannot disinherit TCP fd");
```

Remember that *winman* is only a minimal window manager. It does not perform all the tasks required of window managers as specified by the ICCCM. See Appendix L, *Interclient Communication Conventions*, of Volume Zero, *X Protocol Reference Manual* (as of the second printing), to read about the complete set of requirements for window managers.

A

Specifying Fonts

This appendix describes how to define the names of the default fonts your application will use if the user does not override them. This chapter explains the font service architecture and the use of the scalable fonts. Font service is entirely transparent to the X programmer—it is impossible for the programmer to tell whether a given font came from a font server or from a font file read by the X server. Although there are no new functions or datatypes related to font service, the architecture overview and font server configuration information may be of interest.

In This Appendix:

A
Specifying Fonts

This appendix describes how to specify fonts in application code or in resource files. For all the details on the conventions for font naming, see Appendix M, *Logical Font Description Conventions*, of Volume Zero, *X Protocol Reference Manual* (as of the second printing).

A.1 Font Specification

Most applications that display text allow the user to specify the font via either the `font` resource or the `-fn` and `-font` command line options.

The X Window System supports many different display fonts with different sizes and type styles. (These are *screen* fonts and are not to be confused with *printer* fonts.)

Since Release 3, Adobe Systems, Inc. and Digital Equipment Corporation have jointly contributed several families of screen fonts (Courier, Helvetica, New Century Schoolbook, Symbol, and Times) in a variety of sizes, styles, and weights for 75-dots-per-inch (dpi) monitors. Bitstream, Inc. contributed its Charter font family in the same sizes, styles, and weights for both 75- and 100-dpi monitors. Since Release 4, Bigelow and Holmes, Inc. and Sun Microsystems, Inc. have contributed the Lucida font family and DEC contributed a new terminal emulator font. Since Release 5, Bitstream has contributed several outline fonts to match their contributed bitmap fonts.

Fonts are stored in three directories:

Directory	Contents
/usr/lib/X11/fonts/misc	Several fixed-width fonts, the cursor font
/usr/lib/X11/fonts/75dpi	Fixed- and variable-width fonts, 75 dots per inch
/usr/lib/X11/fonts/100dpi	Fixed- and variable-width fonts, 100 dots per inch

These three directories (in this order) comprise X's default font path. The font path can be changed with the `fp` option to the *xset* client, as described in Volume Three, *X Window System User's Guide*. The font path, together with a great deal of other information about the server defaults, can be listed with *xset query*. All fonts in the font path can be listed with *xlsfonts*, and the characters in a font can be displayed on the screen with *xfd*.

In R5 and later, the font path can include font servers.

An application can modify the font path using **XSetFontPath( )**, to add font directories or font servers. This should be done carefully to make sure the existing font directories are still searched.

The name of each font file in the font directories has a filename extension of *.snf*, which stands for *server natural format*. In R4, fonts were distributed in *binary distribution format* (*bdf*), which needs to be compiled (with a special font compiler) for every different architecture. In R5, fonts are distributed in *portable compiled format* which can be used directly on any architecture. To find out more about the various font file formats, see *The X Resource*, Issue 2.

A.1.1 Font Naming Conventions

Font names are not determined by the names of the files in which they are stored. Instead a font's name is determined by the contents of the font property named FONT*. A font can be referred to by this name or by any of the aliases specified in an alias file in the directory containing the font file.

The syntax of font names is defined in the X Logical Font Description convention, or XLFD. The complete XLFD is reprinted in Volume Zero, *X Protocol Reference Manual*. This appendix tells you the essential information, however.

If you run *xlsfonts*, you will get an intimidating list of names similar to the one shown in Figure A-1 which, upon closer examination, contains a great deal of useful information:

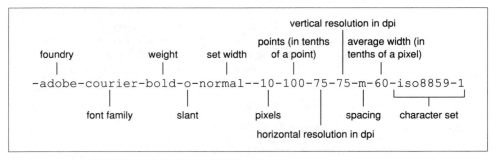

Figure A-1. A fully specified font name

This rather verbose line is actually the name of the font stored in the file *courBO10* (in the *75dpi* directory). This font name specifies the foundry (Adobe), font family (Courier), weight (bold) slant (Oblique), set width (normal), size of the font in pixels (10), size of the font in tenths of a point (100, measured in tenths of a point, thus equals 10 points), horizontal resolution (75 dpi), vertical resolution (75 dpi), spacing (m, for monospace), average width in tenths of a pixel (60, measured in tenths of a pixel, thus equals 6 pixels) and character set (iso8859-1).

The meaning of many of these statistics is obvious. Some of the less obvious information is explained below:

foundry
: The type foundry (in this case, Adobe) that digitized and supplied the font.

set width
: A value describing a font's proportionate width, according to the foundry. Typical set widths include: normal, condensed, narrow, double width. All of the non-misc fonts have the set width *normal*.

pixels and points
: Type is normally measured in points, a printer's unit equal to 1/72 of an inch. The size of a font in pixels depends on the resolution of the display font in pixels. For example, if the display font has 100-dpi resolution, a 12-point font will have a pixel size of 17, while with 75-dpi resolution, a 12-point font will have a pixel size of 12. If both these fields and average width are all zero, the X server or a font server may supply a scalable font, as described in Section A.3.

spacing
: Either m (monospace, i.e., fixed-width) or p (proportional, i.e., variable-width).

horizontal and vertical resolution
: The resolution in dots per inch for which a font is designed. Horizontal and vertical figures are required because a screen may have different capacities for horizontal and vertical resolution.

average width
: Mean width of all characters in the font, measured in tenths of a pixel; in this case, 6 pixels. If this field and pixels and points are all zero, the X server or a font server may supply a scalable font, as described in Section A.3.

character set
: ISO, the International Standards Organization, has defined character set standards for various languages. The iso8859-1 in Figure A-1 represents the ISO Latin-1 character set, which is used by all of the fonts in the *75dpi* and *100dpi* directories. The ISO Latin-1 character set is a superset of the standard ASCII character set, which includes various special characters used in European languages other than English. See Appendix H, *Keysym Reference*, of Volume Two, *Xlib Reference Manual*, for a complete listing and example glyphs of the characters in the ISO Latin-1 character set.

This font naming convention is intended to allow for the unique naming of fonts of any style, resolution, and size. It is powerful but unwieldy.

To display text using the font stored in the file *courBO10*, you could use the resource setting:

```
.yourapp*font:  -adobe-courier-bold-o-normal--10-100-75-75-m-60-iso8859-1
```

Since typing a font name of this length is neither desirable nor practical, the X Window System developers have provided two alternatives: wildcarding and aliasing.

A.1.2 Font Name Wildcarding

Any unnecessary part of a font name can be "wildcarded" by specifying ? for any single character and * for any group of characters.

For example, using a wildcarded font name, the resource specification above could be written:

```
*label:  *courier-bold-o-*-100*
```

(Note that when using wildcards with the −fn command line option, you must take care to quote the font names, since the UNIX shell has special meanings for the wildcard characters * and ?. This can be done by enclosing the entire font name in quotes or by escaping each wildcard character by typing a backslash before it.)

If more than one font in a given directory matches a wildcarded font name, the server chooses the font to use. If fonts from *more than one directory* match the wildcarded name, the server will always choose a font from the directory that is earlier in the font path. Thus, if a wildcarded font name matches a font from both the *75dpi* and the *100dpi* directories and the *75dpi* directory comes first in the font path, the server chooses the font from that directory.

In creating a wildcarded font name, you need to decide which parts of the standard font name must be explicit and which parts can be replaced with wildcards. As the previous example illustrates, you can use a single wildcard character for multiple parts of the font name. For instance, the final asterisk in the example stands for the sequence:

```
−75−75−m−60−iso8859−1
```

in the explicit font name. The idea is to specify enough parts of the font name explicitly so that the server gives you the font you have in mind.

It is helpful to familiarize yourself with the available font families, weights, slants, and point sizes. The following list gives these statistics for the fonts in the directories *75dpi* and *100dpi* in the standard X distribution from MIT.* (The fonts in the *misc* directory are hold-overs from Release 2 and have short, manageable names that should not require wildcarding.)

Font families	Charter, Courier, Helvetica, New Century Schoolbook, Symbol, Times
Weights	Medium, bold
Slants	Roman (r), an upright design Italic (i), an italic design, slanted clockwise from vertical Oblique (o), an obliqued upright design, slanted clockwise from vertical
Point sizes	8, 10, 12, 14, 18, 24

If you are unfamiliar with general appearance of a particular font family, try displaying one of the fonts with *xfd*, as described in Volume Three, *X Window System User's Guide*.

---

*For fonts other than those shipped by MIT, other families, weights, slants, point sizes, etc. may apply.

As a general rule, we suggest you type the following parts of a font name explicitly:

- Font family
- Weight
- Slant
- Point size

Note that it is better to match the point size field, which is measured in tenths of a point (the 100 in the previous example, equal to 10 points), than the pixel field (the 10). This allows your wildcarded font name to work properly with monitors of different resolutions. For example, say you use the following name to specify a 24-point (size), medium (weight), Italic (slant), Charter (family) font:

```
*charter-medium-i-*-240-*
```

This will match either of the following two font names (the first for 75-dpi monitors and the second for 100-dpi monitors):

```
-bitstream-charter-medium-i-normal--25-240-75-75-p-136-iso8859-1
-bitstream-charter-medium-i-normal--33-240-100-100-p-136-iso8859-1
```

depending on which directory comes first in your font path. Specifying font size explicitly in pixels (25 for the first or 33 for the second) rather than in points would limit you to matching only one of these fonts.

Given the complexity of font names and the rules of precedence used by the server, you should use wildcards carefully.

A.1.3 Font Name Aliasing

Another way to abbreviate font names is by aliasing—that is, by associating them with alternative names. You can create a file (or files) called *fonts.alias* in any directory in the font search path to set aliases for the fonts in that directory. The X server uses both *fonts.dir* files (see Section A.2.5) and *fonts.alias* files to locate fonts in the font path.

Be aware that when you create or edit a *fonts.alias* file, the server does not *automatically* recognize the aliases in question. You must make the server aware of newly created or edited alias files by resetting the font path with *xset* as described in Section A.2.4.

The *fonts.alias* file has a two-column format similar to the *fonts.dir* file: the first column contains aliases, the second contains the actual font names. If you want to specify an alias that contains spaces, enclose the alias in double quotes. If you want to include double quotes or other special characters as part of an alias, precede each special symbol with a backslash.

When you use an alias to specify a font in a command line, the server searches for the font associated with that alias in every directory in the font path. Therefore, a *fonts.alias* file in one directory can set aliases for fonts in other directories as well. You might choose to create a single aliases file in one directory of the font path to set aliases for the most commonly used fonts in all the directories. Example A-1 shows a sample *fonts.alias* file.

Example A-1. Sample fonts.alias file

```
xterm12    -adobe-courier-medium-r-normal--12-120-75-75-m-70-iso8859-1
xterm14    -adobe-courier-medium-r-normal--14-140-75-75-m-90-iso8859-1
xterm18    -adobe-courier-medium-r-normal--18-180-75-75-m-110-iso8859-1
```

As the names of the aliases suggest, this sample file contains aliases for three fonts (of different point sizes) that are easily readable in *xterm* windows.

You can also use wildcards within the font names in the right-hand column of an alias file. For instance, the alias file above might also be written:

```
xterm12    *courier-medium-r-*-120*
xterm14    *courier-medium-r-*-140*
xterm18    *courier-medium-r-*-180*
```

Once the server is made aware of aliases, you can specify an alias in resource specifications or on the command line:

```
xterm.font: xterm12
```

or:

```
xterm -fn xterm12
```

If you want each font name to be equivalent to the name of the file in which it is stored, without the *.snf* extension, you can use alias files. In each directory in the font path, create a *fonts.alias* file containing only the following line:

```
FILE_NAMES_ALIASES
```

Each filename (without the *.snf* extension) will then serve as an alias for the font the file contains. Note that an alias file containing this line applies only to the directory in which it is found. To make every font name equivalent to the name of the file in which it is stored, you need to create a *fonts.alias* file such as this in every font directory.

If you have specified FILE_NAMES_ALIASES in an alias file, you can choose the fonts in that directory by means of their filenames, as we did in the resource example at the end of Chapter 2, *X Concepts*.

A.1.4 Making the Server Aware of Aliases

After you create (or update) an alias file, the server does not automatically recognize the aliases in question. You must make the server aware of newly created or edited alias files by "rehashing" the font path with *xset*. Enter:

```
xset fp rehash
```

on the command line. The *xset* option **fp** (font path) with the **rehash** argument causes the server to reread the *fonts.dir* and *fonts.alias* files in the current font path. You need to do this every time you edit an alias file. (You also need to use *xset* if you add or remove fonts. See Volume Three, *X Window System User's Guide*, for details.)

A.1.5 The fonts.dir Files

In addition to font files, each font directory contains a file called *fonts.dir*. The *fonts.dir* files serve, in effect, as databases for the X server. When the X server searches the directories in the default font path, it uses the *fonts.dir* files to locate the font(s) it needs.

Each *fonts.dir* file contains a list of all the font files in the directory with their associated font names in two-column form. (The first column lists the font file and the second column lists the actual font name associated with the file.) The first line in *fonts.dir* lists the number of entries in the file (i.e., the number of fonts in the directory).

Example A-2 shows the *fonts.dir* file from the directory */usr/lib/X11/fonts/100dpi*. As the first line indicates, the directory contains 24 fonts.

Example A-2. fonts.dir file in /usr/lib/X11/fonts/100dpi

```
24
charBI08.snf     -bitstream-charter-bold-i-normal--11-80-100-100-p-68-iso8859-1
charBI10.snf     -bitstream-charter-bold-i-normal--14-100-100-100-p-86-iso8859-1
charBI12.snf     -bitstream-charter-bold-i-normal--17-120-100-100-p-105-iso8859-1
charBI14.snf     -bitstream-charter-bold-i-normal--19-140-100-100-p-117-iso8859-1
charBI18.snf     -bitstream-charter-bold-i-normal--25-180-100-100-p-154-iso8859-1
charBI24.snf     -bitstream-charter-bold-i-normal--33-240-100-100-p-203-iso8859-1
charB08.snf      -bitstream-charter-bold-r-normal--11-80-100-100-p-69-iso8859-1
charB10.snf      -bitstream-charter-bold-r-normal--14-100-100-100-p-88-iso8859-1
charB12.snf      -bitstream-charter-bold-r-normal--17-120-100-100-p-107-iso8859-1
charB14.snf      -bitstream-charter-bold-r-normal--19-140-100-100-p-119-iso8859-1
charB18.snf      -bitstream-charter-bold-r-normal--25-180-100-100-p-157-iso8859-1
charB24.snf      -bitstream-charter-bold-r-normal--33-240-100-100-p-206-iso8859-1
charI08.snf      -bitstream-charter-medium-i-normal--11-80-100-100-p-60-iso8859-1
charI10.snf      -bitstream-charter-medium-i-normal--14-100-100-100-p-76-iso8859-1
charI12.snf      -bitstream-charter-medium-i-normal--17-120-100-100-p-92-iso8859-1
charI14.snf      -bitstream-charter-medium-i-normal--19-140-100-100-p-103-iso8859-1
charI18.snf      -bitstream-charter-medium-i-normal--25-180-100-100-p-136-iso8859-1
charI24.snf      -bitstream-charter-medium-i-normal--33-240-100-100-p-179-iso8859-1
charR08.snf      -bitstream-charter-medium-r-normal--11-80-100-100-p-61-iso8859-1
charR10.snf      -bitstream-charter-medium-r-normal--14-100-100-100-p-78-iso8859-1
charR12.snf      -bitstream-charter-medium-r-normal--17-120-100-100-p-95-iso8859-1
charR14.snf      -bitstream-charter-medium-r-normal--19-140-100-100-p-106-iso8859-1
charR18.snf      -bitstream-charter-medium-r-normal--25-180-100-100-p-139-iso8859-1
charR24.snf      -bitstream-charter-medium-r-normal--33-240-100-100-p-183-iso8859-1
```

The *fonts.dir* files are created by the *mkfontdir* client when X is installed. *mkfontdir* reads the font files in directories in the font path, extracts the font names, and creates a *fonts.dir* file in each directory. If *fonts.dir* files are present on your system, you probably will not have to deal with them or with *mkfontdir* at all. If the files are not present or if you have to load new fonts or remove existing ones, you will have to create files with *mkfontdir*. See Volume Three, *X Window System User's Guide*, for details.

A.2 Font Service

If you have worked with X at a site with workstations from several vendors, you may have encountered frustrating problems with the use of fonts. If fonts have different names on one host than they do on another, an application that performs normally on one display will abort with a "Can't load font" error on another. Or you may have had to maintain separate defaults files for use on different displays.

Ideally, the site administrator could simply place fonts in a directory of a networked file system that is accessible to all hosts at the site. Unfortunately, no binary format for font data has been standardized, and the X servers supplied by different vendors expect data in mutually incompatible formats. If a vendor wishes to support several font formats, the server must include code to parse each one.

R5 provides an elegant solution to these problems in the form of a networked font service. Under this new model, an X server can obtain font data in a simple bitmap format from a *font server* process running somewhere on the network. The font server does the work of parsing font files for any supported format and exports font data in a bitmap format standardized by the X Font Service Protocol (reprinted in Volume Zero, *X Protocol Reference Manual* as of late 1992). X servers that take advantage of font service no longer need to do the work of parsing fonts themselves. In the near future, however, it is likely that workstation-based X servers and X terminals will continue to support file-based fonts along with their support for font servers.

The Font Service Protocol was designed by Jim Fulton of Network Computing Devices. The font server in the MIT distribution was implemented primarily by Dave Lemke, also of NCD. In addition, Apple Computer has donated a font server (which runs only on the Apple Macintosh computer) to export the Apple bitmap fonts, and, if available, the Apple TrueType fonts as well.

Typically, a font server will run on one host per site and will export all the fonts available at the site, but there are a variety of other ways that font service can be configured. A large site may choose to have multiple font servers to prevent overloading of a single server or to protect against service outages caused by network trouble or server crashes. A font server could export fonts parsed from a variety of formats, or a separate server could be used for each format. A vendor of fonts with a custom format might provide a special font server to export those fonts, and might use the special server to implement licensing policies—restricting the maximum number of simultaneous users of a font, for example. Finally, note that in the terminology of X font service, the X server is a *font client*, and that it is perfectly legal to have other font clients such as printer drivers. Figure A-2 shows a font server providing service to a workstation, an X terminal, and a printer driver.

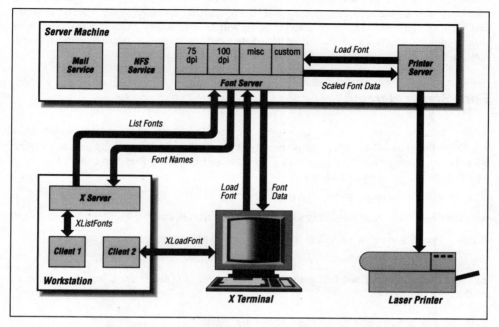

Figure A-2. A typical font server configuration

R5 font service and scalable font support consists of the following components:

- The X Font Service Protocol, a standardized, extensible protocol for communication between a font server and font clients, such as an X display server. This protocol also standardizes the format used for the communication of font data between font server and font client.

- Additions to the X server to allow it to participate in the font service protocol.

- A convention for the naming and inclusion of font servers in the X server font path.

- A bitmap and outline font-scaling algorithm in the X server.

- A set of scalable outline fonts (in Charter and Courier typefaces) from Bitstream, Inc.

- A font server capable of scaling and exporting the new outline fonts as well as the standard X bitmap fonts.

- A font server that runs on an Apple Macintosh computer to export the Apple bitmap fonts and, if available, scaled Apple TrueType fonts to any X servers on the network.

- A respecification of the X server's handling of **XListFonts**, **XLoadFont()**, and **XLoadQueryFont()** to allow pattern matching for scalable fonts.

- An addition to the *X Logical Font Description Conventions* (XLFD) to handle pattern matching for scalable fonts.

There are no new or changed Xlib functions for the support of font service or scalable fonts. There are new conventions for naming and listing scalable fonts, however, and applications that want to make explicit use of scalable fonts will have to follow these conventions. Note that R5 defines a new abstraction, the **XFontSet**, which is used in internationalized applications, but that this has nothing whatsoever to do with font service.

A.2.1 Font Server Naming

To the X server, a font server is just another element in a font path—a place to look when searching for fonts. If a font server is running at your site, you can use it by adding its name (if it is not already there) to your font path with **xset fp**. A font server that runs on a TCP/IP network is named as follows:

> tcp/*hostname*:*port-number*[/*catalogue-list*]

where the optional *catalogue-list* is a list of catalogue names separated with plus signs.

A font server that runs on a DECnet network is named as follows:

> decnet/*nodename*::font$*objname*[/*catalogue-list*]

Example A-3 shows various font paths that might be set in order to use a font server running on the host "ora-server."

Example A-3. X font paths containing font servers

```
tcp/ora-server:7000

tcp/ora-server:7000/75dpi, /usr/lib/X11/fonts/misc

tcp/ora-server:7000/100dpi+misc, /usr/lib/X11/fonts/misc

tcp/ora-server:7000/100dpi+misc, tcp/ora-server:7001/new-fonts
```

Naming a font server is conceptually the same as naming an X display, but obviously the naming schemes used are very different. When naming an X server, a TCP/IP connection is distinguished from a DECnet connection solely by the number of colons that separate the hostname from the display number, and this scheme is not elegantly extensible to other network technologies in the future. Furthermore, an X server communicates over a port which is a relative offset (the display number) from a "hardcoded" base port number, but base port numbers cannot simply be allocated; they must be assigned by the powers that be in the network world. Font server names specify an absolute port number, rather than a relative number. The default is 7000 as in Example A-3, but this can easily be overridden (it is a command-line option) if it conflicts with other services or even other font servers. If X were rewritten today, display names would probably be just like font server names: they would explicitly specify the network type and absolute port number.

A.2.2 Font Server Configuration

The font server shipped as part of the MIT R5 distribution is named `fs`. Generally it is started up automatically on reboot of whatever server machine it is running on. For standalone machines, it may be appropriate to have `xdm` start up the font server when a user logs in. On startup, `fs` reads a configuration file named on the command line, or the default file */usr/lib/X11/fs/config*. This configuration file lists the directories of fonts that the server should export, and controls such things as the maximum number of clients allowed to connect to the server, and the default point size the server should return when a font name does not specify a size. The format of this file is documented in the `fs` man page in the reference section of this book, and the default config file is a good example. Note that this configuration file is not installed by default when R5 is built. Unless you plan to always use the command-line configuration option to `fs`, you should install the configuration file by hand, or add this line at the end of *mit/config/site.def* to have it installed automatically by the build process:

```
#define InstallFSConfig YES
```

The forthcoming O'Reilly & Associates book on X administration will cover font server configuration in more detail.

The R5 distribution from MIT also includes a font server for the Apple Macintosh which will export Apple bitmap fonts (and Apple TrueType fonts if they are available) to X servers on the network. The source code for this server is in *mit/fonts/server/MacFS* and will only build on a Macintosh running A/UX. The *README* file in this directory provides minimal documentation on building and configuring the server. Note that the fonts themselves are not part of the R5 distribution; these must exist on the Macintosh that will be exporting them.

A.3 Scalable Fonts

Another new feature in R5 is font scaling. In previous releases, each font was available only in a limited number of standard point sizes and resolutions. In the MIT distribution of R5, both the X server and the font server implement a simple bitmap font-scaling algorithm that allows fonts to be obtained at any desired point size and resolution. Bitmap fonts are easily scalable, but the resulting scaled font is generally jagged and difficult to read. Fortunately, R5 also provides a set of outline fonts. Outline fonts scale nicely, but the scaling process requires significant computation, so an X server might freeze for several seconds while scaling a large Asian font. This is one of the problems that font servers are intended to address. The fonts and the scaling code were donated by Bitstream, Inc.

Until Release 5, X relied exclusively on non-scalable bitmap fonts. If there was no installed font in the point size and resolution you wanted, then you were out of luck—it is obviously not feasible to provide every font in every point size and for every possible resolution. Bitmap fonts do not scale well, because their pixel-by-pixel specification can only be made smaller by omitting pixels or made larger by making pixels bigger, resulting in a jagged, low-resolution font. The fonts shipped by MIT for Release 5 include several "outline fonts" which describe characters by their component curves rather than by individual pixels. This description allows for successful scaling to any desired point size and resolution. The font server shipped by MIT in Release 5 has the capability to read and scale these outline fonts, and therefore the number of fonts available to the user is greatly increased. (Note, however, that a good bitmap font that is "hand-tuned" to a particular point size and screen resolution will generally be better looking than an outline font scaled to that size and resolution. Font design is an art, and the human touch is still important.)

The following two sections apply equally to all scalable and scaled fonts, whether outline or bitmap, from the X server or the font server.

A.3.1 Finding Scalable Fonts

Supporting scalable fonts raises some important questions about the behavior of the Xlib function `XListFonts()`. First, since there are (theoretically) an infinite number of point sizes and resolutions that a font could be scaled to, it is no longer possible to list all available fonts in *all* available sizes. So some special syntax is needed to indicate that a font is scalable and is available in any desired size, even if that size is not listed. But backwards compatibility is also an issue—the new point sizes provided by scalable fonts should not be hidden from existing pre-R5 applications.

These seemingly contradictory goals are resolved by changing the semantics of the call to `XListFonts()` and by extending the *X Logical Font Description Conventions* slightly.* In R5, scalable fonts are returned by `XListFonts()` with the string "0" in the PIXEL_SIZE, POINT_SIZE, and AVERAGE_WIDTH fields (the seventh, eighth, and twelfth fields of the 14-field XLFD font name). Non-scalable fonts will never have these three fields zero, and therefore these fields are sufficient to distinguish scalable from non-scalable fonts. Most font servers will list a few specific *derived instances* of each scalable font at standard sizes and resolutions for the benefit of older X applications that expect to find font names in this form.

The X server and font server are only required to match scalable fonts when the font name pattern they are passed is a *well-formed* one. A well-formed font name is one that contains all 14 hyphens specified in the XLFD convention. Wildcards are permitted for any field, but may not replace multiple fields—all fields must be present in the name. For example,

```
*-helvetica-bold-o-*-*-*-120-*
```

is not a well-formed name, but

```
-*-helvetica-bold-o-*-*-*-120-75-75-*-*-iso8859-1
```

is well-formed. Shortcut names specified as in the first example have come into common use, but with the increasing variety of display resolutions and fonts with non-standard charsets, it is good practice to specify these extra fields, even if you are not interested in using scaled fonts. If `XListFonts()` is passed a pattern that is not well-formed, it may not include scalable fonts in the search at all.

---

*The XLFD Conventions are printed as Appendix M of *X Protocol Reference Manual*, Volume Zero of the O'Reilly & Associates series of X books.

To list scalable fonts, call **XListFonts()** with a well-formed pattern with "0" or "*" in its PIXEL_SIZE, POINT_SIZE, and AVERAGE_WIDTH fields. Example A-4 shows some queries that will return scalable fonts. You can quickly try them out by replacing the call to **XList-Fonts()** with the client **xlsfonts**.

Example A-4. Listing scalable fonts

```
/* List all Latin-1 fonts.  Returned names of scalable fonts will have
 * "0" for pixel size, point size, and average width
 */
fonts = XListFonts(dpy, "-*-*-*-*-*-*-*-*-*-*-*-*-iso8859-1", 1000, &count);

/* List all scalable courier fonts.  Non-scalable fonts will
 * not be listed.
 */
list = XListFonts(dpy,"-*-courier-*-*-*-*-0-0-*-*-*-0-*-*", 200, &count);
```

A.3.2 Finding Derived Instances of Scalable Fonts

A scalable font name with a point size (and pixel size and average width) of zero is not very useful by itself. If you call **XLoadFont()** on this font name without a size, you will get some implementation-defined default size. Instead of listing scalable Helvetica fonts, for example, you will more often want to list all Helvetica fonts at some particular point size. The list you get may contain non-scaled bitmap fonts as well as derived instances of scalable fonts. In order to include derived instances of scalable fonts in a search, it is necessary to specify some of the size fields explicitly. There are five *scalable fields* in an XLFD font name: PIXEL_SIZE, POINT_SIZE, RESOLUTION_X, RESOLUTION_Y, and AVERAGE_WIDTH (fields 7, 8, 9, 10, and 12.) In order for **XListFonts()** to list a particular scaled size of a scalable font, enough of these scalable fields must be specified so that the font name pattern matches exactly one derived instance of the font. If too few of the scalable fields are specified, there will be no unique match, and if too many are specified, there may not be any possible scaling that meets all of those specified criteria.

When searching for fonts at a particular size, you will typically wildcard the pixel size and average width by setting those fields to "*" and explicitly specify the point size you want along with the x- and y-resolutions of your screen. (You can calculate screen resolutions with macros like **DisplayWidth()** and **DisplayWidthMM()**, as shown in a later example.) These three fields specify all that is needed to correctly scale the font. You need not (and should not) specify the pixel size, because the point size and y-resolution of the screen determine the desired pixel size. You need not specify the average width because the point size and x-resolution of the screen, together with the height to width ratio implicit to the font, determine the desired width. It is also possible to name a single derived instance of a scalable font by specifying a pixel size plus x- and y-resolutions. There are also other combinations of fields that will work, but none are particularly useful in practice. Example A-5 shows font name patterns that will match derived instances of scalable fonts.

Example A-5. Finding derived instances of scalable fonts

```
/* Load a 12-point bold helvetica font defined at a 100x100 dpi
 * resolution.  The actual font loaded might be a derived instance of a
 * scalable font, or it might be a bitmap font--there is no way to
 * distinguish them.
 */
font = XLoadFont(dpy, "-*-helvetica-bold-r-*-*-*-120-100-100-*-*-iso8859-1");

/* Load a 20 pixel high helvetica font defined at 100x100 dpi */
font2 = XLoadFont(dpy, "-*-helvetica-medium-r-*-*-20-*-100-100-*-*-iso8859-1");

/* List all 13-point Latin-1 helvetica fonts defined at a 106x97 dpi
 * resolution.  This pattern will match derived instances of scalable
 * fonts, and will probably only match derived instances of scalable
 * fonts, because there are not likely to be bitmap fonts defined at this
 * particular size and resolution.
 */
list = XListFonts(dpy,"-*-helvetica-*-*-*-*-*-130-106-97-*-*-iso8859-1",
                  50, &count);
```

There are a number of reasons that a font name pattern could fail to match derived instances of scalable fonts. It is difficult to devise an algorithm that will correctly match scalable fonts against any font name pattern. For this reason, the X server or font server is not required to include scalable fonts in its search if the pattern it is given is not well-formed. A well-formed pattern must contain 14 hyphens. Note in particular that the first character in a well-formed name must be a hyphen.

An underspecified font name will not match any derived instances of scalable fonts. This is because your font name could match any number of derived instances, and it is not possible to list them all. When only the point size and pixel size are specified, for example, they are enough together to determine the desired y-resolution for the font, but any x-resolution (and therefore any average width) is still possible. To uniquely match a derived instance, you'd have to specify the x-resolution of your screen or a desired average width for the font. The MIT implementation, however, makes reasonable guesses for unspecified resolution values, so underspecified font names do not occur. If only point size is specified, then default resolutions (75 or 100 dpi) are used. If both point and pixel size are specified as above, then the y-resolution they specify is used for both x- and y-resolution fields.

Similarly, an overspecified font name, one with point size, pixel size, and x- and y-resolutions, for example, may not match any derived instances of scalable fonts: if the specified y-resolution is different from the y-resolution implicitly defined by the combination of point size and pixel size, then there is no way that the font can be scaled to satisfy your request. Example A-6 shows font name patterns that will fail to match any derived instances of scalable fonts.

Example A-6. Font name patterns that don't match scaled fonts.

```
/* List 15-point bold oblique helvetica fonts.  Derived instances of
 * scalable fonts will probably not be included in the list because the
 * pattern does not have all 14 fields.
 */
helvbold15 = XListFonts(dpy,"*-helvetica-bold-o-*-*-*-150-*", 50, &count);

/* List all 17-point, 17-pixel bold oblique helvetica fonts defined at
```

Example A-6. Font name patterns that don't match scaled fonts. (continued)

```
 * 100dpi x- and y-resolutions.  This pattern will not match any derived
 * instances of scalable fonts (nor any font) because a 17 point font
 * at 100dpi is not 17 pixels high.
 */
helvbold17 = XListFonts(dpy,"-*-helvetica-bold-o-*-*-17-170-100-100-*-*-
                        iso8859-1",50, &count);
```

A.3.3 Using Scalable Fonts

Many applications use only a small number of fonts, that are opened at startup and never changed. These applications may leave the choice of fonts to the user. If the user overrides the default with a font that doesn't exist, the application may simply print an error message and exit. Applications such as this need no modification to work with scalable fonts. Users who want to take advantage of scalable fonts, must provide a well-formed and correctly specified font name. Other applications, such as word processors or presentation graphics packages, may allow the user to select fonts from a menu or list at runtime. This kind of application will have to be modified to recognize and make use of scalable fonts. Example A-7 and Example A-8 demonstrate one approach.

Example A-7 shows a procedure that determines whether or not a given font name represents a scalable font. This procedure is intended to be called once for each font returned by `XListFonts()`.

Example A-7. Determining if a font is scalable

```
/*
 * This routine returns True if the passed name is a well-formed
 * XLFD style font name with a pixel size, point size, and average
 * width (fields 7,8, and 12) of "0".
 */
Bool IsScalableFont(name)
char *name;
{
    int i, field;

    if ((name == NULL) || (name[0] != '-')) return False;

    for(i = field = 0; name[i] != '\0'; i++) {
        if (name[i] == '-') {
            field++;
            if ((field == 7) || (field == 8) || (field == 12))
                if ((name[i+1] != '0') || (name[i+2] != '-'))
                    return False;
        }
    }

    if (field != 14) return False;
    else return True;
}
```

Example A-8 shows a procedure that takes a scalable font name and a desired point size and loads the derived instance of that font at the requested size and at the precise resolution of the screen. It is intended to be called with a scalable font name as returned by **XList-Fonts()**.

Example A-8. Loading a derived instance of a scalable font

```
/*
 * This routine is passed a scalable font name and a point size.  It returns
 * an XFontStruct for the given font scaled to the specified size and the
 * exact resolution of the screen.  The font name is assumed to be a
 * well-formed XLFD name, and to have pixel size, point size, and average
 * width fields of "0" and arbitrary x-resolution and y-resolution fields.
 * Size is specified in tenths of points.  Returns NULL if the name is
 * malformed or no such font exists.
 */
XFontStruct *LoadQueryScalableFont(dpy, screen, name, size)
Display *dpy;
int screen;
char *name;
int size;
{
    int i,j, field;
    char newname[ 500 ];    /* big enough for a long font name */
    int res_x, res_y;       /* resolution values for this screen */

    /* catch obvious errors */
    if ((name == NULL) || (name[ 0 ] != '-')) return NULL;

    /* calculate our screen resolution in dots per inch. 25.4mm = 1 inch */
    res_x = DisplayWidth(dpy, screen)/(DisplayWidthMM(dpy, screen)/25.4);
    res_y = DisplayHeight(dpy, screen)/(DisplayHeightMM(dpy, screen)/25.4);

    /* copy the font name, changing the scalable fields as we do so */
    for(i = j = field = 0; name[ i ] != '\0' && field <= 14; i++) {
        newname[ j++ ] = name[ i ];
        if (name[ i ] == '-') {
            field++;
            switch(field) {
            case 7:  /* pixel size */
            case 12: /* average width */
                /* change from "-0-" to "-*-" */
                newname[ j ] = '*';
                j++;
                if (name[ i+1 ] != '\0') i++;
                break;
            case 8:  /* point size */
                /* change from "-0-" to "-<size>-" */
                sprintf(&newname[ j ], "%d", size);
                while (newname[ j ] != '\0') j++;
                if (name[ i+1 ] != '\0') i++;
                break;
            case 9:  /* x-resolution */
            case 10: /* y-resolution */
                /* change from an unspecified resolution to res_x or res_y */
                sprintf(&newname[ j ], "%d", (field == 9) ? res_x : res_y);
                while(newname[ j ] != '\0') j++;
                while((name[ i+1 ] != '-') && (name[ i+1 ] != '\0')) i++;
```

Example A-8. Loading a derived instance of a scalable font (continued)

```
              break;
        }
    }
}
newname[j] = '\0';

/* if there aren't 14 hyphens, it isn't a well formed name */
if (field != 14) return NULL;

return XLoadQueryFont(dpy, newname);
}
```

B

X10 Compatibility

X11 includes a conversion library, so that X10.4 applications can be easily ported to X11, albeit with a loss of performance. In addition, there are a few X10 routines that provide functionality missing in X11, which may still be used. This appendix discusses XDraw ()and related commands and association table routines for data management.

In This Appendix:

X10 Compatibility

These functions are provided for compatibility with X Version 10. They are considered a part of Xlib even though they exist in a separate library. They can be used by including the file *<X11/X10.h>* and linking with the *-loldX* library.

X Version 11 **XDraw** now provides all the functionality of the X Version 10 routines **XDraw**, **XDrawDashed**, and **XDrawPatterned**. X Version 11 **XDrawFilled()** now provides the functionality of the old **XDrawFilled()** and **XDrawTiled**. These routines now use the GC to specify the fill, tile or stipple, line styles, etc.

The association table routines are described next in this appendix. They are also carried over from X10, although their functionality is also provided by the context manager routines described in Chapter 15, *Other Programming Techniques*. However, there are no performance penalties for using association tables if you prefer them.

See Volume Two, *Xlib Reference Manual*, for complete information on using any X10 compatibility function.

B.1 XDraw and XDrawFilled()

XDraw and **XDrawFilled()** call other Xlib routines, not the server directly. If you just have straight lines to draw, using **XDrawLines()** or **XDrawSegments()** is much faster. If you want to draw spline curves in a portable fashion, you currently have no choice but to use **XDraw** until a standard spline extension is adopted.

XDraw draws an arbitrary polygon or curve. The figure drawn is defined by a list of vertices (*vlist*). The points are connected by lines as specified in the flags in the vertex structure. In X Version 11, **XDraw** provides all the functionality of the X Version 10 routines **XDraw**, **XDrawDashed**, and **XDrawPatterned**. **XDrawFilled()** now provides the functionality of the old **XDrawFilled()** and **XDrawTiled**. The fill, pattern, **line_style**, and tile are all controlled by the graphics context. Lines are properly joined according to the GC if they connect and make a closed figure.

The error status returned is the opposite of what it was under X Version 10, conforming to the X Version 11 standard that 0 indicates failure. The **VertexDrawLastPoint** flag and the routines **XAppendVertex** and **XClearVertexFlag** from X Version 10 are not supported.

The *vlist* and *vcount* arguments of **XDraw** and **XDrawFilled( )** control the line or area that is drawn:

vlist   Specifies a pointer to the list of vertices which indicate what to draw.

vcount   Specifies how many vertices are in *vlist*.

Each **Vertex**, as defined in *<X11/Xlib.h>*, is a structure with the following members:

Example B-1. The Vertex structure for XDraw

```
typedef struct _Vertex {
    short x,y;
    unsigned short flags;
} Vertex;
```

The **x** and **y** members are the coordinates of the vertex. These coordinates are interpreted according to the flags.

The **flags** member, as defined in **Xlib.h**, is a mask made by ORing the symbols listed in Table B-1.

Table B-1. Vertex Flags

Flag	Bit	If Not Set
VertexRelative	0	Absolute
VertexDontDraw	1	Draw
VertexCurved	2	Straight
VertexStartClosed	3	Not closed
VertexEndClosed	4	Not closed

XDraw fails (returns 0) only if it runs out of memory or is passed a **Vertex** list which has a vertex with **VertexStartClosed** set not followed by a vertex with **VertexEnd-Closed** set. The **x** and **y** coordinates in **Vertex** are relative to the upper-left inside corner of the drawable if **VertexRelative** is not specified in **flags** or to the previous vertex if **VertexRelative** is specified. The first vertex must be an absolute vertex.

If **VertexDontDraw** is specified in **flags**, no line or curve is drawn from the previous vertex to this one. This is analogous to picking up the pen and moving it to another place before drawing another line.

If **VertexCurved** is specified in **flags**, a spline algorithm is used to draw a smooth curve from the previous vertex through the current one to the next vertex. Otherwise, a straight line is drawn from the previous vertex to the current one. You should set **Vertex-Curved** in **flags** only if a previous and next vertex are both defined, either explicitly or through the definition of a closed curve. If **VertexStartClosed** is specified, then this point marks the beginning of a closed curve. This vertex must be followed later in the array by another vertex whose absolute coordinates are identical and which has **VertexEnd-Closed** specified in its flags.

It is permissible for both the **VertexDontDraw** and the **VertexCurved** bits to be 1. This is useful to define the previous point for the smooth curve, without drawing until the current point.

Example B-2 shows a routine that draws a box on the root window for use by the window manager described in Chapter 16, *Window Management*. Of course, you would want to create the GC in the calling routine if **draw_box** were to be called more than once.

Example B-2. draw_box implemented with X Version 10 XDraw

```
draw_box(display, screen_num, left,top,right,bottom)
Display *display;
int screen_num;
int left,top,right,bottom;
    {
    Vertex corner[5];
    int vertexcount = 5;
    int planes = FIRST_PLANE;
    GC gc;

    /* Create graphics context */
    /* Ignore XGCvalues and use defaults */
    gc = XCreateGC(display, RootWindow(display, screen_num), 0,
            NULL);

    /* Set graphics context to include font */
    XSetFunction(display, gc, GXxor);

    XSetForeground(display, gc, BlackPixel(display,screen_num));

    XSetPlaneMask(display, gc, planes);

    corner[0].x = left;
    corner[0].y = top;
    corner[0].flags = 0;

    corner[1].x = left;
    corner[1].y = bottom;
    corner[1].flags = 0;

    corner[2].x = right;
    corner[2].y = bottom;
    corner[2].flags = 0;

    corner[3].x = right;
    corner[3].y = top;
    corner[3].flags = 0;

    corner[4].x = left;
    corner[4].y = top;
    corner[4].flags = 0;

    XDraw(display, RootWindow(display, screen_num), gc, corner,
            vertexcount);
    XFlush();
    }
```

B.2 Association Tables

Association tables provide a fast lookup table for data that must be searched frequently. They are implemented as a linked list of structures. To use these functions, you must link in *-loldX*, the X10 compatibility library.

Association tables associate arbitrary information with resource IDs. This is similar to the context manager, but the resource IDs used with association tables are existing resources, not created for the purpose of storing data for later retrieval.

An **XAssocTable** can be used to type X resources. For example, the user may wish to have three or four "types" of windows, each with different properties. This can be accomplished by associating each X window ID with a pointer to a window property data structure defined by the programmer. The generic type for resource IDs is **XID**.

There are a few guidelines that should be observed when using an **XAssocTable**:

- All **XID**s are relative to the currently active display. Therefore, if you are using multiple displays, you need to be sure the correct display is active before performing an **XAssocTable** operation. **XAssocTable** imposes no restrictions on the number of **XID**s per table, the number of **XID**s per display, or the number of displays per table.

- Because of the hashing scheme used by the association mechanism, the following rules for determining the size of **XAssocTable**s should be followed. Associations will be made and looked up more efficiently if the table size (number of buckets in the hashing system) is a power of two and if there are not more than eight **XID**s per bucket.

XCreateAssocTable( ) creates an association table. To create an entry in a specific **XAssocTable**, use **XMakeAssoc( )**. Some size suggestions might be: use 32 buckets per 100 objects; a reasonable maximum number of objects per buckets is 8. **XMakeAssoc( )** inserts data into an **XAssocTable** keyed on an **XID**. **XDeleteAssoc( )** deletes an association in an **XAssocTable** keyed on its **XID**. Data is inserted into the table only once. Redundant inserts are meaningless and cause no problems. The queue in each association bucket is sorted from the lowest **XID** to the highest **XID**. Redundant deletes (and deletes of nonexistent **XID**s) are meaningless and cause no problems. Deleting associations in no way impairs the performance of an **XAssocTable**.

XLookUpAssoc( ) retrieves the data stored in an **XAssocTable** by its **XID**. If an appropriately matching **XID** can be found in the table, the routine will return the data associated with it. If the **XID** cannot be found in the table, the routine will return **NULL**.

XDestroyAssocTable( ) frees the memory associated with a specific **XAssocTable**. Using an **XAssocTable** after it has been destroyed is guaranteed to have unpredictable and probably disastrous consequences!

C

Writing Extensions to X

Extensibility is an important part of X. Hooks are provided into Xlib and the protocol so that extensions will have the same performance as the core routines. This appendix provides reference information on how to write extensions and integrate them into Xlib. This appendix is not a tutorial, and you will need to look at existing extensions to figure out how to write one yourself.

In This Appendix:

C

Writing Extensions to X[*]

Extensions can be added to Xlib only with no protocol addition or to both Xlib and the server with a protocol addition. Several extensions are already available that support nonrectangular windows, 3-D graphics, and alternate input devices and multibuffering. See the code for these for examples of writing extensions.

Because X can only evolve by extension to the core protocol, it is important that extensions not be perceivable as second-class citizens. At some point, some extensions may be adopted as parts of the "X Standard."

Therefore, there should be little to distinguish the use of an extension from that of the core protocol. To avoid having to initialize extensions explicitly in application programs, extensions should perform "lazy evaluations" and automatically initialize themselves when called for the first time.

Extensions written according to these instructions will run at essentially the same performance as the core protocol requests.

It is expected that a given extension to X will consist of multiple requests. Defining ten new features as ten separate extensions is a bad practice. Rather, they should be packaged into a single extension and should use minor opcodes to distinguish the requests.

The symbols and macros used for writing stubs to Xlib are listed in *<Xlibint.h>*.

---

*This appendix is lightly edited and reformatted from the original MIT material. Before attempting to write extensions, you should be intimately familiar with the *X Window System Protocol, Version 11*, by Robert Scheifler and Ron Newman, and with the server code.

Unfortunately, this appendix does not currently provide sufficient tutorial or contextual information to allow you to build an extension. We intend to provide a more helpful description of how to write extensions in a forthcoming book about the server. In the meantime, several sample extensions are provided with the X core distribution which can be used as examples.

C.1 Basic Protocol Support Routines

The basic protocol requests for extensions are XQueryExtension() and XList-
Extensions().

```
Bool XQueryExtension(display, name, major_opcode_return, \
first_event_return, first_error_return)
        Display *display;
        char *name;
        int *major_opcode_return;
        int *first_event_return;
        int *first_error_return;
```

display	Specifies the connection to the X server.
name	Specifies the extension name.
major_opcode_return	Returns the major opcode.
first_event_return	Returns the first event code, if any.
	Specifies the extension list.

XQueryExtension() determines if the named extension is present. If the extension is
not present, False is returned; otherwise True is returned. If the extension is present, the
major opcode for the extension is returned to *major_opcode_return*; otherwise, zero
is returned. Any minor opcode and the request formats are specific to the extension. If the
extension involves additional event types, the base event type code is returned to
first_event_return; otherwise, zero is returned. The format of the events is specific
to the extension. If the extension involves additional error codes, the base error code is
returned to *first_error_return*; otherwise, zero is returned. The format of additional
data in the errors is specific to the extension.

If the extension name is not in the Host Portable Character Encoding the result is implementation dependent. Case matters; the strings *thing*, *Thing*, and *thinG* are all considered different names.

C.1.1 XListExtensions

```
char **XListExtensions(display, nextensions_return)
        Display *display;
        int *nextensions_return;
```

display	Specifies the connection to the X server.
nextensions_return	Returns the number of extensions listed.

XListExtensions() returns a list of all extensions supported by the server. If the data
returned by the server is in the Latin Portable Character Encoding, then the returned strings
are in the Host Portable Character Encoding. Otherwise, the result is implementation dependent.

C.1.2 XFreeExtensionList

```
XFreeExtensionList(list)
      char **list;
```

list   Specifies the list of extension names.

XFreeExtensionList() frees the memory allocated by **XListExtensions()**.

C.2 Hooking into Xlib

These functions allow you to hook into the library. They are not normally used by application programmers but are used by people who need to extend the core X protocol and the X library interface. The functions, which generate protocol requests for X, are typically called stubs.

In extensions, stubs first should check to see if they have initialized themselves on a connection. If they have not, they then should call **XInitExtension()** to attempt to initialize themselves on the connection.

If the extension needs to be informed of GC/font allocation or deallocation or if the extension defines new event types, the functions described here allow the extension to be called when these events occur.

C.2.1 XInitExtension

The **XExtCodes** structure returns the information from **XInitExtension()** and is defined in *<Xlib.h>*:

```
typedef struct _XExtCodes {   /* public to extension, cannot be changed */
      int extension;           /* extension number */
      int major_opcode;        /* major op-code assigned by server */
      int first_event;         /* first event number for the extension */
      int first_error;         /* first error number for the extension */
} XExtCodes;

XExtCodes *XInitExtension(display, name)
      Display *display;
      char *name;
```

display   Specifies the connection to the X server.

name   Specifies the extension name.

XInitExtension() determines if the named extension exists. Then it allocates storage for maintaining the information about the extension on the connection, chains this onto the extension list for the connection, and returns the information the stub implementor will need to access the extension. If the extension does not exist, **XInitExtension()** returns NULL.

If the extension name is not in the Host Portable Character Encoding the result is implementation dependent. Case matters; the strings *thing*, *Thing*, and *thinG* are all considered different names.

The extension number in the **XExtCodes** structure is needed in the other calls that follow. This extension number is unique only to a single connection.

C.2.2 XAddExtension

```
XExtCodes *XAddExtension(display)
        Display *display;
```

display   Specifies the connection to the X server.

For local Xlib extensions, **XAddExtension()** allocates the **XExtCodes** structure, bumps the extension number count, and chains the extension onto the extension list. (This permits extensions to Xlib without requiring server extensions.)

C.2.3 Hooks into the Library

These functions allow you to define procedures that are to be called when various circumstances occur. The procedures include the creation of a new GC for a connection, the copying of a GC, the freeing of a GC, the creating and freeing of fonts, the conversion of events defined by extensions to and from wire format, and the handling of errors.

All of these functions return the previous routine defined for this extension.

C.2.3.1 XESetCloseDisplay

```
int (*XESetCloseDisplay(display, extension, proc))()
        Display *display;
        int extension;
        int (*proc)();
```

display   Specifies the connection to the X server.

extension   Specifies the extension number.

proc   Specifies the routine to call when the display is closed.

You use this procedure to define a procedure to be called whenever **XCloseDisplay()** is called. This procedure returns any previously defined procedure, usually NULL.

When `XCloseDisplay()` is called, your routine is called with these arguments:

```
(*proc)(display, codes)
    Display *display;
    XExtCodes *codes;
```

C.2.3.2 XESetCreateGC

```
int (*XESetCreateGC(display, extension, proc))()
    Display *display;
    int extension;
    int (*proc)();
```

display   Specifies the connection to the X server.

extension   Specifies the extension number.

proc   Specifies the routine to call when a GC is closed.

You use this procedure to define a procedure to be called whenever a new GC is created. This procedure returns any previously defined procedure, usually NULL.

When a GC is created, your routine is called with these arguments:

```
(*proc)(display, gc, codes)
    Display *display;
    GC gc;
    XExtCodes *codes;
```

C.2.3.3 XESetCopyGC

```
int (*XESetCopyGC(display, extension, proc))()
    Display *display;
    int extension;
    int (*proc)();
```

display   Specifies the connection to the X server.

extension   Specifies the extension number.

proc   Specifies the routine to call when GC components are copied.

You use this procedure to define a procedure to be called whenever a GC is copied. This procedure returns any previously defined procedure, usually NULL.

When a GC is copied, your routine is called with these arguments:

```
(*proc)(display, gc, codes)
    Display *display;
    GC gc;
    XExtCodes *codes;
```

Writing Extensions to X

C.2.3.4 XESetFreeGC

```
int (*XESetFreeGC(display, extension, proc))()
        Display *display;
        int extension;
        int (*proc)();
```

display   Specifies the connection to the X server.

extension   Specifies the extension number.

proc   Specifies the routine to call when a GC is freed.

You use this procedure to define a procedure to be called whenever a GC is freed. This procedure returns any previously defined procedure, usually NULL.

When a GC is freed, your routine is called with these arguments:

```
(*proc)(display, gc, codes)
        Display *display;
        GC gc;
        XExtCodes *codes;
```

C.2.3.5 XESetCreateFont

```
int (*XESetCreateFont(display, extension, proc))()
        Display *display;
        int extension;
        int (*proc)();
```

display   Specifies the connection to the X server.

extension   Specifies the extension number.

proc   Specifies the routine to call when a font is created.

You use this procedure to define a procedure to be called whenever **XLoadQueryFont()** and **XQueryFont()** are called. This procedure returns any previously defined procedure, usually NULL.

When **XLoadQueryFont()** or **XQueryFont()** is called, your routine is called with these arguments:

```
(*proc)(display, fs, codes)
        Display *display;
        XFontStruct *fs;
        XExtCodes *codes;
```

C.2.3.6 XESetFreeFont

```
int (*XESetFreeFont(display, extension, proc))()
     Display *display;
     int extension;
     int (*proc)();
```

display   Specifies the connection to the X server.

extension   Specifies the extension number.

proc   Specifies the routine to call when a font is freed.

You use this procedure to define a procedure to be called whenever **XFreeFont( )** is called. This procedure returns any previously defined procedure, usually NULL.

When **XFreeFont( )** is called, your routine is called with these arguments:

```
(*proc)(display, fs, codes)
     Display *display;
     XFontStruct *fs;
     XExtCodes *codes;
```

C.2.4 Defining New Events and Errors

The next three functions allow you to define new events to the library. An **XEvent** structure always has a type code (type **int**) as the first component. This uniquely identifies what kind of event it is. The second component is always the serial number (type **unsigned long**) of the last request processed by the server. The third component is always a boolean (type **BoolP**) indicating whether the event came from a **SendEvent** protocol request. The fourth component is always a pointer to the display the event was read from. The fifth component is always a resource ID of one kind or another, usually a window, carefully selected to be useful to toolkit dispatchers. The fifth component should always exist, even if the event does not have a natural "destination"; if there is no value from the protocol to put in this component, initialize it to zero.

NOTE

There is an implementation limit such that your host event structure size cannot be bigger than the size of the **XEvent** union of structures. There also is no way to guarantee that more than 24 elements or 96 characters in the structure will be fully portable between machines.

Writing Extensions to X

C.2.4.1 XESetWireToEvent

```
int (*XESetWireToEvent()(display, event_number, proc))()
    Display *display;
    int event_number;
    Status (*proc)();
```

display	Specifies the connection to the X server.
event_number	Specifies the event code.
proc	Specifies the routine to call when converting an event.

You use this procedure to define a procedure to be called when an event needs to be converted from wire format (**xEvent**) to host format (**XEvent**). The event number defines which protocol event number to install a conversion routine for. This procedure returns any previously defined procedure.

NOTE

You can replace a core event conversion routine with one of your own, although this is not encouraged. It would, however, allow you to intercept a core event and modify it before being placed in the queue or otherwise examined.

When Xlib needs to convert an event from wire format to host format, your routine is called with these arguments:

```
Status (*proc)(display, re, event)
    Display *display;
    XEvent *re;
    xEvent *event;
```

Your routine must return status to indicate if the conversion succeeded. The *re* argument is a pointer to where the host format event should be stored, and the *event* argument is the 32-byte wire event structure. In the **XEvent** structure you are creating, you must fill in the five required members of the event structure. You should fill in the **type** member with the type specified for the **xEvent** structure. You should copy all other members from the **xEvent** structure (wire format) to the **XEvent** structure (host format). Your conversion routine should return **True** if the event should be placed in the queue or **False** if it should not be placed in the queue.

C.2.4.2 _XSetLastRequestRead

To initialize the serial number component of the event, call **_XSetLastRequestRead()** with the event and use the return value.

```
unsigned long _XSetLastRequestRead(display, rep)
    Display *display;
    xGenericReply *rep;
```

display	Specifies the connection to the X server.
rep	Specifies the wire event structure.

This function computes and returns a complete serial number from the partial serial number in the event.

C.2.4.3 XESetEventToWire

```
Status (*XESetEventToWire()(display, event_number, proc))()
    Display *display;
    int event_number;
    int (*proc)();
```

display   Specifies the connection to the X server.

event_number   Specifies the event code.

proc   Specifies the routine to call when converting an event.

You use this procedure to define a procedure to be called when an event needs to be converted from host format (**XEvent**) to wire format (**xEvent**) form. The event number defines which protocol event number to install a conversion routine for. This procedure returns any previously defined procedure. It returns zero if the conversion fails or nonzero otherwise.

NOTE

You can replace a core event conversion routine with one of your own, although this is not encouraged. It would, however, allow you to intercept a core event and modify it before being sent to another client.

When Xlib needs to convert an event from host format to wire format, your routine is called with these arguments:

```
(*proc)(display, re, event)
    Display *display;
    XEvent *re;
    xEvent *event;
```

The *re* argument is a pointer to the host format event, and the *event* argument is a pointer to where the 32-byte wire event structure should be stored. You should fill in the type with the type from the **XEvent** structure. All other members then should be copied from the host format to the **xEvent** structure.

C.2.4.4 XESetWireToError

```
Bool (*XESetWireToError()(display, error_number, proc)()
    Display *display;
    int error_number;
    Bool (*proc)();
```

display   Specifies the connection to the X server.

error_number   Specifies the error code.

proc   Specifies the routine to call when an error is received.

This function defines a procedure to be called when an extension error needs to be converted from wire format to host format. The error number defines which protocol error code to install the conversion routine for. This procedure returns any previously defined procedure.

Use this function for extension errors that contain additional error values beyond those in a core X error, when multiple wire errors must be combined into a single Xlib error, or when it is necessary to intercept an X error before it is otherwise examined.

When Xlib needs to convert an error from wire format to host format, the routine is called with these arguments:

```
Bool (*proc)(display, he, we)
    Display *display;
    XErrorEvent *he;
    xError *we;
```

The *he* argument is a pointer to where the host format error should be stored. The structure pointed at by he is guaranteed to be as large as an **XEvent** structure, and so can be cast to a type larger than an **XErrorEvent( )**, in order to store additional values. If the error is to be completely ignored by Xlib (for example, several protocol error structures will be combined into one Xlib error), then the function should return **False**; otherwise it should return **True**.

C.2.4.5 XESetError

```
int (*XESetError()(display, extension, proc))()
    Display *display;
    int extension;
    int (*proc)();
```

display   Specifies the connection to the X server.

extension   Specifies the extension number.

proc   Specifies the routine to call when an error is received.

Inside Xlib, there are times that you may want to suppress the calling of the external error handling when an error occurs. This allows status to be returned on a call at the cost of the call being synchronous (though most such routines are query operations, in any case, and are typically programmed to be synchronous).

When Xlib detects a protocol error in **_XReply( )**, it calls your procedure with these arguments:

```
int (*proc)(display, err, codes, ret_code)
    Display *display;
    xError *err;
    XExtCodes *codes;
    int *ret_code;
```

The *err* argument is a pointer to the 32-byte wire format error. The *codes* argument is a pointer to the extension codes structure. The *ret_code* argument is the return code you may want **_XReply** returned to.

If your routine returns a zero value, the error is not suppressed, and the client's error handler is called. (For further information, see Section 11.8.2.) If your routine returns nonzero, the error is suppressed, and _XReply returns the value of *ret_code*.

C.2.4.6 XESetErrorString

```
char  *(*XESetErrorString()(display, extension, proc))()
      Display *display;
      int extension;
      char *(*proc)();
```

display   Specifies the connection to the X server.

extension   Specifies the extension number.

proc   Specifies the routine to call to obtain an error string.

The XGetErrorText() function returns a string to the user for an error. XESet-ErrorString() allows you to define a routine to be called that should return a pointer to the error message. The following is an example.

```
(*proc)(display, code, codes, buffer, nbytes)
      Display *display;
      int code;
      XExtCodes *codes;
      char *buffer;
      int nbytes;
```

Your procedure is called with the error code for every error detected. You should copy *nbytes* of a null-terminated string containing the error message into **buffer.**

C.2.4.7 XESetPrintErrorValues

```
void (*XESetPrintErrorValues()(display, extension, proc))()
      Display *display;
      int extension;
      void (*proc)();
```

display   Specifies the connection to the X server.

extension   Specifies the extension number.

proc   Specifies the routine to call when an error is printed.

This function defines a procedure to be called when an extension error is printed, to print the error values. Use this function for extension errors that contain additional error values beyond those in a core X error. This function returns any previously defined procedure.

When Xlib needs to print an error, the routine is called with these arguments:

```
void (*proc)(display, ev, fp)
      Display *display;
      XErrorEvent *ev;
      void *fp;
```

Writing Extensions to X

The structure pointed at by *ev* is guaranteed to be as large as an **XEvent** structure, and so can be cast to a type larger than an **XErrorEvent()**, in order to obtain additional values set by using **XESetWireToError()**. The underlying type of the *fp* argument is system dependent; on a POSIX-compliant fp should be cast to type **FILE***.

C.2.4.8 XESetFlushGC

```
int (*XESetFlushGC()(display, extension, proc))()
        Display *display;
        int extension;
        int *(*proc)();
```

display   Specifies the connection to the X server.

extension   Specifies the extension number.

proc   Specifies the routine to call when a GC is flushed.

The **XESetFlushGC()** procedure is identical to **XESetCopyGC()** except that **XESet-FlushGC** is called when a GC cache needs to be updated in the server.

C.2.5 Hooks onto Xlib Data Structures

Various Xlib data structures have provisions for extension routines to chain extension sup-plied data onto a list. These structures are **GC**, **Visual**, **Screen**, **ScreenFormat**, **Display**, and **XFontStruct**. Because the list pointer is always the first member in the structure, a single set of routines can be used to manipulate the data on these lists.

The following structure is used in the routines in this section and is defined in *<Xlib.h>*:

```
typedef struct _XExtData {
        int number;                 /* number returned by XInitExtension() */
        struct _XExtData *next;     /* next item on list of data for structure */
        int (*free_private)();      /* if defined,  called to free private */
        XPointer private_data;      /* data private to this extension. */
} XExtData;
```

When any of the data structures listed above are freed, the list is walked, and the structure's free routine (if any) is called. If free is NULL, then the library frees both the data pointed to by the **private_data** member and the structure itself.

```
union {   Display *display;
        GC gc;
        Visual *visual;
        Screen *screen;
        ScreenFormat *pixmap_format;
        XFontStruct *font } XEDataObject;
```

C.2.5.1 XEHeadOfExtensionList

```
XExtData **XEHeadOfExtensionList(object)
      XEDataObject object;
```

object   Specifies the object.

`XEHeadOfExtensionList()` returns a pointer to the list of extension structures attached to the specified object. In concert with

C.2.5.2 XAddToExtensionList

`XAddToExtensionList()`, `XEHeadOfExtensionList()` allows an extension to attach arbitrary data to any of the structures of types contained in `XEDataObject()`.

```
XAddToExtensionList(structure, ext_data)
      XExtData **structure;
      XExtData *ext_data;
```

structure   Specifies the extension list.

ext_data   Specifies the extension data structure to add.

The *structure* argument is a pointer to one of the data structures enumerated above. You must initialize `ext_data->number` with the extension number before calling this routine.

C.2.5.3 XFindOnExtensionList

```
XExtData *XFindOnExtensionList()(structure, number)
      struct _XExtData **structure;
      int number;
```

structure   Specifies the extension list.

number   Specifies the extension number from `XInitExtension()`.

`XFindOnExtensionList()` returns the first extension data structure for the extension numbered number. It is expected that an extension will add at most one extension data structure to any single data structure's extension data list. There is no way to find additional structures.

C.2.5.4 XAllocID

The `XAllocID()` macro, which allocates and returns a resource ID, is defined in *<Xlib.h>*.

```
XAllocID(display)
      Display *display;
```

display   Specifies the connection to the X server.

Writing Extensions to X

This macro is a call through the **Display** structure to the internal resource ID allocator. It returns a resource ID that you can use when creating new resources.

C.3 GC Caching

GCs are cached by the library to allow merging of independent change requests to the same GC into single protocol requests. This is typically called a write-back cache. Any extension routine whose behavior depends on the contents of a GC must flush the GC cache to make sure the server has up-to-date contents in its GC.

The **FlushGC( )** macro checks the dirty bits in the library's GC structure and calls **_XFlushGCCache** if any elements have changed. The **FlushGC( )** macro is defined as follows:

    FlushGC(display, gc)
          Display *display;
          GC gc;

display   Specifies the connection to the X server.

gc   Specifies the GC.

Note that if you extend the GC to add additional resource ID components, you should ensure that the library stub sends the change request immediately. This is because a client can free a resource immediately after using it, so if you only stored the value in the cache without forcing a protocol request, the resource might be destroyed before being set into the GC. You can use the **_XFlushGCCache** procedure to force the cache to be flushed. The **_XFlushGCCache** procedure is defined as follows:

    _XFlushGC()Cache(display, gc)
          Display *display;
          GC gc;

display   Specifies the connection to the X server.

gc   Specifies the GC.

C.4 Graphics Batching

If you extend X to add more poly graphics primitives, you may be able to take advantage of facilities in the library to allow back-to-back single calls to be transformed into poly requests. This may dramatically improve performance of programs that are not written using poly requests. A pointer to an **xReq( )**, called **last_req** in the display structure, is the last request being processed. By checking that the last request type, drawable, gc, and other options are the same as the new one and that there is enough space left in the buffer, you may be able to just extend the previous graphics request by extending the length field of the request and appending the data to the buffer. This can improve performance by five times or more in naive programs. For example, here is the source for the **XDrawPoint()** stub. (Writing extension stubs is discussed in the next section.)

```
#include "copyright.h"

#include "Xlibint.h"

/* precompute the maximum size of batching request allowed */

static int size = sizeof(xPolyPointReq) + EPERBATCH * sizeof(xPoint);

XDrawPoint()(dpy, d, gc, x, y)
    register Display *dpy;
    Drawable d;
    GC gc;
    int x, y; /* INT16 */
{
    xPoint *point;
    LockDisplay()(dpy);
    FlushGC()(dpy, gc);
    {
    register xPolyPointReq *req = (xPolyPointReq *) dpy->last_req;
    /* if same as previous request, with same drawable, batch requests */
    if (
            (req->reqType == X_PolyPoint)
        && (req->drawable == d)
        && (req->gc == gc->gid)
        && (req->coordMode == CoordModeOrigin)
        && ((dpy->bufptr + sizeof (xPoint)) <= dpy->bufmax)
        && (((char *)dpy->bufptr - (char *)req) < size) ) {
        point = (xPoint *) dpy->bufptr;
        req->length += sizeof (xPoint) >> 2;
        dpy->bufptr += sizeof (xPoint);
        }

    else {
        GetReqExtra(PolyPoint, 4, req); /* 1 point = 4 bytes */
        req->drawable = d;
        req->gc = gc->gid;
        req->coordMode = CoordModeOrigin;
        point = (xPoint *) (req + 1);
        }
    point->x = x;
    point->y = y;
    }
    UnlockDisplay()(dpy);
    SyncHandle();
}
```

To keep clients from generating very long requests that may monopolize the server, there is a symbol defined in *<Xlibint.h>* of EPERBATCH on the number of requests batched. Most of the performance benefit occurs in the first few merged requests. Note that **FlushGC()** is called *before* picking up the value of **last_req**, because it may modify this field.

C.5 Writing Extension Stubs

All X requests always contain the length of the request, expressed as a 16-bit quantity of 32 bits. This means that a single request can be no more than 256K bytes in length. Some servers may not support single requests of such a length. The value of `dpy->max_request_size` contains the maximum length as defined by the server implementation. For further information, see "X Window System Protocol."

C.5.1 Requests, Replies, and Xproto.h

The *<Xproto.h>* file contains three sets of definitions that are of interest to the stub implementor: request names, request structures, and reply structures.

You need to generate a file equivalent to *<Xproto.h>* for your extension and need to include it in your stub routine. Each stub routine also must include *<Xlibint.h>*.

The identifiers are deliberately chosen in such a way that, if the request is called X_DoSomething, then its request structure is xDoSomethingReq, and its reply is xDoSomethingReply. The GetReq family of macros, defined in *<Xlibint.h>*, takes advantage of this naming scheme.

For each X request, there is a definition in *<Xproto.h>* that looks similar to this:

```
#define X_DoSomething   42
```

In your extension header file this will be a minor opcode, rather than a major opcode.

C.5.2 Request Format

Every request contains an 8-bit major opcode and a 16-bit length field expressed in units of four bytes. Every request consists of four bytes of header (containing the major opcode, the length field, and a data byte) followed by zero or more additional bytes of data. The length field defines the total length of the request, including the header. The length field in a request must equal the minimum length required to contain the request. If the specified length is smaller or larger than the required length, the server should generate a **BadLength** error. Unused bytes in a request are not required to be zero. Extensions should be designed in such a way that long protocol requests can be split up into smaller requests, if it is possible to exceed the maximum request size of the server. The protocol guarantees the maximum request size to be no smaller than 4096 units (16384 bytes).

Major opcodes 128 through 255 are reserved for extensions. Extensions are intended to contain multiple requests, so extension requests typically have an additional minor opcode encoded in the "spare" data byte in the request header, but the placement and interpretation of this minor opcode as well as all other fields in extension requests are not defined by the core protocol. Every request is implicitly assigned a sequence number (starting with one) used in replies, errors, and events.

To help but not cure portability problems to certain machines, the **B16** and **B32** macros have been defined so that they can become bitfield specifications on some machines. For example, on a Cray, these should be used for all 16-bit and 32-bit quantities, as discussed below.

Most protocol requests have a corresponding structure typedef in *<Xproto.h>*, which looks like:

```
typedef struct _DoSomethingReq {
    CARD8 reqType;          /* X_DoSomething */
    CARD8 someDatum;        /* used differently in different requests */
    CARD16 length B16;      /* total # of bytes in request, divided by 4 */
    ...
    /* request-specific data */
    ...
} xDoSomethingReq;
```

If a core protocol request has a single 32-bit argument, you need not declare a request structure in your extension header file. Instead, such requests use *<Xproto.h>*'s **xResourceReq** structure. This structure is used for any request whose single argument is a **Window**, **Pixmap**, **Drawable**, **GContext**, **Font**, **Cursor**, **Colormap**, **Atom**, or **VisualID**.

```
typedef struct _ResourceReq {
    CARD8 reqType;      /* the request type, e.g., X_DoSomething */
    BYTE pad;           /* not used */
    CARD16 length B16;  /* 2 (= total # of bytes in request, divided by 4) */
    CARD32 id B32;      /* the Window, Drawable, Font, GContext, etc. */
} xResourceReq;
```

If convenient, you can do something similar in your extension header file.

In both of these structures, the **reqType** field identifies the type of the request (for example, X_MapWindow or X_CreatePixmap). The length field tells how long the request is in units of 4-byte longwords. This length includes both the request structure itself and any variable length data, such as strings or lists, that follow the request structure. Request structures come in different sizes, but all requests are padded to be multiples of four bytes long.

A few protocol requests take no arguments at all. Instead, they use *<Xproto.h>*'s **xReq** structure, which contains only a **reqType** and a length (and a pad byte).

If the protocol request requires a reply, then *<Xproto.h>* also contains a reply structure typedef:

```
typedef struct _DoSomethingReply {
    BYTE type;                      /* always X_Reply */
    BYTE someDatum;                 /* used differently in different requests */
    CARD16 sequenceNumber B16;      /* # of requests sent so far */
    CARD32 length B32;              /* # of additional bytes, divided by 4 */
    ...
    /* request-specific data */
    ...
} xDoSomethingReply;
```

Most of these reply structures are 32 bytes long. If there are not that many reply values, then they contain a sufficient number of pad fields to bring them up to 32 bytes. The length field is the total number of bytes in the request minus 32, divided by 4. This length will be nonzero only if:

- The reply structure is followed by variable length data such as a list or string.

- The reply structure is longer than 32 bytes.

Only `XGetWindowAttributes()`, `XQueryFont()`, `XQueryKeymap()`, and `XGetKeyboardControl` have reply structures longer than 32 bytes in the core protocol.

A few protocol requests return replies that contain no data. *<Xproto.h>* does not define reply structures for these. Instead, they use the `xGenericReply` structure, which contains only a type, length, and sequence number (and sufficient padding to make it 32 bytes long).

C.5.3 Starting to Write a Stub Routine

An Xlib stub routine should always start like this:

```
#include "Xlibint.h"

XDoSomething (arguments, ... )
/* argument declarations */
{

register XDoSomethingReq *req;
```

If the protocol request has a reply, then the variable declarations should include the reply structure for the request. The following is an example:

```
xDoSomethingReply rep;
```

C.5.4 Locking Data Structures

To lock the display structure for systems that want to support multithreaded access to a single display connection, each stub will need to lock its critical section. Generally, this section is the point from just before the appropriate GetReq call until all arguments to the call have been stored into the buffer. The precise instructions needed for this locking depend upon the machine architecture. Two calls, which are generally implemented as macros, have been provided.

```
LockDisplay(display)
      Display *display;

UnlockDisplay(display)
      Display *display;
```

display　　　　　Specifies the connection to the X server.

C.5.5 Sending the Protocol Request and Arguments

After the variable declarations, a stub routine should call one of four macros defined in *<Xlibint.h>*: `GetReq()`, `GetReqExtra()`, `GetResReq()`, or `GetEmptyReq()`. All of these macros take, as their first argument, the name of the protocol request as declared in *<Xproto.h>* except with X_ removed. Each one declares a `Display` structure pointer, called dpy, and a pointer to a request structure, called req, which is of the appropriate type. The macro then appends the request structure to the output buffer, fills in its type and length field, and sets req to point to it.

If the protocol request has no arguments (for instance, X_GrabServer), then use `GetEmptyReq()`.

```
GetEmptyReq (DoSomething, req);
```

If the protocol request has a single 32-bit argument (such as a `Pixmap`, `Window`, `Drawable`, `Atom`, and so on), then use `GetResReq()`. The second argument to the macro is the 32-bit object. X_MapWindow is a good example.

```
GetResReq (DoSomething, rid, req);
```

The *rid* argument is the `Pixmap`, `Window`, or other resource ID.

If the protocol request takes any other argument list, then call `GetReq()`. After the `GetReq()`, you need to set all the other fields in the request structure, usually from arguments to the stub routine.

```
GetReq (DoSomething, req);
/* fill in arguments here */
req->arg1 = arg1;
req->arg2 = arg2;
```

A few stub routines (such as `XCreateGC()` and `XCreatePixmap()`) return a resource ID to the caller but pass a resource ID as an argument to the protocol request. Such routines use the macro `XAllocID` to allocate a resource ID from the range of IDs that were assigned to this client when it opened the connection.

```
rid = req->rid = XAllocID();
return (rid);
```

Finally, some stub routines transmit a fixed amount of variable length data after the request. Typically, these routines (such as `XMoveWindow()` and `XSetBackground()`) are special cases of more general functions like `XMoveResizeWindow()` and `XChangeGC()`. These special case routines use `GetReqExtra()`, which is the same as `GetReq` except that it takes an additional argument (the number of extra bytes to allocate in the output buffer after the request structure). This number should always be a multiple of four.

C.5.6 Variable Length Arguments

Some protocol requests take additional variable length data that follow the xDo-
SomethingReq structure. The format of this data varies from request to request. Some
requests require a sequence of 8-bit bytes, others a sequence of 16-bit or 32-bit entities, and
still others a sequence of structures.

It is necessary to add the length of any variable length data to the length field of the request
structure. That length field is in units of 32-bit longwords. If the data is a string or other
sequence of 8-bit bytes, then you must round the length up and shift it before adding:

```
req->length += (nbytes+3)>>2;
```

To transmit variable length data, use the **Data** macros. If the data fits into the output buffer,
then this macro copies it to the buffer. If it does not fit, however, the **Data** macro calls
_XSend( ), which transmits first the contents of the buffer and then your data. The **Data**
macros take three arguments: the Display, a pointer to the beginning of the data, and the
number of bytes to be sent.

```
Data(display, (char *) data, nbytes);

Data16(display, (short *) data, nbytes);

Data32(display, (long *) data, nbytes);
```

Data( ), Data16( ), and Data32( ) are macros that may use their last argument more
than once, so that argument should be a variable rather than an expression such as
"nitems*sizeof(item)". You should do that kind of computation in a separate statement before calling them. Use the appropriate macro when sending byte, short, or long data.

If the protocol request requires a reply, then call the procedure _XSend instead of the **Data**
macro. _XSend takes the same arguments, but because it sends your data immediately
instead of copying it into the output buffer (which would later be flushed anyway by the following call on _XReply( )), it is faster.

C.5.7 Replies

If the protocol request has a reply, then call _XReply after you have finished dealing with
all the fixed and variable length arguments. _XReply flushes the output buffer and waits
for an xReply packet to arrive. If any events arrive in the meantime, _XReply places
them in the queue for later use.

```
Status _XReply(display, rep, extra, discard)
       Display *display;
       xReply *rep;
       int extra;
       Bool discard;
```

display   Specifies the connection to the X server.

rep   Specifies the reply structure.

extra   Specifies the number of 32-bit words expected after the replay.

discard   Specifies if beyond the "extra" data should be discarded.

`_XReply` waits for a reply packet and copies its contents into the specified rep. `_XReply` handles error and event packets that occur before the reply is received. `_XReply` takes four arguments:

- A `Display` * structure

- A pointer to a reply structure (which must be cast to an `xReply` *)

- The number of additional 32-bit words (beyond sizeof(*xReply*) = 32 bytes) in the reply structure

- A Boolean that indicates whether `_XReply` is to discard any additional bytes beyond those it was told to read

Because most reply structures are 32 bytes long, the third argument is usually 0. The only core protocol exceptions are the replies to `XGetWindowAttributes()`, `XQuery-Font()`, `XQueryKeymap()`, and `XGetKeyboardControl()`, which have longer replies.

The last argument should be `False` if the reply structure is followed by additional variable length data (such as a list or string). It should be `True` if there is not any variable length data.

NOTE

This last argument is provided for upward-compatibility reasons to allow a client to communicate properly with a hypothetical later version of the server that sends more data than the client expected. For example, some later version of `XGetWindowAttributes` might use a larger, but compatible, `xGet-WindowAttributesReply` that contains additional attribute data at the end.

`_XReply` returns `True` if it received a reply successfully or `False` if it received any sort of error.

For a request with a reply that is not followed by variable length data, you write something like:

```
_XReply(display, (xReply *)&rep, 0, True);
*ret1 = rep.ret1;
*ret2 = rep.ret2;
*ret3 = rep.ret3;
UnlockDisplay()(dpy);
SyncHandle();
return (rep.ret4);
}
```

If there is variable length data after the reply, change the **True** to **False**, and use the appropriate **_XRead** function to read the variable length data.

```
_XRead(display, data_return, nbytes)
        Display *display;
        char *data_return;
        long nbytes;
```

display　　　　Specifies the connection to the X server.

data_return　　Specifies the buffer.

nbytes　　　　Specifies the number of bytes required.

_XRead reads the specified number of bytes into ***data_return***.

C.5.7.1 _XRead16

```
_XRead16(display, data_return, nbytes)
        Display *display;
        short *data_return;
        long nbytes;
```

display　　　　Specifies the connection to the X server.

data_return　　Specifies the buffer.

nbytes　　　　Specifies the number of bytes required.

_XRead16 reads the specified number of bytes, unpacking them as 16-bit quantities, into the specified array as shorts.

C.5.7.2 _XRead32

```
_XRead32(display, data_return, nbytes)
        Display *display;
        long *data_return;
        long nbytes;
```

display　　　　Specifies the connection to the X server.

data_return　　Specifies the buffer.

nbytes　　　　Specifies the number of bytes required.

_XRead32 reads the specified number of bytes, unpacking them as 32-bit quantities, into the specified array as longs.

C.5.7.3 _XRead16Pad

```
_XRead16Pad(display, data_return, nbytes)
        Display *display;
        short *data_return;
        long nbytes;
```

display   Specifies the connection to the X server.

data_return   Specifies the buffer.

nbytes   Specifies the number of bytes required.

_XRead16Pad reads the specified number of bytes, unpacking them as 16-bit quantities, into the specified array as shorts. If the number of bytes is not a multiple of four, _XRead16Pad reads and discards up to three additional pad bytes.

C.5.7.4 _XReadPad

```
_XReadPad(display, data_return, nbytes)
        Display *display;
        char *data_return;
        long nbytes;
```

display   Specifies the connection to the X server.

data_return   Specifies the buffer.

nbytes   Specifies the number of bytes required.

_XReadPad reads the specified number of bytes into **data_return**. If the number of bytes is not a multiple of four, **_XReadPad** reads and discards up to three additional pad bytes.

Each protocol request is a little different. For further information, see the Xlib sources for examples.

C.5.8 Synchronous Calling

To ease debugging, each routine should have a call, just before returning to the user, to a routine called **SyncHandle()**. This routine generally is implemented as a macro. If synchronous mode is enabled (see **XSynchronize()**), the request is sent immediately. The library, however, waits until any error the routine could generate at the server has been handled.

C.5.9 Allocating and Deallocating Memory

To support the possible reentry of these routines, you must observe several conventions when allocating and deallocating memory, most often done when returning data to the user from the window system of a size the caller could not know in advance (for example, a list of fonts or a list of extensions). The standard C library routines on many systems are not protected against signals or other multithreaded uses. The following analogies to standard I/O library routines have been defined:

Xmalloc( )   Replaces `malloc( )`.

XFree( )   Replaces `free( )`.

Xcalloc( )   Replaces `calloc( )`.

These should be used in place of any calls you would make to the normal C library routines.

If you need a single scratch buffer inside a critical section (for example, to pack and unpack data to and from the wire protocol), the general memory allocators may be too expensive to use (particularly in output routines, which are performance critical). The routine below returns a scratch buffer for your use:

```
char *_XAllocScratch(display, nbytes)
    Display *display;
    unsigned long nbytes;
```

display   Specifies the connection to the X server.

nbytes   Specifies the number of bytes required.

This storage must only be used inside of the critical section of your stub.

C.5.10 Portability Considerations

Many machine architectures, including many of the more recent RISC architectures, do not correctly access data at unaligned locations; their compilers pad out structures to preserve this characteristic. Many other machines capable of unaligned references pad inside of structures as well to preserve alignment, because accessing aligned data is usually much faster. Because the library and the server use structures to access data at arbitrary points in a byte stream, all data in request and reply packets *must* be naturally aligned; that is, 16-bit data starts on 16-bit boundaries in the request and 32-bit data on 32-bit boundaries. All requests *must* be a multiple of 32 bits in length to preserve the natural alignment in the data stream. You must pad structures out to 32-bit boundaries. Pad information does not have to be zeroed unless you want to preserve such fields for future use in your protocol requests. Floating point varies radically between machines and should be avoided completely if at all possible.

This code may run on machines with 16-bit ints. So, if any integer argument, variable, or return value either can take only nonnegative values or is declared as a CARD16 in the protocol, be sure to declare it as unsigned int and not as int. (This, of course, does not apply to Booleans or enumerations.)

Similarly, if any integer argument or return value is declared CARD32 in the protocol, declare it as an unsigned long and not as int or long. This also goes for any internal variables that may take on values larger than the maximum 16-bit **unsigned int**.

The library currently assumes that a *char* is 8 bits, a *short* is 16 bits, an *int* is 16 or 32 bits, and a *long* is 32 bits. The **PackData** macro is a half-hearted attempt to deal with the possibility of 32 bit shorts. However, much more work is needed to make this work properly.

C.5.11 Deriving the Correct Extension Opcode

The remaining problem a writer of an extension stub routine faces that the core protocol does not face is to map from the call to the proper major and minor opcodes. While there are a number of strategies, the simplest and fastest is outlined below.

1. Declare an array of pointers, _NFILE long (this is normally found in *<stdio.h>* and is the number of file descriptors supported on the system) of type **XExtCodes( )**. Make sure these are all initialized to NULL.

2. When your stub is entered, your initialization test is just to use the display pointer passed in to access the file descriptor and an index into the array. If the entry is NULL, then this is the first time you are entering the routine for this display. Call your initialization routine and pass it to the display pointer.

3. Once in your initialization routine, call **XInitExtension( )**; if it succeeds, store the pointer returned into this array. Make sure to establish a close display handler to allow you to zero the entry. Do whatever other initialization your extension requires. (For example, install event handlers and so on.) Your initialization routine would normally return a pointer to the **XExtCodes** structure for this extension, which is what would normally be found in your array of pointers.

4. After returning from your initialization routine, the stub can now continue normally, because it has its major opcode safely in its hand in the **XExtCodes** structure.

D

The basecalc Application

This appendix lists the complete source code for the basecalc application described in Chapter 12. Source code for all examples in this book is available as described in the Preface.

D
The basecalc Application

The X Programmer's Calculator (*basecalc*) was described in Chapter 14, *A Complete Application*.

This appendix presents the complete code for *basecalc*, including the following files and routines that were not shown in Chapter 14.

`basecalc.h`	Include file for this application.
`convButton`	Changes the current base and converts a value, if any.
`digitButton`	Gets a digit and assigns it to the variable `Value`.
`displayVal`	Calculates appropriate format string for base.
`initTty`	Performs system calls to get user's current erase, delete, and interrupt characters.
`keyToWin`	Translates a keycode as if a `pad` had been selected.
`makePixmap`	Makes a pixmap from bitmap data, shown and described in Chapter 6, *Drawing Graphics and Text*.
`operButton`	An operation, either does it or waits for next value and =.
`printInBase`	Composes the string that should be displayed. Called from `Sprintf`.
`specButton`	Clears a digit, an entry, or all, or toggles unsigned mode.
`Sprintf`	A modified version of the standard C utility `sprintf`, which does not print in binary. `Sprintf` calls `printInBase`.
`winPressed`	Determines whether `pad` pressed was a digit, an operator, a conversion, or a special `pad`.

Example D-1 shows the *basecalc.h* include file. This include file sets up the structures and global variables used in the calculator application.

Example D-1. The complete basecalc.h file

```
/* Window flags */
#define WTYP_OPER 0x01          /* Operator, +, -, =, etc */
#define WTYP_DIG 0x02           /* Digit 0-9, A-F */
#define WTYP_DISP 0x04          /* Display Window */
#define WTYP_CONV 0x08          /* Converter -- hex, oct, dec, bin */
#define WTYP_SPEC 0x10          /* Special, CE, CA, CD */

/* Operators */
#define OPR_ADD         1
#define OPR_SUB         2
#define OPR_MUL         3
#define OPR_DIV         4
#define OPR_MOD         5
#define OPR_OR                6
#define OPR_AND         7
#define OPR_XOR         8
#define OPR_SHL         9
#define OPR_SHR         10
#define OPR_CLRE        11
#define OPR_CLRD        12
#define OPR_CLRA        13
#define OPR_ASGN        14
#define OPR_NEG         15
#define OPR_NOT         16
#define OPR_UNS         17

/* Colors */
#define      WHITE      0
#define      BLACK      1
#define      DARKGRAY        2
#define      LIGHTGRAY       3

static XrmDatabase commandlineDB, rDB;

int pressedColor =              WHITE;
int unpressedColor =    BLACK;
int disabledColor =             LIGHTGRAY;
int displayColor =              WHITE;

char myDisplayName[ 256 ];
char *myFontName =      "8x13";

char             *calcName;

Display          *display;
int              screen_num;
Visual           *visual;
Colormap         colormap;
XFontStruct *theFont;
Cursor           theCursor;
Window           calcWin;
Window           iconWin;
Window           dispWin;
Pixmap           lgrayPixmap;
Pixmap           grayPixmap;
```

Example D-1. The complete basecalc.h file (continued)

```
Pixmap             iconPixmap;

int                foreground;
int                background;

GC                 fgGC;
GC                 bgGC;

/* Calculator variables */
int        Base = 10;          /* Default base, updated to command line
                                * or .Xdefaults */
int        Winbase;            /* windata offset for current base, set
                                * in InitCalc, used in ConvButton */

int        Digit = 0;
long       Value = 0;          /* Current pressed value */
long       Accum = 0;          /* Current results */
Bool       Unsigned = True;    /* Default for U/S key */
int        LastOpt = OPR_ADD;      /* Initial previous operator */
int        CalcReset = 0;
char       Hexmeasure[ ] = "  .   .   .   .   .   .   .  ";
char       Octmeasure[ ] = " .  .  .  .  .  .  .  .  .  .  ";


/* Startup options */
Bool iconOnly = False;

char Geostr[ 20 ];
char iconGeostr[ 20 ];


/* Command line options table; only resources are entered here...
 * there is a pass over the remaining options after XrmParseCommand
 * is let loose; we don't do anything with many of these resources,
 * but the program is ready for expansion */

#define GEOMETRY          "*geometry"
#define ICONGEOMETRY      "*iconGeometry"
#define UNSIGNED          "*unsigned"
#define BASE              "*base"
#define ICONSTARTUP       "*iconStartup"

static int opTableEntries = 25;
static XrmOptionDescRec opTable[ ] = {
{"-unsigned",      UNSIGNED,          XrmoptionNoArg,     (caddr_t)   "off"},
{"-x",             BASE,              XrmoptionNoArg,     (caddr_t)   "16"},
{"-hex",           BASE,              XrmoptionNoArg,     (caddr_t)   "16"},
{"-dec",           BASE,              XrmoptionNoArg,     (caddr_t)   "10"},
{"-oct",           BASE,              XrmoptionNoArg,     (caddr_t)   "8"},
{"-binary",        BASE,              XrmoptionNoArg,     (caddr_t)   "2"},
{"-geometry",      GEOMETRY,          XrmoptionSepArg,    (caddr_t)   NULL},
{"-iconGeometry",  ICONGEOMETRY,      XrmoptionSepArg,    (caddr_t)   NULL},
{"-iconic",        ICONSTARTUP,       XrmoptionNoArg,     (caddr_t)   "on"},
{"-background",    "*background",     XrmoptionSepArg,    (caddr_t)   NULL},
{"-bg",            "*background",     XrmoptionSepArg,    (caddr_t)   NULL},
{"-fg",            "*foreground",     XrmoptionSepArg,    (caddr_t)   NULL},
{"-foreground",    "*foreground",     XrmoptionSepArg,    (caddr_t)   NULL},
{"-xrm",           NULL,              XrmoptionResArg,    (caddr_t)   NULL},
{"-display",       ".display",        XrmoptionSepArg,    (caddr_t)   NULL},
/* Remainder not currently supported: */
```

```
{"-bd",             "*borderColor",   XrmoptionSepArg,   (caddr_t)   NULL},
{"-bordercolor",    "*borderColor",   XrmoptionSepArg,   (caddr_t)   NULL},
{"-borderwidth",    ".borderWidth",   XrmoptionSepArg,   (caddr_t)   NULL},
{"-bw",             ".borderWidth",   XrmoptionSepArg,   (caddr_t)   NULL},
{"-fn",             "*font",          XrmoptionSepArg,   (caddr_t)   NULL},
{"-font",           "*font",          XrmoptionSepArg,   (caddr_t)   NULL},
{"-name",           ".name",          XrmoptionSepArg,   (caddr_t)   NULL},
{"-title",          ".title",         XrmoptionSepArg,   (caddr_t)   NULL},
};

/* Keyboard equivalents */
struct KeyCode {
      int   kc_char;
      char *kc_func;
      int   kc_len;
} KeyCodes[ ] = {
      { CERASE,  "CD", 2 },
#ifdef SYSV
      { 027,     "CE", 2 },
#else
      { CWERASE,"CE",  2 },
#endif SYSV
      { CKILL,   "CE", 2 },
      { CINTR,   "CA", 2 },
      { 0,       0,    0 },
};
char  QuitChar = CQUIT;

#include "bitmaps/xcalc.icon"
#include "bitmaps/lgray"
#include "bitmaps/gray"

/* Placement variables */
XSizeHints sizehints = {
      PMinSize | PMaxSize | PPosition | PSize | USSize,
      400, 100,       /* x, y */
      300, 139,       /* Width, height */
      300, 139,       /* min_width and min_height */
      300, 139,       /* max_width and max_height */
      0, 0,           /* Width and height increments, not set */
      0, 0, 0, 0,     /* Aspect ratio, not set */
};
XSizeHints iconsizehints = {
      PMinSize | PMaxSize | PPosition | PSize,
      150, 2,
      icon_width, icon_height,
      icon_width, icon_height,
      icon_width, icon_height,
      0, 0,
      0, 0, 0, 0,
};
XWMHints wmhints = {
      InputHint | StateHint | IconWindowHint,
      True,           /* Input model */
      NormalState,    /* Starts up in normal state */
      0,              /* Icon pixmap -- set later */
      0,              /* Icon window -- created later */
```

```
      150, 2,          /* Icon position of icon */
      0,               /* Icon mask pixmap -- not used */
};

/* Configuration of subwindows */
typedef struct _OpaqueFrame {
      Window self;                     /* Window ID, filled in later */
      int x, y;                        /* Where to create the window */
      unsigned int width, height;  /* Width and height */
} OpaqueFrame;

#define NBUTTONS 38
OpaqueFrame Buttons[NBUTTONS] = {
      { 0, 3, 5, 292, 18},   /* Display area */

      { 0, 10, 35, 19, 18},  /* c d e f */
      { 0, 37, 35, 19, 18},
      { 0, 63, 35, 19, 18},
      { 0, 91, 35, 19, 18},

      { 0, 10, 60, 19, 18},  /* 8 9 a b */
      { 0, 37, 60, 19, 18},
      { 0, 63, 60, 19, 18},
      { 0, 91, 60, 19, 18},

      { 0, 10, 85, 19, 18},  /* 4 5 6 7 */
      { 0, 37, 85, 19, 18},
      { 0, 63, 85, 19, 18},
      { 0, 91, 85, 19, 18},

      { 0, 10, 110, 19, 18}, /* 0 1 2 3 */
      { 0, 37, 110, 19, 18},
      { 0, 63, 110, 19, 18},
      { 0, 91, 110, 19, 18},

      { 0, 261, 110, 28, 18},/* ca ce, cd, = */
      { 0, 187, 110, 28, 18},
      { 0, 224, 110, 28, 18},
      { 0, 131, 110, 46, 18},

      { 0, 131, 60, 19, 18}, /* + — * / % */
      { 0, 158, 60, 19, 18},
      { 0, 185, 60, 19, 18},
      { 0, 212, 60, 19, 18},
      { 0, 239, 60, 19, 18},

      { 0, 131, 85, 19, 18}, /* | & << >> ^ */
      { 0, 158, 85, 19, 18},
      { 0, 185, 85, 19, 18},
      { 0, 212, 85, 19, 18},
      { 0, 239, 85, 19, 18},

      { 0, 131, 35, 32, 18}, /* hex oct bin dec */
      { 0, 165, 35, 31, 18},
      { 0, 198, 35, 32, 18},
      { 0, 232, 35, 31, 18},

      { 0, 269, 35, 20, 18}, /* UNS */
      { 0, 269, 60, 20, 18}, /* NEG */
      { 0, 269, 85, 20, 18}, /* NOT */
};
```

```
struct windata {
      int   color;      /* Color */
      char  *text;      /* Pointer to the text string */
      int   x;          /* x coordinate of text */
      int   y;          /* y coordinate of text */
      int   value;      /* 0-16 for number, symbol for operator */
      int   type; /* Number, operator, display */
} windata[NBUTTONS] = {
      { 1, "                              0 ", 2, 3, 0, WTYP_DISP },

      { 0, "C", 5, 3, 12, WTYP_DIG },
      { 0, "D", 5, 3, 13, WTYP_DIG },
      { 0, "E", 5, 3, 14, WTYP_DIG },
      { 0, "F", 5, 3, 15, WTYP_DIG },

      { 0, "8", 5, 3,  8, WTYP_DIG },
      { 0, "9", 5, 3,  9, WTYP_DIG },
      { 0, "A", 5, 3, 10, WTYP_DIG },
      { 0, "B", 5, 3, 11, WTYP_DIG },

      { 0, "4", 5, 3, 4, WTYP_DIG },
      { 0, "5", 5, 3, 5, WTYP_DIG },
      { 0, "6", 5, 3, 6, WTYP_DIG },
      { 0, "7", 5, 3, 7, WTYP_DIG },

      { 0, "0", 5, 3, 0, WTYP_DIG },
      { 0, "1", 5, 3, 1, WTYP_DIG },
      { 0, "2", 5, 3, 2, WTYP_DIG },
      { 0, "3", 5, 3, 3, WTYP_DIG },

      { 0, "CA", 6, 3, OPR_CLRA, WTYP_SPEC },
      { 0, "CE", 6, 3, OPR_CLRE, WTYP_SPEC },
      { 0, "CD", 6, 3, OPR_CLRD, WTYP_SPEC },
      { 0, "=", 17, 2, OPR_ASGN, WTYP_OPER },

      { 0,  "+", 5, 3, OPR_ADD, WTYP_OPER },
      { 0,  "-", 5, 3, OPR_SUB, WTYP_OPER },
      { 0,  "*", 5, 4, OPR_MUL, WTYP_OPER },
      { 0,  "/", 5, 3, OPR_DIV, WTYP_OPER },
      { 0,  "%", 5, 3, OPR_MOD, WTYP_OPER },

      { 0,  "|", 5, 3, OPR_OR,  WTYP_OPER },
      { 0,  "&", 5, 3, OPR_AND, WTYP_OPER },
      { 0,  ">>",1, 3, OPR_SHR, WTYP_OPER },
      { 0,  "<<",0, 3, OPR_SHL, WTYP_OPER },
      { 0,  "^", 5, 3, OPR_XOR, WTYP_OPER },

      { 0, "HEX", 2, 3, 16, WTYP_CONV },
      { 0, "DEC", 2, 3, 10, WTYP_CONV },
      { 0, "OCT", 2, 3,  8, WTYP_CONV },
      { 0, "BIN", 2, 3,  2, WTYP_CONV },

      { 0, "U",  5, 3,  OPR_UNS, WTYP_SPEC },
      { 0, "'",  5, 3,  OPR_NEG, WTYP_OPER },
      { 0, "~",  5, 3,  OPR_NOT, WTYP_OPER },
};
```

Example D-2 is the complete source for the calculator application described in Chapter 14, *A Complete Application.*

Example D-2. Remaining code for basecalc

```
/* X Version 11 Integer Programmer's Calculator, written by
 * Alan Greenspan, modified slightly by Adrian Nye */
#include <X11/Xlib.h>
#include <X11/Xutil.h>
#include <X11/Xresource.h>
#include <X11/cursorfont.h>

#include <stdio.h>

#ifdef SYSV
#include <termio.h>
#else
#include <sgtty.h>
#include <sys/ttychars.h>
#endif SYSV

#include <ctype.h>
#include <pwd.h>

#include "basecalc.h"

/* Programmer's calculator with number base conversions */
main (argc, argv)
int argc;
register char *argv[ ];
{
    /* So we can use the resource manager data merging functions */
    XrmInitialize();

    /* Parse command line first so we can open display,
     * store any options in a database  */
    parseOpenDisp (&argc, argv);

    /* Get server defaults, program defaults, .Xdefaults,
     * command line, etc. and merge them */
    mergeDatabases();

    /* Extract values from database for use */
    extractOpts ();

    /* Load font, make pixmaps, set up arrays of windows */
    initCalc ();

    /* Get keyboard settings for interrupt, delete, etc. */
    initTty ();

    /* Make a standard cursor */
    makeCursor ();

    /* Set standard properties, create and map windows */
    makeWindows (argc, argv);

    /* Get events */
    takeEvents ();

    /* Bow out gracefully */
    XCloseDisplay(display);
    exit (1);
```

```
}

static char *getHomeDir( dest )
char *dest;
{
    int uid;
    extern char *getenv();
    extern int getuid();
    extern struct passwd *getpwuid();
    struct passwd *pw;
    register char *ptr;

    if((ptr = getenv("HOME")) != NULL) {
        (void) strcpy(dest, ptr);

    } else {
        if((ptr = getenv("USER")) != NULL) {
            pw = getpwnam(ptr);
        } else {
            uid = getuid();
            pw = getpwuid(uid);
        }
        if (pw) {
            (void) strcpy(dest, pw->pw_dir);
        } else {
            *dest = ' ';
        }
    }
    return dest;
}

/* Get program's and user's defaults */
mergeDatabases()
{
    XrmDatabase homeDB, serverDB, applicationDB;

    char filenamebuf[ 1024 ];
    char *filename = &filenamebuf[ 0 ];
    char *environment;
    char *classname = "Basecalc";
    char name[ 255 ];

    (void) strcpy(name, "/usr/lib/X11/app-defaults/");
    (void) strcat(name, classname);
    /* Get application defaults file, if any */
    applicationDB = XrmGetFileDatabase(name);
    (void) XrmMergeDatabases(applicationDB, &rDB);

    /* MERGE server defaults, these are created by xrdb,
     * loaded as a property of the root window when the server
     * initializes, and loaded into the display structure
     * on XOpenDisplay; if not defined, use .Xdefaults */
    if (XResourceManagerString(display) != NULL) {
        serverDB = XrmGetStringDatabase(XResourceManagerString(display));
    } else {
        /* Open .Xdefaults file and merge into existing data base */
        (void) getHomeDir(filename);
        (void) strcat(filename, "/.Xdefaults");
```

```
        serverDB = XrmGetFileDatabase(filename);
    }
    XrmMergeDatabases(serverDB, &rDB);

    /* Open XENVIRONMENT file or, if not defined, the ~/.Xdefaults,
     * and merge into existing data base */
    if ((environment = getenv("XENVIRONMENT")) == NULL) {
        int len;
        environment = getHomeDir(filename);
        (void) strcat(environment, "/.Xdefaults-");
        len = strlen(environment);
        (void) gethostname(environment+len, 1024-len);
    }
    homeDB = XrmGetFileDatabase(environment);
    XrmMergeDatabases(homeDB, &rDB);

    /* Command line takes precedence over everything */
    XrmMergeDatabases(commandlineDB, &rDB);
}

/* Get command line options */
parseOpenDisp (argc, argv)
int *argc;
register char *argv[ ];
{
    XrmValue value;
    char *str_type[20];

    myDisplayName[0] = ' ';

    XrmParseCommand(&commandlineDB, opTable, opTableEntries, argv[0],
            argc, argv);

    /* Check for any arguments left */
    if (*argc != 1) Usage();

    /* Get display now, because we need it to get other databases*/
    if (XrmGetResource(commandlineDB, "basecalc.display", "Basecalc.Display",
            str_type, &value)== True) {
        (void) strncpy(myDisplayName, value.addr, (int) value.size);
    }

    /* Open display */
    if (!(display = XOpenDisplay(myDisplayName))) {
        (void) fprintf(stderr, "%s: Can't open display '%s'\n",
            argv[0], XDisplayName(myDisplayName));
        exit(1);
    }

    screen_num = DefaultScreen(display);
    visual = DefaultVisual(display, screen_num);
    colormap = DefaultColormap(display, screen_num);
}

extractOpts()
{
    char *str_type[20];
    char buffer[20];
```

```
long flags;
XrmValue value;
int x, y, width, height;
XColor screen_def;

/* Get geometry (actually, this is currently ignored) */
if (XrmGetResource(rDB, "basecalc.geometry", "Basecalc.Geometry",
        str_type, &value)== True) {
    (void) strncpy(Geostr, value.addr, (int) value.size);
} else {
    Geostr[ 0 ] = NULL;
}

if (XrmGetResource(rDB, "basecalc.iconGeometry", "Basecalc.IconGeometry",
        str_type, &value)== True) {
    (void) strncpy(iconGeostr, value.addr, (int) value.size);
} else {
    iconGeostr[ 0 ] = NULL;
}

if (XrmGetResource(rDB, "basecalc.unsigned", "Basecalc.Unsigned",
        str_type, &value)== True)
    if (strncmp(value.addr, "False", (int) value.size) == 0)
            Unsigned = False;

if (XrmGetResource(rDB, "basecalc.base", "Basecalc.Base", str_type,
        &value)== True) {
    (void) strncpy(buffer, value.addr, (int) value.size);
    buffer[value.size ] = NULL;
    Base = atoi(buffer);
} else Base = 10;

if (XrmGetResource(rDB, "basecalc.foreground", "Basecalc.Foreground",
        str_type, &value)== True) {
    (void) strncpy(buffer, value.addr, (int) value.size);
    if (XParseColor(display, colormap, buffer,
        &screen_def) == 0)  {
        (void) fprintf(stderr, "basecalc: fg color specification %s \
                invalid", buffer);
        foreground = BlackPixel(display, screen_num);
    } else {
        if ((visual->class == StaticGray) || (visual->class ==
                GrayScale))

            foreground = BlackPixel(display, screen_num);
        else if (XAllocColor(display, colormap, &screen_def) == 0) {
            foreground = BlackPixel(display, screen_num);
            (void) fprintf(stderr, "basecalc: couldn't allocate color: \
                    %s.\n", buffer);
        }
        else
            foreground = screen_def.pixel;
    }
} else {
    foreground = BlackPixel(display, screen_num);
}

if (XrmGetResource(rDB, "basecalc.background", "Basecalc.Background",
```

```
            str_type, &value)== True) {
    (void) strncpy(buffer, value.addr, (int) value.size);
    if (XParseColor(display, colormap, buffer,
        &screen_def) == 0)  {
        (void) fprintf(stderr, "basecalc: bg color specification %s \
                invalid", buffer);
        background = WhitePixel(display, screen_num);
    } else {
        if ((visual->class == StaticGray) || (visual->class ==
                GrayScale))
            background = WhitePixel(display, screen_num);
        else if (XAllocColor(display, colormap, &screen_def) == 0) {
            background = WhitePixel(display, screen_num);
            (void) fprintf(stderr, "basecalc: couldn't allocate color: \
                    %s.\n", buffer);
        }
        else
            background = screen_def.pixel;
    }
} else {
    background = WhitePixel(display, screen_num);
}

/* One last check to make sure the colors are different! */
if (background == foreground) {
    background = WhitePixel(display, screen_num);
    foreground = BlackPixel(display, screen_num);
}


/*   Could add a command line option for initial state:
 *   iconOnly[ 0 ] = NULL; */

/* Get window geometry information */
if (Geostr != NULL) {
    flags = XParseGeometry(Geostr,
        &x, &y, &width, &height);
    if ((WidthValue|HeightValue) & flags)
        Usage ();
    if (XValue & flags) {
        if (XNegative & flags)
            x = DisplayWidth(display, screen_num) +
                x - sizehints.width;
        sizehints.flags |= USPosition;
        sizehints.x = x;
    }
    if (YValue & flags) {
        if (YNegative & flags)
            y = DisplayHeight(display, screen_num) +
                x - sizehints.width;
        sizehints.flags |= USPosition;
        sizehints.y = y;
    }
}

/* Get icon geometry information */
if (iconGeostr != NULL) {
    iconGeostr[ 0 ] = '=';
```

```
        flags = XParseGeometry(iconGeostr,
            &x, &y, &width, &height);
        if ((WidthValue|HeightValue) & flags)
            Usage ();
        if (XValue & flags) {
            if (XNegative & flags)
                x = DisplayWidth(display, screen_num) +
                    x - iconsizehints.width;
            iconsizehints.flags |= USPosition;
            wmhints.flags |= IconPositionHint;
            wmhints.icon_x = x;
            iconsizehints.x = x;
        }
        if (YValue & flags) {
            if (YNegative & flags)
                y = DisplayHeight(display, screen_num) +
                    x - iconsizehints.width;
            iconsizehints.flags |= USPosition;
            wmhints.flags |= IconPositionHint;
            wmhints.icon_y = y;
            iconsizehints.y = y;
        }
    }
}

/* Print message to stderr and exit */
Usage ()
{
    (void) fprintf (stderr,
        "%s: [-iconic] [-unsigned] [-hex|x|dec|oct|binary] \
        [-display <display>] [-geometry <geometrystring>] \
        [-iconGeometry <icongeometrystring>\n",
        calcName ? calcName : "basecalc");
    exit (1);
}

/* Make a pixmap */
Pixmap
makePixmap(data, width, height)
char *data;
unsigned int width, height;
{
    Pixmap pid;

    pid = XCreatePixmapFromBitmapData(display, DefaultRootWindow(display),
            data, width, height, foreground, background,
            DefaultDepth(display, screen_num));
    return(pid);
}

/* Initialize calculator options */
initCalc ()
{
    register int win;
    register int found = -1;
    XGCValues values;
```

```
    extern char lgray_bits[ ];

    if ((theFont = XLoadQueryFont (display, myFontName)) == NULL) {
        (void) fprintf(stderr, "basecalc: can't open font %s\n",
                myFontName);
        exit(-1);
    }

    /* Make the utility pixmaps */
    grayPixmap = makePixmap(gray_bits, gray_width, gray_height);
    lgrayPixmap = makePixmap(lgray_bits, lgray_width, lgray_height);

    /* Make the utility gc's */
    values.font = theFont->fid;
    values.foreground = foreground;
    fgGC = XCreateGC(display, DefaultRootWindow(display),
        GCForeground|GCFont, &values);
    values.foreground = background;
    values.function = GXcopy;
    bgGC = XCreateGC(display, DefaultRootWindow(display),
        GCForeground|GCFont|GCFunction, &values);

    /* Loop through buttons, setting disabled buttons to Color
     * Light Gray; also find the window which corresponds to the
     * starting display base; also add ascent to y position of text */
    for (win = 1; win < NBUTTONS; win++) {
        if (windata[win].type == WTYP_CONV &&
            windata[win].value == Base) {
            found = win;
        } else
            if (windata[win].type == WTYP_DIG &&
                windata[win].value >= Base) {
                windata[win].color = disabledColor;
            }
            else
                if (windata[win].type == WTYP_SPEC &&
                    windata[win].value == OPR_UNS) {
                    if (Unsigned)
                        windata[win].text = "U";
                    else
                        windata[win].text = "S";
                    windata[win].color = pressedColor;
                }
                else
                    windata[win].color = unpressedColor;
        windata[win].y += theFont->max_bounds.ascent;
    }
    windata[0].y += theFont->max_bounds.ascent;
    if (found >= 0) {
        Winbase = found;
        windata[found].color = pressedColor;
    } else {
        (void) fprintf(stderr, "basecalc: can't use base %d\n", Base);
        exit(-1);
    }
    windata[0].color = displayColor;
}
```

```
/* Get the user's tty special chars; this is currently 4.2 specific */
initTty ()
{
    register struct KeyCode *KeyCodePtr;
    register int fd;
#ifdef SYSV
    struct termio term;
#else
    struct sgttyb tty;
    struct tchars tchars;
    struct ltchars ltchars;
#endif SYSV

    if (!isatty(0)) {
        if ((fd = open ("/dev/console", 0)) < 0)
            return;
    } else
        fd = 0;
#ifdef SYSV
    (void) ioctl  (fd, TCGETA,    &term);
#else
    (void) ioctl  (fd, TIOCGETP, &tty);
    (void) ioctl  (fd, TIOCGETC, &tchars);
    (void) ioctl  (fd, TIOCGLTC, &ltchars);
#endif SYSV
    if (fd)
        (void) close (fd);

    KeyCodePtr = KeyCodes;
#ifdef SYSV
    KeyCodePtr++->kc_char = term.c_cc[VERASE ];
    KeyCodePtr++;
    KeyCodePtr++->kc_char = term.c_cc[VKILL ];
    KeyCodePtr->kc_char = term.c_cc[VINTR ];
    QuitChar = term.c_cc[VQUIT ];
#else
    KeyCodePtr++->kc_char = tty.sg_erase;
    KeyCodePtr++->kc_char = ltchars.t_werasc;
    KeyCodePtr++->kc_char = tty.sg_kill;
    KeyCodePtr->kc_char = tchars.t_intrc;
    QuitChar = tchars.t_quitc;
#endif SYSV
}


/* Make the cursor */
makeCursor ()
{
    theCursor = XCreateFontCursor (display, XC_hand1);
}


/* Set up the selection of events */
selectEvents ()
{
    int win;

    XSelectInput (display, calcWin, KeyPressMask|KeyReleaseMask);
```

```
    XSelectInput (display, dispWin, ExposureMask);
    for (win = 1; win < NBUTTONS; win++)
        XSelectInput (display, Buttons[win].self,
            ExposureMask|
            ButtonPressMask|ButtonReleaseMask|
            EnterWindowMask|LeaveWindowMask);
}

/* Get events and process them */
takeEvents ()
{
    XEvent Event;
    register int win;
    register int Pressed = False;
    register int InWindow = False;
    char buffer[10];
    register char *KeyChars = buffer;
    register int WasKeyDown = False;
    unsigned i, nbytes;

    while (1) {
        if (!WasKeyDown)
            XNextEvent (display, &Event);
        else
            Event.type = KeyRelease;

        /* Map keyboard events to Window events */
        if (Event.type == KeyPress || Event.type == KeyRelease) {
            nbytes = XLookupString (&Event, buffer,
                sizeof(buffer), NULL, NULL);
            if (Event.type == KeyPress) {
                Event.type = ButtonPress;
                WasKeyDown = 1;
            } else {
                for (i=0; i<60000; i++)
                    ;
                Event.type = ButtonRelease;
            }
            if ((Event.xbutton.window =
                keyToWin (KeyChars, nbytes)) == None){
                WasKeyDown = 0;
                continue;
            }
        }
        for (win=0; win < NBUTTONS; win++)
            if (Buttons[win].self == Event.xbutton.window)
                break;
        switch (Event.type) {
        case ButtonPress:
            if (windata[win].color == disabledColor)
                break;
            Pressed = win;
            if (!WasKeyDown)
                InWindow = True;
            windata[win].color = pressedColor;
            drawButton (win, 0);
            break;
```

```
        case LeaveNotify:
            if (Pressed != win)
                break;
            InWindow = False;
            windata[win].color = unpressedColor;
            drawButton (win, 0);
            break;
        case EnterNotify:
            if (Pressed != win)
                break;
            InWindow = True;
            windata[win].color = pressedColor;
            drawButton (win, 0);
            break;
        case ButtonRelease:
            if (windata[win].color == disabledColor ||
                Pressed != win) {
                WasKeyDown = False;
                break;
            }
            Pressed = False;
            windata[win].color = unpressedColor;
            if (WasKeyDown || InWindow)
                winPressed (win);
            WasKeyDown = False;
            InWindow = False;
            drawButton (win, 0);
            break;
        case Expose:
            drawButton (win, 1);
            break;
        }
        XFlush(display);
    }
}

/* Make the calculator windows */
makeWindows (argc, argv)
int argc;
char *argv[ ];
{
    register int i;
    XSetWindowAttributes attributes;
    char *window_name = "Programmer's Calculator";
    char *icon_name = "basecalc";
    XClassHint class_hints;
    XTextProperty windowName, iconName;

    /* Define the border and background for the main window --
     * black border and a patterned background */
    attributes.border_pixel = foreground;
    attributes.background_pixmap = grayPixmap;
    /* Create the main window (calculator frame) as a child of
     * the root window */
    attributes.cursor = theCursor;
    calcWin = XCreateWindow(display, DefaultRootWindow(display),
```

```
        sizehints.x, sizehints.y, sizehints.width, sizehints.height,
        1, DefaultDepth(display, screen_num), InputOutput,
        CopyFromParent, CWBorderPixel|CWBackPixmap|CWCursor,
        &attributes);

    /* Create the icon window and associate it with the calculator */
    iconPixmap = makePixmap(icon_bits, icon_width, icon_height);
    attributes.border_pixel = foreground;
    attributes.background_pixmap = iconPixmap;
    iconWin = XCreateWindow(display, DefaultRootWindow(display),
        iconsizehints.x, iconsizehints.y,
        iconsizehints.width, iconsizehints.height,
        1, DefaultDepth(display, screen_num), InputOutput,
        CopyFromParent, CWBorderPixel|CWBackPixmap,
        &attributes);
wmhints.icon_window = iconWin;
wmhints.initial_state = iconOnly ? IconicState : NormalState;
wmhints.input = True;
wmhints.flags |= InputHint | StateHint | IconWindowHint;
XSetWMHints(display, calcWin, &wmhints);

    /* These calls store window_name and icon_name into XTextProperty
     * structures and set their other fields properly */
    if (XStringListToTextProperty(&window_name, 1, &windowName) == 0) {
        (void) fprintf( stderr, "%s: structure allocation for windowName \
                failed.\n", argv[0]);
        exit(-1);
    }

    if (XStringListToTextProperty(&icon_name, 1, &iconName) == 0) {
        (void) fprintf( stderr, "%s: structure allocation for iconName \
                failed.\n", argv[0]);
        exit(-1);
    }

class_hints.res_name = argv[0];
class_hints.res_class = "Basicwin";

XSetWMProperties(display, calcWin, &windowName, &iconName,
        argv, argc, &sizehints, &wmhints,
        &class_hints);

    /* Create the buttons as subwindows */
attributes.background_pixmap = lgrayPixmap;
attributes.border_pixel = foreground;
for (i = 0; i < NBUTTONS; i++)
    switch (windata[i].color) {
    case WHITE:
        Buttons[i].self = XCreateSimpleWindow(display, calcWin,
            Buttons[i].x, Buttons[i].y,
            Buttons[i].width, Buttons[i].height,
            1, foreground, background);
        break;
    case BLACK:
        Buttons[i].self = XCreateSimpleWindow(display, calcWin,
            Buttons[i].x, Buttons[i].y,
```

basecalc Application

```
                    Buttons[i].width, Buttons[i].height,
                    1, background, foreground);
              break;
         case LIGHTGRAY:
              Buttons[i].self = XCreateWindow(display, calcWin,
                    Buttons[i].x, Buttons[i].y,
                    Buttons[i].width, Buttons[i].height,
                    1, CopyFromParent, InputOutput, CopyFromParent,
                    CWBorderPixel|CWBackPixmap, &attributes);
              break;
         }

    /* The display window is distinguished */
    dispWin = Buttons[0].self;

    /* Initialize event catching */
    selectEvents ();

    /* Map the calculator and subwindows */
    XMapSubwindows(display, calcWin);
    XMapWindow(display, calcWin);
}


/* Draw a single button with its text */
drawButton (win, exposeEvent)
register int win;
{
    register char *string;
    register int x, y;
    struct windata *winp;
    char *measure;
    XSetWindowAttributes attributes;
    unsigned long valuemask;
    GC gc;

    winp = &windata[win];
    x = winp->x;
    y = winp->y;
    string = winp->text;

    switch (windata[win].color) {
    case WHITE:
        gc = fgGC;
        attributes.background_pixel = background;
        attributes.border_pixel = foreground;
        valuemask = CWBackPixel|CWBorderPixel;
        break;
    case BLACK:
        gc = bgGC;
        attributes.background_pixel = foreground;
        attributes.border_pixel = background;
        valuemask = CWBackPixel|CWBorderPixel;
        break;
    case LIGHTGRAY:
        gc = bgGC;
        attributes.background_pixmap = lgrayPixmap;
        attributes.border_pixel = foreground;
        valuemask = CWBackPixmap|CWBorderPixel;
```

```
        break;
    }
    if (!exposeEvent){
        XChangeWindowAttributes(display, Buttons[win].self,
            valuemask, &attributes);
        XClearWindow(display, Buttons[win].self);
    }
    XDrawString (display, Buttons[win].self, gc, x, y, string,
            strlen (string));
    if (win == 0) {
        switch (Base) {
        case 10:
        case 8:
            measure = Octmeasure;
            break;
        default:
        case 16:
        case  2:
            measure = Hexmeasure;
            break;
        }
        XDrawString (display, dispWin, gc, 7, 6, measure, 31);
    }
}

static unsigned int LastDisp = 1;
/* Do the operation corresponding to a key press */
winPressed (win)
{
    register int type;

    type = windata[win].type;
    switch (type) {
    case WTYP_CONV:
        convButton (win);
        displayVal (LastDisp == 1 ? Value : Accum);
        break;
    case WTYP_DIG:
        digitButton (win);
        displayVal (Value);
        LastDisp = 1;
        break;
    case WTYP_OPER:
        if (operButton (win) == 0) {
            displayVal (Accum);
            LastDisp = 2;
        } else {
            displayVal (Value);
            LastDisp = 1;
        }
        break;
    case WTYP_SPEC:
        specButton (win);
        displayVal (LastDisp == 1 ? Value : Accum);
        LastDisp = 1;
    }
```

Example D-2. Remaining code for basecalc (continued)

```
}

/* Handle a conversion button */
convButton (win)
{
    register int i, NewBase, Diff, Digit;
    register int HiBase, LowBase;

    NewBase = windata[win].value;
    windata[Winbase].color = unpressedColor;
    drawButton (Winbase, 0);
    windata[win].color = pressedColor;

    Diff = NewBase - Base;
    if (Diff) {
        if (NewBase > Base) {
            LowBase = Base;
            HiBase = NewBase;
        } else {
            LowBase = NewBase;
            HiBase = Base;
        }
        for (i = 1; i < NBUTTONS; i++) {
            if (windata[i].type == WTYP_DIG) {
                Digit = windata[i].value;
                if (Digit >= LowBase && Digit < HiBase) {
                    if (Diff < 0)
                        windata[i].color = disabledColor;
                    else
                        windata[i].color = unpressedColor;
                    drawButton (i, 0);
                }
            }
        }
    }
    Winbase = win;
    Base = NewBase;
}

/* Handle a digit button */
digitButton (win)
{
    register unsigned long Temp;

    if (CalcReset) {
        CalcReset = 0;
        Accum = 0;
        Value = 0;
        LastOpt = OPR_ADD;
    }
    Digit = windata[win].value;
    if (Unsigned)
        Temp = (unsigned)Value * (unsigned)Base + Digit;
    else
        Temp = Value * Base + Digit;
    if ((unsigned)Temp/Base != (unsigned)Value) {     /* Overflow? */
        /* Flash the display since the character didn't register */
```

```
        windata[ 0 ].color =
            (displayColor == WHITE) ? BLACK : WHITE;
        drawButton (0, 0);
        XFlush(display);
        Delay ();
        windata[ 0 ].color = displayColor;
        drawButton (0, 0);
        return;
    }
    Value = Temp;
}

/* Handle a special operator */
specButton (win)
{
    register int oper;

    oper = windata[ win ].value;

    switch (oper) {
    case OPR_CLRD:
        if (LastOpt == OPR_ASGN)
            break;
        Value = (unsigned)Value / Base;
        break;
    case OPR_CLRE:
        Value = 0;
        break;
    case OPR_CLRA:
        Accum = 0;
        Value = 0;
        LastOpt = OPR_ADD;
        break;
    case OPR_UNS:
        Unsigned = !Unsigned;
        windata[ win ].text = Unsigned ? "U" : "S";
        windata[ win ].color = pressedColor;
        drawButton (win, 0);
        break;
    }
}

/* Handle an operator */
operButton (win)
{
    register int oper;

    oper = LastOpt;
    LastOpt = windata[ win ].value;

    CalcReset = 0;
    switch (LastOpt) {
    case OPR_NEG:
        Value = -Value;
        if ((LastOpt = oper) == OPR_ASGN)
            Accum = Value;
        return 1;
```

```
    case OPR_NOT:
        Value = ~Value;
        if ((LastOpt = oper) == OPR_ASGN)
            Accum = Value;
        return 1;
    }

    switch (oper) {
    case OPR_ADD:
        if (Unsigned)
            Accum = (unsigned)Accum + (unsigned)Value;
        else
            Accum += Value;
        break;
    case OPR_SUB:
        if (Unsigned)
            Accum = (unsigned)Accum - (unsigned)Value;
        else
            Accum -= Value;
        break;
    case OPR_MUL:
        if (Unsigned)
            Accum = (unsigned)Accum * (unsigned)Value;
        else
            Accum *= Value;
        break;
    case OPR_DIV:
        if (Value == 0)
            break;
        if (Unsigned)
            Accum = (unsigned)Accum / (unsigned)Value;
        else
            Accum /= Value;
        break;
    case OPR_MOD:
        if (Value == 0)
            break;
        if (Unsigned)
            Accum = (unsigned)Accum % (unsigned)Value;
        else
            Accum %= Value;
        break;
    case OPR_OR:
        Accum |= Value;
        break;
    case OPR_AND:
        Accum &= Value;
        break;
    case OPR_SHR:
        if (Unsigned)
            Accum = (unsigned)Accum >> (unsigned)Value;
        else
            Accum >>= Value;
        break;
    case OPR_SHL:
        if (Unsigned)
```

```
            Accum = (unsigned)Accum << (unsigned)Value;
        else
            Accum <<= Value;
        break;
    case OPR_XOR:
        Accum ^= Value;
        break;
    case OPR_ASGN:
        break;
    }
    if (LastOpt == OPR_ASGN) {
        Value = Accum;
        CalcReset = 1;
        return 1;
    }
    Value = 0;
    return 0;
}

/* Display a number in the display window */
displayVal (number)
register long number;
{
    register char *Fmt;
    register char *cp;
    register int i;

    switch (Base) {
    case 16:
        Fmt = "%32x";
        break;
    case 10:
        Fmt = "%32d";
        break;
    case 8:
        Fmt = "%32o";
        break;
    case 2:
        Fmt = "%032b";
        break;
    }
    cp = windata[ 0 ].text;
    for (i=32; --i >= 0; )
        *cp++ = ' ';
    *cp = ' ';
    Sprintf (windata[ 0 ].text, Fmt, number);
    drawButton (0, 0);
}

/* Translate a key code to a corresponding window */
keyToWin (str, n)
register char *str;
register unsigned n;
{
    register int value = -1;
    register struct KeyCode *KeyCodePtr;
```

```
register char ch;
register int i;

if (n > (unsigned) 0) {
    ch = *str;
    if (islower(ch) && isxdigit(ch))
        value = 10 + ch - 'a';
    else
        if (isdigit(ch))
            value = ch - '0';
    if (value >= 0) {
        for (i = 1; i < NBUTTONS; i++)
            if (windata[i].type == WTYP_DIG &&
                windata[i].value == value)
                return Buttons[i].self;
    } else {
        /* Do some translations -- these should be driven
         * from the user's terminal erase, kill, etc */
        switch (ch) {
        case 'U':
            if (Unsigned)
                return -1;
            str = "S";
            n = 1;
            break;
        case 'S':
            if (!Unsigned)
                return -1;
            str = "U";
            n = 1;
            break;
        case '\r':
        case '\n':
            str = "=";
            n = 1;
            break;
        default:
            if (ch == QuitChar) {
                XCloseDisplay(display);
                exit (1);
            }
            KeyCodePtr = KeyCodes;
            while ((n = KeyCodePtr->kc_len) > (unsigned) 0) {
                if (ch == KeyCodePtr->kc_char) {
                    str = KeyCodePtr->kc_func;
                    break;
                }
                KeyCodePtr++;
            }
            if (n == 0)
                n = 1;
            break;
        }
        for (i = 1; i < NBUTTONS; i++) {
            if (windata[i].type != WTYP_DIG &&
                strncmp (windata[i].text, str, (int) n) == 0)
```

```
                    return Buttons[i].self;
            }
        }
    }
    return None;
}
/*
 * Specialized version of C Library sprintf.
 *
 * %u %d %o %x %b (binary) are recognized.
 * %0W... — where 0 means pad with zeros otherwise blanks
 *        - if W, the minimum field width is larger than
 *        - the number
 */
Sprintf(cp, fmt, x1)
register char *cp;
register char *fmt;
unsigned x1;
{
    register int c, b, sign;
    register char    *s;
    register unsigned short fw;
    char *printInBase();
    char pad;

    while ((c = *fmt++) != '%') {
        if (c == ' ') {
            *cp = c;
            return;   /* to displayVal */
        }
        *cp++ = c;
    }
    c = *fmt++;
    if (c == '0') {
        pad = '0';
        c = *fmt++;
    } else
        pad = ' ';

    /* Calculate minimum field width */
    fw = 0;
    while (c >= '0' && c <= '9') {
        fw = fw * 10 + (c - '0');
        c = *fmt++;
    }
    sign = 0;
    switch (c) {
    case 'x':
        b = 16;
        break;
    case 'd':
        if (!Unsigned)
            sign = 1;
        /*  falls through into 'u' case */
    case 'u':
        b = 10;
```

basecalc Application

```
        break;
    case 'o':
        b = 8;
        break;
    case 'b':
        b = 2;
        break;
    default:
        /*
         * Unknown format
         */
        b = 0;
        break;
    }
    if (b)
        cp = printInBase (cp, x1, b, fw, pad, sign);
    break;

/* Print a number n in base b into string cp;
 * minimum field width = fw, pad character = pad */
char *
printInBase (cp, n, b, fw, pad, sign)
register char *cp;
register long n;
register b;
register int fw, pad;
{
    register i, nd, c;
    int     flag;
    int     plmax;
    char d[ 33 ];

    c = 1;
    if (sign)
        flag = n < 0;
    else
        flag = 0;
    if (flag)
        n = (-n);
    if (b==2)
        plmax = 32;
    else if (b==8)
        plmax = 11;
    else if (b==10)
        plmax = 10;
    else if (b==16)
        plmax = 8;
    if (b==10) {
        if (flag == 0)
            sign = 0;
        flag = 0;
    }
    for (i=0;i<plmax;i++) {
        if (flag == 0)
            nd = (unsigned)n%b;
        else
            nd = n%b;
```

```
        if (flag) {
            nd = (b - 1) - nd + c;
            if (nd >= b) {
                nd -= b;
                c = 1;
            } else
                c = 0;
        }
        d[ i ] = nd;
        if (flag == 0)
            n = (unsigned)n/b;
        else
            n = n/b;
        if ((n==0) && (flag==0))
            break;
    }
    if (i==plmax)
        i--;
    if (sign) {
        fw--;
        if (pad == '0')
            *cp++ = '-';
    }
    if (fw > i+1) {
        for (fw -= i+1; fw > 0; fw--)
            *cp++ = pad;
    }
    if (sign && pad != '0')
        *cp++ = '-';
    for (;i>=0;i--)
        *cp++ = "0123456789ABCDEF"[d[ i ] ];
    *cp = ' ';
    return cp;
}

/* Delay a little while */
Delay ()
{
    long tic;

    for (tic = 0; tic < 50000; tic++)
        ;
}
```

E

Event Reference

This appendix provides a detailed description of each event type in a reference page format. The information provided here is essential for a full understanding of the events, how they are selected and propagated, and the intracies of their operation.

In This Appendix:

E

Event Reference

This appendix describes each event structure in detail and briefly shows how each event type is used. It covers the most common uses of each event type, the information contained in each event structure, how the event is selected, and the side effects of the event, if any. Each event is described on a separate reference page.

E.1 Meaning of Common Structure Elements

Example E-1 shows the **XEvent** union and a simple event structure that is one member of the union. Several of the members of this structure are present in nearly every event structure. They are described here before we go into the event-specific members (see also Section 8.2.2).

Example E-1. XEvent union and XAnyEvent structure

```
typedef union _XEvent {
    int type;                    /* Must not be changed; first member */
    XAnyEvent xany;
    XButtonEvent xbutton;
    XCirculateEvent xcirculate;
    XCirculateRequestEvent xcirculaterequest;
    XClientMessageEvent xclient;
    XColormapEvent xcolormap;
    XConfigureEvent xconfigure;
    XConfigureRequestEvent xconfigurerequest;
    XCreateWindowEvent xcreatewindow;
    XDestroyWindowEvent xdestroywindow;
    XCrossingEvent xcrossing;
    XExposeEvent xexpose;
    XFocusChangeEvent xfocus;
    XNoExposeEvent xnoexpose;
    XGraphicsExposeEvent xgraphicsexpose;
    XGravityEvent xgravity;
    XKeymapEvent xkeymap;
    XKeyEvent xkey;
    XMapEvent xmap;
    XUnmapEvent xunmap;
    XMappingEvent xmapping;
    XMapRequestEvent xmaprequest;
```

Event Reference

```
    XMotionEvent xmotion;
    XPropertyEvent xproperty;
    XReparentEvent xreparent;
    XResizeRequestEvent xresizerequest;
    XSelectionClearEvent xselectionclear;
    XSelectionEvent xselection;
    XSelectionRequestEvent xselectionrequest;
    XVisibilityEvent xvisibility;
} XEvent;

typedef struct {
    int type;
    unsigned long serial;        /* # of last request processed by server */
    Bool send_event;             /* True if this came from SendEvent
                                  * request */
    Display *display;            /* Display the event was read from */
    Window window;               /* window on which event was requested
                                  * in event mask */
} XAnyEvent;
```

The first member of the **XEvent** union is the type of event. When an event is received (with **XNextEvent**, for example), the application checks the **type** member in the **XEvent** union. Then the specific event type is known and the specific event structure (such as **xbutton**) is used to access information specific to that event type.

Before the branching depending on the event type, only the **XEvent** union is used. After the branching, only the event structure which contains the specific information for each event type should be used in each branch. For example, if the **XEvent** union were called **report**, the **report.xexpose** structure should be used within the branch for **Expose** events.

You will notice that each event structure also begins with a **type** member. This member is rarely used, since it is an identical copy of the **type** member in the **XEvent** union.

Most event structures also have a **window** member. The only ones that do not are certain selection events (**SelectionNotify** and **SelectionRequest**) and events selected by the **graphics_exposures** member of the GC (**GraphicsExpose** and **No-Expose**). The **window** member indicates the event window that selected and received the event. This is the window where the event arrives if it has propagated through the hierarchy as described in Section 8.3.2. One event type may have two different meanings to an application, depending on which window it appears in.

Many of the event structures also have a **display** and/or **root** member. The **display** member identifies the connection to the server that is active. The **root** member indicates which screen the window that received the event is linked to in the hierarchy. Most programs only use a single screen and therefore do not need to worry about the **root** member. The **display** member can be useful, since you can pass the display variable into routines by simply passing a pointer to the event structure, eliminating the need for a separate display argument.

All event structures include a `serial` member that gives the number of the last protocol request processed by the server. This is useful in debugging, since an error can be detected by the server but not reported to the user (or programmer) until the next routine that gets an event. That means several routines may execute successfully after the error occurs. The last request processed will often indicate the request that contained the error.

All event structures also include a `send_event` flag, which, if `True`, indicates that the event was sent by `XSendEvent` (i.e., by another client rather than by the server).

The following pages describe each event type in detail. The events are presented in alphabetical order, each on a separate page. Each page describes the circumstances under which the event is generated, the mask used to select it, the structure itself, its members, and useful programming notes. Note that the description of the structure members does not include those members common to many structures. If you need more information on these members, please refer to this introductory section.

ButtonPress, ButtonRelease

When Generated

There are two types of pointer button events: `ButtonPress` and `ButtonRelease`. Both contain the same information.

Select With

May be selected separately, using `ButtonPressMask` and `ButtonReleaseMask`.

XEvent Structure Name

```
typedef union _XEvent {
    . . .
    XButtonEvent xbutton;
    . . .
} XEvent;
```

Event Structure

```
typedef struct {
int type;                        /* of event */
unsigned long serial;            /* # of last request processed by server */
Bool send_event;                 /* True if this came from a SendEvent request */
Display *display;                /* Display the event was read from */
Window window;                   /* event window it is reported relative to */
Window root;                     /* root window that the event occurred under */
Window subwindow;                /* child window */
Time time;                       /* when event occurred, in milliseconds */
int x, y;                        /* pointer coordinates relative to receiving
                                  * window */
int x_root, y_root;              /* coordinates relative to root */
unsigned int state;              /* mask of all buttons and modifier keys */
unsigned int button;             /* button that triggered event */
Bool same_screen;                /* same screen flag */
} XButtonEvent;
typedef XButtonEvent XButtonPressedEvent;
typedef XButtonEvent XButtonReleasedEvent;
```

Event Structure Members

subwindow   If the source window is the child of the receiving window, then the `subwindow` member is set to the ID of that child.

time   The server time when the button event occurred, in milliseconds. `Time` is declared as `unsigned long`, so it wraps around when it reaches the maximum value of a 32-bit number (every 49.7 days).

x, y   If the receiving window is on the same screen as the root window specified by `root`, then `x` and `y` are the pointer coordinates relative to the receiving window's origin. Otherwise, `x` and `y` are zero.

When active button grabs and pointer grabs are in effect (see Section 9.4), the coordinates relative to the receiving window may not be within the window (they may be negative or greater than window height or width).

x_root, y_root   The pointer coordinates relative to the root window which is an ancestor of the event window. If the pointer was on a different screen, these are zero.

state   The state of all the buttons and modifier keys just before the event, represented by a mask of the button and modifier key symbols: Button1Mask, Button2Mask, Button3Mask, Button4Mask, Button5Mask, ControlMask, LockMask, Mod1Mask, Mod2-Mask, Mod3Mask, Mod4Mask, Mod5Mask, and ShiftMask. If a modifier key is pressed and released when no other modifier keys are held, the ButtonPress will have a state member of 0 and the ButtonRelease will have a nonzero state member indicating that itself was held just before the event.

button   A value indicating which button changed state to trigger this event. One of the constants: Button1, Button2, Button3, Button4, or Button5.

same_screen   Indicates whether the pointer is currently on the same screen as this window. This is always True unless the pointer was actively grabbed before the automatic grab could take place.

Notes

Unless an active grab already exists or a passive grab on the button combination that was pressed already exists at a higher level in the hierarchy than where the ButtonPress occurred, an automatic active grab of the pointer takes place when a ButtonPress occurs. Because of the automatic grab, the matching ButtonRelease is sent to the same application that received the ButtonPress event. If OwnerGrabButtonMask has been selected, the ButtonRelease event is delivered to the window which contained the pointer when the button was released, as long as that window belongs to the same client as the window in which the ButtonPress event occurred. If the ButtonRelease occurs outside of the client's windows or OwnerGrabButtonMask was not selected, the ButtonRelease is delivered to the window in which the ButtonPress occurred. The grab is terminated when all buttons are released. During the grab, the cursor associated with the grabbing window will track the pointer anywhere on the screen.

If the application has invoked a passive button grab on an ancestor of the window in which the ButtonPress event occurs, then that grab takes precedence over the automatic grab, and the ButtonRelease will go to that window, or it will be handled normally by that client depending on the owner_events flag in the XGrabButton() call.

Event Reference

CirculateNotify

When Generated

A `CirculateNotify` event reports a call to change the stacking order, and it includes whether the final position is on the top or on the bottom. This event is generated by `XCirculateSubwindows()`, `XCirculateSubwindowsDown()`, or `XCirculate-SubwindowsUp()`. See also the `CirculateRequest` and `ConfigureNotify` reference pages.

Select With

This event is selected with `StructureNotifyMask` in the `XSelectInput()` call for the window to be moved or with `SubstructureNotifyMask` for the parent of the window to be moved.

XEvent Structure Name

```
typedef union _XEvent {
    . . .
    XCirculateEvent xcirculate;
    . . .
} XEvent;
```

Event Structure

```
typedef struct {
    int type;
    unsigned long serial;       /* # of last request processed by server */
    Bool send_event;            /* True if this came from SendEvent request */
    Display *display;           /* Display the event was read from */
    Window event;
    Window window;
    int place;                  /* PlaceOnTop, PlaceOnBottom */
} XCirculateEvent;
```

Event Structure Members

event   The window receiving the event. If the event was selected by `Structure-NotifyMask`, event will be the same as window. If the event was selected by `SubstructureNotifyMask`, event will be the parent of window.

window   The window that was restacked.

place   Either `PlaceOnTop` or `PlaceOnBottom`. Indicates whether the window was raised to the top or bottom of the stack.

CirculateRequest

When Generated

A CirculateRequest event reports when XCirculateSubwindows(), XCirculateSubwindowsDown(), XCirculateSubwindowsUp(), or XRestack-Windows() is called to change the stacking order of a group of children.

This event differs from CirculateNotify in that it delivers the parameters of the request before it is carried out. This gives the client that selects this event (usually the window manager) the opportunity to review the request in the light of its window management policy before executing the circulate request itself or to deny the request. (CirculateNotify indicates the final outcome of the request.)

Select With

This event is selected for the parent window with SubstructureRedirectMask.

XEvent Structure Name

```
typedef union _XEvent {
    ...
    XCirculateRequestEvent xcirculaterequest;
    ...
} XEvent;
```

Event Structure

```
typedef struct {
    int type;
    unsigned long serial;      /* # of last request processed by server */
    Bool send_event;           /* True if this came from SendEvent request */
    Display *display;          /* Display the event was read from */
    Window parent;
    Window window;
    int place;                 /* PlaceOnTop, PlaceOnBottom */
} XCirculateRequestEvent;
```

Event Structure Members

parent   The parent of the window that was restacked. This is the window that selected the event.

window   The window being restacked.

place   PlaceOnTop or PlaceOnBottom. Indicates whether the window was to be placed on the top or on the bottom of the stacking order.

Event Reference

ClientMessage

When Generated

A ClientMessage event is sent as a result of a call to XSendEvent() by a client to a particular window. Any type of event can be sent with XSendEvent(), but it will be distinguished from normal events by the send_event member being set to True. If your program wants to be able to treat events sent with XSendEvent() as different from normal events, you can read this member.

Select With

There is no event mask for ClientMessage events, and they are not selected with XSelectInput(). Instead XSendEvent() directs them to a specific window, which is given as a window ID: the PointerWindow or the InputFocus.

XEvent Structure Name

```
typedef union _XEvent {
    ...
    XClientMessageEvent xclient;
    ...
} XEvent;
```

Event Structure

```
typedef struct {
    int type;
    unsigned long serial;    /* # of last request processed by server */
    Bool send_event;         /* True if this came from SendEvent request */
    Display *display;        /* Display the event was read from */
    Window window;
    Atom message_type;
    int format;
    union {
        char b[ 20 ];
        short s[ 10 ];
        long l[ 5 ];
    } data;
} XClientMessageEvent;
```

Event Structure Members

message_type   An atom that specifies how the data is to be interpreted by the receiving client. The X server places no interpretation on the type or the data, but it must be a list of 8-bit, 16-bit, or 32-bit quantities, so that the X server can correctly swap bytes as necessary. The data always consists of twenty 8-bit values, ten 16-bit values, or five 32-bit values, although each particular message might not make use of all of these values.

format   Specifies the format of the property specified by message_type. This will be on of the values 8, 16, or 32.

ColormapNotify

When Generated

A `ColormapNotify` event reports when the colormap attribute of a window changes or when the colormap specified by the attribute is installed, uninstalled, or freed. This event is generated by `XChangeWindowAttributes()`, `XFreeColormap()`, `XInstall-Colormap()`, and `XUninstallColormap()`.

Select With

This event is selected with `ColormapChangeMask`.

XEvent Structure Name

```
typedef union _XEvent {
    ...
    XColormapEvent xcolormap;
    ...
} XEvent;
```

Event Structure

```
typedef struct {
    int type;
    unsigned long serial;      /* # of last request processed by server */
    Bool send_event;           /* True if this came from SendEvent request */
    Display *display;          /* Display the event was read from */
    Window window;
    Colormap colormap;         /* a colormap or None */
    Bool new;
    int state;                 /* ColormapInstalled, ColormapUninstalled */
} XColormapEvent;
```

Event Structure Members

window   The window whose associated colormap or attribute changes.

colormap   The colormap associated with the window, either a colormap ID or the constant `None`. It will be `None` only if this event was generated due to an `XFree-Colormap` call.

new   `True` when the colormap attribute has been changed, or `False` when the colormap is installed or uninstalled.

state   Either `ColormapInstalled` or `ColormapUninstalled`; it indicates whether the colormap is installed or uninstalled.

Event Reference

ConfigureNotify

When Generated

A `ConfigureNotify` event announces actual changes to a window's configuration (size, position, border, and stacking order). See also the `CirculateRequest` reference page.

Select With

This event is selected for a single window by specifying the window ID of that window with `StructureNotifyMask`. To receive this event for all children of a window, specify the parent window ID with `SubstructureNotifyMask`.

XEvent Structure Name

```
typedef union _XEvent {
    ...
    XConfigureEvent xconfigure;
    ...
} XEvent;
```

Event Structure

```
typedef struct {
    int type;
    unsigned long serial;      /* # of last request processed by server */
    Bool send_event;           /* True if this came from SendEvent request */
    Display *display;          /* Display the event was read from */
    Window event;
    Window window;
    int x, y;
    int width, height;
    int border_width;
    Window above;
    Bool override_redirect;
} XConfigureEvent;
```

Event Structure Members

event	The window that selected the event. The `event` and `window` members are identical if the event was selected with `Structure-NotifyMask`.
window	The window whose configuration was changed.
x, y	The final coordinates of the reconfigured window relative to its parent.
width, height	The width and height in pixels of the window after reconfiguration.
border_width	The width in pixels of the border after reconfiguration.
above	If this member is `None`, then the window is on the bottom of the stack with respect to its siblings. Otherwise, the window is immediately on top of the specified sibling window.

override_redirect   The override_redirect attribute of the reconfigured window. If True, it indicates that the client wants this window to be immune to interception by the window manager of configuration requests. Window managers normally should ignore this event if override_redirect is True.

ConfigureRequest

When Generated

A `ConfigureRequest` event reports when another client attempts to change a window's size, position, border, and/or stacking order.

This event differs from `ConfigureNotify` in that it delivers the parameters of the request before it is carried out. This gives the client that selects this event (usually the window manager) the opportunity to revise the requested configuration before executing the `XConfigureWindow()` request itself or to deny the request. (`ConfigureNotify` indicates the final outcome of the request.)

Select With

This event is selected for any window in a group of children by specifying the parent window with `SubstructureRedirectMask`.

XEvent Structure Name

```
typedef union _XEvent {
    ...
    XConfigureRequestEvent xconfigurerequest;
    ...
} XEvent;
```

Event Structure

```
typedef struct {
    int type;
    unsigned long serial;     /* # of last request processed by server */
    Bool send_event;          /* True if this came from SendEvent request */
    Display *display;         /* Display the event was read from */
    Window parent;
    Window window;
    int x, y;
    int width, height;
    int border_width;
    Window above;
    int detail;               /* Above, Below, BottomIf, TopIf, Opposite */
    unsigned long value_mask;
} XConfigureRequestEvent;
```

Event Structure Members

parent   The window that selected the event. This is the parent of the window being configured.

window   The window that is being configured.

x, y   The requested position for the upper-left pixel of the window's border relative to the origin of the parent window.

width, height   The requested width and height in pixels for the window.

`border_width`	The requested border width for the window.
`above`	The sibling specified in the `XConfigureWindow()` call, or `Above` if no sibling was specified.
`detail`	`None`, `Above`, `Below`, `TopIf`, `BottomIf`, or `Opposite`. Specifies the sibling window on top of which the specified window should be placed. If this member has the constant `None`, then the specified window should be placed on the bottom.
`value_mask`	A bit mask representing which elements of configuration are to be changed.

Notes

The geometry is derived from the `XConfigureWindow()` request that triggered the event.

Event Reference

CreateNotify

When Generated

A CreateNotify event reports when a window is created.

Select With

This event is selected on children of a window by specifying the parent window ID with SubstructureNotifyMask. (Note that this event type cannot be selected by StructureNotifyMask).

XEvent Structure Name

```
typedef union _XEvent {
    ...
    XCreateWindowEvent xcreatewindow;
    ...
} XEvent;
```

Event Structure

```
typedef struct {
    int type;
    unsigned long serial;      /* # of last request processed by server */
    Bool send_event;           /* True if this came from SendEvent
                                * request */
    Display *display;          /* Display the event was read from */
    Window parent;             /* parent of the window */
    Window window;             /* window ID of window created */
    int x, y;                  /* window location */
    int width, height;         /* size of window */
    int border_width;          /* border width */
    Bool override_redirect;    /* creation should be overridden */
} XCreateWindowEvent;
```

Event Structure Members

parent   The ID of the created window's parent.

window   The ID of the created window.

x, y   The coordinates of the created window relative to its parent.

width, height   The width and height in pixels of the created window.

border_width   The width in pixels of the border of the created window.

override_redirect   The override_redirect attribute of the created window. If True, it indicates that the client wants this window to be immune to interception by the window manager of configuration requests. Window managers normally should ignore this event if override_redirect is True.

Notes

For descriptions of these members, see the `XCreateWindow()` function and the `XSet-WindowAttributes` structure.

DestroyNotify

When Generated

A `DestroyNotify` event reports that a window has been destroyed.

Select With

To receive this event type on children of a window, specify the parent window ID and pass `SubstructureNotifyMask` as part of the `event_mask` argument to `XSelect-Input()`. This event type cannot be selected with `StructureNotifyMask`.

XEvent Structure Name

```
typedef union _XEvent {
    ...
    XDestroyWindowEvent xdestroywindow;
    ...
} XEvent;
```

Event Structure

```
typedef struct {
    int type;
    unsigned long serial;    /* # of last request processed by server */
    Bool send_event;         /* True if this came from SendEvent request */
    Display *display;         /* Display the event was read from */
    Window event;
    Window window;
} XDestroyWindowEvent;
```

Event Structure Members

event   The window that selected the event.

window   The window that was destroyed.

EnterNotify, LeaveNotify

When Generated

EnterNotify and LeaveNotify events occur when the pointer enters or leaves a window.

When the pointer crosses a window border, a LeaveNotify event occurs in the window being left and an EnterNotify event occurs in the window being entered. Whether or not each event is queued for any application depends on whether any application selected the right event on the window in which it occurred.

In addition, EnterNotify and LeaveNotify events are delivered to windows that are *virtually crossed*. These are windows that are between the origin and destination windows in the hierarchy but not necessarily on the screen. Further explanation of virtual crossing is provided two pages following.

Select With

Each of these events can be selected separately with EnterWindowMask and Leave-WindowMask.

XEvent Structure Name

```
typedef union _XEvent {
    ...
    XCrossingEvent xcrossing;
    ...
} XEvent;
```

Event Structure

```
typedef struct {
    int type;                  /* of event */
    unsigned long serial;      /* # of last request processed by server */
    Bool send_event;           /* True if this came from SendEvent request */
    Display *display;          /* Display the event was read from */
    Window window;             /* event window it is reported relative to */
    Window root;               /* root window that the event occurred on */
    Window subwindow;          /* child window */
    Time time;                 /* milliseconds */
    int x, y;                  /* pointer x,y coordinates in receiving
                                * window */
    int x_root, y_root;        /* coordinates relative to root */
    int mode;                  /* NotifyNormal, NotifyGrab, NotifyUngrab */
    int detail;                /* NotifyAncestor, NotifyInferior,
                                * NotifyNonLinear, NotifyNonLinearVirtual,
                                * NotifyVirtual */
    Bool same_screen;          /* same screen flag */
    Bool focus;                /* boolean focus */
    unsigned int state;        /* key or button mask */
} XCrossingEvent;
typedef XCrossingEvent XEnterWindowEvent;
typedef XCrossingEvent XLeaveWindowEvent;
```

Event Structure Members

The following list describes the members of the `XCrossingEvent` structure.

subwindow	In a `LeaveNotify` event, if the pointer began in a child of the receiving window, then the `child` member is set to the window ID of the child. Otherwise, it is set to `None`. For an `EnterNotify` event, if the pointer ends up in a child of the receiving window, then the `child` member is set to the window ID of the child. Otherwise, it is set to `None`.
time	The server time when the crossing event occurred, in milliseconds. Time is declared as `unsigned long`, so it wraps around when it reaches the maximum value of a 32-bit number (every 49.7 days).
x, y	The point of entry or exit of the pointer relative to the event window.
x_root, y_root	The point of entry or exit of the pointer relative to the root window.
mode	Normal crossing events or those caused by pointer warps have mode `NotifyNormal`, events caused by a grab have mode `NotifyGrab`, and events caused by a released grab have mode `NotifyUngrab`.
detail	The value of the `detail` member depends on the hierarchical relationship between the origin and destination windows and the direction of pointer transfer. Determining which windows receive events and with which `detail` members is quite complicated. This topic is described in the next section.
same_screen	Indicates whether the pointer is currently on the same screen as this window. This is always `True` unless the pointer was actively grabbed before the automatic grab could take place.
focus	If the receiving window is the focus window or a descendant of the focus window, the `focus` member is `True`; otherwise, it is `False`.
state	The state of all the buttons and modifier keys just before the event, represented by a mask of the button and modifier key symbols: `Button1Mask`, `Button2Mask`, `Button3Mask`, `Button4Mask`, `Button5Mask`, `ControlMask`, `LockMask`, `Mod1Mask`, `Mod2-Mask`, `Mod3Mask`, `Mod4Mask`, `Mod5Mask`, and `ShiftMask`.

Virtual Crossing and the detail Member

Virtual crossing occurs when the pointer moves between two windows that do not have a parent-child relationship. Windows between the origin and destination windows in the hierarchy receive `EnterNotify` and `LeaveNotify` events. The `detail` member of each of these events depends on the hierarchical relationship of the origin and destination windows and the direction of pointer transfer.

Virtual crossing is an advanced topic that you should not spend time figuring out unless you have an important reason to use it. We have never seen an application that uses this feature, and we know of no reason for its extreme complexity. With that word of warning, proceed.

Let's say the pointer has moved from one window, the origin, to another, the destination. First, we'll specify what types of events each window gets and then the detail member of each of those events.

The window of origin receives a `LeaveNotify` event and the destination window receives an `EnterNotify` event, if they have requested this type of event. If one is an inferior of the other, the `detail` member of the event received by the inferior is `NotifyAncestor` and the detail of the event received by the superior is `NotifyInferior`. If the crossing is between parent and child, these are the only events generated.

However, if the origin and destination windows are not parent and child, other windows are *virtually crossed* and also receive events. If neither window is an ancestor of the other, ancestors of each window, up to but not including the least common ancestor, receive `Leave-Notify` events, if they are in the same branch of the hierarchy as the origin, and `Enter-Notify` events, if they are in the same branch as the destination. These events can be used to track the motion of the pointer through the hierarchy.

- In the case of a crossing from a parent to a child of a child, the middle child receives a `LeaveNotify` with detail `NotifyVirtual`.

- In the case of a crossing between a child and the parent of its parent, the middle child receives an `EnterNotify` with detail `NotifyVirtual`.

- In a crossing between windows where there is no direct ancestral relationship, both the origin and destination windows receive events with detail `NotifyNonlinear`. The windows between the origin and the destination in the hierarchy, up to but not including their least common ancestor, receive events with detail `NotifyNonlinearVirtual`. The least common ancestor is the lowest window from which both are descendants.

- If the origin and destination windows are on separate screens, the events and details generated are the same as for two windows not parent and child, except that the root windows of the two screens are considered the least common ancestor. Both root windows also receive events.

Event Reference

Table E-1 shows the event types generated by a pointer crossing from window *A* to window *B* when window *C* is the least common ancestor of *A* and *B*.

Table E-1. Border Crossing Events and Window Relationship

LeaveNotify	EnterNotify
Origin window (*A*)	Destination window (*B*)
Windows between *A* and *B*, exclusive, if *A* is inferior	Windows between *A* and *B*, exclusive, if *B* is inferior
Windows between *A* and *C*, exclusive	Windows between *B* and *C*, exclusive
Root window on screen of origin if different from screen of destination	Root window on screen of destination if different from screen of origin

Table E-2 lists the `detail` members in events generated by a pointer crossing from window *A* to window *B*.

Table E-2. Event detail Member and Window Relationship

detail Flag	Window Delivered To
NotifyAncestor	Origin or destination when either is descendant
NotifyInferior	Origin or destination when either is ancestor
NotifyVirtual	Windows between *A* and *B*, exclusive, if either is descendant
NotifyNonlinear	Origin and destination when *A* and *B* are two or more windows distant from least common ancestor *C*
NotifyNonlinearVirtual	Windows between *A* and *C*, exclusive, and between *B* and *C*, exclusive, when *A* and *B* have least common ancestor *C*; also on both root windows if *A* and *B* are on different screens

For example, Figure E-1 shows the events that are generated by a movement from a window (window *A*) to a child (window *B1*) of a sibling (window *B*). This would generate three events: a LeaveNotify with detail NotifyNonlinear for the window *A*, an EnterNotify with detail NotifyNonlinearVirtual for its sibling window *B*, and an EnterNotify with detail NotifyNonlinear for the child (window *B1*).

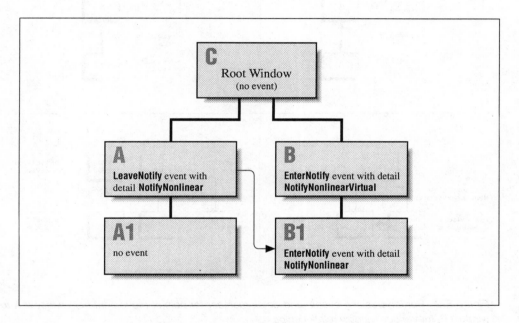

Figure E-1. Events generated by a move between windows

EnterNotify and LeaveNotify events are also generated when the pointer is grabbed, if the pointer was not already inside the grabbing window. In this case, the grabbing window receives an EnterNotify and the window containing the pointer receives a LeaveNotify event, both with mode NotifyUngrab. The pointer position in both events is the position before the grab. The result when the grab is released is exactly the same, except that the two windows receive EnterNotify instead of LeaveNotify and vice versa.

Event Reference

Figure E-2 demonstrates the events and details caused by various pointer transitions, indicated by heavy arrows.

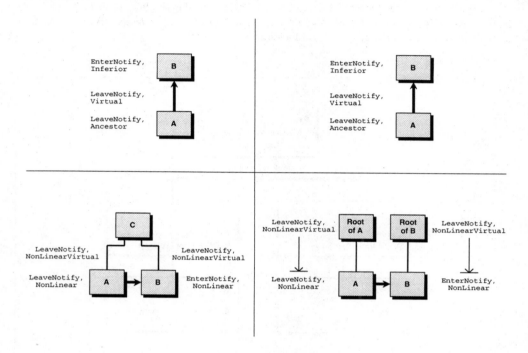

Figure E-2. Border crossing events and detail member for pointer movement from window A to window B, for various window relationships

Expose

When Generated

An `Expose` event is generated when a window becomes visible or a previously invisible part of a window becomes visible. Only `InputOutput` windows generate or need to respond to `Expose` events; `InputOnly` windows never generate or need to respond to them. The `Expose` event provides the position and size of the exposed area within the window and a rough count of the number of remaining exposure events for the current window.

Select With

This event is selected with `ExposureMask`.

XEvent Structure Name

```
typedef union _XEvent {
    ...
    XExposeEvent xexpose;
    ...
} XEvent;
```

Event Structure

```
typedef struct {
    int type;
    unsigned long serial;      /* # of last request processed by server */
    Bool send_event;           /* True if this came from SendEvent request */
    Display *display;          /* Display the event was read from */
    Window window;
    int x, y;
    int width, height;
    int count;                 /* If nonzero, at least this many more */
} XExposeEvent;
```

Event Structure Members

x, y   The coordinates of the upper-left corner of the exposed region relative to the origin of the window.

width, height   The width and height in pixels of the exposed region.

count   The approximate number of remaining contiguous `Expose` events that were generated as a result of a single function call.

Notes

A single action such as a window movement or a function call can generate several exposure events on one window or on several windows. The server guarantees that all exposure events generated from a single action will be sent contiguously, so that they can all be handled before moving on to other event types. This allows an application to keep track of the rectangles specified in contiguous `Expose` events, set the `clip_mask` in a GC to the areas specified in

Event Reference

the rectangle using `XSetRegion()` or `XSetClipRectangles()`, and then finally redraw the window clipped with the GC in a single operation after all the `Expose` events have arrived. The last event to arrive is indicated by a `count` of 0. In Release 2, `XUnionRect-WithRegion()` can be used to add the rectangle in `Expose` events to a region before calling `XSetRegion()`.

If your application is able to redraw partial windows, you can also read each exposure event in turn and redraw each area.

FocusIn, FocusOut

When Generated

FocusIn and FocusOut events occur when the keyboard focus window changes as a result of an XSetInputFocus() call. They are much like EnterNotify and LeaveNotify events except that they track the focus rather than the pointer.

When a focus change occurs, a FocusOut event is delivered to the old focus window and a FocusIn event to the window which receives the focus. In addition, windows in between these two windows in the window hierarchy are virtually crossed and receive focus change events, as described below. Some or all of the windows between the window containing the pointer at the time of the focus change and the root window also receive focus change events, as described below.

Select With

FocusIn and FocusOut events are selected with FocusChangeMask. They cannot be selected separately.

XEvent Structure Name

```
typedef union _XEvent {
    ...
    XFocusChangeEvent xfocus;
    ...
} XEvent;
```

Event Structure

```
typedef struct {
    int type;                  /* FocusIn or FocusOut */
    unsigned long serial;      /* # of last request processed by server */
    Bool send_event;           /* True if this came from SendEvent request */
    Display *display;          /* Display the event was read from */
    Window window;             /* Window of event */
    int mode;                  /* NotifyNormal, NotifyGrab, NotifyUngrab */
    int detail;                /* NotifyAncestor, NotifyDetailNone,
                                * NotifyInferior, NotifyNonLinear,
                                * NotifyNonLinearVirtual, NotifyPointer,
                                * NotifyPointerRoot, NotifyVirtual*/
} XFocusChangeEvent;
typedef XFocusChangeEvent XFocusInEvent;
typedef XFocusChangeEvent XFocusOutEvent;
```

Event Structure Members

mode   For events generated when the keyboard is not grabbed, mode is Notify-Normal; when the keyboard is grabbed, mode is NotifyGrab; and when a keyboard is ungrabbed, mode is NotifyUngrab.

Event Reference

detail   The detail member identifies the relationship between the window that receives the event and the origin and destination windows. It will be described in detail after the description of which windows get what types of events.

Notes

The *keyboard focus* is a window that has been designated as the one to receive all keyboard input irrespective of the pointer position. Only the keyboard focus window and its descendants receive keyboard events. By default, the focus window is the root window. Since all windows are descendants of the root, the pointer controls the window that receives input.

Most window managers allow the user to set a focus window to avoid the problem where the pointer sometimes gets bumped into the wrong window and your typing does not go to the intended window. If the pointer is pointing at the root window, all typing is usually lost, since there is no application for this input to propagate to. Some applications may set the keyboard focus so that they can get all keyboard input for a given period of time, but this practice is not encouraged.

Focus events are used when an application wants to act differently when the keyboard focus is set to another window or to itself. FocusChangeMask is used to select FocusIn and FocusOut events.

When a focus change occurs, a FocusOut event is delivered to the old focus window and a FocusIn event is delivered to the window which receives the focus. Windows in between in the hierarchy are virtually crossed and receive one focus change event each depending on the relationship and direction of transfer between the origin and destination windows. Some or all of the windows between the window containing the pointer at the time of the focus change and that window's root window can also receive focus change events. By checking the detail member of FocusIn and FocusOut events, an application can tell which of its windows can receive input.

The detail member gives clues about the relationship of the event receiving window to the origin and destination of the focus. The detail member of FocusIn and FocusOut events is analogous to the detail member of EnterNotify and LeaveNotify events but with even more permutations to make life complicated.

Virtual Focus Crossing and the detail Member

We will now embark on specifying the types of events sent to each window and the detail member in each event, depending on the relative position in the hierarchy of the origin window (old focus), destination window (new focus), and the pointer window (window containing pointer at time of focus change). Don't even try to figure this out unless you have to.

Table E-3 shows the event types generated by a focus transition from window A to window B when window C is the least common ancestor of A and B. This table includes most of the events generated, but not all of them. It is quite possible for a single window to receive more than one focus change event from a single focus change.

Table E-3. FocusIn and FocusOut Events and Window Relationship

FocusOut	FocusIn
Origin window (A)	Destination window (B)
Windows between A and B, exclusive, if A is inferior	Windows between A and B, exclusive, if B is inferior
Windows between A and C, exclusive	Windows between B and C, exclusive
Root window on screen of origin if different from screen of destination	Root window on screen of destination if different from screen of origin
Pointer window up to but not including origin window if pointer window is descendant of origin	Pointer window up to but not including destination window if pointer window is descendant of destination
Pointer window up to and including pointer window's root if transfer was from `PointerRoot`	Pointer window up to and including pointer window's root if transfer was to `PointerRoot`

Table E-4 lists the `detail` members in events generated by a focus transition from window *A* to window *B* when window *C* is the least common ancestor of *A* and *B*, with *P* being the window containing the pointer.

Table E-4. Event detail Member and Window Relationship

`detail` Flag	Window Delivered To
`NotifyAncestor`	Origin or destination when either is descendant
`NotifyInferior`	Origin or destination when either is ancestor
`NotifyVirtual`	Windows between *A* and *B*, exclusive, if either is descendant
`NotifyNonlinear`	Origin and destination when *A* and *B* are two or more windows distant from least common ancestor *C*
`NotifyNonlinearVirtual`	Windows between *A* and *C*, exclusive, and between *B* and *C*, exclusive, when *A* and *B* have least common ancestor *C*; also on both root windows if *A* and *B* are on different screens
`NotifyPointer`	Window *P* and windows up to but not including the origin or destination windows
`NotifyPointerRoot`	Window *P* and all windows up to its root, and all other roots, when focus is set to or from `Pointer-Root`
`NotifyDetailNone`	All roots, when focus is set to or from `None`

Figure E-3 shows all the possible combinations of focus transitions and of origin, destination, and pointer windows and shows the types of events that are generated and their `detail` member. Solid lines indicate branches of the hierarchy. Heavy arrows indicate the direction of transition of the focus. At each end of this arrow are the origin and destination windows, windows *A* to *B*. Arrows ending in a bar indicate that the event type and detail described are delivered to all windows up to the bar.

In any branch, there may be windows that are not shown. Windows in a single branch between two boxes shown will get the event types and details shown beside the branch.

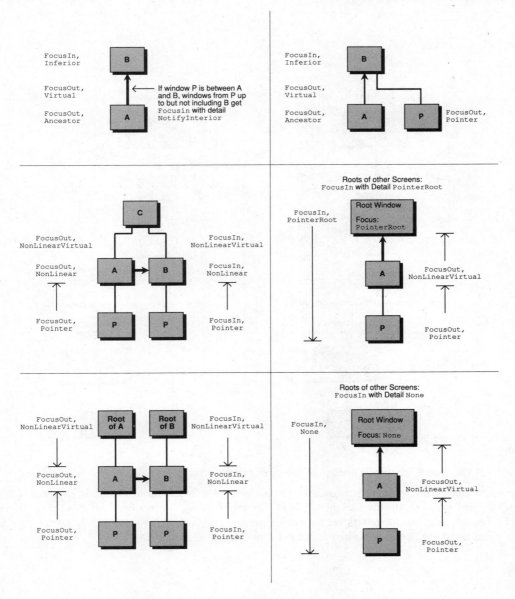

Figure E-3. FocusIn and FocusOut event schematics

Event Reference

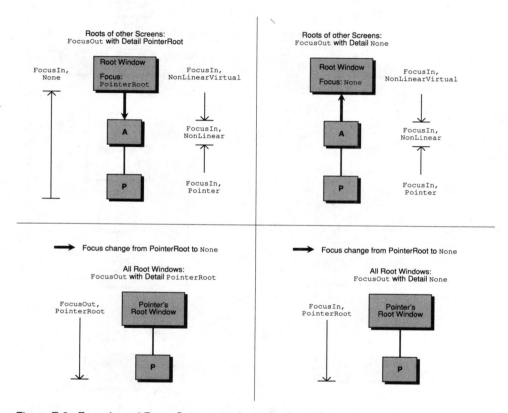

Figure E-3. FocusIn and FocusOut event schematics (cont'd)

FocusIn and FocusOut events are also generated when the keyboard is grabbed, if the focus was not already assigned to the grabbing window. In this case, all windows receive events as if the focus was set from the current focus to the grab window. When the grab is released, the events generated are just as if the focus was set back.

GraphicsExpose, NoExpose

When Generated

GraphicsExpose events indicate that the source area for a XCopyArea() or XCopy-Plane() request was not available because it was outside the source window or obscured by a window. NoExpose events indicate that the source region was completely available.

Select With

These events are not selected with XSelectInput() but are sent if the GC in the XCopy-Area() or XCopyPlane() request had its graphics_exposures flag set to True. If graphics_exposures is True in the GC used for the copy, either one NoExpose event or one or more GraphicsExpose events will be generated for every XCopyArea() or XCopyPlane() call made.

XEvent Structure Name

```
typedef union _XEvent {
    ...
    XNoExposeEvent xnoexpose;
    XGraphicsExposeEvent xgraphicsexpose;
    ...
} XEvent;
```

Event Structure

```
typedef struct {
    int type;
    unsigned long serial;   /* # of last request processed by server */
    Bool send_event;        /* True if this came from SendEvent request */
    Display *display;        /* Display the event was read from */
    Drawable drawable;
    int x, y;
    int width, height;
    int count;              /* if nonzero, at least this many more */
    int major_code;         /* core is X_CopyArea or X_CopyPlane */
    int minor_code;         /* not defined in the core */
} XGraphicsExposeEvent;

typedef struct {
    int type;
    unsigned long serial;   /* # of last request processed by server */
    Bool send_event;        /* True if this came from SendEvent request */
    Display *display;        /* Display the event was read from */
    Drawable drawable;
    int major_code;         /* core is X_CopyArea or X_CopyPlane */
    int minor_code;         /* not defined in the core */
} XNoExposeEvent;
```

Event Reference

Event Structure Members

drawable — A window or an off-screen pixmap. This specifies the destination of the graphics request that generated the event.

x, y — The coordinates of the upper-left corner of the exposed region relative to the origin of the window.

width, height — The width and height in pixels of the exposed region.

count — The approximate number of remaining contiguous GraphicsExpose events that were generated as a result of the XCopyArea() or XCopy-Plane() call.

major_code — The graphics request used. This may be one of the symbols X_Copy-Area or X_CopyPlane or a symbol defined by a loaded extension.

minor_code — Zero unless the request is part of an extension.

Notes

Expose events and GraphicsExpose events both indicate the region of a window that was actually exposed (x, y, width, and height). Therefore, they can often be handled similarly. The symbols X_CopyPlane and X_CopyArea are defined in *<X11/Xproto.h>*. These symbols are used to determine whether a GraphicsExpose or NoExpose event occurred because of an XCopyArea() call or an XCopyPlane() call.

GravityNotify

When Generated

A GravityNotify event reports when a window is moved because of a change in the size of its parent. This happens when the win_gravity attribute of the child window is something other than StaticGravity or UnmapGravity.

Select With

This event is selected for a single window by specifying the window ID of that window with StructureNotifyMask. To receive notification of movement due to gravity for a group of siblings, specify the parent window ID with SubstructureNotifyMask.

XEvent Structure Name

```
typedef union _XEvent {
    ...
    XGravityEvent xgravity;
    ...
} XEvent;
```

Event Structure

```
typedef struct {
    int type;
    unsigned long serial;    /* # of last request processed by server */
    Bool send_event;         /* True if this came from SendEvent request */
    Display *display;        /* Display the event was read from */
    Window event;
    Window window;
    int x, y;
} XGravityEvent;
```

Event Structure Members

event   The window that selected the event.

window   The window that was moved.

x, y   The new coordinates of the window relative to its parent.

KeymapNotify

When Generated

A KeymapNotify event reports the state of the keyboard and occurs when the pointer or keyboard focus enters a window. KeymapNotify events are reported immediately after EnterNotify or FocusIn events. This is a way for the application to read the keyboard state as the application is "woken up," since the two triggering events usually indicate that the application is about to receive user input.

Select With

This event is selected with KeymapStateMask.

XEvent Structure Name

```
typedef union _XEvent {
    ...
    XKeymapEvent xkeymap;
    ...
} XEvent;
```

Event Structure

```
typedef struct {
    int type;
    unsigned long serial;    /* # of last request processed by server */
    Bool send_event;         /* True if this came from SendEvent request */
    Display *display;        /* Display the event was read from */
    Window window;
    char key_vector[ 32 ];
} XKeymapEvent;
```

Event Structure Members

window   Reports the window which was reported in the window member of the preceding EnterNotify or FocusIn event.

key_vector A bit vector or mask, each bit representing one physical key, with a total of 256 bits. For a given key, its keycode is its position in the keyboard vector. You can also get this bit vector by calling XQueryKeymap().

Notes

The serial member of KeymapNotify does not contain the serial number of the most recent protocol request processed, because this event always follows immediately after EnterNotify or FocusIn events in which the serial member is valid.

KeyPress, KeyRelease

When Generated

`KeyPress` and `KeyRelease` events are generated for all keys, even those mapped to modifier keys such as Shift or Control.

Select With

Each type of keyboard event may be selected separately with `KeyPressMask` and `KeyReleaseMask`.

XEvent Structure Name

```
typedef union _XEvent {
    ...
    XKeyEvent xkey;
    ...
} XEvent;
```

Event Structure

```
typedef struct {
    int type;                  /* of event */
    unsigned long serial;      /* # of last request processed by server */
    Bool send_event;           /* True if this came from SendEvent request */
    Display *display;          /* Display the event was read from */
    Window window;             /* event window it is reported relative to */
    Window root;               /* root window that the event occurred on */
    Window subwindow;          /* child window */
    Time time;                 /* milliseconds */
    int x, y;                  /* pointer coordinates relative to receiving
                                * window */
    int x_root, y_root;        /* coordinates relative to root */
    unsigned int state;        /* modifier key and button mask */
    unsigned int keycode;      /* server-dependent code for key */
    Bool same_screen;          /* same screen flag */
} XKeyEvent;
typedef XKeyEvent XKeyPressedEvent;
typedef XKeyEvent XKeyReleasedEvent;
```

Event Structure Members

subwindow   If the source window is the child of the receiving window, then the `subwindow` member is set to the ID of that child.

time   The server time when the button event occurred, in milliseconds. `Time` is declared as `unsigned long`, so it wraps around when it reaches the maximum value of a 32-bit number (every 49.7 days).

x, y   If the receiving window is on the same screen as the root window specified by `root`, then `x` and `y` are the pointer coordinates relative to the receiving window's origin. Otherwise, `x` and `y` are zero.

Event Reference

When active button grabs and pointer grabs are in effect (see Section 9.4), the coordinates relative to the receiving window may not be within the window (they may be negative or greater than window height or width).

x_root, y_root The pointer coordinates relative to the root window which is an ancestor of the event window. If the pointer was on a different screen, these are zero.

state The state of all the buttons and modifier keys just before the event, represented by a mask of the button and modifier key symbols: Button1Mask, Button2Mask, Button3Mask, Button4Mask, Button5Mask, ControlMask, LockMask, Mod1Mask, Mod2-Mask, Mod3Mask, Mod4Mask, Mod5Mask, and ShiftMask.

keycode The keycode member contains a server-dependent code for the key that changed state. As such, it should be translated into the portable symbol called a keysym before being used. It can also be converted directly into ASCII with XLookupString. For a description and examples of how to translate keycodes, see Section 9.1.1.

Notes

Remember that not all hardware is capable of generating release events and that only the main keyboard (a-z, A-Z, 0-9), Shift, and Control keys are always found.

Keyboard events are analogous to button events, though, of course, there are many more keys than buttons and the keyboard is not automatically grabbed between press and release.

All the structure members have the same meaning as described for ButtonPress and ButtonRelease events, except that button is replaced by keycode.

MapNotify, UnmapNotify

When Generated

The X server generates `MapNotify` and `UnmapNotify` events when a window changes state from unmapped to mapped or vice versa.

Select With

To receive these events on a single window, use `StructureNotifyMask` in the call to `XSelectInput()` for the window. To receive these events for all children of a particular parent, specify the parent window ID and use `SubstructureNotifyMask`.

XEvent Structure Name

```
typedef union _XEvent {
    ...
    XMapEvent xmap;
    XUnmapEvent xunmap;
    ...
} XEvent;
```

Event Structure

```
typedef struct {
    int type;
    unsigned long serial;       /* # of last request processed by server */
    Bool send_event;            /* True if this came from SendEvent request */
    Display *display;           /* Display the event was read from */
    Window event;
    Window window;
    Bool override_redirect;     /* boolean, is override set */
} XMapEvent;

typedef struct {
    int type;
    unsigned long serial;       /* # of last request processed by server */
    Bool send_event;            /* True if this came from SendEvent request */
    Display *display;           /* Display the event was read from */
    Window event;
    Window window;
    Bool from_configure;
} XUnmapEvent;
```

Event Structure Members

event   The window that selected this event.

window   The window that was just mapped or unmapped.

override_redirect (XMapEvent() only)
            `True` or `False`. The value of the `override_redirect` attribute of the window that was just mapped.

`from_configure`(XUnmapEvent( ) only)

> True if the event was generated as a result of a resizing of the window's parent when the window itself had a `win_gravity` of UnmapGravity. See the description of the `win_gravity` attribute in Section 4.3.4. `False` otherwise.

MappingNotify

When Generated

A `MappingNotify` event is sent when any of the following is changed by another client: the mapping between physical keyboard keys (keycodes) and keysyms, the mapping between modifier keys and logical modifiers, or the mapping between physical and logical pointer buttons. These events are triggered by a call to `XSetModifierMapping()` or `XSet-PointerMapping()`, if the return status is `MappingSuccess`, or by any call to `XChangeKeyboardMapping()`.

This event type should not be confused with the event that occurs when a window is mapped; that is a `MapNotify` event. Nor should it be confused with the `KeymapNotify` event, which reports the state of the keyboard as a mask instead of as a keycode.

Select With

The X server sends `MappingNotify` events to all clients. It is never selected and cannot be masked with the window attributes.

XEvent Structure Name

```
typedef union _XEvent {
    ...
    XMappingEvent xmapping;
    ...
} XEvent;
```

Event Structure

```
typedef struct {
    int type;
    unsigned long serial;    /* # of last request processed by server */
    Bool send_event;         /* True if this came from SendEvent request */
    Display *display;         /* Display the event was read from */
    Window window;            /* unused */
    int request;             /* one of MappingMapping, MappingKeyboard,
                              * MappingPointer */
    int first_keycode;       /* first keycode */
    int count;               /* range of change with first_keycode*/
} XMappingEvent;
```

Event Structure Members

request
: The kind of mapping change that occurred: `MappingModifier` for a successful `XSetModifierMapping()` (keyboard Shift, Lock, Control, Meta keys), `MappingKeyboard` for a successful `XChange-KeyboardMapping` (other keys), and `MappingPointer` for a successful `XSetPointerMapping()` (pointer button numbers).

first_keycode
: If the `request` member is `MappingKeyboard` or `Mapping-Modifier`, then `first_keycode` indicates the first in a range of keycodes with altered mappings. Otherwise, it is not set.

count   If the request member is MappingKeyboard or Mapping-
                                 Modifier, then count indicates the number of keycodes with altered
                                 mappings. Otherwise, it is not set.

Notes

If the request member is MappingKeyboard, clients should call XRefreshKeyboard-
Mapping().

The normal response to a request member of MappingPointer or MappingModifier
is no action. This is because the clients should use the logical mapping of the buttons and
modifiers to allow the user to customize the keyboard if desired. If the application requires a
particular mapping regardless of the user's preferences, it should call XGetModifier-
Mapping() or XGetPointerMapping() to find out about the new mapping.

MapRequest

When Generated

A `MapRequest` event occurs when the functions `XMapRaised()` and `XMapWindow()` are called.

This event differs from `MapNotify` in that it delivers the parameters of the request before it is carried out. This gives the client that selects this event (usually the window manager) the opportunity to revise the size or position of the window before executing the map request itself or to deny the request. (`MapNotify` indicates the final outcome of the request.)

Select With

This event is selected by specifying the window ID of the parent of the receiving window with `SubstructureRedirectMask`. (In addition, the `override_redirect` member of the `XSetWindowAttributes` structure for the specified window must be `False`.)

XEvent Structure Name

```
typedef union _XEvent {
    ...
    XMapRequestEvent xmaprequest;
    ...
} XEvent;
```

Event Structure

```
typedef struct {
    int type;
    unsigned long serial;    /* # of last request processed by server */
    Bool send_event;         /* True if this came from SendEvent request */
    Display *display;        /* Display the event was read from */
    Window parent;
    Window window;
} XMapRequestEvent;
```

Event Structure Members

parent   The ID of the parent of the window being mapped.

window   The ID of the window being mapped.

MotionNotify

When Generated

A MotionNotify event reports that the user moved the pointer or that a program warped the pointer to a new position within a single window.

Select With

This event is selected with ButtonMotionMask, Button1MotionMask, Button2-MotionMask, Button3MotionMask, Button4MotionMask, Button5MotionMask, PointerMotionHintMask, and PointerMotionMask. These masks determine the specific conditions under which the event is generated.

See Section 8.3.3.3 for a description of selecting button events.

XEvent Structure Name

```
typedef union _XEvent {
    ...
    XMotionEvent xmotion;
    ...
} XEvent;
```

Event Structure

```
typedef struct {
    int type;                  /* of event */
    unsigned long serial;      /* # of last request processed by server */
    Bool send_event;           /* True if this came from SendEvent request */
    Display *display;          /* Display the event was read from */
    Window window;             /* event window it is reported relative to */
    Window root;               /* root window that the event occurred on */
    Window subwindow;          /* child window */
    Time time;                 /* milliseconds */
    int x, y;                  /* pointer coordinates relative to receiving
                                * window */
    int x_root, y_root;        /* coordinates relative to root */
    unsigned int state;        /* button and modifier key mask */
    char is_hint;              /* is this a motion hint */
    Bool same_screen;          /* same screen flag */
} XMotionEvent;
typedef XMotionEvent XPointerMovedEvent;
```

Event Structure Members

subwindow   If the source window is the child of the receiving window, then the subwindow member is set to the ID of that child.

time   The server time when the button event occurred, in milliseconds. Time is declared as unsigned long, so it wraps around when it reaches the maximum value of a 32-bit number (every 49.7 days).

x, y	If the receiving window is on the same screen as the root window specified by root, then x and y are the pointer coordinates relative to the receiving window's origin. Otherwise, x and y are zero.
	When active button grabs and pointer grabs are in effect (see Section 9.4), the coordinates relative to the receiving window may not be within the window (they may be negative or greater than window height or width).
x_root, y_root	The pointer coordinates relative to the root window which is an ancestor of the event window. If the pointer was on a different screen, these are zero.
state	The state of all the buttons and modifier keys just before the event, represented by a mask of the button and modifier key symbols: Button1Mask, Button2Mask, Button3Mask, Button4Mask, Button5Mask, ControlMask, LockMask, Mod1Mask, Mod2-Mask, Mod3Mask, Mod4Mask, Mod5Mask, and ShiftMask.
is_hint	Either the constant NotifyNormal or NotifyHint. NotifyHint indicates that the PointerMotionHintMask was selected. In this case, just one event is sent when the mouse moves, and the current position can be found by calling XQueryPointer() or by examining the motion history buffer with XGetMotionEvents(), if a motion history buffer is available on the server. NotifyNormal indicates that the event is real, but it may not be up to date, since there may be many more later motion events on the queue.
same_screen	Indicates whether the pointer is currently on the same screen as this window. This is always True unless the pointer was actively grabbed before the automatic grab could take place.

Notes

If the processing you have to do for every motion event is fast, you can probably handle all of them without requiring motion hints. However, if you have extensive processing to do for each one, you might be better off using the hints and calling XQueryPointer() or using the history buffer if it exists. XQueryPointer() is a round-trip request, so it can be slow.

EnterNotify and LeaveNotify events are generated instead of MotionNotify events if the pointer starts and stops in different windows.

Event Reference

PropertyNotify

When Generated

A `PropertyNotify` event indicates that a property of a window has changed or been deleted. This event can also be used to get the current server time (by appending zero-length data to a property). `PropertyNotify` events are generated by `XChangeProperty()`, `XDeleteProperty()`, `XGetWindowProperty()`, or `XRotateWindowProperties()`.

Select With

This event is selected with `PropertyChangeMask`.

XEvent Structure Name

```
typedef union _XEvent {
    ...
    XPropertyEvent xproperty;
    ...
} XEvent;
```

Event Structure

```
typedef struct {
    int type;
    unsigned long serial;      /* # of last request processed by server */
    Bool send_event;           /* True if this came from SendEvent request */
    Display *display;          /* Display the event was read from */
    Window window;
    Atom atom;
    Time time;
    int state;                 /* Property NewValue, PropertyDeleted */
} XPropertyEvent;
```

Event Structure Members

window   The window whose property was changed, not the window that selected the event.

atom   The property that was changed.

state   Either `PropertyNewValue` or `PropertyDelete`. Whether the property was changed to a new value or deleted.

time   The `time` member specifies the server time when the property was changed.

682   Xlib Programming Manual

ReparentNotify

When Generated

A ReparentNotify event reports when a client successfully reparents a window.

Select With

This event is selected with SubstructureNotifyMask by specifying the window ID of the old or the new parent window or with StructureNotifyMask by specifying the window ID.

XEvent Structure Name

```
typedef union _XEvent {
    ...
    XReparentEvent xreparent;
    ...
} XEvent;
```

Event Structure

```
typedef struct {
    int type;
    unsigned long serial;      /* # of last request processed by server */
    Bool send_event;           /* True if this came from SendEvent request */
    Display *display;          /* Display the event was read from */
    Window event;
    Window window;
    Window parent;
    int x, y;
    Bool override_redirect;
} XReparentEvent;
```

Event Structure Members

window   The window whose parent window was changed.

parent   The new parent of the window.

x, y   The coordinates of the upper-left pixel of the window's border relative to the new parent window's origin.

override_redirect   The override_redirect attribute of the reparented window. If True, it indicates that the client wants this window to be immune to meddling by the window manager. Window managers normally should not have reparented this window to begin with.

ResizeRequest

When Generated

A ResizeRequest event reports another client's attempt to change the size of a window. The X server generates this event type when another client calls XConfigureWindow( ), XMoveResizeWindow( ), or XResizeWindow( ). If this event type is selected, the window is not resized. This gives the client that selects this event (usually the window manager) the opportunity to revise the new size of the window before executing the resize request or to deny the request itself.

Select With

To receive this event type, specify a window ID and pass ResizeRedirectMask as part of the event_mask argument to XSelectInput( ). Only one client can select this event on a particular window. When selected, this event is triggered instead of resizing the window.

XEvent Structure Name

```
typedef union _XEvent {
    . . .
    XResizeRequestEvent xresizerequest;
    . . .
} XEvent;
```

Event Structure

```
typedef struct {
    int type;
    unsigned long serial;    /* # of last request processed by server */
    Bool send_event;         /* True if this came from SendEvent request */
    Display *display;        /* Display the event was read from */
    Window window;
    int width, height;
} XResizeRequestEvent;
```

Event Structure Members

window   The window whose size another client attempted to change.

width, height   The requested size of the window, not including its border.

SelectionClear

When Generated

A `SelectionClear` event reports to the current owner of a selection that a new owner is being defined.

Select With

This event is not selected. It is sent to the previous selection owner when another client calls `XSetSelectionOwner()` for the same selection.

XEvent Structure Name

```
typedef union _XEvent {
    ...
    XSelectionClearEvent xselectionclear;
    ...
} XEvent;
```

Event Structure

```
typedef struct {
    int type;
    unsigned long serial;      /* # of last request processed by server */
    Bool send_event;           /* True if this came from SendEvent request */
    Display *display;          /* Display the event was read from */
    Window window;
    Atom selection;
    Time time;
} XSelectionClearEvent;
```

Event Structure Members

window   The window that is receiving the event and losing the selection.

selection   The selection atom specifying the selection that is changing ownership.

time   The last-change time recorded for the selection.

SelectionNotify

When Generated

A SelectionNotify event is sent only by clients, not by the server, by calling XSend-Event(). The owner of a selection sends this event to a requestor (a client that calls XConvertSelection() for a given property) when a selection has been converted and stored as a property or when a selection conversion could not be performed (indicated with property None).

Select With

There is no event mask for SelectionNotify events, and they are not selected with XSelectInput(). Instead XSendEvent() directs the event to a specific window, which is given as a window ID: PointerWindow, which identifies the window the pointer is in, or InputFocus, which identifies the focus window.

XEvent Structure Name

```
typedef union _XEvent {
    ...
    XSelectionEvent xselection;
    ...
} XEvent;
```

Event Structure

```
typedef struct {
    int type;
    unsigned long serial;      /* # of last request processed by server */
    Bool send_event;           /* True if this came from SendEvent request */
    Display *display;          /* Display the event was read from */
    Window requestor;
    Atom selection;
    Atom target;
    Atom property;             /* Atom or None */
    Time time;
} XSelectionEvent;
```

Event Structure Members

The members of this structure have the values specified in the XConvertSelection call that triggers the selection owner to send this event, except that the property member either will return the atom specifying a property on the requestor window with the data type specified in target or will return None, which indicates that the data could not be converted into the target type.

SelectionRequest

When Generated

A `SelectionRequest` event is sent to the owner of a selection when another client requests the selection by calling `XConvertSelection()`.

Select With

There is no event mask for `SelectionRequest` events, and they are not selected with `XSelectInput()`.

XEvent Structure Name

```
typedef union _XEvent {
    ...
    XSelectionRequestEvent xselectionrequest;
    ...
} XEvent;
```

Event Structure

```
typedef struct {
    int type;
    unsigned long serial;    /* # of last request processed by server */
    Bool send_event;         /* True if this came from SendEvent request */
    Display *display;        /* Display the event was read from */
    Window owner;
    Window requestor;
    Atom selection;
    Atom target;
    Atom property;
    Time time;
} XSelectionRequestEvent;
```

Event Structure Members

The members of this structure have the values specified in the `XConvertSelection` call that triggers this event.

The owner should convert the selection based on the specified `target` type, if possible. If a property is specified, the owner should store the result as that property on the requestor window and then send a `SelectionNotify` event to the requestor by calling `XSendEvent`. If the selection cannot be converted as requested, the owner should send a `SelectionNotify` event with `property` set to the constant `None`.

VisibilityNotify

When Generated

A VisibilityNotify event reports any change in the visibility of the specified window. This event type is never generated on windows whose class is InputOnly. All of the window's subwindows are ignored when calculating the visibility of the window.

Select With

This event is selected with VisibilityChangeMask.

XEvent Structure Name

```
typedef union _XEvent {
    ...
    XVisibilityEvent xvisibility;
    ...
} XEvent;
```

Event Structure

```
typedef struct {
    int type;
    unsigned long serial;    /* # of last request processed by server */
    Bool send_event;         /* True if this came from SendEvent request */
    Display *display;        /* Display the event was read from */
    Window window;
    int state;               /* VisibilityFullyObscured,
                              * VisibilityPartiallyObscured,
                              * VisibilityUnobscured*/
} XVisibilityEvent;
```

Event Structure Members

state   A symbol indicating the final visibility status of the window: Visibility-FullyObscured, VisibilityPartiallyObscured, or VisibilityUnobscured.

Notes

Table E-5 lists the transitions that generate VisibilityNotify events and the corresponding state member of the XVisibilityEvent structure.

Table E-5. State Element of the XVisibilityEvent Structure

Visibility Status Before	Visibility Status After	State Member
Partially obscured, fully obscured, or not viewable	Viewable and completely unobscured	`VisibilityUnobscured`
Viewable and completely unobscured, Viewable and completely obscured, or not viewable	Viewable and partially obscured	`VisibilityPartially-Obscured`
Viewable and completely unobscured, or viewable and partially obscured, or not viewable	Viewable and partially obscured	`VisibilityPartially-Obscured`

Event Reference

F

The Xmu Library

The Xmu library provides a number of functions that combine Xlib functions in useful ways. This appendix summarizes the available functions. See Appendix J of Volume Two, Xlib Reference Manual, *for detailed reference pages for each function. (After mid-1992, these reference pages may be moved to a new volume,* Extensions and Utilities.)

In This Appendix:

F

The Xmu Library

The Xmu Library is a collection of miscellaneous (some might say random) utility functions that have been useful in building various applications and Xt Toolkit widgets. Though not defined by any X Consortium standard, this library is written and supported by MIT in the core distribution and therefore should be available on most machines.

The functions in Xmu are briefly described here in several categories: atom manipulation, error handlers, system utilities, window utilities, cursor utilities, color utilities, pixmap utilities, graphics functions, selection functions, character set functions, compound text functions, close display functions, event queue functions, and standard colormap functions. For detailed calling sequences for these functions, see Appendix J, *The Xmu Library*, of Volume Two, *Xlib Reference Manual*.

At each release, the number and variety of functions in this library have increased dramatically. Even if you are familiar with the contents of Xmu in an earlier release, it is worthwhile skimming this appendix.

Each of the groups of functions listed below has its own header file. The Xmu header files are located (by default on UNIX-based systems) in */usr/include/X11/Xmu*.

F.1 Atom Functions

These functions allow an application to use various properties that do not have predefined atoms, without having to maintain a global variable to store the atom. Instead Xmu handles calling `XInternAtom()` on the first reference and caches the value for all further references. For example, after initializing Xmu's atom-caching facility (with the arcane invocation `XmuInternAtom(display, XmuMakeAtom("NULL"))`), you can get the atom for any property that Xmu knows about, such as CLIPBOARD, simply by using the phrase `XA_CLIPBOARD(`*display*`)`.

F.2 Error Handler Functions

`XmuPrintErrorMessage()` prints an error message equivalent to Xlib's default error message for protocol errors. It returns a nonzero value if the caller should consider exiting; otherwise, it returns 0. This function can be used when you need to write your own error handler but need to print out an error from within that handler.

`XmuSimpleErrorHandler()` is an error handler function you can use in place of the default protocol error handler. It ignores **BadWindow** errors for **XQueryTree()** and **XGetWindowAttributes()** and ignores **BadDrawable** errors for **XGet-Geometry()**; it returns 0 in those cases. Otherwise, it prints the default error message and returns a nonzero value if the caller should consider exiting and 0 if the caller should not exit.

F.3 System Utility Functions

`XmuGetHostname()` provides an operating-system-independent interface for getting the hostname of the system on which the client is running. This is useful for setting the WM_CLIENT_MACHINE property for the window manager.

F.4 Window Utility Functions

`XmuScreenOfWindow()` returns a pointer to the **Screen** structure that describes the screen on which the window was created.

`XmuClientWindow()` finds a window at or below the specified window which has a WM_STATE property. If such a window is found, it is returned; otherwise, the argument window is returned. This is used by window managers.

`XmuUpdateMapHints()` is a convenience routine for setting (by applications) and reading (by the window manager) the **XA_WM_NORMAL_HINTS** property. It clears the **PPosition** and **PSize** flags and sets the **USPosition** and **USSize** flags in the hints structure and then stores the hints for the window using **XSetWMNormalHints()** and returns **True**. If **NULL** is passed for the hints structure, then the current hints are read back from the window using **XGetWMNormalHints()** and are used instead and **True** is returned; otherwise, **False** is returned.

F.5 Cursor Utility Functions

XmuCursorNameToIndex takes the name of a standard cursor and returns its index in the standard cursor font. The cursor names are formed by removing the XC_ prefix from the symbolic constants for cursors listed in Appendix I, *The Cursor Font*, of Volume Two, *Xlib Reference Manual*.

F.6 Color Utilities

XmuDistinguishableColors compares two or more sets of RGB values and determines whether the colors are distinguishable.

XmuDistinguishablePixels compares two or more pixel values and determines whether the colors in the corresponding colormap cells are distinguishable.

F.7 Pixmap Utilities

XmuLocatePixmapFile creates a pixmap from a file located in a relative or absolute directory, possibly specified in an environment variable.

F.8 Graphics Functions

XmuDrawRoundedRectangle draws a rounded rectangle, given x, y, width, height dimensions of the overall rectangle, and ew and eh sizes of a bounding box that the corners are drawn inside of. This function simply calls Xlib's drawing routines.

XmuFillRoundedRectangle simply fills a shape similar to that drawn by **XmuDraw-RoundedRectangle**, in the same way that **XFillRectangle( )** fills.

XmuDrawLogo draws the "official" X Window System logo. The bounding box of the logo is given by x, y, width, and height.

XmuCreateStippledPixmap creates a two- by two-pixel pixmap of specified depth on the specified screen, with the top-left and bottom-right pixels drawn in the foreground pixel value and the other two drawn in the background. The pixmap is cached so that multiple requests share the same pixmap. The pixmap should be freed with **XmuRelease-StippledPixmap** to maintain correct reference counts.

XmuReadBitmapData reads a standard bitmap file description from the specified stream and returns the parsed data in a format suitable for passing to **XCreateBitmapFrom-Data( )**

XmuReadBitmapDataFromFile reads a standard bitmap file description from the specified file and returns the parsed data in a format suitable for passing to **XCreate-BitmapFromData()**.

XmuLocateBitmapFile reads a file in standard bitmap file format, using **XRead-BitmapFile()**, and returns the created bitmap. The filename may be absolute or relative to the global resource named **bitmapFilePath** with class **BitmapFilePath**. If the resource is not defined, the default value is the build symbol **BITMAPDIR**, which is typically */usr/include/X11/bitmaps*.

XmuCreatePixmapFromBitmap creates a pixmap of the specified width, height, and depth on the same screen as the specified drawable and then performs an **XCopyPlane()** from the specified bitmap to the pixmap, using the specified foreground and background pixel values.

F.9 Selection Functions

XmuConvertStandardSelection converts the following standard selections: CLASS, CLIENT_WINDOW, DECNET_ADDRESS, HOSTNAME, IP_ADDRESS, NAME, OWNER_OS, TARGETS, TIMESTAMP, and USER. It returns **True** if the conversion was successful, else it returns **False**.

F.10 Character Set Functions

XmuCopyISOLatin1Lowered copies a null-terminated string (including the null), changing all Latin-1 uppercase letters to lowercase. **XmuCopyISOLatin1Uppered** copies a null-terminated string (including the null), changing all Latin-1 lowercase letters to uppercase. **XmuCompareISOLatin1** compares two null-terminated Latin-1 strings, ignoring case differences, and returns an integer greater than, equal to, or less than 0, according to whether first is lexicographically greater than, equal to, or less than second. In all three of these routines, the string is assumed to be encoded using ISO 8859-1.

The following functions have the same arguments and function as **XLookupString()**, except that they convert to keysyms in different sets.

Function	Converts To
XmuLookupAPL	APL string
XmuLookupArabic	Latin/Arabic (ISO 8859-6) or ASCII control!
XmuLookupCyrillic	Latin/Cyrillic (ISO 8859-5) or ASCII control
XmuLookupGreek	Latin/Greek (ISO 8859-7) or ASCII control
XmuLookupHebrew	Latin/Hebrew (ISO 8859-8) or ASCII control string
XmuLookupJISX0201	JIS X0201-1976 encoding, including ASCII control

Function	Converts To
XmuLookupKana	Latin-1 (ISO 8859-1) and ASCII control in the Graphics Left half (values 0 to 127) and Katakana in the Graphics Right half (values 128 to 255), using the values from JIS X201-1976.
XmuLookupLatin1	Latin-1 (ISO 8859-1) or ASCII control (synonym for XLookupString)
XmuLookupLatin2	Latin-2 (ISO 8859-2) or ASCII control
XmuLookupLatin3	Latin-3 (ISO 8859-3) or ASCII control
XmuLookupLatin4	Latin-4 (ISO 8859-4) or ASCII control

F.11 Compound Text Functions

These functions are for parsing Compound Text strings, decomposing them into individual segments. Four functions are provided for this purpose: **XctCreate, XctFree, XctNextItem, XctReset**. For more information on these functions, see Appendix J, *The Xmu Library*, of Volume Two, *Xlib Reference Manual*.

F.12 CloseDisplay Hook Functions

XmuAddCloseDisplayHook adds a function that will be called with the given arguments when **XCloseDisplay()** is called. **XmuRemoveCloseDisplayHook** deletes the function that has been added with **XmuAddCloseDisplayHook**. More than one such function can be added.

XmuLookupCloseDisplayHook determines if a function is installed.

These functions use the Display Queue Functions internally, which are described next.

F.13 Display Queue Functions

XmuDQCreate creates and returns an empty **XmuDisplayQueue** (which is really just a linked list of displays; it is called a queue for historical reasons). The queue is initially empty, but displays can be added using **XmuDQAddDisplay**. Functions can be added for each display, to be called when the display connection is closed. These are called close callbacks. Functions can also be added to be called when the last display connection is closed. These are called free callbacks. The application is responsible for actually freeing the queue, by calling **XmuDQDestroy**.

XmuDQAddDisplay does not attempt to prevent duplicate entries in the queue; the caller should use **XmuDQLookupDisplay** to determine if a display has already been added to a queue. The **XmuDQNDisplays** macro returns the number of displays in the specified queue. `XmuDQRemoveDisplay` removes the specified display from the specified queue, without calling its close callbacks. `XmuDQDestroy` releases all memory associated with the specified queue and optionally calls the close callbacks for each display.

F.14 Standard Colormap Functions

`XmuAllStandardColormaps` creates all of the appropriate standard colormaps for every visual of every screen on a given display. If the property of any standard colormap is already defined, this function will redefine it. This function is intended to be used by window managers or a special client at the start of a session.

`XmuVisualStandardColormaps` creates all of the appropriate standard colormaps for a given visual on a given screen.

`XmuLookupStandardColormap` creates a standard colormap if one does not currently exist or replaces the currently existing standard colormap. Given a screen, a visual, and a property, this function will determine the best allocation for the property under the specified visual and whether to create a new colormap or use the default colormap of the screen.

`XmuGetColormapAllocation` determines the best allocation of reds, greens, and blues in a standard colormap. It is assumed that the visual is appropriate for the colormap property.

`XmuStandardColormap` creates any one standard colormap, given a visual, a standard colormap atom, and other input, and returns an `XStandardColormap` structure. `XmuCreateColormap` creates any one colormap, given an `XStandardColormap` structure.

All colormaps are created with read-only allocations, with the exception of read-only allocations of colors, which fail to return the expected pixel value, and these are individually defined as read/write allocations. This is done so that all the cells defined in the colormap are contiguous, for use in image processing. This typically happens with White and Black in the default map.

Colormaps of static visuals are considered to be successfully created if the map of the static visual matches the definition given in the standard colormap structure.

`XmuDeleteStandardColormap` removes any standard colormap property, also releasing any resources used by the colormap(s) specified in the property, if possible.

G

Sources of Additional Information

This appendix describes where you can get more information about Xlib and about X in general, including other books on the subject and the various ways to get the source code for X.

In This Appendix:

G

Sources of Additional Information

This appendix lists a few of the official and unofficial sources for information about the X Window System and associated software.

Note that some of this detailed information may become dated rather quickly. The best source of current information is the *comp.windows.x* network news group, described later in this appendix.

G.1 Getting the X Software

At this writing, the current public release level is Release 5. This book documents Release 4 and Release 5. Many people will continue to use R4 for a while, since there is a considerable lag time between the date that MIT distributes a new release and the date by which vendors integrate that release into their own products and issue updates. All changes to Xlib in R5 are backwards compatible, although there are many new interfaces that provide additional capabilities.

You can get the X software directly from MIT on three 9-track 1600-BPI magtapes written in UNIX *tar* format or on one 9-track 6250-BPI magtape, along with printed copies of MIT's manuals, by sending a check in U.S. currency for U.S. $400 to:

> MIT Software Distribution Center
> Technology Licensing Office
> MIT E32-300
> 77 Massachusetts Avenue
> Cambridge, MA 02139

Their telephone number is (617) 253-6966, and the "X Ordering Hotline" is (617) 258-8330. If you want the tapes and manuals shipped overseas, the price is $500. The manual set alone is $125, including U.S. shipping, or $175, including overseas shipping.

Other distribution media or formats are not available from the MIT Software Distribution Center but are from other independent vendors such as ICS, mentioned later. The Release tape comes with source code for sample servers for Apollo, DEC, HP, IBM, Sony, Sun, and several other workstations, source code for clients written by MIT, sources for the toolkits Xt, XView, Interviews, and Andrew, contributed software written outside MIT, and sources and Postscript files for all MIT's documentation. Note that the servers supplied are sample servers only; commercial vendors typically release optimized (faster) servers for the same machines.

Sites that have access to the Internet can retrieve the distribution from the following machines using anonymous *ftp*. Here are the current sites:

Location	Hostname	Address	Directory
Western USA	*gatekeeper.dec.com*	16.1.0.2	*pub/X11/R5*
Eastern USA	*ftp.uu.net*	192.48.96.9	*X/R5*
		137.39.1.9	*X/R5*
Northeastern USA	*export.lcs.mit.edu*	18.24.0.12	*pub/R5*
	crl.dec.com	192.58.206.2	*pub/X11/R5*
Central USA	*mordred.cs.purdue.edu*	128.10.2.2	*pub/X11/R5*
	giza.cis.ohio-state.edu	128.146.8.52	*pub/X.V11R5*
Southern USA	*wuarchive.wustl.edu*	129.252.135.4	*packages/X11R5*
UK (Janet)	*src.doc.ic.ac.uk*	146.169.2.1	*X*
Australia	*munnari.oz.au*	128.250.1.21	*X.V11/R5*
		192.43.207.1	*X.V11/R5*

DO NOT do anonymous *ftp* during normal business hours, and please use the machine nearest you.

The distribution is also available by UUCP from UUNET for sites without Internet access. The files are split up to be small enough for UUCP distribution.

G.1.1 Bug Fixes

Critical bug fixes as well as a limited number of important new features are available from the archive server *xstuff@expo.lcs.mit.edu*. Electronic mail sent to this address is forwarded to a program which responds with the requested information. The rest of this section and the two sections that follow it explain how to use *xstuff*.

The *xstuff* server is a mail-response program. This means that you mail it a request and it mails back the response.

The *xstuff* server is a very dumb program. It does not have much error checking. If you do not send it commands that it understands, it will just answer "I don't understand you."

The *xstuff* server reads your entire message before it does anything, so you can have several different commands in a single message. It treats the "Subject:" header line just like any other line of the message. You can use any combination of upper and lowercase letters in the commands.

The archives are organized into a series of directories and subdirectories. Each directory has an index, and each subdirectory has an index. The top-level index gives you an overview of what is in the subdirectories, and the index for each subdirectory tells you what it contains.

If you are bored with reading documentation and just want to try something, then send the server a message containing the line:

```
send index fixes
```

When you get the index back, it will contain the numbers of all of the fixes and batches of fixes in the archive. Then you can send the server another message asking it to send you the fixes that you want:

```
send fixes 1 5 9 11-20
```

If you are using a mailer that understands "@" notation, send to *xstuff@expo.lcs.mit.edu*. If your mailer deals in "!" notation, try sending to *{someplace}!eddie!expo.lcs.mit.edu!xstuff*. For other mailers, you're on your own.

The server has four commands. Each command must be the first word on a line.

help   The command *help* or *send help* causes the server to send you the help file. No other commands are honored in a message that asks for help (the server figures that you had better read the help message before you do anything else).

index   If your message contains a line whose first word is *index*, then the server will send you the top-level index of the contents of the archive. If there are other words on that line that match the names of subdirectories, then the indexes for those sub-directories are sent instead of the top-level index. For example, you can say:

```
index
```

or:

```
index fixes
```

You can then send back another message to the *xstuff* server, using a *send* command (see below) to ask it to send you the files whose names you learned from that list.

index fixes and *send index fixes* mean the same thing: you can use *send* instead of *index* for getting an index.

If your message has an *index* or a *send index* command, then all other *send* commands will be ignored. This means that you cannot get an index and data in the same request. This is so that index requests can be given high priority.

send   If your message contains a line whose first word is *send*, then the *xstuff* server will send you the item(s) named on the rest of the line. To name an item, you give its directory and its name. For example:

```
send fixes 1-10
```

Once you have named a category, you can put as many names as you like on the rest of the line. They will all be taken from that category. For example:

```
send fixes 1-10 11-20 21-30
```

Each *send* command can reference only one directory. If you would like to get one fix and one of something else, you must use two *send* commands.

You may put as many *send* commands as you like into one message to the server, but the more you ask for, the longer it will take to receive. See Section G.1.1.2 for an explanation. Actually, it is not strictly true that you can put as many *send* commands as you want into one message. If the server must use UUCP mail to send your files, then it cannot send more than 100K bytes in one message. If you ask for more than it can send, then it will send as much as it can and ignore the rest.

path   The *path* command exists to help in case you do not get responses from the server when you mail to it.

Sometimes the server is unable to return mail over the incoming path. There are dozens of reasons why this might happen, and if you are a true wizard, you already know what those reasons are. If you are an apprentice wizard, you might not know all the reasons, but you might know a way to circumvent them.

If you put in a *path* command, then everything that the server mails to you will be mailed to that address rather than to the return address on your mail. The server host *expo.lcs.mit.edu* does not have a direct UUCP connection to anywhere; you must go through *mit-eddie* (the UUCP name of *eddie.mit.edu*) or somewhere else.

G.1.1.1 Notes

The *xstuff* server acknowledges every request by return mail. If you do not get a message back in a day or two, you should assume that something is going wrong and perhaps try a *path* command.

The *xstuff* server does not respond to requests from users named *root*, *system*, *daemon*, or *mailer*. This is to prevent mail loops. If your name is "Bruce Root" or "Jane Daemon" and you can document this, we will happily rewrite the server to remove this restriction. Yes, we know about Norman Mailer and Waverley Root. Norman doesn't use netmail and Waverley is dead.

G.1.1.2 Fairness

The *xstuff* server contains many safeguards to ensure that it is not monopolized by people asking for large amounts of data. The mailer is set up so that it will send no more than a fixed amount of data each day. If the work queue contains more requests than the day's quota, then the unsent files will not be processed until the next day. Whenever the mailer is run to send its day's quota, it sends the shortest requests out first.

If you have a request waiting in the work queue and you send in another request, the new request is added to the old one (thereby increasing its size) rather than being filed anew. This prevents you from being able to send in a large number of small requests as a way of beating the system.

The reason for all of these quotas and limitations is that the delivery resources are finite, and there are many people who would like to make use of the archive.

G.2 Netnews

The Usenet network newsgroup and mailing lists are probably the most valuable source of information abouta X. The current list of public mailing lists that discuss X is as follows:

News Group	Description
motif@lobo.gsfc.nasa.gov	People interested in the OSF's Motif X toolkit This mailing list is also gatewayed to the Usenet newsgroup *comp.windows.x.motif*. If you receive that newsgroup, you don't need to get this mailing list.
x11-3D@x.org	People interested in X and 3-D graphics
x-ada@x.org	X and ada
ximage@x.org	People interested in image processing and X
xpert@x.org	General discussion of X This mailing list is also gatewayed to the Usenet newsgroup *comp.windows.x*. If you receive that newsgroup, you don't need to get this mailing list.
openlook@unify.com	Discussion of the OPEN LOOK graphical user interface, and its various implementations. This mailing list is also gatewayed to the Usenet newsgroup *comp.windows.open-look*. If you receive that newsgroup, you don't need to get this mailing list.
xvideo@x.org	Discussion of video extensions for X

First ask your site administrator whether you can get these news groups locally. Requests to have the motif mailing list mailed directly to you should be sent to *motif-request*@lobo.gsfc.nasa.gov. Requests to have the OPEN LOOK mailing list mailed directly to you should be sent to *openlook*-request@unify.com. Requests for all the other lists should be sent to *mailing-list-name*-request@x.org, or uunet!x.org!*mailing-list-name*-request (for example, to join the ximage mailing list, send mail to ximage-request@x.org).

The newsgroup *comp.window.x* (which is the same as *xpert*), is where users and developers around the world ask and answer questions.

G.3 Training, Consulting, and Support

Numerous independent vendors provide courses on X programming. Several sources that we are aware of include:

- *Integrated Computer Solutions*, 201 Broadway, Cambridge, MA 02139; (617) 621-0060. Courses on Xlib, Motif, strategic overviews of X. Also provides consulting services and manages an X user's group.

- *Hands-On Learning*, 27 Cambridge Street, Burlington, MA 01803; (617) 272-0088. Courses on Xlib and Xt.

- X tutorials are now a regular feature of UNIX conventions, such as the UNIX EXPO, Usenix, Uniforum, Xhibition, and the annual X conference at MIT. Also contact hardware vendors for information on courses they offer.

- Dyksen Associates offers training in X including courses on Xlib, the Intrinsics, the Motif toolkit, and the OPEN LOOK toolkit. Contact them at (317) 497-7613.

Training companies wishing to be listed here should send us information on the courses they offer.

There are currently no telephone support lines at the X Consortium, because X was developed by a university, not a system manufacturer or software house. Some vendors such as OSF offer support for a fee.

ICS provides telephone support for a fee. See Section G.3 for their telephone number.

G.4 The X Consortium

The X Consortium can be reached at:

    X Consortium, Inc.
    One Memorial Drive
    Cambridge, MA 02142-1301

The Consortium's telephone number is (617) 374-1000; its current members are shown below.

Table G-1. Consortium Members

Apple Computer, Inc.	NCR Corporation
AT&T UNIX System Laboratories	NEC Corporation
BULL	Network Computing Devices, Inc.
Control Data Corporation	Nippon Telegraph and Telephone Corporation
Convex Computer Corporation	Oki Electric Industry Co., Ltd.
Cray Research, Inc.	Olivetti Systems & Networks
Data General	OMRON Corp.
Digital Equipment Corporation	Prime Computer, Inc.
Du Pont Imaging System	The Santa Cruz Operation, Inc.
Fujitsu America, Inc.	Sequent Computer Systems Inc.
Hewlett-Packard Company	Siemens Nixdorf Informationssysteme AG
Hitachi	Silicon Graphics Computer Systems
Hughes Aircraft Co.	Sony Corporation
IBM Corporation	Sun Microsystems, Inc.
Intergraph Corporation	Tandberg Data A/S
Eastman Kodak Company	Tektronix, Inc.
Kubota Pacific	Texas Instruments, Inc.
Matsushita Electric Industrial CO., LTD.	Unisys Corp.
Mitsubishi Electric Corporation	Xerox Corporation
Motorola, Inc.	

Table G-2. Consortium Affiliates

Adobe Systems
AGE Logic, Inc.
Aptronix, Inc.
ASTEC, Inc.
Athenix Corp.
Bitstream, Inc.
CETIA
Chromatics
Codonics, Inc.
Industrial Technology Research Institute
    (China)
Data Connection Ltd.
Evans & Sutherland
Frame Technology Corp.
GIPSI S.A. (France)
GfxBase
HaL Computer Systems
Institute for Information Industry (Taiwan)
Integrated Computer Solutions, Inc.
Interactive Systems Corp.
Ithaca Software
IXI Limited
Japan Computer Corporation
Jupiter Systems
KAIST (Korea Advanced Institute
    of Science and Technology)
Labtam Australia
Liant Software Corporation
Locus Computing Corporation
University of Lowell
Megatek Corp.
Metro Link, Inc.

Metheus Corp.
MIPS Computer Systems
MITRE Corp.
Objectivity, Inc.
Open Software Foundation
O'Reilly & Associates, Inc.
PCS Computer Systeme GmbH (Germany)
Peritek Corp.
PsiTech, Inc.
Quarterdeck Office Systems

Ramtek Corp.
Samsung Software America
ShoGraphics, Inc.
Snitily Graphics Consulting Services
Solbourne Computer Inc.
SOUM Corporation (Japan)
SPARC International
SpectraGraphics Corp.
Stanford University
Strategic Research Institute Inc. (Japan)
Sumitomo Electric Workstation Corp.
Tatung Science and Technology
Tyan Computer
Unipalm XTech

VisionWare Ltd.
Visix Software, Inc.
Visual Information Technologies, Inc.
Visual Technology, Inc.
Widget, Inc. (Japan)
X/Open Company Ltd.

Most of these companies are preparing products based on X. It should not be long before many different products are available that support X.

G.5 Finding Out for Yourself

X is unusual in that the source code is freely copyable by anyone as long as the copyright notices are observed. It should be possible for most X programmers to get a copy of the X source code from the sources listed above. Once you understand how the code is organized, you can look up certain details about how X works as long as you have a good knowledge of C and a little persistence. In "Star Wars," the saying was "Use the Force, Luke." In X, it is "Use the Source, Luke."

Xlib and the server are two distinct chunks of code. Each contains code for sending and receiving information to and from the other over the network using protocol requests, replies, events, and errors. The source tree as supplied on the X distribution tape places the Xlib source in the directory *base/lib/X*, where *base* is the top of the entire source tree. Their server source is placed in *base/server*.

The procedure for finding out something about an Xlib routine is normally to search for the routine in the Xlib code and then figure out what it does. Sometimes the answer can be found there. Many of the routines, however, simply place their arguments in a protocol request and send it to the server. Then you will have to look in the server code for the answer. To find the correct place in the server code, you will need the symbol for the protocol request, which is the first argument in the `GetReq` call.

The server code is much more involved than Xlib itself. The device-dependent portions are in *base/server/ddx*, and the device-independent portions are in *base/server/dix*. The device-independent code should be your first stop, because it is here that protocol requests from Xlib arrive and are dispatched to the appropriate code. Search for the protocol request symbol you found in Xlib. It will appear in several source files. Start with the occurrence in *dispatch.c*, and try to figure out what the code does. This will require following leads to other routines.

If you do not find a routine in *base/server/dix*, then it must be in the device-dependent code. *base/server/ddx* has one directory in it for each brand of hardware to which a sample server has been ported. It also contains the directories */cfb*, */mfb*, */mi*, and */snf*, which contain routines used in writing the sample server device-dependent code. Note that servers may include code ostensibly for other machines. For example, the Sun sample server appears to use code in several of the directories for other servers such as *dec* and *hp*.

Xlib and the X protocol are both defined by specification documents, not by any particular implementation. Never depend on the implementation details of the Xlib or server code. If you do, your code may not run on a machine that has optimized X software. This manual documents only those features of Xlib and X in general that are governed by X Consortium standard specifications. If you follow the guidance you find in this volume and the details in Volume Two, *Xlib Reference Manual*, you will be in good shape.

H

Release Notes

This appendix describes the changes between recent releases of X Version 11. It begins with the changes in the most recent version and works back. There were no changes in the underlying X protocol.

In This Appendix:

Release Notes

H.1 Changes from Release 4 to Release 5

The major additions in Release 5 were support for internationalization and support for device-independent color (the X Color Management System). There were also a few new resource management functions added mainly to support the R5 changes in the Xt Intrinsics.

H.1.1 Internationalization

The largest new part of X11R5 is the support for writing *internationalized* programs. An internationalized application is one that runs, without changes to the binary, in any given "locale." Among other things, this means that a program must display all text in the user's language, accept input of all text in that same language, and display times, dates, and numbers in the user's accustomed format.

The internationalization of terminal-based programs is a problem that has been satisfactorily solved where terminals exist that can display and accept input for a particular language. The ANSI-C library contains mechanisms for this terminal-based internationalization, and X11R5 internationalization is based on these mechanisms. Internationalized text input is based on the concept of an "input method," which is a specialized program that allows user input of a particular language. Input methods are essential for Asian languages where there are more symbols than can appear on a keyboard.

Before beginning, note that the internationalization features of X11R5 are not self contained, and therefore may not work on all systems. If your system does not have the ANSI-C internationalization features, you may be able to make do with alternatives provided with the Xlib sample distribution and by contributed libraries, but these have not been thoroughly tested and you may encounter difficulties. In ANSI-C internationalization, the C library reads a "localization database" customized for each locale. Many systems (systems sold in the U.S., at least) support ANSI-C internationalization, but do not ship databases for any but a default locale.

Xlib now provides:

- Simple locale management functions.

- Routines for internationalized text-drawing.
  - Font set handling functions.
  - Font set metric and string measuring functions.
  - String drawing functions.

- Respecification of many Xlib functions to clarify their handling of strings in internationalized applications.

- New functions to support internationalized window manager and text properties for inter-client communication.

- New resource manager functions to support localized databases.

- Respecifications of many resource manager functions to make their behavior in internationalized applications clear.

- New support for internationalized text input through input methods.

- Two sample implementations of all the new Xlib internationalization functions.

The X11R5 distribution provides two different implementations of the new internationalization functions. The default implementation is named "Xsi" and is from the OMRON Corporation; the MIT distribution builds Xsi by default on all but Sony machines. Sony systems build the "Ximp" implementation from Fujitsu, Sony, and others. Both "Xsi" and "Ximp" implement the same specification,* but are mutually incompatible. In particular, the localization files they read are in very different formats.

H.1.2 X Color Management System

Xcms defines a new syntax for the color strings used throughout Xlib, and provides a programming interface that allows extremely precise control over the allocation of colors. One feature of Xcms is the provision for a database that maps color names to device-independent color specifications. This database is read by Xlib rather than by the X server. No sample Xlib-side database is provided in the MIT distribution. There is also a new part of the ICCCM, the X Device Color Characterization Conventions (XDCCC), which are a standard format for new root window properties that contains the information about the physical characteristics of the screen necessary to support the conversion of device-independent color specifications into device-dependent values.

Several existing Xlib functions were modified to support this new standard syntax for color strings. The syntax allows color specification in several international standard color spaces including CIElab, CIEluv, and a simple color space called TEKhvc. RGB is also still supported.

---

*These names probably stand for "X sample implementation" and "X input method protocol."

H.1.3 Resource Management

The character ? may now be used in resource files to wildcard a single component of a resource name. This allows greater flexibility in the specification of resources.

Resource files may now include other files with a C-like #include syntax.

A new function, XrmSetDatabase(), associates a resource database with a display, and another new function, XrmGetDatabase(), queries the database of a display.

A function, XrmLocaleOfDatabase(), returns the locale of a resource database.

Two new functions, XrmCombineDatabase() and XrmCombineFile-Database(), merge the contents of two resource databases. They are more flexible than the existing XrmMergeDatabase.

A new function, XrmEnumerateDatabase(), iterates through the items in a resource database.

H.1.4 Scalable Font Support

Because the font server was introduced in R5, the server's handling of XListFonts(), XLoadFont(), and XLoadQueryFont() was changed to allow pattern matching for scalable fonts.

H.2 Miscellaneous Xlib Changes

A new type, XPointer, has been defined to replace caddr_t, which is not a standard type and is therefore not necessarily portable. (The type XtPointer was added to the X11R4 X Toolkit for the same reason.) An XPointer is a typedef for a char *, and occurs most noticeably in the XrmValue and XrmOptionDescRec structures.

The X11R5 distribution installs the file XKeysymDB in *usr/lib/X11*. This file contains a list of vendor-private keysyms names and their corresponding values. It is required for the correct operation of many Motif applications and any application that wants to make use of vendor-specific keys on a keyboard. This file was in the X11R4 distribution, but was not installed by default.

A new function, XFlushGC(), forces Xlib to write its cached GC changes to the X server. For efficiency, Xlib combines multiple GC changes into a single server request whenever multiple changes to a GC occur before a use of that GC. It is possible for extensions to X to use GCs in ways that Xlib is not aware of, and this can mean that requests made by the extension client library may not operate with the expected contents of the GC. XFlushGC() is provided to address this problem.

The XErrorEvent structure used by Xlib contains only 32 bits of data specific to the error, which is usually used to return a resource ID. This is sufficient for all core X errors, but may not be enough for extensions (notably PEX). There is plenty of room in the protocol error structure that is transmitted between server and client, but Xlib truncates this information when converting the protocol error into an **XErrorEvent** structure. Since the **XError-Event** structure is smaller than the **XEvent** union of which it is a part, an **XErrorEvent** can be cast into a larger structure with more room for error values, and the workaround provided by X11R5 takes advantage of this fact. X11R5 provides two new functions, **XSet-WireToError()** and **XSetPrintErrorValues()**, which allow an extension library to register a function to convert a protocol error into some type longer than an **XErrorEvent**, and to display an error message that makes use of the additional data in the special error message.

H.3 Changes from Release 3 to Release 4

We will begin by describing the new functions, and then we will describe the small existing interface changes.

H.3.1 New Routines

Because of the adoption of the ICCCM (*Inter-Client Communication Conventions Manual*) as an X Consortium standard, several Xlib structures had to be changed, and therefore, several of the R3 routines are now superceded by new routines. All R3 routines are still supported, but the superceded routines should not be used in new applications because they do not meet the current conventions. Table H-1 lists the old and new routines.

Table H-1. Superceded R3 Routines and New R4 Routines

Superceded Routine	New Routine	Change
XSetStandardProperties	XSetWMProperties	Added **WM_HINTS** and **WM_CLASS**, format changes
XSetNormalHints	XSetWMNormalHints	New fields in **XSizeHints**
XGetNormalHints	XGetWMNormalHints	New fields in **XSizeHints**
XSetZoomHints	(No replacement)	No longer part of ICCCM
XGetZoomHints	(No replacement)	No longer part of ICCCM
XSetSizeHints	XSetWMSizeHints	New fields in **XSizeHints**
XGetSizeHints	XGetWMSizeHints	New fields in **XSizeHints**
XStoreName	XSetWMName	Property format change
XFetchName	XGetWMName	Property format change
(No R3 equivalent)	XGetCommand	Convenience routine for **XGetWindowProperty**
XSetIconName	XSetWMIconName	Property format change
XGetIconName	XGetWMIconName	Property format change
XGeometry	XWMGeometry	New fields and arguments

Superceded Routine	New Routine	Change
XGetStandardColormap	XGetRGBColormaps	New fields in **XStandard-Colormap**
XSetStandardColormap	XSetRGBColormaps	New fields in **XStandard-Colormap**

XSetWMProperties() is the new interface for setting all required window manager properties. This function now sets the WM_HINTS and WM_CLASS properties, in addition to the properties set under R3 by **XSetStandardProperties()**. Furthermore, the window name and icon name arguments are now **XTextProperty** structures that can be filled with the new function **XStringListToTextProperty()**, described below.

All string properties to be set for the window manager have been changed to use **XTextProperty** structures so that they can use non-Western encodings (which require more than the eight bits of data provided in the R3 STRING property). For this reason, **XGetWMIconName()** replaces **XGetIconName()**, **XSetWMIconName()** replaces **XSetIconName()**, **XGetWMName()** replaces **XFetchName()**, and **XSetWMName()** replaces **XStoreName()**.

XGetCommand() was added to make it easier for window managers to read the XA_WM_COMMAND property. In R3, **XSetCommand()** was provided but no **XGetCommand()**.

Three new fields have been added to the **XSizeHints** structure. Two, **base_width** and **base_height**, basically supercede the **min_width** and **min_height** fields. The **x**, **y**, **width**, and **height** fields of **XSizeHints** are no longer used. Instead these values are simply set when creating the top-level window (and the window manager gets these values through substructure redirection in **CreateNotify** and **MapNotify** events). The other new field, **win_gravity**, allows an application to specify that some other portion of the window is to be placed when the window manager allows the user to place windows. The purpose of this, for example, is to allow users that display languages that read from right to left to position the top-right corner of these terminals instead of their top-left corner.

XWMGeometry replaces **XGeometry**. **XWMGeometry** calculates geometry values for the top-level window, given a possibly incomplete user-specified geometry string and a complete application default geometry specified using an **XSizeHints** structure. **XWMGeometry** also returns a **win_gravity** value based on which corner of the top-level window the user or application specified, suitable for setting into the **XSizeHints** structure.

New fields have been added to the **XStandardColormap** structure to return the visual associated with the colormap and also to provide information about who is allowed to delete the colormap. To use the new fields, **XGetStandardColormap()** is superceded by **XGetRGBColormaps()** and **XSetStandardColormap()** is superceded by **XSetRGBColormaps()**.

The following routines are completely new in R4.

XSetWMClientMachine() is used by clients to set a new property to be read with **XGetWMClientMachine()** by window or session managers. The property stores the name of the machine on which the client is running, as seen from the server, so that the session manager can stop and restart the client on the right machine. See Chapter 12, *Interclient Communication*.

XSetWMProtocols() is used by clients to set a new property to be read with **XGetWMProtocols()** by the window manager. This property indicates which of a number of window manager-client protocols the client would like to take part in. Under these protocols, the window manager sends synthetic events to the client to notify the client of certain impending conditions, such as that the client has been granted the keyboard focus or is about to have one of its windows destroyed or that the entire client is about to be killed. See Chapter 12.

XSetWMColormapWindows() is used by clients to set a new property to be read with **XGetWMColormapWindows()** by the window manager. This property tells the window manager that certain subwindows of the client have custom colormaps that will need installing. See Chapter 12.

Five new routines are provided that allocate and zero the fields of structures used in setting the window manager hints: **XAllocClassHint()**, **XAllocIconSize()**, **XAllocSizeHints()**, **XAllocStandardColormap()**, and **XAllocWMHints()**. When using these routines, an application declares only a pointer to the structure and then uses one of these routines to allocate the memory. The purpose of doing this is to avoid having compiled-in structure sizes, so that fields can be added to these structures in later releases without causing binary incompatibility. See Chapter 12.

XGetGCValues() reads most GC component values out of Xlib's local cache. It does not read the dash list or clip mask. See Chapter 5, *The Graphics Context*.

XIconifyWindow() is to be called by the client to tell the window manager to iconify a window. Similarly, **XWithdrawWindow()** tells the window manager to unmap a window without iconifying it. These two routines were added to simplify compliance with the new ICCCM. **XReconfigureWMWindow()** is used by clients to reconfigure top-level windows—it works like **XConfigureWindow()** except that it handles stacking order changes correctly even if the window or some of its siblings have been reparented. See Chapter 12.

As mentioned above, all of the R3 functions that write or read string properties have been superceded by R4 functions that provide a more flexible property format. All these new functions use the **XTextProperty** structure. Several routines that manipulate these structures are now provided: **XFreeStringList()**, **XGetTextProperty()**, **XSetTextProperty()**, **XStringListToTextProperty()**, and **XTextPropertyToStringList()**. See Chapter 12.

XListDepths() and **XListPixmapFormats()** extract information from the **Display** structure. These are useful when you want to create a window or a pixmap that is not the default depth and not a depth of one plane.

`XrmDestroyDatabase()` destroys a resource database, a function that was missing in earlier releases.

The `XScreenNumberOfScreen()` function has also been added. It simply returns the screen integer corresponding to the specified pointer to a `Screen` structure. This function is listed with the macros in Appendix C, *Macros*, of Volume Two, *Xlib Reference Manual*.

H.3.2 Existing Interface Changes

The following sections describe the changes in the areas of `XOpenDisplay()`, error handlers, nonstandard keysyms and keyboard groups, `XReadBitmapFile()`, resource specification syntax, and `XrmParseCommand()`.

H.3.2.1 XOpenDisplay()

The use of *unix* as a hostname in the DISPLAY environment variable read by `XOpen-Display()` is no longer part of the specification (for trademark reasons); use an empty hostname. In other words, setting DISPLAY to ":0.0" will instruct Xlib to make the best local connection to the server running on the same system as this client.

H.3.2.2 Error Handlers

`XSetErrorHandler()` and `XIOSetErrorHandler` now return the previous error handler.

```
int (*XSetErrorHandler(handler))()
    int (*handler)(Display *, XErrorEvent *)
int (*XSetIOErrorHandler(handler))()
    int (*handler)(Display *);
```

In `XGetErrorDatabaseText()`, for an extension request, the extension name (as given by `XInitExtension()`) followed by a period (.) and the minor request protocol number is used for the *message* argument.

H.3.2.3 Nonstandard Keysyms

Keysyms that are not part of the Xlib standard can now be obtained by using `XString-ToKeysym()` and `XKeysymToString()`. Note that the set of keysyms that are available in this manner and the mechanisms by which Xlib obtains them is implementation-dependent. (In the MIT sample implementation, the resource file */usr/lib/X11/XKeysymDB* is used starting in R4. The keysym name is used as the resource name, and the resource value is the keysym value in uppercase hexadecimal.)

H.3.2.4 XReadBitmapFile()

In `XReadBitmapFile()`, the ability to read X10 format is no longer required of an implementation. The ability to read other than the standard format is implementation-dependent.

H.3.2.5 Resource Specification Syntax

As of R4, the BNF notation of a resource specification is now specified:

ResourceLine	=	Comment | ResourceSpec
Comment	=	"!" string | <empty line>
ResourceSpec	=	WhiteSpace ResourceName WhiteSpace ":" WhiteSpace value
ResourceName	=	[Binding] ComponentName {Binding ComponentName}
Binding	=	"." | "*"
WhiteSpace	=	{" " | "Tab"}
ComponentName	=	{"a"–"z" | "A"–"Z" | "0"–"9" | "_" | "-"}
value	=	string
string	=	{<any character not including "\n">}

Note that elements enclosed in curly braces ({...}) indicate zero or more occurrences of the enclosed elements.

To allow values to contain arbitrary octets, the four-character sequence *nnn*, where *n* is a digit in the range of 0 through 7 is recognized and replaced with a single byte that contains this sequence interpreted as an octal number. For example, a value containing a **NULL** byte can be stored by specifying \000.

H.3.2.6 XrmParseCommand()

In `XrmParseCommand()`, a new value, `XrmoptionSkipNArgs`, has been added to the `XrmOptionKind` enum. Note that `XrmoptionSkipArg` is equivalent to `XrmoptionSkipNArgs` with the `XrmOptionDescRec.value` field containing the value one. Note also that the value zero for `XrmoptionSkipNArgs` indicates that only the option itself is to be skipped.

H.3.2.7 Keyboard Groups

In R4, the concept of keyboard groups has been introduced, and `XLookupString()` implements new semantics to support keyboard groups. Keyboard groups support having two complete sets of keysyms for a keyboard. Which set will be used can be toggled using a particular key. This is implemented by using the first two keysyms in the list for a key as one set and the next two keysyms as the second set.

The standard rules for obtaining a keysym from a **KeyPress** event make use of only the Group 1 and Group 2 keysyms; no interpretation of other keysyms in the list is given here. Which group to use is determined by modifier state. Switching between groups is controlled by the keysym named MODE SWITCH, by attaching that keysym to some keycode and attaching that keycode to any one of the modifiers Mod1 through Mod5. This modifier is called the "group modifier." For any keycode, Group 1 is used when the group modifier is off and Group 2 is used when the group modifier is on.

Within a group, which keysym to use is also determined by modifier state. The first keysym is used when the Shift and Lock modifiers are off. The second keysym is used when the Shift modifier is on, when the Lock modifier is on and the second keysym is uppercase alphabetic, or when the Lock modifier is on and is interpreted as Shift Lock. Otherwise, when the Lock modifier is on and is interpreted as Caps Lock, the state of the Shift modifier is applied first to select a keysym, but if that keysym is lowercase alphabetic, then the corresponding uppercase keysym is used instead.

If the list of Keysyms (ignoring trailing `NoSymbol` entries) is a single keysym "K," then the list is treated as if it were the list "K NoSymbol K `NoSymbol`." If the list (ignoring trailing `NoSymbol` entries) is a pair of keysyms "$K1\ K2$," then the list is treated as if it were the list "$K1\ K2\ K1\ K2$." If the list (ignoring trailing `NoSymbol` entries) is a triple of keysyms "$K1\ K2\ K3$," then the list is treated as if it were the list "$K1\ K2\ K3$ `NoSymbol`." When an explicit "void" element is desired in the list, the value `VoidSymbol` can be used.

The first four elements of the list are split into two groups of keysyms. Group 1 contains the first and second keysyms; Group 2 contains the third and fourth keysyms. Within each group, if the second element of the group is `NoSymbol`, then the group should be treated as if the second element were the same as the first element, except when the first element is an alphabetic keysym "K" for which both lowercase and uppercase forms are defined. In that case, the group should be treated as if the first element were the lowercase form of "K" and the second element were the uppercase form of "K."

No spatial geometry of the symbols on the key is defined by their order in the keysym list, although a geometry might be defined on a vendor-specific basis. The X server does not use the mapping between keycodes and keysyms. Rather it stores it merely for reading and writing by clients.

The modifier named Lock is intended to be mapped to either a Caps Lock or a Shift Lock key, but which one is left as application-specific and/or user-specific. However, it is suggested that the determination be made according to the associated keysym(s) of the corresponding keycode.

Glossary

Glossary

This glossary is an expanded version of the glossary in the *Xlib–C Language X Interface*, by Jim Gettys, Ron Newman, and Bob Scheifler.

access control list

X maintains lists of hosts that are allowed access to each server controlling a display. By default, only the local host may use the display, plus any hosts specified in the *access control list* for that display. This access control list can be changed by clients on the local host. Some server implementations may implement other authorization mechanisms in addition to or instead of this one. The list can currently be found in */etc/X#.hosts*, where # is the number of the display. The access control list is also known as the host access list.

active grab

Keyboard keys, the keyboard, pointer buttons, the pointer, and the server can be *grabbed* for exclusive use by a client, usually for a short time period. An active grab causes pointer and keyboard events to be sent to the grabbing window regardless of the current position of the pointer. See **passive grab**.

ancestor

If window *W* is an inferior of window *A*, then *A* is an *ancestor* of *W*. The parent window, the parent's parent window, and so on are all ancestors of the given window. The root window is the ancestor of all windows on a given screen.

association table

Association tables provide a fast lookup table for data that must be searched frequently. Association tables associate arbitrary information with resource IDs. This is similar to the context manager, but the resource IDs used with association tables are existing resources, not created for the purpose of storing data for later retrieval.

atom

An *atom* is a unique numeric ID corresponding to a string name. Atoms are used to identify properties, types, and selections in order to avoid the overhead of passing arbitrary length property name strings.

background

>The **background** member of a GC defines a window's background, which consists of either a solid color or a tile pattern. If a window has a background, it will be repainted automatically by the server whenever there is an **Expose** event on the window. If a window does not have a background, it will be transparent. **background** can be set using the **GCBackground** mask, when the GC is created, or by a call to **XSetBackground( )**. Default is 1. See also **foreground**.

backing store

>When a server maintains the contents of a window, the off-screen saved pixels are known as a *backing store*. This feature is not available on all servers. Use the **DoesBackingStore( )s** macro to determine if this feature is supported.

base font name

>A font name used to select a family of fonts whose members may be encoded in various charsets. The **CharSetRegistry** and **CharSetEncoding** fields of an XLFD name identify the charset of the font. A base font name may be a full XLFD name, with all fourteen '-' delimiters, or an abbreviated XLFD name containing only the first 13 fields of an XLFD name, up to but not including **CharSet-Registry**, with or without the thirteenth '-', or a non-XLFD name. Any XLFD fields may contain wild cards. When creating an **XFontSet**, Xlib accepts from the client a list of one or more base font names which select one or more font families. They are combined with charset names obtained from the encoding of the locale to load the fonts required to render text.

bit gravity

>When a window is resized, the contents of the window are not necessarily discarded. It is possible to request the server (though no guarantees are made) to relocate the previous contents to some region of the resized window. This attraction of window contents for some location of a window is known as *bit gravity*. For example, an application that draws a graph might request that the contents be moved into the lower-left corner, so that the origin of the graph will still appear in the lower-left corner.

bit plane

>On a color or gray-scale display, each pixel has more than one bit defined. Data in display memory can be thought of either as pixels (multiple bits per pixel) or as bit planes (one bit plane for each usable bit in the pixel). The *bit plane* is an array of bits the size of the screen.

bitmap

>A *bitmap* is a pixmap with a depth of one bit. There is no bitmap type in X11. Instead use a pixmap of depth 1.

border

A window can have a *border* that is zero or more pixels wide. If a window has a border, the border can have a solid color or a tile pattern, and it will be repainted automatically by the server whenever its color or pattern is changed or an `Expose` event occurs on the window.

button grab

Specifies a pointer grab that occurs only when a specified set of keys and/or buttons is held down. This is analogous to a key grab. See **mouse grab**.

byte order

The order in which bytes of data are stored in memory is hardware-dependent. For pixmaps and bitmaps, *byte order* is defined by the server, and clients with different native byte ordering must swap bytes as necessary. For all other parts of the protocol, the byte order is defined by the client, and the server swaps bytes as necessary.

character

A member of a set of elements used for the organization, control, or representation of text (ISO2022, as adapted by XPG3). Note that in ISO2022 terms, a character is not bound to a coded value until it is identified as part of a coded character set.

character glyph

The abstract graphical symbol for a character. Character glyphs may or may not map one-to-one to font glyphs, and may be context-dependent, varying with the adjacent characters. Multiple characters may map to a single character glyph.

character set

A collection of characters.

charset

An encoding with a uniform, state-independent mapping from characters to codepoints. In the ISO2022 framework, this means a coded character set that does not use any shift sequences. (An encoding which uses single shifts is state-independent, but is not uniform.) For display in X, there can be a direct mapping from a charset to one font, if the width of all characters in the charset is either one or two bytes. A text string encoded in an encoding such as Shift-JIS cannot be passed directly to the X server, because the text imaging requests accept only single-width charsets (either 8 or 16 bits). Charsets which meet these restrictions can serve as "font charsets". Font charsets strictly speaking map font indices to font glyphs, not characters to character glyphs. Note that a single font charset is sometimes used as the encoding of a locale, for example, ISO8859-1.

children

The *children* of a window are its first-level subwindows. All of these windows were created with the same window as parent. A client creates its top-level window as a child of the root window.

class

There are two uses of the term *class* in X: window class and visual class. The window class specifies whether a window is `InputOnly` or `InputOutput`. See Chapter 2, *X Concepts*, for details. The visual class specifies the color model that is used by a window. See Chapter 7, *Color*, for details.

client

An application program connects to the window system server by an interprocess communication (IPC) path such as a TCP connection or a shared memory buffer. This program is referred to as a *client* of the window system server. More precisely, the client is the IPC path itself; a program with multiple paths open to the server is viewed as multiple clients by the protocol. Server resources survive only as long as the connection remains intact, not as long as a client program remains running. Normally the connection and the program terminate concurrently, but the client's resources may live on if `XChangeCloseDownMode` has been called.

clip mask

In many graphics routines, a bitmap or list of rectangles can be specified to restrict output to a particular region of the window. The image defined by the bitmap or rectangles is called a *clip mask* or *clipping region*. Output to child windows is automatically clipped to the borders of the parent unless `subwindow_mode` of the GC is `IncludeInferiors`. Therefore, the borders of the parent can be thought of as a clip mask or clipping region.

clipping region

See **clip mask**.

coded character

A character bound to a codepoint.

coded character set

A set of unambiguous rules that establishes a character set and the one-to-one relationship between each character of the set and its bit representation. (ISO2022, as adapted by XPG3) A definition of a one-to-one mapping of a set of characters to a set of codepoints. Some encodings, such as Compound Text, have more than one bit representation for a given character, and thus are not considered coded character sets.

codepoint

The coded representation of a single character in a coded character set.

colorcell

An entry in a colormap is known as a *colorcell*. An entry contains three values specifying red, green, and blue intensities. These values are always 16-bit unsigned numbers, with zero being minimum intensity. The values are truncated or scaled by the server to match the display hardware. See also **colormap**.

colormap

A *colormap* consists of a set of colorcells. A pixel value indexes into the colormap to produce intensities of red, green, and blue to be displayed. Depending on hardware limitations, one or more colormaps may be installed at one time, such that windows associated with those maps display with true colors. Regardless of the number of installable colormaps, any number of virtual colormaps can be created. When needed, a virtual colormap can be installed and the existing installed colormap might have to be deinstalled. The colormap on most systems is a limited resource that should be conserved by allocating read-only colorcells whenever possible and by selecting RGB values from the predefined color database. Read-only cells may be shared between clients. See also **colorcell**, **DirectColor**, **GrayScale**, **PseudoColor**, **StaticColor**, **StaticGray**, and **TrueColor**.

connection

The IPC path between the server and client is known as a *connection*. A client usually (but not necessarily) has one connection to the server over which requests and events are sent.

containment

A window *contains* the pointer if the window is viewable and the hotspot of the cursor is within a visible region of the window or a visible region of one of its inferiors. The border of the window is included as part of the window for containment. The pointer is in a window if the window contains the pointer but no inferior contains the pointer.

coordinate system

The *coordinate system* has X horizontal and Y vertical pixels, with the origin (0,0) at the upper left. Coordinates are discrete. Each window and pixmap has its own coordinate system. For a window with a border, the origin is inside the border.

cursor

A *cursor* is the visible shape of the pointer on a screen. It consists of a hotspot, a shape bitmap, a mask bitmap, and a pair of pixel values. The cursor defined for a window controls the visible appearance of the pointer when the pointer is in that window.

cut buffer

Cut buffers are a simple but limited method of client communication, sometimes used instead of the selection mechanism. Cut buffers are properties of the root window of screen 0 of a display. They rely on a prior agreement between the two clients regarding the format of the data to be placed in the cut buffers. The data that can be placed in a single cut buffer is limited to the maximum size of a single property. See **selection**.

depth

The *depth* of a window or pixmap is the number of planes that are to be used to represent gray scales or color within a window.

descendants

See **inferiors**.

device

Keyboards, mice, tablets, track-balls, button boxes, etc. are all collectively known as input *devices*.

DirectColor

`DirectColor` is a visual class in which a pixel value is decomposed into three separate subfields for colormap indexing. One subfield indexes an array to produce red intensity values; the second subfield indexes a second array to produce blue intensity values; and the third subfield indexes a third array to produce green intensity values. The RGB (red, green, and blue) values in the colormap entry can be changed dynamically. This visual class is normally found on high performance color workstations. (`XGetVisualInfo()`, `XMatchVisualInfo()`)

display

A *display* is a set of one or more screens that are driven by a single X server. The Xlib `Display` structure contains all information about the particular display and its screens as well as the state that Xlib needs to communicate with the display over a particular connection.

display function

See **logical function**.

drawable

Both windows and pixmaps may be used as destinations in graphics operations. These are collectively known as *drawables*.

encoding

A set of unambiguous rules that establishes a character set and a relationship between the characters and their bit representations. The character set does not have to be fixed to a finite pre-defined set of characters. Examples are an ISO2022 graphic set, a state-independent or state-dependent combination of graphic sets, possibly including control sets, and the X Compound Text encoding. In X, encodings are identified by a string which appears as: the `CharSetRegistry` and `CharSetEncoding` components of an XLFD name; the name of a charset of the locale for which a font could not be found; or an atom which identifies the encoding of a text property or which names an encoding for a text selection target type. Encoding names should be composed of characters from the X Portable Character Set.

escapement

The escapement of a string is the distance in pixels in the primary draw direction from the drawing origin to the origin of the next character (that is, the one following the given string) to be drawn.

event

Clients are informed of device input or client request side effects asynchronously via *events*. Events are grouped into types; events are never sent to a client by the server unless the client has specifically asked to be informed of that type of event. However, other clients can force events of any type to be sent to any clients. Events are typically reported relative to a window.

event mask

Events are requested relative to a window. The set of event types a client requests relative to a window is described using an *event mask*. See **do_not_propagate_mask** and **event_mask**.

event propagation

Device-related events *propagate* from the source window to ancestor windows until a window that has selected that type of event is reached or until the event is discarded explicitly in a **do_not_propagate_mask** attribute.

event source

The smallest window containing the pointer is the *source* of a device-related event.

event window

An *event window* specifies the ID of the window in which an event appears to have occurred. See **source window**.

exposure

Window *exposure* occurs when a window is first mapped or when another window that obscures it is unmapped, resized, or moved. Servers do not guarantee to preserve the contents of windows when windows are obscured or reconfigured. **Expose** events are sent to clients to inform them when contents of regions of windows have been lost and need to be regenerated.

extension

Named *extensions* to the core protocol can be defined to extend the system. Extension to output requests, resources, and event types are all possible and expected. Extensions can perform at the same level as the core Xlib.

font

The **font** member of a GC specifies which font to use in graphics requests. A font is an array of characters or other bitmap shapes such as cursors. **font** can be set using the **GCFont** mask, when the GC is created, or by a call to **XSet-Font()**. The default font is installation dependent.

font glyph

The abstract graphical symbol for an index into a font.

foreground

The `foreground` member of a GC defines the pixel value that will actually be used for drawing pictures or text. `foreground` can be set using the `GCForeground` mask, when the GC is created, or by a call to `XSetForeground()`. Default is 0. See also **background**.

frozen events

Clients can *freeze* event processing while they change the screen by grabbing the keyboard or pointer with a certain mode. These events are queued in the server (not in Xlib) until an `XAllowEvents()` call with a counteracting mode is given.

GC

The term *GC* is used as a shorthand for graphics context. See **graphics context**.

glyph

An *glyph* is an identified abstract graphical symbol independent of any actual image. (ISO/IEC/DIS 9541-1) An abstract visual representation of a graphic character, not bound to a codepoint.

glyph image

An image of a glyph, as obtained from a glyph representation displayed on a presentation surface. (ISO/IEC/DIS 9541-1)

grab

Keyboard keys, the keyboard, pointer buttons, the pointer, and the server can be *grabbed* for exclusive use by a client, usually for a short time period. In general, these facilities are not intended to be used by normal applications but are intended for various input and window managers to implement various styles of user interfaces. See **active grab** and **passive grab**.

graphics context

Various information for graphics output is stored in a *graphics context* (GC), such as foreground pixel, background pixel, line width, clipping region, etc. Everything drawn to a window or pixmap is modified by the GC used in the drawing request. GCs are created or altered with `XChangeGC()`, `XCopyGC()`, and `XCreateGC()`.

gravity

Controls the repositioning of a resized window's contents (bit gravity) or of a resized parent window's subwindows (window gravity). See **bit gravity** and **window gravity**.

GrayScale

`GrayScale` is a visual class in which the red, green, and blue values in any given colormap entry are equal, thus producing shades of gray. The gray values can be changed dynamically. `GrayScale` can be viewed as a degenerate case of `PseudoColor`. (`XGetVisualInfo()`, `XMatchVisualInfo()`)

hint

Certain properties, such as the preferred size of a window, are referred to as *hints*, since the window manager makes no guarantee that it will honor them. See **XA_WM_HINTS**, **XA_WM_NORMAL_HINTS**, **XA_WM_SIZE_HINTS**, and **XA_WM_ZOOM_HINTS**.

host access list

See **access control list**.

host portable character encoding

The encoding of the X Portable Character Set on the host. The encoding itself is not defined by this standard, but the encoding must be the same in all locales supported by Xlib on the host. If a string is said to be in the Host Portable Character Encoding, then it only contains characters from the X Portable Character Set, in the host encoding.

hotspot

A cursor has an associated *hotspot* that defines the point in the cursor which corresponds to the coordinates reported for the pointer.

icon

An *icon* is a small marker window that indicates that a larger "main" window exists and is available but is not currently mapped on the screen.

identifier

Each resource has an *identifier* or *ID*, a unique value that clients use to name the resource. Any client can use a resource if it knows the resource ID.

inferiors

The *inferiors* of a window are all of the subwindows nested below it: the children, the children's children, etc. The term *descendants* is a synonym.

input focus

See **keyboard focus**.

input manager

Control over keyboard input may be provided by an *input manager* client. This job may also be done by the window manager.

InputOnly window

A window that cannot be used for graphics requests is called an `InputOnly` window. `InputOnly` windows are invisible and can be used to control such things as cursors, input event generation, and grabbing. `InputOnly` windows cannot have `InputOutput` windows as inferiors.

InputOutput window

The normal kind of window that is used for both input and output is called an `InputOutput` window. It usually has a background. `InputOutput` windows can have both `InputOutput` and `InputOnly` windows as inferiors.

internationalization

The process of making software adaptable to the requirements of different native languages, local customs, and character string encodings. Making a computer program adaptable to different locales without program source modifications or recompilation.

ISO2022

ISO standard for code extension techniques for 7-bit and 8-bit coded character sets.

Latin-1

The coded character set defined by the ISO8859-1 standard.

latin portable character encoding

The encoding of the X Portable Character Set using the Latin-1 codepoints plus ASCII control characters. If a string is said to be in the Latin Portable Character Encoding, then it only contains characters from the X Portable Character Set, not all of Latin-1.

locale

The international environment of a computer program defining the "localized" behavior of that program at run-time. This information can be established from one or more sets of localization data. ANSI C defines locale-specific processing by C system library calls. See ANSI C and the X/Open Portability Guide specifications for more details. In this specification, on implementations that conform to the ANSI C library, the "current locale" is the current setting of the LC_CTYPE `setlocale` category. Associated with each locale is a text encoding. When text is processed in the context of a locale, the text must be in the encoding of the locale. The current locale affects Xlib in its:

- Encoding and processing of input method text

- Encoding of resource files and values

- Encoding and imaging of text strings

- Encoding and decoding for inter-client text communication

localization

The process of establishing information within a computer system specific to the operation of particular native languages, local customs and coded character sets. (XPG3)

locale name

The identifier used to select the desired locale for the host C library and X library functions. On ANSI C library compliant systems, the locale argument to the `set-locale` function.

key grab

Specifies a keyboard *grab* that occurs only when a certain key or key combination is pressed. This is analogous to a button grab. See **keyboard grab**.

keyboard focus

The *keyboard focus* is the window that receives main keyboard input. By default, the focus is the root window, which has the effect of sending input to the window that is being pointed to by the mouse. It is possible to attach the keyboard input to a specific window with `XSetInputFocus()`. Events are then sent to the window independent of the pointer position or, if the `owner_events` argument is `True`, to the window containing the pointer if it is owned by the same client as the focus window.

keyboard grab

All keyboard input is sent to a specific window (or client, depending on `owner_events`) when the keyboard is *grabbed*. This is analogous to a mouse grab. This is very much like a temporary keyboard focus window.

keyboard vector

A *keyboard vector* represents, in the event structure, the state of the keyboard; the vector consists of 32 bytes of data, with one bit for each keyboard key.

keycode

A *keycode* is a code in the range [8,255], inclusive, that represents a physical or logical key on the keyboard. The mapping between keys and keycodes cannot be changed. A list of keysyms is associated with each keycode.

keysym

A *keysym* is a `#defined` symbol which is a portable representation of the symbol on the cap of a key. Each key may have several keysyms, corresponding to the key when various modifier keys are pressed. You should interpret key events according to the keysym returned by `XLookupString()` or `XLookupKeysym()`, since this translates server-dependent keycodes into portable keysyms. See **keycode**.

listener

A *listener*-style window manager sets the keyboard focus to a particular window when that window is clicked on with a pointer button. This is the window manager style used with the Apple Macintosh ™.

logical function

Logical functions control how the *source* pixel values generated by a graphics request are combined with the *old destination* pixel values already present on the screen or drawable to result in the *final destination* pixel values. A logical function can be changed by a call to `XSetFunction()`. Sometimes called raster operations, raster ops, or display functions.

mapping

A window is said to be *mapped* if a `XMapWindow()` or `XMapRaised()` call has been performed on it. Unmapped windows are never viewable. Mapping makes a window eligible for display. The window will actually be displayed if the following conditions are met: (1) all its ancestors are mapped and (2) it is not obscured by siblings.

mask

A *mask* specifies which values in a specified structure should be read when updating the resource values. One bit in the mask is assigned to every member of its corresponding structure. For example, `CWBackgroundPixmap` mask is used to indicate that the `background_pixmap` member of the specified window attributes structure is to be read and the corresponding member in the resource changed. See **structure**.

modifier key

A key such as Shift or Control that can modify the meaning of a key event. Shift, Control, Meta, Super, Hyper, Alt, Compose, Apple, Caps Lock, Shift Lock, and similar keys are called *modifier keys*.

monochrome

A *monochrome* screen has only two colors: black and white. Monochrome is a special case of the `StaticGray` visual class, in which there!!! are only two colormap entries.

mouse grab

All mouse input is sent to a specific window (or client, depending on `owner_events`) when the mouse is *grabbed*. This is analogous to a keyboard grab.

multibyte

A character whose codepoint is stored in more than one byte; any encoding which can contain multibyte characters; text in a multibyte encoding. The "char *" null-terminated string datatype in ANSI C. Note that references in this document to multibyte strings imply only that the strings *may* contain multibyte characters.

obscures

Window *A obscures* window *B* if *A* is higher in the global stacking order and the rectangle defined by the outside edges of *A* intersects the rectangle defined by the outside edges of *B*.

occludes

Window *A occludes* window *B* if both are mapped, if *A* is higher in the global stacking order, and if the rectangle defined by the outside edges of *A* intersects the rectangle defined by the outside edges of *B*. The (fine) distinction between the terms *obscures* and *occludes* is that for *obscures*, the windows have to be mapped, while for *occludes*, they do not. Also note that window borders are included in the calculation. Note that `InputOnly` windows never obscure other windows but can occlude other windows.

owner client

Selections transfer arbitrary information between two clients. An *owner client* owns the data representing the value of a selection, and a requestor client wants it. See **selection**.

padding

Some bytes are inserted in the data stream to maintain alignment of the protocol requests on natural boundaries. This *padding* increases ease of portability to some machine architectures.

parent window

Each new window is created with reference to another previously created window. The new window is referred to as the child, and the reference window as the *parent*. If *C* is a child of *P*, then *P* is the parent of *C*. Only the portion of the child that overlaps the parent is viewable.

passive grab

Keyboard keys, the keyboard, pointer buttons, the pointer, and the server can be grabbed for exclusive use by a client, usually for a short time period. A *passive grab* causes an active grab to begin when a certain key or button combination is pressed. The grab becomes active when the key or button is actually pressed. Before the active grab takes place, nothing has changed. See **active grab**.

pixel value

A *pixel value* is an *N*-bit value, where *N* is the number of bit planes used in a particular window or pixmap. For a window, a pixel value indexes a colormap to derive an actual color to be displayed. For a pixmap, a pixel value will be interpreted as a color in the same way when it is copied into a window.

pixmap

A *pixmap* is a three-dimensional array of bits. A pixmap is normally thought of as a two-dimensional array of pixels, where each pixel can be a value from 0 to $(2^N - 1)$, where *N* is the depth (z-axis) of the pixmap. A pixmap can also be thought of as a stack of *N* bitmaps.

plane

When a pixmap or a window is thought of as a stack of bitmaps, each bitmap is called a *plane*.

plane_mask

Graphics operations can be restricted to affect only a subset of bit planes in a drawable. The `plane_mask` member of a GC is a bit mask describing which planes are to be modified. Default is all ones. `plane_mask` can be set using the `GCPlaneMask` mask, when the GC is created, or it can be changed by a call to `XSetPlaneMask()`.

pointer

The *pointer* is the pointing device currently attached to the cursor and tracked on the screens. This may be a mouse, tablet, track-ball, or joystick, among other things.

pointer grab

A client can actively *grab* control of the pointer, causing button and motion events to be sent to the grabbing client rather than to the client indicated by the pointer.

pointing device

A *pointing device* is typically a mouse or tablet or some other device with effective two-dimensional motion. There is only one visible cursor defined by the core protocol, and it tracks whatever pointing device is currently attached as the pointer.

position

A window has a *position*, which locates its upper-left corner relative to its parent's corner.

POSIX

Portable Operating System Interface, ISO/IEC 9945-1 (IEEE Std 1003.1).

POSIX Portable Filename Character Set

The set of 65 characters which can be used in naming files on a POSIX-compliant host that are correctly processed in all locales. The set is:

```
a..z A..Z 0..9 ._-
```

shift sequence

ISO2022 defines control characters and escape sequences which temporarily (single shift) or permanently (locking shift) cause a different character set to be in effect ("invoking" a character set).

property

Windows may have associated *properties*, each consisting of a name, a type, a data format, and some data. The protocol places no interpretation on properties; they are intended as a general purpose data storage and intercommunication mechanism for clients. There is, however, a list of predefined properties and property types so that clients might share information such as resize hints, program names, and icon formats with a window manager via properties. In order to avoid passing arbitrary length property name strings, each property name is associated with a corresponding integer value known as an atom. See also **atom**.

property list

The *property list* of a window is the list of properties that have been defined for that window.

PseudoColor

PseudoColor is a visual class in which a pixel value indexes the colormap entry to produce independent red, green, and blue values. That is, the colormap is viewed as an array of triples (RGB values). The RGB values can be changed dynamically. (`XGetVisualInfo()`, `XMatchVisualInfo()`)

quark

A *quark* is an integer ID that identifies a name, class, or type string for the resource manager. Like atoms and resource IDs, quarks eliminate the need to pass strings of arbitrary length over the network. The quark type is `XrmQuark`, and the types `XrmName`, `XrmClass`, and `XrmRepresentation` are also defined to be `XrmQuark`.

raise

Changing the stacking order of a window so as to occlude all sibling windows is to *raise* that window.

raster operation

See **logical function**.

real estate

A window management style characterized by the input being sent to whichever window the pointer is in. This is the most common style of input management used in X.

rectangle

A *rectangle* specified by [x,y,w,h] has an (infinitely thin) outline path with corners at [x,y], [x+w,y], [x+w,y+h] and [x,y+h]. When a rectangle is filled, the lower-right edges are not drawn. For example, if w=h=0, nothing would be drawn. For w=h=1, a single pixel would be drawn.

redirect

Window managers (or other clients) may wish to enforce window layout policy in various ways. When a client attempts to change the size or position of a window, the operation may be *redirected* to the window manager, rather than actually being performed. Then the window manager (or other client that redirected the input) is expected to decide whether to allow, modify, or deny the requested operation before making the call itself.

reparenting

The window manager often *reparents* the top-level windows of each application in order to add a titlebar and perhaps resize boxes. In other words, a window with a titlebar is inserted between the root window and each top-level window. See also **save-set**.

reply

Information requested by a client, by routines whose names include the word Query, is sent back to the client with a *reply*. Both events and replies are multiplexed on the same connection. Requests that require replies are known as *round-trip requests*. Most requests do not generate replies. Some requests generate multiple replies. See **round-trip request**.

request

A command to the server is called a *request*. It is a single block of data sent over the connection to the server.

requestor client

Selections transfer arbitrary information between two clients. An owner client owns the data representing the value of a selection, and a *requestor client* wants it. See **selection**.

resource

Windows, pixmaps, cursors, fonts, graphics contexts, and colormaps are known as *resources*. They all have unique identifiers (IDs) associated with them for naming purposes. The lifetime of a resource is bounded by the lifetime of the connection over which the resource was created.

resource manager

Every application should provide command line options that allow users to set colors or patterns for the window border and background; set foreground colors for drawing; start the application at a desired size, position, and configuration; select fonts; and so on. An application must also allow users to specify their own default values (user preferences) for each of these options. There are three and sometimes four sets of options that need to be read and merged: the program's defaults, the user's defaults stored in the root window's XA_RESOURCE_MANAGER property or in the user's *.Xdefaults* file, and the command line arguments. The order in which the various options are merged is important. A value for an option in the user's defaults should override the program's default for that option, but a value on the command line would override both the program's and the user's default value. The routines and database structures used for managing user preferences are collectively referred to as the *resource manager*.

RGB values

Red, green, and blue intensity values are used to define a color. These values are always represented as 16-bit unsigned numbers, with 0 the minimum intensity and 65535 the maximum intensity. The X server scales these values to match the display hardware.

root

The *root* of a window, pixmap, or graphics context (GC) is the same as the root of whatever drawable was used when the window, pixmap, or GC was created. These resources can be used only on the screen indicated by this window. See **root window**.

root window

Each screen has a *root window* covering it. It cannot be reconfigured or unmapped but otherwise acts as a full-fledged window. A root window has no parent.

round-trip request

A request to the server that generates a reply is known as a *round-trip request*. Requests that require replies should be avoided when possible since they introduce network delays. See **reply**.

save-set

The *save-set* of a client is a list of other clients' windows which, if they are inferiors of one of the client's windows at connection close, should not be destroyed and which should be reparented and remapped if the client is unmapped. Save-sets are typically used by window managers to avoid lost windows if the manager should terminate abnormally. See **reparenting** for more background information.

scan line

A *scan line* is a list of pixel or bit values viewed as a horizontal row (all values having the same Y coordinate) of an image, with the values ordered by increasing X coordinate values.

scan line order

An image represented in *scan line order* contains scan lines ordered by increasing Y coordinate values.

screen

A server may provide several independent *screens*, which may or may not have physically independent monitors. For instance, it is possible to treat a color monitor as if it were two screens, one color and the other black and white. There is only a single keyboard and pointer shared among the screens. A `Screen` structure contains the information about that screen and is a member of the `Display` structure.

selection

Selections are a means of communication between clients using properties and events. From the user's perspective, a selection is an item of data which can be highlighted in one instance of an application and pasted into another instance of the same or a different application. The client that highlights the data is the owner, and the client into which the data is pasted is the requestor. Properties are used to store the selection data and the type of the data, while events are used to synchronize the transaction and to allow the requestor to indicate the type it prefers for the data and to allow the owner to convert the data to the indicated type if possible. See **cut buffer**.

server

The *server* provides the basic windowing mechanism. It handles IPC connections from clients, demultiplexes graphics requests onto the screens, and multiplexes input back to the appropriate clients. It controls a single keyboard and pointer and one or more screens that make up a single display.

server grab

The server can be *grabbed* by a single client for exclusive use. This prevents processing of any requests from other client connections until the grab is complete. This is typically a transient state to perform such tasks as rubber-banding and pop-up menus or to execute requests indivisibly.

sibling

Children of the same parent window are known as *sibling* windows.

source window

A *source window* specifies the ID of the window in which an event originally happens. See **event window**.

stacking order

Sibling windows may stack on top of each other, obscuring lower windows. This is similar to papers on a desk. The relationship between sibling windows is known as the *stacking order*. The first window in the stacking order is the window on top.

state-dependent encoding

An encoding in which an invocation of a charset can apply to multiple characters in sequence. A state-dependent encoding begins in an "initial state" and enters other "shift states" when specific "shift sequences" are encountered in the byte sequence. In ISO2022 terms, this means use of locking shifts, not single shifts.

state-independent encoding

Any encoding in which the invocations of the charsets are fixed, or span only a single character. In ISO2022 terms, this means use of at most single shifts, not locking shifts.

STRING encoding

Latin-1, plus tab and newline.

StaticColor

`StaticColor` is a visual class which represents a multiplane color screen with a predefined and read-only hardware colormap. It can be viewed as a degenerate case of `PseudoColor`. (`XGetVisualInfo()`, `XMatchVisualInfo()`)

StaticGray

`StaticGray` is a visual class which represents a multiplane monochrome screen with a predefined and read-only hardware colormap. It can be viewed as a degenerate case of `GrayScale`, in which the gray values are predefined and read-only. Typically, the values are linearly increasing ramps. (`XGetVisualInfo()`, `XMatchVisualInfo()`)

Status

Many Xlib functions return a `Status` of zero if it fails and nonzero if it succeeds. If the function does not succeed, its arguments are not changed.

stipple

The `stipple` member of a GC defines a single-plane pixmap that is used to tile a region. Bits set to 1 in the stipple are drawn with the `foreground` pixel value; bits set to 0, with the `background` pixel value. `stipple` can be set using the `GCStipple` mask, when the GC is created, or by a call to `XSetStipple()`. Default is the pixmap filled with ones. See **tile**.

STRING encoding

Latin-1, plus tab and newline.

structure

Pointers to *structures* are the major way of specifying data to and returning data from Xlib routines. If the routine returns data, the returned value will be a pointer to the data structure, unless the routine returns more then one structure, in which case one or all of the structures will be arguments. When setting the characteristics of an X resource, such as a set of window attributes or a graphics context, both a structure and a mask are specified as arguments. See **mask**.

subwindow_mode

The `subwindow_mode` member of a GC controls whether subwindows obscure their parent. `subwindow_mode` can be set using the `GCSubwindowMode` mask, when the GC is created, or by a call to `XSetSubwindowMode()`. Possible values are `ClipByChildren` (the default) or `IncludeInferiors`.

tile

The `tile` member of a GC defines a pixmap used for patterning an area. A tile has the same depth as the drawable it is used to pattern. `tile` can be set using the `GCTile` mask, when the GC is created, or by a call to `XSetTile()`. Default is the pixmap is filled with the foreground pixel. See **stipple**.

time

A *time* value in X is expressed in milliseconds, typically since the last server reset. Time values wrap around (after about 49.7 days). One time value, represented by the constant `CurrentTime`, is used by clients to represent the current server time.

top-level window

A child of the root window is referred to as a *top-level window*.

TrueColor

`TrueColor` is a visual class which represents a high performance multiplane display with predefined and read-only RGB values in its hardware colormap. It can be viewed as a degenerate case of `DirectColor`, in which the subfields in the pixel value directly encode the corresponding RGB values. Typically, the values are linearly increasing ramps. (`XGetVisualInfo()`, `XMatchVisual-Info()`)

type property

A *type property* is used to identify the interpretation of property data. Types are completely uninterpreted by the server; they are solely for the benefit of clients.

viewable

A window is *viewable* if it and all of its ancestors are mapped. This does not imply that any portion of the window is actually visible, since it may be obscured by other windows.

visible

A region of a window is *visible* if someone looking at the screen can actually see it; that is, the window is viewable and the region is not obscured by any other window.

visual

The specifications for color handling for a drawable, including visual class, depth, RGB/pixel, etc., are collectively referred to as a *visual* and are stored in a structure of type `Visual`. The visual accounts for the differences between various types of hardware in determining the way pixel values are translated into visible colors within a window. A screen may support only one of several types of visuals.

visual class

This attribute accounts for the differences between various types of display hardware in determining the way in which pixel values are translated into visible colors within a particular window. See **DirectColor**, **GrayScale**, **PseudoColor**, **StaticColor**, **StaticGray**, and **TrueColor**.

whitespace

Any spacing character. On implementations that conform to the ANSI C library, whitespace is any character for which `isspace` returns `True`.

window

An X server controls a bitmapped screen. In order to make it easier to view and control many different tasks at the same time, this screen can be divided up into smaller areas called windows. A window is a rectangular area of any size that works in several ways like a miniature screen. Windows in the screen can be arranged so they all are visible or so they cover each other completely or partially. Each window can be involved in a different activity, and the windows currently in use are placed so they are at least partially visible.

window gravity

When windows are resized, subwindows may be repositioned automatically relative to an edge, a corner, or the center of the window. This attraction of a subwindow to some part of its parent is known as *window gravity*.

window manager

Manipulation of windows on the screen is provided by a *window manager* client. The window manager has authority over the arrangement of windows on the screen and the user interface for selecting which window receives input. See also **redirect**.

X Portable Character Set

A basic set of 97 characters which are assumed to exist in all locales supported by Xlib. This set contains the following characters:

```
a..z A..Z 0..9
!"#$%&'()*+,-./:;<=>?@[\\]^_'{|}~
<space>, <tab>, and <newline>
```

This is the left/lower half (also called the G0 set) of the graphic character set of ISO8859-1 plus <space>, <tab>, and <newline>. It is also the set of graphic characters in 7-bit ASCII plus the same three control characters. The actual encoding of these characters on the host is system dependent; see the Host Portable Character Encoding.

XLFD The X Logical Font Description Conventions that define a standard syntax for structured font names.

XYPixmap

`XYPixmap` specifies the format for an image. The data for an image is said to be in `XYPixmap` format if it is organized as a set of bitmaps representing individual bit planes. (`XCreateImage()`, `XGetImage()`, `XPutImage()`)

zoomed window

Some applications not only have a normal size for their top-level window and an icon but also have a *zoomed window* size. This could be used in a painting program (similar to the MacPaint™ fat bits). The zoomed window size preferences can be specified in the window manager hints.

ZPixmap

`ZPixmap` specifies the format for an image. The data for an image is said to be in `ZPixmap` format if it is organized as a set of pixel values in scan line order. (`XGetImage()`, `XPutImage()`)

References

ANSI Programming Language — C: ANSI X3.159-1989, December 14, 1989.

Draft Proposed Multibyte Extension of ANSI C, Draft 1.1, November 30, 1989 SC22/C WG/SWG IPSJ/ITSCJ Japan.

X/Open Portability Guide, Issue 3, December 1988 (XPG3), X/Open Company, Ltd, Prentice-Hall, Inc. 1989. ISBN 0-13-685835-8. (See especially Volume 3: XSI Supplementary Definitions.)

POSIX: Information Technology — Portable Operating System Interface (POSIX) - Part 1: System Application Program Interface (API) [C Language], ISO/IEC 9945-1.

ISO2022: Information processing — ISO 7-bit and 8-bit coded character sets — Code extension techniques.

ISO8859-1: Information processing — 8-bit single-byte coded graphic character sets — Part 1: Latin alphabet No. 1.

Text of ISO/IEC/DIS 9541-1, Information Processing — Font Information Interchange — Part 1: Architecture.

Index

attributes (cont'd)
    description, 93
    do_not_propagate_mask, 39,
        107, 263, 266
    event_mask, 35, 39, 107, 263,
        266
    input context, 374-378
    input methods, 367
    InputOnly windows, 97
    override_direct, 513
    override_redirect, 108, 417
    Preedit, 375
    root window, 38
    save_under, 35, 106, 417
    setting, 93-110
    Status area, 375
    substructure redirect override,
        35
    symbols, 94
    win_gravity, 34, 103
    XIC, 372
authentication, 60, 497
authorization protocols, 497
automatic grab, between button
    events, 314
automatically selected events,
    279
auto_repeat_mode, 321
Auxiliary area, 360
AVERAGE_WIDTH, 567

                    B

B16, 597
B32, 597
back-end input method, 359
background, 146-147
    attributes, 34
    definition, 723
    GC component, 138
    specifying, 97
background_pixel attribute, 99
background_pixmap attribute,
    98
backing store, 34, 105
    definition, 29, 724
    in exposure handling, 79
backing_pixel attribute, 105
backing_planes attribute, 105
BadLength, 596

BadMatch error, in drawing, 151
base font name, definition, 724
base font name list, 338
basecalc application, 201,
        469-491, 609-635
    basecalc.h include file, 610-615
    code for calculator application,
        615-635
    description of, 469
    drawButton routine, 489-490
    example, 477
    example database for, 474
    extractOpts routine, 479
    getting user defaults, 473
    GetUsersDataBase routine,
        477-478
    how to use, 470
    include files, 472
    initCalc routine, 485-486
    main, 472
    parseOpenDisp routine, 474
    parsing command line, 474
    portability of, 470
    selectEvents routine, 487
    Usage routine, 482
basicwin program, 56-89
    connecting to server, 59
    creating icon pixmap, 66
    creating windows, 64
    include files, 57
    main of, 57
    mapping window, 72
    setting standard properties, 69
beep volume, 320
bell volume, 320-321
bindings, loose, 456, 459
    tight, 456
bit gravity, definition, 724
bit plane, definition, 724
bit_gravity attribute, 34, 101
    constants, 102
bitmap, fonts, 565
    font-scaling algorithm, 563
bitmap client, 66
bitmap file format, 66, 156-157,
        695
bitmaps, creating, 156
    definition, 32, 724
bits per pixel, 30
bitwise OR, combining mask sym-
    bols, 262

black background, 65
BlackPixel macro, 31, 64-65, 200
border attributes, 34
border crossing events, 312,
    655-660
border_pixel attribute, 101
border_pixmap attribute, 100
borders, clipping to, 27
    color, specifying, 99
    definition, 724
    pattern, specifying, 99
    width, 24, 35, 425
BSD functions, header files for,
    504
buffering, 17-18
    affect on screen, 80
button, example, 535
    grab between, 314
    mapping, 311, 677
button grab, definition, 725
ButtonMotionMask event mask,
    264, 272-273
ButtonPress event, 266, 314,
    642-643
ButtonPressMask event mask,
    272
ButtonRelease event, 266, 314,
    642-643
ButtonReleaseMask event mask,
    272
byte order, 507
    definition, 725
    for pixmaps, 507
    in image, 178

C

C++, header files, 504
caching of GCs in display hard-
    ware, 122
caddr_t, 713
calculator example, 469, 482-486
callbacks, geometry, 381-382
    Preedit, 378, 381-382
    Status, 378, 381
CapButt cap_style, 125
CapNotLast cap_style, 125
CapProjecting cap_style, 125
CapRound cap_style, 125
cap_style, GC component,
    122-123, 125

CCC, **234**, 238
    default, 238
    of colormap, 238
changeable colormaps, 199
    versus immutable colormaps,
    198
character compound, 288
character glyph, definition, 725
character set, 332
    definition, 725
    functions in Xmu library,
    696-697
character width, versus string
    width, 340
characters, accented, displaying,
    329
    definition, 725
    format, 160
    metrics, 162
    unconvertible, 350
charset, 332
    definition, 725
child processes, 522, 552
child windows, 27
    drawing through, 145
    moving with parent, 24
    of root window, 26
    stacking relative to parent, 28
children, definition, 725
Chinese text, 329, 358
choosing colors, 206
Chroma, color space, 232, 239
CIELab, gamut-querying func-
    tions for, 240
CIELuv, gamut-querying func-
    tions for, 240
circle drawing, 132, 152
CirculateNotify event, 277, 530,
    644
CirculateRequest event, 278,
    513, 645
circulating windows, 28
class, and portability, 506
    definition, 726
class (resource), choosing, 460
    names, 458
    property, 418
    versus instance, 456
class (window), 26
    InputOnly, 36
    InputOutput, 36

clearing windows, 158
client, definition, 10, 726
  owner, 428
  properties, 406
  requestor, 428
client resources, killing, 224
client_data, 381
ClientMessage event, 266, 279,
  517, 646
client-side, color name database,
  192
client-to-client, communication,
  428-436
  internationalization, 344
client-to-window-manager, internationalization, 344
client-window manager, communication, 516-518
clip mask, 115
  definition, 726
  GC component, 133, 139
clip origin of GC, 139
  setting, 133
CLIPBOARD selection, 435
ClipByChildren, subwin-
  dow_mode, 145
clipping region, definition, 726
clipping to parent borders, 27
close down mode, 499
close on fork, 522
close operations, 500
closing the display, 81
coded character, definition, 726
coded character set, definition,
  726
codepoint, definition, 726
codeset, 330, 332
collation, 331
color, 240
  aliases, 192
  allocating (description), 188
  allocating read-only, 201
  allocating read/write, 206-217
  and pixels, 30
  choosing, 206
  concepts, 187
  conversion, 238
  device-independent, 230-241
  for a 24-plane workstation, 223
  highlighting, 531
  lookup order, 193
  naming, 192
  new features, 230

  number available versus pos-
    sible, 188
  reversing foreground and back-
    ground, 384
  terms, 187
  user preference for, 206
  values; obtaining, 235
  (see also device depen-
    dent/independent color.)
color conversion context, (see
  CCC)
color mapping on mid-range
  color screen, 188
color name database, 189-190
color names, ISO Latin encoding,
  190
color spaces, 191, 232-233
color specification, hexadecimal,
  193
color utility, functions in Xmu
  library, 695
colorcells, 188
  allocating read/write, 211-216,
    216-217
  allocating with XAllocColor-
    Cells, 211-216
  allocating with XAllocColor-
    Planes, 216-217
  compared to colormaps, 199
  counting free, 200
  definition, 30, 726
  read/write, 199, 206-217
  setting color of, 235
colorimetry, 231
Colormap, 597
colormap attribute, 35, 108
colormap cells, querying, 234
colormap index, definition, 31
ColormapChangeMask, 243, 276
ColormapNotify event, 243-244,
  276, 647
colormaps, and window manager,
  108, 242
  atoms, 221
  changeable versus immutable,
    198
  creating, 242
  definition, 30, 188, 727
  differences of in display hard-
    ware, 193-199

cursor position, moving, 384-385
Cursor type, 597
cursor utility, functions in Xmu
    library, 695
cursorfont.h include file, 181
cut buffers, 436-437
    communication through, 403
    definition, 727

D

dashes, and fill_style, 137
    example of setting, 128
    GC component, 122-123, 128
dash_list, XSetDashes argument,
    128
dash_offset, GC component, 122,
    128
Data, 600
data communication, 403
data management, 495, 501
data structures, display, 728, 740
    see also structures, 740
data transfers, 434, 436
Data16, 600
Data32, 600
database, 351
    color name, 189-190
    loading, 477
    resource manager, 453-461
    storing into, 462
    using values directly, 462
    (see also resource databases.)
dates, displaying in international-
    ized applications, 328, 331
dbx, 48
debugging, tools for, 48
    tricks for, 48
    X applications, 47-51
decimal separators, 331
DECnet, 5
    font servers, naming, 564
default, attributes for InputOutput
    window, 110
DefaultColormap, example, 202
DefaultDepth, example, 202
DefaultScreen macro, 60-61
DefaultVisual macro, 196
    example, 202
defined symbols, 46

delta for horizontal offset, 168
depth, 36, 136-137, 157, 160, 197
    and GC, 118
    and pixel values, 30
    default, 204
    definition, 26, 727
    of InputOnly, 36
derived instances, 567
    of scalable fonts, 566-567
DES (Data Encryption Stan-
    dard), and securing access
    control, 497
descendants, 28
    definition, 728
descent of character, definition,
    162
    in placing text, 166
design requirements for applica-
    tions, 42
destination drawable, 116, 139,
    159
destination of graphics request,
    140
DestroyAll close mode, 499
DestroyNotify event, 277, 516,
    654
device, definition, 728
device events, selecting, 268
device gamut, 233, 239-240
device-dependent color, 231
device-independent color,
    230-241
    allocating, 234, 237
    color name database, 230
    converting to device dependent,
    233
    device gamut, 233
    gamut compression, 233
    motivation for, 230
    naming; aliases, 192;
        client database, 192;
        examples, 192
    new features, 230
    querying device gamut,
    239-240
device-independent color spaces,
    232
dialog boxes, 288-291
    implementing, 288
dimensions, of root window, 62
    of screen, 62

Index

errors, 49
  definition, 16
  events and, 17
  synchronizing, 50
  through returned value, 49
escapement, definition, 729
event loops, 41
event mask, attribute, 35, 39, 107
  definition, 262-263, 729
  description of each, 271
  to event correspondence, 264
  XNFilterEvents, 375
event mask symbols, 262-264
  table of, 262
event members, 640
event propagation, definition, 729
event queues, 18, 40
event source, definition, 729
event structure, 41
  common members, 251
event types, 41
  handling, 531
  selecting, 71
event window, 266
  definition, 729
event_mask attribute, 263, 266
events, 38, 249, 251
  accessing specific data, 639
  automatically selected, 279
  border crossing, 312, 655-660
  ButtonPress, 266, 314, 642-643
  ButtonRelease, 266, 314,
    642-643
  CirculateNotify, 277, 530, 644
  CirculateRequest, 278, 513
  CirculateRequest , 645
  clearing duplicates, 530
  ClientMessage, 266, 279, 517,
    646
  ColormapNotify, 243-244, 276,
    647
  ConfigureNotify, 55, 81, 277,
    279, 530, 648
  ConfigureRequest, 278, 513,
    650-651
  CreateNotify, 277, 652-653
  definition, 8, 16, 38, 59, 729
  DestroyNotify, 277, 516, 654
  display member, 251
  duplicate, 40, 530

EnterNotify, 273-274, 312, 315,
  655-660
errors and, 17
Expose, 40, 55, 75, 274,
  661-662
filtering, 362, 388-389
FocusIn, 264, 270, 273, 312,
  315, 663-668
FocusOut, 264, 270, 273, 312,
  315, 663-668
GraphicsExpose, 116, 143-144,
  160, 280, 669-670
GravityNotify, 277, 671
handling, 73-81, 107, 250,
  253-257
KeymapNotify, 274, 313. 322,
  672
KeyPress, 264, 266, 271, 285,
  673-674, 718
KeyRelease, 266, 271, 285,
  673-674
LeaveNotify, 273-274, 312,
  315, 655-660
loops for getting, 75
MapNotify, 277, 675-676
MappingNotify, 265, 279,
  677-678
MapRequest, 278, 513, 679
MotionNotify, 264, 266, 304,
  311, 531, 535, 680-681
NoExpose, 116, 143, 160, 280,
  669-670
predicate procedures, 260
printing the type, 256
processing, example of,
  487-489
propagation, 39, 266, 269
PropertyNotify, 276, 436, 682
queue, 253
receiving, 268
ReparentNotify, 277, 683
ResizeRequest, 279, 684
root member, 251
routines, getting for, 257,
  257-262
selecting, 39, 262-280;
  by grabbing, 271;
  by multiple clients, 40;
  example, 487
SelectionClear, 280, 429, 431,
  685

Index

Index

modifier keys, 294
    changing mapping, 299
    definition, 734
    table of typical mapping, 294
monetary quantities, formatting, 331
monochrome display, 65, 194, 204
    definition, 734
    gray effects, 484
    highlighting, 205, 531
motion events, getting all, 301
motion history buffer, 306
    checking whether it exists, 306
    getting motion events, 306
MotionNotify event, 264, 266, 304, 311, 531, 680-681
    example, 535
    getting all, 301
mouse clicks, handling, 386
mouse cursor, specifying, 377
mouse grab, definition, 734
multi-byte, definition, 734
multi-byte input, obtaining, 389
multi-byte strings, 334
    freeing, 349
    reading, 335
    writing, 335
multiple processes, 19
multiple screens, 61
multiple windows, and input focus, 361
multi-processing, 51

N

naming conventions, 45-46
naming font servers, examples, 564
NeedFunctionPrototypes, 504
NeedNestedPrototypes, 505
NeedVarargsPrototypes, 505
negotiating geometries, 378-381
nested, argument lists, 365
    function prototypes, 505
netnews, 705
networked font service, (see font service)
networks, efficiency, 17
    permission, 42

supported by X, 5
new, (as structure name), and portability, 506
NoExpose event, 116, 143, 280, 669-670
    and XCopyArea or XCopyPlane, 160
Nonconvex, shape flag for XFillPolygon, 155
None, background_pixmap, 98
    border_pixmap, 100
nonstandard keysysm, 717
normal hints, 409
NotUseful, backing_store attribute, 106
NTSC standard, 220
NULL, passing to XOpenDisplay, 60

O

obscures, definition, 735
obscuring windows, 28
obsolete routines, XSetIconName, 403
    XSetNormalHints, 403
    XSetStandardProperties, 403
    XSetWMHints, 403
    XSetZoomHints, 403
    XStoreName, 403
occludes, definition, 735
off-screen memory, 32
offset from parent, 24
off-the-spot interaction style, 360
opaque structures, Visual, 196
opening displays, 477
operating systems, portability between, 58
optimizing performance, 47
    redrawing, 77
    with bit gravity, 101
option styles (command line), 476
options table for XrmParseCommand, 474
OR operator, 262
order, byte, 507
    code steps, 82
origin, definition, 24
outline fonts, 563, **565**

Index

type property, definition, 742
type-ahead, 316

U

underlining, 384
underspecified font names, 568
union, XEvent, 59, 251
UNIX variable DISPLAY, 59-61
unloading fonts, 81
UnlockDisplay, 598
UnmapGravity win_gravity, 104
UnmapNotify event, 105, 275,
    277, 530, 675-676
unmapping windows, 29-30
usage messages, 482
Usage routine, 482
Usenet network news, see net-
    news, 705
user defaults, 44
    getting, 473-482
user interface, designing, 43
    lack of policy, 16
user preferences, 44, 441
    managing, 441
user resource specifications, 441
user versus program size hints,
    70
USG, 506
uwm window manager, 512

V

Value color space, 232, 239
valuemask argument, 94, 118
values argument, 118
variable argument lists, in C, 505
Version 10 functions, 575
versions of X, 3
vertical text, 171
viewable, definition, 742
virtual colormap, 194, 198
    definition of, 241
    versus hardware, 241
virtual crossing, 657
visibility, before event handling,
    250
    conditions for, 29, 72
    monitoring, 112

VisibilityChangeMask, 275-276
VisibilityNotify event, 275,
    688-689
visible, definition, 743
Visual, 592
visual class, comparisons of, 197
    definition, 743
    versus window class, 197
Visual structure, 196
VisualID, 597
visuals, 36, 196-198, 217-220
    choosing, 219
    classes of, 197
    definition, 26, 196, 743
    GrayScale, 220, 224
    VisualInfo structure, 218

W

waiting before drawing, 79
wchar_t, 334
well-formed font names, 566
WhenMapped, backing_store
    attribute, 106
white background, 65
WhitePixel macro, 31, 64-65, 200
whitespace, definition, 743
wide lines, definition, 123
wide-character input, obtaining,
    389
wide-character strings, 334
    drawing, 342
    freeing, 349
wide-character type, 334
width of window, 35
width_inc size hint, 70
wildcards, 459
    and resource component names,
    457
    in font names, 558
    in scalable fonts, 566
Window, 597, 599
window, definition, 743
    event component, 251, 266
    InputOutput, 661
    keyboard focus, 663
    visibility, 72
window attributes, 34
    default, 110
    definition, 26
    querying, 110

Index

Index

About the Author

Adrian Nye is a senior technical writer at O'Reilly & Associates. In addition to the X Window System programming manuals, he has written user's manuals for data acquisition products, and customized UNIX documentation for Sun Microsystems and Prime. Adrian has also worked as a programmer writing educational software in C, and as a mechanical engineer designing offshore oilspill cleanup equipment. He has long-term interests in using his technical writing skills to promote recycling and other environmentally sound technologies. He graduated from the Massachusetts Institute of Technology in 1984 with a B.S. in Mechanical Engineering.

More Titles from O'REILLY™

X Window System

Volume 0: X Protocol Reference Manual

Edited by Adrian Nye
4th Edition January 1995
458 pages, ISBN 1-56592-083-X

This manual describes the X Network Protocol, which underlies all software for Version 11 of the X Window System. It provides not only a practical demonstration of what is involved in a client session, but also an extensive set of reference pages for each protocol request and event. Reference pages, alphabetized for easy access, include encoding of requests and replies.

The fourth edition of *X Protocol Reference Manual* includes protocol clarifications of X11 Release 6 and can be used with any release of X. Note: This edition does not contain the Inter-Client Communication Conventions Manual (ICCCM) or the X Logical Font Description Convention (XLFD). This material will be included in an upcoming O'Reilly book.

Volume 1: Xlib Programming Manual

By Adrian Nye
3rd Edition July 1992
824 pages, ISBN 1-56592-002-3

Covering X11 Release 5, the *Xlib Programming Manual* is a complete guide to programming the X library (Xlib), the lowest level of programming interface to X. It includes introductions to internationalization, device-independent color, font service, and scalable fonts.

Includes chapters on:

- X Window System concepts
- A simple client application
- Window attributes
- The graphics context
- Graphics in practice
- Color
- Events
- Interclient communication
- Internationalization
- The Resource Manager
- A complete client application
- Window management
- Other programming techniques

This manual is a companion to *Volume 2, Xlib Reference Manual*.

Volume 2: Xlib Reference Manual

By Adrian Nye
3rd Edition June 1992
1138 pages, ISBN 1-56592-006-6

Volume 2, Xlib Reference Manual, is a complete programmer's reference for Xlib. Covers X11 Release 4 and Release 5.

Contents include:

- Reference pages for Xlib functions
- Reference pages for event types
- Permuted index to Xlib functions
- Description of macros and reference pages for their function versions
- Listing of the server-side color database
- KeySyms and their meaning
- Illustration of the standard cursor font
- Function group index to the right routine for a particular task
- Reference pages for Xlib-related Xmu functions (miscellaneous utilities)
- Four single-page reference aids for the GC and window attributes

Volume 3M: X Window System User's Guide

Motif Edition
By Valerie Quercia & Tim O'Reilly
2nd Edition January 1993
956 pages, ISBN 1-56592-015-5

The *X Window System User's Guide, Motif Edition* orients the new user to window system concepts and provides detailed tutorials for many client programs, including the xterm terminal emulator and the twm, uwm, and mwm window managers. Later chapters explain how to customize the X environment. Revised for Motif 1.2 and X11 Release 5.

Volume 4M: X Toolkit Intrinsics Programming Manual

Motif Edition
By Adrian Nye & Tim O'Reilly
2nd Edition August 1992
674 pages, ISBN 1-56592-013-9

A complete guide to programming with the *X Toolkit Intrinsics*, the library of C language routines that facilitates the design of user interfaces with reusable components called widgets. This book provides concepts and examples that show how to use the various X Toolkit routines. The first few chapters are devoted to using widgets; the remainder of the book covers the more complex task of writing new widgets.

For information: **800-998-9938**, 707-829-0515; **info@ora.com; http://www.ora.com/**
To order: **800-889-8969** (credit card orders only); **order@ora.com**

X Window System *(continued)*

Volume 5: X Toolkit Intrinsics Reference Manual

 Edited by David Flanagan
3rd Edition April 1992
916 pages, ISBN 1-56592-007-4,

The *X Toolkit Intrinsics Reference Manual* is a complete programmer's reference for the X Toolkit. This volume is based on Xt documentation from the X Consortium and has been reorganized and expanded for X11 Release 5. It provides reference pages for each of the Xt functions, as well as the widget classes defined by Xt and the Athena widgets, and many useful appendices.

This manual is a companion to *Volume 4M, X Toolkit Intrinsics Programming Manual.*

Volume 6A: Motif Programming Manual

 By Dan Heller, Paula Ferguson & David Brennan
2nd Edition February 1994
1016 pages, ISBN 1-56592-016-3

 The *Motif Programming Manual* is a source for complete, accurate, and insightful guidance on Motif application programming. There is no other book that covers the ground as thoroughly or as well as this one.

The *Motif Programming Manual* describes how to write applications using the Motif toolkit from the Open Software Foundation (OSF). The book goes into detail on every Motif widget class, with useful examples that will help programmers to develop their own code. Anyone doing Motif programming who doesn't want to have to figure it out alone needs this book.

In addition to information on Motif, the book is full of tips about programming in general and about user interface design. It includes a tutorial on UIL; coverage of drag-and-drop, tear-off menus, and internationalization as implemented in the Motif widgets such as Text and TextField; plus the entire book has been checked for accuracy with Motif 1.2 (while remaining usable with Motif 1.1). Complements *Volume 6B, Motif Reference Manual.*

Volume 6B: Motif Reference Manual

 By Paula Ferguson & David Brennan
1st Edition June 1993
920 pages, ISBN 1-56592-038-4

A complete programmer's reference for the Motif toolkit. This book provides reference pages for the Motif functions and macros, the Motif and Xt widget classes, the Mrm functions, the Motif clients, and the UIL file format, data types, and functions. Covers Motif 1.2. This manual is a companion to *Volume 6A, Motif Programming Manual.*

Volume 6C: Motif Tools

 By David Flanagan
1st Edition August 1994
1024 pages, Includes CD-ROM ISBN 1-56592-044-9

 *Motif Tools* and the Xmt programming library that accompanies it on CD-ROM offer resources that will empower Motif programmers and dramatically speed up application development with the X Toolkit and Motif. While the book is a complete programmer's guide and reference manual for the Xmt library, it is not just a dry volume about programming mechanics; it also describes a holistic philosophy of development of a complete application: from first conception, through design and implementation, and on to the finishing stylistic touches.

The X Window System in a Nutshell

Edited by Ellie Cutler, Daniel Gilly & Tim O'Reilly
2nd Edition April 1992
424 pages, ISBN 1-56592-017-1

 Indispensable companion to the X Window System series. Experienced X programmers can use this single-volume desktop companion for most common questions, keeping the full series of manuals for detailed reference. This book has been updated to cover R5, but is still useful for R4.

"If you have bought a notebook computer and write X code while backpacking the Pennine Way or flying the Atlantic, this is the one for you!"
—*Sun UK User*

Stay in touch with O'REILLY™

Visit Our Award-Winning World Wide Web Site

http://www.ora.com/

VOTED

"Top 100 Sites on the Web" —*PC Magazine*
"Top 5% Websites" —*Point Communications*
"3-Star site" —*The McKinley Group*

Our Web site contains a library of comprehensive product information (including book excerpts and tables of contents), downloadable software, background articles, interviews with technology leaders, links to relevant sites, book cover art, and more. File us in your Bookmarks or Hotlist!

Join Our Two Email Mailing Lists

LIST #1 **NEW PRODUCT RELEASES:** To receive automatic email with brief descriptions of all new O'Reilly products as they are released, send email to: listproc@online.ora.com and put the following information in the first line of your message (NOT in the Subject: field, which is ignored): **subscribe ora-news "Your Name" of "Your Organization"** (for example: **subscribe ora-news Kris Webber of Fine Enterprises)**

List #2 **O'REILLY EVENTS:** If you'd also like us to send information about trade show events, special promotions, and other O'Reilly events, send email to: **listproc@online.ora.com** and put the following information in the first line of your message (NOT in the Subject: field, which is ignored): **subscribe ora-events "Your Name" of "Your Organization"**

Visit Our Gopher Site

* Connect your Gopher to **gopher.ora.com**, or
* Point your Web browser to **gopher://gopher.ora.com/**, or
* telnet to **gopher.ora.com** (login: **gopher**)

Get Example Files from Our Books Via FTP

There are two ways to access an archive of example files from our books:

REGULAR FTP — ftp to: **ftp.ora.com** (login: **anonymous**—use your email address as the password) or point your Web browser to: **ftp://ftp.ora.com/**

FTPMAIL — Send an email message to: **ftpmail@online.ora.com** (write "help" in the message body)

Contact Us Via Email

order@ora.com — To place a book or software order online. Good for North American and international customers.

subscriptions@ora.com — To place an order for any of our newsletters or periodicals.

software@ora.com — For general questions and product information about our software.
   • Check out O'Reilly Software Online at **http://software.ora.com/** for software and technical support information.
   • Registered O'Reilly software users send your questions to **website-support@ora.com**

books@ora.com — General questions about any of our books.

cs@ora.com — For answers to problems regarding your order or our products.

booktech@ora.com — For book content technical questions or corrections.

proposals@ora.com — To submit new book or software proposals to our editors and product managers.

international@ora.com — For information about our international distributors or translation queries.
   • For a list of our distributors outside of North America check out:
   http://www.ora.com/www/order/country.html

O'REILLY™

101 Morris Street, Sebastopol, CA 95472 USA
TEL 707-829-0515 or 800-998-9938 (6 A.M. to 5 P.M. PST)
FAX 707-829-0104

Listing of Titles from O'REILLY™

INTERNET PROGRAMMING

CGI Programming on the
   World Wide Web
Designing for the Web
Exploring Java
HTML: The Definitive Guide
Web Client Programming with Perl
Learning Perl
Programming Perl, 2nd.Edition
   (Fall '96)
JavaScript: The Definitive Guide, Beta
   Edition (Summer '96)
Webmaster in a Nutshell
The World Wide Web Journal

USING THE INTERNET

Smileys
The Whole Internet User's Guide
   and Catalog
The Whole Internet for Windows 95
What You Need to Know:
   Using Email Effectively
Marketing on the Internet (Fall 96)
What You Need to Know: Bandits on the
   Information Superhighway

JAVA SERIES

Exploring Java
Java in a Nutshell
Java Language Reference
   (Fall '96 est.)
Java Virtual Machine

WINDOWS

Inside the Windows '95 Registry

SOFTWARE

WebSite™ 1.1
WebSite Professional™
WebBoard™
PolyForm™

SONGLINE GUIDES

NetLearning
NetSuccess for Realtors
NetActivism (Fall '96)

SYSTEM ADMINISTRATION

Building Internet Firewalls
Computer Crime:
   A Crimefighter's Handbook
Computer Security Basics
DNS and BIND
Essential System Administration,
   2nd ed.
Getting Connected:
   The Internet at 56K and Up
Linux Network Administrator's Guide
Managing Internet Information Services
Managing Usenet (Fall '96)
Managing NFS and NIS
Networking Personal Computers
   with TCP/IP
Practical UNIX & Internet Security
PGP: Pretty Good Privacy
sendmail
System Performance Tuning
TCP/IP Network Administration
termcap & terminfo
Using & Managing UUCP (Fall '96)
Volume 8: X Window System
   Administrator's Guide

UNIX

Exploring Expect
Learning GNU Emacs, 2nd Edition
   (Fall '96 est.)
Learning the bash Shell
Learning the Korn Shell
Learning the UNIX Operating System
Learning the vi Editor
Linux in a Nutshell (Fall '96 est.)
Making TeX Work
Linux Multimedia Guide (Fall '96)
Running Linux, 2nd Edition
Running Linux Companion
   CD-ROM, 2nd Edition
SCO UNIX in a Nutshell
sed & awk
Unix in a Nutshell: System V Edition
UNIX Power Tools
UNIX Systems Programming
Using csh and tsch
What You Need to Know:
   When You Can't Find Your
   UNIX System Administrator

PROGRAMMING

Applying RCS and SCCS
C++: The Core Language
Checking C Programs with lint
DCE Security Programming
Distributing Applications Across
   DCE and Windows NT
Encyclopedia of Graphics File
   Formats, 2nd ed.
Guide to Writing DCE Applications
lex & yacc
Managing Projects with make
ORACLE Performance Tuning
ORACLE PL/SQL Programming
Porting UNIX Software
POSIX Programmer's Guide
POSIX.4: Programming for
   the Real World
Power Programming with RPC
Practical C Programming
Practical C++ Programming
Programming Python (Fall '96)
Programming with curses
Programming with GNU Software
   (Fall '96 est.)
Pthreads Programming
   (Fall '96)
Software Portability with imake
Understanding DCE
Understanding Japanese Information
   Processing
UNIX Systems Programming for SVR4

BERKELEY 4.4 SOFTWARE DISTRIBUTION

4.4BSD System Manager's Manual
4.4BSD User's Reference Manual
4.4BSD User's Supplementary Docs.
4.4BSD Programmer's Reference Man.
4.4BSD Programmer's Supp. Docs.

X PROGRAMMING
THE X WINDOW SYSTEM

Volume 0: X Protocol Reference Manual
Volume 1: Xlib Programming Manual
Volume 2: Xlib Reference Manual
Volume. 3M: X Window System
   User's Guide, Motif Ed.
Volume. 4: X Toolkit Intrinsics
   Programming Manual
Volume 4M: X Toolkit Intrinsics
   Programming Manual, Motif Ed.
Volume 5: X Toolkit Intrinsics
   Reference Manual
Volume 6A: Motif Programming Man.
Volume 6B: Motif Reference Manual
Volume 6C: Motif Tools
Volume 8 : X Window System
   Administrator's Guide
Programmer's Supplement for Release 6
X User Tools (with CD-ROM)
The X Window System in a Nutshell

HEALTH, CAREER, & BUSINESS

Building a Successful Software Business
The Computer User's Survival Guide
Dictionary of Computer Terms
The Future Does Not Compute
Love Your Job!
Publishing with CD-ROM

TRAVEL

Travelers' Tales: Brazil (Summer '96 est.)
Travelers' Tales: Food (Summer '96)
Travelers' Tales: France
Travelers' Tales: Hong Kong
Travelers' Tales: India
Travelers' Tales: Mexico
Travelers' Tales: San Francisco
Travelers' Tales: Spain
Travelers' Tales: Thailand
Travelers' Tales: A Woman's World

International Distributors

Customers outside North America can now order O'Reilly & Associates books through the following distributors. They offer our international customers faster order processing, more bookstores, increased representation at tradeshows worldwide, and the high-quality, responsive service our customers have come to expect.

EUROPE, MIDDLE EAST AND NORTHERN AFRICA *(except Germany, Switzerland, and Austria)*

INQUIRIES
International Thomson Publishing Europe
Berkshire House
168-173 High Holborn
London WC1V 7AA, United Kingdom
Telephone: 44-171-497-1422
Fax: 44-171-497-1426
Email: **itpint@itps.co.uk**

ORDERS
International Thomson Publishing Services, Ltd.
Cheriton House, North Way
Andover, Hampshire SP10 5BE,
United Kingdom
Telephone: 44-264-342-832 (UK orders)
Telephone: 44-264-342-806 (outside UK)
Fax: 44-264-364418 (UK orders)
Fax: 44-264-342761 (outside UK)
UK & Eire orders: **itpuk@itps.co.uk**
International orders: **itpint@itps.co.uk**

GERMANY, SWITZERLAND, AND AUSTRIA

International Thomson Publishing GmbH
O'Reilly International Thomson Verlag
Königswinterer Straße 418
53227 Bonn, Germany
Telephone: 49-228-97024 0
Fax: 49-228-441342
Email: **anfragen@arade.ora.de**

AUSTRALIA

WoodsLane Pty. Ltd.
7/5 Vuko Place, Warriewood NSW 2102
P.O. Box 935, Mona Vale NSW 2103
Australia
Telephone: 61-2-9970-5111
Fax: 61-2-9970-5002
Email: **info@woodslane.com.au**

NEW ZEALAND

WoodsLane New Zealand Ltd.
21 Cooks Street (P.O. Box 575)
Wanganui, New Zealand
Telephone: 64-6-347-6543
Fax: 64-6-345-4840
Email: **info@woodslane.com.au**

ASIA *(except Japan & India)*

INQUIRIES
International Thomson Publishing Asia
60 Albert Street #15-01
Albert Complex
Singapore 189969
Telephone: 65-336-6411
Fax: 65-336-7411

ORDERS
Telephone: 65-336-6411
Fax: 65-334-1617

JAPAN

O'Reilly Japan, Inc.
Kiyoshige Building 2F
12-Banchi, Sanei-cho
Shinjuku-ku
Tokyo 160 Japan
Telephone: 81-3-3356-5227
Fax: 81-3-3356-5261
Email: **kenji@ora.com**

INDIA

Computer Bookshop (India) PVT. LTD.
190 Dr. D.N. Road, Fort
Bombay 400 001
India
Telephone: 91-22-207-0989
Fax: 91-22-262-3551
Email: **cbsbom@giasbm01.vsnl.net.in**

THE AMERICAS

O'Reilly & Associates, Inc.
101 Morris Street
Sebastopol, CA 95472 U.S.A.
Telephone: 707-829-0515
Telephone: 800-998-9938 (U.S. & Canada)
Fax: 707-829-0104
Email: **order@ora.com**

SOUTHERN AFRICA

International Thomson Publishing Southern Africa
Building 18, Constantia Park
240 Old Pretoria Road
P.O. Box 2459
Halfway House, 1685 South Africa
Telephone: 27-11-805-4819
Fax: 27-11-805-3648

O'REILLY™

TO ORDER: **800-889-8969** (CREDIT CARD ORDERS ONLY); **order@ora.com; http://www.ora.com**
OUR PRODUCTS ARE AVAILABLE AT A BOOKSTORE OR SOFTWARE STORE NEAR YOU.

O'Reilly & Associates, Inc.
101 Morris Street
Sebastopol, CA 95472-9902
1-800-998-9938

Visit us online at:
http://www.ora.com/
orders@ora.com

O'REILLY™

O'REILLY WOULD LIKE TO HEAR FROM YOU

Which book did this card come from?

_____

Where did you buy this book?
- ❑ Bookstore
- ❑ Direct from O'Reilly
- ❑ Bundled with hardware/software
- ❑ Other _____
- ❑ Computer Store
- ❑ Class/seminar

What operating system do you use?
- ❑ UNIX
- ❑ Windows NT
- ❑ Other _____
- ❑ Macintosh
- ❑ PC(Windows/DOS)

What is your job description?
- ❑ System Administrator
- ❑ Network Administrator
- ❑ Web Developer
- ❑ Other _____
- ❑ Programmer
- ❑ Educator/Teacher

❑ Please send me O'Reilly's catalog, containing a complete listing of O'Reilly books and software.

Name _____ Company/Organization _____

Address _____

City _____ State _____ Zip/Postal Code _____ Country _____

Telephone _____ Internet or other email address (specify network) _____

Nineteenth century wood engraving
of a bear from the O'Reilly &
Associates Nutshell Handbook®
Using & Managing UUCP.

POST CARD

BUSINESS REPLY MAIL

FIRST CLASS MAIL   PERMIT NO. 80   SEBASTOPOL, CA

Postage will be paid by addressee

O'Reilly & Associates, Inc.
101 Morris Street
Sebastopol, CA 95472-9902